# Mental Health Aspects of Mental Retardation

# Mental Health Aspects of Mental Retardation

PROGRESS IN ASSESSMENT AND TREATMENT

*Edited by*

## Robert J. Fletcher
## Anton Dosen, M.D.

LEXINGTON BOOKS
*An Imprint of Macmillan, Inc.*
NEW YORK
Maxwell Macmillan Canada
TORONTO
Maxwell Macmillan International
NEW YORK   OXFORD   SINGAPORE   SYDNEY

**Library of Congress Cataloging-in-Publication Data**

Mental health aspects of mental retardation : progress in assessment
    and treatment / edited by Robert J. Fletcher and Anton Dosen.
        p.   cm.
    ISBN 0-669-28077-1
    1. Mentally handicapped—Mental health.   2. Mental illness—
Treatment.   I. Fletcher, Robert J. (Robert Jonathan)  II. Dosen,
Anton.
    [DNLM: 1. Mental Retardation—psychology.   2. Mental Disorders—
diagnosis.   3. Mental Disorders—therapy.   4. Psychotherapy—
methods.   WM 307.M5 M5485 1993]
RC451.4.M47M463   1993
616.85'88—dc20
DNLM/DLC
for Library of Congress                                              93-27741
                                                                          CIP

Lexington Books
An Imprint of Macmillan, Inc.
866 Third Avenue, New York, N.Y. 10022

Maxwell Macmillan Canada, Inc.
1200 Eglinton Avenue East
Suite 200
Don Mills, Ontario M3C 3N1

Macmillan, Inc. is part of the Maxwell Communication Group of Companies.

Printed in the United States of America

printing number
1   2   3   4   5   6   7   8   9   10

*This book is dedicated to*
*Frank J. Menolascino*
*5/25/30–4/3/92*

This individual was a giant among giants and an exceptional human being—both professionally and personally. He was a leading advocate of humane and dignified community-based services for mentally retarded persons. His career-long interest in mental illness among persons with mental retardation impacted on the lives of millions of people world-wide. The field of dual diagnosis was largely unexplored before his research and clinical work.

Frank Menolascino dedicated his professional life to the field of mental health care in persons who have mental retardation. He was a prolific writer in this field and an authority in every aspect of it. He was a friend and mentor to many people, including the editors of this book. Frank will be missed deeply by all of us, but his memory and spirit will live on.

We dedicate this book as a tribute to Frank.

# Contents

# Introduction

The progress made in the last two decades in the assessment, diagnostics, and treatment of behavioral and psychiatric disorders among mentally retarded individuals has been formidable. One of the first extensive volumes on psychiatric disorders in the mentally retarded, *Psychiatric Approaches to Mental Retardation,* appeared in 1970, edited by Frank J. Menolascino. Menolascino wrote in the preface of the book, "There has been a recent renaissance of interest in the behavioral dimensions of mental retardation. It is the editor's opinion that a book is needed which will literally corral some major representatives of the current psychiatric ferment and activity in the area of mental retardation"

Since then, a number of books on the subject of mental illness among the mentally retarded have appeared. Most of them have attempted to give a broad overview of the present knowledge of assessment, diagnostics, and treatment and in this way have offered a base upon which a psychiatric view on the problems encountered among the mentally retarded could be formed. Many of these books have served as psychiatric handbooks in this field.

At this time, more knowledge of different issues in this area of research has been accumulated and deepened. Specific assessment approaches and treatment methods applicable to particular diagnostic categories have been developed. There is no doubt anymore that mental health approaches to the mentally retarded are developing in their own right, in their own directions, and are being recognized as a scientific discipline as well. In order to follow these developments, an appropriate dissemination of information on the state of the field is needed from time to time.

This book defines the current views on particular diagnostic categories and treatment possibilities. A number of distinguished scientists from the United States and Europe, known to be specialists in particular behavioral and psychiatric disorders, have been asked to give their views on the theoretical and practical aspects of particular disorders. In order to make the material as suitable as possible for practicing clinicians and scientists, whenever possible, the same authors have been asked to give their views on assessment and diagnosis as well as on treatment.

Some more recent treatment methods that do not belong to a particular diagnostic category are also presented. These methods may be suitable for treatment of various diagnostic entities when applied in connection with a careful analysis of the situation.

As you can see from the book's contents, the intent of the editors was not to give a broad survey of psychopathology, but to focus on particular entities that, on the one hand, are most frequently diagnosed among the mentally retarded and, on the other hand, are currently the topic of animated discussions among scientists and practitioners. The book aims to meet the needs of various professionals working in the field of mental health and mental retardation.

Because of the speed with which knowledge in this area is being gathered, a regular circulation of the information on new scientific developments is needed. That is why it is the intention of the editors of this volume to continue their efforts to compile the knowledge available and regularly edit new volumes with up-to-date information on the progress being made in the field of assessment and treatment.

# Part I
# Overview

At a recent conference of European experts on mental health and mental retardation (Veldhoven, 1992), also attended by delegates from the United States, the differences in the concepts about the mental health of mentally retarded individuals in different countries were striking. An important task of the European association for mental health in mental retardation, which was founded by that conference, is to promote the use of the same terminology, understandable to all members of the association, independent of the significant differences in various other aspects of the care of the mentally retarded.

Understanding the terms being used is the basis of good communication. That is why a discussion of the terminology takes place at the beginning of this volume. Internationally accepted concepts and terms are also needed for establishing good cooperation between the associations in this field on different continents. The editors of this volume hope that in this way, the cooperation between (NADD) and the recently founded European association will be stimulated.

A critical review of the terminology and the meanings of the terms is also needed because of the rapidly changing opinions and attitudes within this field.

The professionals should be atuned to the questions concerning terms, concepts, and constructs being used: Are they still adequate and do they give enough leeway for further developments? A clear definition of the term *mental health* may lead to a better insight into the specificities of this concept within the framework of mental retardation, on which more appropriate aims for further development may be built.

# 1

# Mental Health and Mental Illness in Persons with Retardation: What We Are Talking About?

*Anton Dosen*

The term *mental health of mentally retarded individuals* has recently and frequently been used in particular countries, especially the United States and the United Kingdom and is becoming familiar to workers in the field of mental retardation (Stark et al., 1988). However, the meaning of the term may differ from professional discipline to professional discipline. For example, a psychiatrist is inclined to comprehend this term in the context of the combating of mental illness, while a pedagogue or educator relates it to problems of rearing, and a social worker links the term to the life problems associated with unfavorable social circumstances. In most cases, practitioners in the field are inclined to think in terms of the various difficulties encountered while interacting with the mentally retarded individuals whom they are usually confronted with in day-to-day practice.

Obviously professionals are still not accustomed to thinking positively when speaking of the mental health of this population. One speaks of mental health but thinks of disturbance. This attitude may probably be related to traditional thinking (that is, in terms of abnormalities, disorders, and defects) when speaking of mentally retarded persons.

The same attitude is, consciously or unconsciously, more-or-less present even in reference to particular existential and psychosocial aspects of mentally retarded individuals that are not necessarily linked to their abnormalities, for example, joy, happiness, sadness, and similar emotional and social features.

By way of the normalization movement, important changes in residential, vocational, educational, and several other aspects of life of the mentally retarded have taken place. The mental health issue has, however, been only marginally touched by the normalization movement so far. Until recently, the propagators of normalization were more concerned with behavioral and psychiatric disorders than with a structured approach to the promotion of mental health.

This situation is currently visible in practice in several European countries. Because of the normalization process that has been taking place in the past few decades, many big institutions in these countries have been closed, and many mentally retarded persons, formerly living in psychiatric hospitals, have been placed in group homes or small institutions for the mentally retarded. One of the most disputed problems encountered among these persons since the early 1970s is the problem of behavioral disorders. Attempts directed toward finding a solution for this problem have led, particularly since the early 1980s, to the insight that not only behavioral disorders but also psychiatric disorders are often present among these individuals. (Int. experts' conference 1992). According to a recent discussion held at a European experts' conference on the mental health of the mentally retarded (Int. experts' conference 1992), in different countries the problem of behavioral and psychiatric disorders is currently very real. However, the subject of mental health is just coming into focus. In most countries, professionals are still unfamiliar with this concept.

It is apparent from the above that, at this stage in the care of the mentally retarded, the mental health of mentally retarded individuals needs to be discussed in more detail. Despite the growing number of specialized services for mental health care in individual countries (Braddock, 1992; Bouras & Drummond, 1989), there is still the question of a good definition of the term and what the proper objectives of the mental health care of this population are.

## The Mental Health of the Mentally Retarded

The concept of the mental health of mentally retarded individuals has, so far, not been clarified enough in the professional literature. In the following comments by Frank Menolascino (1988), some important facets of this concept come to the fore: "The mentally retarded/mentally ill can teach us that the goal of treatment is not to eliminate disruptive or destructive behaviors, but rather to teach new sets of humanizing behaviors that focus on our solidarity with all persons, leads us to open ourselves up to the bonding, and gives us deep insight into the elemental human need for mutual love" (Menolascino 1988, p. 122). Basic human needs like social acceptance, social relationships, and positive affection have been stressed by Menolascino as elements of mental health.

The definition of health of the World Health Organization (WHO; 1978) is as follows: "Health is a state of physical, mental and social wellbeing and not merely the absence of disease or infirmity" (p. 2). For mental health, the same definition could be used.

The question "Can a mentally retarded person be mentally healthy?" has been answered to a great extent by the statement that mental retardation is not an illness but a developmental disturbance. However, if we keep in mind the specificities of biological abnormalities, a lack of mental consolidation, and a poverty of social interactions, the concept of mental health as related to mentally retarded persons may be questionable. From this point of view, it is necessary to make some additions to the WHO definition when speaking of the mentally retarded.

From the developmental, psychodynamic, and systemic theoretical approaches, the following factors that are important in the mental health of the nonretarded, as well as the retarded, deserve to be discussed.

- A balanced, developed personality
- A place of one's own and a role in the surroundings
- Functioning in accordance with one's own abilities (Dosen, 1990)

A balanced personality develops when all aspects of the personality develop equally well and reach the same developmental level. Which level is not considered in the concept of balance. Thus, a mentally retarded person whose developmental rate is slower, and who eventually reaches a lower developmental level than a nonretarded individual, may show parallel development in cognitive, emotional, social, and other areas and may thus have a balanced personality. Such a person may have his or her own recognizable place or territory and may pursue activities having a meaningful significance for other people in the surroundings. When such persons are involved in interaction according to their abilities, they can function in a way that is satisfactory to themselves and to others. It may be expected that such persons can feel safe and satisfied within their surroundings.

If we add these components to the WHO definition of mental health, the accent is on the positive subjective experiences of mentally retarded individuals. Feelings of satisfaction and happiness should not be strange to these individuals and are basic components of mental health.

From this consideration two important questions arise:

- How can one adequately stimulate a person's development?
- How can the environmental conditions that are optimal for a healthy life be created and maintained?

In order to answer these questions, forming a mental-health-care system for mentally retarded children and adults is necessary. This care is of great importance in the prevention as well as the combating of behavioral disorders and mental illness. However, before such a system of mental health care can be established, it is necessary to be precisely aware of what the term *mental health of the mentally retarded* means.

A successful mental health care system for the mentally retarded should, in my opinion, focus on the following three tasks:

- the stimulation of healthy mental development and the protection of a healthy mental life
- the prevention of behavioral and psychiatric disorders
- the treatment of behavioral disorders and mental illness

## Mental Illness in the Mentally Retarded

Various investigators have discovered that behavioral and psychiatric disorders prevail more among mental retardates than among the nonretarded. The percentages found vary from 20 to 64 percent of the cases (Rutter, et al., 1970; Corbett, 1979; Reid, 1980; Eaton & Menolascino, 1982; Szymanski, 1977; Ineichen, 1984; Gillberg et al., 1986). It appears that prevelance increases as the intellectual level decreases (Gillberg et al., 1986). Gualtieri (1988) quotes two widely accepted reasons for the high prevalence of psychiatric disorders among the mentally retarded:

- Persons with mental retardation, by dint of endowment and training, have limited capacity to cope with the pressures and demands of day-to-day life.
- Day-to-day life challenges retarded persons to an extraordinary degree. A person with mental retardation rarely experiences what might be called a developmentally appropriate environment (Gualtieri, 1988, p. 174).

According to Gualtieri there are, in addition to these two reasons, two more important factors that play a role in the occurrence of psychiatric problems:

- Malformations or brain damage
- Deficiencies in the mental health care of the mentally retarded

The early work of authors in the field of mental illness and mental retardation, like that of Menolascino (1970, 1977), Balthazar and Stevens (1975), and James and Smith (1979) as well as subsequent literature in this area by Szymanski and Tanguay (1980), Reid (1982), and Matson and Barrett (1982), are directed toward an assessment of the problems of the mentally retarded that corresponds with the diagnostics that mental health professionals use with the population in general. In their attempts to apply the same diagnostics and the same classification systems to the mentally retarded as to nonretarded individuals, the above authors faced a number of problems. Most of them revolve around the following questions:

- What role does low IQ play in the onset and appearance of behavioral disorders and mental illness?

- Do the symptoms have the same diagnostic significance in the mentally retarded as in the nonretarded?
- Does the same psychopathology occur among the mentally retarded as among nonretardates?
- Does the etiology of mental illness of the retarded differ from that of nonretarded individuals?

The high percentage of disorders and the diagnostic and classification difficulties mentioned above, as well as other unresolved problems in the understanding of these disorders, have led some scientists in this field to develop specific theoretical approaches to the explanation of the differences and similarities found among the mentally retarded.

Achenbach and Zigler (1968) pointed to the importance of the social incompetence of the mentally retarded in the onset of interactional and intrapsychic problems. This theoretical approach has been supported by later investigations (Zigler & Spitz, 1978; Reiss & Benson, 1984; Reiss, Levitan, & McNelly, 1982), in which the discrepancies between the self-image, expectations in the surroundings, and what the person would like to be are accentuated. According to these authors, this is fertile ground for the onset of psychopathology.

Menolascino (1970, 1977) developed a theoretical direction that could be termed *biodevelopmental theory* (Matson & Frame, 1986). The accent is placed on the neurophysiological and psychological developmental processes, which, in mentally retarded persons, may have different timing and may take different directions, causing deviations from normal development.

Matson (1985) proposed the so-called biosocial theory, in which it is stated that, in addition to specific biological factors (neurological, biochemical, genetic, etc.), specific social aspects (family interactions and cultural and other environmental variables) and specific psychological processes (cognitive development and personality variables) also lead to differences in the psychopathology of the retarded and the nonretarded.

Other authors (Szymanski, 1988; Tanguay, 1984; Gilson & Levitas, 1987; Dosen, 1989, 1990; Gaedt and Gärtner, 1990) have chosen a so-called developmental theoretical approach. Tanguay proposed the use of a developmental model based on Piaget's stages of cognitive development for a better understanding of psychopathology and for a more appropriate classification. Gilson and Levitas stressed crisis periods during the process of personality development in the mentally retarded and the related psychosocial problems. Some other authors (e.g., Dosen, 1990; Gaedt and Gärtner, 1990) have proposed a link between psychopathology and disturbances in psychosocial development, applying a psychodynamic model of thinking to diagnostic differentiation.

Furthermore, attempts have been made, on the one hand, to distinguish behavioral disorders from mental illness and, on the other, to understand the symptoms of the psychopathology within the specific context of the life of a mentally retarded individual and to define appropriate diagnostic and syndromal entities.

Diverse attempts have been made to apply the diagnostic categories of traditional psychiatry to the psychopathology of the mentally retarded. Corbett (1979) and Reid (1980), for example, applied diagnoses from the ninth edition of WHO's *International Classification of Diseases* (ICD-9) to their mentally retarded population, whereas Menolascino (1990) began from the third edition of the American Psychiatric Association (APA) Diagnostic and Statistical Manual (DSM-III, 1980) diagnostic system. Senatore, Matson, and Kazdin (1985) developed a scale for detecting the psychopathology, the (PIMRA), and Reiss (1987) made a similar effort with his Reiss Screen for Maladaptive Behavior Test Manual. Both scales are based on DSM-III typology.

The applicability of psychiatric classification systems to the mentally retarded, however, has been critically discussed by more investigators (Hucker et al., 1979; Szymanski, 1988; Sovner & Des Noyers-Hurley 1986; Levitas & Gilson, 1990; Jacobson, 1990). It seems probable that ICD-9 and DSM-III criteria can be applied with no modifications or with only minor modifications to persons with mild retardation, but for the more severely retarded, the utility of these criteria is doubtful.

Recently, diagnosticians have been looking for a broadening of or for modifications in the standard psychiatric systems so that they can be applied to mentally retarded patients. Ballinger et al. (1991) applied ICD-9 diagnostic categories to the adult residents of a hospital for the mentally handicapped, concluding that, in 80 percent of the cases, establishing a diagnosis was possible. However, to approximately 35 percent of the residents, the investigators applied diagnostic groupings normally used in child psychiatry, like childhood psychosis, conduct disorder, and hyperkinetic syndrome (Ballinger et al 1991). Sovner and his associates (Sovner & Lowry, 1990; Sovner & Hurley, 1990) have pointed out the need for objective behavioral measurement in the case of the mentally ill mentally retarded. These authors have emphasized that an experienced diagnostician who looks carefully at a specific global behavioral phenomena may find symptoms having the same meaning for mentally retarded and nonretarded mentally ill individuals. This standpoint led Sovner to propose a modification of the symptoms that serve as criteria for the DSM-III diagnostics, so that they could be applied to the mentally retarded. This is an example of an adapted phenomenological approach to the mentally retarded that uses traditional psychiatric diagnoses.

As mentioned earlier, the so-called developmental approach to the psychopathology of the mentally retarded has recently been growing. The accent is placed on distorted psychosocial development and its relationship to psychopathology. Corbett (1985) stated that most forms of psychiatric disorders among the mentally retarded stem from developmental impairments occurring during childhood. Behavioral disturbances rooted in childhood tend to remain unchanged during adolescence, whereas emotional problems like anxiety, fearfulness, and unhappiness seem to decrease.

Levitas and Gilson (1990) pointed out the developmental impairments in the personality of the mentally retarded. They wrote of a secondary psychosocial deficit. The psychiatric clinical pictures of these individuals may, to differing extents, be colored by the specificity of their personality development. Keeping the developmental history of such a person in mind, the diagnostician can better understand particular behavioral features and symptoms and, in this way, may come to a more reliable diagnosis.

Gaedt and coworkers (Gaedt and Gartner, 1990; Gaedt, Jäkel and Kischkel, 1987), German psychodynamically oriented psychiatrists, have stressed a range of developmental aspects in the psychopathology of the mentally retarded. Early childhood development and particularly the mother–child interaction are unfavorably influenced, primarily by the factors responsible for retardation and, secondarily, by retardation itself. These impairments may be of decisive importance in the onset of problems of social adaptation and in ego development and often lead to psychopathology.

In the Netherlands, Dosen (1989, 1990) used the so-called developmental dynamic approach to the diagnosis and treatment of behavioral and psychiatric disorders of the mentally retarded. In many respects, this approach is similar to that of Gaedt. Both approaches emphasize that symptoms depend on the developmental level. Within the developmental dynamic approach, the importance of the phase of socioemotional development during which the disorder occurs has been stressed. Also, within the developmental dynamic approach, an attempt has been made to develop some specific developmental diagnostic entities as a remedial tool that will shed more light on the complexity of the psychopathology of the mentally retarded.

Also, with no particular theoretical backdrop, but for practical reasons, some investigators have made attempts to establish special diagnoses for a number of complex behavioral features frequently encountered among particular population groups. In doing so, Lund (1986) found that autistic psychosis had frequently been detected in the institutionalized mentally retarded. Szymanski and Biederman (1984) reported that depression was found relatively often in combination with anorexia nervosa in Down syndrome persons. Also, particular psychiatric syndromes are linked to specific genetic, organic cerebral or metabolic disorders. For example, in persons with fragile-X syndrome, autisticlike and hyperkinetic conditions have been described (Bregman et al., 1987); in tuberosclerosis patients, psychotic states and disruptive behavior have been found relatively often (Reid, 1985; Parsons et al., 1984); and in PKU (Phenylketonuria) persons, depressive conditions have been reported (Realmuto et al., 1986).

The pedagogical schools in the Dutch, Swiss, and German tradition have extensive experience with the directive pedagogical approach to the mentally retarded (Gennep, 1990; Reukauf, 1985; Bradl, 1987). Establishing a child's developmental needs is an important motive in this technique. Three elements of this approach are of essential importance: a pedagogical climate, a structuring of the activities, and the establishment of appropriate relationships (Gennep, 1990). After a person's needs have been established, the totality of the person's existence may be involved in a process aimed at changing some and learning other sorts of behaviors and skills. In this way, appropriate development can be stimulated, and reeducation may take place.

The treatment potentialities of the pedagogical approach are promising, particularly as a possible treatment form intended to prevent behavioral and psychiatric disorders at all levels of retardation.

## Mental Health Care of the Mentally Retarded Population

There is no doubt that mentally retarded persons, because of their specific psychobiological composition, particular social aspects, and characteristic development, need special care to achieve optimal mental activity and a feeling of well-being in their surroundings. Professionals in the field are aware of the necessity of special knowledge in order to stimulate adequately the development of mentally retarded persons and to keep them in healthy balance with their surroundings.

As stressed earlier, such care should focus on the stimulation of healthy development and on the prevention and treatment of behavioral and psychiatric disorders.

The problems that the professionals working on the realization of this care are facing are threefold:

- Difficulties in the organizing the proper care.
- Problems regarding the correct professional approach, especially with respect to diagnostics and treatment.
- Problems in adapting the cultural attitude of the surroundings to the mental health needs of the mentally retarded. (Dosen, 1992)

### Difficulties in Organization

There are difficulties in interpreting the principles of normalization when one is caring for the behaviorally and psychiatrically disturbed.

In some countries, professionals are predominantly of the opinion that the creation of a special sort of care is antagonistic to the idea of normalization. From day-to-day practice, however, it is clear that the movement toward establishing a special system for mental health care should be seen not as a contradictory but as a complementary component of the actualization of the philosophy of normalization. Mental health care, that is, means not only combating behavioral and psychiatric disorders but also understanding the different aspects of the inner life and motivations of the mentally retarded, as well as their interactions with the outside world. In terms of normalization, we should first discover what the normal and healthy life of the mentally retarded individual is.

Unfortunately, except for the knowledge we have of cognitive development, we know very little about the development and functioning of other psychic aspects of mentally retarded individuals. Knowledge regarding the forming of the personality of the mentally retarded is wanting. There is a lack of insight into the characteristics of the life system functioning of these persons. The roots of behavioral and psychiatric disorders are often unclear. There are obvious diagnostic and classification problems, as well as treatment difficulties. Hardly any work has been done on the prevention of these disorders. In addition, it is becoming increasingly clear that the knowledge we have of the traditional psychiatry and psychology of the population in general is not sufficient to give answers to all the relevant questions involved in caring for a mentally retarded individual. It is obvious that the existing mental health care of the general population offers an insufficient amount of knowledge that is applicable to the mental health care of the mentally retarded.

In order to gain more appropriate knowledge in this field, it is necessary that specialization in working with this population be stimulated. These specialists would form a bridge between the workers in the field of mental retardation and those who work in the mental health care of the population in general.

In a tentative model of the mental health care of the mentally retarded in the Netherlands, a number of services are being provided for the general care of the mentally retarded:

- Social pedagogical services concerned with the social care and counseling of parents and practical pedagogical home training
- special schools for the mentally retarded
- special workshops
- special housing (institutions and group homes)

Mental health care should be provided to all mentally retarded persons within all these services. Organizationally, the care should take place in a center for mental health care, divided into three sections: outreaching team, day treatment, and a clinic. The center should be designed to meet the needs of chidren as well as of adults.

The center should develop its activities at the following four levels:

- the clinical level: the diagnosis and treatment of mental illness and behavioral disorders
- the institutional level: the organization and maintenance of care within the institutions and group homes in cooperation with the internal professionals
- the community level: the provision of mental health care at home, at school, or at a workshop, in cooperation with all concerned$vparents, caregivers, educators, planners, and others.
- the regional and national public policy level: advice and assistance in the creation of conditions in which efficient mental health services can be carried out.

The center's professionals would act on calls from the services for general care. In most cases, aid could be given by the outreaching team at the place where the problem emerges. In more complex cases, day treatment or a clinical admission would be necessary. In addition, support and counseling would be given to the professionals at the general care facilities in their work on the healthy side of the psychic life of the mentally retarded. The education of new professionals as well as scientific research activities would also be the task of the center. The center should cooperate with the mental health care services for the general population and with university centers.

In practice, the idea of such a center is, at the moment, limited to the practitioners in a particular region of the country.

Menolascino (1991A) proposed a similar model of a regional treatment center, accentuating balanced diagnostic and treatment services. The developmentally oriented approach and the prevention of mental illness would be the focus of this center.

## The Problem of the Correct Professional Approach

The role and place of the different professional disciplines within the totality of mental retardation care may be decisive in the theory and practice of the care. In some countries, psychiatric approaches prevail; in others, the approach is pedagogical, and in still others, psychological. The positions held by these disciplines may determine the development of care. In particuliar countries at particular times, the collision of professional disciplines has become a severe obstacle to the search for a constructive approach to the care of the mentally retarded.

If one keeps the complexity of the psychophysical problems of the mentally retarded in mind, it is obvious that proper mental health care must be multidisciplinary in organization and must be multidimensionally directed. For example, for a mentally retarded child with the risk of aberrant development, prompt aid by professionals specialized in neurophysiology, developmental psychiatry, pedagogy, psychology, and so on is necessary. After an adequate assessment and a multidisciplinary diagnosis, further guidance and stimulation of the child's development may be placed in the hands of pedagogical or psychological professionals. In the case of evident behavioral or psychiatric disorders, the role of the psychiatrist, after establishing the diagnosis, might be accentuated during treatment.

Overlaps and cooperation of different disciplines cannot be avoided. In my experience, these overlaps have served as a meeting point and a place for a better understanding of each other's work.

A lack of specific knowledge about the diagnosis and treatment of the mentally retarded is more-or-less present in all disciplines. As a result, one may be inclined toward a gratuitous application to the mentally retarded of the knowledge obtained from studies of the general population. Misunderstandings and faulty decisions may be the consequence of such an approach.

The necessity of educating and training professionals for this special task is obvious. It is remarkable, however, that in different European countries (Int. experts' conference 1992), the universities pay very little attention to the mentally retarded population. The educational possiblities for professionals are limited and often depend on initiative taken by those practicing in the field. The same can be said of scientific research in the area of mental retardation. Apparently, these universities are not yet familiar with the movement toward normalization in the field of mental retardation. An urgent change is needed.

## Problems of Cultural Attitude

The cultural attitude taken toward the mentally retarded differs from country to country. Besides the intercountry differences in the awareness and acceptance of the existence of mental retardation, there are also similarities in the reactions of the general population. Mental retardation is still generally seen as a negative, painful, and even frightening phenomenon. There are different sorts of taboos, prejudices, and projections among the general population leading to inappropriate attitudes, reactions, and interactions. Even widely accepted ideologies like normalization are not likely to be strong enough to bring about a change in such cultural patterns. This problem obviously calls for widespread and systematic work on changing cultural concepts.

The economic factor has not been mentioned as being important because it is always present in all countries when new developments and innovations in community care are the issue. According to Menolascino (1991), money should not be the problem; the problem is how to use it properly. Apparently, the course of further development of care for this population will be determined rather by the cultural attitude of the community and professionals than by the economic factor.

## Summary

The mental health care of the mentally retarded has been the focus of professionals for some time. However, the term *mental health,* when it is used with regard to this population, is still controversial. In the definition of the mental health of the mentally retarded, the subjective feelings of the individual deserve an important place.

Within the focus of mental health care, a long-term priority should be given to promoting mental health. Combating mental illness deserves only a short-term priority.

Mental illness in the mentally retarded, however, is still a challenging subject. Various questions are linked to a lower IQ, like questions about symptomatology, pathogenesis, and diagnostic entities. The specific biological and psychosocial conditions present in the mentally retarded may cause some differences in the clinical picture of mental illness. Diagnostic differentiation is the focus of various investigators in this field.

There is no doubt that mentally retarded individuals, because of the specificities of their development and their psychiatric disorders, deserve specialized mental health care. This care should be incorporated into the existing general care of the mentally retarded and should be linked to the mental health care of the population in general. This care can be seen as complementary to the realization of the idea of normalization.

A model of mental health care has been presented, and the organizational, professional, and other aspects of the care have been discussed.

## References

Achenbach, T. M., & Zigler, E. F. (1968). Cue-learning and problem-learning strategies in normal and retarded children. *Child Devel., 39,* 827–848.

Ballinger, B. R., Ballinger, C. B., Reid, A., & McQueen, E. (1991). The psychiatric symptoms, diagnoses and care needs of 100 mentally handicapped patients. *Br. J. Psychiatr., 158,* 251–254.

Balthazar, E. E., & Stevens, H. A. (1975). The emotionally disturbed mentally retarded. Englewood Cliffs, NJ: Prentice-Hall.

Bouras, N., & Drummond, K. (1989). Community psychiatric services in mental handicap: Six years experiences. London: NVPRD.

Braddock, D. (1992). Community mental health and mental retardation services in the United States. *Am. J. Psychiatr., 149,* 175–183.

Bradl, Ch. (1987). Geistigbehinderte und Psychiatrie. In W. Dreher, Th. Hofmann, & Ch. Bradl (Eds.), *Geistig behnderte zwichen Pädagogik und Psychiatrie.* Bonn: Psychiatrie Verlag.

Bregman, J. D., Deykens, E., Wetson, M., Ort, S., & Leckman, J. (1987). Fragile-x syndrome: Variability of phenotypic expression. *J. Am. Acad. Child Psychiatr., 26(4),* 463–471.

Corbett, J. A. (1985). Mental retardation, psychiatric aspects. In M. Rutter & L. Hersov (Eds.), *Child and adolescent psychiatry: Modern approaches.* London: Basil Blackwell.

Corbett, J. A. (1979). Psychiatric morbidity and mental retardation. In F. E. James & R. P. Snaith (Eds.), *Psychiatric illness and mental handicap* (pp. 11–25). London: Gaskell.

Dosen, A. (1989). Diagnostic and treatment of mental illness in mentally retarded children: A development model. *Child Psychiatr. Human Devel., 20(1),* 73–84.

Dosen, A. (1990). *Psychische en gedragsstoornissen bij zwakzinnigen.* Amsterdam: Boom.

Dosen, A. (1992). The European scene. In N. Bouras (Ed.), *Mental retardation and mental health; A way ahead,* in Press.

Dosen, A., & Menolascino, F. J. (1990). *Depression in the mentally retarded children and adults.* Leiden: Logon.

DSM III (1980). *Diagnostical and Statistical Manual of Mental Disorders* (3rd edition), Am. Psychiat. Ass. Washington, D.C.

Eaton, L. F., & Menolascino, F. J. (1982). Psychiatric disorders in the mentally retarded: Types problems and challenges. *Am. J. Psychiatr. 139,* 10, 1297–1303.

Gaedt, Ch. (1986). *Besonderheiten der Behandelung psychisch gestörter geistig Behinderter mit Neuroleptika.* Neuerkeröder forum Neuerkeröder Anstalten.

Gaedt, Ch., & Gärtner, D. (1990). *Depressive Grundprozesse-Reinszenierung der Selbstentwertung.* Neuerkeröder Forum 4, Neuerkeröder Anstalten.

Gaedt, Ch., Jäkel, D., & Kischkel, W. (1987). Psychotherapie bei geistig Behinderten. In Ch. Gaedt (Ed.), *Psychotherapie bei geistig Behinderten,* Neuerkeröder Forum 2 Neuerkeröder Anstalten.

Gennep, A. van (1990). Treatment of persons with a mental handicap: Trends in orthopedagogy. In A. Dosen, A. van Gennep, & G. Zwanikken (Eds.), *Treatment of mental illness and behavioral disorders in the mentally retarded.* Leiden: Logon.

Gillberg, C., Presson, E., Grufman, N., & Themmer, V. (1986). Psychiatric disorders in mildly and severely mentally retarded urban children and adolescents: Epidemiological aspects. *Br. J. Psychiatr., 149,* 68–74.

Gilson, S. F., & Levitas, A. S. (1987). Psychosocial crisis in the lives of mentally retarded people. *Psychiatr. Aspects Ment. Retard. Rev., 6,* 27–32.

Gualtieri, C. Th. (1988). Mental health of persons with mental retardation. In Stark, J. A., Menolascino F. J., Albarelli, M. H., Gray, Y. C. (Eds.), *Mental retardation and mental health,* New York: Springer, Verlag.

Hucker, S. J., Day, K. A., Gerorge, S., & Roth, M. (1979). Psychosis in mentally handicapped adults. In F. E. James & R. P. Snaith (Eds.), *Psychiatric illness and mental handicap.* London: Gaskell.

JICD-9 (1980). *International Classification of Diseases* (9th revision). U.S. Depart. of Health and Human Services, Washington, D.C.

Ineichen, B. (1984). Prevalence of mental illness among mentally handicapped people (discussion paper). *J. R. Soc. Med., 77,* 761–765.

Jacobson, J. W. (1990). Assessing the prevalence of psychiatric disorders in a developmentaly disabled population. In E. Dibble, D. B. Gray (ed) National Institute of Mental Health, *Assessment of behavioral problems in persons with mental retardation living in the community.* Rockville, MD: Author.

James, F. E., & Snaith, R. P. (1979). *Psychiatric illness and mental handicap.* London: Gaskell.

Levitas, A., & Gilson, S. (1990). Towards the developmental understanding of the impact of mental retardation on assessment and psychopathology. In E. Dibble, D. B. Gray (Ed) *National Institute of Mental Health assessment of behavioral problems in persons with mental retardation living in the community,* Rockville, MD: Author.

Lund, J. (1986). Behavioral symptoms and autistic psychosis in the mentally retarded adult. *Acta Psychiatr. Scand., 71,* 429–436.

Matson, J. L. Barrett R. P. (1982). *Psychopathology in the mentally retarded,* New York: Grunne and Stratton.

Matson, J., & Frame, C. (1986). *Psychopathology among mentally retarded children and adolescents.* Beverly Hills, CA: Sage.

Matson, J. L. (1985). Biosocial theory of psychopathology: A three-by-three factor model. *Appl. Res. Ment. Retard., 6,* 199–227.

Menolascino, F. J. (1970). *Psychiatric approach to the mental retardation.* New York: Basic Books.

Menolascino, F. J. (1977). Challenges in mental retardation: Progressive ideologies and services. New York: Human Sciences Press.

Menolascino, F. J. (1988). Mental illness in the mentally retarded: Diagnostic and treatment issues. In J. A. Stark, Menolascino, F. J., Albarelli, M. H., Gray, V. C. (Ed.). *Mental retardation and mental health. New York: Springer Verlag.*

Menolascino, F. J. (1990). Mental retardation and the risk, nature and types of mental illness. In A. Dosen & F. J. Menolascino (Eds.), *Depression in mentally retarded children and adults.* Leiden: Logon.

Menolascino, R. J. (1991a). Mental illness in persons with mental retardation. *NADD News., 8,* 4.

Menolascino, F. J. (1991b). International conference, Mental retardation and mental health–A way ahead. Canterbury. 1991 (unpublished paper)

Parsons, J. A., May, J. G., Menolascino, F. Y. (1984). The nature and incidence of mental illness in mentally retarded individuals. In F. Y. Menolascino, J. A. Stark (eds.), *Handbook of mental illness in the mentally retarded* New York: Plenum Press.

Realmuto, G. M., Garfinkel, B. D., Tuchman, M., Tsai, M. W., Chang, P., Fisch, R. O., & Shapiro, S. (1986). Psychiatric diagnosis and behavioral characteristics of phenylketonuric children. *J. Nerv. Ment. Dis., 9,* 536–540.

Reid, A. H. (1980). Psychiatric disorders in mentally handicapped children: A clinical and follow-up study. *J. Dent. Defic. Res., 24*(4), 287–198.

Reid, A. H. (1982). *The psychiatry of mental handicap.* London: Basil Blackwell.

Reid, A. H. (1985). Psychiatry and mental handicap. In M. Craft, J. Bicknell, & S. Hollins (Eds.), *Mental handicap: A multi-disciplinary approach.* London: Ballière Tindall.

Reiss, S. (1987). *Reiss Screen Test Manual.* Chicago: University of Illinois.

Reiss, S., & Benson, B. A. (1985). Psychosocial correlates of depression in mentally retarded adults: Minimal social support and stimatization. *Am. J. Ment. Defic., 89,* 331–337.

Reiss, S., Levitan, G. W., & McNally, R. J. (1982). Emotionally disturbed mentally retarded people: An underserved population. *Am. Psychol., 37,* 361–367.

Reukauf, W. (1985). Zur Praxis der Kooperation zwischen Psychotherapeuten und Heilpädagogen aus psychologischer Sicht. *Schweiz. Heilp;auad. Rundsch.,* 7(11), 265–268.

Rutter, M., Grahan, P., & Yule, W. (1970). *A neuropsychiatric study in childhood.* Clinics in Developmental Medicine, *Nos. 35/36. London: Heinemann/Spastics.*

Senatore, V,, Matson, J. L., & Kazdin, A. E. (1985). An inventory to assess psychopathology of mental retarded adults. *Am. J. Ment. Defic., 89,* 459–466.

Sovner, R., & Des Noyers-Hurley, A. (1986). Four factors affecting the diagnosis of psychiatric disorders in mentally retarded persons. *Psychiatr. Aspects Ment. Retard. Rev., 5, 9.*

Sovner, R., & Hurley, A. (1990). Assessment tools which facilitate psychiatric evaluations and treatment. *Habilitative Ment. Health Care News., 9,* 11.

Sovner, R., & Lowry, M. A. (1990). A behavioral methodology for dignosing affective disorders in individuals with mental retardations. *Habiltative Ment. Health Care News., 9,* 7.

Stark, J. A., Menolascino, F. J., Albarelli, M. H., & Gray, V. C. (1988). *Mental retardation and mental health.* New York: Springer Verlag.

Szymanski, L. S. (1977). Psychiatric diagnostic evaluation of mentally retarded individuals. *J. Am. Ac. Child. Psichiat. 16,* 67–87.

Szymanski, L. S. (1988). Integrative approach to diagnosis of mental disorders in retarded persons. In J. A. Stark, F. J. Menolascino, M. H. Albarelli, & V. C. Gray (Eds.), *Mental retardation and mental health.* New York: Springer.

Szymanski, L. S., & Biederman, J. (1984). Depression and anorexia nervosa of persons with Down syndrome. *Am. J. Ment. Defic., 89,* 246–251.

Szymanski, L. S., & Tanguay, P. E. (1980). *Emotional disorders of mentally retarded persons.* Baltimore: University Park Press.

Tanguay, P. E. (1984). Toward a new classification of serious psychopathology in childr. *J. Am. Acad. Child Psychiatr., 23,* 373–384.

International experts' conference on mental health in mental retardation (1992), Veldhoven, in press.

World Health Organization. (1978). International conference on primary health care, Alma-Ata, HFA Leadership M2.

Zigler, E. F., & Spitz, V. (1978). Changing trends in socialization theory and research. *Am. Behav. Sci., 21,* 731–756.

# 2
# Mental Health Care in Persons with Mental Retardation: Past, Present, and Future

*Frank J. Menolascino*
*Mark H. Fleisher*

> If we could first know where we are, and whither we are tending, we could better judge what to do and how to do it.
> —Abraham Lincoln

Individuals with mental retardation are nearly twice as likely as the general population to manifest severe behavioral problems or to experience mental illness. This heightened risk results from a variety of factors, including allied medical, physical, or sensorial difficulties; actual organic problems; the inability of some persons with mental retardation to communicate their feelings; impaired memory and transfer of learning; delayed language development; low self-esteem; and society's basic, and occasionally caustic, nonacceptance of the "differentness" of these individuals. Life events can also exert a negative influence on the behavioral and emotional responses of persons with mental retardation. While maladaptive behavior can be provoked by life events that are far less stressful than caregivers would tend to expect, it is also important to keep in mind that the psychological stress experienced by familial caregivers is greater than that found in the general population (Ghaziuddin, 1988; Whittick, 1988). Collectively, we need to become more sensitized to the at-risk nature of these individuals *and* their families, and to realize that the psychological risks they face are related to a variety of factors, both intrinsic and extrinsic. Just as important, we must understand that any clustering of behaviors that equates with a major mental illness in a person with mental retardation requires active intervention, and that persons with special needs require increased integration and support, not less, if they are to live in sound mental health in a normalized community setting.

18

Since the first of Jean Itard's work with Victor, the Wild Boy of Aveyron (Itard [1801] 1932), mental retardation has provided psychiatry with a special pathway toward the understanding of human existence and its existential concerns. Before the 1960s, however, persons with mental retardation were faced with appalling treatment, including segregation and sterilization. They were entombed by the fallacy of untrainability and untreatability. If they became aggressive or self-injurious because of mental illness, their behaviors were viewed as the result of mental retardation and, thus, unalterable. Long-term abandonment in institutional back wards became the norm for the dually diagnosed, and simplistic solutions to aggravated behaviors revolved around punishment and restraint. Beginning with the U.S. Community Mental Health and Mental Retardation Facilities Construction Act of 1963, however, profound and far-reaching changes have occurred in America involving the integration of these individuals into the mainstreams of family and community life.

## Community Issues for Persons with a Dual Diagnosis

The array of programs and services that are currently being developed in the United States to facilitate the challenge of mental illness in persons with mental retardation include models for the care and treatment of acute psychiatric disorders, specialized education and vocational programs, group homes, and supportive services such as day hospitals, individual and group therapy, and family support programs. Nevertheless, a high number of these individuals remain in state institutions. Often, the dually diagnosed are shuffled from institutions for the mentally retarded to institutions for the mentally ill in a lifelong cycle of nontreatment. Although they have the same rights and privileges as other citizens, when diagnoses are combined their rights are often obscured, the result being interagency conflicts that leave them poorly served by both systems. Perhaps the increasing use of computer-based technology along with innovations in comprehensive expert systems will help prevent these individuals from "falling through the cracks" of our human service systems (Walls, 1989). Currently, however, the best approach is to treat their acute psychiatric needs in psychiatric settings and to meet their long-term needs in community programs with secondary support provided by the mental health system (Fletcher & Menolascino, 1989; Menolascino, 1989).

The reality-based difficulties, for which persons with mental retardation are always more at risk, present us with the continuing professional challenge that we have as complete a grasp on the existential setting of these individuals as possible. For example, deinstitutionalized retarded citizens tend to be ill equipped to understand or adjust to the complexities of life in the community. Whether based on the passive conformity fostered in lare public institutions or the limited capacities of these individuals to manage more demanding sets of psychosocial expectancies, the response is too often the same: bewilderment, poor adjustment, and, at times, major and prolonged emotional turmoil resulting in severe behavioral disorders.

### Community Services

Recognizing the need for decent and responsive programs and services for persons with mental retardation and mental illness, whether institution- or community-based, is one thing, but putting our values into practice can be quite another, as is evident from the unfortunately persistent professional issues that surround the institution-based versus the community-based array of services. Nevertheless, persons who are mentally retarded and mentally ill do often require quite a full range of programs and supports. The two extremes on this continuum are *prevention* and *acute care,* and both are greatly needed. Prevention includes simple, low-cost supports, such as respite care, in-home services, and parent training, which serve to lessen the impact of mental illness or to prevent it entirely. At the other end of the continuum is acute care: short-term inpatient psychiatric care such as we have provided at the University of Nebraska and Affiliated Hospital, for over twenty years. The average length of stay for persons with mental retardation and mental illness who are admitted to our hospital for acute care is two weeks, after which they typically return to their community programs.

In order to serve all individuals in the community, the Eastern Nebraska Community Office of Retardation (ENCOR) was established in 1969; it is a regional program serving a population base of approximately 500,000 (Casey et al., 1985). Within this region, ENCOR serves nearly 1,050 persons with mental retardation, including those with a diagnosis of mental illness. ENCOR has a policy of *zero rejection:* no one can be refused services because of the severity or complexity of his or her allied psychiatric needs. The system currently serves 135 approx. persons with a dual diagnosis (19 percent of the total).

### The Cost of Caring

From its inception, ENCOR has been concerned about the cost–benefit dimensions of its programs. We have discovered that institutionalization costs an inordinate amount of money (its annual costs range from $43,000 to $55,000 per client) and provides precious little benefit. We have also learned that for the provision of residential and full-day programs identical to those provided in an institution, ENCOR's annual costs are less than half: from $12,000 to $20,000 per client. Most significantly, supporting the family rather than supplanting it is the most cost-effective option available, ranging from $4,000 to $8,000 per client per year.

Two significant aspects of the continuing success of ENCOR have been its willing recognition and active treatment of the dual diagnosis and the strong linkages that it has forged between local mental retardation and mental health programs so as to provide for both acute and ongoing care. This relationship is one of the few in our nation in which the developmental model and the medical model have been synthesized in the best interests of the client. In place of the continuing theoretical professional competitiveness that have been known to exist between these two models, we have successfully established a combined treatment–management approach to mental retardation-mental illness. While ENCOR provides basic community services, local psychiatric professionals provide inpatient, transitional, and outpatient follow-up care. Although it would be misleading to suggest that there have not been barriers, disagreements, and failures in this relationship of shared services, the focus has always been on the mobilization of whatever means are necessary to meet the individual needs of the dually diagnosed.

## Smoothing Community Integration

Yet the question remains: Are individuals with mental retardation and mental illness who used to be "protected" in an institutional environment actually better off within communities whose citizens devalue their presence? Although an enhanced quality of life following deinstitutionalization is possible, it is *not* inevitable (Allen, 1989). Certainly the "dumping" of persons into the community in the name of normalization must be utterly rejected, as it only fuels the risk that mental illness will develop. We need to do more in the future to ensure that the community placement of individuals with mental retardation will be smooth, and that supportive structures will be in place and will remain active. Initial and ongoing support is vital to success. Further, preparatory steps within the community can go a long way toward removing the irrational fears that some individuals have regarding the establishment of a group home in their neighborhood, fears that have actually led to vandalism and arson in some cases (Singh & Balasubramaniam, 1989).

Not only is informing and involving new neighbors a successful technique for refuting irrational prejudice and smoothing community integration, the close involvement of the family is vital to the entire process. Booth, Booth, and Simons (1989), in a study of forty-five individuals and their families, found that the majority of the families had not been taken into consideration when the decision was made to relocate their mentally retarded family members, nor had they been consulted when the transfer took place. The irony associated with this ill-conceived practice is that the social workers who made the decisions were basing their actions on what they thought were sound professional principles: Their clients were adults and were to be treated as adults. Considering the vital importance of ongoing social support for persons with mental retardation so as to prevent mental illness from emerging once they have been placed independently in the community, such "professional practices," however well-intentioned, are sadly misguided. In this instance, failure to ensure that relatives would be involved in relocation decisions resulted in breakdowns in the relationships between the families and the professionals, and in upsets or complications in relationships between parents and their adult children.

### New Community Ideologies

Some believe that concern regarding the quality of life of persons with mental retardation and mental illness will actually replace the principle of normalization in the coming decade because of a number of current trends, including the reemergence of the holistic perspective and the increasing importance of client rights and satisfaction (Wiener, 1990). Schalock et al. (1989) have developed a questionnaire to be used as an assessment of the goodness of fit between individuals and their environments. This test has been conducted in the State of Nebraska, and the results thus far indicate a higher quality of life for individuals who live independently and work part time, as well as a lower quality of life for those who live in mental health facilities or with their parents.

Thus, we have moved from warehousing the dually diagnosed in institutional back wards to integrating these citizens into our communities. Although the transition is neither perfect nor complete, the modern array of services available is impressive (see Table 1). We are certainly heading in the right direction, but challenges remain. For example, there is an ongoing debate regarding whether special units should be established for individuals with mental retardation and severe behavioral challenges. While it is true that behavioral disorders continue to constitute a major barrier to community placement (Gardner & Moffatt, 1990), the creation of segregated settings stands in direct contrast to the ideology of normalization. It is our belief that homogeneous groups in recently established dual-diagnosis units need to be dismantled.

**Table 1**
**The Modern Array of Services for Persons with Mental Retardation and Mental Illness**

| | | |
|---|---|---|
| Respite services | Financial Subsidies | Self-care training |
| Recreation | Parent training | Counseling |
| Developmental services | Transportation | Out-of-home care |
| In-home staff support | Health services | |

Although the vast majority of service systems for persons with mental retardation are not saturated with persons with a concurrent mental illness, there will exist a relatively small number of such individuals who will require specialized services (Hoefkens & Allen, 1990; Krisnamurti, 1990). There are no easy answers for meeting the unique requirements of these individuals, but certain of the treatment practices in these settings are unacceptable, including locked doors, locked windows, alarm systems, increased use of punishment, mechanical and chemical restraint, and lack of movement outside the unit itself. We also need to explore options regarding community placement and support for the dually diagnosed who are elderly, individuals who challenge the legal system, those who live in rural areas, and persons who have severe to profound mental retardation and multiple physical handicaps.

## The Complex Dually Diagnosed

It is interesting that the individuals with a dual diagnosis who currently present the most complex sets of clinical challenges have behavioral or personality difficulties as one of their core problems. Although their primitive behaviors often emanate from their extremely restricted use of delayed special sensory and language abilities to deal with the external world, it is instructive that these limitations have direct repercussions on their families, their caregivers, and society in general. These complex individuals tend to exhaust their parents, both physically and emotionally. They also represent a huge dosage of reality to overzealous treatment personnel, who literally cannot seem to wait for or tolerate the typically slow developmental timetables often noted in these patients. Individuals with severe retardation and mental illness forcibly demand a careful rethinking of *where* they should be served. For example, should they be served within their family, a community-based facility, or an institution? Also, *how* should they be served: in full-day programs, in individually tailored partial-day programs, or in daily treatment programs involving recreational rather than developmental or vocational issues? Far from being resolved, these issues of location and the allocation of society's resources remain a challenge to all professionals in both the mental retardation and the mental health fields.

## The Legal Offender

Similar professional challenges surround the issue of attempting to provide modern service for the chronically delinquent adolescent or an adult with mental retardation who displays maladaptive, aggressive, or unacceptable sexual proclivities. Indeed, the difficulties in providing effective treatment are demonstrably marked in this population because the corrections systems have a much weaker base of involvement on ongoing parental support than do the developmental-educational mental-health systems of care. Although the number of mentally retarded adolescent delinquents is numerically not great, they do tend to tie up excessive amounts of staff time, and their behavioral volatility has an ever-present disruptive influence on general programs of service. It is a truism that the adolescent delinquent can and should be treated via the current models of care in adolescent psychiatry, but this truism awaits fuller implementation as increasing numbers of mental health personnel become actively involved. The adult with mental retardation who consistently has legal entanglements secondary to his or her poor impulse control does not, however, tend to respond to mental-health-treatment approaches. The future trend may be to involve these individuals more directly in the correctional systems of care, while providing mental health inputs and mental retardation services on an ongoing consultation basis.

Allied issues regarding the rehabilitative treatment of the offender with mental retardation, particularly the sex offender, continue to concern mental health professionals and public officials alike, especially in light of the recent U.S. Supreme Court decision that persons with mental retardation are not to be granted blanket exemption from the death penalty by virtue of their mental disability. Despite this decision by a conservative Court, it makes little sense to punish any individual beyond his or her capacity to comprehend the crime. It is our experience that the majority of sex offenders with mental retardation are people who do not appreciate the severity of their crime. The developmental histories of these persons are extraordinarily deficient in experiences that might promote the active mastery of their emotional and sexual impulses. Several educational programs for the sex offender with retardation currently exist, and most of these individuals can be easily redirected if presented with appropriate alternatives (Swanson & Garwick, 1990). There are those, however, who do exhibit a pattern of repeated nonconsensual sexual acts and who respond to such education with increased arousal and repetition.

Day (1988) described the results of an inpatient treatment program that used both practical and social education within a token-based economy to rehabilitate twenty sex and property offenders with mental retardation. The average age of these patients was twenty-one years. Over one-half of those involved in the hospital-based program demonstrated an extremely favorable response. As one might expect in a system based, at least in part, on rewards involving the ownership of property, a concept that is seemingly poorly understood by property offenders, the sex offenders emerged with the better prognosis.

## The Elderly

The elderly individual with mental retardation and their mental status and adjustment have been a topic of growing concern in the United States in view of this group's expanding numbers and age-related vulnerability to the development of mental illness. While some persons with mental handicaps begin to show signs of aging at an accelerated rate, such as those with Down syndrome, many age in a manner that parallels that of the general population. A gradual decline in physical abilities, a dampening of sensory acuteness, and an increase in episodes of psychosocial loss are borne by all elderly individuals. However, persons with mental retardation run a greater risk of excessive diminution of their already limited coping abilities and may experience intolerable repercussions from the "normal aging process."

The quality of life of a small number of older individuals (up to the age of sixty) with mental retardation living in the community, as determined by Donegan and Potts (1988), suggests that increased support and encouragement are needed if these individuals are to live out their lives fruitfully, with grace, and without an increased risk of mental illness. This knowledge has become practically axiomatic since the deinstitutionalization movement took hold, and yet it remains particularly true for the elderly who can no longer maintain an active vocational life. It is estimated that approximately 150,000 mentally retarded individuals in the United States alone are currently age sixty and above, but very limited national attention has been given them, and resources that would enhance their quality of life remain scant to nonexistent. It is hoped that our nation will concentrate a bit more keenly on this often disenfranchised—and growing—subpopulation (Menolascino & Potter, 1989a, 1989b).

*The Key Community Challenge*

By far the most important community issue for the dually diagnosed in the 1990s is entitlement to services. Institutions should continue to close down in favor of supported family or familylike alternative settings in the community, and our central challenge will be to ensure that *all* individuals with mental retardation will have the right to basic living, schooling, and vocational opportunities. The current service-delivery system has become bureaucratically driven. Regulations are rigid, and the battle for funding sources has taken precedence over the fulfillment of human needs. Accounting to officials has often become more important than accountability to individuals, and substantive systemic changes are greatly needed. Waiting lists need to be reasonable, and supervision needs to ensure that the services provided will be appropriate to each person's age and developmental requirements. The system should be transformed into one that is client-driven, with financial subsidies dispersed directly to families where appropriate. We see this transformation as a key political struggle in the near future and will emerge from the state level, as outlined in Table 2.

## Table 2
## The Role of the Legislature in Service Delivery Transformation

1. The creation of a separate department of developmental disabilities
2. Regional core programs and services to be distributed by private, nonprofit service providers for case advocacy, information and referral, and local and regional financing and monitoring
3. Mandated core services for all persons with developmental disabilities, with a minimum of bureaucratic entanglements
4. The requirement that case advocates report to the department of developmental disabilities on a periodic basis regarding the individuals served, the quality of the services, and the needs not met
5. State departments that have authority over all programs and services; the flow of federal, state, and local monies; the coordination of regulations; research and development; and monitoring
6. The establishment of regional programs as the conduit for the above, as well as for case advocacy.
7. The establishment of a distributive service-delivery system in which regional programs create a range of service providers
8. The assurance of direct subsidies to all families when the client resides within the home
9. Assurance that the flow of monies will emanate from the regional programs
10. The assurance of financing sufficient for the delivery of core services

## The Differential Diagnosis

Although we have come a long way in translating normalization and deinstitutionalization from ideologies into realities, deinstitutionalized retarded citizens tend to be ill equipped to understand or adjust to the complexities of their new homes in the community. The challenge has today become acute as the population of public institutions for the retarded began to decrease dramatically during the 1980s.

### At-Risk Criteria

The existence of mental retardation in conjunction with a wide range of cognitive, communicative, emotional, physical, and developmental disabilities requires that a delicate balance be struck in the lives of persons with mental retardation, for it does not take a great deal to push these individuals into cognitive and emotional turmoil. In 1970, an excellent contribution was made by Webster, who delineated by level of retardation the most common risk factors for mental illness. For example, persons with *severe* retardation are burdened by their lack of linguistic competence as well as by a veritable host of allied medical, neurological, and special sensory deficits, which can easily leave these individuals unable to reach out or to express their needs and feelings. Disabilities of this nature can result in an ingrained repetition of primitive behaviors (for example, autistic hand movements, skin picking, and body rocking) unless active and ongoing programmatic support is provided. Persons with moderate retardation are at risk mainly because their façade of linguistic integrity is coupled with an inability to process little other than concrete information. They typically have sufficient linguistic ability to communicate their basic needs, but not enough to describe their feelings in any depth. Finally, persons with mild retardation experience societal prejudice, exploitation, and very often a personal knowledge and painful recognition of their own "differentness."

*Diagnostic Assessment*

The relatively recently issued revised third edition of the *Diagnostic and Statistical Manual of Mental Disorders* (DSM III-R; American Psychiatric Association, 1987) by the American Psychiatric Association (APA) includes two major changes that inspired some controversy during the year following its appearance: The symptom of mental retardation was placed in a seondary position on Axis II, and the possible presence of a concurrent mental illness (i.e., the principle reason for patient presentation) became an Axis I assignment. This change in nomenclature has helped to reverse what Reiss (1988) termed "diagnostic overshadowing," referring to those situations in which the syndrome of mental retardation tended to overshadow the presence, or even the possibility, of an accompanying mental illness (Reiss, Levitan, & Szyszko, 1982; Sovner, 1986). Thus, there is an increasing focus today on the descriptive diagnosis, that is, on what is clinically present, rather than on the possible causative mechanisms of the indirect dynamic formulations typical of the recent past. The measurement and recording of bizarre behaviors on an objective descriptive scale are replacing the hypothesized presence of difficulties associated with reality testing. For example, the Self-Report Depression Questionnaire (Reynolds & Baker, 1988), which can be much more rapidly administered than the Hamilton Depression Rating Scale, holds promise as a preliminary screening device for ascertaining the possible presence of remedial depression in patients with mental retardation, a disorder that has been overlooked far too frequently in this population (Dosen & Menolascino, 1990). One need only reflect on the language and communication problems of persons with mental retardation, as well as their limited social skills and lack of social networks, to realize that all of the hallmarks of loneliness may be present in their lives and that they are genuinely at risk of developing an affective disorder. Many of the assessment techniques developed in recent years have intentionally centered on the detection of mental illness in adults with mental retardation. Similar rating scales for children, which would allow the early identification of mental illness, rapid treatment intervention, and appropriate special education so vital to the healthy development of the child with mental retardation, are greatly needed.

While clinicians today seem more comfortable viewing and describing multiple symptom phenomena, the challenge of diagnosing a special-needs person, who may well display six to eight major presenting symptoms, can be bewildering. Nevertheless, the evolving postures of descriptive diagnostic clarification will continue to clear away the aura of bewilderment that has clouded mental health professionals' vision of the dually diagnosed person in the past. Included in this vision are the many professional myths regarding the behavior of persons with mental retardation, which lead to psychotoxic treatment interventions or rigid prognostic expectations. For example, many professionals were trained to believe (or had fixed their personal views before ever starting advanced training) that, in contrast to the norm, individuals with mental retardation displayed qualitative or quantitative differences in their expression of the signs and symptoms of mental illness. A clear instance of this excessive focus on extraneous factors has commonly been noted in the stereotypical assumption that persons with Down syndrome were inevitably charming, friendly, affable, given to mimicry, and devoid of personality conflicts. Unfortunately, this particular behavioral stereotype has caused generations of professionals to be blind to what was directly before them, and to concentrate instead on the traditional interpretation of expected behaviors. An article by Lund (1988) takes its place in this long debate about whether persons with Down syndrome are or are not more prone to psychiatric disorders than those with etiologically disparate conditions. Lund's findings strongly suggest specific psychopathological vulnerability in individuals with Down syndrome.

## Behavioral Parameters

There are three broad types of behaviors that most frequently confront the psychiatrist working with persons who are mentally retarded. *Primitive* behaviors, such as finger flicking, arm waving, and self-injury, are frequently seen in individuals with severe retardation and become particularly prominent if early intevention is not provided. If the person is simply tossed into an environment with no supports, these primitive behaviors increase in severity and persist until they virtually consume the individual's whole being. *Atypical* behaviors are indistinct clusters of behavioral signs or symptoms, rather than syndromes (or prodromes) of psychosis. They are often akin to slowly solidifying personality disorders and may present clinically as adjustment disorders. *Abnormal* behaviors, such as bizarreness of manner, gesture, and posture of the display of deviant affective expression, encompass the entire range of DSM-III-R diagnoses. Our understanding of these behaviors is becoming increasingly astute, particularly as we continue to explore those techniques that will enable us to diagnose mental illness with greater specificity in persons with severe retardation.

Table 3 illustrates the findings we accept from our repeated professional experiences in diagnosing several psychiatric disorders in individuals with severe mental retardation who are essentially nonverbal. The diagnostic parameters shown in this table highlight the recent attention that has been given to the formulation of objective criteria for diagnosing complex persons with mental retardation. In our examination of over 2,450 patients, schizophrenia has been the most frequent diagnosis, followed by organic brain disorder with psychosis. However, with the development of more sensitive and objective diagnostic procedures, the profile of diagnostic categories is beginning to shift. We also recognize that many clinicians would not diagnose schizophrenia or other disorders in nonverbal severely retarded individuals.

## Future Directions in Diagnosis

In the future, we should arrive at a deeper understanding of the signs and symptoms of mental illness in individuals with severe levels of mental retardation. This understanding will involve ongoing study of the primitive and atypical behaviors seen in nonverbal persons. More comprehensive examinations of the interactional nature of mental illness and mental retardation also need to be pursued; Axis IV and V dimensions in the DSM-III-R are often preludes to future *transitional* diagnoses, such as adjustment disorders and brief reactive psychoses.

In addition, we must strive for increased and varied analyses of the role of mental illness in individuals with self-injurious behaviors. Researchers need to take a closer look at the environmental and psychosocial dimensions of the lives of vulnerable individuals: Are challenging behaviors "driven" or "volitional"? If truly volitional components exist, self-training protocols should be initiated. A narrowing of clusters of symptoms (for example, the DSM-III-R atypical versus descriptive diagnosis) would prove extremely beneficial in differential diagnoses. Finally, research should move forward in behavioral psychopharmacology, genetics, and distinct chronological age groupings, which may reveal different diagnostic spectrums of mental illness in persons with mental retardation. The rapid growth of the multidisciplinary concept in the field of mental health and mental retardation, which has brought together professionals with a wide range of talents and skills, should help us to further clarify these complex diagnostic challenges.

The dual diagnosis of mental illness and mental retardation does pose major diagnostic difficulties. For example, the differential diagnostic issues involved in separating the social-adaptive behavioral indices of an individual with moderate retardation from his or her concurrent problems in interpersonal transactions are extremely challenging. Yet, a resolution of these difficulties clarifies the treatment considerations, such as *what* technique, appropriate for *which* person, with what *specific* problems in living will most effectively restabilize his or her mental health status.

Table 3
Diagnostic Criteria for Three Types of Mental Illness in Persons with
Mental Retardation

MAJOR DEPRESSION (Sovner, 1986)
  I.  A disturbance of mood characterized by sadness, withdrawal, agitation
  II. Any 4 of the following 9 symptoms (only 3 symptoms needed if there is a positive
      history of depression in a first-degree relative):
          change in sleep patterns
          change in appetite and/or weight
          onset or increase in the severity of self-injurious behavior
          apathy
          psychomotor retardation
          loss of daily living skills (e.g., onset of urinary incontinence)
          catagonic stupor and/or rigidity
          spontaneous crying
          fearfulness

MANIA (Sovner, 1986)
  I.  A disturbance of mood characterized by elation, irritability, or excitability
  II. Any 4 of the following 7 symptoms (only 3 symptoms needed if there is a postive history
      of bipolar disorder in a first-degree relative):
          decreased sleep
          overactivity
          biphasic course
          onset or increase in severity of distractibility
          onset or increase in severity of aggressiveness
          onset or increase in severity of noncompliance
          increase in rate or frequency of verbalizations

SCHIZOPHRENIA (Menolascino, 1990)
  I.  A disturbance of thought and feeling characterized by personality disorganization,
      bizarre behaviors, and social/adaptive regression
  II. Any 5 of the following 8 symptoms (only 4 symptoms needed if there is a positive
      history of schizophrenia in a first-degree relative):
          flat, blunted, or incongruous affect
          marked personal/interpersonal withdrawal
          regression in self-care and social and work skills
          behavior indicating hallucinations
          prodrome of marked isolation, withdrawal, or anergia
          marked suspicion or paranoia
          the ruling out of schizoaffective disorder, unipolar depression, and bipolar
              affective disturbance.
          duration of 6 months (R/O reactive psychosis)

# The Treatment and Management of the Dually Diagnosed

A particularly strong antidote to the past and ongoing overreliance on the
stereotype of mental retardation noted above has been the behavioral analysis approach and its direct treatment aspect: behavior modification. One can
treat only what is *present,* whether in a patient who is mentally retarded and
mentally ill, or in one who is nonretarded and mentally ill. Although psy-

choanalysts would scoff at such a simplistic view of human behavior, they would have to concede that behavioral improvement is what most conflicted or mentally ill persons are requesting today, and that the psychoanalytical goal of reeducation of the personality is increasingly viewed as a rare luxury, both in its attainment and in terms of patient interest. In other words, most people want to obtain prompt relief of their disturbed feelings and are not overly interested in knowing the symbolic basis of them. The professional posture of using a wide variety of direct treatment approaches to described behaviors specifically will be more actively extended into the episodes of mental illness in the lives of persons with mental retardation.

## Psychopharmacology

The exposure of the fraudulent work of Stephen E. Breuning, who generated nearly one-third of the literature on psychopharmacology for persons with mental retardation during the last several years (Sprague, 1987; Garfield & Welljams-Dorof, 1990), has brought a new vigor to this topic. Recently published books (Gadow & Poling, 1988; Ratey, 1991) and articles (Langee, 1989; Ratey et al., 1989; Reudrich, Grush, & Wilson, 1990; Sovner, 1989; Thinn, Clarke, & Corbett, 1990), as well as a series of national workshops, have kept the interest in this topic well elevated, and principled research is moving forward.

A major challenge across our nation in the recent past has been to decrease the use of psychotropic medications as mere chemical restraints for singular behaviors, such as aggression, and as cheap substitutes for enhanced staffing or appropriate programs. For example, the average use of psychoactive medications in the State of Nebraska has historically been quite high (over 60 percent) in both institutional and community settings. However, the use of these medications has decreased substantially because of improved diagnostic procedures, an insistence that drugs be linked to specific DSM-III-R diagnostic entities, the creation of markedly improved full-day programs, and the threat of federal lawsuits. Today, in ENCOR's community programs, no psychoactive medications can be administered without a formal psychiatric diagnosis and an assurance that developmental treatment will be active and concurrent. The percentage of psychoactive drug use in ENCOR today is about 9 percent, which is an impressive percentage in view of the total number of persons with mental retardation and mental illness served.

Our primary purpose in administering any psychoactive medication should be to assist the patient in moving forward toward meaningful interpersonal interactions within the least restrictive of physical settings—an aim that simply cannot be attained if the patient remains in a condition of semi-sedation. Our complex retarded citizens truly require remediation over time and not the "quick fix" of crisis-to-crisis phamacological intervention.

Debates regarding short- and long-term treatment highlight certain associated dangers, such as incorrect diagnoses and poor monitoring of treatment. As the dually diagnosed are cared for over time, the clinician must rely increasingly on psychosocial and educational-vocational approaches to long-term personality change.

With more precise diagnostic procedures being developed, ranging from clinical checklists to neuroimaging procedures, the use of psychoactive medication will be increasingly targeted to specific biochemical dysfunctions. Thus the use of pharmacological interventions will have more specific targets and more exact monitoring, and the time allowed for their remedial effects will be shortened. The improvement and expansion of community services for persons with mental retardation will also serve as preventive mechanisms and will eventually decrease psychosocial pharmacological use. Improved intervention procedures will have a similar impact. We predict, therefore, that the use of psychoactive medication may decline to between 5 and 10 percent as the above trends continue.

Currently, publications concerning the evolving psychopharmacology for persons with mental retardation and mental illness illustrate a renewed interest in the single-case-study approach. As a result, the need for increased research interaction, a national pooling of study results, and the rapid dissemination of novel treatment approaches remains great.

## Behavioral Modification Techniques

There has been continuing professional argument concerning the need for aversive behavioral-modification techniques in treating persons with mental retardation and mental illness. Viewpoints are polarized, and the argument involving "life-and-death behavioral change" is often used to justify harsh and aversive treatment approaches (LaVigna & Donnellan, 1986; Matson & DiLorenzo, 1984; Menolascino & Stark, 1984). As psychiatry more strongly embraces the biopsychosocial model, it has become increasingly clear that the complexity of diagnostic entities *must* be matched by equally complex and/or definitive treatment inteventions. Yet severe behavioral challenges in persons with mental retardation and mental illness may bring out the best as well as the worst in those who provide them with care. In certain instances, "behavioral intevention" is nothing more than a euphemism for what would be objectively evaluated by global human-rights groups as torture. Other methods, such as Gentle Teaching (McGee et al., 1987) maintain the dignity of the individual. Yet professionals who use non-aversive techniques have yet to report on a client who may have failed to respond to reciprocal human warmth and solidarity.

Self-injurious and disruptive behaviors challenge us all, and the debate involving "aversive" and "nonaversive" interventions is far from over. There have recently been heated debates concerning the acceptability of aversive therapeutic interventions based on an analysis of their scientific and ideological paradigms (Guess, Turnball, & Helmstetter, 1990; Mulick, 1990a, 1990b), as well as concerning the feasibility of prohibiting aversive procedures entirely (Evans & Meyer, 1990; Horner et al., 1990a, 1990b). A critical issue here is whether such point–counterpoint disagreements have seriously stalled the development and implementation of research approaches to helping persons with mental retardation and self-injurious behaviors.

Just what "aversive procedures" actually consist of constitutes yet another facet of this debate. Is physical pain included in the definition? Is emotional pain? Does either aspect escape inclusion in the definition but become obvious in practice? Are intrusive interventions occasionally necessary? How are guidelines to be established? The arguments continue unabated, and the challenges are assessed from a variety of viewpoints since the fundamental philosophy of the caregiver or the institution does make a difference in whether a particular intervention is viewed as helpful or heinous (Tarnowski, Mulick, & Rasnake, 1990). Rather than a clinging to one antithetical position or the other, it is being increasingly voiced that a *balanced* treatment approach is what is needed most.

## Long-Term Treatment Issues

The home and work environments in which individuals with mental retardation are involved, often against a backdrop of complicated social interactions, may become an additional challenge in terms of the development of a concurrent mental illness. As longevity increases, one must also consider the implications of sexual drives, courtship, marriage, and childbearing juxtaposed to the hostility often encountered when these desires are expressed. For example, in 1940, the mortality rate of individuals with Down syndrome at five years of age was 60 percent. Today, the rate has plummeted to 10 percent, although transcultural and geographical factors continue to affect the prognosis of this biologically based disorder (Gompertz, 1990). The impact that this declining mortality rate has and will continue to have on our communities and families, as well as on the individuals with Down syndrome themselves, is worthy of considerable thought. Treatment options, such as individual or group therapy, although readily available to the general public, are often still denied to individuals with mental handicaps. Increasing numbers of middle-aged individuals with mental retardation will require unique consideration and service. Only if sensitive and active mental health clinics are available can these individuals receive appropriate care.

Although local mental-health-treatment resources, such as the community mental-health center and private mental-health practitioners, come readily to mind, a more energetic outreach will be needed in the future. Considering the demonstrated difficulties associated with motivating nonre-

tarded citizens with mental illness to use these community resources, the dually diagnosed individual is in need of a far more direct linkage. We foresee
an increase in mobile mental-health services to provide service in group
homes or group therapy at sheltered places of employment. We also foresee
an enhanced focus on the training of mental retardation personnel in mental-health-treatment techniques so that they can use their new skills as an
ongoing part of their daily work in educational, training, and residential facilities. Thus, the direct and indirect components of modern mental-health-
consultation practice can and should be accomplished concurrently.

## Health and Disease

Another important factor in both the diagnosis and the treatment of individuals with mental retardation is the range of medical disorders found in
this population. In a study conducted at the University of Nebraska a number of years ago, nearly 48 percent of the patients referred to our dual-diagnosis unit had an associated medical disorder that had been incorrectly
diagnosed in the past. A major medical disorder, such as a seizure disorder,
exacerbates the already complex coexistence of mental retardation and mental illness, as the postseizure confusion state makes the individual additionally incapable of interpersonal transactions.

The occurrence of cancer in persons with mental retardation remains
a serious concern in itself, as well as in terms of its relationship to depression in the dually diagnosed. Cancer in these patients is difficult to detect
and difficult to manage, primarily because of communication deficits, and
the number of patients who die of cancer of the gastrointestinal tract continues to rise, particularly in women (Jancar, 1990). Beyond the general
health challenges that have been with us for decades, new ones, such as
HIV infection, are emerging. The rights of both clients and caretakes who
are exposed to individuals infected with HIV have been argued in the
courts of law and in local clinics. How does a philosophy of the "least-re-
strictive" environment mesh with ethical decision making when one is
dealing with an infectious and lethal disease? Although the exact guidelines
remain vague, policies have been suggested in the literature for dealing
with the remote possibility of transmission in special populations (Kastner,
et al., 1990).

## Future Trends

The care and treatment of the dually diagnosed has been identified as a primary national concern by the President's Committee on Mental Retardation
(Stark et al., 1988). As we move forward in our continuous search for more

responsive and creative ways to help persons with mental retardation–mental illness and their families, probably one of the most fascinating and promising technologies that will aid us is positron emission tomography (PET).

## Positron Emission Tomography

For psychiatric applications in general, a PET scan creates both quantitative and pictorial descriptions of cerebral blood flow and volume as well as precise measurements of the metabolic extraction and consumption of such key biochemicals as oxygen and glucose. PET also provides highly sensitive and accurate measurements of the density of the brain's various neurotransmitters, imbalances of which are implicated in schizophrenia. For example, PET has already revealed that when dopamine receptors are blocked, hallucinations and delusions tend to be controlled; this finding verifies the long-standing clinical hypothesis that an excess of D2 receptors constitutes a major foundation of this psychosis (Jacobson, 1989).

Currently, there is scant evidence that this breakthrough technology is being used to explore the many and varied dimensions of the dual diagnosis. However, at the Creighton/Nebraska Department of Psychiatry, the PET scan will form an intricate part of our diagnoses, treatment and monitoring procedures, and research endeavors. It is hoped that within the next decade, this technology will be available and of benefit to all who serve persons with a dual diagnosis. At present, several researchers are using PET technology to explore the syndrome of mental retardation. For example, Horwitz et al. (1990) found that young adults with Down syndrome, when compared with normal controls, had smaller correlations of region pairs within and between the frontal and parietal lobes. The thalamus also had smaller correlations with the temporal and occipital regions in the Down syndrome group. These results suggest that Down syndrome is accompanied by a functional disruption of the neural circuits associated with directed attention.

Epilepsy is often a concomitant disorder in the dually diagnosed. Because cerebral dysfunction in epilepsy is rarely attended by structural abnormalities detectable by traditional anatomical scans, remedial surgery is infrequently performed, and even excellent medical management may fail to relieve the seizures. Many potential candidates for surgery would benefit greatly if the precise site in which their seizures originate could be clearly identified. Without recourse to invasive exploration, the PET scan's depiction of regional glucose and oxygen utilization pinpoints the exact location of lesions and clearly identifies those individuals most appropriate for surgery, as well as those for whom surgery would be inappropriate (Wagner, 1988). Chugani et al. (1990) found that PET findings were superior to radiological findings in identifying unsuspected focal cortical dysplasia in infants with cryptogenic spasms.

Further, anatomical imaging technologies have never succeeded in clearly identifying the presence, the exact extent, or the progress of Alzheimer's disease or the related dementias. Yet PET differentiates among Alzheimer's disease and some of the other forms of dementia and serves as an invaluable aid in the diagnosis of degenerative disease such as Huntington's disease, Parkinson's disease, normal pressure hydrocephalus, subdural hematoma, pernicious anemia, multi-infarct dementia, Wilson's disease, and Jacob-Creutzfeldt disease (Hawkins, 1986). Cutler (1986) compared the cerebral metabolism in Alzheimer's disease (AD) and Down syndrome (DS) subjects and found that brain metabolism remained invariant in healthy subjects twenty-one to eighty-three years of age. It remained unchanged in the mild to moderate AD group but was significantly reduced throughout the brain in the late-severe AD group. Marked elevations in young adult DS individuals, age-related declines in middle-aged DS subjects, and further declines in demented DS individuals were also observed. Schapiro et al. (1990) suspected that DS adults over the age of forty-five have reduced parietal and temporal glucose metabolism in comparison with younger DS adults, and they found that the subjects studied did not have alterations in either regional or global cerebral glucose metabolism before the age at which the neuropathological changes in AD had been reported to occur.

PET's utility is currently being expanded to include the diagnosis and treatment of posttraumatic stress disorder, the affective disorders, anxiety disorders (e.g., panic and obsessive-compulsive disorders), language acquisition disorders, and the attention-deficit disorders of childhood (Lou et al., 1989; Martinot & Peron-Magnon, 1987; Reiman, 1988). In addition, since disruptions in cerebral blood flow and glucose metabolism can be detected before cognitive disturbances clearly appear, PET's potential as an effective screening and assessment device for certain diseases of the brain is cause for optimism regarding baseline studies that will compare new and earlier treatment interventions.

## Summary

Since the early 1960s, major advances have been made in the diagnosis and treatment of mental illness in persons with mental retardation. Historically, the diagnostic procedures for this population often resulted in ambiguous syndromes that recognized descriptive clusters of atypical or abnormal behaviors but failed to achieve specific psychiatric diagnoses. The psychiatrist's use of diagnoses such as "early infantile autism," "organic brain syndrome with psychotic reaction," or "childhood schizophrenia" offered little help to individuals with complex problems. As increasing professional attention to specific diagnostic criteria has emerged, there has been a concurrent development in treatment rationales, the use of more specific intervention procedures, and significant changes in treatment sites. Likewise, a more concentrated focus on the biological, psychological, and social dimensions of mental retardation has inspired a closer analysis of the specific descriptors in the DSM-III-R and other diagnostic systems.

Concurrently with these changes, strong parental advocacy efforts for integrated treatment and service-delivery systems, most notably regarding in-home support and community-based programs, have made substantial headway. The consequent rise of community-based educational, vocational, and residential programs has also increased family and community expectations, and active monitoring by local advocacy groups has resulted in major changes in both the types and the locations of these services. As community-based programs increasingly become the option of choice, four subpopulations will present substantial challenges to the psychiatrist, including the mentally retarded offender and the elderly with mental retardation. Each of these subpopulations requires sensitive diagnostic procedures, the active involvement of parents and significant others in the treatment process, and adaptable programs and services.

The care and treatment of persons with mental retardation require that some basic questions be asked; the answers bring insight to the psychiatrist. The emotional vulnerability of this population, as a group, is most evident. Their relative lack of language, their difficulty in expressing their needs, and their lowered defense mechanisms make them more at risk of developing a mental illness than persons who are not mentally retarded. By examining the nature and types of psychiatric illnesses seen in persons with mental retardation, we can deepen our diagnostic insight and expand our treatment practices by adapting some of our traditional procedures to meet their unique needs. As mental health professionals, we must enhance our understanding of the at-risk nature of mental retardation, develop a thorough working knowledge of the nature and types of mental illness in persons with mental retardation, and examine our fundamental treatment goals and the range of our treatment techniques.

The future is likely to bring even greater challenges and insights. The use of positron emission tomography (PET) to confirm the mind–brain interactions that are at the very core of mental retardation offers remarkable promise concerning objective diagnostic clarification and individualized treatment intervention. Research efforts are rapidly progressing into the area of secondary prevention, that is, the reversal and even the "cure" of mental retardation. As the biochemical individuality of a growing number of the major psychiatric disorders is being illuminated, little doubt can remain that the traditional subtleties of clinical psychiatry are moving rapidly into the scientific arena of objective verification.

# References

Allen, D. (1989). The effects of deinstitutionalization on people with mental handicaps: A review. *Ment. Handicap Res., 2,* 18–37.

American Psychiatric Association. (1987). *Diagnostic and statistical Manual (3rd ed., rev.;* (DSM-III-R). Washington, DC: Author.

Booth, T., Booth, W., & Simons, K. (1989). Clients and partners: The role of families in relocating people from mental handicap hospitals and hostels. *Br. J. Ment. Subnorm., 35,* 40–49.

Casey, K., McGee, J., Stark, J., & Menolascino, F. J. (1985). *A community-based system for the mentally retarded: The ENCOR experience.* Lincoln: University of Nebraska Press.

Chugani, H. T., Shields, W., Shewnon, D., Olson, D., Phelps, M., & Peacock, W. (1990). Infantile spasms: PET identifies focal cortical dysgenesis in cryptogenic cases for surgical treatment. *Ann. Neurol., 27,* 406–413.

Cutler, N. R. (1986). Cerebral metabolism as measured with PET and 18F 2-deoxy-D-glucose: healthy aging, Alzheimer's disease and Down syndrome. *Prog. Neurophychopharacol. Biol. Psychiatr., 10,* 309–321.

Day, K. (1988). A hospital-based treatment programme for male mentally handicapped offenders. *Br. J. Psychiatr., 153,* 635–644.

Donegan, C., & Potts, M. (1988). People with mental handicap living alone in the community: A pilot study of their quality of life. *Br. J. Ment. Subnorm., 34,* 10–22.

Dosen, A. & Menolascino, F. J. (1990). *Depression in mentally retarded children and adults.* Leiden, Netherlands: Logon.

Evans, I. A., & Meyer, L. H. (1990). Toward a science in support of meaningful outcomes: A response to Horner et al. *J. Assn. Ser. Handicap., 15,* 133–135.

Fletcher, R., & Menolascino, F. J. (1989). *Mental retardation and mental illness: Assessment, treatment, and service for the dually diagnosed.* Lexington, MA: Lexington Books.

Gadow, K. D., & Poling, A. G. (1988). *Pharmacotherapy and Mental Retardation.* Boston: Little, Brown.

Gardner, W. I., & Moffatt, C. W. (1990). Aggressive behavior: Definition, assessment, treatment. *Int. Rev. Psychiatr., 2,* 91–100.

Garfield, E., & Welljams-Dorof, A. (1990). The impact of fraudulent research on the scientific literature. The Stephen E. Breuning case. *JAMA, 9;* 263 (10):1424–6; 26; 264(24):3145–6.

Ghaziuddin, M. (1988). Behavioural disorder in the mentally handicapped: The role of life events. *Br. J. Psychiatr., 152,* 683–686.

Gompertz, J. (1990). Improving communication in Down syndrome. *Lancet, 335,* 1278.

Guess, D., Turnball, H., & Helmstetter, E. (1990). Science, paradigms, and values: A response to Mulick. *Am. J. Ment. Regard., 95,* 157–163.

Hawkins, R. A. (1986, August). Diagnosis and management merge in clinical PET. *Diagn. Imaging,* pp. 106–114.

Hoefkens, A. & Allen, D. (1990). Evaluation of a special behavior unit for people with mental handicaps and challenging behavior. *J. Ment. Defic. Res., 34,* 213–228.

Horner, R. H., Dunlap G., Koegel, R. L. Carr, E. G., Sailor, W., & Anderson J. (1990a). In support of integration for people with severe problem behaviors: A response to four commentaries. *J., 15*, 145–147.

Horner, R. H., Dunlap, G., Koegel, R. L., Carr, E. G., Sailor, W., & Anderson, J. (1990b). Toward a technology of "nonaversive" behavioral support. *J., 15*, 125–132.

Horwitz, B., Schapiro, M., Grady, C., & Rapoport, S. (1990). Cerebral metabolic pattern in young adult Down's syndrome subjects: Altered intercorrelations between regional rate of glucose utilization. *J. Ment. Defic. Res., 34*, 237–252.

Itard, J. (1932). *The wild boy of Aveyron.* (Original title: *De l'education d'un homme sauvage,* 1801). New York: Century Press.

Jacobson, H. G. (1989). Positron emission tomography—A new approach to brain chemistry. *J. Am. Med. Assoc., 260*(18), 2704–2710.

Jancar, J. (1990). Cancer and mental handicap: a further study (1976–85). *Br. J. Psychiatr., 156*, 531–533.

Kastner, T., DeLotto, P., Scagnelli, B., & Testa, W. R. (1990). Proposed guidelines for agencies serving persons with developmental disabilities and HIV infection. *Ment. Retard., 28*, 139–145.

Krishnamurti, D. (1990). Evaluation of special behavior unit for people with mental handicaps and challenging behavior: A riposte. *J. Ment. Defic. Res., 34*, 229–231.

Langee, H. R. (1989). Retrospective study of mentally retarded patients with behavioral disorders who were treated with carbamazepine. *Am. J. Ment. Retard., 93*, 640–643.

LaVigna, R., & Donnellan, P. (1986). *Alternatives to punishment: Solving behavior problems with non-aversive strategies.* Boston: Irvington.

Lou, H., Henriksen, L., Bruhn, P., Borner, H., & Nielsen, J. (1989). Striatal dysfunction in attention deficit and hyperkinetic disorder. *Arch. Neurol., 46*, 48–52.

Lund, J. (1988). Psychiatric aspects of Down's syndrome. *Acta Psychiatr. Scand., 78*, 369–374.

Martinot, J. L., & Peron-Magnon, P. (1987). Cerebral imaging and depressive disorder. *Encephale, 13*, 273–277.

Matson, R., & DiLorenzo, F. (1984). *Punishment and its alternatives: A new perspective for behavior modification.* New York: Springer-Verlag.

McGee, J., & Menolascino, F. J. (1991). *Beyond gentle teaching.* New York: Plenum Press.

McGee, J., Menolascino, F., Hobbs, D., & Menousek, P. (1987). *Gentle teaching: A non-aversive approach to helping persons with mental retardation.* New York: Human Sciences Press.

Menolascino, F. J. (1989). Model services for treatment/management of the mentally retarded-mentally ill. *Com. Ment. Health, J., 25*, 145–155.

Menolascino, F. J., & Potter, J. (1989a). Delivery of services in rural settings to the elderly mentally retarded-mentally ill. *Int. J. Aging Hum. Dey, 28*, 261–275.

Menolascino, F. J., & Potter, J. (1989b). Mental illness in the elderly mentally retarded. *J. Appl. Gerontol., 8*, 192–202.

Menolascino, F. J., & Stark, J. (1984). *Handbook of mental illness in the mentally retarded.* New York: Plenum Press.

Mulick, J. A. (1990a). Ideology and punishment reconsidered. *Am. J. Ment. Retard.,* *95,* 173–181.

Mulick, J. A. (1990b). The ideology and science of punishment in mental retardation. *Am. J. Ment. Retard., 95,* 142–156.

Ratey, J. J. (1991). *Mental retardation: Developing pharmacotherapies.* Progress in Psychiatry Series. Washington, DC: American Psychiatric Association.

Ratey, J. J., Sovner, R., Mikkelsen, E., & Chmielkinski, H. E. (1989). Bupirone therapy for maladaptive behavior and anxiety in developmentally disabled persons. *Clin. Psychiatr., 50,* 382–384.

Reiman, E. M. (1988). The quest to establish the neural substrates of anxiety. *Psychiatr. Clin. North. Am., 11,* 295–307.

Reiss, S. (1988). Dual diagnosis in the United States. *Aus. N.Z. J. Psychiatr., 14,* 43–48.

Reiss, S., Levitan, G., & Szyszko, J. (1982). Emotional disturbance and mental retardation: Diagnostic overshadowing. *Am. J. Ment. Defic., 86,* 567–574.

Reynolds, W. M., & Baker, J. A. (1988). Assessment of depression in persons with mental retardation. *Am. J. Ment. Retard., 93,* 93–103.

Reudrich, S. L., Grush, L., & Wilson, J. (1990). Beta adrenergic blocking medications for aggressive or self-injurious retarded persons. *Am. J. Ment. Retard., 95,* 110–119.

Schalock, R., Keith, K., Hoffman, K., & Karan, O. (1989). Quality of life: Its measurement and use. *Ment. Regard., 27,* 25–31.

Schapiro, M., Grady, C., Kusar, A., Herscovitch, P., Haxby, J., Moore, A., White, B., Friedland, R., & Rapoport, S. (1990). Regional cerebral glucose metabolism in normal young adults with Downs syndrome. *J. Cereb. Blood Flow Metab., 10,* 199–206.

Singh, T., & Balasubramaniam, S. (1989). Hospital to community: A pilot rehabilitation project for elderly mentally retarded. *J. Ment. Defic. Res., 33,* 25–29.

Sovner, R. (1986). Limiting factors in the use of DSM-III criteria with mentally ill/mentally retarded persons. *Psychopharm. Bull., 22,* 1055–1060.

Sovner, R. (1989). The use of valproate in the treatment of mentally retarded persons with typical and atypical bipolar disorders. *J. Clin. Psychiatr., 50* (3, Suppl.) 40–43.

Sprague, R. L. (1987). Quoted in *Time,* June 1, p. 59.

Stark, J., Menolascino, F. J., Albarelli, M. H., & Gray, V. (1988). *Mental retardation and mental illness: Classification, diagnosis, treatment, services.* New York: Springer-Verlag.

Swanson, C. K., & Garwick, G. B. (1990). Treatment for low-functioning sex offenders: Group therapy and interagency coordination. *Ment. Retard., 28,* 155–161.

Tarnowski, K. J., Mulick, J., & Rasnake, L. (1990). Acceptability of behavioral interventions for self-injurious behavior: Replication and interinstitutional comparison. *Am. J. Ment. Retard., 95,* 182–187.

Thinn, K., Clarke, D. J., & Corbett, J. A. (1990). Psychotropic drugs and mental retardation: A comparison of psychoactive drug use before and after discharge from hospital to community. *J. Ment. Defic. Res., 34,* 397–407.

Wagner, H. N. (1988). The society of Nuclear Medicine 35th Annual Meeting: Scientific highlight 1988: The future is now. *J. Nucl. Med., 29,* 1329–1335.

Walls, R. (1989). Expert systems for human service programs. *Am. J. Ment. Retard.*, *94*, 152–160.

Webster, T. G. (1970). Unique aspects of emotional development in mentally retarded children. In F. J. Menolascino (Ed.), *Psychiatric approaches to mental retardation*. New York: Basic Books.

Whittick, J. E. (1988). Dementia and mental handicap: Emotional distress in carers. *Br. J. Clin. Psychol.*, *27*, 167–172.

Wiener, R. (1990). Looking for quality. *Ment. Handicap, 18,* 166–168.

# Part II
# Diagnosis and Assessment

In the next seven chapters are discussed the most challenging issues in the contemporary diagnosis of the psychiatric and behavioral disorders. The diagnostic categories include both those most frequently observed, like the behavioral disorders and depression, and many disputable syndromes, like schizophrenia and the personality disorders.

Distinguished scientists from several countries give a survey of the current status of the topic, as well as their own views of it. Gardner and Graeber (Chapter 3) take an interesting approach to the behavioral disorders, accentuating an integrative perspective on the problem. Such an approach is very welcome at this moment, not only because of its usefulnes in day-to-day practice, but also because it accentuates the multidisciplinary and multidimensional model of mental health care.

Reid (Chapter 5) discusses the very old but still controversial subject of schizophrenia in the mentally retarded. It is interesting that the prevalence of this disorder varies from country to country. For example, in the United States, schizophrenia ranks first among psychiatric disorders (see Menolascino and Fleisher, Chapter 2 of this book), while in the United Kingdom, hardly any difference is reported in its occurrence among the retarded and among the nonretarded. Probably the criteria used for establishing the diagnosis are different. Reid's assessment of the criteria undoubtedly deserves broader discussion by international experts.

Depression and bipolar disorder (Dosen and Gielen, Chapter 4; Ruedrick, Chapter 6) are currently a focus of diagnosticians in the field of mental retardation. Recognizing the symptoms and establishing the diagnosis are as important as discovering the roots and mechanisms by which the disorder emerges and is maintained, and the diagnostician needs experience and specific knowledge of the psychopathology of the mentally retarded. The progress being made in the assessment of these disorders is encouraging.

Personality disorders (Dana, Chapter 7) and dementia (Harper, Chapter 9) have recently attracted the attention of professionals. The assessment and diagnostics of these disorders are mediocre at the moment. The advances made in investigations in this area, however, are promising.

Self-injurious behavior in the mentally retarded (Dosen, Chapter 8) remains little understood. The various hypotheses concerning the onset and maintenance of this behavior tend to give an oversimplified explanation of this very complex phenomenon. The integrative look offered here gives no simple answers; it presents a broad starting point from which further investigations in this area may take off.

It was difficult to avoid some overlap in these chapters, but the overlaps may serve the purpose of comparison as the reader contrasts the views of different authors on the same issues. Thus, the reader is given an additional opportunity to form her or his own opinion.

# 3

# Severe Behavior Disorders in Persons with Mental Retardation: A Multimodal Behavioral Diagnostic Model

*William I. Gardner*
*Janice L. Graeber*

In persons with mental retardation, most chronic psychological symptoms, such as aggression, self-injury, negativism, generalized irritability, and anxiety, occur in clusters of symptoms rather than as isolated responses. Typically, these and similar aberrant behaviors are viewed as reflecting learned modes of reacting and are treated by behavior therapy procedures. In some instances, however, these and similar clusters of problem behaviors may be symptomatic expressions of specific physical influences, such as hyperthyroidism (Kastner et al., 1990), or other more pervasive organic or mental disorders, such as Alzheimer's disease or schizophrenia. In the latter case, such behaviors as agitated and disruptive episodes or self-injury and negativism are presumed to reflect impairments of behavioral expression that result from these underlying neurological or biochemical abnormalities (Sovner & Hurley, 1984).

In view of the potential multiple determinants of behavioral symptoms, the development of an effective client-specific intervention program depends on a diagnostic understanding of the specific and unique constellation of physical, psychological, and socioenvironmental factors present in each individual. Thus, diagnostic efforts addressing both external and internal contributors are undertaken to produce a functional explanation of the presenting symptoms. In specific illustration of the need for a multidimensional and uniquely individualized assessment, one person's episodes of aggression may reflect the absence of effective alternative means of communicating his or her fearfulness or frustration (Durand, 1990). In another person, similar aggressive responding may reflect the influence of schizophrenia or a major mood disorder (Sovner, 1990). Aggression in a third individual may be a functional behavior and may reflect a learned mode of obtaining desired consequences, such as an immediately increased level of social attention or the removal of aversive or potentially painful conditions such as a taunting peer or a dentist's needle (Mace, et al., 1986). Of significance, even within the same person, highly similiar symptoms, such as agitated and disruptive behaviors or self-injurious acts, may serve different functions at different times or may reflect the influence of highly disparate conditions, for example, pain-elicited aggression on one occasion and aggression on another to create distress in an authority figure (Mulick, Hammer, & Dura, 1991).

In sum, the heuristic value of a comprehensive individualized diagnostic assessment reflects the reality that there is no single or simple physical or psychological cause and thus no single or specific effective treatment, psychological or medical, for most aberrant behaviors of those with mental retardation. As most behavior difficulties are predominantly interpersonal, they are best understood and treated in the context of social interactions. Diagnostic activities thus include the assessment of interpersonal and other environmental influences as well as unique personal physical and psychological characteristics.

Chronic problems, as noted, may accompany various other aberrant physical and psychological conditions. Therefore, behavioral assessment should closely interface with medical and psychiatric diagnostic efforts. To elaborate, the thought and perceptual difficulties of a person with a schizophrenic disorder may impair her or his judgment about the consequences of aberrant behaviors. This impairment, in combination with emotional lability and impaired impulse control, may result in severe aggressive and self-injurious behaviors under otherwise innocuous conditions of external provocation. An attempt to treat the behavioral symptoms independent of an understanding of the underlying contributing factors would at best bring only temporary remission of the symptoms.

Additional examples of medical conditions that may influence behavioral symptoms are provided by the person with temporal lobe epilepsy, who may engage in episodes of self-injury and/or assaultive behaviors, and the individual with a nonspecific seizure disorder, who may present generalized irritability (Gedye, 1989a, 1989b; Rapport et al., 1983). When behavioral symptoms are associated with these and other psychiatric and physical conditions, such as mania, agitated depression, generalized anxiety, or akathisia, the medical treatment of these underlying clinical conditions may result in concomitant decreases in the behavioral symptoms (Dosen, 1984; Sovner, 1990; Sovner & Hurley, 1986).

## Multicomponent Assessment and Treatment Model

A multicomponent assessment and treatment model, depicted in Figure 1, provides a guide not only to the needed areas of diagnostic activities but also

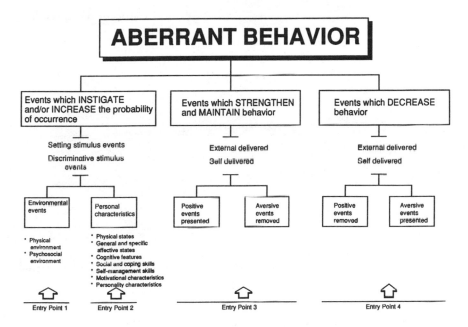

**Figure 1. Multicomponent Functional Diagnostic and Treatment Protocol**

to the resulting interpretation and to the translation of the information obtained into client-specific treatment approaches.

This model, reflecting a *biopsychosocial* perspective as depicted in Figure 2, is based on constructs and empirical data from various contemporary behavioral and related systems of a biological, psychological, and social nature concerned with behavior development, pathology, and treatment. The model emphasizes that behavioral symptoms represent the combined influences of the person's psychological and physical features and her or his current physical and social environments. It thus recognizes that the recurring behavioral symptoms present in those with a dual diagnosis are typically influenced by multiple internal and external factors, including those of a physical nature.

As an illustration of the nature of the interactions or interrelationships of biological, psychological, and social influences, a biologically based psychiatric condition such as schizophrenia or a bipolar disorder may result in changes in cognitive functions, mood and affective states, emotional regulation, and psychomotor behaviors. These changing psychological and physical characteristics may result in new behavioral or emotional difficulties or may influence the occurrence or increase the severity of problems that predated the current episode of the psychiatric disorder. These symptoms, in turn, create changes in the manner in which the social environment responds to and interacts with the person and his or her problem behaviors. These

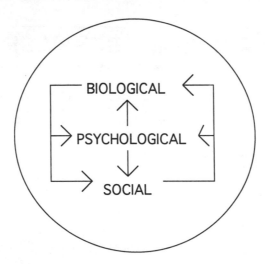

**Figure 2. Depicting the Interrelationship Among Biological, Psychological, and Social Influences.**

experiences with the social environment may reciprocally reinforce the problem behaviors, intensify the emotional arousal, and change the person's perceptions of this social feedback. To be most effective, diagnostic and related intervention efforts must be sensitive to these interrelationships and must give attention to each set of influences.

The biopsychosocial perspective, as depicted in Figure 3, also recognizes the interactive nature of the psychological elements of this triad. Any predominant *behavioral* symptoms, such as self-injury or aggression, frequently have *cognitive* and *affective* components that either result from or contribute to the frequency and severity of the overt behavioral symptoms. These cognitive and affective components, presumed in individual cases to contribute to the behavioral symptoms, may become the primary focus of treatment, as illustrated by anger management training (Benson, 1986), self-management training (Cole, Gardner, & Karan, 1985), and anxiety reduction procedures (Spencer & Conrad, 1989). More specifically, although the person's behavioral symptoms, such as aggression or self-injurious acts, are frequently those that create the most concern, the multimodal behavioral approach recognizes the interactive effects of behaviors, emotions, and cognitions. What a person *feels* (for example, anger or anxiety) as well as what the person *thinks* (for example, "He deserved that") potentially influences what the person *does* (for example, hits a caregiver who provides a directive for low-preference behavior).

Psychological intervention may be directed toward changing any one of these interactive components:

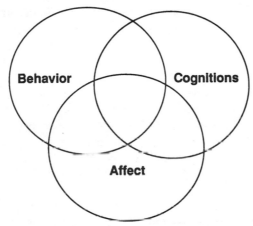

**Figure 3. Depicting an Interactive Psychological Model**

If it is assumed that a person behaves aggressively under the conditions of increased anger, interventions may focus on teaching the person to control or reduce his anger relative to specific provocative events and, as a result, to reduce the likelihood of aggressive behavior. In other instances, a person may become angry and thus behave aggressively as a result of his repetitively thinking that a person is dangerous and attempting to harm him. Modifying the ruminative thinking behaviors either through medication or psychological therapy will in turn decrease the level of anger and thus remove a critical condition contributing to the aggressive acts. Finally, a person's aggressive behaviors may be followed immediately by negative consequences. These experiences may result in inhibition of the impulses to be aggressive, changes in the person's cognitions (e.g., "I'll not hit because I'll get in trouble"), and a reduction in the level of anger as the person selects alternative means of coping with the source of provocation.

In sum, regardless of the specific focus of intervention, it is recognized that other components of a person's psychological triad (behaviors, emotions, and cognitions) will be influenced. In view of this perspective, psychological assessment and intervention efforts should consider each component.

As suggested, the objective of behavioral diagnostics is to obtain information from which a client-specific intervention program can be devised. Assessment focuses on identifying those biopsychosocial variables contributing to the *instigation* of aberrant behavioral symptoms as well as those influencing the *acquisition* and *persistent* recurrence of these problem symptoms. This functional diagnostics represents a three-step process of (1) gathering information about the variables that contribute to the likelihood of the instigation, acquisition, and persistent occurrence of aberrant behaviors; (2) developing client-specific hypotheses about the specific contributing factors following an analysis and interpretation of these assessment data; and (3) developing client-specific intervention procedures consistent with these hypotheses.

Assessment information may be obtained through (1) repeated direct observation of and interaction with the client in the actual situations in which the target behaviors occur; (2) interviews of client, staff, family members, and peers; (3) a review of case records; and (4) exposure to analogue conditions (Gardner & Cole, 1990). The reader is encouraged to consult Carr and Durand (1985b), Repp, Felce, and Barton (1988), and Mace, Lalli, and Lalli (1991) for illustrations of the analogue procedure. Briefly, the client, either in a controlled or in an *in vivo* setting, is exposed to events assumed to set the occasion for and/or to strengthen the target aberrant behaviors. Based on the client's differential reactions to these events, an individualized intervention program is designed and implemented.

Functional diagnostic information, in summary, provides the basis for developing a series of hunches about the current biological, psychological, and socioenvironmental factors that contribute to occurrences of an individual's aberrant behaviors. These hypotheses, in turn, form the basis for an individualized treatment plan. In most instances of chronic behavior disorders, multiple hypotheses about the contributing factors may result in the prescription of multiple person-specific intervention approaches. This process is illustrated in the case study described in Chapter 10.

## Functional Diagnostic Assessment

### External Factors Correlated with Aberrant Behaviors

An initial focus of assessment is the identification of those preceding interpersonal and other potential influences of the psychosocial and physical environments that instigate or otherwise increase the likelihood of occurrence of the target symptoms. These social and physical environmental events producing aberrant behaviors are obviously person-specific and can be identified only through systematic and objective observation of an individual in those particular situations in which the target symptoms occur (Gardner, 1988). These conditions may include such general sources of environmental stimulation as a high noise level, overcrowding, excessively demanding performance standards, or disruptive peer models (Boe, 1977; Rago, Parker, & Cleland, 1978; Schroeder, 1990; Talkington & Altman, 1973); and such specific instigating events as a reduction in the frequency of staff attention (Carr & Durand, 1985a), the presentation of demands (Carr & Newsom, 1985), and the removal of positive conditions (Mace et al., 1986). That the assessment must be individualized is emphasized by findings reported by Mace et al. (1986) and Carr and Durand (1985b), which reveal obvious individual differences among persons with developmental disabilities in the types of antecedent conditions that serve to instigate their aberrant behaviors. These clinicians have demonstrated that conditions such as social disapproval, adult demands, and reduced social attention resulted in varying effects on the aberrant behaviors of different persons.

### Client Characteristics

Various client characteristics have been suggested as influential variables in the occurrence of problem behaviors (Gardner & Cole, 1987, 1990, 1993; Gualtieri, Matson, & Keppel, 1989; Lowry & Sovner, 1991). These variables include conditions that may instigate or may serve as setting events and thus increase the likelihood of aberrant responses to other specific instigating external events (Schroeder, 1990). These conditions may involve both transitory and more enduring *physical-sensory* factors, such as drug effects, chronic pain, fatigue, seizure activity, hearing impairment, neurological impairment, and premenstrual discomfort, (Podboy & Mallery, 1977; Rapport et al., 1983; Gedye 1989a; Gualtiere et al., 1989); *affective states*, such as anger, major depressed mood, generalized anxiety, and chronic sadness (Benson, 1986; Dosen, 1984; Fahs, 1989); and *cognitive* variables, such as provocative covert verbal ruminations and paranoid ideation (Gardner, Clees, & Cole, 1983). Also of interest are those *deficit skill* areas, such as social communication, anger management, self-management, and related problem-solving and coping skills, that, because of their low strength or absence, contribute to the *vulnerability* of the person engaging in aggression under conditions of provocation (Carr & Durand, 1985a; Gardner & Cole, 1989; LaVigna, Willis, & Donnellan, 1989; Talkington, Hall, & Altman, 1971).

Evidence that supports a relationship between client features and an increased inclination toward aberrant responding comes from a variety of sources. As specific illustrations, Podboy and Mallery (1977) suggested a relationship between levels of caffeine intake and aggressive incidents among persons with severe mental retardation residing in an institution. A reduction in caffeine level through the substitution of decaffeinated coffee correlated with a reduction in aggression as well as in the number of nocturnal awakenings. Rapport et al. (1983) noted that the physical aggression, consisting of grabbing, biting, kicking, and hair pulling, of a young adolescent client was related to prodomal and postictal seizure activity. Talkington and Riley (1971) reported a relationship between an imposed reduction diet and aberrant behavior among institutionalized adults with mild and moderate levels of mental retardation. Following the imposition of the reduction diet, the number of aggressive incidents toward peers and staff increased substantially.

In a study of persons with mental retardation and differing levels of communication skills, Talkington et al. (1971) found that those with severe communication difficulties engaged in more destructive outbursts, such as breaking windows, overturning furniture, and ripping clothing, than did matched peers who had adequate communication skills. These writers speculated that the aggressive acts served to reduce the arousal level produced by difficulties in communicating wishes and needs. Gardner et al. (1983) described the potential role that verbal ruminations assumed in producing an increased inclination toward disruptive outbursts in an adult with moderate mental retardation. Finally, LaVigna et al. (1989) and Durand (1990) have provided illustrations of the therapeutic effectiveness of teaching communication skills as functional equivalents to various aggressive and self-injurious acts in persons with a deficit in the means of making their wishes known.

Other variables of significance in understanding chronic problem behaviors include the individual's *motivational and personality features*. A knowledge of the events that serve as positive reinforcers (for example, adult approval, peer acceptance, having control over others, and aggravating others), as well as of the variety and relative effects of the aversive events that influence the person's behaviors (for example, rejection by peers, noise level, crowding conditions, difficult task demands, and adult reprimand) is important in behavioral assessment and the related treatment planning. As an illustration of the potential influence of personality traits, an individual who is ritualistic has an increased likelihood of aberrant responding under conditions that require frequent and sudden changes in routine.

In sum, some personal characteristics, such as excessive negative emotional arousal, may *by their presence* increase the likelihood of aberrant behaviors in those inclined to behave disruptively. Other variables, such as communication skills and motivation to please others, *by their absence or low strength* render the person more vulnerable to inappropriate behaviors under conditions of provocation.

### Setting Events: Combining External and Internal Influences

In assessing the events that instigate various problem behaviors, it would be highly unusual for such behaviors always to follow the occurrence of any specific external and internal stimuli. In most cases, a *stimulus complex* sets the occasion for these reactions (Gardner et al., 1986; Schroeder, 1990). This complex frequently involves sources of internal as well as external stimulation. As an illustration, an adolescent with mild mental retardation who is prone to engaging in aggression and other agitated and disruptive acts under conditions of social provocation may, when in a state of positive emotional arousal, behave appropriately when taunted by a peer. When in a state of negative arousal, such as anger or anxiety, this same adolescent, under the same external provocation, may behave aggressively. This diagnostic information would suggest that the critical variable requiring treatment is the person's lack of coping skills in the dual conditions of negative emotional arousal and peer teasing.

Gardner and associates (Gardner, Karan, & Cole, 1984; Gardner et al., 1986) described an expanded behavioral-assessment model that highlights this stimulus complex. The traditional behavior-analysis assessment model, consisting of immediately preceding stimulus events–behavior–consequences, was expanded to include an assessment of *setting events*. These events are defined as those circumstances that influence which specific stimulus–response relationships will occur out of all those that currently make up a person's behavioral repertoire. These setting events may consist of (1) *physiological conditions*, such as sleep deprivation or the presence or absence of drugs; (2) *durational events*, such as the presence of a specific staff member or the specific work requirements of a vocational training program; and (3) *behavioral histories*, which represent temporally distant stimulus–response interactions wholly separate in space and time from the current stimulus conditions, such as an argument with one's mother before arriving at school (Schroeder, 1990). The effects of setting events are presumed either to *facilitate* or to *inhibit* the occurrence of specific stimulus–response combinations.

Setting events are not constant across persons and thus must be individually defined and identified. As an illustration, the mere presence of a large male staff person (as a durational setting event) may serve to inhibit aggressive behavior in a client who is likely to behave aggressively when reprimanded by other staff. However, this same staff member may have no such "setting" effect on another client in the same stimulus conditions.

The expansion of the applied-behavior-analysis assessment and intervention model to include a consideration of setting events (i.e., setting event–immediate-antecedent–behavior–consequence) holds the promise of providing a more complete and functional description of the combination of physiological, durational, temporally historical, and temporally immediate events that influence the aberrant behaviors of persons with mental retardation. Data reported by Brown, Gardner, and Davidson (1992), Davidson, Gardner, and Brown (1992), W. I. Gardner et al. (1986), and J. M. Gardner et al. (1985) support the usefulness of this expanded protocol. With groups of persons with lengthy histories of conduct difficulties and mild to profound levels of mental retardation, the identification of person-specific setting events resulted in significant improvement in predicting the occurrence of aberrant behaviors. In each case, the problem behaviors were more likely to occur in the presence of specific discriminative conditions when these occurred in combination with a setting event when this setting condition was absent. Thus, including an assessment of setting events greatly increased the predictability that these problems would occur in the presence of the immediately preceding discriminative event. Identification of the conditions that contribute to the likelihood of aberrant behaviors offers a number of potentially useful intervention strategies (W. I. Gardner et al., 1986; Schroeder, 1990).

## Functionality of Aberrant Behaviors

The final set of variables evaluated and treated are those that may contribute to the functionality of problem behaviors. Problems of aggression, pica, psychogenic vomiting, stereotypy, and self-injury are used here to illustrate this relationship.

### Functionality of Aggression

**Reinforcement-Motivated Aggression.** Some recurring acts of aggression may be functional as they result in an occurrence of or an increase in positive consequences (reinforcement-motivated aggression). Consequences suggested by various writers as positive reinforcers for behavioral symptoms include (1) various aspects of the victim's behavior; (2) various aspects of the behavior of others in the social environment who may verbally or physically intervene or otherwise react; and (3) either attaining or avoiding loss of material reinforcers or other items or activities of value, such as winning a fight or regaining a denied reinforcer (Martin & Foxx, 1973; Matson & Gorman-Smith, 1986). This hypothesis suggests interventions consisting of (1) removing the functionality of the aggression through extinction, that is, removing the reinforcing consequences (Forehand, 1973); (2) teaching specific alternative (functionally equivalent) ways of obtaining the same or similar reinforcers (Carr & Durand, 1985b); (3) reducing aggression through providing reinforcement following periods of nonoccurrence of the aggressive behavior (Luiselli & Slocumb, 1983); and (4) suppressing aggressive acts through presenting contingent aversive consequences (St. Lawrence & Drabman, 1984).

**Escape-Motivated Aggression.** Aggression also may be functional in reducing or terminating sources of aversiveness (for example, taunting from peers or unwanted task demands by a caregiver). In this case, aggression represents a form of escape-motivated behavior maintained by negative reinforcement (Carr & Newsom, 1985; Carr & Durand, 1985b). Recent empirical demonstrations (for example, Carr & Newsom, 1985) support our clinical observations that aggressive behaviors are most frequently strengthened by the effects of removing or reducing aversive events. This hypothesis suggests interventions consisting of (1) removing or reducing the aversiveness of the provoking events or conditions; (2) removing the functionality of the aggression through extinction (Carr, Newsom, & Binkoff, 1980); or (3) teaching specific skills that are functionally equivalent to the aggression (Bird et al., 1989; Carr & Durand, 1985a).

### Functionality of Pica

**Positive Reinforcement: Social and Sensory Consequences.** Pica may be strengthened and maintained by the social and sensory feedback produced. Pica behavior, like any appropriate or inappropriate behavior, may occur because it results in social attention from staff and peers. If staff observe a person mouthing and ingesting such items as cigarette butts, paper, leaves, or feces, the typical reaction is exaggerated concern. The individual may be yelled at or otherwise reprimanded for the pica behavior, provided physical contact in the process of attempts to remove the item being ingested, or provided other attention by staff or family concerned about possible physical harm resulting from the ingested substance. If the person lives in, or has a lengthy history of living in, a setting that provides inadequate social stimulation, such social feedback may be quite reinforcing. It may represent one of the few means of obtaining social attention, especially by persons with mental retardation with a limited behavioral repertoire. In addition, staff may provide desired physical contact and sensory stimulation, potentially reinforcing consequences, in an effort to retrieve the ingested substance from the person's mouth, or to clean the person's face and hands, especially following episodes of feces smearing and coprophagy (Mace & Knight, 1986).

**Positive Reinforcement: Food.** Pica may be strengthened and maintained through infrequent food reinforcers. Because the person, in scavenging and ingesting a variety of substances such as trash or cigarette butts, may find food particles, such as cracker or cookie crumbs or sweet substances from gum or candy wrappers, the pica behavior may be reinforced and thus maintained on an infrequent schedule of reinforcement. The ingestion of the discarded food provides immediate reinforcement (Singh, 1983).

**Positive Reinforcement: Chemical.** Pica may be strengthened and maintained by chemical reinforcers. The ingestion of cigarette butts and other tobacco products and coffee grounds may be maintained by the nicotine or caffeine obtained from these items (Donnelly & Olczak, 1990).

**Positive Reinforcement: Oral Stimulation and Stimulus Deprivation.** Some authorities suggest that pica represents an attempt to obtain increased oral stimulation and/or to satisfy a hunger need. As the availability of food in a closely supervised environment is highly controlled, the person whose appetite is not satisfied, or who does not obtain sufficient oral stimulation from the food that is provided, may engage in pica behavior in an attempt to gain this desired stimulation. Other persons, because of profound sensory, motoric, and developmental handicaps, may be in a chronic state of stimulus deprivation. In these instances, pica may represent an available means of providing the needed sensory stimulation (McAlpine & Singh, 1986).

**Negative Reinforcement.** Pica may be strengthened and maintained because it results in the removal or reduction of aversive conditions. In some instances, the pica may result in removal of the person from an aversive situation. For example, a person in a work activities program that he does not enjoy may ingest small items, such as nuts and paper clips, that are available in the workshop area. On observing the pica, staff may remove the client from the work program. After a few similar experiences, pica may become more frequent as a result of negative reinforcement.

**Nutritional Deficiencies.** Some authorities suggest a relationship between nutritional deficiencies and pica. In this view of etiology, a person with mental retardation may engage in pica because of nutritional deficiencies involving the vitamins C and D, phosphorus, iron, thiamine, calcium, niacin, or zinc and/or because of inadequate total caloric intake. Of the nutritional trace elements, zinc is most often linked with pica behavior. It is theorized that a zinc deficiency may reach a certain low level and thus instigate pica as a means of obtaining zinc from various sources. Studies support the value of treatment with trace elements in reducing the frequency of pica behavior (Lofts, Schroeder, & Maier, 1990).

*Functionality of Psychogenic Vomiting and Rumination*

**Positive Reinforcement:** Sensory Stimulation. Vomiting and rumination may occur as a means of obtaining the sensory stimulation produced by eating, chewing, and swallowing. Some authorities suggest that individuals may engage in ruminative vomiting in order to obtain oral stimulation. The person may be a rapid eater and may obtain minimal oral stimulation during the process of eating. In other instances, the texture of the person's diet may produce minimal oral stimulation. For example, many persons with profound levels of mental retardation are fed pureed food for a variety of medical reasons. There is some evidence that, in such instances, a reduction in chronic rumination may be realized by increasing the amount of oral activity and stimulation during feeding. Clinical experience has demonstrated that having the person actively bite the spoon to remove the food or chew a nipple to receive milk may result in dramatic reductions in chronic rumination in persons with profound mental retardation who have previously been hand-fed pureed food with no active participation required (Rast et al., 1988).

**Positive Reinforcement: Condition of Satiation.** A body of research supports the possibility that rumination may represent an attempt to produce a state of satiation. Persons residing in institutions are frequently restricted both in how much food they can consume and in the amount of time available for eating. Additionally, food is typically not available between meals. The person may thus be in a state of food deprivation and may have no effective means of communicating this hunger. In this instance, ruminative vomiting may contribute to a state of satiation (Yang, 1988).

**Positive Reinforcement: Social Attention.** Vomiting and rumination may occur as a result of the positive consequences produced by this behavior. In some instances, these behaviors may be reinforced and maintained by positive social consequences, such as attention. It is difficult not to attend to a person who vomits food or who regurgitates, rechews, and then swallows the vomitus. Although the attention provided by family, staff, or peers is typically of a negative social quality, it should be noted that persons with severe to profound mental retardation may have a limited number of alternative behaviors that consistently produce more positive social feedback. Vomiting and rumination may thus be one of the few behaviors that consistently produce this valued form of reinforcement (Holvoet, 1984).

**Negative Reinforcement.** Vomiting may occur because it results in the removal of some aversive condition. A child may discover that a nonpreferred food or an unpleasant program demand, such as a school or work task, may be avoided or terminated following vomiting. As a result, the behavior is strengthened and maintained through negative reinforcement. Again, this behavior must be viewed in the context of the person's restricted means of influencing his or her environment in a more socially acceptable manner (Wolf et al., 1970).

*Functionality of Stereotyped Behaviors*

**Reduction in Aversive Overstimulation.** Stereotypy may represent expressions of tension, anxiety, discomfort, unsatisfied needs, or attempts to reduce excessive environmental stimulation. In support of this position, studies have reported stereotyped behaviors to be more frequent when individuals are placed in novel or unfamiliar situations than when these same individuals are in more familiar surroundings. Other studies have demonstrated an increase in stereotyped acts when the person is exposed to high noise levels like those in many overcrowded and understaffed residential living areas, is suffering food deprivation, and in the presence of specific peers. These findings suggest that when fearful of or disturbed, excited, or overstimulated by external or internal sources, some persons may engage in repetitive actions, presumably as a means of coping with this uncomfortable overstimulation. These undifferentiated motor behaviors may be a result of the person's highly limited behavioral repertoire; the person may not have other more appropriate ways of expressing his or her uncomfortable overstimulation (Rojahn & Sisson, 1990).

**Primitive Frustration Reaction.** Stereotyped behaviors may reflect a primitive frustration reaction. Because of the limited repertoire of skills that those with severe and profound mental retardation have to cope with problem situations, frustration may be expressed by immediate stereotyped reactions. For example, when a person's schedule is changed so that expected or routine reinforcement is not provided (for example, if the canteen is closed, a bus ride is canceled, a favorite staff person does not come to work, or reinforcing objects or possessions are taken or lost), stereotypy may be the resulting frustration response. Other instances of frustration, such as interference with goal-directed activities, failure to obtain what is desired (for example, seeing a favorite staff person interact with someone else), and changes in the frequency of reinforcement (for example, providing praise every ten minutes instead of the usual five minutes on a work training task), have been reported to produce various forms of stereotyped actions (Wiesler et al., 1988).

**Increase in General Sensory and Social Stimulation.** Stereotyped behaviors may reflect a need for increased levels of general sensory and social stimulation. This stimulus deprivation or arousal position is based on the hypothesis that every human has a basic need to achieve and maintain a minimal level of stimulation. If this level of stimulation is not provided by external sources, the person gains it from self-stimulation. In support of this position, studies have reported an increase in stereotyped behaviors when individuals are exposed to settings relatively devoid of general sensory stimulation. Other studies have demonstrated, in support of this position, a decrease in stereotyped behaviors among individuals with severe and profound levels of mental retardation when they are provided additional environmental stimulation. Because of the boredom or lack of arousal arising from a nonstimulating environment, the unavailability of objects to manipulate or activities to engage in, and a severely impoverished social and cognitive repertoire, a person may engage in stereotyped actions as a means of providing the sensory input needed for central nervous system stimulation (Buyer et al., 1987).

It should be noted that persons with severe and profound levels of mental retardation and with lengthy histories of residence in large institutions spend long periods in situations in which routine opportunities for meaningful interactions are limited or even absent. Many spend numerous hours each day in dayrooms with other individuals with similar limitations, who provide minimal, if any, social stimulation. Toys and other objects are often limited or nonexistent, or if they are present, the person may lack the skills to independently seek and maintain active engagement with the items. As many persons with severe and profound disabilities fail to reach a level where spontaneous initiation of appropriate social interaction with staff or other aspects of their environments is possible, the person is left with minimal environmental stimulation unless it is routinely provided by others. Direct-care personnel most frequently are kept busy with the physical care of such persons (for example, dressing, toileting, and bathing) and may have minimal time to provide active social stimulation. Structured program experiences designed specifically for the unique psychological and physical characteristics of each person are typically lacking. In these circumstances, and considering the limited behavioral repertoire present, many individuals with severe and profound levels of mental retardation may engage in various stereotyped activities as a means of providing themselves with valued stimulation.

**Increase in Specific Sensory and Perceptual Stimulation.** Stereotyped acts may be acquired and maintained because these behaviors produce specific preferred tactile, proprioceptive, and other sensory and perceptual feedback. This explanation, an elaboration of the previously discussed stimulus-deprivation hypothesis, emphasizes the specific self-stimulatory nature of the repetitive behaviors. In fact, this hypothesis assumes that self-stimulatory behaviors are maintained by the reinforcing perceptual stimuli that are produced. For example, one study (Lovaas, Newsom, & Hickman, 1987) demonstrated that a child's stereotyped object-spinning was maintained by the auditory stimulation produced. When this auditory feedback was eliminated by the carpeting of the surface of the table, the stereotyped behavior disappeared.

Such stereotyped activities are presumed to produce preferred sensory feedback and thus to become dominant behavior patterns that actively interfere with learning other, more socially adaptive behaviors. This explanation would account for the range of stereotyped behaviors observed in different individuals. Some engage in activities that produce *visual* stimulation, such as waving their hands or twirling a string in front of their eyes, staring at lights or rotating fans, or repeatedly assembling the same puzzle. Others engage in predominantly *auditory* acts, such as repetitive screaming or clicking or grinding their teeth. Still others produce *vestibular* stimulation through repetitive head nodding, body rocking, or spinning while standing up or *tactile* stimulation through repetitive rubbing, stroking, pinching, or poking themselves or rubbing objects such as textured sweaters or smooth tabletops (Rincover, 1978).

**Positive and Negative Reinforcement.** Stereotyped actions may reflect the effects of the specific social or physical consequences that these behaviors produce. This position suggests that stereotyped behaviors are strengthened by positive reinforcement because they produce positive social (for example, parent, staff, or peer) feedback, or by negative reinforcement because they reduce or terminate some unpleasant source of stimulation. As an example, an individual may find that whenever she begins to body-rock and bang against the wall, staff attention is forthcoming. After a number of such reinforcing experiences, the person begins to body-rock as a means of gaining staff attention. In other instances, studies have demonstrated that when presented with difficult task demands, children may engage in such stereotyped behaviors as body rocking and hand flapping as a means of escape from these aversive conditions. Following a number of experiences involving negative reinforcement, the child's stereotypy may become a predominant response when difficult or otherwise nonpreferred task demands are presented (Repp et al., 1988).

*Functionality of Self-Injurious Behaviors*

**Positive Reinforcement: Physical and Social Consequences.** Self-injurious behaviors (SIBs) may represent learned behavior that has been strengthened and maintained by positive consequences. This position is known as the discriminative stimulus hypothesis. SIBs may occur in some persons because they serve to signal such reinforcing social events as attention, concern, or physical contact. It is not unusual, especially following severe self-abuse, for staff or family to comfort the person or to attempt to distract her or him by providing special attention, food, or a favored object or activity. As a result, an SIB may become functional in ensuring desired attention, physical contact, or other forms of social interaction. In many individuals with severe mental retardation, limited communication skills, and few alternative social behaviors. SIBs may be one of the few consistent means of ensuring social feedback or of communicating their needs (Carr, 1977).

Mark, a twenty-seven-year-old adult with profound mental retardation, without speech and with limited social skills, engaged in episodic bouts of agitated face slapping, head banging, and screaming. Following close observation of the conditions in which these behaviors occurred, it was noted that they occurred following periods of isolation from social contact. It was speculated that Mark's SIBs occurred because they ensured immediate staff attention and thus met his need for social stimulation. A program of ensuring that no period in excess of twenty minutes elapsed throughout the day without personalized social stimulation resulted in a significant reduction in Mark's SIBs. Following the demonstration that this was the function or purpose served by the SIBs, a program was initiated to teach Mark alternative skills for obtaining social attention.

This explanation of SIBs emphasizes the need, as noted, to replace the SIBs with alternative skills for obtaining positive consequences. The individual with minimal functional verbal skills should be taught specific other means of communicating his or her needs or wishes.

**Positive Reinforcement: Sensory Stimulation.** Self-injury may be strengthened by sensory stimulation. Such behaviors as poking and pressing on the eye produce visual stimulation; head banging and face slapping produce auditory, proprioceptive, and tactile stimulation, as do such behaviors as scratching or pinching. Some persons with severe or profound levels of mental retardation, with limited social behaviors, and/or with sensory and neurological difficulties may resort to SIBs to provide valuable sensory stimulation (Rincover & Devany, 1982).

Some theorists suggest that violent contact, as in face slapping or head banging, increases the sensory sensitivity of the tissue involved. Repeated contact thus ensures immediately heightened sensory input and reinforcement. Finally, it has been suggested that repeated self-injurious behaviors may produce nerve damage, which, in turn, necessitates more intense hitting, scratching, or pinching if one is to experience the sensory feedback. As a result, the self-injurious acts become more intense over time (Blankensmith & Lamberts, 1989).

**Negative Reinforcement: Removal of Aversive Conditions.** SIBs may represent learned behavior that is strengthened and maintained by the reduction or termination of unpleasant situations or events. This escape or avoidance hypothesis suggests that SIBs represent a means of escaping or avoiding unpleasant situations, such as periods of minimal reinforcement, staff or task demands, training tasks that have minimal value to the person, or reduced social contact. The person with limited alternative means of expression or of communicating his or her displeasure may discover that, whenever SIB occurs, the deprivation or demand is reduced or removed (Oliver & Head, 1990). For example, a person may find social contact, a specific staff member, and specific work task, periods of minimal stimulation, or an activity such as class participation to be unpleasant. These aversive conditions may typically produce strong emotional responses, which in turn may add to the aversiveness of the demands or deprivations. These unwanted social events, deprivation states, or demands for low-preference activities and the associated negative emotional arousal may be reduced or removed, even though only temporarily, following an episode of SIB. As a result, the SIB is strengthened through negative reinforcement. In this manner, the person learns that SIB, although potentially painful, will result in escape from or avoidance of other unpleasant experiences.

> Katherine, a fifteen-year-old adolescent with profound mental re-
> tardation and minimal communication and social skills, wore a hel-
> met, unless closely supervised, to protect her from self-injury during
> her frequent agitated and disruptive episodes. Close observation of
> Katherine's severe episodes of face slapping, scratching, and associ-
> ated loud screaming suggested that these activities were being main-
> tained because they removed her from various unpleasant
> situations. As one example, following ten to fifteen minutes in pro-
> gram activities that required her to remain seated and to engage in
> prevocational tasks, Katherine frequently engaged in agitated and
> disruptive behaviors that resulted in her removal from the room. A
> program designed to teach Katherine alternative means of commu-
> nicating her dislikes, combined with providing her with the option
> of selecting her prevocational activities from among the variety of
> available ones, resulted in a significant reduction in her agitated,
> disruptive, and self-injurious episodes.

In summary, this escape explanation for SIBs suggests a specific program emphasis on decreasing the aversive features (persons, situations, or activities) that result in SIB, teaching specific skills of coping with the aversive conditions, and/or teaching the person alternative means of communicating or expressing his or her needs or wishes (Carr & Durand, 1985a).

It is interesting that some individuals who display SIBs appear to enjoy physical restraints, such as arm splints or hand and arm restraints. When these are removed, the person becomes upset and seems to welcome a reapplication of the restraints following periods of freedom from them. Such behavior may be explained by the negative reinforcing function of such restraints. SIBs following staff-imposed demands that have resulted in restraints may, in turn, effectively remove the unpleasant demands. The SIBs may thus result in an escape from the demands of staff and into the restraint condition (Favell, 1982).

**Neurotransmitter Disturbance.** Finally, some writers have suggested an association between SIB and various other less-well-defined biological conditions involving neurotransmitter disturbances. As an example, it has been suggested that SIB results in the release of endorphins, which may either act as a positive reinforcer or decrease sensitivity to the pain produced by the SIB. This and similar hypotheses relating to neurotransmitter disturbances, while receiving some support in carefully controlled studies, currently offer no specific empirically documented treatment direction for the clinician. These hypotheses and the accumulating supportive data, nonetheless, support the possibility that organic factors make significant contributions to the functionality of SIB in some persons (Farber, 1987).

## Development of Hypotheses Based on Assessment

These assessment data provide the basis for developing a series of hunches about the current factors that contribute to the person's problems. As noted, hypotheses have been developed about (1) current environmental conditions (for example, task demands and threats from peers); (2) personal characteristics (for example, a deficit in communication skills, dysphoria, limited awareness of the social acceptability of behaviors, chronic fatigue, and anger) that increase the likelihood of aberrant behavior; and (3) the functions served by the behavior (for example, SIBs may result in the removal of task demands, aggression may produce staff distress and peer approval, or aggression may "punish those who are attempting to poison my food"). In most instances of chronic aberrant behaviors, multiple hypotheses are developed about the contributing factors in each of these areas (Gardner & Moffatt, 1990).

## Selection of Client-Specific Treatment Procedures

Hypotheses about contributing factors are used in the selection of the specific procedures that make up a psychosocial treatment program addressing these client-specific influences. As an illustration, an adolescent who demonstrates increased aggression following the nonattainmnent of a valued reward, and whose assessment data reveal deficit coping skills in this circumstance, would be provided a program designed to teach him alternative means of coping with this failure. If physical factors or specific psychological-psychiatric disorders are hypothesized to contribute to the aggressive episodes, an integrated treatment program is designed to ensure a close interface among the different treatment modalities.

The following illustrates the translation of assessment information into intervention approaches:

> Jack, a young adult with profound mental retardation and severe physical disabilities, vomited following every meal. Observation of Jack in his living area indicated that, immediately following each meal, he would sit in the dayroom across from the staff office and would stick his hand into his throat until he regurgitated a small amount of his meal. He would then rub the vomitus on his face and hands and finally wipe it on his clothing. After chewing the remaining vomitus for a few minutes, he would reswallow it. These activities were repeated until staff intervened or until he had vomited four or five times. Eventually, staff would approach Jack, make some comment about his mess, and then take him to his room to clean and change him. At other times, Jack was typically ignored, as he appeared content to sit in his chair and observe staff and peers. Jack responded positively when he was provided attention by staff or peers but made minimal attempts to initiate or maintain interaction.

These observations suggested an intervention program of consistent structured program experiences immediately following each meal, frequent social attention throughout the waking hours, regular participation in structured programs away from the living area, and teaching Jack alternative skills for obtaining valued sensory and social stimulation.

## Use of Aversive Procedures

The selection of aversive procedures in the treatment of aberrant behaviors poses some particular problems for the behavioral diagnostician. In most cases, such procedures are selected for the purpose of suppressing excessively occurring aberrant behaviors. This selection, however, is usually not based on diagnostic information about the factors that contribute to the instigation or strength of the person's undesired actions. On the contrary, the use of punishment as a treatment procedure too frequently is based on the supposition that the aversive properties associated with the treatment will be sufficient to suppress the problem behavior by overcoming the effects of whatever may be producing or maintaining the behavior.

The rationale typically used for the selection of aversive procedures is that (1) the aberrant behavior poses a distinct danger to the client or others and interferes significantly with the person's involvement in his or her social and habilitation environments, and (2) other less intrusive treatment procedures have been attempted and found ineffective. In practice, it is not unusual for highly intrusive punishment procedures to be used, based on the *a priori* conclusion that the personnel resources are not available to effectively evaluate the treatment efficacy of other procedures, such as differential reinforcement and extinction. In any event, the severity of the problem behaviors and the relative effectiveness and efficiency of procedures involving aversive consequences are typically used as a justification for the use of these approaches, rather than their selection based on conceptually derived diagnostic information.

While space constraints do not permit a discussion of the empirical and ethical issues involved in the use of punishment, the reader is encouraged to consult Gardner (1989) and Repp and Singh (1990) for a range of contemporary perspectives.

## Summary

Behavior disorders among persons with mental retardation result from and are maintained by a variety of external and internal biopsychosocial variables. The effective management and treatment of these disorders can be attained only following a diagnostic understanding of these multiple influences and their relative effects. The functional diagnostic model presented provides the initial step in formulating and implementing an intervention plan. The translation of diagnostic information into specific procedures is described in Chapter 10.

## References

Benson, B. A. (1986). Anger management training. *Psychiatr. Aspects Ment. Retard. Rev., 5,* 51–55.

Bird, F., Dores, P. A., Moniz, D., & Robinson, J. (1989). Reducing severe aggressive and self-injurious behaviors with functional communication training. *Am. J. Ment. Retard., 94,* 37–48.

Blankenship, M. D., & Lamberts, F. (1989). Helmet restraint and visual screening as treatment for self-injurious behavior in persons who have profound mental retardation. *Behav. Residential Treat., 4,* 253–265.

Boe, R. B. (1977). Economical procedures for the reduction of aggression in a residential setting. *Ment. Retard., 15,* 25–28.

Brown, M. G., Gardner, W. I., & Davidson, D. P. (1993). *A setting event analysis of aggression in persons with profound mental retardation.* Manuscript submitted for publication.

Buyer, L. S., Berkson, G., Winnga, M. A., & Morton, L. (1987). Stimulation and control as components of stereotyped body rocking. *Am. J. Ment. Defic., 91*, 543–547.

Carr, E. G. (1977). The motivation of self-injurious behavior: A review of some hypotheses. *Psychol. Bull., 84*, 800–816.

Carr, E. G., & Durand, V. M. (1985a). Reducing behavior probelms through functional communication training. *J. Appl. Behav. Anal., 18*, 111–126.

Carr, E. G., & Durand, V. M. (1985b). The social-communicative basis of severe behavior problems in children. In S. Reiss & R. P. Bootzin (Eds.), *Theoretical issues in behavior therapy* (pp. 219–254). New York: Academic Press.

Carr, E. G., & Newsom, C. (1985). Demand-related tantrums conceptualization and treatment. *Behav. Modif., 9*, 403–426.

Carr, E. G., Newsom, C. D., & Binkoff, J. A. (1980). Escape as a factor in the aggressive behavior of two retarded children. *J. Appl. Behav. Anal., 13*, 101–117.

Cole, C. L., Gardner, W. I., & Karan, O. C. (1985). Self-management training of mentally retarded adults presenting severe conduct difficulties. *Appl. Res. Ment. Retard., 6*, 337–347.

Danforth, J. S., & Drabman, R. S. (1989). Aggressive and disruptive behavior. In E. Cipani (Ed.), *The treatment of severe behavior disorders: Behavior analysis approaches* (pp. 111–127). Washington, DC: American Association on Mental Retardation.

Davidson, D. P., Gardner, W. I., & Brown, M. G. (1993). *Factors influencing conduct difficulties in persons with mental retardation: A setting event analysis.* Manuscript submitted for publication.

Donnelly, D. R., & Olczak, P. V. (1990). The effects of differential reinforcement of incompatible behaviors (DRI) on pica for cigarettes in persons with intellectual disabilities. *Behav. Modif., 14*, 81–89.

Dosen, A. (1984). Depressive conditions in mentally handicapped children. *Acta Paedopsychiatr., 50*, 29–40.

Durand, V. M. (1990). *Severe behavior problems: A functional communication training approach.* New York: Guilford Press.

Fahs, J. J. (1989). Anxiety disorders. In *Treatment of psychiatric disorders* (Vol. 1, pp. 14–19). Washington, DC: American Psychiatric Association.

Farber, J. M. (1987). Psychopharmacology of self-injurious behavior in the mentally retarded. *J. Am. Acad. Child Adol. Psychiatr., 26*, 296–302.

Favell, J. E. (Task Force Chairperson). (1982). The treatment of self-injurious behavior. *Behav. Ther., 13*, 529–554.

Forehand, R. (1973). Teacher recording of deviant behavior: A stimulus for behavior change. *J. Behav. Ther. Exp. Psychiatr., 4*, 39–40.

Gardner, J. M., Souza, A., Scabbia, A., & Breuer, A. (1985). Using microcomputers to help staff reduce violent behavior. *Computers in Human Services, 1*, 53–61.

Gardner, W. I. (1988). Behavior therapies: Past, present, and future. In J. Stark, F. Menolascino, M. Albarelli, & V. Gray (Eds.), *Mental retardation and mental health: Classification, diagnosis, treatment, services* (pp. 161–172). New York: Springer-Verlag.

Gardner, W. I. (1989). In the meantime: A client perspective of the controversy over the use of aversive/intrusive procedures. *Behav. Ther., 12*, 179–182.

Gardner, W. I., Clees, T. J., & Cole, C. L. (1983). Self-management of disruptive verbal ruminations by a mentally retarded adult. *Appl. Res. Ment. Retard., 4,* 41–58.

Gardner, W. I., & Cole, C. L. (1987). Managing aggressive behavior: A behavioral diagnostic approach. *Psychiatr. Aspects Ment. Retard. Rev., 6,* 21–35.

Gardner, W. I., & Cole, C. L. (1989). Self-management approaches. In E. Cipani (Ed.), *The treatment of severe behavior disorders* (pp. 19–36). Washington, DC: American Association on Mental Retardation.

Gardner, W. I., & Cole, C. L. (1990). Aggression and related conduct difficulties. In J. L. Matson (Ed.), *Handbook of behavior modification with mentally retarded* (2nd cd., pp. 225–254). New York: Plenum Press.

Gardner, W. I., & Cole, C. L. (1993). Aggression. In J. L. Matson & R. P. Barrett (Eds.), *Psychopathology in the mentally retarded* (2nd ed., pp. 213–252). Boston: Allyn & Bacon.

Gardner, W. I., Cole, C. L., Davidson, D. P., & Karan, O. C. (1986). Reducing aggression in individuals with developmental disabilities: An expanded stimulus control, assessment, and intervention model. *Educ. Training Ment. Retard., 21,* 3–12.

Gardner, W. I., Karan, O. C., & Cole, C. L. (1984). Assessment of setting events influencing functional capacities of mentally retarded adults with behavior difficulties. In A. S. Halpern & M. J. Fuhrer (Eds.), *Functional assessment in rehabilitation* (pp. 171–185). Baltimore: Brookes.

Gardner, W. I., & Moffatt, C. W. (1990). Aggressive behaviour: Definition, assessment, treatment. *Int. Rev. Psychiatr., 2,* 91–100.

Gedye, A. (1989a). Episodic rage and aggression attributed to frontal lobe seizure. *J. Ment. Defic. Res., 33,* 369–379.

Gedye, A. (1989b). Extreme self-injury attributed to frontal lobe seizures. *Am. J. Ment. Retard., 94,* 20–26.

Gualtieri, C. T., Matson, J. L., & Keppel, J. M. (1989). Psychopathology in the mentally retarded. In *Treatment of psychiatric disorders* (Vol. One, pp. 4–8). Washington, DC: American Psychiatric Association.

Holvoet, J. F. (1984). The etiology and management of rumination and psychogenic vomiting: A review. In J. H. Hollis & C. E. Meyers (Eds.), *Life-threatening behavior: Analysis and intervention.* Washington, DC: American Association on Mental Deficiency.

Kastner, T., Friedman, D. L., O'Brien, D. R., & Pond, W. S. (1990). Health care and mental illness in persons with mental retardation. *Habilitative Ment. Healthcare Newsl., 9,* 17–24.

LaVigna, G. W., Willis, T. J., & Donnellan, A. M. (1989). The role of positive programming in behavioral treatment. In E. Cipani (Ed.), *The treatment of severe behavior disorders* (pp. 59–84). Washington, DC: American Association on Mental Retardation.

Lofts, R. H., Schroeder, S. R., & Maier, R. H. (1990). Effects of serum zinc supplementation on pica behavior of persons with mental retardation. *Am. J. Ment. Retard., 95,* 103–109.

Lovaas, I., Newsom, C., & Hickman, C. (1987). Self-stimulatory behavior and perceptual reinforcement. *J. Appl. Behav. Anal., 20,* 45–68.

Lowry, M., & Sovner, R. (1991). The functional significance of problem behavior: A key to effective treatment. *Habilitative Ment. Health Newsl., 10,* 59–63.

Luiselli, J. K., & Slocumb, P. R. (1983). Management of multiple aggressive behaviors by differential reinforcement. *J. Behav. Ther. Exp. Psychiatr., 14,* 343–347.

Mace, F. C., & Knight, D. (1986). Functional analysis and treatment of severe pica. *J. Appl. Behav. Anal., 19,* 411–416.

Mace, F. C., Lalli, J. S., & Lalli, E. P. (1991). Functional analysis and treatment of aberrant behavior. *Res. Devel. Disabilities, 12,* 155–180.

Mace, F. C., Page, T. J., Ivancic, M. T., & O'Brien, S. (1986). Analysis of environmental determinants of aggression and disruption in mentally retarded children. *Appl. Res. Ment. Retard., 7,* 203–221.

Martin, P. L., & Foxx, R. M. (1973). Victim control of aggression of an institutionalized retardate. *J. Behav. Ther. Exp. Psychiatr., 4,* 161–165.

Matson, J. L., & Gorman-Smith, D. (1986). A review of treatment research for aggressive and disruptive behavior in mentally retarded. *Appl. Res. Ment. Retard., 7,* 95–103.

McAlpine, C., & Singh, N. N. (1986). Pica in institutionalized mentally retarded persons. *J. Ment. Defic. Res., 30,* 171–178.

Mulick, J. A., Hammer, D., & Dura, J. R. (1991). Assessment and management of antisocial and hyperactive behavior. In J. L. Matson & J. A. Mulick (Eds.), *Handbook of mental retardation* (2nd ed.). New York: Pergamon Press.

Oliver, O., & Head, D. (1990). Self-injurious behavior in people with learning disabilities: Determinants and interventions. *Int. Rev. Psychiatr., 2,* 101–116.

Podboy, J. W., & Mallery, W. A. (1977). Caffeine reduction and behavior change in the severely retarded. *Ment. Retard., 15,* 40.

Rago, W. V., Parker, R. M., & Cleland, C. C. (1978). Effect of increased space on the social behavior of institutionalized profoundly retarded male adults. *Am. J. Ment. Defic., 82,* 554–558.

Rapport, M. D., Sonis, W. A., Fialkov, M. J., Matson, J. L., & Kazdin, A. E. (1983). Carbamazepine and behavior therapy for aggressive behavior: Treatment of a mentally retarded, postencephalatic adolescent with seizure disorders. *Behav. Modif., 7,* 255–265.

Rast, J., Johnston, J. M., Lubin, D., & Ellinger-Allen, J. (1988). Effects of premeal chewing on ruminative behavior. *Am. J. Ment. Retard., 93,* 67–74.

Repp, A. C., Felce, D., & Barton, L. E. (1988). Basing the treatment of stereotypic and self-injurious behaviors on hypotheses of their causes. *J. Appl. Behav. Anal., 21,* 281–289.

Repp, A. C., & Singh, N. N. (Eds.). (1990). *Perspectives on the use of nonaversive and aversive interventions for persons with developmental disabilities.* Sycamore, IL: Sycamore Press.

Rincover, A. (1978). Sensory extinction: A procedure for eliminating self-stimulatory behavior in psychotic children. *J. Abnorm. Child Psychol., 6,* 299–310.

Rincover, A., & Devany, J. (1982). The application of sensory extinction procedures to self-injury. *Anal. Intervention Devel. Disabilities, 2,* 67–81.

Rojahn, J., & Sisson, L. A. (1990). Stereotyped behavior. In J. L. Matson (Ed.), *Handbook of behavior modification with the mentally retarded* (pp. 181–223). New York: Plenum Press.

St. Lawrence, J. S., & Drabman, R. S. (1984). Suppression of chronic high frequency spitting in a multiply handicapped and mentally retarded adolescent. *Child Fam. Behav. Ther., 6,* 45–55.

Schroder, S. R. (Ed.). (1990). *Ecobehavioral analysis and developmental disabilities.* New York: Springer-Verlag.

Singh, N. N. (1983). Behavior treatment of pica in mentally retarded persons. *Psychiatr. Aspects Ment. Retard. Newsl., 2,* 33–36.

Sovner, R. (1990). Bipolar disorder in persons with developmental disorders: An overview. In A. Dosen & F. J. Menolascino (Eds.), *Depression in mentally retarded children and adults.* Leiden: Logon.

Sovner, R., & Hurley, A. D. (1984). The role of the medical model in psychiatry. *Psychiatr. Aspects Ment. Retard. Rev., 5,* 51–55.

Sovner, R., & Hurley, A. (1986). Managing aggressive behavior: A psychiatric approach. *Psychiatr. Aspects Ment. Retard. Rev., 5,* 16–21.

Spencer, C. R., & Conrad, P. L. (1989). Treatment of acrophobia of an institutionalized adult with mental retardation. *Ment. Retard., 27,* 1–4.

Talkington, L. W., & Altman, R. (1973). Effects of film-mediated aggressive and affectual models on behavior. *Am. J. Ment. Defic., 77,* 420–425.

Talkington, L., Hall, S., & Altman, R. (1971). Communication deficits and aggression in the mentally retarded. *Am. J. Ment. Defic., 76,* 235–237.

Talkington, L., & Riley, J. (1971). Reduction diets and aggression in institutionalized mentally retarded patients. *Am. J. Ment. Defic., 76,* 235–237.

Wiesler, N. A., Hanson, R. H., Chamberlain, T. P., & Thompson, T. (1988). Stereotypic behavior of mentally retarded adults adjunctive to a positive reinforcement schedule. *Res. Devel. Disabilities, 9,* 393–403.

Wolf, M. M., Birnbrauer, J., Lawler, J., & Williams, T. (1970). The operant extinction, reinstatement, and re-extinction of vomiting behavior in a retarded child. In R. Ulrich, T. Stanick, & T. Mabry (Eds.), *Control of human behavior: From cure to prevention* (Vol. 2, pp. 146–149). Clearview, IL: Scott Foresman.

Yang, L. (1988). Elimination of habitual rumination through the strategies of food satiation and fading: A case study. *Behav. Residential Treatment, 3,* 223–234.

# 4

# Depression in Persons with Mental Retardation: Assessment and Diagnosis

*Anton Dosen*
*Jan J. M. Gielen*

Recently, most of the psychiatric diagnostic categories have been recognized as being present among the mentally retarded at all levels of mental retardation. However, the prevalence and recognition of depression remain a challenging issue. The reasons are, among others, the differences in the symptomatology and, to a certain extent, diagnosticians' lack of familiarity with the concept of depression in the mentally retarded.

The symptomatology is thought to be strongly influenced by the low cognitive abilities of the mentally retarded as well as by their lack of proficiency in expressing themselves verbally (Dosen, 1990a; Gillberg et al., 1986). In general, the ability to verbally express the grief, sadness, and hopelessness experienced is found only among the less severely retarded. Often, at the lower levels, the clinician must rely on indices other than verbal expression that are more related to the "masked" symptoms of depression, such as agitation, irritability, neurovegetative phenomena, mood swings, periodicity, and eating and sleeping disturbances.

Furthermore, atypical manifestations of depression, especially among the more severely retarded, may lead to diagnostic uncertainty. Particularly with psychotic depressives, the presentation of symptoms varies greatly, and atypical manifestations are common (Day, 1990). When these atypical symptoms dominate, the underlying depressive state may remain invisible.

In addition to the problem of the specificity of the symptomatology, there may also be the problem of a differential diagnosis in cases of coexisting mental illnesses. Some authors (Menolascino & Weiler, 1990; Day, 1990) have pointed out the difficulty of differentiating between paranoid psychosis or schizophrenia, on the one hand, and depressive illness, on the other. Especially with the more severely handicapped, this distinction may be very difficult to make. Furthermore, hypochondriacal complaints may sometimes be mistaken for physical illness and may serve as a detour in the diagnosing of depression. Diagnostic problems in differentiating between depression and hypothyroidism or early dementia may occur, especially

70

with sufferers of Down syndrome (Day, 1990). In cases of twofold diagnoses, when one is focusing on the "primary" diagnosis of developmental or behavioral disorder, the presence of a depressive illness may easily be missed. One example is when depression is superimposed on a pervasive developmental disorder (Berney & Jones, 1988; Dosen, 1990b).

With respect to a lack of clarity in the conceptualization of depression among the mentally retarded, the discussion centers on the differences between the postulates made by the traditional psychoanalytic, individual-oriented theorists and those advocated later by authors oriented to psychodynamic social relations. Early psychoanalysts (Freud, 1957; Abraham, 1927) argued that, for depression to occur, the superego had to be developed, and thus, depression could not occur in children younger than four years old or, translated into terms of developmental age, could not occur in mentally retarded persons who are severely or profoundly retarded. Later, psychodynamically oriented authors (Spitz, 1946; Bowlby, 1973; Arieti, 1977; Sandler & Joffee, 1965; Yalom, 1980) hypothesized that the loss of socioemotional and existential security may cause depression irrespective of the developmental level of the person. Similar discussions have taken place with regard to the occurrence of depression during childhood, with the result that the protagonists of psychodynamic concepts have been inclined to discover depression among children at a younger and younger age (Dosen, 1990a).

In line with this tradition, Nissen (1980) referred to an underlying course of psychic development in pointing to the diversity of the symptoms of depressive illness present in infants, preschoolers, school-aged children, and adolescents. It is Nissen's view that this course of development should be seen as the ordering principle when one is examining the multifold expression of depressive symptoms exhibited throughout the developmental stages of childhood. Like Nissen (1980), Gaedt and Gärtner (1990) stressed the relevance of the disparity in developmental ages with regard to the expression of depressive symptomatology in the mentally retarded.

In addition to the difficulties mentioned above, there are also problems related to the diagnosis of depression that are linked to the specific behavioral and social-interactional patterns of the mentally retarded. Sovner and Lowry (1990) summarized several diagnostic methodological problems related to these specifics. First, the subjective changes associated with depression are expressed only at the higher cognitive levels. Therefore, it is difficult to use self-reports to determine the presence of diagnostically relevant behavior and symptoms. Second, the presence of an affective disorder may be missed when the onset presents itself as an increase in the severity of preexisting maladaptive responses. Third, an affective disorder may represent a comorbid psychopathological state, for example, fragile-X syndrome or autism. Finally, the diagnostic significance of nonspecific behaviors will be overlooked if the association with depressive illness is not recognized.

Furthermore, there are difficulties in speaking about depression among the mentally retarded in the terms of the recent classification systems. The phenomenological-descriptive classification of psychotic and neurotic forms of depression—according to the revised third edition of the American Psychiatric Association (APA, 1987) *Diagnostic and Statistical Manual* (DSM-III-R), major depressive syndrome and dysthymia—among the mentally retarded is plagued with a number of problems with regard to the recognition and interpretation of symptoms and establishing a clear-cut diagnosis. Despite these difficulties, in most investigations in the field of the mental health care of the mentally retarded an attempt is made to adapt diagnostic thinking to the framework of diagnoses as applied to the population in general. Additionally, attempts are being made to shed more light on these problems by making use of the developmental approach. Apparently, this approach offers some possibilities for a better understanding of some of the specific mechanisms that lead to depression as well as for differentiating some of its manifest forms.

In the following section we elaborate more on these two diagnostic approaches. In addition, some types of depressive illness that appear to be connected with particular forms of mental retardation are discussed.

## Phenomenological-Descriptive Diagnostics

### Psychotic Depression

In general, psychotic depression is characterized by severe impairments in four dimensions of life: vitality, behavior, mood, and thought content. Symptoms of delayed vitality, or so-called vital symptoms (Praag et al., 1965) are sleep disturbance, loss of appetite, diurnal variation of mood and activity, obstipation, loss of libido, loss of energy and interest, and disturbance of the vegetative nervous system. Impairment of behavior usually consists of aggression, temper tantrums, obsessive behavior, agitation, deterioration of personal habits, psychomotor retardation, social withdrawal, and so on. The mood is usually depressed or dysphoric. Thought content is characteristically colored by delusions of guilt, suicidal ideation, paranoid delusions, hallucinations, anxiety symptoms, and so on. This sort of depression is also known as *major depression, affective psychosis, vital depression, endogenous depression,* and *melancholia.*

The traditional psychiatric literature has viewed this sort of depression as being etiologically and qualitatively detached from the neurotic form. Recently, however, scientists have been more inclined to distinguish these two forms quantitatively only. They place both depressions on a continuum of severity, considering the psychotic depression a severe form and neurotic depression a lighter form of a similar psychopathology (APA, 1987; Dosen,

1990a). From this point of view, when the neurotic form lasts a long time, or when the causative factors worsen, it may take on the form of a psychotic depression.

In this section, we focus on the most severe form of depression as well as on manic-depressive psychoses. The prevalence of the psychotic form of depression and the manic-depressive state among the mentally retarded has been estimated to be similiar to the prevalance encountered in the general population. Various investigators (Reid, 1972; Heaton-Ward, 1977; Corbett, 1979; Lund, 1985; Hucker et al., 1979; Gostason, 1985) have found the prevalence to be between 1.2 and 3.2 percent in the adult mentally retarded population. In mentally retarded children, the frequency varies from 1.5 to 2 percent (Gillberg et al., 1986; Way, 1983; Dosen, 1990a).

The symptoms exhibited by the mentally retarded may differ from those exhibited by the nonretarded population. Persons with a low level of intelligence and nonspeaking patients present a more varied symptomatology than do nonretarded patients (Dosen, 1990a).

In a survey of the clinical features of psychotic depression that are recognized frequently in the mildly and moderately mentally retarded, Day (1990) summed up the following symptoms:

1. reduced appetite and loss of weight, as well as sleep disturbance, including waking up very early in the morning

2. complaints of sadness or a depressed mood, often traceable in facial expression, general demeanor, or tearfulness

3. social withdrawal and loss of interest

4. psychomotoric retardation with depressive stupor and mutism or irritability and agitation, sometimes expressed as aggressiveness and temper tantrums

5. delusions of bodily dysfunction and somatic complaints like headache, abdominal pain, or vomiting

6. delusions of guilt and persecution, sometimes accompanied by auditory hallucinations

7. feelings of hopelessness, self-blame, and thoughts of death and suicide, sometimes to be inferred from general demeanor or the content of delusional material

8. suicidal attempts

9. atypical features, like regression with attention seeking, childish clinging behavior, return of incontinence, deterioration of personal habits and social skills, hysterical symptoms, negativism, robotlike responsiveness, or elective mutism

Other authors have tried to develop diagnostic criteria that are less dependent on the expression of subjective feelings and based more and more on the behavioral components of depressive illness. Sovner's attempts (1986), based on the DSM-III-R criteria, to construct such free diganostic criteria for differentiating affective illness among the mentally retarded are a good example. More recently, Sovner and Lowry (1990) operationalized these criteria into observable equivalents for mentally retarded persons that can be measured in terms of concrete behaviors. Sovner and Lowry distinguished the following symptoms among mentally retarded depressed patients in comparison to the DSM-III-R symptoms: apathetic facial expressions (instead of depressed mood); withdrawal and lack of reinforcers (instead of loss of interest or pleasure); aggressive or autoaggressive behavior or decreased activity (instead of psychomotoric activity and retardation); change in workshop performance (instead of decreased concentration); dwelling on the subject of death (instead of suicidal ideation); and so on.

Menolascino and Weiler (1990) focused on severely mentally retarded depressed patients. They distinguished the following symptoms:

- mood disorder, in which sadness, apathy, withdrawal, agitation, and crying spells may predominate
- property destruction and temper tantrums
- sleeping disorders
- appetite disorder and weight loss
- onset of or increase in self-injurious behavior
- motoric retardation and decrease of activity
- catatonic stupor
- hallucinations
- anxiety
- suicidal actions or ideations

Among mentally retarded children diagnosed as suffering from depression, the following constant symptoms were signalized (Dosen, 1990a):

- disphoria and sadness (observed or verbalized)
- changes in the vital functions (disorders of sleeping, eating, and so on)
- changes in motoric activity
- irritability

For the severely and profoundly retarded, the following symptoms could be added as well:

- autoagression
- stereotypy
- constipation

For the mildly and moderately retarded, the additional symptoms were:

- death wishes
- low self-esteem
- somatic complaints
- hallucinations
- delusions

Some authors have focused on bipolar, manic-depressive disorder occurring among the mentally retarded. Two authors (Reid, 1982; Sovner, 1990), have pointed to the difficulties in recognizing the symptoms of mania in the mentally retarded. Euphoric mood, particularly at the lower levels of mental retardation, may be less accentuated. Boisterousness or excitement may be the predominant state. Instead of flights of ideas and pressured speech, the mentally retarded may exhibit increased vocalization and disorganized speech. Symptoms that are characteristic of the mentally retarded and that serve as equivalents of the DSM-III-R criteria for the manic state were specified by Sovner (1990) and are presented in Table 1. Cases of chronic mania have also been described (Sovner, 1990; Steingard & Biederman, 1987).

Table 1
Behavioral Equivalents in the Mentally Retarded of DSM-III-R Diagnostic Criteria for Mania

| DSM-III-R Criteria | Behavioral Equivalents in Developmentally Disabled Persons |
| --- | --- |
| Mood/Symptom criteria | Boisterousness or excitement may be the predominant mood state. Self-injury may be associated with irritability. |
| Euphoric/elevated/irritable mood (no minimum duration necessary) | |
| At least three symtoms must be present if patient has euphoric mood. Four symptoms must be present, if patient has only irritable mood: | Behaviors represent manifestations of manic symptoms in developmentally disabled persons. |
| | Thought content may center on mastery of daily living skills. |
| 1. inflated self-esteem/grandiosity | Maladaptive behavior increases at usual bedtime or in early morning. Patient is dressed for work at 5.00 A.M. |
| 2. decreased need for sleep | |
| 3. more talkative/pressured speech | |
| 4. flight of ideas/racing thoughts | Frequency of vocalization increases irrespective of whether patient has usual speech. |
| 5. distractibility | Speech is disorganized. |
| 6. increased goal-directed activity/ psychomotor agitation | Workshop performance decreases. |
| 7. excessive involvement in pleasurable activities | Aggressive behavior and negativism may be present. |
| | Teasing behavior, fondling others, publicly masturbating. |

*Source:* R. Sovner. (1990). "Bipolar Disorder in Persons with Developmental Disorders: An Overview." In A. Dosen and F. J. Menolascino (Eds.), *Depression in Mentally Retarded Children and Adults.* Leiden, the Netherlands: Logon Publications.

Among these patients long-standing behavioral problems dominate the clinical picture, making it difficult to establish a diagnosis.

The investigators in this field agree that the recognition of the depressive and manic-depressive periods of the severely and the profoundly mentally retarded is far more difficult than is so for the mildly retarded because of a nonspecific symptomatology predominantly characterized by behavioral difficulties. Especially in cases of agitated depression in severely nonspeaking mentally retarded persons, the differentiation of manic and depressive states may be difficult. An elevation or decrease in the vitality and mood of these patients is not usually expressed in a recognizable fashion, and the striking feature is a global change in activity and behavior. Also, a diagnosis differentiating the manic or depressive condition from other organic or psychopathological states associated with restlessness, irritability, and aggressive and disruptive behavior may be difficult.

Various authors (Reid & Naylor, 1976; Dosen, 1979; Reid, 1982; Day, 1990) have reported a shorter duration of depressive and manic periods among the mentally retarded than among the nonretarded. In the mentally retarded, these periods may last anywhere from several days to several weeks. In these cases, some authors have written of a rapid-cycling psychosis (Day, 1990; Sovner, 1990). Some investigators (Reid & Naylor, 1976; Berney & Jones, 1989; Sovner, 1990) have linked this sort psychotic state with organic disorders of the CNS, neuroendocrine dysfunctions, thyroid abnormalities, or with the side effect of anti-depressant medication.

There are case reports (Day, 1990; Reid, 1985) of a mixed type of manic and depressive disorder. Either there is a simultaneous presence of manic and depressive features or these features follow each other rapidly. Establishing a proper diagnosis in these cases may be difficult for the inexperienced diagnostician.

Sovner (1990) suggested that daily behavioral ratings of activity, sleep, and maladaptive behaviors may be helpful in establishing characteristic dramatic exacerbations and remissions that cannot be explained by external events or somatic illness. Reid (1982) pointed out the usefulness of a good history of illness, including previous episodes of mania or depression, and stressed how helpful a knowledge of family histories of mental illness can be.

Recognizing the following specific features of manic-depressive psychosis in the mentally retarded can be useful in establishing a diagnosis (Dosen, 1990b):

1. Distinct expression of depressive or manic mood is not obligatory.
2. Episodes of depression or mania do not generally last as long as in nonretarded individuals.
3. Less pronounced intra- and more interpersonal problems are present.
4. There is a frequent presentation of autoaggression.

5. Loss of decorum is often present.

6. Very often, there is a regression in behavior.

### Neurotic Depression

Globally, neurotic depression is characterized by a milder form of the symptoms of depression. Psychotic symptoms are absent. Vital and vegetative symptoms are minimal, and the clinical picture is dominated more by neurotic signs like anxiety, obsessions, and hypochondriasis. The diagnosis is established predominantly among persons at mild and moderate levels of cognitive functioning. Neurotic depression is generally associated with varying degrees of characterological vulnerability and a dependent personality. These features are also often found among the mentally retarded (Day, 1990; Dosen & Gielen, 1990). Additionally, specific social circumstances or the particular course of development of the mentally retarded may heighten their vulnerability to this sort of depression. This form of depression is also known as *dysthymia, reactive depression, psychogenic depression,* and personal depression.

Until recently, the neurotic form of depression occurring among the mentally retarded has received little attention by investigators, the consequence being that the prevalence was underestimated. The attitude of the professionals is undoubtably linked to the traditional theoretical question of whether a neurosis and a depression of this type may occur among persons functioning at low cognitive levels and with weak personality formation.

Since the late 1970s, however, investigators (Day, 1985, 1990; Lund, 1985; Richardson et al., 1979; Menolascino et al., 1986) have been pointing out how high the frequency of this disorder is among the mentally retarded, stressing that this sort of depression is probably far more frequent among the retarded than among the nonretarded. Day (1990) found neurotic depression in 33 percent of the patients admitted to a psychiatric unit for the mentally retarded. Benson (1985) reported an anxious-depressed withdrawal disorder in 15 percent of the adolescents referred to an outpatient mental-health clinic. Among mentally retarded children referred for psychiatric care, the diagnosis of neurotic depression was established in 16 percent of the cases (Way, 1983; Dosen, 1984).

Summarizing the clinical features of twenty-six adults with mild and moderate handicap who were diagnosed as having neurotic depression, Day (1990) found the following symptoms:

1. depressed mood: fluctuating often, reactive and elevating rapidly when a change of environment takes place

2. suicidal ideation or attempts: rarely life-threatening, accompanied by

suicidal threats, often having the function of drawing attention to the illness

3. vegetative symptoms: much less pronounced and, if occurring, mainly in the form of reduced appetite
4. anxiety and other neurotic symptoms: frequently occurring as tension, panicky feelings, overbreathing, sweating, pallor, shakiness, concerns about physical health, and bodily complaints
5. initial insomnia and general sleep disturbance, but not early-morning awakening
6. behavioral problems, like aggressiveness, temper tantrums, and irritability

Additionally, the following characteristic symptoms of a neurotic depression in the mildly and moderately mentally retarded have been reported (Dosen, 1990a): weak control of aggressive impulses; strongly varying moods, ranging from sadness or apathy to an indifferent mood; obsessive behaviors; and attention seeking in a socially positive or negative way.

Often, the onset of the illness is acute and is precipitated by stressful events like the death or serious illness of a caring relative, or relational or other family problems. Changes in the life situation, like placement in an institution or in a group home or moving from one residential facility to another, may cause severe psychogenic reactions with symptoms of depression.

In cases of reactive behavioral and psychic disorders, the profoundly and severely retarded do not exhibit the same range of neurotic symptomatology as those at the higher levels of mental retardation do. If occurring, reactions to the changes in life circumstances are usually massive and accompanied by symptoms of severe behavioral disturbances like aggression, self-injurious behavior, anxiety, panic attacks, withdrawal, and apathy. Such catastrophic reactions may be elicited by changes in the environment or by other events of great personal impact. This reaction type is, to a certain extent, similar to Spitz's anaclitic depression (Dosen, 1990b).

Labeling the characteristics of thirty-one children with a wide range of intellectual capacities who were diagnosed as having a neurotic depression, Dosen (1990a) was able to distinguish the following symptoms:

1. behavioral disorders like hyperactivity, aggression, passivity, and inhibition
2. marked affective hunger
3. fear of failure

4. depressed or indifferent mood

5. arrest of or regression in cognitive development

6. sleeping and appetite disorders, constipation, encopresis and enuresis

7. somatic complaints

In general, this group of children could be characterized as having behavioral problems, often due to shortcomings in frustration toleration. Their mood was often characterized by affective emptiness, passing into strong affective hunger with strong bonding tendencies once psychotherapy was started. Somatic complaints were found less frequently than among the depressed nonretarded. Encopresis, enuresis, and problems with eating and sleeping did occur but were considered a neurotic rather than a depressive symptom. Weak self-concept, feelings of guilt, and suicidal ideation were hardly ever found. In Dosen's view, the explanation may be that, because of the lower cognitive levels, no sufficient cognitive representation of the self had been established.

## Developmentally Oriented Diagnostics

The developmental approach to depression is strongly linked to the psychodynamic point of view and is related to the notion of the loss of a loved object or the loss of self or self-representation that takes place throughout the psychogenesis of the ego. From this point of view, depression is a basic psychobiological reaction to these losses. The earlier conceptualization of anaclitic depression, formulated by Spitz (1946), described the withdrawal reaction of very young children after continuous traumatic separation from their mothers. Sandler and Joffee (1965) formulated a theory that the loss of the previous state of the self was the precondition for the onset of depression. Others (Bowlby, 1952; Bemporad & Wilson, 1978) have defined depression as being a negative consequence of repeated frustrations stemming from the separation–individuation phase. Furthermore, depressive personalities are seen as having invested too much of their self-esteem in a significant other, and detachment, psychological differentiation, individuation, and autonomy have not been established. Unconditional availability of and appraisal by the significant other have become a prerequisite for the sense of self experienced. However, as a consequence, the depressive personality has a strong dependency on the significant other, risking a strong "devaluing of the self" (Gaedt & Gärtner, 1990).

Threats to the loss of the self mobilize behavioral tendencies to possess the loved object, symbolizing the symbiotic attachment phase of early childhood. Clownish behavior and theatricality are defense mechanisms when the subject experiences helplessness and impotence. Aggression and autoaggression are often a forceful protest against the sensed separation. Thumb sucking, moving the body up and down, fantasies of omnipotence, and obsessional rituals are defenses against depressive affect, accompanied by feelings of self-worthlessness and being unworthy of love. Clinging behavior is an attempt to restore symbiotic attachment (Gaedt & Gärtner, 1990).

Many problem behaviors associated with development during the stages of separation and individuation occur even when the process of detachment from the bonding figure is taking the usual course with the usual developmental timing. These behaviors, however, become pathognomic when the developmental process deviates from the time schedule and once the person acquires the characteristics of the unstable self. In this context, Gaedt and Gärtner (1990) postulated a typology of depressive personalities in the mentally retarded, in which the psychogenesis of depression is governed by the psychodynamic paradigm, and with which the pertinent specific psychobiological and social relational aspects of mentally retarded individuals have been integrated. These authors pointed out the following characteristics of mentally retarded persons that have an impact on the onset and expression of depressive conditions:

1. Limited cognitive, sensoric and motoric functions may influence perception and communication with regard to the depressive state. Specific aspects of cerebral lesions may influence the expression of depression in a particular fashion.

2. A retarded person with limited verbal ability to communicate feelings of helplessness is inclined to express these feelings in concrete behavioral action.

3. The limited verbal capacities of the retarded individual are generally the expression of an immature psychic structure and serve as a complicating factor in understanding the individual's feelings.

4. Mentally retarded persons exhibit psychic defense mechanisms similar to those used by normal children. They are more inclined to externalize their tensions and conflicts in the form of acting-out behavior directed toward the environment.

5. Because of the immaturity of their ego functions, mentally retarded persons are only partly differentiated from their object representations. This may be the reason for their turning the aggression toward themselves and exhibiting self-injurious behavior.

6. Vegetative and somatic reactions as a kind of affective discharge may be caused by immature psychic structures or motoric disabilities.

7. Limited possibilities in life and within social relationship may further negatively influence the possibilities of self-actualization and may strengthen the feeling of hopelessness.

On the grounds of the formation of a characteristic depression-prone personality, Gaedt and Gärtner (1990) distinguished the following three types of depression:

1. *Unstable self-depression (selbst Labilen).* These depression-prone persons generally exhibit behaviors that are fairly typical of the frustration experienced during the separation–individuation phase. This condition is similar to Bowlby's protest phase (1952). The following symptoms may be identified:

- Sudden dip in the mood. Sadness and crying are often symptoms, although this sort of mood is not always present.
- Arrest of playing behaviors and the slowing down of motoric functions.
- Flight into omnipotence and fantasy.
- Hyperactivity.
- Attacks of rage.
- Autoaggressive masturbation.
- Anhedonia, apathy, and helplessness.
- Chronic indecisiveness and ambivalence.
- Reactivity of symbiotic attachment behaviors such as: provocative running away, hiding away, provocative self-injury, a shift from extreme attachment to aggressive turning away, regression into symbiotic behavior, clinging behavior

2. *Self-distorted depression (selbst Zerstören).* The behaviors of these depressives are the final result of failing to regain the love of the important bonding figure. The starting point is Mahler's thesis (Mahler, Pine, & Bergmann, 1975); the three stages of this process are

- Once a situation arises that threatens self-esteem, strong tendencies to possess the loved person arise. The desire for love emerges as a strong dependency and demanding behaviors in attempts to fuse with the omnipotent other.
- When these efforts to regain love are not responded to, the depressive person behaves in such a way that punishment and submission become inevitable.
- Once these behaviors do not restore homeostasis or symbiosis, complete withdrawal from the environment, often accompanied by heavy autoaggression and a total helplessness, is the result. Gaedt and Gärtner

postulated here the final and most extreme form of depreciating the self, in which the self is completely destroyed.

3. *Still depression (stille Depression)*. Persons with still depression are comparable to children suffering from Spitz's anaclitic depression. These persons typically blend into the background of groups of the mentally retarded. They are easily overlooked by caregivers when it comes to giving attention. Their phenotype is characterized by an empty gaze, a resigned facial expression, depressed motoric functions, minimal self-initiative, low body weight, problems with eating and sleeping, and avoidance of eye contact.

Gaedt and Gärtner (1990) pointed out that all three types of depressives are inclined to relive their experiences in their social interactions. They seem to be trying to organize their social situation in such a way that early conflicts stemming from the separation–individuation stage are repeated, often causing feelings of impotence in the caregivers. In relationships with caregivers and important others, similar childhood disturbances are reexpressed, and the risk is that these individuals will feel rejected and continue to devalue themselves, the ultimate results being depressive illness. Insight into these mechanisms of projection and the transference of early experiences may serve as a valuable entry point for therapeutic strategies.

Based on the psychodynamic point of view, Kischkel et al. (1990) presented diagnostic criteria for recognizing depression in the profoundly and severely retarded. In their view of the underlying dynamics that cause depression, these authors referred to disturbances in the subtle reciprocal schemes of interactions between the mother and the baby. Normally, vocal, tactile, and visual cues play a very important role in the synchronic rhythmic cycles of communicative exchange. In the normal mother and child dyad, there should be a tuning in to each others' behaviors. However, experiments with simulated depression show that, after repeated exposures to a depressed mother, the child gives up its efforts to restore communication. It gradually falls into passivity and helplessness as it is unable to redirect the mother's communication. Loss of interest, withdrawal, and lengthy mood disturbances are the corresponding phenomena. In Kischkel et al.'s view, many profoundly and severely retarded persons have been involved in a similar situation, in which their communication signals were not responded to. The authors suggested the following criteria for depression in severely and profoundly retarded individuals:

1. a sad, unhappy, and depressed outward appearance
2. serious withdrawal behavior, in which signals in the environment are hardly responded to
3. phases of prolonged states of displeasure

4. difficulty in maintaining lasting social contacts
5. minimal or no efforts to regulate social contact and avoidance, as well as neglect of eye contact.
6. sleeping, eating, and psychosomatic disorders

In the conception of Dosen and Bojanin (1990), the phenomenology of depression is explicitly associated with the developmental age. These authors proposed a model of normal social-emotional development consisting of three developmental stages, each associated with specific developmental tasks:

1. first adaptation phase (0–6 months)
   a. integration of sensory stimuli
   b. integration of the structure of place, time, and persons
2. first socialization phase (6–18 months)
   a. bonding
   b. creating a secure base
3. first individuation phase (18–36 months)
   a. separation
   b. individuation

According to Dosen and Bojanin, this model of socioemotional development can be seen as the underlying basis of the developmentally-specific manifestations of depression among the mentally retarded. When this model is applied to depressive symptoms, the following global scheme may be helpful in understanding the phenomenology of depression in terms of developmental age:

1. First adaptation phase. When there is inappropriate stimulation or a loss of acquired structure in space, time, and persons, the following may occur:
   a. phenomena of developmental deprivation (Bemporad & Wilson, 1978)
   b. phenomena like "conservation withdrawal" (Engel & Reichsman, 1956)
   c. general impairment of the autonomic homeostatic regulatory process accompanied by, among other things, disorders in sleeping, eating, and motoric activities, as well as a failure to thrive phenomena similar to those in anaclitic depression (Spitz, 1946)
2. First socialization phase. When a loss of an established affective bond

occurs (phenomenon of protest phase; Bowlby, 1952), the following ensue:

a. feelings of hopelessness

b. despair

c. disregulation of mood

3. First individuation phase. When a loss of a previous state of the self (in the sense of Sandler & Joffee, 1965) takes place, the result may be:

a. low self-esteem

b. depressed mood

c. aggressiveness and destructiveness

d. psychomotoric retardation

e. disorders of vegetative functioning

In line with the developmental-dynamic view, Dosen (1990a) introduced the concept of developmental depression elsewhere. Etiological factors may be found in a disturbed process of secure attachment in the second or third year of life. Because there is a growth in the ego structure and in the cognitive representation of the self, it is suggested that symptoms occurring after the individuation phase (after the third year of life) will differ from those manifested at an earlier age. Therefore, under the developmental age of four, primitive aspecific symptoms dominate, such as autoaggression, withdrawal, passivity, and self-stimulation. At a higher developmental level, the symptomatology is more differentiated, more depressively colored, and often accompanied by neurotic symptoms, like fear of failure and somatic complaints. These suggestions may be useful in recognizing the depressive symptoms of the severely and profoundly mentally retarded.

In light of the observations made by the developmentally oriented authors, a few general remarks can be made. First, reactions of the individual to changes in personal and material surroundings at a very early developmental age seem to be more global than at higher developmental levels. In addition, these reactions are nonspecific; the person acts in the same way whether the changes are due to special changes in the environment, separation from the caregiver, or somatic illness. Disturbances in psychomotoric and vegetative functions are usually concomitant symptoms at this level. Second, when depression occurs at a later developmental age, a sort of regression may occur, incorporating the symptoms characteristic of earlier developmental ages.

# Depression Linked with Particular Forms of Mental Retardation

While Reid (1982) stressed that there are no particular associations between the physical pathology of the mentally retarded and depressive or manic-depressive psychosis, there are authors who described specific clinical pictures and a specific course of this disorder in a number of patients with particular forms of mental retardation. On the basis of experiences with persons suffering from organic brain dysfunctions and treatment-resistant mood and behavior disorder, Sovner (1990) hypothesized that the CNS pathology producing a patient's developmental disabilities may also affect those limbic system structures that may mediate the symptomatology of the affective disorders. Szymanski and Biederman (1984) and Warren and coworkers (1989) have described several cases of Down syndrome persons suffering from depression with a specific course.

In our practice (Dosen, 1990b), the depressive states of Down syndrome patients have often been characterized by mutism, passivity, and apathy. These conditions have often been elicited by the loss of a loved one, by moving from the parental home to a residential setting, by other multiple changes, or by changes in a living pattern that was important for the person. The depressive state of these patients could exacerbate, lasting for several months. In other cases, the depression might take on a chronic character, lasting for several years with little variation. Several authors (Singh, 1988; Hucker, 1985; Sovner, Hurley & Labrie, 1985) have pointed to the fact that mania is seldom seen in Down syndrome. Sovner (1990) proposed that persons with Down syndrome are unable to develop mania because the neurotransmitter systems that mediate bipolar disorders are affected.

In individuals with fragile-X syndrome, the symptoms of the affective disorders have also been seen. Reis et al. (1988) described depression and Sovner (1990) described chronic mania in fragile-X adults. Depression has also been reported in those suffering from Klinefelter's syndrome (Sorensen & Nielsen, 1977) and PKU (phenylketonuria) syndrome (Realmuto et al., 1986), and with neurological impairments causing dysfunction of the right hemisphere (Brumback & Staton, 1982). Although the presence of affective psychosis in these particular syndromes of mental retardation may suggest that there is a link between physical disorder and mental illness, it would be premature to draw a conclusion about the etiological mechanisms without further epidemiological investigations of this population. However, the aforementioned findings suggest that the clinical picture of affective psychosis may prevail in different organic or genetic syndromes, and that diagnosticians must be attuned to this possibility in order to recognize the symptoms.

In the literature, depressive or manic-depressive illness has been observed to be a comorbid state in cases of autism (APA, 1987; Sovner, 1990;

Wright, 1982; Burd & Kerbeshian, 1988). In our clinical practice (Dosen, 1990b) with adult mentally retarded persons suffering from autism and pervasive developmental disorders, episodes of depressive psychosis have been recognized in a number of cases. Furthermore, in a number of depressed patients, the history of disturbed physical contact with the mother in the first three years of life was reported without there being evidence of autism or pervasive developmental disorder. In our opinion, the clinical findings of depression in both kinds of patients may be related to a weak emotional-security base in these individuals, caused by a lack of attachment development (Dosen, 1990b).

Speculations on the role of attachment development and physical contact in depressed mentally retarded persons have been supported by recent investigations on physical contact experiences and the occurrence of depression in the general population. The hypothesis that the tactile relationship of the child with the mother is the basis of trust and confidence has been explored by a number of investigators of the early infant–mother relationship (Harlow, 1958; Frank, 1957; A. Freud, 1965; Montague, 1971). Recent investigations in this field (Cochrane, 1990) suggest that unsatisfactory physical contact experiences during childhood, as well as at the present, may be closely linked to several psychiatric disorders, among which depression has frequently been signaled. The psychopathological mechanism hypothesized is that there is a lack of social support present in the persons with physical contact disorder, causing a decrease in the ability to cope with stress and triggering the onset of a depressive condition (Cochrane, 1990). Similar mechanisms for the onset of depressive states in mentally retarded persons suffering from physical contact disorder, no matter what the etiology is, are conceivable. Usually, in these people, the onset of depression can be linked to events that apparently had a stressful impact on the person.

Considering the relatively frequent feature of disturbed physical contact during early childhood, particularly among more severely mentally handicapped children, it might be speculated that severely and profoundly mentally retarded persons are more depression-prone. So far, investigations in this field have been scarce and do not allow verification of this proposition. However, when one is assessing a severely mentally retarded person with behavioral disorders, the possibility of a link between depression and contact disturbance should be kept in mind.

Mixtures of depression and other types of psychiatric disorders are well known in the psychiatry of the general population. In mentally retarded persons, mixtures are, diagnostically, less clear-cut because of their less specific symptomatology. Day (1990) reported states of so-called schizoaffective psychosis with a mixture of both schizophrenic and affective symptoms. Szymanski and Biederman (1984) described several cases of depression and anorexia. In our clinical practice, the diagnosis of depression has sometimes been established conjointly with conduct disorder, hyperkinetic syndrome,

Tourette sydrome, anxiety disorders, and obsessive-compulsive disorder (Dosen, 1990b). By means of a cautious exploration of the developmental history, we have often discovered that depression occurs as a secondary illness within the domain of the developmental, psychiatric, or behavioral disorders that already existed. Often, this secondary disorder has been found to be caused by additional stressful events or by long-standing unfavorable environmental circumstances.

## Assessment

Various authors agree the psychiatric assessment of the mentally retarded should be multidisciplinary and multidimensional (Szymanski, 1988; Dosen, 1990b). The variety and complexity of physical and psychic abnormalities call for a dependable examination by various professionals. The results of all these examinations should lead to a twofold diagnostic insight—appraisal of the person's general biopsychosocial state and the functioning of the person within his or her environment—that establishes a psychopathological diagnosis.

In order to get this diagnostic insight a holistic integration of the different findings obtained by various examiners is needed. For this difficult task, diagnosticians should have a wide range of biological, psychological, and developmental knowledge at their disposal. Szymanski (1988) considered child psychiatrists the best trained in this sense. In our opinion, a new profile of psychiatrists should be created for this task: subspecialists in mental retardation. In our practice, we focus in assessment on the following aspects:

- a detailed developmental history
- a family history
- medical examinations (general somatic, genetic, neurological, biochemical, and so on)
- a psychological examination (cognitive development, social development, and personality development)
- a neuropsychological examination
- a detailed psychiatric examination
- a milieu examination
- other examinations (didactic, physiotherapeutic, and so on)

Starting from a broad holistic perspective, the diagnostician focuses on the symptoms of psychopathology and attempts to place the symptoms within the framework of a complete picture. Detailed information about the course of the developmental process of the person is of great importance in the search for the roots of depression.

As mentioned earlier, detecting the symptoms of depression may be difficult. Various investigators in this area have made attempts to develop a strategy or a method that will be helpful in the diagnostic process. Some of these are described here.

## Observation of Behavior

Recently, Sovner and Lowry (1990) proposed a behavioral assessment methodology that is particularly well suited to the diagnosis of affective disorders among the mentally retarded. The authors distinguished five departure points for this behavioral methodology:

1. Behavioral equivalents of some of the manic and depressive symptoms are recognizable (for example, manic overactivity) and are therefore quantifiable.
2. Many data systems commonly used in applied behavior analysis are suitable for measuring behavior associated with an affective disorder.
3. Direct-service staff, who provide caregiving supervision to mentally retarded persons at home and work, can be trained to become reliable observers and data collectors.
4. Behavioral data, collected in several different settings and at different times of day, can be pooled to provide a comprehensive picture of an individual's functioning.
5. The data collected provide a baseline with which treatment efficacy can be compared.

The proposed behavioral methodology was further elaborated by Sovner and Lowry in a six-step behavior-monitoring program:

1. Give an operational definition of the behaviors to be measured.
2. Choose appropriate data-collection systems.
3. Frequency counting should be based on manageable and discrete units of the behavior as it occurs.
4. Frequency counting should be based on partial interval recording; that is, the length of time in which the specific behaviors occur should be divided into series of intervals of equal duration.
5. Staff members who work in the client's residence and in the workshop need to be trained by a clinician to use the system.
6. The partial-interval and frequency-recording system permits multiple behavior analyses across hours, days, weeks, or months. Statistical

analysis and graphic techniques can bring behavioral patterns or correlations to light.

Matson and Barrett (1982) advocated a diagnostic methodology based on observable, operationally defined behaviors rather than on inferred behaviors. The proposition of these authors is that three systems are of value in obtaining objectively measurable information about the behavioral characteristic of depression:

1. Recorded information obtained from interviews with mildly or moderately mentally retarded persons. Sometimes, the oral rating scales used for depression in nonretarded population are applicable.
2. Ratings by significant others or the most knowledgeable informant, referred to as the *third-party method.*
3. Assessment by operationally defined behavior that can be directly observed in either analogue or naturalistic environments.

*Rating Scales*

Love and Matson (1990) made an inventory of the diagnostic instruments used to assess depression among the mentally retarded. However, the authors and others (Beck et al., 1987) have stressed that, as most of these instruments were developed for the nonretarded population, ratings based on self-reports are limited to the mildly retarded. When administering these tests to very young individuals or to the severely mentally retarded, one has to rely increasingly on ratings by others or on direct behavioral observation. Sometimes, modification of the instruments is useful, for example, reading the instrument to the subject, changing the wording, or using shortened forms of the instrument. The diagnosis of depression is usually based on a certain cutoff score. Sometimes, the severity of the illness is indicated by the total score.

We have summarized Love and Matson's survey, including their psychometric qualities, in Tables 2 and 3. Instruments for both adults and children have been noted separately.

*Biological Markers*

Recently, investigators in the field of depression have increasingly been searching for biological markers of this disorder. Considering the difficulties encountered in recognizing the symptomatology of depression among the

## Table 2
### Instruments for Diagnosis of Depression in Mentally Retarded Adults

| Name | Reliability | Validity | Administration |
|------|-------------|----------|----------------|
| Beck Depression Inventor | Split-half, .86–.93; internal consistency high | Construct val. good Concurrent val. good; discriminant val. weak | Statements can be read by clinician. Short form available. |
| Zung Self-Rating Scale | Split-half, .82–.93; internal consistency high | Concurrent val. good | Statements can be read by clinician. |
| Depression Adjective Checklists | Internal consistency acceptable or less; split-half, .65–.88; test–retest adequate stability or less; coefficient alpha, .83 | Not fully validated Concurrent val. good | Both informant and self-report versions available. Informant ratings. Statements can be read by clinician. |
| Psychopathology Instrument for M.R. Adults (PIMRA), incl. Affective Subscale | | | |
| Hamiliton Psychiatric Rating Scale for Depression | Internal consistency adequate; interrater score excellent | | |
| Minnesota Multiphasic Personality Inventory, incl. Depression Scale (MMPI-D) | Split-half for MMPI-D, .35–.84; test–retest for MMPI-D moderate | | |

Source: S. R. Love and J. L. Matson. (1990). "Diagnostic Instruments for Depression in the Mentally Retarded." In A. Dosen and F. J. Menolascino (Eds.), *Depression in Mentally Retarded Children and Adults*. Leiden, The Netherlands: Logon Publications.

mentally retarded, finding biological markers would be of great importance to the diagnostician. However, because of the biological abnormalities of the mentally retarded, a question arises about whether finding specific biochemical aberrations in depressed retarded persons would have the same diagnostic significance it would in nonretarded individuals. The opinions of various investigators diverge on this issue.

The dexamethasone suppression test (DST) has shown that 40 to 70 percent of nonretarded psychotic depressed patients fail to suppress plasma cortisol, compared to only 5 percent of controls (Ruedrich, 1990). However, this nonsuppression has also been reported in various organic, developmental, and psychiatric disorders. Studies making use of the DST with the mentally retarded are scarce. Some investigators (Pirodsky et al., 1985; Reudrich et al., 1987) have found that the DST may be a valuable instrument for diagnosing depression in the mentally retarded when it is used in combination with other information concerning the clinical picture, family history, and other relevant features. Sireling (1986) questioned how helpful this test is because of the negative outcome of the test with a number of clinically

Table 3
Instruments for Diagnosis of Depression in Mentally Retarded Children

| Name | Reliability | Validity | Administration |
|------|-------------|----------|----------------|
| Bellevue Index of Depression<br>Child Depression Inventory<br>Child Behavior Checklist, incl. Depression Subscale | Test–retest relatively stable for shorter time interval: split-half, .85. Test–retest, .82–.90 | Convergent val. good; concurrent val. good. Construct val. favorable. | Appropriate for ages 6–12. Patient + parent interview + school data are used in making ratings.<br>Appropriate for ages 7–17. Both self- and informant-report versions.<br>Appropriate for ages 4–16. Ratings preferably based on in- |

Source: S. R. Love and J. L. Matson. (1990). "Diagnostic Instruments for Depression in the Mentally Retarded." In A. Dosen and F. J. Menolascino (Eds.), *Depression in Mentally Retarded Children and Adults*. Leiden, The Netherlands: Logon Publications.

depressed patients. Also, relatively often, false-positive nonsuppressions may make the application of the DST with these individuals questionable.

Ruedrich (1990) reported that the baseline hypercortisolemia of the mentally retarded patients examined correlated significantly with the symptomatology of psychiatric and behavioral disorders and older age. Ruedrich stressed that all symptoms found were not depression-specific, and that, apparently, the same biochemical findings may be encountered in other psychiatric and behavioral disorders.

Investigators of nonretarded depressive patients have made attempts to find other, more reliable biological markers of depression, like blunted TSH (thyroid-stimulating hormone) and changes in the level of particular neurotransmitters.

Unfortunately, it is rare that this sort of research is carried out on the mentally retarded population. This rarity undoubtedly represents the small amount of interest that scientists have nowadays in investigating the affective disorders of the mentally retarded.

## Summary and Conclusion

The diagnosis of depression among the mentally retarded is a great challenge to clinicians working on the mental health care of the dually diagnosed. Diagnostic overshadowing (Reiss & Szyszko, 1983) is certainly related to the affective illness of the mentally retarded.

There are no particular diagnostic problems in light forms of retardation with the more severe forms of depression (that is, psychotic depression), in which sad facial expression, vital characteristics, periodicity, psychomotoric retardation, or agitation dominate the clinical picture. More diagnostic uncertainty arises in more severe forms of retardation and when atypical symptoms of a "masked" (neurotic or reactive) depression come to the fore. Differential diagnostic questions come up when affective symptoms coexist with organic brain damage, early dementia, symptoms of early schizophrenia, or pervasive developmental disorders. Traditionally, research on the affective diseases of the mentally retarded has dealt largely with the differential criteria for the psychotic-neurotic dichotomy.

Modifications of the DSM-III-R criteria for establishing the diagnosis of major affective disorder have proved to be useful in clinical practice. Self-report or other-report rating scales have been an aid in operationalizing depressive symptoms into overt measurable behaviors. These instruments may give more (differential) diagnostic certainty to the clinician. A sophisticated behavioral methodology has become available for the assessment of changes in symptomatology and treatment efficacy. The psychodynamic approach has pointed out the developmentally specific symptomatology of depression. According to this point of view, the phenomenology of depression reflects psychobiological consequences specific to the associated socioemotional level. This developmental approach concedes that the behavioral manifestations are not necessarily related only to psychotic or neurotic depression. It suggests that individual behavioral manifestations may have the meaning of reflecting or even reiterating the mechanisms that have contributed to the experiences of the loss of the bonding figure, the loss of self-representation, or the loss of the sense of self. In addition, there are questions about the relation of depression to particular types of mental retardation, certain dysfunctions of the central nervous system, and particular biological failures.

It is obvious that the cognitive level has an influence on the presentation of the symptoms. However, it is not clear to what extent delayed cognitive development plays a role in the onset and the type of depression. Also, it is not clear to what extent the personality characteristics of the mentally retarded play a role in the onset of depression. The specific environmental circumstances and characteristic interactional patterns of the mentally retarded person and his or her surroundings have been hypothesized as predisposing the mentally retarded to depression. However, all these hypotheses and speculations lack scientific verification. Many more investigations are necessary in this field before we attain insight into the various specificities of the phenomenon of depression among the mentally retarded. These insights are essential for the adequate treatment and prevention of this disorder.

For practical purposes, integrative or holistic assessment methods are proposed. A number of diagnostic instruments are now being used or are being developed. The suitability of these instruments for all levels of retardation is, however, still questionable.

The search for new psychological as well as biological markers of depression is promising.

## References

Abraham, K. (1927). Notes on the psychoanalytic investigation and treatment of manic-depressive insanity and allied conditions. In E. Jones (Ed.), *Selected Papers*. London: Hogarth Press.

American Psychiatric Association. (1987). *Diagnostic and statistical manual of mental disorders* (3rd ed., rev.; DSM-III-R). Washington, DC: Author.

Aricti, S. (1977). Psychotherapy of severe depression. *Am. J. Psychiatr., 134,* 864–868.

Beck, C. B., Carlson, G. A., Russel, A., & Brownfield, F. E. (1987). Use of depression rating instruments in developmentally and educationally delayed adolescents. *J. Am. Acad. Child Adol. Psychiatr., 26*(1), 97–100.

Bemporad, J. R., & Wilson, A. (1978). A developmental approach to depression in childhood and adolescence. *J. Am. Psychoanal., 6*(3), 325–352.

Benson, B. A. (1985). Behavior disorder and mental retardation: Association with age, sex and level of functioning in an outpatient clinic sample. *Appl. Res. Ment. Retard., 6,* 79–88.

Berney, T. P. & Jones, P. M. (1989). Manic-depressive disorder in the mentally handicapped. Australia and New Zealand *J. Develop. Disabil.* 19, 219–225.

Bowlby, J. (1952). Maternal care and mental health. Genf: WHO Monograph Series No. 2.

Bowlby, J. V. (1973). *Attachment and loss: Vol. 2. Separation.* New York: Basic Books.

Brumback, R. A., & Staton, R. D. (1982). A hypothesis regarding the commonality of right hemisphere involvement in learning disability, attentional disorder, and childhood major depressive disorder. *Percept and Motor Skills, 55,* 1091–1097.

Burd, L., & Kerbeshian, J. (1988). Psychogenic and neurodevelopmental factors in autism. *J. Am. Child Psychol., 27*(2) 252–253.

Carlson, G. A. (1987). The impact of the pathoplastic effects of mental retardation on the phenomenology of depression. Paper presented at International Research Conference on the Mental Retardation, Chicago.

Cochrane, N. (1990). Physical contact experiences and depression. *Acta Psychiatr. Scand.,* Suppl. 357, 82.

Corbett, J. A. (1979). Psychiatric morbidity and mental retardation. In F. E. James & R. P. Snaith (Eds.), *Psychiatric illness and mental handicap* (pp. 11–25). London: Gaskell.

Day, K. A. (1990). Depression in mildly and moderately retarded adults. In A. Dosen & F. J. Menolascino (Eds.), *Depression in mentally retarded children and adults.* Leiden: Logon.

Day, K. A. (1985). Psychiatric disorder in the middle-aged and elderly mentally handicapped. *B. J. Psychiat. 197,* 660–667.

Dellisch, H. von (1983). Das symbiotisch-psychotisches Syndrom (M. S. Mahler). *Prax. Kinderpsychol., 32,* 305–310.

Dosen, A., (1979). Manisch-depressieve ziekte bij kinderen. *Ned. T. Geneesk., 123,* 4.

Dosen, A. (1984). Depressive conditions in mentally retarded children. *Acta Paedopsychiatr., 50,* 29–40.

Dosen, A. (1988). The developmental approach to the diagnosis of psychiatric disorders among mentally retarded adults. Paper to the Regional Symposium World Psychiatric Association, Washington, DC.

Dosen, A. (1990a). Depression in mentally retarded children and adults. In A. Dosen & F. J. Menolascino (Eds.), *Depression in mentally retarded children and adults.* Leiden: Logon.

Dosen, A. (1990b). *Psychische en gedragsstoornissen bij zwakzinnigen.* Amsterdam: Boom Meppel.

Dosen, A., & Bojanin, S. (1990). Developmental and biological factors in the mentally retarded and vulnerability to depression. In A. Dosen & F. J. Menolascino (Eds.), *Depression in mentally retarded children and adults.* Leiden: Logon.

Dosen, A., & Gielen, J. J. M. (1990). Psychological characteristics of mentally retarded persons and the risk of depression. In A. Dosen & F. J. Menolascino (Eds.), *Depression in mentally retarded children and adults.* Leiden: Logon.

Engel, G. L., & Reichsman, F. (1956). Spontaneous and experimentally induced depressions in an infant with a gastric fistula. *J. Am. Psychoanal. Assoc., 4,* 428–452.

Frank, L. K. (1957). Tactile communication. *Genet. Psychol. Monogr., 56,* 209–225.

Freud, A. (1965). *Normality and pathology in childhood.* New York: International Universities Press.

Freud, S. (1957). *Mourning and melancholia.* London: Hogarth Press. (First edition, 1927.)

Gaedt, Ch., & Gärtner, D. (1990). Depressive Grundprozesse: Reinszenierungen des Selbstentwertung. In Ch. Gaedt (Ed.), *Selbstentwertung—depressieve Inszenierungen bei Menschen mit geistiger Behinderung.* Neuerkerode: Neuerkeröder Forum 4.

Gillberg, C., Presson, E., Grufman, N., & Themmer, V. (1986). Psychiatric disorders in mildly and severely mentally retarded urban children and adolescents: epidemiological aspects. *Brit. J. Psychiatr., 149,* 68–74.

Gostason, R. (1985). Psychiatric illness among the mentally retarded: A Swedish population study. *Acta Psychiatr. Scand., 71,* (Suppl. 318), 1–117.

Harlow, H. F. (1958). The nature of love. *Am. Psychol., 13,* 673–685.

Heaton-Ward, A. (1977). Psychosis in mental handicap, *B. J. Psychiatr. 130,* 525–533.

Hucker, S. J. (1985). Is mania incompatible with Down's syndrome. *Br. J. Psychiatr., 147,* 93–94.

Hucker, S. J., Day, K. A., George, S., & Roth, M. (1979). Psychosis in mentally handicapped adults. In F. E. James & R. P. Snaith (Eds.), *Psychiatric illness and mental handicap.* London: Gaskell.

Kischkel, W., Pohl, K., Rüster, K., Schultz, R. Sievers, R., & Störmer, N. (1990). Therapeutischer Ansätze bei Menschen mit schwerergeistiger Behinderung und depressieven Symptomen. In Ch. Gaedt (Ed.), *Selbstentwertung—depressieve Inszenierungen bei Menschen mit geistiger Behinderung.* Neuerkerode: Neuerkeröder Forum 4.

Levitas, A., & Gilson, S. F. (1990). Toward the developmental understanding of the impact of mental retardation on the assessment of psychopathology. In E. Dibble & D. B. Gray (Eds): *Assessment of behavior problems in persons with mental retardation living in the community;* Rockville, MD: National Institute of Mental Health.

Love, S. R., & Matson, J. L. (1990). Diagnostic instruments for depression in the mentally retarded. In A. Dosen & F. J. Menolascino (Eds.), *Depression in mentally retarded children and adults.* Leiden: Logon.

Lund, J. (1985). Behavioral symptoms and autistic psychosis in the mentally retarded adult. *Acta Psychiatr. Scand., 71,* 429–436.

Mahler, M. S., Pine, F., & Bergman, A. (1975). *The psychological birth of the human infant.* New York: Basic Books.

Matson, J. L., & Barrett, R. P. (1982a). Affective disorders. In J. L. Matson & R. P. Barrett (Eds.), *Psychopathology in the mentally retarded.* New York: Grune & Stratton.

McGee, J. (1989). *Being with others: Toward a psychology of interdependence.* Omaha, NE: Creighton University.

Menolascino, F. J. (1988). Reflections on depression in the severely retarded: Diagnostic and treatment challenges. Unpublished paper.

Menolascino, F. J. (1990). Mental retardation and the risk, nature and types of mental illness. In A. Dosen & F. J. Menolascino (Eds.), *Depression in mentally retarded children and adults.* Leiden: Logon.

Menolascino, F. J., Levitas, A., & Greiner, C. (1986). The nature and types of mental illness in the mentally retarded. *Psychopharmacol. Bull., 22,* 1060–1071.

Menolascino, F. J., & Weiler, M. A. (1990). The challenge of depression and suicide in severely mentally retarded adults. In A. Dosen & F. J. Menolascino (Eds.), *Depression in mentally retarded children and adults.* Leiden: Logon.

Montagu, A. (1971). *Touching: the humane significance of the skin.* New York: Columbia University Press.

Nissen, G. (1980). Psychogene Störungen mit vorweigend psychischer Symptomatik. In J. Harbauer, R. Lempp, G. Nissen, & P. Strunck (Eds.), *Lehrbuch der speziellen Kinder- und Jugendpsychiatrie.* New York, Berlin, Heidelberg: Springer.

Pawlarcyzk, D., & Beckwith, B. E. (1987). Depressive symptoms displayed by persons with mental retardation: A review. *Ment. Retard., 25*(6)325–330.

Pirodsky, D. M., Gibbs, J. W., Hesse, R. A., Hseih, M. C., Krause, R. B., & Rodriguez, W. H. (1985). Use of the dexamethasone suppression test to detect depressive disorders of mentally retarded individuals. *Am. J. Ment. Defic., 90,* 245–252.

Praag, H. M. van, Uleman, A. N., & Spitz, J. C. (1965). The vital syndrome interview for the recognition and registration of the vital depressive symptom complex. *Psychiatr., Neurol., Neurochir., 68,* 329.

Realmuto, G. M., Garfinkel, B. D., Tuchman, M., Tsai, M. Y., Chang, P., Fisch, R. O., & Shapiro, S. (1986). Psychiatric diagnosis and behavioral characteristics of phenylketonuric children. *J. Nerv. Ment. Dis., 9,* 536–540.

Reid, A. H. (1972). Psychoses in adult mental defectives: 1. Manic depressive psychosis. *Br. J. Psychiatr., 120,* 205–212.

Reid, A. H. (1982). *The psychiatry of mental handicap.* London: Basil Blackwell.

Reid, A. H. (1985). Psychiatry and mental handicap. In M. Craft, J. Bicknell, & S. Hollins (Eds.), Mental handicap, a multi-disciplinary approach. London: Balliére Tindall.

Reid, A. H., & Naylor, G. J. (1976). Short-cycle manic depressive psychosis in mental defectives: A clinical and physiological study. *J. Ment. Defic. Res., 20,* 67–76.

Reid, A. H., Swanson, A. J. G., Jain, A. S., Spowart, G., & Wright, A. F. (1987). Manic depressive psychosis with mental retardation and flexion deformities: A clinical and cytogenetic study. *Br. J. Psychiatr., 150,* 92–97.

Reiss, A. L., Feinstein, C., Toomey, K. E., Goldsmith, B., Rosenbauw, K., & Caruso, M. A. (1988). Psychiatric disability associated with the fragile X chromosome. *Am. J. Med. Gen., 23,* 393–401.

Reiss, S., & Szyszko, J. (1983). Diagnostic overshadowing and professional experience with mentally retarded persons. *Am. J. Ment. Defic., 87,* 396–402.

Richardson, S. A., Katz, M., Koller, H., McLaren L., & Rubinstein, B. (1979). Some characteristics of a population of mentally retarded young adults in a British city: A basis for estimating some service needs. *J. Ment. Defic. Res., 23,* 275–283.

Ruedrich, S. L. (1990). Biochemical findings in mentally retarded persons with depressive disorder. In A. Dosen & F. J. Menolascino (Eds.), *Depressive illness in mentally retarded persons.* Leiden: Logon.

Ruedrich, S. L., Wadke, C. V., Sallach, H., Hahn, R., & Menolascino, F. J. (1987). Adrenocortical function and depressive illness in mentally retarded patients. *Am. J. Psychiatr., 144,* 537–602.

Sandler, A., & Joffee, W. G. (1965). Notes on childhood depression. *Int. J. Psychoanal., 46,* 89–96.

Singh, I. (1988). Down's syndrome with mania. *Br. J. Psychiatr., 152,* 436–437.

Sireling, L. (1986). Depression in mentally handicapped patients: Diagnostic and neuroendocrine evaluation. *Br. J. Psychiatr., 149,* 274–278.

Sorensen, K., & Nielsen, J. (1977). Twenty psychotic males with Klinefelter's syndrom. *Acta Psychiatr. Scand., 56,* 249–255.

Sovner, R. (1986). Limiting factors in the use of DSM-III criteria with mentally ill/mentally retarded persons. *Psychopharm. Bull., 22,* 1055–1060.

Sovner, R. (1990). Bipolar disorder in persons with developmental disorders: An overview. A. Dosen & F. J. Menolascino (Eds.), *Depression in mentally retarded children and adults.* Leiden: Logon.

Sovner, R., & Hurley, A. D. (1990, December). Affective disorder update. *Habilatative Ment. Healthcare Newsl., 9*(12), 103–108.

Sovner, R., Hurley, A. D., & Labrie, R. (1985). Is mania incompatible with Down's syndrome? *Br. J. Psychiatr., 46,* 319–320.

Sovner, R., & Lowry, M. A. (1990). A behavioral methodology for diagnosing affective disorders in individuals with mental retardation. *Habilitative Ment. Healthcare Newsl., 9*(7), 55–61.

Spitz, R. (1946). Anaclitic depression. *Psychoanal. Study Child, 2,* 113–117.

Steingard, R., & Biederman, J. (1987). Lithium responsive manic-like symptoms in two individuals with autism and mental retardation. *J. Am. Acad. Child Adol. Psychiatr., 26,* 932–935.

Szymanski, L. S. (1988). Integrative approach to diagnosis of mental disorders in retarded persons. In J. Stark, F. J. Menolascino, N. Albarelli, & V. Gray (Eds.), *Mental retardation and mental health.* New York: Springer.

Szymanski, L. S., & Biederman, J. (1984). Depression and anorexia nervosa of persons with Down syndrome. *Am. J. Ment. Defic., 89,* 246–251.

Warren, A. C., Holroyd, S., & Folstein, M. F. (1989). Major depression in Down's syndrome. *Br. J. Psychiatr., 155,* 202–205.

Way, M. C. (1983). The symptoms of affective disorder in severely retarded children. Paper presented at IASSMD Congress, Toronto. Not published.

Wright, E. C. (1982). The presentation of mental illness in mentally retarded adults. *Br. J. Psychiatr., 141,* 496–502.

Yalom, I. (1980). *Existential psychotherapy.* New York: Basic Books.

# 5

## Schizophrenic and Paranoid Syndromes in Persons with Mental Retardation: Assessment and Diagnosis

*Andrew Reid*

Distinctions have been drawn between mental illness and mental handicap for centuries, but no one has put it more succinctly than Esquirol who, in 1845, commented, "A man in a state of dementia is deprived of advantages which he formerly enjoyed: he was a rich man who has become poor. The idiot, on the other hand, has always been in a state of want and misery" (p. 447). Around the same time as Esquirol drew this seminal distinction, Wells, also in 1945, noted the presence of "Mania in cretins as well as a particular suicidal form of the affliction which prompts the wretched maniac to attempt self-destruction by throwing himself in the fire" (cited in Ireland, 1898, p. 281).

In 1866, Seguin divided psychoses in idiot children into hyperkinetic and hypokinetic types. In 1867, Griesinger retained Seguin's groupings but renamed them "apathetic" and "excited" types. In 1888, Hurd commented that the attacks occurring in the lower grades could not be considered insanity, but that the psychoses of the higher grades were similar in type and progression to those in previously normal individuals. He identified cases of mania, melancholia, attempted suicide or homicide, persistent delusions, and *"folie circulaire"* in mentally retarded patients. In 1898, Ireland gave a good description of melancholia in a small series of mentally retarded females. And Clouston, also in 1898, commented:

> Congenital imbeciles may have attacks of maniacal excitement or melancholic depression—in fact, are subject to them. They may become impulsive, dangerous and even homicidal: they may, after an attack, have secondary stupor, or may become demented as compared with their primitive condition.

By the turn of the century, therefore, a distinction had been drawn between mental illness and mental handicap, and the concept of hyperkinetic/hypokinetic or excited/apathetic types had emerged. There were descriptions of melancholia, mania, *folie circulaire,* and persistent delusions, and also of behavior disorders and associated aggressiveness.

It was Kraepelin who attempted to bring system and order into clinical psychiatry in the earlier years of the twentieth century by studying the natural history of groups of patients over many years. His was part of the German fascination with nosology and classification, and it was he who introduced the concepts of manic-depressive insanity and dementia praecox (1896, 1919), concepts that were reflected in the writings of Gordon (1916, 1918) in the United States.

Kraepelin (1896) took the view that approximately 7 percent of cases of dementia praecox arose on the basis of imbecility. He also suggested that "certain forms of idiocy with developed mannerisms and stereotypies might be early cases of dementia praecox," and he proposed the term *"Pfropfschizophrenie"* to denote "eine besonders früh entstandene Schizophrenie." Although he later modified his views and agreed that the rhythmic movements seen in some idiots did not, in fact, signify dementia praecox, he continued to believe that dementia praecox beginning in the first decade could produce "states of weakness . . . regarded as imbecility or idiocy."

This suggestion opened up a lively debate. Bleuler (1916) disagreed and stated that "the stereotyped behaviour of idiots is basically different from catatonia" (p. 287). Beier (1919, p. 95) believed that dementia praecox "is frequently a cause of mental infeeblement which passes for imbecility" and Greene (1930) suggested that intrauterine, perinatal, or infantile damage to the brain could produce in one individual (congenital) feeblemindedness and in another dementia praecox at a later stage. Critchley and Earl (1932) described twenty-nine cases of tuberose sclerosis and claimed that they showed "a primitive type of catatonic schizophrenia," basing their diagnosis on "a variety of complex hand and finger movements, mannerisms and stereotypes, as well as other signs." Earl followed this paper in 1934 with a further description of thirty-eight idiots; using diagnostic criteria rather similar to those in the previous paper, he maintained that the patients showed a primitive catatonic psychosis, "a form of schizophrenia played out upon the psychomotor level rather than the symbolic." Glaus (1936) tried to introduce a further subdivision; he wished to retain the term *Pfropfschizophrenie* for mental defectives in whom a schizophrenic psychosis appeared in the third or fourth decade, and he suggested that the term *"schizophrene Fruhdemenz"* be used to accommodate the view that "certain forms of idiocy with mannerisms and stereotypies might be cause by infantile forms of dementia praecox."

Neustadt (1927), however, placed little diagnostic weight on "catatonic" disturbance of motility in mental defectives, and Brugger (1928) and

Katzenfuss (1935) also argued against retaining the term, maintaining that there was nothing particularly distinctive about schizophrenic psychoses in mental defectives.

By the late 1930s, therefore, the term *Pfropfschizophrenie* was under attack. It had come to mean so many things to so many different investigators that is ceased to be of clinical use, and it gradually withered away.

Hayman (1939) opened a new phase with his particularly well-documented review. He maintained that the lowest grades showed an undifferentiated psychosis, with a constitutional periodicity in some cases. With increasing levels of intelligence, reactions suggestive of adult forms of mental illness emerged. Herskovitz and Plesset (1941) followed this assertion by suggesting that schizophrenia could not be diagnosed on clinical grounds in patients with an IQ much below 50. Penrose (1963) also confined the diagnosis of schizophrenia to high grade mental defectives.

Most contemporary investigators would now agree in confining the diagnosis of schizophrenia to the mild range of mental retardation (IQ 50–70) and to patients who have a reasonable degree of verbal fluency (Reid, 1972; Heaton-Ward, 1977; Hucker et al., 1979; Day, 1985). Flickers of the old debate still appear, however, in the works of O'Gorman (1970) and McGee et al. (1984), who have speculated on the possibility of diagnosing schizophrenia in some severely retarded patients on the grounds of motility phenomena alone.

The motor disorders of mental handicap have been the subject of a scholarly and wide-ranging review by Rogers et al. (1991), who studied 236 residents in a hospital for the mentally handicapped in the Bristol area. They found widespread motor disorder in this population and showed that it correlated with the degree of retardation, the presence of epilepsy, the diagnosis of psychiatric disorder (unspecified), and the use of neuroleptic medication. They commented, however, that comparable motor disorders were also found in those patients who were, and had always been, neuroleptic-free. They suggested that most of these motor disorders were essentially extrapyramidal phenomena and related to the underlying cerebral disorder.

The historical background of the issue of schizophrenia in mental retardation has been summarized by Reid (1971) and Turner (1989).

## Diagnosis

Systems of classification come and go and have their advocates and detractors. The third edition of the American Psychiatric Association (APA, 1980) *Diagnostic and Statistical Manual* (DSM-III) followed the ninth edition of the World Health Organization (WHO, 1975) *International Classification of Diseases* (ICD-9) and will itself be followed by the ICD-10. The clinical symptoms of schizophrenia persist unchanged, however, and the diagnosis is still based on the descriptive psychopathology summarized by Batchelor (1964) as follows:

> The diagnosis of schizophrenia is clinical and based on various symptoms which tend to be language-based. The significance of these symptoms has to be evaluated against the background of previous personality, the mode of onset of the disability, and the course of the illness. The main symptoms include ideas of influence, made experiences, auditory hallucinations, thought disorder, primary delusions and abnormalities of affect and of motility.

The diagnosis is clinical and firmly rooted in language-based phenomenology, and a certain level of intelligence is required for the patient to be able to describe the key diagnostic concepts. For that reason, it remains my view that the diagnosis can be established with any degree of conviction only in mentally retarded adults with an IQ of above 45 (that is, the upper end of the moderate range of mental retardation).

Moreover, the limited verbal competence that usually accompanies mental retardation of any significant degree inevitably makes interviewing difficult in that there may be problems with suggestibility and lack of concentration. As a result, it may be necessary to rely on frequent shorter interviews, carried out over a longer time span, and supplemented in all cases by a reliable third-party account.

## Prevalence

There have been no convincing prevalence studies based on a widespread ascertainment of the number of mentally retarded people in both residential and community settings, accompanied by a systematic assessment of intelligence and defined diagnostic criteria for schizophrenia. The issue is bedeviled by the fact that the condition of mild mental retardation is established in the United Kingdom on the combined grounds of intellectual retardation and social incompetence of such a degree as to require special services. The prevalence rates of mild mental retardation in the United Kingdom are, therefore, low for preschool children; reach a peak during school age, when special educational facilities are required; and then trail off rapidly in adult life, when the mildly retarded person usually succeeds in leading a relatively independent life. As a result, most prevalence studies of schizophrenia in mild mental retardation refer only to that segment of the mildly mentally retarded adult population that requires services. This problem is illustrated in Table 1.

Even so, several investigators have tried their best to estimate prevalence rates, and Table 2 summarizes the results of these investigations.

## Table 1
### Estimated Numbers of Mentally Retarded Persons
(*rates per thousand population*)

|  | Severe | Mild |
|---|---|---|
| Preschool | 3.0 | — |
| School age | 3.6 | 8.7 |
| Adult | 2.0 | 2.5 |

Source: After SHHD and SED (1979).

Despite the variety of methods, aims, ascertainment, and diagnostic criteria, among all these surveys, there is a surprising consensus around a point prevalence rate of some 3 percent of mentally handicapped adults with a schizophrenic illness. This is above the rate in the general population and raises the question of whether there is an increased liability to schizophrenia in mentally retarded adults. Two large Swedish community surveys (Hallgren & Sjogren, 1959; Larsson & Sjogren, 1954) give indirect support to this view with the finding of a 10.5 percent rate of "mental deficiency" among a registered cohort of schizophrenics.

Perhaps a more likely explanation, however, derives from the fact that only one-third, or thereabouts, of adults with an IQ in the range of 50–70 are in contact with services (see Table 1). Since schizophrenia is probably one of the reasons that people in this intelligence range require services, there would accordingly be a very significant overrepresentation of schizophrenia among that segment of the mildly retarded population that is known to the statutory services. The issue will not be resolved until there is a convincing whole-population survey.

## Clinical Features

Historically, four main subtypes of schizophrenia have been recognized: simple, hebephrenic, catatonic, and paranoid. Simple schizophrenia is a clinical syndrome with few distinctive or convincing diagnostic features, and it is my own view that it cannot be identified with any degree of certainty among mentally retarded people. The main varieties of hebephrenic, catatonic, and paranoid syndromes are all seen in retarded people, however, although these types are not mutually exclusive and admixtures and transitional forms are common.

Some schizophrenic syndromes may develop out of a previous schizoid personality configuration (Wolff, 1991), but more often there is no such association.

Overall, the clinical symptomatology is unremarkable. Disorders of

## Table 2
## Prevalence Surveys of Schizophrenia in Mentally Retarded Adults

| Author | Population Studied | Total Numbers in Study | Nature of Study | Rate % |
|---|---|---|---|---|
| Reid (1972) | Hospital residents | 500 | Point prevalence | 3.2 |
| Heaton-Ward (1977) | Hospital residents | 1,251 | Period prevalence (1yr) | 3.4 |
| Corbett (1979)[a] | Community | 402 | Period prevalence (3 yrs) | 6.2 |
| Wright (1982)[b] | Hospital residents | 1,507 | Point prevalence | 1.8 |
| Day (1985) | Hospital residents | 357 | Not stated | 3.1 |
| Lund (1985)[c] | Community | 302 | Not stated | 1.3 |
| Gostason (1985) | Community | 131 | Point prevalence | 3.0 |

[a]Includes patients with a history of schizophrenia.
[b]Excludes paranoid syndromes.
[c]3.3% in the IQ range 68–85 and 2.6% in the IQ range 52–67.

affect occur, including incongruity and facile cheerfulness. Volition and drive are frequently impaired, but it is difficult to know how much significance to attach to this in mentally retarded people, in whom problems of this sort may be common and quite unrelated to mental illness. Thought disorder occurs in mentally retarded people with schizophrenia and is expressed in abnormalities of speech. These include combinations of echolalia, flitting from subject to subject, tangential replies, incoherence, vorbeireden, verbigeration, perseveration, neologisms, and the incorporation of chance external stimuli from the environment (Reid, 1972). The significance of such symptoms as echolalia has, of course, to be evaluated against the background of the patient's level of development.

Ideas of influence and of self-reference may be expressed with great vividness. Patients may feel that their thoughts can be read by "just looking" or that their thoughts are controlled by a variety of external agencies, including television, radio, and machines of various sorts. The belief that one's speech, behavior, or actions are controlled by an outside agency, and that thoughts are stolen, inserted, broadcast, or visible, is very suggestive of schizophrenia.

Delusions may be grandiose, naive, and at times wish-fulfilling. Sometimes, they are extensive and well ramified and show rationalization, but more often they are featureless, fragmentary, and unconvincing, and their presence can be established with certainty only through repeated interviewing and a following of their evolution. Hallucinations are common, paticularly of hearing, but also of sight. Hucker et al. (1979) found that some patients experience tactile hallucinations as well. Voices may threaten, shout obscenities, discuss, criticize, accuse, talk rubbish, or insert thoughts. They may consist of noises, music, or sounds. Patients may answer back, adopt a listening posture, or even seek to block them out by inserting their fingers in their ears.

Disorders of motility, including recurrent periods of extreme excitement or stupor, flexibilitas cerea, catalepsy, automatic obedience, and negativism, are associated with, but not exclusively confined to, a catatonic schizophrenic presentation.

Some patients with acute schizophrenic symptomatology are very disturbed, impulsively aggressive, noisy, and unpredictable. Assaultive behavior may be associated with hallucinatory instructions, or with the incorporation of carers or relatives in delusional patterns of thinking and experiencing.

> Jean is forty-nine years old and has an IQ of around 60. She comes from an itinerant (Gypsy) family but was extruded even from that relatively undemanding lifestyle in her late teens because of her social incompetence, unreliability, and tendency to pilfer and to prostitute herself. She was seen at that time and noted to be facile and irrational in her replies, and over the years, she has gone on to develop a frank schizophrenic psychosis. She has become grandiose, believing that she is related to the queen and a distinguished surgeon, naval officer, air force commander, and politician, all in one. She is persistently auditorily hallucinated. At the age of forty-seven, she developed grand mal epilepsy, and a brain scan suggested that this had been caused by a brain stem microinfarct. It caused a disturbance of thirst regulation, and she developed polydipsia, leading on to water retention, acute confusional episodes, further fits, and a rapid deterioration in her schizophrenic symptomatology, with problems of noisiness and impulsive aggression. She has now been stabilized at a more acceptable level on a substantial dose of a depot preparation, along with careful monitoring of her fluid intake, and an anticonvulsant.

## Natural History and Prognosis

The hebephrenic and catatonic varieties of schizophrenia typically affect a younger age group, with onset in the second and third decade; the paranoid syndromes are associated more with an older age group, with onset in the fifth decade and onward (Reid, 1972; Day, 1985). The sex distribution in the hebephrenic and catatonic forms appears to be approximately equal, although Reid (1989), by amalgamating the results of several previous investigations, suggested that there may be a female preponderance in the paranoid forms.

Untreated, the psychosis runs a variable course in the early-onset, hebephrenic forms in particular, tending to be more persistent, intrusive, and damaging. Some psychoses run a remittent course in which periods of relative normality are interspersed with acute flare-ups of symptomatology. May (1931) and Milici (1937) felt that, on the whole, schizophrenia is a more benign psychosis in retarded people than in the general population. It is generally agreed now that the paranoid syndromes are characterized by a later and more acute onset, run a more benign course, and are less intrusive and damaging to the personality (Fenton & McGlashan, 1991).

## Differential Diagnosis

In earlier years, there was diagnostic confusion between childhood psychosis and schizophrenia. This was a natural sequel to Kraepelin's earlier work and reflected the undue diagnostic significance that was attached to some of the complex motility disorders encountered, particularly in more severely retarded people. It was Kanner who in 1943 recognized and defined the clinical features of early childhood autism. Subsequent investigators have shown it to be a separate condition from schizophrenia, with a different age of onset, family history of mental illness, genetic pathway, and treatment approach (Rutter, 1985). More recently Cox (1991) and Wolff (1991) have studied the related conditions of Asperger's syndrome and schizoid personality.

Some schizophrenic psychoses present acutely with components of clouding of consciousness and confusional symptoms that may be difficult to distinguish from mixed affective states.

Acute paranoid reactions are sometimes seen in mentally handicapped people, particularly under conditions of stress, threat, and unfamiliarity, for example, custody, questioning, and imprisonment. These acute paranoid syndromes are psychogenically determined and usually settle down quickly on removal from the stressful environment.

Some paranoid syndromes in mentally retarded people turn out eventually to be arising on the basis of an incipient dementing process, which becomes apparent through time.

Some schizophrenic syndromes are unconvincing initially, and the symptomatology fragmentary, and it is only through time that a picture of a progressive schizophrenic psychosis emerges.

George is thirty-five and mildly mentally retarded, with an IQ of around 55. He is an only son, and his parents are elderly and come from a professional background. They have endeavored throughout to maximize his abilities and intellectual potential, and he has a certain verbal competence that belies the underlying degree of retardation. His parents sought advice about him first when he was in his middle twenties and had started to shout out loud and talk in a worried way about disasters and impending catastrophes. At interview, he described seeing "doubles," by which he meant people in the streets masquerading as well-known personalities. There was a suspicion that he was developing a schizophrenic psychosis, but it was unconvincing. No medication was prescribed, but he was noted even then to have abnormal mouth and tongue movements suggestive of a developing orofacial dyskinesia. He has been followed up for some years now and has gone on to develop frank and obvious schizophrenic symptomatology. The "doubles" have persisted and have become more intrusive, and he has started to hear voices emanating from two "spirit" women who talk about him between themselves and prompt, criticize, and instruct him. Sometimes, he answers them back. He realizes that no one else sees them, but to him, they have the conviction of absolute reality. He has become progressively more sluggish and apathetic, although he remains gentle by nature and his social graces are intact. Treatment with trifluoperazine has probably delayed the rate of progression of his symptomatology.

Some mentally retarded people have vivid and prominent fantasy lives, and it is important not to mistake these fantasies for delusional beliefs and not to regard them as pathognomic of schizophrenia (Heaton-Ward, 1977). For example, the statement in midsummer by a middle-aged, moderately retarded man, that it is Christmas today and Santa Claus brought him a present down the chimney, is obviously wish-fulfilling and not a symptom of mental illness.

Finally, isolated cataleptic phenomena are common in mentally retarded patients, particularly among the more severe degrees of mental retardation, and are of uncertain significance; they do not form an acceptable basis for the diagnosis of catatonic schizophrenia (see the historical overview at the beginning of this chapter).

## Physical Abnormalities

A body of research is beginning to build up suggesting that some schizophrenic psychoses, particularly those that run a malignant course and go on to an end-state schizophrenic dementia, are of genetically determined neurodevelopmental origin with pathology affecting the medial temporal lobe (Roberts, 1991). A few cases may be associated with a history of brain damage due to birth injury or perinatal infection, but these cases form a minority. This recent research has tended to place schizophrenia firmly as a biologically determined, organic psychosis.

Paranoid syndromes, especially those occurring in later life, are associated disproportionately frequently with abnormalities of hearing, in particular, and also of vision (Cooper, 1976).

There are no convincing links between chromosomal abnormalities and schizophrenia, and schizophrenic and paranoid syndromes have been reported in association with a range of chromosomal disorders, including the 47 XXY (Klinefelter's syndrome), 47 XXX, 48 XXYY, partial trisomy 5 (Barrett et al., 1988), a balanced translocation on Chromosome II (St. Clair et al., 1990), trisomy 21 and both Down and Turner's syndrome mosaics. In only a minority of these cases has there been coexisting mental retardation, and these cases are summarized in Table 3.

There has been a long debate about the possible association of epilepsy and schizophrenia (Slater, Beard, & Glithero, 1963). Epilepsy is common among mentally retarded people and is related to severity of retardation and multiple handicap. Penrose (1938) quoted an overall prevalence rate of 28 percent for epilepsy in his Colchester survey of 1,280 mentally retarded people. Reid (1989) commented that, against this background, there were no convincing data from previous prevalence studies to support the suggestion that there is a particular association between epilepsy and schizophrenia in retarded people. More recently, Deb and Hunter (1991) carried out a careful study and showed a reverse association between epilepsy and psychiatric disorder in a retarded population, in that there was an increased incidence of psychiatric illness in the nonepileptic, as opposed to the epileptic, groups in their hospital- and community-based study in Leicester.

Table 3
**Chromosomal Abnormalities in Mentally Retarded Adults with Schizophrenia**

| IQ Range | Nature of Chromosomal Abnormality | Psychiatric Diagnosis | Reference |
|----------|-----------------------------------|-----------------------|-----------|
| Moderate | Trisomy 21 | Paranoid schizophrenia | Reid |
| Moderate | 48XXYY | Paranoid schizophrenia | (1972) |
| Mild | 46XX/47XX (Down syndrome mosaic) | Paranoid schizophrenia | |
| Mild | 47XXY (Klinefelter's syndrome) | Paranoid schizophrenia | Wakeling (1972) |
| Moderate | 45XO/46XXY (Turner mosaic) | Paranoid schizophrenia | Heaton-Ward (1977) |
| Moderate | Trisomy 21 | Schizophrenia | Hucker et al. (1979) |
| Mild | 47XXX | Schizoaffective psychosis | Woodhouse et al. (1992) |

# Conclusion

Schizoprenia is a small but important aspect of the psychiatry of mental retardation. The diagnosis is a clinical one, and the same diagnostic parameters apply in mentally retarded people as in people of normal intelligence. There are no particular associations with other disorders, and the natural history and prognosis are along the same lines as in mainstream psychiatry. Treatment is considered in Chapter 12.

# References

American Psychiatric Association. (1987). *Diagnostic and statistical manual of mental disorders* (3rd ed., rev.; DSM-III-R). Washington, DC: Author.

Barrett, A. S., McGillivray, B. C., Jones, B. D., & Tapio Panzar, J. (1988). Partial trisomy chromosome 5 cosegregating with schizophrenia. *Lancet, 1,* 799–800.

Batchelor, I. R. C. (1964). The diagnosis of schizophrenia. *Proc. R. Soc. Med., 57,* 417–19.

Beier, A. L. (1919). The incidence of dementia praecox among the feeble minded. *J. Psychoasthenics, 24,* 89–98.

Bleuler, E. (1916). *Lehrbuch der Psychiatrie.* Trans. A. A. Brill, as *Textbook of psychiatry* (1924). New York: Dover.

Brugger, C. (1928). Die erbbiologische Stellung der Pfropfschizophrenie. *Z. Neurol. Psychiatr., 113,* 348–78.

Clouston, T. S. (1898). *Clinical lectures on mental diseases.* London: Churchill.

Cooper, A. F. (1976). Deafness and psychiatric illness. *Br. J. Psychiatr., 129,* 216–226.

Corbett, J. A. (1979). Psychiatric morbidity and mental retardation. In F. E. James & R. P. Snaith (Eds.), *Psychiatric illness and mental handicap.* London: Gaskell.

Cox, A. D. (1991). Is Asperger's syndrome a useful diagnosis? *Arch. Dis. Childhood, 66,* 259–262.

Critchley, M., & Earl, C. J. C. (1932). Tuberous sclerosis and allied conditions. *Brain, 55,* 311–346.

Day, K. A. (1985). Psychiatric disorder in the middle-aged and elderly mentally handicapped. *Br. J. Psychiat., 147,* 660–667.

Deb, S., & Hunter, D. (1991). Psychopathology of people with mental handicap and epilepsy: 2. Psychiatric illness. *Br. J. Psychiatr., 159,* 826–830.

Earl, C. J. C. (1934). The primitive catatonic psychosis of idiocy. *Br. J. Med. Psychol., 14,* 231–253.

Esquirol, J. E. D. (1845). *Mental maladies: A treatise on insanity.* Trans. E. K. Hunt. Philadelphia: Lea & Blanchard.

Fenton, W. S., & McGlashan, T. H. (1991). Natural history of schizophrenia subtypes: 1. Longitudinal study of paranoid, hebephrenic and undifferentiated schizophrenia. *Arch. Gen. Psychiatr., 48,* 969–977.

Glaus, A. (1936). Üxber Pfropfschizophrenie und schizophrene Fruhdemenz. *Schweiz. Arch. Neurol. Psychiatr., 37,* 238–252; *38,* 37–68.

Gordon, A. (1916). Psychoneuroses, psychoses and mental deficiency in 2000 cases considered especially from the standpoint of etiological incidents and sex. *Trans. Am. Med. Psychiatr. Assoc., 23*, 439–454.

Gordon, A. (1918). Psychoses in mental defects. *Am. J. Insanity, 75*, 489–499.

Gostason, R. (1985). Psychiatric illness among the mentally retarded: A Swedish population study. *Acta Psychiatr. Scand.* (Suppl. 318).

Greene, R. A. (1930). Psychoses and mental deficiencies, comparisons and relationships. *J. Psychoasthenics 35*, 128–147.

Griesinger, W. (1867). *Mental pathology and therapeutics*. London.

Hallgren, B., & Sjogren, T. (1959). A clinical and genetico-statistical study of schizophrenia and low-grade mental deficiency in a large Swedish rural population. *Acta Psychiatr. Neurol. Scand.* (Suppl. 140). Copenhagen: Munksgaard.

Hayman, M. (1939). The interrelations of mental defect and mental disorder. *J. Ment. Sci., 85*, 1183–1193.

Heaton-Ward, A. (1977). Psychosis in mental handicap. *Br. J. Psychiatr., 130*, 525–533.

Herskovitz, H. H., & Plesset, M. R. (1941). Psychoses in adult mental defectives. *Psychiatr. Q., 15*, 574–588.

Hucker, S. J., Day, K. A., George, S., & Roth, M. (1979). Psychosis in mentally handicapped adults. In F. E. James & R. P. Snaith (Eds.), *Psychiatric illness and mental handicap*. London: Gaskell.

Hurd, H. M. (1888). Imbecility with insanity. *Am. J. Insanity, 45*, 261–269.

Ireland, W. W. (1898). *The mental affections of children: Idiocy, imbecility and insanity*. London: Churchill.

Kanner, L. (1943). Autistic disturbances of affective contact. *Nerv. Child, 2*, 217–250.

Katzenfuss, H. (1935). Beitrag zum Problem der Pfropfschizophrenie. *Schweiz. Arch. Neurol. Psychiatr., 35*, 295–316.

Kraepelin, E. (1896). Psychiatrie. Trans. as *Clinical psychiatry* 1902). New York: A. R. Deferndorf.

Kraepelin, E. (1919). *Dementia: Praecox and paraphrenia*. Trans. R. M. Barclay. Edinburgh: Livingstone.

Larsson, T., & Sjogren, T. (1954). A methodological psychiatric and statistical study of a large Swedish rural population. *Acta Psychiatr. Neurol. Scand.* (Suppl. 89). Copenhagen: Munksgaard.

Lund, J. (1985). The prevalence of psychiatric morbidity in mentally retarded adults. *Acta Psychiatr. Scand., 72*, 563–570.

May, J. V. (1931). The dementia praecox–schizophrenia problem. *Am. J. Psychiatr., 11*, 401–446.

McGee, J. J., Folk, L., Swanson, D. A., & Menolascino, F. J. (1984). A model inpatient psychiatric programme: Its relationship to a continuum of care for the mentally retarded–mentally ill. In F. J. Menolascino & J. A. Stark (Eds.), *Handbook of mental illness in the mentally retarded*. New York: Plenum Press.

Milici, P. (1937). Pfropfschizophrenia: Schizophrenia engrafted upon mental deficiency. *Psychiatr. Q., 11*, 190–212.

Neustadt, R. (1927). Über Pfropfschizophrenie. *Arch. Psychiatr., 82*, 78–84.

O'Gorman, G. (1970). *The nature of childhood autism* (2nd ed.). London: Butterworths.

Penrose, L. S. (1963). *The biology of mental defect* (3rd ed.). London: Sidgwick & Jackson.

Reid, A. H. (1971). *Mental illness in adult mental defectives with special reference to psychosis.* MD thesis, University of Dundee.

Reid, A. H. (1972). Psychoses in adult mental defectives: 1. Manic-depressive psychosis. 2. Schizophrenic and paranoid psychoses. *Br. J. Psychiatr., 120,* 205–212, 213–218.

Reid, A. H. (1989). Schizophrenia in mental retardation: Clinical features. *Res. Devel. Disabilities, 10,* 241–249.

Roberts, G. W. (1991). Schizophrenia: A neuropathological perspective. *Br. J. Psychiatr., 158,* 8–17.

Rogers, D., Karki, C., Bartlett, C., & Pocock, P. (1991). The motor disorders of mental handicap. *Br. J. Psychiatr., 158,* 97–102.

Rutter, M. (1985). Infantile autism and other pervasive developmental disorders. In M. Rutter & L. Hersov (Eds.), Child and adolescent psychiatry: Modern approaches. Oxford: Blackwell Scientific Publications.

St. Clair, D., Blackwood, D., Muir, W., Carothers, A., Walker, M., Spowart, G., Gosden, C., & John Evans, H. (1990). Association within a family of a balanced autosomal translocation with major mental illness. *Lancet, 336,* 13–16.

Seguin, E. (1866). Idiocy and its treatment by the physiological method. New York: Wood.

SHHD and SED (1979). *A better life: Report on services for the mentally handicapped in Scotland.* Edinburgh: HMSO.

Slater, E., Beard, A. W., & Glithero, E. (1963). The schizophrenia-like psychoses of epilepsy. *Br. J. Psychiatr., 109,* 95–150.

Turner, T. H. (1989). Schizophrenia and mental handicap: An historical review with implications for further research. *Psychol. Med., 19,* 301–314.

Wakeling, A. (1972). Comparative study of psychiatric patients with Klinefelter's syndrome and hypogonadism. *Psychol. Med., 2,* 139–154.

Wolff, S. (1991). Schizoid personality in childhood and adult life: 1. The vagaries of diagnostic labelling. *Br. J. Psychiatr., 159,* 615–620.

Woodhouse, W. J., Holland, A. J., McLean, G., & Reveley, A. (1992). The association between Triple X and psychosis. *Br. J. Psychiatr., 160,* 554–557.

Wright, E. C. (1982). The presentation of mental illness in mentally retarded adults. *Br. J. Psychiatr., 141,* 496–502.

N.B. The terminology in the Introduction and literature review is used in its historical context and is not intended to be contemporary.

# 6

# Bipolar Mood Disorders in Persons with Mental Retardation: Assessment and Diagnosis

*Stephen Ruedrich*

"**D**o bipolar mood disorders (BMDs) occur in mentally retarded persons?" In 1993, this question would be answered with a resounding and nearly universal yes, by all persons with any experience in the development disability field. However, two other obvious questions would quickly follow and would produce much more controversy among mental health clinicians and other caregivers:

1. How often, and in what form and manner?
2. How are bipolar disorders diagnosed and/or otherwise assessed?

This chapter undertakes to highlight these two areas, examining first the prevalence of bipolar illness in persons with mental retardation, and then current diagnostic thinking about symptomatology and course, with a discussion of various models for characterizing this illness in the developmentally disabled. Finally, treatment options and guidelines will be discussed in Chapter 13. Discussion of all of the above is restricted to the area of BMD, in that similar approaches to the incidence, assessment, and therapy of unipolar depressive disorders has been comprehensively addressed in Chapters 4 and 11.

## Background

Information regarding the incidence and form of BMD among developmentally disabled persons appears in the literature in several separate forums. The first involves survey data, in which the frequencies of mood disorder diagnoses are reported for various samples of retarded individuals, based in both institutional and community settings. Such reports vary widely in the

111

diagnostic methodology utilized, reflecting not only the focus of the report but also the date of publication, given the continuous evolution of diagnostic and descriptive psychiatry. An additional survey method for incidence and prevalence data, somewhat less satisfying, is available in survey reports regarding psychotropic practices with developmentally disabled persons, with the retrospective assumption that certain therapies are more-or-less indicative of specific diagnostic categories. The second source of information regarding BMD in developmental disability is contained in the single- or multiple-case report literature, in which specifics regarding the diagnosis and/or treatment of individuals selected on the basis of their bipolar illness are reported, and which address more the form and manner of the illness than its incidence or prevalence.

## How Often Bipolar Mood Disorders Occur in Retarded Persons

The lifetime risk of bipolar illness is thought to be approximately 1 percent worldwide, with a roughly equal gender distribution (Keller, 1987). This percentage is reported for nonretarded individuals, and little large-scale epidemiological information is available that addresses prevalence among developmentally disabled persons. Three true epidemiological studies of this issue are available. In the first, Corbett (1979), using the criteria from the eighth edition of the World Health Organization (WHO,) *International Classificiation of Diseases* (ICD-8), reported a 1.5 percent prevalence of BMD among 402 retarded residents of an English population sample. In 1985, Lund reported that 3 of 302 (1.0 percent) developmentally disabled residents of a Danish county had BMD. Finally, Göstason (1985) found no one with bipolar illness among 122 mentally retarded residents of a Swedish county, but reported that 2 of 122 (1.6 percent) had cyclothymic disorder. Both of the latter studies employed the criteria from the third edition of the American Psychiatric Association (APA, 1980) *Diagnostic and Statistical Manual* (DSM-III) in their diagnostic assessments.

Viewed from a different epidemiological perspective, a number of authors have described rates of bipolar illness among retarded patients seen in referral or inpatient settings. In a seminal article reviewing the literature to that point, Reid (1972) reported a 1.2 percent prevalence of BMD among the more than 500 inpatients at an English hospital for the handicapped. Heaton-Ward (1977) noted a 2.0 percent prevalence among four English hospitals. No specific mood abnormalities were reported by Eaton and Menolascino (1982) in a sample of 114 community-based individuals referred for psychiatric evaluation. The latter group were assessed with both DSM-II (APA, 1968) and DSM-III (APA, 1980) criteria, however, so that some persons identified with adjustment disorders, psychoneurotic disorders, or psychotic illnesses were not specifically identified as having mood abnormalities.

Wright (1982) wrote of 42 of 1,507 (2.8 percent) of mentally retarded inpatients who had "typical affective" illness, with an additional 41 (2.7 percent) demonstrating "atypical" affective illness superimposed on childhood psychosis. Day (1985) surveyed both long-stay hospital residents and new admissions to a specialized mental-retardation–developmental-disability psychiatric unit in England and found that 15 of 572 (2.6 percent) had "cyclic mood swings or hypomania." Myers (1986) found that three of 62 (4.8 percent) of retarded persons admitted to a *general* psychiatric hospital had BMD, and Menolascino, Levitas, and Greiner (1986) found that 5 of 543 (0.9 percent) of retarded patients admitted to a *specialized* developmental-disability unit were bipolar; interestingly, another 7 of 543 (1.3 percent) were identified as unipolar manic. This recognition of a separate group with unipolar mania remains somewhat controversial (Keller, 1987). Poindexter (1989) noted that 6 of 474 (1.3 percent) of residents seen in psychiatric consultation over a ten-year period had BMD. Finally, Glue (1989) found that 10 of 100 (10 percent) of retarded persons in a long-stay psychiatric hospital had rapid-cycling BMD, and another 2 patients had some other mood diagnosis.

Several authors have surveyed the utilization of psychopharmacological agents in large populations of retarded persons and compared the use of specific medications with the presence of psychiatric diagnosis or diagnoses. Huessy and Ruoff (1984) noted only 1 patient (1/320; 0.3 percent) receiving lithium in a Vermont training school, but no diagnostic categories were specified. Burd et al. (1991) reported that 15 of 809 (1.8 percent) residents of mental retardation group homes in North Dakota were receiving lithium, and although all but 1 had a psychiatric diagnosis, specific diagnoses were not reported. Presumably, most had bipolar disorder. Burd et al. noted that anticonvulsants have been increasingly used in recent years for psychiatric and/or behavioral disorders in retarded persons, so that some subset of persons receiving anticonvulsants in their sample may also have had BMD. In 140 retarded residents in an institutional setting, Hancock et al. (1991) found 2 residents (1.4 percent) receiving "antimanic medication" during the surveyed interval, and Buck and Sprague (1989) reported a similar frequency (73/166; 1.3 percent) receiving lithium treatment.

When we turn to the case reports and series literature, there are more than twenty reports totaling at least sixty patients in the English literature since the early 1970s. Again, the diagnostic system utilized in such reports is often not specified or is assumed to be the prevalent system in use at the time the report was written. This specification is important in view of the significant difficulty of assessing BMD in retarded persons (Sovner, 1986), which leaves open to interpretation the reported results of any treatment intervention when the diagnostic criteria have not been specified.

This literature begins with a report by Adams, Kirowitz, and Ziskind (1970) of an eighteen-year-old female with mild mental retardation, BMD, and a family history positive for bipolar illness, as well as a positive response to lithium treatment.

In two separate papers, Naylor et al. (1976) and Reid and Naylor (1976) described 4 retarded adults with BMD with "short-cycle" symptomatology involving fluctuations of motor activity and verbal productivity, accompanied by apparent mood swings. All 4 appears to have a family history of bipolar illness.

Rivinus and Harmatz (1979) described 5 institutionalized retarded adults. Hasan and Mooney (1979) described 3 more, all with BMD, 2 with clearly positive family histories of mood disorders.

Carlson (1979) reviewed the cases above and found 5 more single-case reports of adolescents with mental retardation and bipolar illness, 4 of whom had "responses to lithium" (no treatment was noted for the fifth case). Wallace (1983) noted 3 patients with BMD among more than 500 institutionalized retarded individuals seen over fifteen years of psychiatric consultation. No specifics were given regarding treatment, other than a "gratifying" response in these patients.

Since 1980, BMD in retarded persons has been described in a number of additional case reports, each highlighting a specific issue: concurrent illness, age of onset, clinical course, or treatment. Regarding the presence of concomitant illness, BMD in retarded persons has been described in autistic individuals by several authors (Komoto, Usui, & Hirata, 1984; Steingard & Biederman, 1987; Kerbeshian, Burd, & Fisher, 1987; Sovner, 1990) as well as in individuals with pervasive developmental disorders (Kaminer, Feinstein, & Barrett, 1986), and in relationship to fragile-X syndrome (Sovner, 1990). Others have noted BMD in mentally retarded adolescents (Linter, 1987; Kaminer et al., 1986; McCracken & Diamond, 1988) and in older mentally retarded adult patients (Mayer, 1985; Kadambari, 1986). Several reports have focused on BMD in retarded individuals that first appeared after tricyclic treatment for depression (Akuffo, MacSweeney, & Gajwani, 1986; Sovner, 1990) and with *seasonal* mood variation (springtime exacerbation of apparent mania); Arumainayagam & Kumar, 1990). In a provocative report, Reid et al. (1987) examined 6 retarded adult patients with known BMD and found all 6 to have varying degrees of flexion deformities of the fingers. Of the 6, 4 represented two sibling pairs. The authors speculated that such deformities could be related to long-standing medication management (all 6 had received lithium; several had also received neuroleptics and anticonvulsants) or two other factors (epilepsy in 3 of the 6) or chromosomal anomalies (based on the sibling clusters).

One area of particular interest regarding the comorbidity of BMD and other pathological states in retarded persons has focused on the relationship between BMD and Down syndrome (DS). Sovner, Hurley, and Labrie (1985) presented a review of 31 patients with Down syndrome and mood disorders; all 31 had depressive symptomatology only. Based on the statistical improbability that this might occur randomly, the authors postulated that DS may be incompatible with the development of mania and speculated that this seeming mutual exclusivity was based in abnormalities of neuronal amine activity in Down patients that precluded mania. Hucker (1985) agreed, finding no cases of DS among 16 patients with affective psychosis. McLaughlin (1987) seemed to refute this contention with his report of a twenty-six-year-old male with DS who had developed a depressive disorder and, when treated with amitriptyline, became hyperactive, giddy, and sleepless. The author noted that the patient had received only three weeks of tricyclic antidepressant treatment and had been medication-free for six weeks before the onset of the manic symptoms. This report was followed by a second case report (Cook & Leventhal, 1987) of a twenty-three-year-old male with DS and BMD manifested by recurrent mania. Singh (1988) felt that the previously presented patient had more likely been hypomanic than manic and speculated that the apparent loss of noradrenergic activity in the brain of DS patients would tend to modify (lessen) the manic presentation in these persons. Finally, Singh and Zolese (1986) found that only 1 of 60 DS patients in a hospital population had cyclic mood change and felt that this lower-than-expected rate did reflect reduced nonadrenergic function in this group. Sovner et al. (1985), Sovner (1991), and others have called for prospective studies of DS patients that would further exmaine this apparent relationship.

In summary, not only standard epidemiological surveys but also surveys of inpatient and outpatient systems serving retarded persons, as well as an extensive case-report literature, support the fact that persons with mental retardation experience BMD. Prevalence rates within the retarded population range from 0.9 percent to 4.8 percent, and therefore this form of psychiatric illness appears to be more common in retarded persons than in nonretarded groups. Such figures are even more impressive if viewed in the context of what is agreed on is diagnostic uncertainty in many retarded individuals (see below). Several authors have attempted to address this propensity by noting the several additional clinical conditions with which BMD may be associated (for example, autism and DS). As a result, one must now inquire into the specific constellation of symptoms that characterize BMD in retarded persons and how to organize an appropriate diagnostic assessment.

## How Bipolar Mood Disorders Can Be Diagnosed in Mentally Retarded Persons

### Introduction

A global review of the available information regarding the diagnosis of BMD in retarded persons seems to separate broadly into three major approaches to assessment:

1. The direct application of the current diagnostic systems widely used in mainstream psychiatry.

2. An extrapolation and/or minor revision of current diagnostic schemes for application to persons with mental retardation, or to specific subgroups of disabled persons based on the severity of retardation or the presence or absence of communicative language.

3. The development of derived diagnostic systems, or others developed de novo, for specific application to mentally retarded persons, on the assumption that the appearance and presentation of such illnesses in retarded persons are distinctly different, or that the features of developmental disabilities make the utilization of standard systems impossible.

### Direct Applications of Current Systems

Accurate diagnosis has long been the cornerstone of modern medicine and the basis on which any and all treatment decisions are based. A number of authors have noted, however, that this basic medical approach—that is, considering and ultimately arriving at an accurate diagnostic hypothesis—has been underutilized and occasionally ignored in the treatment of retarded persons (Sovner & Hurley, 1989; Menolascino, Ruedrich, & Kang, 1991; Gaultieri, 1989). Rather, treatment, both behavioral and pharmacological, has often focused on single symptoms (for example, self-injurious behavior or hyperactivity) or multiple behavioral problems (for example, noncompliance, short attention span, and aggression).

Among many others, Menolascino et al. (1991) have called for diagnostic "clarity" as a necessary precursor of appropriate psychopharmacological intervention. Unfortunately, many others have noted the difficulty of attaining such clarity in diagnosing retarded persons (Sovner, 1986; Campbell & Malone, 1991). Reiss and Szyszko (1983) used the term "diagnostic overshadowing" to describe the process of ascribing all symptomatology in a retarded person to the developmental disability itself, and Sovner (1986) outlined several issues that make current standard diagnostic systems less than optimally functional in the assessing of retarded persons. In the same paper, Sovner also stated, however, that mood disorders should be one area of relatively less diagnostic distortion, because of the presence in mood disorders of several neurovegetative signs and more specific responses to pharmacological treatments. In fact, it does seem that the current criteria for BMD can be reliably applied to the diagnosis of many mildly retarded individuals. A number of authors have highlighted the feasibility of making BMD diagnoses on "usual clinical grounds" in persons who have a disability in the borderline and mild range, and who have sufficient communicative language with which to describe the largely subjective DSM-III-R (APA, 1987) criteria (Sovner & Hurley, 1983; Campbell & Malone, 1991).

*Extrapolated Diagnostic Systems*

Even so, it is clear that a developmental disability of necessity limits the strict application of diagnostic systems such as the DSM-III-R for the diagnosis of many retarded persons. This circumstance has led to attempts by several authors to modify the diagnostic criteria to address the level of intellectual and communicative ability of the mentally retarded (Hucker et al., 1979; Sovner & Hurley, 1983). Huckner et al. (1979) modified the criteria for mania only slightly; they include a "resentment of restraint" alongside the more traditional elevated or irritable mood, overactivity, increased libido, pressured speech, flight of ideas, grandiosity, and reduced sleep. Sovner and coauthors, in a series of reports, outlined modifications in the DMS-III (APA, 1980) criteria, which they specially adapted to retarded persons (Sovner & Hurley, 1983; Sovner, 1986), as well as behavioral equivalents that may correspond to each DSM-III criterion. This outline can be seen in Tables 1 and 2.

Several points are worthy of discussion. In the DSM-III-R (and proposed in the DSM-IV), in addition to elevated or expansive mood, three manic symptoms are necessary for the diagnosis. Four symptoms are necessary if the pervasive mood state is irritability rather than euphoria. Several authors have reported that retarded persons with BMD-mania are more likely to have irritable as opposed to elevated mood (Reid, 1972). In Sovner's extrapolated system (1986), four rather than three of such symptoms would be necessary for diagnosis, unless the individual has a first-degree relative with BMD. No similar "family" history criterion exists in the DSM-III-R, but it makes intuitive sense that such a positive history should add to diagnostic certainty in both retarded and nonretarded persons. Sovner also added "biphasic course," "onset/increase in aggressivity," and "onset/increase in self-injury" as diagnostic criteria, although these types of behaviors are not specifically noted in BMD criteria for nonretarded populations. However, both aggression and self-injury *have* been described in manic retarded patients (McCracken & Diamond, 1988; Steingard & Biederman, 1987); a key point appears to be that one or both behaviors may

Table 1
DSM-III-R Diagnostic Criteria for Mania and Behavioral Equivalents in
the Mentally Retarded

| | DSM-III-R Criteria | Observed Equivalents in Mentally Retarded Persons | Objective Behaviors Which Might Be Monitored |
|---|---|---|---|
| Mood state | Euphoric/elevated/irritable mood (no minimum duration necessary) | Boisterousness or excitement may be the predominant mood state. Self-injury may be associated with irritability. Thought content may center on mastery of daily-living skills. Increased maladaptive behavior at usual bedtime or in early morning. Patient is dressed for work at 5 A.M. Increased frequency of vocalization irrespective of whether patient has usable speech. Disorganized speech. Decrease in workshop performance. Aggressive behavior and negativism may be present. Teasing behavior, fondling others, publicly masturbating. | Measure rates of smiling and/or laughing. Measure inappropriate remarks. Monitor sleep pattern using 30-minute intervals. Measure rates of swearing, singing, screaming. Use workshop performance data. Measure aggressions, request refusals per week, pacing, etc. Measure intervals in which the behavior occurs. |
| Symptom criteria | At least three symptoms must be present if patient has euphoric mood. Four symptoms must be present if patient only has irritable mood: (1) inflated self-esteem/grandiosity (2) decr. need for sleep (3) more talkative/pressured speech (4) flight of ideas/racing thoughts (5) distractibility (6) incr. goal-directed activity/psychomotor agitation (7) excessive involvement in pleasurable activitites | | |

Source: R. Sovner & A. D. Hurley. (1983). "Do the Mentally Retarded Suffer from Affective Illness?" Archives of General Psychiatry, 40, 61–67.

increase in frequency and/or severity in conjunction with the onset of the manic episode. As in nonretarded manic patients, the onset of mania may result in a new onset of some activity not previously seen, or in an exaggeration of a well-established constellation of symptoms.

Special note must be taken of some retarded individuals with BMD who have what has been referred to as *atypical bipolar syndromes*. These include rapid-cycling BMD, mixed states with features of mania and depression appearing simultaneously, and unipolar mania. Rapid-cycling BMD is defined as greater than three or four mood episodes occurring in a calendar year and is often more treatment-resistant than more typical BMD. It is noted that rapid cycling in nonretarded persons is associated with both specific neuro-

Table 2
DSM-III-R Diagnostic Criteria for Major Depression and Behavioral
Equivalents in the Mentally Retarded

| | DSM-III-R Criteria (Five or more of the following symptoms must be present for a minimum of two weeks. Symptom (1) or (2) must be one of the five.) | Observed Equivalents in Mentally Retarded Persons | Objective Behaviors Which Might Be Measured |
|---|---|---|---|
| Mood state | (1) Depressed mood, irritable mood in children or adolescents | Apathetic facial expression with lack of emotional re-activity. Withdrawal, lack of re-inforcers. | Measure rates of smiling, responses to preferred activities, crying episodes. |
| Symptom criteria | (2) Generalized decrease in interest or pleasure by self-report or observed apathy | Change in total sleep time | Measure time spent in room, etc. |
| | (3) significant decrease in appetite or weight loss (5% body weight in one month) or significant increase in appetite or weight gain (5% of body weight in one month) | Agitation may present as self-injurious behavior or aggression. Retardation may present as decreased energy, passivity. Statements such as, "I'm retarded." | Measure meal refusals, change in weight. Use sleep chart to record sleep. Time spent in bed, spontaneous verbalizations, pacing. Requires expressive language to determine if symptom is present. |
| | (4) insomnia or hypersomnia | Change in workshop performance. Perseveration of the deaths of family members and friends, preoccupation with funerals. | Use workshop performance data. Requires expressive language to determine if symptom is present. |
| | (5) psychomotor activity or retardation | | |
| | (6) fatigue or loss of energy | | |
| | (7) feelings of worthlesness/inappropriate guilt | | |
| | (8) decreased concentration/indecisiveness/diminished ability to think | | |
| | (9) recurrent thoughts of death/suicidal ideation | | |

Source: R. Sovner & A. D. Hurley. (1983). "Do the Mentally Retarded Suffer from Affective Illness?" Archives of General Psychiatry, 40, 61–67.

logical and endocrinological (thyroid) abnormalities; in this regard, retarded persons may be particularly susceptible to this BMD subtype (Sovner, 1990). Glue (1989) found that 10 of 12 cases of BMD in his group of mood-disordered retarded patients had rapid-cycling illness, but to date there have been no substantive epidemiological data to address this question. It should be noted that the DSM-IV is likely to recognize rapid cycling as a "course specifier," probably requiring at least four distinct mood episodes per year, so that the investigation of this phenomenon in retarded persons can be facilitated in conjunction with other research (APA, 1991).

"Mixed" BMD is also described in developmentally disabled persons (Naylor et al., 1974) and is also thought to be relatively treatment-resistant in comparison to typical BMD. In the DSM-IV, the "mixed" subtype is likely to be a specific subtype of manic episode, rather than a type of episode. The "mixed" category will no longer include rapid cycling and will require that the person have a clear manic episode, with features of depression also present at least half the time.

Finally, controversy continues regarding the validity of unipolar mania as a BMD diagnostic subtype. In the DSM-IV, mania occuring in any form will probably be seen as a symptom of BMD, occurring either singly or recurrently. In the nonretarded, both single episodes of mania and recurrent mania without depressive episodes are thought to be rare (Keller, 1987). However, several authors have noted "chronic" mania in developmentally disabled patients (Sovner, 1988, 1989, 1990; Steingard & Biederman, 1987), with episodes of manic symptomatology lasting continuously for several years in some patients. Whatever its ultimate designation or diagnostic validity, what this presentation of BMD seems to share with other "atypical" subtypes is its relative treatment resistance, at least to conventional approaches.

In summary, this second diagnostic approach—that is, using extrapolation from and interpretation of the current diagnostic systems for specific applications to retarded persons—is a valid and thoughtful approach to delineating BMD in retarded populations. Because such extrapolated systems are easily applicable, they are probably the methods most frequently utilized by clinicians working in the field.

## Derived or Novel Diagnostic Systems

For many of the reasons outlined in the preceding section, a number of researchers have attempted a third method of assessing psychiatric disorders in retarded persons. This approach involves the development of de novo diagnostic systems, which are not based on, or extrapolated directly from, other widely accepted systems. Several are based loosely on the DSM-III-R or other systems, and others have no intrinsic relationship and also vary as to whether they are intended to serve as diagnostic approaches or as methods for assessing treatment response. Currently, there are at least five such systems available: the Psychopathology Instrument for Mentally Retarded Adults (PIMRA), the Reiss Screen, the Diagnostic Assessment for the Severely Handicapped (DASH), the Problem Behavior Scale (PBS), and the Aberrant Behavior Checklist (ABC). Each wll be discussed briefly in turn, particularly with regard to its specific utility in assessing retarded persons for the presence of BMD.

The PIMRA is a DSM-III–derived system consisting of fifty-six statements that are answered dichotomously (presence/absence) (Matson, Kazdin, & Senatore, 1984). There are two versions : One is administered to the individual with developmental disability (self-report), and the other is completed by the staff caregiver in direct contact with the patient (informant version). In initially presenting the PIMRA, its authors (Matson et al., 1984) reported test–retest reliabilities within acceptable ranges (better for the informant than for the self-report versions) and diagnostic validity across the two versions. Following factor analysis, several subscales were apparent, including one the researchers delineated affective disorder. Examples of items loading on this particular subscale include:

"Are you real happy some days, and real sad on other days?"

"Do you feel sad?"

"Mood swings and moodiness."

"Decreased energy—mental and/or physical fatigue."

"Death wishes and/or hypersensitivity that results in the person crying easily."

These items can be seen to reflect both depressive and manic symptomatology. Others (Aman et al., 1986) have reported interrater reliability in the 70 to 95 percent range, with varied opinions regarding the robustness of other psychometric characteristics. One area that did seem to be replicable across these subsequent studies appears to be the Affective subscale, which may reflect some relative ease of identifying some of the neurovegetative symptoms that may accompany mood disorders in retarded persons. It should be noted that the PIMRA is intended to be a screening exam for the assessment of general psychopathology and does not provide a measure of severity, nor can it be applied to treatment outcome (Sturmey, Reed, & Corbett, 1991). It focuses on current (recent) behavioral findings and, like the DSM-III-R is "cross-sectional," providing a snapshot assessment of current function without information regarding longitudinal course, family history, and so on.

The Reiss Screen for maladaptive behavior consists of thirty-eight potentially problem-causing areas of symptomatology and behaviors often seen in mentally retarded individuals (Reiss & Szyszko, 1983). Informant raters are asked to report on whether each area or issue presents "no problem," "problem," or "major problem," based on information given for each rating. These definitions attempt to include both the frequency and the severity of the symptomatology, as well as the distress or discomfort it causes on the individual under assessment. Several Reiss items are thought to reflect depression, including ratings for anxiety, crying spells, fearfulness, sensitivity, sadness, somatic complaints, eating problems, no energy, and sleep disturbance. This screen does not include a subscale specifically identifying mania or BMD, but it does provide for a rating of "euphoria." Like the PIMRA, the Reiss Screen is intended as a broad screening assessment for the presence or absence and several subtypes of psychopathology, *but* it also provides for an assessment of the severity of the illness.

A recurrent theme in developing assessment instruments, whether derived or novel, is the difficulty in applying them—and the consequent validity concerns—to persons at the lower end of the developmental disability scale. To address this, Matson et al. (1991) recently developed the DASH (Diagnostic Assessment for the Severely Handicapped), an eighty-three-item instument in which raters address the frequency, duration, and severity of each rated item, following interviews with direct-care staff knowledgeable about the client. The DASH is also derived from the DSM-III-R; its eighty-three items contain many DSM-III-R symptom and sign criteria and are grouped into thirteen subscales corresponding to DSM-III-R categories. The DASH offers subscales for both depression and mania and requires endorsement of more than 50 percent of the items in order to render either diagnosis. The criteria offered for "mood disorder—mania" include:

1. has decreased need for sleep
2. is restless or agitated
3. talks loudly
4. is extremely happy or cheerful for no obvious reason
5. is cranky or irritable
6. is easily distracted
7. talks quickly

Matson et al. presented data regarding the utilization of the DASH on a sample of 506 profoundly retarded and severely retarded persons. Globally, residents who were retarded, but ambulatory, had higher ratings than severely retarded individuals or nonambulatory clients. The interrater reliability was quite high; internal consistency of the thirteen sub-scales ranged from .20 to .84 (mania = .52). In their sample, 39 of 506 individuals (7.7

percent) demonstrated mania by criteria, and 91 percent of the sample exhibited at least one psychiatric condition.

In a subsequent factor-analytic study of the same data base, six factors were statistically apparent. These were categories entitled "emotional lability," "antisocial behavior," "language disorder," "social withdrawal/ stereotypy," "eating disorder," and "sleeping disorder." The "manic" criteria listed above did not congregate in any of the six factor-derived groupings. The authors concluded both reports by highlighting the need for combining factor-analytic and clinically extrapolated systems into coherent systems for retarded persons, and then investigating the validity of such systems in comparison to that of the extant systems.

Weiseler, Campbell, and Sonis (1988) reported on their use of an instrument specifically attempting to characterize and follow BMD in retarded persons. The scale contains eight items, each rated in Likert fashion, with a five-option format, and it is completed by direct-care staff. The authors reported good interrater reliability when the test was performed by knowledgeable staff and acceptable interrater agreement even for inexperienced users.

Espie, Montgomery, and Gillies (1988) described their development of a rating instrument, the Problem Behavior Scale (PBS), for application to developmentally disabled patients with "hysterical" responses (meaning dramatic, manipulative, and attention-seeking behaviors associated with "pseudoseizure" activity). Several items load on a factor that the authors entitled "passivity/dominance" and indicate that persons with high scores on the PBS are likely to conform to the caricature associated with "hysterical personality." Apparently no attempt was made to relate the PBS to any other specific psychiatric diagnoses; further research might conceivably address its utility in addressing BMD in retarded persons.

One additional psychometric method used to diagnose this population has focused not on general surveys for the presence of specific psychiatric disorders, but on methods of assessing responses to treatment. Aman et al. (1985) developed the Aberrant Behavior Checklist (ABC), a fifty-eight-item factor-analytically derived system originally involving some 1,000 residents of several mental-retardation–developmental-disability institutions in New Zealand. The initial and subsequent statistically derived samples excluded nonambulatory, blind, and mildly retarded persons, so that the final study sample was felt to be more homogeneous. Each item is rated on a scale of 0 to 3 (0 = not a problem; 3 = severe problem). The authors reported five factors (irritability/crying/agitation, lethargy/social withdrawal, stereotypy, hyperactivity/noncompliance, and inappropriate speech) and reported acceptable levels of internal consistency, test–retest, and interrater reliability. Test items that have typically been associated with mania seem to load on the hyperactivity and inappropriate speech factors, but since the ABC was developed mostly as a method of following treatment response, few direct comparisons have been made to other syndromal or descriptive systems addressing specific diagnostic disorders.

## Summary

It is clear that mentally retarded persons suffer both typical and atypical forms of BMD, and that diagnostic assessment for these disorders is aided both by the application of mainstream diagnostic systems and by the development of extrapolated or derived assessment instruments and diagnostic schemata. In the use of such systems, modifications of usual diagnostic strategies are helpful, and often necessary, for success. These modifications can be summarized as follows:

1. The diagnostic assessment of retarded persons often resembles the process found in the fields of child psychiatry and pediatrics, in that the individual in question is generally not viewed as the most reliable or useful source of historical information. Retarded persons *are* often able to report their mood state and to engage in limited reflection on their circumstances, but they are generally unable to detail a step-by-step evolution of their illness over time. For this, the clinician must look to secondary sources, such as parents, siblings, direct caregivers, workshop supervisors, and teachers, much as in child psychiatry or pediatrics.

2. Therefore, the efficacy of the traditional patient-centered interview as the primary source of information must be modified to allow an appreciation of the full diagnostic picture.

3. In comparison to persons with borderline and mild retardation, individuals with more severe intellectual and social deficits and thus more limited communication skills require the clinician to rely even more heavily on corroborating historians and less on direct examination, and to utilize diagnostic schemes that are more sign- than symptom-based. Sovner and Lowry (1990) outlined a behavioral methodology that they feel is necessary for assessing BMD in such persons. It assumes that systems already utilized in the behavioral analysis field can be modified to measure behaviors associated with BMD, and it affirms that direct-care staff can be trained to become the "eyes, ears, and recorders" for such systems. Sovner and Hurley (1990) took this approach one step further, presenting five assessment tools (biographical time line, sleep chart, behavioral incident chart, bipolar mood chart, and psychotropic drug profile) that can be systematically employed both to organize diagnosis and to follow treatment response. One of these, the bipolar mood chart, calls for staff caregivers to rate the retarded pa-

tients' mood state on a daily basis, an especially important activity for patients with rapid-cycling illness. Only in this manner can clinicians hope to make valid and reliable diagnoses in patients with severe and profound retardation.

4. Although rarely stated, it is also generally believed by most clinicians in this area that the level of diagnostic confidence regarding BMD diagnoses varies in rough approximation to the *valid* application of any diagnostic system. Generally, this belief indicates a lower level of diagnostic confidence in the severe or profound range of retardation.

5. Sovner (1990) noted that there is currently no set of *validated* criteria which can be uniformly applied irrespective of the level of disability. For better or worse, this statement seems to characterize diagnostic systems that extrapolate and/or derive criteria for specific application to retarded persons. Lest this stance seems too therapeutically pessimistic, however, it should be noted that *all* of diagnostic psychiatry is clinical in its approach, and that, with the rarest exception, there is little or no pathological or laboratory confirmation available for *any* psychiatric diagnosis, in either retarded or nonretarded persons. It is hoped that recent developments in neurodiagnostic, particularly neuroradiological, examinations in psychiatry, such as magnetic resonance imaging (MRI) and positron-emission tomography (PET), will soon allow much needed diagnostic validity studies for the first time.

# References

Adams, G. L., Kivowitz, J., & Ziskind, E. (1970). Manic depressive psychosis, mental retardation, and chromosomal rearrangement, *Arch. Gen. Psychiatr., 23,* 305–309.

Akuffo, E., MacSweeney, D. A., & Gajwani, A. K. (1986). Multiple pathology in a mentally handicapped individual. *Br. J. Psychiatr., 149,* 377–378.

Aman, M. G., Singh, N. N., Stewart, A. W., & Field, C. J. (1985). The Aberrant Behavior Checklist: A behavior rating scale for the assessment of treatment effects. *Am. J. Ment. Defic., 89*(5), 485–491.

Aman, M. G., Watson, J. E. Singh, N. N., Turbott, S. H., & Wilsher, C. P. (1986). Psychometric and demographic characteristics of the psychopathology instrument for mental retarded adults. *Psychopharmacol. Bull., 22,* 1072–1076.

American Psychiatric Assocciation. (1987). *Diagnostic and Statistical Manual of Mental Disorders (3rd. ed., rev.; DSM-III-R).* Washington, DC: Author.

American Psychiatric Association. (1991). *DSM-IV Options Book: Work in Progress.* Washington, DC: Author.

Arumainayagam, M., & Kumar, A. (1990). Manic-depressive psychosis in a mentally handicapped person. Seasonality: A clue to a diagnostic problem. *Br. J. Psychiatr., 156,* 886–889.

Benson, (1990). Behavioral treatment of depression. In A. Dosen & F. J. Menolascino (Eds.), *Depression in mentally retarded children and adults* (pp. 309–330). Leiden: Logon.

Bojanin, S., & Ispanovic-Radojkovic, V. ( ). Treatment of depression in mentally retarded children: A developmental approach. In A. Dosen & F. J. Menolascino (Eds.), *Depression in mentally retarded children and adults* (pp. 265– 280). Leiden:Logon.

Buck, J. A., & Sprague, R. L. (1989). Psychotropic medication of mentally retarded residents in community long-term care facilities. *Am. J. Ment. Retard., 93*(6), 618–623.

Burd, L., Fisher, W., Vesely, B. A., Williams, M., Kerbeshian, J., & Leech, C. (1991). Prevalence of psychoactive drug use among North Dakota group home residents. *Am. J. Ment. Retard., 96,* 119–126.

Campbell, M., & Malone, R. P. (1991). Mental retardation and psychiatric disorders. *Hosp. Commun. Psychiatr., 42*(4), 374–379.

Carlson, G. (1979). Affective psychoses in mental retardates, *Psychiatr. Clin. N. Am., 2,* 499–510.

Cook, E. H., Jr., & Leventhal, B. L. (1987). Down's syndrome with mania. *Br. J. Psychiatr., 150,* 249–250.

Corbett, J. A. (1979). Psychiatric morbidity and mental retardation. In F. E. James & R. P. Snaith (Eds.), *Psychiatric illness and mental handicap,* (pp. 11–25). London: Gaskell.

Day, K. (1985). Psychiatric disorders in the middle-aged and elderly handicapped. *Br. J. Psychiatr., 147,* 600–667.

Dosen, A., & Gielen, J. (1993). Depression in the mentally retarded: Assessment and prognosis. In R. J. Fletcher & A. Dosen (Eds.), *Mental health aspects of mental retardation.*

Dosen, A., & Petry, D. (1992). Treatment of depression in the mentally retarded. In R. J. Fletcher, & A. Dosen (Eds.), *Mental health aspects of mental retardation.*

Eaton, L. F., & Menolascino, F. J. (1982). Psychiatric disorders in the mentally retarded: Types, problems, and challenges. *Am. J. Psychiatr., 139,* 1297–1303.

Espie, L. A., Montgomery, J. M., & Gillies, J. B. (1988). The development of a psychosocial behavior scale for the assessment of mentally handicapped people. *J. Ment. Defic. Res, 32,* 395–403.

Gaultieri, C. T. (1989). Affective disorders. In American Psychiatric Association, *Treatment of psychiatric disorders* (pp. 10–13). Washington, DC: Author.

Glue, P. (1989). Rapid cycling affective disorders in the mentally retarded. *Biol. Psychiatr., 26,* 250–256.

Göstason, R. (1985). Psychiatric illness among the mentally retarded: A Swedish population study. *Acta Psychiatr. Scand., 71,* 1–117.

Griffiths, D. (1990). The social skills game, Parts 1 and 2. *Habitative Ment. Healthcare Newsl., 9,* 1–13.

Hancock, R. D., Weber, S. L., Ramarao, K., & Her, K. S. (1991). Changes in psychotropic drug use in long-term residents of an ICF/MR facility. *Am. J. Ment. Retard., 96,* 137–141.

Hasan, M. R., & Mooney, R. P. (1979). Three cases of manic-depressive illness in mentally retarded adults. *Am. J. Psychiatr., 136,* 1069–1071.

Heaton-Ward, A. (1977). Psychosis in mental handicap. *Br. J. Psychiatr., 130,* 525–533.

Hucker, S. J. (1985). Is mania incompatible with Down's syndrome? *Br. J. Psychiatr., 147,* 93.

Hucker, S. J., Day, K. A., George, S., & Roth, M. (1979). Psychosis in mentally handicapped adults. In F. E. James & R. P. Smith (Eds.), *Psychiatric illness and mental handicap,* (pp. 27–35). London: Gaskell.

Huessy, H. R., & Ruoff, P. A. (1984). Towards a rational drug usage in a state institution for retarded individuals. *Psychiatr. J. Univ. Ottawa, 9*(2), 56–58.

Hurley, A. D. (1989). Behavior therapy for psychiatric disorders in mentally retarded individuals. In R. J. Fletcher & F. J. Menolascino (Eds.), *Mental retardation and mental illness: Service and treatment for dually diagnosed.* Lexington, MA: Lexington Books, D. C. Heath.

James, D. H. (1986). Psychiatric and behavioural disorders amongst older severely mentally handicapped inpatients. *J. Ment. Defic. Res., 30,* 341–345.

Kadambari, S. R. (1986). Manic-depressive psychosis in a mentally handicapped person: Diagnosis and management. *Br. J. Psychiatr., 148,* 595–596.

Kaminer, Y., Feinstein, C., & Barrett, R. P. (1986). A relationship between pervasive developmental disorders and affective disorders? *J. Am. Acad. Child Psychiatr., 25,* 434–435.

Keller, M. B. (1987). Differential diagnosis, natural course, and epidemiology of bipolar disorders. In R. E. Hales & A. J. Frances (Eds.), *American Psychiatric Association Annual Review* (Vol. 6, pp. 10–28). Washington, DC: American Psychiatric Press.

Kerbeshian, J., Burd, L., & Fisher, W. (1987). Lithium carbonate in the treatment of two patients with infantile autism and atypical bipolar symptomatology. *J. Clin. Psychopharmacol., 7*(6), 401–405.

Komoto, J., Usui, S., & Hirata, J. (1984). Infantile autism and affective disorder. *J. Autism Devel. Disorders, 14,* 81–84.

Linter, C. M. (1987). Short-cycle manic-depressive psychosis in a mentally handicapped child without family history. *Br. J. Psychiatr., 151,* 554–555.

Lund, J. (1985). The prevalence of psychiatric morbidity in mentally retarded adults. *Acta Psychiatr. Scand., 72,* 563–567.

Matson, J. L., Gardner, W. I., Koe, D. A., & Sovner, R. (1991). A scale for evaluating emotional disorders in severely and profoundly mentally retarded persons: Development of the Diagnostic Assessment for the Severely Handicapped (DASH) Scale. *Br. J. Psychiatr., 159,* 404–409.

Matson, J. L., Kazdin, A. E., & Senatore, V. (1984). Psychometric properties of the psychopathology instrument for mentally retarded adults. *Appl. Res. Ment. Retard., 5,* 81–89.

Mayer, C. (1985). Mental handicap, psychosis and thyrotoxicosis: A demonstration' of the usefulness of an integrated community and hospital science. *J. Ment. Defic. Res., 29,* 275–280.

McCracken, J. T., & Diamond, R. P. (1988). Case study: Bipolar disorder in mentally retarded adolescents. *J. Am. Acad. Child Adol. Psychiatr., 27,* (4), 494–499.

McLaughlin, M. (1987). Bipolar affective disorder in Down's syndrome. *Br. J. Psychiatr., 151,* 116–117.

Menolascino, F. J., Levitas, A., & Greiner, C. (1986). The nature and types of mental illness in the mentally retarded. *Psychopharmacol. Bull., 22,* 1060–1071.

Menolascino, F. J., Ruedrich, S. L., & Kang, J. S. (1991). Mental illness in the mentally retarded: Diagnostic clarity as a prelude to psychopharmacological interventions. In J. J. Ratey (Ed.), *Mental retardation: Developing phamacotherapies,* (pp. 19–34)., Washington, DC: American Psychiatric Press.

Myers, B. A. (1986). Psychopathology in hospitalized developmentally disabled individuals. *Compr. Psychiatr., 27,* 115–126.

Naylor, G. J., Donald, J. M., Le Poidevin, D., & Reid, A. H. (1974). A double-blind trial of long-term lithium therapy in mental defectives. *Br. J. Psychiatr., 124,* 52–57.

Naylor, G. J., Reid, A. H., Dick, D. A. T., & Dick, E. G. (1976). A biochemical study of short-cycle manic depressive psychosis in mental defectives. *Br. J. Psychiatr., 128,* 169–180.

Poindexter, A. R. (1989). Psychotropic drug patterns in a large ICF/MR facility: A ten year experience. *Am. J. Ment. Retard., 93*(6), 624–626.

Reid, A. H. (1972). Psychoses in adult mental defectives: 1. Manic depressive psychosis. *Br. J. Psychiatr., 120,* 205–212.

Reid, A. H., & Naylor, G. J. (1976). Short cycle manic depressive psychosis in mental defectives: A clinical and psychological study. *J. Ment. Defic. Res., 20*(1), 67–76.

Reid, A. H., Swanson, A. J. G., Jain, A. S., Spowart, G., & Wright, A. F. (1987). Manic depressive psychosis with mental retardation and flexion deformities: A clinical and cytogenetic study. *Br. J. Psychiatr., 87,* 396–402.

Reiss, S. & Szyszko, J. (1983). Diagnostic overshadowing and professional experience with mentally retarded persons. *Am. J. Ment. Defic.,* 87; 396–402.

Rivinus, T. M., & Harmatz, J. S. (1979). Diagnosis and lithium treatment of affective disorder in the retarded: Five case studies. *Am. J. Psychiatr., 136,* 551–554.

Ruedrich, S. L., Des Noyers-Hurley, A. D., & Sovner, R. (in press). Treatment of mood disorders in mentally retarded persons. In A. Dosen & K. Day (Eds.), *Treatment of mental illness and behavioral disorders in mentally retarded children and adults.*

Signer, S. F., Benson, D. F., & Rudnick, F. D. (1986). Undetected affective disorders in the developmentally retarded. *Am. J. Psychiatr., 143*(2), 259.

Singh, I. (1988). Down's syndrome with mania. *Br. J. Psychiatr., 152,* 436–437.

Singh, I., & Zolese, G. (1986). Is mania really incompatible with Down's syndrome? *Br. J. Psychiatr., 148,* 613–614.

Sovner, R. (1986). Limiting factors in the use of DSM-III criteria mentally retarded persons. *Psychopharmacol. Bull., 22,* 1055–1059.

Sovner, R. (1988). Anticonvulsant drug therapy of neuropsychiatric disorders in mentally retarded persons. In S. L. McElroy & H. G. Pope (Eds.), *Use of anticonvulsants in psychiatry: Recent advances,* (pp. 169–181). Clifton, NJ: Oxford Health Care, Inc.

Sovner, R. (1989). The use of valproate in the treatment of mentally retarded persons with typical and atypical bipolar disorders. *J. Clin. Psychiatr., 50*(3, Suppl.), 40–43.

Sovner, R. (1990). Bipolar disorder in persons with developmental disorder: An overview. In A. Dosen & J. Menolascino (Eds.), *Depression in Mentally Retarded Children and Adults*, (pp. 175–198). Leiden: Logon.

Sovner, R. (1991). Divalproex-responsive rapid cycling bipolar disorder in a patient with Down's syndrome: Implications for the Down's syndrome-mania hypothesis. *J. Ment. Defic. Res., 35,* 171–173.

Sovner, R., & Hurley, A. D. (1983). Do the mentally retarded suffer from affective illness? *Arch. Gen. Psychiatr., 40,* 61–67.

Sovner, R., & Hurley, A. D. (1989). Ten diagnostic principles for recognizing psychiatric disorders in mentally retarded persons. *Psychiatr. Aspects Ment. Retard. Rev., 8,* 9–16.

Sovner, R., & Hurley, A. D. (1990). Assessment tools which facilitate psychiatric evaluations and treatment. *Habilitative Ment. Healthcare Newsl., 9*(11), 91–100.

Sovner, R., Hurley, A. D., & Labrie, R. (1985). Is mania incompatible with Down's syndrome? *Br. J. Psychiatr., 146,* 319–320.

Sovner, R., & Lowry, M. A. (1990). A behavioral methodology for diagnosing affective disorders in individuals with mental retardation. *Habilitative Ment. Healthcare Newsl., (7),* 55–64.

Steingard, R., & Biederman, J. (1987). Lithium responsive manic-like symptoms in two individuals with autism and mental retardation. *J. Am. Acad. Child Adol. Psychiatr., 26,* 932–935.

Sturmey, P., Reed, J., & Corbett, J. (1991). Psychometric assessment of psychiatric disorders in people with learning difficulties (mental handicap): A review of measures. *Psychol. Med., 21,* 143–155.

Wallace, J. G. (1983). Affective disorder in the mentally retarded. *Am. J. Psychiatr., 140,* 1539–1540.

Weiseler, N. A., Campbell, G. J., & Sonis, W. (1988). Ongoing use of an affective rating scale in the treatment of a mentally retarded individual with rapid-cycling bipolar affective disorder. *Res. Devel. Disabilities, 9,* 47–53.

World Health Organization. (1969). *International Classification of Diseases* (8th ed.; ICD-8). Chicago, Illinois.

Wright, E. C. (1982). The presentation of mental illness in mentally retarded adults. *Br. J. Psychiatr., 141,* 496–502.

# 7

# Personality Disorder in Persons with Mental Retardation: Assessment and Diagnosis

*Lawrence Dana*

Personality disorder is defined by the revised third edition of the *Diagnostic and Statistical Manual* (DSM-III-R) of the American Psychiatric Association (APA, 1987) as "inflexible and maladaptive patterns of sufficient severity to cause either significant impairment in adaptive functioning or subjective distress." (p. 335). According to Rutter (1987, p. 450), three "unifying features" are typically used to make the diagnosis of personality disorder: (1) onset in childhood; (2) long-standing persistence over time without marked remission or relapses; and (3) "abnormalities that seem to constitute a basic aspect of the individual's usual functioning."

Before one gets into specific applications of this diagnosis to a developmentally disabled population, some important ethical and practical concerns need to be addressed.

One must respect the fact that developmentally handicapped persons have had (in many cases) life experiences that would negatively affect *anyone's* personality. These range from the horrors of inhumane institutions (Blatt, 1970, 1973) to simply trying to survive in a nonhandicapped world.

One of the best treatments of this issue is an article by Zigler and Burack (1989), which concludes:

> Zigler and colleagues have shown that mentally retarded individuals often share similar experiential histories that lead to certain personality or motivational characteristics. They have found the personality makeup of mentally retarded persons to be characterized by dependency on others, approval seeking behavior, wariness of strangers, outerdirected problem solving styles, low expectancy of success, low aspiration level, and a low ideal self image. *It is likely these personality characteristics are responsible for the high rate of mental unhealth in mentally retarded persons.* (p. 236; italics added)

A link between depressed mood, low social support, and poor social skills was found among mildly retarded persons (Laman & Reiss, 1987). This link was further found to be associated with inept social interactions. And inept and inappropriate social interactions are among the key diagnostic criteria for personality disorders.

One would expect that persons who are developmentally disabled *and* currently institutionalized would show very high rates of personality disorders. This expectation is clearly borne out in a study by Reid and Ballinger (1987). More than half (56 percent) of a sample of mild and moderately retarded adults in a hospital setting showed clear signs of personality disorder. Of this group, 22 percent were markedly disabled by personality disorder. Significantly, those disorders most associated with violent behavior were seen predominantly.

We must recall that the two key discriminators in making a diagnosis of personality disorders are "inflexible" and "maladaptive." For many developmentally disabled persons labeled as having personality disorders, these two discriminators can rightly be applied to the world around them, too.

More than perhaps any other psychiatric diagnosis, the determination that a developmentally handicapped person has a personality disorder should *always* be a tentative one, subject to constant periodic review.

Disabled persons with extraordinarily disordered behaviors, easily fitting the diagnostic criteria of any number of personality disorders, have had dramatic positive behavior changes once exposed to a functional and normalized world. This reaction has been noted in the literature repeatedly for almost thirty years (Dybwad, 1964; Wolfensberger, 1972). Also, one very prominent psychiatrist, Robert Sovner, has repeatedly stated in his workshops that the severity of a behavior problem is *not* necessarily related to its prognosis.

These factors do not suggest that making the diagnosis of personality disorder among developmentally disabled persons is impossible. They do strongly indicate the need for extreme caution, as well as much professional modesty and restraint.

## Making the Diagnosis

Having said all that, let us examine the DSM-III-R system of classification of personality disorders.

The DSM-III-R organizes personality disorders into three general "clusters." As one works with developmentally disabled persons, some with very limited verbal abilities, diagnoses finer than the "cluster" level may be quite difficult (and possibly unnecessary). The clusters include:

These clusters are organized around the following behavior patterns:

## DSM-III-R Personality Disorders

| Cluster A | Cluster B | Cluster C |
|-----------|-----------|-----------|
| Paranoid | Antisocial | Avoidant |
| Schizoid | Borderline | Dependent |
| Schizotypal | Histrionic | Obsessive-compulsive |
| | Narcissistic | Passive-aggressive |

Cluster A, "persons who are odd or eccentric"; Cluster B, "persons who are dramatic, emotional or erratic"; and Cluster C, "persons who appear anxious or fearful" (APA, 1987, p. 337).

Somewhat superimposed over these diagnostic categories are two rather controversial clinical issues related to developmental disabilities and the well-documented personality changes due to brain injury or anomaly.

First, the existence of personality problems associated with epilepsy has had a long history marked by much professional disagreement. In his article, Trimble (1988) stated, "It is suggested that patients with limbic system dysfunction are most susceptible to undergo changes of personality, and that the latter reflect a chronic organic personality change" (p. 99). The behaviors associated with this purported limbic system dysfunction would tend to be associated with Cluster B diagnoses because behaviors involving hypersexuality, fearfulness and aggression are the ones most commonly cited in Trimble's review.

Consistent with the Trimble article, Benson (1991) also traced the history of the relationship between personality problems and epilepsy. More specifically, he discussed the work of Norman Geschwind, who described a constellation of behaviors among some persons with epilepsy that has been dubbed "the *Geschwind syndrome.* These behaviors include excessive verbal and written output, altered sexuality, and exaggerated cognitive and emotional responses (Benson, 1991). If such a syndrome exists (Benson tended to support its existence but acknowledged the need for more studies), then its prognosis is quite poor. Benson wrote in the 1991 article, "Unlike the patient with frontal lobe behavior who will understand the problem and the treatment but who cannot act on this knowledge, the patient with the Geschwind syndrome is unlikely to accept either criticism or advice. They are not amenable to insight psychotherapy" (p. 420).

There is also some scientific support for a specific personality disorder associated with autism. It is called *Asperger's syndrome* and is named for the Austrian physician who first described this disorder. The syndrome apparently appears among high-functioning persons with autism and includes stereotyped and lengthy speech, poor nonverbal communication, peculiar social interactions, poor empathy, resistance to change, clumsy and stereotyped motor movement, and low interest levels (Kerbeshian, Burd, & Fisher, 1990). Violence may also be a factor (Mauson et al., 1985). Although rare (1 in 10,000; Volkmar, Paul, & Cohen, 1985), the syndrome has drawn significant scientific support.

Organic personality syndrome, characterized by temper outbursts, socially inappropriate behavior, and exaggerated responses to stimuli (APA, 1987) has been associated with some forms of epilepsy. These symptoms are usually associated with diagnosed brain pathology and often improve with antiseizure medications.

There are a number of steps a clinician should consider in order to make a reasonably accurate, if tentative, diagnosis. An important first step is considering those disorders mentioned above. The following suggestions are offered to the clinician to facilitate the diagnostic process:

1. Although it may seem obvious, a good knowledge of the DSM-III-R is crucial. The use of vague or outdated terms such as *psychopath* are not helpful and may easily be used pejoratively. Since many developmentally disabled persons may not fit neatly into a single category, consider describing which features do exist to support the claim of "inflexible" and "maladaptive" patterns of behavior.

Sometimes a developmentally disabled person says things that, if said by someone of normal capacity, would lead a clinician to consider "antisocial personality disorder" as a possible diagnosis. But persons who are mentally retarded sometimes say things that more closely reflect their developmental age and emotional immaturity than a clear-cut disorder of personality.

For example, late one evening, while I was visiting a living unit in a developmental center, a young man eluded the staff and attempted to attack me. Suddenly, we both lost our footing, and I landed on top of him, with my right arm pinned beneath him. As help arrived, I said to the staff, "Please be careful. I think my right arm is broken." As he was being led away, the young fellow turned to me and said, grinning, "Good!, I did that." Fortunately, the arm wasn't broken, but his comment made it difficult for me not to feel angry.

This person had a habit of making remarks like this and had, over his history of institutionalization since age six, been diagnosed as having "psychopathic tendencies" on many occasions. This diagnosis had led to an escalating series of punishment-based treatments, which only worsened his *actual* condition of rapid-cycling bipolar disorder. Once he was properly diagnosed, the frequency of his severe behavior outbursts dropped to almost zero.

2. Persons who function below the "mild" range of mental retardation should not be diagnosed as having personality disorder. Such a diagnosis would be most unhelpful, as virtually anyone who functions at this level and who has a behavior problem would be subject to such a diagnosis.

In fact, a major epidemiological study done in Sweden found no evidence of personality disorder in this population, other than those behaviors clearly associated with brain damage (Göstason, 1987).

3. Do not rely solely on clinical observation or interview. In a study by Zimmerman et al. (1986), almost one diagnosis in five was changed once further information from an informant was included.

For example, I was asked to see a mildly retarded man who was being held in the psychiatric ward of a New York City hospital because of violent episodes at home. This man had a history of suddenly losing behavior control with almost no warning. He also frequently refused to leave his parents' apartment and flew into a rage when it became necessary. He was initially diagnosed as having a "dependent personality disorder" and also an "intermittent explosive disorder." However, these diagnoses were eliminated once new information became available. It seemed he had been the victim of a mugging in which his life had been threatened by a man with a gun. His maladaptive behaviors, which began shortly after the mugging, were more likely the result of severe anxiety attacks than of a disorder of personality.

4. Consider using one of the commercially available assessment tools. These include the Reiss Screen for Maladaptive Behavior (Reiss, 1987), the Psychopathology Inventory for Mentally Retarded Adults (PIMRA; Matson, 1988), and the Prout-Strohmer Assessment System (Prout & Strohmer, 1989).

The Reiss Screen, as its name implies, is very helpful in making tentative diagnoses of mentally retarded persons whose behavior is raising significant concerns. The screen is completed by knowledgeable caretakers and can be used to gauge differences of perception by two or more groups of caretakers. For example, it would be most helpful to find out if residential staff rate an individual the same way as do program staff.

The PIMRA was designed by Matson as a follow-up of the Reiss Screen. The PIMRA has two forms, one administered to the individual and another administered to caretakers. When the results are taken together, if personality disorder is present, a diagnosis of antisocial, avoidant, and/or dependent personality can be facilitated, since the items related to personality disorder are directed in these areas.

The Prout-Strohmer is designed to assess those mild to borderline retarded persons in whom personality disorder is suspected. Although the scoring does not lead directly to DSM-III-R diagnoses, it is extremely helpful in giving the clinician a systematic data base on which a diagnosis can be developed.

For an especially helpful review of these assessment tools, see Hurley and Sovner (1992).

Using these more formalized tools will help clinicians guard against a phenomenon called *diagnostic overshadowing,* in which clinicians sometimes overlook the presence of mental illness among mentally retarded persons (Reiss & Szysyko, 1983). These tools are especially useful in forensic evaluations because they allow the clinician to back up his or her clinical impressions with a systematic instrument.

I was asked to evaluate a man with borderline intelligence who had been caught setting a number of fires in a small Upstate New York town. Not only was the combined administration of the Prout-Strohmer and the PIMRA very helpful in estabishing a diagnosis of antisocial personality disorder, but it also helped confirm the motive for these very serious, life-threatening fires. It seemed he enjoyed listening to an emergency band scanner as a hobby. When it broke, he set fires so he could steal one from one of the responding emergency vehicles.

5. Once you have gathered your data, try first to identify which "cluster" your person falls into. You may discover that this may be as far as your analysis will take you. Consider using the DSM-III-R Code 301.90, "Personality Disorder Not Otherwise Specified," if that is the best you can do.

6. Possibly the most crucial issue in making a diagnosis of personality disorder among developmentally disabled persons is respecting what has been called the *developmental factor* (Matson & Frame, 1983, cited in Wagner, 1991, p. 87). Compared with persons of normal development, retarded persons almost always appear somewhat immature, impulsive, and uninformed: it is the very nature of the cognitive handicap. So these characteristics need to be factored out in order to prevent spurious diagnoses. Wagner (1991) made two suggestions that may be helpful. He resurrected the old concept of mental age and argued that it is useful in this context. He then used projective tests (an instrument like the Thematic Apperception Test) to elicit responses on which he made a diagnosis.

While one may quibble with Wagner's methods, certainly it is patently unfair to expect a retarded person to react to a social and environmental demand as competently as a nonhandicapped person would. The clinician is cautioned, therefore, to gauge the responses of the person being evaluated in the context of what can reasonably be expected from a person of that developmental level.

## Differential Diagnosis

The literature, including the items on the three available assessment tools, suggests that six personality disorders exist most often among mentally retarded persons: antisocial, avoidant, schizoid, borderline, dependent, and obsessive-compulsive. Special treatment is given to antisocial personality disorder because the literature is virtually silent about treatment strategies for this disorder, but the disorder presents an extraordinary challenge to the clinician.

Here are some descriptions to help the clinician establish a more precise diagnosis. Once again, the reader is cautioned that many developmentally disabled persons do not fall neatly into DSM-III-R categories, and that a more general diagnostic statement may be the best that can be done.

### Antisocial Personality

Probably more than any other personality disorder, antisocial personality represents the most clinically challenging. It is also very likely the disorder most clinicians have in mind when using the term *personality disorder* generically.

Over 150 years ago, Pritchard described a syndrome in which "the moral and active principles of mood are strongly impaired and the individual is found to be incapable, not of talking or reasoning upon any subject proposed to him, but of conducting himself with decency and propriety in the business of life" (quoted by Doren, 1987).

The term *psychopath* or *sociopath* still persists for this disorder and suggest the continued pervasive notion of a moral failure among the persons so afflicted.

This attitude is clearly reflected currently in the DSM-III-R diagnostic description (301.70). Not only is the person described as irritable and irresponsible, but pejorative descriptors such as "lying" and "conning" are part of the diagnostic criteria. Significant additional criteria include persistent criminal behavior, poor ability to maintain interpersonal relationships, recklessness, and the real potential for violence.

As with all personality disorders, care must be taken to ensure that these behaviors are *not* simply reflective of inadequate social learning but exist *despite the individual's clear ability to know better.*

### Avoidant Personality Disorder and Schizoid Personality Disorder

The advoidant and schizoid personality disorders are discussed in the same section because they are easily confused, as the observable behavior for both is the same. In both cases, the person appears to be a loner, has few friends and no intimate relationships, and may appear shy, aloof, and hypersensitive to attempts at friendship. Differential diagnosis depends on the clinician's judgment of the person's *desires* to have close relationships (APA, 1987). Persons with schizoid personality disorder express very little, or no, desire to relate to other persons. The problem, of course, is that many people will indicate they do not want what they cannot have.

Developmentally disabled persons, especially those with a history of institutional living, may have been repeatedly betrayed by persons claiming to be friends. The clinician also needs to be sensitive to the poorly developed language skills that many developmentally disabled persons demonstrate, which may easily create situations in which a person is unable to communicate his or her desire to develop a relationship.

## Borderline Personality Disorder

Borderline personality disorder is one of the most vexing personality disorders. It is described in the DSM-III-R as "a pervasive pattern of instability of self-image, interpersonal relationships, and mood" (p. 346). This disorder presents, among borderline and mildly retarded persons, as a personality that is either not well organized or has been fragmented because of extraordinarily stressful life experiences.

One outstanding feature of persons with borderline personality disorder is their almost uncanny ability to infuriate their caregivers. One such person whom I know, waits for a holiday like Christmas to get drunk, present himself to the police, and have them call his harried caseworker for help. If he is ignored, he sometimes threatens suicidal or other dangerous behaviors and may partially carry them out.

Another very common characteristic is the person's virtual inability to see how behavior is connected to its consequences. Programs based on rewards and punishments, therefore, are rarely effective with persons with borderline personality.

## Dependent Personality Disorder

Retarded persons often have been rewarded for subservience to the demands of others and have been punished for showing too much independence (Zigler & Burack, 1989; Zigler & Bolla, 1977). The hallmark of this disorder is fearfulness in social situations, particularly fear of making decisions, or of hurting someone else's feelings. There is a marked lack of self-advocacy, and much submissive behavior (APA, 1987).

One way this disorder presents among the developmentally disabled is an extraordinary vulnerability to being taken advantage of by others.

Sometimes behaviors that appear at first sight to be hypersexuality are the sad efforts of a developmentally disabled person who has an exaggerated desire to please everyone with whom he or she comes in contact.

## Obsessive-Compulsive Personality Disorder

Obsessive-compulsive personality disorder describes a person who is consumed by the need for perfection and an internal focus on compliance with rules and regulations (APA, 1987). This disorder is rarely cited in the literature as representing a serious source of interfering behaviors. However, the disorder is similar, and may be associated with, a much more disabling condition called *obsessive-compulsive disorder.*

My own experience with developmentally disabled persons suggests that lack of literature may be misleading. Many developmentally handicapped persons have lived in places where a rigid regimen of scheduling and an insistence on almost antiseptic cleanliness are the day-to-day routine. Such persons often become quite uncomfortable when finding themselves in a more normalized environment.

Also, some persons with relatively mild autism may be more likely to demonstrate an obsessive-compulsive personality disorder than the much more pathological obsessive-compulsive rituals associated with more severe forms of autism.

The remaining personality disorders have not been predominently mentioned in the developmental disability literature. Whether this lack of mention represents a problem with case-finding techniques or truly reflects the epidemiology of these disorders is an open question.

## Summary

Diagnosing personality disorders among persons who are mentally retarded needs to be carried out with great respect for both ethical and practical considerations.

The late Burt Blatt brought a New York City audience to tears some years ago. He told a story about how a little retarded boy experienced Christmas in a large state institution. If that child survived, he would most likely carry a diagnosis of personality disorder today.

One must guard against using the diagnosis of personality disorder as an excuse either to withhold services to someone or to use interventions that are not culturally normative.

This chapter urges the reader always to consider the diagnosis of personality disorder as a tentative one, given the dramatic positive changes people make when their world changes.

A menu of services, ranging from functional skills training to intensive supervision and structure, needs to be made available to this population. This group of people will test the will of both the clinician and the community to do the right thing. It is quite likely that creative links between diverse parts of the human services system will need to be developed to serve this population.

In their book, *Gentle Teaching* (1987), John McGee and his coauthors advised the clinician to remain "serene." When working with persons with personality disorder, this advice is well taken.

# References

American Psychiatric Association. (1987). *Diagnostic and Statistical Manual of Mental Disorders* (3rd ed., rev.; DSM-III-R). Washington, DC.: Author.

Benson, F. D. (1991). The Geschwind syndrome. *Adv. Neurol., 55,* 411–421.

Blatt, B. (1970). *Exodus from pandemonium: Human abuse and a reformation of public policy.* Boston: Allyn & Bacon.

Blatt, B. (1973). *Souls in extremis: An anthology on victims or victimizers.* Boston: Allyn & Bacon.

Doren, D. M. (1987). *Understanding and treating the psychopath.* New York: Wiley.

Durand, M. (1985). Reducing behavior problems through functional communication training. *J. Appl. Behav. Anal., 18,* 111–126.

Dybwad, G. (1964). *Challenges in mental retardation.* New York: Columbia University Press.

Göstason, R. (1987). Psychiatric illness among the mildly mentally retarded. *Upsala J. Med. Sci.,* Suppl. 44, 115–124.

Hurley, A. D., & Sovner, R. (1992). Inventories for evaluating psychopathology in developmentally disabled individuals, *The Habilitative Mental Healthcare Newsletter, 11,* Nos. 7, 8, 45–54.

Kerbeshian, J., Burd, L. & Fisher, W. (1990). Asperger's syndrome: To be or not to be? *Br. J. Psychiatr., 156,* 721–725.

Lamon, D., & Reiss, S. (1987) Social skill deficiencies associated with depressed mood of mentally retarded adults. *Am. J. Men. Def., 92*(2), 224–229.

Matson, Johnny L. (1988). *The Psychopathology Inventory for Mentally Retarded Adults.* Orland Park: International Diagnostic Systems.

Mawson, D., Grounds, A., & Tantam, D. (1985). Violence and Asperger's Syndrome: A Case Study. *Br. J. Psychiatr., 147,* 566–569.

McGee, J., Menolascino, F., Hobbs, D., & Menousek, P. (1987). *Gentle teaching: A nonaversive approach for helping persons with mental retardation.* New York: Human Services Press Texas PROED.

Prout, H. T., & Strohmer, D. C. (1989). *The Prout Strohmer Assessment System.* Schenectady: Genium.

Reid, A. H., & Ballinger, B. R. (1987). Personality disorder in mental handicap. *Psychol. Med., 17,* 983–987.

Reiss, S. (1987). *Reiss Screen for Maladaptive Behavior.* Orland Park: International Diagnostic Systems.

Reiss, S., Leviton, G. W., & Szyszko, J. (1982). Emotional disturbance and mental retardation: Diagnostic overshadowing. *Am. J. Ment. Defic., 86,* 567–574.

Reiss, S., & Szyszko, J. (1983). Diagnostic overshadowing and professional experience with mentally retarded persons. *Am. J. Ment. Defic., 87,* 396–402.

Rutter, M. (1987). Temperament, personality and personality disorder. *Br. J. Psychiatr., 150,* 443–458.

Trimble, M. R. (1988). Personality disorder and epilepsy. *Acta Neurochir.* (Suppl. 44), 98–101.

Volkman, F. R., Paul, R., & Cohen, D. J. (1985). The use of "Asperger's syndrome": Letter to the editor. *J. Autism Devel. Disorders, 15,* 437–439.

Wagner, P. (1991). Developmentally based personality assessment. *Ment. Retard.,* 29, 87–92.

Wolfersberger, W., (1972). *The principles of normalization in human services.* Toronto: National Institute on Mental Retardation.

Zigler, E., & Bolla, D. (1977). Impact of institutional experience on the behavior and development of retarded persons. *Am. J. Ment. Defic., 82,* 1–11.

Zigler, E., & Burack, J. A. (1989). Personality development and the dually diagnosed person. *Res. Devel. Disabilities, 10,* 225–240.

Zimmerman, M., Pfohl, B., Stange D., & Lorenthal, C. (1986). Assessment of DSM III personality disorders: the importance of interviewing an informant. *J. Clin. Psychiatr., 47,* 261–263.

# 8

# Self-Injurious Behavior in Persons with Mental Retardation: A Developmental Psychiatric Approach

*Anton Dosen*

S elf-injurious behavior (SIB) is defined as chronic repetitive behavior causing external trauma on a mechanical basis and occurring in cognitively impaired persons (Rojahn, 1986). Among the inhabitants of institutes for the mentally retarded, SIB is reported in 8 to 14 percent of the cases (Farber, 1987; Oliver, Murphy, & Corbett, 1987). The severity of the behavior may vary from light to very severe, causing organ damage and even being life-threatening. Most cases however involve repetitive soft-tissue injury with an apparently low risk of "serious" sequelae. Nevertheless, intervention to reduce or prevent even this behavior from occurring is necessary because it interferes with the emotional and ethical concerns of the caregivers and is incompatible with the person's ongoing training in self-care skills.

Self-injurious behavior occurs markedly more often among persons at the moderate and lower levels of retardation (IQ less than 50) than among the mildly retarded (IQ > 50). It is also reported that profoundly and severely retarded persons exhibit this behavior more frequently than do the moderately retarded (Oliver et al., 1987; Rojahn, 1986). This behavior emerges most frequently between the ages of ten and thirty, with a peak between fifteen and twenty years of age (Oliver et al., 1987).

Until recently, SIB attracted remarkably little attention from professionals. In addition, it was common practice for each of the disciplines to view SIB separately, making no attempt to attain a mutual insight into the totality of the individual life and health problems of the mentally retarded.

Furthermore, the focus of the assessment and treatment was the symptom. The examiners were less concerned about psychopathological, pathophysiological, social, systemic, and other aspects. This narrow focus led to only partial examination of SIB in the mentally retarded, and so it remained a phenomenon about which very little was known. In this chapter, an attempt is made to integrate the present theories and facts in the hope that, in this way, the relevant questions will come to light and will serve as a guide to new directions in further investigations.

## Current Etiological Considerations

There are many theories and hypotheses concerning the etiology of SIB in the mentally retarded. However, this disorder may occur among animals and nonretarded persons when they are faced with extreme circumstances as well. In persons with a normal level of intelligence, SIB is described in cases in which the persons involved are suffering from various psychiatric problems or are being exposed to particularly severe stressful life circumstances. When this form of behavior occurs in the nonretarded population, it is usually called *automutilation*.

In studies of intellectually normal individuals exhibiting SIB, a link has been found between a history of childhood sexual abuse (Shapiro, 1987) and self-injurious behavior. This behavior has often also been found in those with borderline personality disorders. In addition, links have been made between eating disorders and SIB (Winchel & Stanley, 1991). Psychotic patients, usually in response to command hallucinations or delusions of punishing themselves as a result of feelings of guilt, may inflict injury on themselves as well.

The same behavior may be found in prison populations. Investigations of prisoners have revealed a significantly high rate of fighting, outbursts of rage, drug abuse, and anxiety coupled with self-injurious behavior (Winchel & Stanley, 1991).

In all these cases, a depersonalization, implying very high levels of anxiety, is commonly seen (Jones, 1982). Experiences of social isolation during developmental periods are often reported in the histories of these individuals.

Studies of animals in captivity have revealed that isolation increases aggressivity in various species (Jones, 1982). "Fearfulness" was estimated to be the underlying state of these animals. Because of this fearfulness, the animal becomes agitated, and that fearfulness, in turn, induces self-injurious behavior. Severe self-injury is seen when aggressive behavior is provoked by threats and, at the same time, the animal is prevented from fighting back. Mild self-injury is seen in animals frustrated by isolation and all its consequences. Once started, this behavior tends to become stereotyped.

Jones (1982) concluded that similar forms and causes of SIB are to be found in animals and in human beings. Severe forms occur because of agitation and rage, and mild forms of stereotyped SIB are caused by unfavorable social factors and distress. Feelings of anxiety and anger are common when one is subjected to social isolation. Disturbances in social bonding during development, resulting later predominantly in feelings of social isolation and loneliness, may play an important role in the occurrence of this sort of behavior in both animals and humans.

These findings and speculations will be discussed further within the context of the appearance of SIB among mentally retarded individuals.

The most disputed hypotheses about SIB are those dealing with biological impairments and psychological abnormalities. There are also psychodynamic considerations. However, psychodynamic thinking is utilized more often to explain cases of automutilation among nonretarded individuals.

## Biological Aspects

The protoype of biologically caused SIB is the Lesch-Nyhan syndrome, which is an X-linked enzyme-deficiency disorder characterized by mental retardation, spasticity, choreoathetosis, and compulsive and stereotyped self-injurious behavior. SIB among Lesch-Nyhan sufferers usually involves biting the fingers, lips, and oral tissue.

Self-injurious behavior is also present in other congenital forms of mental retardation, like Cornelia de Lange's syndrome and PKU (phenylketonuria). In some cases, frontal lobe seizures have also been reported as causing SIB (Gedye, 1989).

Recently, the attention of investigators has been focused on the neurobiochemical aspects of the CNA of the SIB patients. In Lesch-Nyhan syndrome, a dysregulation of dopaminergic activity and dopamine receptor supersensitivity has been found (Lloyd et al., 1981). Other psychopharmacological studies of SIB patients (Gualtieri & Schroeder, 1989), however, do not, as yet, permit definite conclusions about the involvement of dopaminergic mechanisms in this behavioral disorder.

The serotonin hypothesis about SIB is based on the observation that patients with various kinds of violent impulsive or autoaggressive behavior have a significantly lower cerebrospinal fluid concentration of serotonin metabolite 5-hydroxyindoleacetic acid (5-HIAA) (Brown, Linnoila, & Goodwin, 1990; Roy & Linnoila, 1990). In SIB patients, depressed plasma serotonin levels have also been found. Some psychopharmacological studies (Gualtieri, 1989; Rasmussen et al., 1989) have suggested that SIB can be reduced by using serotonin reuptake inhibitors or serotonin-enhancing compounds.

Current studies of the role of the opiate system in SIB suggest that the opiate system of SIB individuals may be altered in such a way that an increased release of endogenous opiates (B-endorphin) is necessary to maintain homeostasis. According to this theory, the self-injurious behavior in these individuals serves as a mediator to increase the B-endorphin level in the CNS. The positive results obtained among a number of patients to whom opiate antagonists (naltrexone and naloxone) were administered

(Kars et al., 1990) support this theory. Although there have been a limited number of biochemical studies and reports of pharmacologically treated patients, there appears to be sufficient evidence to warrent biologically oriented studies of SIB patients (see also Chapter 15 in this book).

## Psychological Theories

The most popular psychological theory about SIB is that it creates self-stimulation. The theory begins with the assumption that an SIB person suffers from an inability to process stimuli adequately. There are two alternatives to such a condition: hypoarousal and hyperarousal. In both cases, the individual attempts to find compensation for the impairment by way of her or his own activities. In the case of hypoarousal, tactile, vestibular, and kinesthetic modalities are practiced in the form of stereotypical movements or SIB, the aim being to increase sensory stimulation. In cases of hyperarousal, the person engages in SIB to change the situation and reduce discomfort by inflicting other sorts of stimuli upon herself or himself.

Another theory is that of learned behavior. This theory will be discussed later.

On the grounds of these theoretical approaches, various treatment methods have been developed, the most well-known of which are sensory stimulation (Edelson, 1984; Mason & Newson, 1990) and behavior therapies (Mulick & Kedesdy, 1988; Matson & Keyes, 1990).

## Psychodynamic Considerations

As mentioned above psychodynamic thinking has been utilized primarily to explain the automutilative behavior of nonretarded persons. The reason is, presumably, not that these theories cannot be utilized with the mentally retarded, but that there is a shortage of knowledge of the personality development of the mentally retarded. Speaking of automutilation in intellectually normal individuals, we make a link between this symptom and preoedipal developmental pathology (Kafka, 1969; Graff & Mallin, 1967; Kernberg, 1987). Disorders in early ego development, predisposing the individual to dissociation and to other primitive defenses, may, according to our experiences (Dosen, 1990), also be taken into consideration in cases of mentally retarded individuals suffering from SIB.

## An Integrative Developmental Psychiatric Look at SIB

So far, the studies of SIB have been mainly of the analytic kind, searching for isolated causes of the phenomenon and trying to explain the behavior from a single essential impairment at the biological or psychosocial level. Recently accumulated knowledge suggests that this behavior may also occur in certain psychiatric disorders in which both biological and psychosocial impairments are obvious. The occurrence of SIB has, in particular cases, also been related to adverse environmental and organismic conditions (for example, hospitalization and somatic illness) and to the particular developmental levels.

These problems call for a holistic approach to the problem of an SIB individual. Not isolated aspects, but the totality of the organismic and environmental existence should be placed within the scope of the investigator. For this complex problem, a developmental psychiatric approach is likely to be most appropriate. Such an approach is integrative rather than selective, synthesizing rather than analyzing the mechanisms and processes that may lead to this behavior. From the developmental psychiatric point of view, it may be beneficial to shed light on the following issues:

1. developmental impairments
2. the effects of stress
3. anxiety and SIB
4. the relationship between psychiatric disorders and SIB

*Developmental Impairments*

In most cases, self-injurious behavior begins at the developmental age. In addition to SIB, these persons usually also exhibit particular behavioral patterns that reflect earlier age-appropriate behavior. Among these mentally retarded individuals, there is often a disturbance in the ability to make social contact via touch, ambiguity when making affective bonding, excitation as a reaction to changes in the surroundings, a lack of affect control, stereotypy, withdrawal, and an inclination toward self-stimulative behavior. It is also remarkable how accentuated the dependence of these persons is on environmental structures and how hypersensitive they are to particular sensory stimuli. There is usually a severe retardation in the cognitive as well as the socioemotional development of the individuals who have these behavioral characteristics. The discrepancy between the cognitive and the socioemotional developmental levels is striking among some of them. Usually, the cognitive level is higher than the socioemotional level. Speech is usually underdeveloped among these individuals, and when it is developed, its purpose is more instrumental than socially communicative.

Since all these behavioral characteristics occur mostly at an early developmental age in the life of the mentally retarded person, it is necessary for the diagnostician to attain an appropriate insight into different developmental aspects.

From this description, it may be clear that SIB persons show some psychosocial characteristics by means of which a particular personality type may be determined. Here, we discuss some of the physiological, neuroendocrinological, psychological, and socioemotional aspects of such a personality. In this context it is important to focus on the following issues:

- disturbed maturation of cerebral tissue
- disturbances at the biological and neurobiochemical levels
- primitive reaction types at the lower developmental levels
- disturbances in phasic socioemotional development
- adaptive (learned) behavior

**Disturbances in Maturation.** There is no doubt that most mentally retarded infants begin their postnatal development with a tendency toward discrepant maturation of the diverse CNS areas (Luria, 1973; Coulter, 1988; Huttenlocher, 1984). Not only are there neurohystological (Ebels, 1980) and neurophysiological differences but also neurobiochemical (Huttenlocher, 1984) differences between a mentally retarded infant and a normally developing child. The developmental variations may lead to disturbed psychosocial development at various ages and in various developmental phases (Menolascino, 1977). Usually, one speaks of a developmental-phase-specific sensitivity and vulnerability. For example, when there is a problem with sensory integration (lack of adequate psychophysiological processing of the stimuli), it causes difficulties in adapting to the living environment and, consequently, has a negative impact on the stimulation of psychosocial development (for example, a blind infant usually shows retarded early psychosocial development), resulting in a risk of stagnation in socioemotional development. Disturbances in maturation of the CNS may also cause problems in the attachment-forming phase or may make it difficult to establish an emotional security base. From the other side, diverse studies of the issue of early developmental disorders (Spitz, 1946; Engel & Schmale, 1973; Bemporad & Wilson, 1978) have suggested that inappropriate processing of stimuli (for example, understimulation or overstimulation ) and a lack or loss of attachment behavior may cause disengagement from active interaction with the surroundings at both the motor and the perceptual levels and possibly metabolic rearrangement as well.

From these considerations, one may expect that a mentally retarded infant will have difficulties in attaining a psychophysiological homeostasis and will be distress-prone.

**Disturbances at the Biological and Neurobiochemical Levels.** As mentioned above, neuroendocrinological disorders in SIB persons are apparent. Usually, investigators have paid more attention to the link between SIB mechanisms and opioid system activity and have so far overlooked the consequences of the dysfunctioning of this system for the functioning of other neurobiological systems and for the psychosocial development of the child as well.

The neuropeptides and endogenous opioids seem to influence pre- and postnatal brain maturation. Increased opioids seem to decrease the maturational rate (Zadrian et al., 1985; Strand et al., 1989). Additionally, a range of behavioral specificities are linked to increased activity of the opioid system, like impaired attachment behavior (a decrease in contact behavior and a reduction in social interactions), diminished novelty behavior, a decrement in learning and memory, an increase in stereotyped behavior, and a decrease in the ability to cope with stress (Buitelaar, 1991). Also, there is evidence that the endogenous opioid system influences other neurobiochemical systems, for example, the modulation of catecholamine and acetylcholine activity in the CNS (Buitelaar, 1991).

It is obvious that a change in neuroendocrine activity influences the development of the child in such a way that a spectrum of developmental disturbances may occur. Seemingly, different pathological factors may lead, by different neurophysiological pathways, to disturbances in different endocrinological and neurobiochemical systems at different levels, resulting finally in the same symptoms. It is not clear what should be seen as the cause and what as the consequence. Is it the endocrinological disorder that causes psychological, behavioral, and other disorders, or are there environmental influences and psychophysical problems that cause endocrinological changes, or do all these factors together determine the sort of disturbance? Scientists are aware that neuroendocrinological disorders do occur in SIB and that this phenomenon needs to be investigated further. However, the complexity of the disorder calls for an integrated approach, within which SIB should be seen as a product of a multidimensional disorder in which biological, developmental, and psychosociological factors interact.

**Primitive Reaction Types.** Scientific investigations of mentally retarded infants are insufficient. All we know about the development of mentally retarded infants is deduced from investigations of nonretarded infants, and it is presumed that development may also occur along the same lines in the mentally retarded. Keeping not only the slower rate of psychosocial development, but also other specific aspects of a mentally retarded child in mind, such as a specific biological constellation, characteristic environmental changes during the acceptation process of the child, and physiological and interactional specificities as well, one may assume that comparisons with nonretarded children are prone to various limitations.

The comparisons of developmental and chronological age may serve as a basis for forming a global judgment concerning the severity of the handicap and the level of intellectual functioning, but they cannot give sufficient insight into various personality aspects or explain all the interaction and re-action patterns of the mentally retarded. Nevertheless, the observations made of nonretarded children may serve as a starting point from which speculations or hypothetical thinking may take off.

The speculations and hypotheses that are discussed here should be seen and understood as attempts to broaden and deepen thinking on various developmental factors that may play a role in SIB.

When there is psychomotor excitement in nonretarded infants, autoaggressive activities are common. This feature has been explained by psychodynamically oriented investigators to be a reaction specific to the differentiation phase of self–other (according to Mahler, Pine and Bergman, 1975), and to the phase of separation from symbiotic bonding. Such an infant is in transition between the reality of separation and the fantasy of symbiosis. In cases of frustration, autoaggressivity emerges as an anxiety-diminishing phenomenon (Gaedt, Jäkel, & Kischkel, 1987). This sort of SIB in the mentally retarded can be seen as a primitive behavioral pattern in a state of distress and as occurring because of an undifferentiated sense of the self and others. Also, it has been suggested that such a highly emotional repetitive event can cause neurobiochemical changes on the hormonal and CNS levels (Tuinier, 1989).

**Disturbance in Socioemotional Development.** A comparison between autistic and severely mentally retarded children exhibiting SIB may provide more material for this discussion.

Recent investigations (Chamberlain & Herman, 1990; Buitelaar, 1991) show that there is increased opioid activity in both autistic and severely mentally retarded SIB children. In autistic children, SIB is a relatively frequent feature. In both sorts of SIB children, the following common psychophysiological impairments are striking: difficulties with sensory integration, problems with attachment and social interaction (withdrawal), problems with adaptation to changed surroundings, a high degree of anxiety, and sterotypical and self-stimulative activities. Remarkable differences between these SIB children can be found in their cognitive levels. Autistic SIB children usually have higher cognitive levels than the mentally retarded. Furthermore autistic children show specific impairments, like disturbed language development, an insistence on sameness, and specific sensory abnormalities, that make them different from an average mentally retarded child.

Keeping in mind the similarities and dissimilarities between SIB autistic and nonautistic mentally retarded children, one may differentiate factors that apparently are related to SIB from those that are not. The factors possibly related to SIB are difficulties in adapting to the surroundings, problems with social bonding, problems with social communication, and anxiety.

Because the same factors play an important role in socioemotional development, one may speculate that SIB is linked to disturbances in socioemotional development. A similar train of thought may be deduced from the fact that, in most cases, SIB occurs after the age of two. Oliver et al. (1987) found that, within a group of 506 SIB individuals, only 3 percent were younger than five. The largest group was made up of individuals between the ages of fifteen and twenty.

It is likely from these findings that a certain level of socioemotional, rather than cognitive, development is necessary for the onset of SIB. It is conceivable that its occurrence is linked to a particular developmental phase. Apparently, distortion in the forming of secure attachment and emotional security bases may be of great importance in the onset of SIB.

**Adaptive (Learned) Behavior.** SIB as an adaptive (learned) behavior is seen as being a consequence of developmental delay (Guess & Carr, 1991; Repp et al., 1990). A motoric developmental lag among the mentally retarded is one of the reasons why these children exhibit rhythmic movements far longer than nonretarded children do. Rhythmic behavior is a normal behavior pattern for infants during the first months of life and precedes the acquisition of motoric skills. Motoric delay, accompanied by difficulties in sensory integration, leads to sterotypical movements aimed at compensating for sensory under- or overstimulation. Let it be well understood that this is a mechanism for increasing or decreasing arousal and, in this way, for serving to attain a physiological homeostasis. By doing so, the person may adapt to the given environmental circumstances. In cases in which the stereotypy is reinforced by the environmental circumstances, it may evolve into self-injurious behavior. Guess and Carr (1991) distinguished two ways in which SIB emerges in these persons:

- as a controlling function, modulating arousal and controlling the behavior of other people in the surroundings
- as a nonverbal mode of communication

In the first case, SIB is explained as an attempt to reduce the high level of arousal resulting from stress or anxiety. In the second case, the SIB mechanism is maintained by means of a conditioned positive reinforcer (receiving attention from others) or a negative reinforcer (escaping or avoiding an overload of stimuli).

### Stress and SIB

Stress was defined by Maccoby (1983) as follows: "it begins with an arousing event which disrupts the organism's equilibrium; altering responses occur, which are usually accompanied by strong affect, and the organism engages in a set of problem-solving efforts, which either return the organism to the prior organisational status or produce a new organisation. In the worst case a state of disorganisation persists" (p. 218).

Little is known about the effects of stress on mentally retarded children. Somewhat more is known about stress in nonretarded children. Work done by Rutter (1983) shed more light on this issue. Rutter found that the child's reaction to stressful events depends on age, sex, temperament, social networks, cognitive appraisal, genetic factors, protective factors, and coping processes.

The most frequently occurring important psychosocial stressful events that take place during childhood are loss of a parent, hospitalization, birth of a sibling, parental divorce, chronic environmental adversities (for example, an abusive environment, family adversities, and chronic threatening) and cataclysmic events (for example, earthquake or war). In unfavorable circumstances, the consequences of such stressful events may be changes visible at diverse levels—the socioemotional level, the developmental level, and the physiological level—additionally causing psychiatric disturbances.

At the socioemotional level, a stressful event can cause fearfulness and anxiety accompanied by an increase in arousal and activation meant to avoid the stressful situation. The younger the child, the greater the likelihood of extensive behavioral disorganization (Maccoby, 1983; Terr, 1991).

At the developmental level, regressive behavior may be marked, sometimes causing a long-lasting arrest in psychosocial development (Rutter, 1983).

At the physiological level, specific neuroendocrinological changes may occur (Ciarnello, 1983). Henry (1980) proposed a model of stress, neuroendocrine response, and coping that differentiates two basic sorts of outcomes. The perceiving of a stressful stimulus depends on interactions between genetic, early experiental, and learned coping patterns. If a stimulus is perceived as being a challenge to control, then the fight–flight mechanism is triggered. This is associated with the noradrenergic arousal system and results in an increased secretion of noradrenalin and adrenalin. If the stressful stimulus is associated with loss of control and helplessness, activation of the hypothalamic-pituitary-adrenal (HPA) system occurs. An elevation of the adrenocorticotropic hormone (ACTH) and cortisol levels is the consequence. In the first case, because of the increase of noradrenalin, the person's mobility and aggression are marked. In the case of cortisol increase, a so-called conservation withdrawal (Engel & Schmale, 1973) takes place accompanied by a sort of depression.

Despite a severe shortage in the number of studies of the SIB population, some speculations on this hypothesis are conceivable. Heightened levels of opioids in the CNS apparently diminish the secretion of ACTH and cortisol. This lower sensitivity of the HPA axis may mean that these children are less capable of reacting to stress by activating the HPA axis and are thus less able to cope with stressful events. It is most likely that these children react predominantly with an activation of the noradrenergic arousal system leading to restlessness and aggression. Disturbances at the opioid level may also cause diminished learning from one's own experiences, leading to repetition of the behavioral pattern in the unchanged circumstances, and to an inability to adapt to the changed situation. Stress-proneness is probably increased in such cases.

With regard to psychiatric disorders, long-lasting or perpetual stressful circumstances have been related to the onset of depression, dissociation, personality disorders, and psychosomatic disorders (Rutter, 1983; Sanders & Giolas, 1991).

The effect of particular stressful events depends on, among other factors, the age of the child. For example, fearfulness of strange people in an infant does not occur earlier than the approximate age eight months. Separation of the child from the mother is most stressful in the period between eight and thirty-six months. Grief reactions are both milder and of shorter duration in young children than in adolescents.

There is evidence that early stressful events may influence and alter sensitivity to stress or may modify the style of coping in such a way that a sort of sensitization to later similar stressors occurs (Rutter, 1983). For example, the first short-term hospital admission usually has no harmful effect, whereas the child may react with psychological problems or even symptoms of psychiatric disorder to the next admissions. Adverse reactions may occur immediately after the stressful event or may be triggered later by another similar event (for example, separation from the mother) or a different severe adverse event.

Long-lasting or repeated exposure to extreme external events evoke the emotions of fear, rage, or sadness and activate defense and coping mechanisms, among which aggression and autoaggression often come to the fore (Jones, 1982; Shapiro, 1987). For example, rage, including anger directed toward the self, is a striking finding among children who are victims of prolonged abuse. Self-mutilations or suicide attempts are relatively frequent among these children and adolescents (Terr, 1991; Sanders & Giolas, 1991).

From these considerations concerning the effects of stress on nonretarded children, some parallels may be drawn between them and mentally retarded children. Undoubtedly the mentally retarded child is subjected to the same stressful events as the nonretarded, but the reactions of such a child may be different in many ways. The differences may be influenced at the least by altered intellectual abilities and specific coping processes. Other differences in retarded children, like their social networks, their specific vulnerabilities, and their later development of particular psychosocial skills, may also play a role in the effect that stressful events have.

Studies in prematurely born children (Levine, 1983; Leiderman, 1983) suggest that these children are less capable of coping with unfavorable events, which often cause behavioral and developmental difficulties. This coping impairment is explained as being a consequence of an early distortion of the mother–child interaction (due to hospitalization of the child and fearful concerns of the mother), rather than as being a result of physical problems of the child.

In mentally handicapped infants, social interactions are established at a slower rate than in normal children. Since a normal attachment process is seen as being a very important aspect of the development of defensive mechanisms for stressful occurrences (Lipsitt, 1983), it may be expected that mentally retarded children with attachment disturbances are stress-prone. This may mean that events that have no significant consequences for children growing up normally may cause psychophysical difficulties among mentally retarded contact-disturbed children.

In SIB children, a number of previously mentioned stressful events may play a role. Their attachment behavior is often not adequate for developing a stable emotional security base. The problems of interaction with their surroundings lead to their being unable to be part of a trustful relationship; they can therefore not be protected by other people. Their sensory problems and cognitive inabilities are the reason why they have severe difficulties in adapting to their environmental circumstances. Their low level of socioemotional development usually does not allow for them to develop a unique personality and to achieve a stable sense of themselves. Additionally, frequent somatic illnesses, hospitalizations, institutionalization, and other changes, as well as other unfavorable environmental events, may lead these children to suffer from stress.

In this context, SIB may be seen as a form of defense against the extensive fear and rage that occur in the stressful situation. As mentioned above, similar behavior is reported in chronically abused children, imprisoned persons, and frustrated captive animals. Apparently, anxiety and rage may be diminished or suppressed by SIB.

On the other hand, when the intensity and frequency of SIB are increased, the SIB itself may become a frightening and stressful event. Thus, SIB and stress become entangled in a casual spiral, worsening and maintaining each other.

Can such a conflict situation lead to further psychosocial distortion and the occurrence of one or another psychiatric illness? Theoretically, this question can probably be answered positively. However, further evidence from day-to-day practice and research on this issue is indispensable.

The stress hypothesis of SIB calls for an extensive and broad investigation on the psychological as well as the developmental psychiatric and neuroendocrinological fronts. The findings could have important consequences for treatment and prevention.

*Anxiety and SIB*

Cannon (1929) described anxiety as a psychological and physiological state in which the person is prepared either to combat danger or to take flight—the fight-or-flight syndrome. Dangerous and threatening environmental circumstances induce anxiety, which in turn may lead to the "fight" response, or aggression. This "fear-induced" aggression (Moyer, 1976) is related to self-defense and apparently diminishes anxiety. However, this behavior is not always adaptive in dealing with fear. Highly anxious states diminish the ability to assess the situation and to pursue alternative courses of action; thus, they may lead to maladaptive behavior. Kashani, Deuser, and Reid (1991) found that aggression is one way of dealing with anxiety; on the other hand, in highly aggressive subjects, a greater degree of various psychopathologies was found (Kashani et al., 1991).

The neurobiochemical and neuroendocrinological aspects of anxiety and antisocial behavior are currently the focus of scientists. Gray (1982, 1987) proposed a two-factor theory of the origin of antisocial behavior; the behavioral inhibition system (BIS) and the behavioral activating system (BAS). Within the BIS, anxiety plays an important role, serving to inhibit behavior in the presence of punishment or extinction. This behavior is primarily mediated by the related serotonergic system. The BAS serves to activate the escape from punishment. This system is mediated by the sympathetic nervous system.

McBurnett et al. (1991) found that children with conduct disorder and anxiety show inhibited behavior. Among these children, an elevated level of urine and saliva cortisol was found. This behavior is mediated by the BIS. In conduct-disturbed children without anxiety, an activated behavior was established. Among these children, a lower level of cortisol was found. These children also showed a lower blood serotonine level than the inhibited children.

Despite increased cortisol secretion due to anxiety, the investigators very rarely found positive Dexamethasone Suppression Test (DST) among patients with anxiety disorders (Lieberman et al., 1983; Sheehon et al., 1983; Bridges et al., 1986). These findings suggest that the underlying pathophysiology of anxiety does not necessarily have an impact on the HPA axis as measured by DST. This seldomly positive DST among persons with an anxiety disorder seems to be an important biological feature in differentiating these individuals and patients suffering from depression. According to investigations of patients with attacks of panic (Boer, 1988), a reduced 5-HT receptor sensitivity was found. These findings suggest that there is a serotonergic dysfunction in the anxiety disorder. Higher plasma adrenalin and noradrenalin levels in these patients have also been reported (Liebowitz, 1987).

Investigations of the neurobiochemical and neuroendocrinological aspects of anxiety in the mentally retarded are very rare. In reference to the favorable results achieved with some SIB patients by administrating antidepressants that induce predominantly serotonergic activation (Dosen, 1990a), one might consider the possibility of the impact of this medication not only on depressive but also on anxiety disorders. Also, good results with SIB have been reported when B-adrenergic blockers were administered (Gualtieri, 1991). The clinical observation of anxiety among SIB patients, comparative studies of the neurobiochemical findings in nonretarded persons having anxiety disorders, and medication results in the SIB individuals—all these data emphasize the importance of a scientific approach to the phenomenon of anxiety among these patients.

Anxiety as phenomenon among the mentally retarded has attracted the attention of investigators. In a review of the literature on anxiety states among the mentally retarded, Ollendick and Ollendick (1982) concluded that: "Anxiety at least in its general pervasive form is more prevalent in the mentally retarded than in nonretarded persons, is more likely to be observed earlier in more severely retarded persons than in mildly retarded or normal individuals, and is equally prevalent in males and females" (p. 83).

Among the mildly and moderately retarded, forms of anxiety disorders similar to those in nonretarded persons may be diagnosed. Although an accurate classification of anxiety subtypes among the severely and profoundly mentally retarded may be very difficult, the presence of general anxiety may be determined by sharp-sighted behavioral observation (Crabbe, 1989). It is striking how little attention has been paid in the scientific literature to anxiety in SIB patients. In clinical practice, when cautiously observed, anxiety may often be recognized at different stages of the SIB activity and in different forms. In some clinical cases, anxiety may be marked when SIB is triggered (for example, by sudden, unexpected stimuli or changes in the environment). In inflicting injuries on themselves, such persons usually exhibit anger, which gradually dominates the clinical picture. Eventually, anger decreases with a transition into a sort of desperation and helplessness. At this stage, anxiety appears again. In the case of punching oneself with one's own fists, such a person may show anxiety toward his or her own hands and may feel released when someone holds the hands or when he or she can restrain or hide them.

With regard to excitement at the onset of SIB, most investigators qualify this emotional state by the rather undifferentiated term *frustration*. However, to achieve a better understanding of this term, this state should be more appropriately qualified. For example, in cases of so-called hyperarousal, unfamiliar stimuli that cannot be adequately processed should be distinguished from familiar stimuli having negative connotations. With the latter, one can expect an increase in anxiety, which should not be understood as simple frustration. Also, in cases of low basic emotional security, when confronted with separation and the emergence of SIB, the diagnostician should recognize separation anxiety and speak of an existential anxiety, rather than in terms of behavioral concepts.

## Psychiatric Clinical Pictures and SIB

Recently, the attention of scientists has been more attuned to the occurrence of depression among mentally retarded persons (see Dosen & Menolascino, 1990). A number of authors (Menolascino, 1990; Sovner, 1990; Dosen, 1990b) have reported SIB among the mentally retarded suffering from depression. Individuals at lower developmental levels (severely and profoundly retarded) suffering from depression exhibited SIB more frequently than those at higher levels (Dosen, 1990b). This behavior has been found in children as well as in adults.

Self-abusive behavior has been described in both the psychotic and the neurotic forms of depression. The intensity and frequency may vary from light tissue damage, as a reaction to frustration that passes, to constant and severe activity, in which particular organs are damaged, this behavior becoming the most striking and even the main symptom in the clinical picture. In some cases, this behavior emerges at the onset of the depressive state; in other cases, the behavior is already present before the depressive disorder occurs but increases significantly at the onset of depression. The onset of the depressive condition has often been related to important happenings in the environment or to changes in the biological or psychological homeostasis of the person (for example, changes in the family, somatic illness, being placed in an institute, or the loss of an important caregiver).

The onset of depression and SIB after puberty is found relatively often. Besides accompanying the psychotic and neurotic types of depression, the SIB has also been described together with prolonged passive, apathetic, and socially deprived states. These conditions are usually rooted in disturbances in the emotional bonding of the child, causing an insecure emotional base (Dosen & Bojanin, 1990). This so-called developmental depression is usually a constant psychological state of the person. An acute depression may be superincluded in these persons as a reaction to unfavorable life circumstances. Among these individuals, the proneness to exhibit SIB is marked (Dosen, 1990b). Similar findings with regard to a prolonged depressionlike state, in which there is a proneness to exhibit SIB, were reported by some psychodynamically oriented investigators (Gaedt & Gärtner, 1990). Within this context, it is interesting to note that autistic persons and those suffering from pervasive developmental disorder are predisposed to depression (APA, 1987; Sovner, 1990; Dosen, 1990b). In this condition, SIB and even suicidal inclinations may be an important symptom (Sovner, 1990; Dosen, 1990b).

SIB is often reported in the mentally retarded suffering from psychotic states of various origins. The most frequent are reactive psychotic conditions in which anxiety, excitement, anger, aggression, and autoaggression predominate. In more specific psychotic states like schizophrenia, different autoaggressive activities are possible. However, no specific data concerning SIB and schizophrenia are reported. Obviously, one of the reasons for this lack of knowledge is the problems related to the diagnosis of schizophrenia among the severely and profoundly mentally retarded.

Light forms of SIB (for example, biting in one's own hand or hair pulling) may be found in neurotic states. These persons usually function at a lightly mentally retarded level and exhibit this behavior in states of frustration or excitement.

Neuroendocrinological investigations of persons exhibiting SIB and suffering from one or another psychiatric disorder are rare. Ruedrich (1990) pointed out that baseline hypercortisolemia is often found among the mentally retarded with behavioral and psychiatric problems. Depressive symptoms and aggressive and autoaggressive behavior occur frequently among these individuals. Concerning SIB patients, it would be meaningful to examine the functioning of the HPA axis as well as the hormonal changes in the thyroid axis.

Until recently, a psychiatric diagnosis was neglected in cases of SIB. The behavioral phenomenon was seen as being isolated from the totality of the person, and psychiatric diagnostics was not seen as being of any importance. With the developing of new psychiatric views of the mentally retarded population, the necessity of a basic psychiatric examination became obvious. In addition to clinical experience, various diagnostic tools (such as rating scales) should be utilized, and biochemical and neurophysiological examinations should be made. In the case of psychiatric disorder and SIB, treatment should be directed at the basic psychiatric disorder, and not only at the symptom of SIB.

## An Integrative Developmental Model

All the theoretical approaches described above may be seen within the framework of the ontogenetic development of a child and are interlinked. Each theory starts with a particular significant developmental aberration of a mentally retarded child, and, together, they all express the complexity of SIB.

Apparently, there is no sole reason or sole onset mechanism for this phenomenon. Instead, this disorder emerges within a disturbed developmental process in which various unfavorable factors—biological, psychological, and enviornmental—are involved and are interrelated.

If one unites these interrelated factors, an integrative model of SIB emerges (see Figures 1 and 2):

1. Disturbances at biological and neurobiochemical levels cause a delay in maturation and a slow developmental rate. This disorder is usually pre-

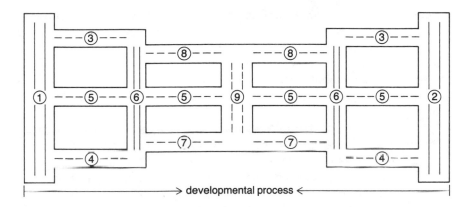

(1) biological disorders; (2) environmental disturbances; (3) motoric disorders; (4) sensoric integration disorders; (5) adaptive behavior; (6) disorders in socio-emotional development; (7) anxiety; (8) psychiatric disorders; (9) stress

**Figure 1. Causal spiral of SIB.**

sent at the beginning of postnatal life. However, it may be recognized later in childhood via the onset of behavioral problems.

2. Environmental problems are also present from the beginning of postnatal life. These problems are usually caused by biological disorders because of which the child cannot adapt adequately to the environment and cannot process stimuli in an appropriate way. Both biological and environmental factors form the basis for a range of other developmental dis-

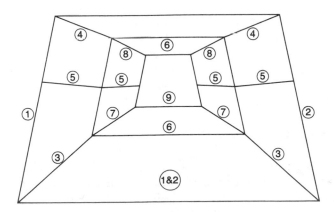

(1) biological disorders; (2) environmental disturbances; (3) motoric disorders; (4) sensoric integration disorders; (5) adaptive behavior; (6) disorders in socio-emotional development; (7) anxiety; (8) psychiatric disorders; (9) stress

**Figure 2. Developmental Pyramid and SIB.**

orders. Particularly important in the onset of SIB are the following deviations: (a) disorders in motoric development with a prolongation of the period of rhythmic patterns and the onset of stereotypy, (b) disorders in the processing of sensory stimuli with hypo- or hyperarousal resulting in self-stimulation and stereotypy, and (c) adaptive behavior learned in order to attain physiological homeostasis, reinforced by reactions from the surroundings.

These three sorts of disorders usually lead to disturbances in psychosocial homeostasis consisting of an aberration in socioemotional development and disturbed personality development.

3. Disorders in socioemotional development, with an arrest during a particular phase or deviation in personality development, may serve as a basis for other sorts of emotional aberrations and for psychiatric disorders.

4. Anxiety disorder may occur as a consequence of disturbed socioemotional development but may also be the result of a learning process.

5. Psychiatric disorders may emerge as a consequence of disturbed socioemotional development but may also be caused by unfavorable biological and environmental factors.

6. Stress may be caused by an unfavorable interplay of internal (within the person) and external (within the surroundings) factors. It may occur on different developmental levels and may lead to different consequences and symptoms.

SIB may occur at different levels of the developmental pyramid (Figure 2) and may be caused and maintained by different mechanisms.

Since SIB seldom occurs before the age of three, it appears that this behavior usually emerges after the child has made some progress in cognitive and socioemotional development or, in other words, has collected certain experiences in interaction with the surroundings. This consideration points to the involvement of emotional and social factors in the occurrence of SIB as well as to environmental circumstances. It also accentuates the importance of taking the total person within her or his surroundings into consideration when searching for the causes and treatment of SIB.

## Assessment and Diagnosis

From the developmental psychiatric point of view, the roots of behavior are not only in previous maturation, in physical influences, and in the residues of early experiences, but also in the modulation of that behavior by the present circumstances (Rutter, 1980). If fundamental behavioral skills develop in a balanced, smooth way, the result is integrated and cohesive human behavior, or psychosocial homeostasis. If, because of unfavorable circumstances, fundamental skills develop in an autonomous way, relatively independent of each other, each may also fail to develop, and the result may be a range of levels of developmental handicaps and symptoms of behavioral disturbances (Tanguay, 1984). According to Rutter (1980), it is not only the diminishing or loss of brain function but also an abnormal functioning of particular brain tissue that affects the totality of psychophysical functioning and behavior. Differentiating the quality of various developmental aspects and knowing the degree to which individual elements have developed or are dysfunctioning are essential to understanding the pathogenesis of the disorder. In order to achieve an appropriate insight into all these important factors, multidimensional assessment is necessary. The assessment done in our clinic is performed by a team of various professionals coordinated by a developmental psychiatrist. The following assessment is performed:

1. developmental anamnesis
2. medical examination
    a. general somatic
    b. special neurological: neuromorphological, neurophysiological, and neurobiochemical
    c. genetic
3. psychological assessment
    a. cognitive development
    b. social development
    c. personality forming
    d. neuropsychological examination
    e. analysis of behavioral problem
4. psychiatric examination
    a. establishment of level of emotional development
    b. analysis of disorders in physiological and psychosocial homeostasis
    c. determination of symptoms of psychopathology
    d. psychiatric biochemical examinations
    e. establishment of psychiatric diagnosis
5. milieu examination
    a. assessment of parental and family milieu
    b. assessment of current residential milieu
    c. establishment of systemic diagnosis
6. pedagogical assessment
    a. analysis of interaction with surroundings
    b. establishment of adaptation abilities
    c. establishment of environmental characteristics

7. when needed, other examinations by speech therapist, physiotherapist, and so on

The diagnostician first attempts to gain insight into the biological substrate, the rate of CNS maturation, and the funcitoning of different CNS structures. With the aid of the psychological, psychiatric, and other examinations, the diagnostician makes a reconstruction of the developmental process, focusing on the moments and events that are important in the current psychopathology and behavioral problems. In this way, a twofold psychiatric diagnosis is being made. The first one is conceptualized as a developmental psychiatric assessment, and the second one is an integration of all the facets of the other examinations into a holistic diagnosis. By means of these diagnoses, a range of causative factors for SIB may come to light. The diagnostic considerations should be supported and matched by appropriate tools and instruments, for example, biochemical examinations and checklists for particular issues, like a list for emotional development, anxiety scoring lists, and depression lists. In cases in which the diagnosis remains obscure, explorative treatment should be started on the basis of a hypothetical diagnosis. In our opinion, the diagnostic process should lead to a dynamic view of the past and present processes that play a decisive role in the emergence and maintenance of the disorder. Such a diagnosis should lead to the following three results:

1. an integrative developmental psychiatric diagnosis shedding light on the roots of the disorder and leading to an understanding of the current mechanisms of the phenomenon
2. insight into the physiological and psychosocial needs of the person
3. establishment of the starting point of the treatment

Here is an example:

A four-year-old boy has been exhibiting SIB from his third year onward. He is severely mentally retarded, and it is known from his history that he suffered severe brain damage due to perinatal asphyxia. His whole life, he has often been admitted to the hospital for different somatic problems. In total, he has spent more than half a year in the hospital. At admission, he could not walk or talk and was incontinent (urine and bowel).

Through the assessment it was established that there was an arrest in socioemotional development at the attachment level (age six to eighteen months), probably due to recurrent interruptions during attachment development and the stressful impact of somatic illness and hospitalization.

In addition, symptoms of depression were found. SIB was seen as a symptom of this condition. The disorder has probably been maintained by unfavorable reactions of the surroundings to the child's behavior and by a lack of understanding of the child's basic needs.

The integrative developmental psychiatric diagnosis was

1. Diagnosis: Problems with the integration of sensory stimuli and arrest in socioemotional development at the attachment level, with symptoms of a depressionlike state, among which SIB is pronounced.
2. Needs: Adaptation of sensory stimuli to the child's integrative abilities; providing an attachment process.
3. Treatment: Creation of environmental and personal conditions that could lead to adequate stimulation and an individual therapeutic approach on the basis of the developmental needs; additional treatment, if necessary, consisting of behavioral modification and psychotropic medication.

## The Consequences in Treatment of an Integrative Approach

Currently the treatment of SIB is usually directed toward the symptom itself. As described above, there are several theories concerning SIB, both psychological and biological, to which particular treatment strategies are related. However, in cases in which the treatment methods do not produce the desired effects, professionals are mostly inclined to use aspecific measures like physical restraint and broad-spectrum psychotropic medication. Both kinds of treatment often fail to create a handling structure that can function as an essential aid to the person suffering from SIB. In the symptom-directed methods, SIB is usually treated as such without the other life problems of the patient being taken into account. In the case of global protective attempts, preventive measures against SIB are taken, and the person is usually deprived of interaction with his or her environment and of his or her freedom.

From the developmental psychiatric point of view, the symptom SIB should be treated within the totality of the developmental, existential, and social context of the person. This means, for example, that a self-injurious child with autisticlike withdrawal behavior may be seen as suffering from hypoarousal and insufficient sensory stimulation and, at the same time, may have increased ß-endorphin activity in the CNS and a low level of serotonin in the blood and may be unable to cope with stressful events. The treatment indicated for such a child should be directed toward adequate sensory stimulation supported by a specific medication (see Chapter 15 in this book) and counseling and guidance in his or her daily activities, so that stressful situations can be avoided or coped with. Despite this broadened treatment management, the self-abusive behavior may persist as a learned interactional pattern. In such cases, the treatment should also be geared toward teaching the person to use other interaction forms (for example, by learning particular communication skills).

## Current Problems of Assessment and Future Developments

The still prevailing monotheoretical and monodisciplinary approach to the phenomenon of SIB forms a serious problem in the search for appropriate assessment and diagnostic strategies. In addition, various professionals, in their assessment attempts, miss the special techniques and methods needed for an adequate examination of SIB persons. Also, there is a shortage of special instruments for assessment.

In particular professional areas, the following assessment deficits are striking:

- neurology: lack of special assessment techniques, too little attention to developmental lags, and shortage of insight into the link between neurophysiological and psychosocial aspects
- psychology and pedagogy: lack of assessment instruments for sensory integration problems, lack of tools for neuropsychological examination, lack of insight into specific personality development or into the presence of specific biological and environmental conditions, and lack of techniques for assessing environmental conditions
- psychiatry: the implementation of not enough developmentally oriented and too much traditional phenomenological psychiatric thinking, a lack of insight into the specificity of the psychopathology and into specific diagnostic categories applying to the SIB population, a shortage of adequate neurobiochemical examinations, and a lack of assessment scales and other instruments
- in general: a shortage of multidisciplinary cooperation and integrative thinking

By mentioning the shortages in different professional fields, I am emphasizing the necessity of developing the techniques, methods, and instruments needed in the future. In addition, scientific research in different areas should make it easier to discover what the developmental disorders and conditions are that may lead to the SIB.

Medical examinations, including new technologies like magnetic resonance imaging, positron emission tomography, and specific biochemical examinations, could be utilized to detect early specific biological and maturational aberrations. By a keen observation of the child and her or his surroundings, remarkable interactional conditions should be noted and, in turn, should elicit timely professional intervention, specific stimulation of the child, and counseling and support in the surroundings.

The organization of early detection and intervention methods and techniques is of great importance, on the one hand, for the prevention of SIB and, on the other, for a deepening of insight into the onset mechanisms for this phenomenon.

## Conclusion

An isolated look at the phenomenon of SIB from one theoretical approach or by one treatment method is usually insufficient to determine the appropriate aid to the person suffering from this behavior. This highly complex phenomeon calls for a multidimensional view and a multiprofessional approach.

Since the disorder occurs mostly in childhood and adolescence and is related to various biological as well as psychosocial disturbances, the developmental psychiatric approach is, in my opinion, the most appropriate one. This approach provides one with the possibility of inspecting the problem from different perspectives, of examining the role of various factors, and of discovering the interactional onset mechanisms.

For a better understanding of the onset of SIB at an early developmental age, delving deeper into the specific developmental aspects of the SIB person is inevitable. Various biological maturational and psychosocial developmental processes have to be taken into account if one is to get insight into the different mechanisms that may lead to the forming of specific personality qualities and to self-injurious behavior.

There is no doubt that unfavorable environmental influences may also cause stress in mentally retarded children. However, the effects of stress on this population have been very poorly examined. It is conceivable that there is a relationship between the stressful experiences of a mentally retarded child and SIB.

Anxiety has often been observed among the mentally retarded, but it has rarely been examined closely. The possibility of finding anxiety disorders among the mentally retarded that are similar to those present in the general population cannot be denied. The interreaction between anxiety and SIB has not yet been analyzed.

Various psychiatric clinical pictures are found among nonretarded patients exhibiting self-abusive behavior. Even though there is no reason to suppose that the mentally retarded are immune to the psychopathology occurring in the general population, most investigators of SIB in the mentally retarded have overlooked the possibility of SIB coexisting with particular psychiatric disorders. Recently, more attention has been paid by different investigators to the occurrence of SIB among the depressive and psychotic mentally retarded. The difficulties in managing SIB undoubtedly express, on the one hand, a lack of accurate, specific theoretical considerations involving the totality of the existential and social problems of the SIB individuals and, on the other hand, the lack of appropriate diagnostic. An integrative model of the onset of SIB, like the one presented in this chapter, may serve as a more complete diagnostic guide. It can be expected that the broadening of theoretical views will culminate in a better understanding of the biological, developmental, and psychosocial aspects of the life of the mentally retarded. For clinical purposes, however, the development of new tools and instruments and the gathering and systematizing of clinical experiences are necessary.

Neurobiochemical examinations and an insight into neuroendocrine changes may give important information that can be used in giving more form to diagnostic thinking. However, so far, it is not clear how extensive the influence of psychosocial and environmental factors is on hormonal and neurobiochemical conditions. Instruments such as scales for discovering and measuring symptomatology are badly needed. Above all, an integrative way of thinking is needed, so that findings by all kinds of examiners can be integrated into one picture of a total individual existence.

# References

Bemporad, J. R., & Wilson, A. (1978). A developmental approach to depression in childhood and adolescence. *J. Am. Psychoanal., 6*(3), 325–352.

Boer, J. A. den (1988). *Serotonergic mechanisms in anxiety disorders.* Utrecht: Proefschrift.

Bridges, M., Yeragani, V. K., Rainey, J. M., et al. (1986). Dexamethasone suppression test in patients with panic attacks. *Biol. Psychiatr., 21,* 849–853.

Brown, G. L., Linnoila, M., & Goodwin, F. K. (1990). Clinical assessment of human aggression and impulsivity in relationship to biochemical measures. In H. M. Van Praag, R. Plutchnik, & A. Apter (Eds), *Violence and suicidality* (pp. 184–217). New York: Brunner/Mazel.

Buitelaar, J. K. (1991). *Psychopharmacology of autism.* Utrecht: Proefschrift.

Cannon, W. B. (1929). *Bodily changes in pain, hunger, fear and rage* (2nd ed). New York: Appleton-Century-Crofts.

Chamberlain, R. S., & Herman, B. H. (1990). A novel biochemical model linking dysfunctions in brain melatonin, proopiomelancortin peptides and serotonin in autism. *Biol. Psychiatr., 28,* 773–793.

Ciarnello, R. D. (1983). Neurochemical aspects of stress. In N. Germazy & M. Rutter (Eds.), *Stress, coping and development in children.* New York: McGraw-Hill.

Coulter, D. L. (1988). The neurology of mental retardation. In F. Menolascino & J. Stark (Eds.), *Preventive and curative intervention in mental retardation.* Baltimore: Brookes.

Crabbe, H. F. (1989). *A guidebook for the use of psychotropic medication in persons with mental illness and mental retardation.* New London, State of Connecticut, Department of Mental Retardation.

Dosen, A. (1990a). *Psychische en gedragsstoornissen bij zwakzinnigen.* Amsterdam: Boom.

Dosen, A. (1990b). Depression in mentally retarded children and adults. In A. Dosen & F. J. Menolascino (Eds.), *Depression in mentally retarded persons and adults.* Leiden: Logon.

Dosen, A., & Bojanin, S. (1990). Developmental and biological factors in the mentally retarded and vulnerability to depression. In A. Dosen & F. J. Menolascino (Eds.), *Depression in mentally retarded children and adults.* Leiden: Logon.

Dosen, A., & Menolascino, F. J. (1990). *Depression in the mentally retarded children and adults.* Leiden: Logon.

Ebels, E. I. (1980). Maturation of the central nervous system. In M. Rutter (Ed.), *Scientific foundations of developmental psychiatry.* London: Heinemann Medical Books.

Edelson, S. M. (1984). Implications of sensory stimulation in self-destinative behavior. *Am. J. Ment. Defic., 89*(2), 140–143.

Engel, G. L., Schmale, A. (1973). Conservation-withdrawal, a primary regulatory process for organismic homeostasis. In Ciba Foudnation Symposium 8, *Emotion and psychosomatic illness.* Amsterdam: Elsevier, Excerpta Medica.

Farber, J. M. (1987). Psychopharmacology of self injurious behavior in the mentally retarded. *J. Am. Acad. Child Adol. Psychiatr., 26,* (3), 296–302.

Gaedt, Ch., & Gärtner, D. (1990). *Depressive Grundproxesse—Reinzeniering der Selbstentwertung.* Neuerkeroder Forum 4, Neuerkeröder Anstalten.

Gaedt, Ch., Jäkel, D., & Kischkel, W. (1987). Psychotherapie bei geistig Behinderten. In Ch. Gaedt (Ed.), *Psychotherapie bei geistig Behinderten,* Neuerkeröder 21, Neuerkeröder Anstalten.

Gedye, A. (1989). Extreme self-injury attributed to frontal lobe seizures. *Am. J. Ment. Retard., 91*(1), 20–26.

Graff, H., & Mallin, R. (1967). The syndrome of the wrist cutter. *Am. J. Psychiatr., 124,* 36–42.

Gray, J. A. (1982). *The neuropsychology of anxiety: An enquiry into the functions of the septo-hippocampal system.* Oxford: Oxford University Press.

Gray, J. A. (1987). *The psychology of fear and stress* (2nd ed.). Cambridge: Cambridge University Press.

Gualteri, C. Th., & Schroeder, S. R. (1989). Pharmacotherapy for self-injurious behavior: Preliminary tests of the D1 hypothesis. *Psychopharmacol. Bull., 25,* 365–371.

Gualtieri, C. Th. (1989). The differential diagnosis of self-injurious behavior in mentally retarded people. *Psychopharmacol. Bull., 25,* 358–363.

Gualtieri, C. Th. (1991). B-Blockers as primary treatment for aggression and self-injury in the developmentally disabled. In J. J. Ratey (Ed.), *Mental retardation, developing pharmacotherapies.* Washington, DC: American Psychiatric Press.

Guess, D., Carr, E. (1991). Emergence and maintenance of stereotypy and self-injury, *Am. J. Ment. Retard., 96,* 3, 299–319.

Henry, J. P. (1980). Present concepts of stress theory. In E. E. A. Usdin (Ed.), *Catecholamines and stress; Recent advances.* New York: Elsevier.

Huttenlocher, P. H. (1984). Synapse elimination and plasticity in developing human cerebral cortex. *Am. J. Ment. Def., 88,(5),* 488–496.

Jones, I. (1982). Self-injury: Toward a biological basis. *Perspect. Biol. Med., 26,* 137–150.

Kafka, J. A. (1969). The body as transitional object: A psychoanalytic study of a self-mutilation patient. *Br. J. Med. Psychol., 42,* 207–212.

Kars, H. Broekema, W., Glaudemans-van Gelderen, I., Verhoven, W. M. A., & van Ree, J. M. (1990). Naltrexone attenuates self-injurious behavior in mentally retarded subjects. *Biol. Psychiatr., 27,* 741–746.

Kashani, J. H., Deuser, W., & Reid, J. (1991). Aggression and anxiety; A new look at an old notion. *J. Am. Acad. Child Adol. Psychiatr., 30,(2),* 218–223.

Kernberg, O. F. (1987). A psychodynamic approach. *J. Pers. Disorders, 1,* 344–346.

Leiderman, P.H. (1983). Social ecology and childbirth. In N. Garmezy & N. Rutter (Eds.), *Stress, coping and development in children.* New York: McGraw-Hill.

Levine, S. (1983). A psychobiological approach to the ontogeny of coping. In R. Garmezy & M. Rutter (Eds.), *Stress, coping and development in children.* New York: McGraw-Hill.

Lieberman, J. A., Brenner, R., Lesser, M., et al. (1983). Dexamethasone suppression tests in patients with panic disorder. *Am. J. Psychiatr., 140,* 917–919.

Liebowitz, M. R. (1987a). A medication approach. *J. Pers. Disorders, 2,* 181–190.

Liebowitz, M. R. (1987b). Social phobia. *Mod. Probl. Pharmacopsychiatr.* (Karger, Basel), *22,* 141–173.

Lipsitt, L. (1983). Stress in infancy. In N. Garmezy & N. Rutter (Eds.), *Stress, coping and development in children.* New York: McGraw-Hill.

Lloyd, K. G., Hornykiewicz, O., Davidson, L., Shannak, K., Farley, I., Goldstein, M., Shibaya, M., Kelley, W. N., & Fox, I. H. (1981). Biochemical evidence of dysfunction of brain neurotransmitters in the Lesch-Nyhan syndrome. *N. E. J. Med., 305,* 1106–1111.

Luria, A. R. (1974). *The working brain.* London: Penguin Press.

Maccoby, E. E. (1983). Social-emotional development and response to stressors. In N. Garmezy & M. Rutter (Eds.), *Stress, coping and development in children.* New York: McGraw-Hill.

Mahler, M. S., Pine, F., Bergman, A. (1975). *The psychological birth of the human infant,* New York: Basic Books.

Mason, S. A., & Newson, C. D. (1990). The application of sensory change to reduce stereotyped behavior. *Res. Devel. Disabilities, 11,* 257–271.

Matson, J. L., & Keyes J. B. (1990). A comparison on DRO to movement suppression time-out and DRO with two self-injurious and aggressive mentally retarded adults. *Res. Devel. Disorders,* 11, 111–120.

McBurnett, K., Lahey, B., Frick, P., et al. (1991). Anxiety, inhibition, and conduct in children. *J. Am. Acad. Child Adol. Psychiatr.,* 30,(2), 192–196.

Menolascino, F. J. (1977). *Challenges in mental retardation: Progressive ideologies and services.* New York: Human Sciences Press.

Menolascino, F. J. (1990). Mental retardation and the risk, nature and types of mental illness. In A. Dosen & F. J. Menolascino (Eds.), *Depression in mentally retarded children and adults.* Leiden: Logon.

Moyer, K. E. (1976). *The psychobiology of aggression.* New York: Harper & Row.

Mulick, J. A., & Kedesdy, J. H. (1988). Self-injurious behavior, its treatment, and normalization. *Ment. Retard.,* 26, 223–229.

Oliver, C., Murphy, G. H., & Corbett, J. A. (1987). Self-injurious behavior in people with mental handicap: A total population study. *J. Ment. Defic. Res.,* 31, 147–162.

Ollendick, T. H., & Ollendick, D.G. (1982). Anxiety disorders. In J. Matson & R. Berrett (Eds.), *Psychopathology in the mentally retarded.* New York: Grune Stratton.

Rasmussen, D. L., Olivier, B., Raghoebar, M., & Mos, J. (1989). Possible clinical applications of serenics and some implications of their preclinical profile for their clinical use in psychiatric disorders. In M. Raghoebar, B. Olivier, D. L. Rasmussen & J. Mos (Eds.), *Drug metabolism and drug interactions, Eltoprazine: A serenic compound* (pp. 159–186). London: Freund.

Repp, A. C., Singh, N. N., Olinger, E., & Olson, D. R. (1990). The use of functional analyses to test causes of self-injurious behavior: Rationale, current status and future directions. *J. Ment. Defic. Res.,* 34, 95–105.

Rojahn, J. (1986). Self-injurious and stereotypic behavior of noninstitutionalized mentally retarded people: prevalence and classification. *Am. J. Ment. Def.,* 91, 268–276.

Roy, A., & Linnoila,M. (1990). Monaomines and suicidal behavior. In H. M. van Praag, R. Plutchnick, & A. Apter (Eds.), *Violence and suicidality,* (pp. 141–183). New York: Brunner/Mazel.

Ruedrich, S. L. (1990). Biochemical findings in depressed mentally retarded individuals. In A. Dosen, F. J. Menolascino (Eds.), *Depression in mentally retarded children and adults,* Leiden: Logon.

Rutter, M. (1980). Developmental psychiatry-introduction. In M. Rutter (Ed): Scientific foundations of developmental psychiatry. London: William Heinemann Med. Books Limited.

Rutter, M. (1983). Stress, coping and development. In N. Garmezy & M. Rutter (Eds.), *Stress, coping and development in children.* New York: McGraw-Hill.

Sanders, B., & Giolas, M. H. (1991). Dissociation and childhood trauma in psychologically disturbed adolescents. *Am. J. Psychiatr.,* 148(1), 50–61.

Shapiro, S., (1987). Self-mutilation and self-blame in incest victims. *Am. J. Psychother.,* 41, 46–54.

Sheehon, D. V., Bao, B. Ch., Claycomb, J. B., et al. (1983). Panic attacks and the dexamethasone suppression test. *Am. J. Psychiatr.,* 140, 1063–1064.

Sovner, R. (1990). Bipolar disorder in persons with developmental disorders: An overview. In A. Dosen & F. J. Menolascino (Eds), Depression in mentally retarded children and adults. Leiden: Logon.

Spitz, R. (1946). Anaclitic depression. *Psychoanal. Study Child, 2,* 113–117.

Strand, F. L., Rose, K. J., King, J. A., Segarra, A. C., & Zuccarelli, L. A. (1989). ACTH modulation of nerve development and regeneration. *Prog. Neurobiol., 33,* 44–85.

Tanguay, P. E. (1984). Toward a new classification of serious psychopathology in children. *J. Am. Acad. Child Psychiatr., 23,* 373–384.

Terr, L. C. (1991). Childhood traumas: An outline and overview. *Am. J. Psychiatr., 148*(1), 10–20.

Tuinier, S. (1989). De psychiater en de wilde man; Een veldstudie over de relatie psychiatrisch syndroom en criminaliteit. *Meppel: Proefschrift, Drukkerij Giethoorn.*

Winchel, R. M., & Stanley, M. (1991). Self-injurious behavior: A review of the behavior and biology of self-mutilation. *Am. J. Psychiatr., 148,* 306–315.

Zadrian, J. E., Kastin, A. J., Coy, D. H., & Adinoff, B. A. (1985). Developmental, behavioral and opiate receptor changes after prenatal or postnatal beta-endorphin, CRF or tyr-MIF-1. *Psychoneuroendocrinol., 10,* 367–383.

# 9

# A Primer on Dementia in Persons with Mental Retardation: Conclusions and Current Findings

*Dennis C. Harper*

## Part 1: Aging, Mental Retardation, and Dementia— Basic Processes

### Introduction

Dementia in older adults is a national health concern in the United States. The elderly population with mental retardation are also experiencing this problem; however, they have and are receiving less attention from many community-health providers because of the common bias toward those with mental retardation, that is, the expectations of a general downhill course when there is a history of mental retardation. Because 50 percent of the U.S. population lives to age seventy-five and 25 percent to age eighty-five (American Medical Association, 1986), we have increasing numbers of people exhibiting some form and degree of dementing illness. The prevalence of severe dementia in the general population over age sixty-five is estimated at between 5 and 6 percent, while mild degrees are reported to range from 3 to 15 percent (Mortimer & Schuman, 1981; Office of Technology Assessment, 1987). This variation in prevalence is clearly a function of differences in the methodological studies and the age groups used to compile these figures. The most common cause of dementia is well known as Alzheimer's disease. In those in the general population aged

This work was supported in part by a grant from the Office of Human Development, Association on Developmental Disabilities to the Iowa University Affiliated Facility. Specific support from the Department of Preventative Medicine and Environmental Health and assistance from the Division of Developmental Disabilities, The University of Iowa College of Medicine.

eighty, Alzheimer's is at a 4 percent annual incidence, and at age eighty, the prevalence is approximately 20 percent of the U.S. population (Office of Technology Assessment, 1985; Plum, 1979; Small & Jarvik, 1982; Henderson, 1983; Goldman, 1984). These figures are noted to place the outcomes of dementia in elders with mental retardation in the proper perspective. Some decrement in behavioral competency is expected in all people as they age; however, the most detectable decline is specific and is usually related to a particular organic process, of which there are many (Cummings & Benson, 1983).

An understanding of dementia should begin with a brief review of standard diagnostic criteria. By definition, dementia is a clinical syndrome of acquired intellectual compromise that includes persistent and usually permanent deficits, generally in three or more of the following areas of neuropsychological function: language and communication, memory, visual-spatial skills, cognition, and personality (Cummings & Benson, 1983). Standard psychiatric definitions of dementia (American Psychiatric Association, 1987) specifically exclude disorders of consciousness, such as delirium and confusional states. The emphasis in defining and recognizing dementia is on a change in status, usually a loss in prior skill levels or a worsening of general behavioral functioning. Usually, the lower the level of prior cognitive and adaptive functioning (in all areas), the more difficult it is to detect changes without a detailed history of prior functioning levels. The dementia syndrome, from a functional standpoint, is generally viewed as etiologically nonspecific and may be produced by reversible or irreversible conditions.

A behavioral-clinical assessment of cognitive and adaptive skills is the first crucial step in identifying the diagnosis and etiology of the syndrome. Dementia may be viewed on a continuum where the severity of the disorder may reflect some degree of central nervous system compromise. In the milder forms of dementia or in the earlier stages, the most obvious failing is often in the area of immediate memory. However, in the adult with moderate to severe mental retardation and limited verbal expressive skills, these changes or decrements in memory may be difficult to detect and, at the very least, are variable during clinical assessment. Reid & Aungle (1974) noted that changes in (loss of) temporal orientation may not be a sensitive indicator of the early onset of dementia in a person with mental retardation. Furthermore, Reid reported that isolated psychotic episodes, especially in Down syndrome, may portend the beginning of an organic dementia. Clearly, the early signs of dementia may be noted as the failure to carry out normal daily routines or previously completed simple tasks. Such beginning changes are subtle, and documentation by knowledgeable individuals is an important, if not the major, key in this identification or first step of the diagnostic process. In severe or end-stage dementia, memory loss is frequently global, and there often follows a course of general incontinence and behavioral deterioration. As deterioration continues, seizures may develop, and the person often dies of an intercurrent infection of cardiovascular disease.

This brief and devastating scenario represents the common sequence of dementive loss, but the time line of these events, their relative rates of progression, and the associated deficits are highly variable from individual to individual. Earlier demise in the Alzheimer's patient is somewhat equivocal at this time with respect to the disease process itself. That is, it is unclear if it is the disease process or the associated poor self-care as well that leads to earlier mortality. Generally speaking, in those individuals with mental retardation, as well as in the non-mentally-retarded elderly, dementia usually develops insidiously as the result of a primary brain disease or systemic diseases, in association with psychiatric disorders, and also as a toxic reaction to chronic psychotropic drug therapies. It is possible that the frequency of dementia in reaction to drug therapy may be somewhat higher in the elderly with mental retardation because of the general high use of psychotropic drugs within this population (Aman, 1985, 1990). However, specific data on this process of cognitive loss related to medication use are yet to be determined in those with mental retardation.

## Diagnosis and Etiology of the Dementias

Two broadly and clinically distinct patterns of mental status change are reported to occur within the dementia syndrome. Cummings and Benson (1983) reported a categorization of dementias associated with (1) a primary dysfunction of the cerebral cortex or (2) subcortical features. It should be emphasized that this nosological distinction is not totally accepted either by neuropsychologists or by neuropathologists at this time, but it is useful for discussion and initial diagnostic purposes. Dementias associated with a primary dysfunction of the cerebral cortex often produce aphasias, amnesias, and apraxia-agnosia, and judgment and insight are frequently impaired. Such common types of the cortical dementias are Alzheimer's disease and Pick's disease. Again, in these neurogenerative diseases, the cognitive process is slowed gradually, forgetfulness appears, and, according to Cummings and Benson (1983), concurrent affective disorders are not uncommon as well. Personality style and behavior (early stages) may be relatively well preserved in the cortical dementias until late in the disease. Loss of inhibitions and increases in behavioral impulsivity are also recognized features. The subcortical dementias include the vast majority of all the remaining dementive disorders. A partial listing includes multi-infarct episodes, movement disorders (Huntington's chorea and Parkinson's disease), psychiatric disorders and associated psychiatric-based dementias, hydrocephalus, and metabolic- and toxic-based dementias. In these subcortical dementias, neuropsychiatric features and psychiatric disorders are more common as are movement-type disorders. Generally, those individuals with cortical dementias are reported to remain free of motor system involvement until late in the disease. Metabolic and toxic dementias share many features of the acute confusional states, such as fluctuating arousal, slowness, and hallucinations, but they may last for many weeks and months. The pattern of intellectual impairment in the toxic and metabolic conditions often resembles that observed with degenerative disorders of the subcortical brain structures, that is, slowing in responsiveness, cognitive declines, and movement disorders. Rigidity, tremors, and myoclonus are not uncommon in toxic- and metabolic-based dementias (Cummings & Benson, 1983).

Elders with mental retardation may exhibit dementia syndromes that may occur as part of a variety of these aforementioned categories and as well concurrently with psychiatric disturbances, such as depression and schizophrenia. There is considerable debate on whether these psychiatric conditions represent the so-called true dementias. These disorders are most difficult to sort out, especially when they are found in the context of significant mental retardation (such as moderate retardation and below). These psychiatric-associated dementias, or in some cases pseudodementias (Kiloh, 1961), may not show the common cortical features of dementia, that is, problems with naming, memory deficits, apraxias-agnosias, and so on. However, these distinctions between psychiatric-based dementias and cortical dementias are very difficult to make in clinical practice when it is possible and rather common to have neurological disease concurrently with psychiatric disease. These aforementioned syndromes can and do occur in varying combinations in the context of mental retardation and in an aging brain. The implications of these distinctions for differential diagnosis are very complicated and have ramifications for treatment and the subsequent course of decline.

After Alzheimer's disease, multi-infarct dementia is reported as the next most frequent and common cause of dementia in all elders, irrespective of whether or not they exhibit mental retardation. Such multi-infarct dementia is present in individuals who have strokes and in those with a history of ischemia. The overt characteristics of dementia in this particular etiological group are often related to the specific locations of the involved vessels as well as to the amount of infarcted tissue (Cummings & Benson, 1983). The key historical features that identify the likelihood of multi-infarct dementia include hypertension, previous strokes, abrupt onset, stepwise deterioration, focal neurological symptoms, fluctuating course, and, in some cases, nocturnal confusion. Epidemiological features that can help to discriminate between multi-infarct dementia and Alzheimer's disease are the former's age of onset (earlier) and the tendency to affect males more than females.

## Normative Aging Changes in Cognitive Function

The distinction between a specific decline associated with dementia and a decline associated with aging may become somewhat blurred, especially in those with a history of mental retardation. Trying to determine the boundary line between normal decline in cognitive function and dementia may be a problem at the lower levels of intellectual ability and especially in the presence of multiple physical and sensory impairments. In this regard, it is important to clarify normative functional changes in aging for all adults. Generally, all adults are expected to have some cognitive and behavioral changes as they age, usually beginning around the middle of the sixth decade (Botwinick, 1984). These changes are quite variable in their extent and in the type of process that begins such a general behavioral slowing; however, the healthy person generally remains reality-oriented, can reason, and can use good judgment unless very specific disease processes interrupt those functional skills. On the other hand, reaction time tasks reflect a general slowing in most adults as they age. Forgetfulness occurs, which seems to be a decrease in the retrieval of recently learned material. There is also some increase in word-finding problems, usually proper names, and a general slowing of responsiveness or general arousal levels. Personality changes in the older adult are said to reflect lessened drive, diminished interest in novelty, or, conversely, a preference for routines or structure. Changes in the acuteness of all senses is diminished, with sleep reflecting more waking— or less Stage 4 (deep)—sleep. The gait becomes more deliberate, and general balance and stability are impaired as well. All of these are generally viewed as aging characteristics not generally felt to reflect dementia in adults as they age. For the most part, cognition stays intact up to age seventy-five, and then changes become more probable for all elders (Botwinick, 1984).

## Aging and Cognitive Changes in the Adult with Mental Retardation

On a practical level, clinically significant cognitive changes in IQ testing are not based simply on an IQ point drop. Variation in cognitive performance is often related to the efficiency of many underlying processes (attention, memory, and so on) and their mutual relationships. Rather, it is much more important and accurate to determine what specific functions may be declining (memory, abstract thinking, or visual-spatial skills) rather than a nonspecific general lowering of skills or lack of effort during neuropsychological evaluation. More specifically, abrupt decrements are reported to be more pathognomic for some specific central nervous system dysfunction. However, any form of decrement has to be tempered by a number of issues:

(1) the prior cognitive level; (2) when the prior cognitive level was ascertained, (3) the health and sensory level of the individual during the current psychological assessment; and (4) the relative relationship between the decrements and cognitive abstract skills and functional adaptive skills; tested IQ may drop but there may be no consequent or parallel decrement in functional behavior (this depends particularly on the living setting and the amount of structure available for certain elders with mental retardation).

## Differential Diagnosis in Elders with Mental Retardation

There are several major concerns and difficulties in the neuropsychological evaluation of dementia in the elderly person with mental retardation. The following is a partial listing:

1. What is a normal aging-related decline in elders with mental retardation? Currently, this issue is somewhat problematical, given our present state of knowledge. There is disagreement as to what constitutes the definition of aging in this population. Although the definition of developmental disability and mental retardation is generally accepted, where the stages of the aging processes begin in this population with mental retardation is open to debate. Some authors attempting to define aging (as life phases distinct from middle age) have selected either a normative-statistical approach or a biological approach related to the "signs and symptoms" of early decline, such as Alzheimer's disease, in persons with Down syndrome. Many others have used an arbitrary chronological age limit to define the lower limits of aging, some authors suggesting that the social expectations of aging being in those with mental retardation as early as age thirty-five (Dickerson, et al., 1979). However, most contemporary researchers have selected the mid-fifties (e.g., fifty-five) and have based their observations on changing functional status and social expectations of change in a normative age-related model (Janicki & Wisniewski, 1985). Studies of intellectual changes in those who are older and have mental retardation have revealed mixed findings (Janicki & Jacobson, 1986; Walz, Harper, & Wilson, 1986). The problem in interpreting these studies related broadly to the bias of the samples studied and the researchers' particular methodology. Studies have often included a mix of settings; individuals with varying frequencies of multiple disabilities; cross-sectional and longitudinal designs; and global evaluations of cognitive status. Each of these issues can affect morbidity and mortality rates and rate of change in cognitive and adaptive skills. Normative aging is difficult to define from such heterogeneous studies, so that the search for who and what is a healthy elder with significant mental retardation is difficult if not moot.

2. The lower the IQ and/or the initial level of adaptive functioning, the more difficult it becomes to evaluate change and document the process of dementia. Reid (1982) noted that around IQ 25, reflecting severe to pro-

found mental retardation, the task of differential diagnosis is very difficult, especially if no prior neuropsychological data exist.

3. Preexisting cognitive and psychosocial deficits may mask deterioration and changes in those with mental retardation (Hurley & Sovner, 1986). When individuals have a long-standing history of behavioral disabilities and very idiosyncratic responses to the environment as well, sorting out change is often not possible until major deficits appear.

4. Early in a dementia process in the adult, changes in cognitive skill or adaptive behavior, whether they be in those with mental retardation or in the nonmentally retarded, are often quite subtle and very difficult to detect.

5. The bias of many professionals and caretakers toward the elderly with mental retardation in expecting a downhill course often results in not examining their status routinely and only when the symptoms are obvious and quite substantial in their presentation.

6. Differential diagnosis efforts are also hampered by the difficulty of sorting out the long-term lack of environmental stimulation as a potential contributing effect. Little work is available examining the environment's impact on functional skills, except work that categorizes environments by size and location (Harpe, Wadsworth & Michael 1989). More sensitive measures are needed to identify all aspects of living (for example, cognitive, nutritional, physical, and amount of independence.)

7. Diagnosing multiple medical conditions (organic disease, hypertension, and schizophrenia) and trying to sort out the separate effects of a particular dementia process are extremely complicated.

8. The effects of chronic drug treatments on the mental processes are well known as basic iatrogenic factors but are rarely considered clinically.

9. Dementia is often dismissed as a behavior problem in the older person. The unruly older person is often dismissed without clarification or further diagnostic work. When deterioration occurs or irritability surfaces, the outcome is often a placement change or the addition of psychotropic medication or a behavioral intervention rather than an evaluation and treatment.

10. There is a major lack of consistent documentation of prior cognitive and adaptive levels for all elders with mental retardation in most living and treatment settings. Without appropriate baselines, it is virtually impossible to determine decrements until they become extremely pronounced and/or obvious.

11. The lower the functional level (cognitive and adaptive) of the aging individual, the less applicable are the traditional psychometric procedures. More emphasis in evaluation needs to focus on behavioral observations over time in multiple settings or situations (Harper, 1991).

Clearly the major problem in sorting out these issues of differential diagnosis is the multiplicity of medical and environmental factors in combination with the aging process, which generally makes it difficult to pinpoint the presence or status of dementia-type conditions. This problem of the identification of effects extends from the individual to group studies, where investigators are interested in isolating the group-related factors associated with aging and mental retardation as well. These studies (Walz, et al., 1986) are reviewed in the following section.

### Methodological Problems in the Assessment of Aging, Mental Retardation, and Dementia

From a methodological standpoint, there are numerous issues to consider when evaluating research on aging indivduals (fifty-five and older) with mental retardation that are directed at determining the morbidity of dementia. The following list presents a partial review of the issues to consider when reviewing research studies in this area:

1. Data from many studies on normal aging indicate that a decline in cognitive and memory abilities with advancing age is less than previously thought, and it appears to occur later in life, usually in seventh to eighth decades (Benton & Sivan, 1984).

2. The rate of decline (in all types of skills is a specific function of what is being measured (for example, global versus memory skills). In this respect, traditional speed of response will reflect more obvious changes, and assessments of short-term memory will also reflect changes as a function of age (Botwinick, 1984).

3. The rate of decline is also related to how the skill is being measured. This is extremely important when we consider that the majority of methods of cognitive assessment rely on verbal skills, which are often applied to the assessment of moderate and severely to profoundly mentally retarded invididuals with limited expressive language.

4. Interindividual variability of skills and performance increases with age. This increase has been documented by a number of investigators, in the areas of both aging and mental retardation (Botwinick, 1984).

5. Outcome findings are affected by the particular research design and assessment methodology. Cross-sectional designs reflect specific cohort or robust survivor effects. Longitudinal prospective designs are also affected by particular subject attrition (early mortality in an age cohort reduces the overall performances of the aging cohort) and are difficult to sustain over time. Assessment methods vary between and within studies, and most studies use global evaluations (IQ) over specific neuropsychological measures, often obscuring more specific and subtle age changes in function.

6. Differential etilogy (Down syndrome is an exception) is rarely addressed or specified in particular age-related studies on cognitive or adaptive functioning. Information is emerging that identifies the importance of specific etiology in cognitive aging patterns (Burack, Hodapp, & Zigler, 1988).

7. Mental efficiency (accuracy and speed of response) appears to be correlated with general health status. Data are becoming more specific in this respect. The relationship between hypertension (optimal blood pressure levels) and cognitive levels has been documented (Benton & Sivan, 1984). It is important to note that dementia in association with high blood pressure and subsequent multi-infarct dementia is a frequent occurrence in both elders with mental retardation and those without prior intellectual deficits.

8. The impact of psychological distress (state factors) on cognitive efficiency is rarely included as a moderating variable in longitudinal studies of aging and dementia (Benton & Sivan, 1984). The extent of such distress can be reflected as a loss of morale and depression, an important and neglected issue in assessing cognitive functioning and following individuals during various life phases.

### Longitudinal Assessment of Cognitive Changes in Aging and Persons with Mental Retardation

The data available on the cognitive status of elders with mental retardation presents a very mixed picture of the issue of intellectual decline. These studies, many of which date to the 1930s, are replete with a variety of methodological errors as well as questionable assessment orientations. Specifically, a review of these longitudinal IQ studies reveals the following:

1. The majority of these studies of repeated IQ assessment are suspect because of problems in test sequencing. That is, the periodic assessment of these individuals was inconsistent, they were grouped with different age bands between testing, and there were virtually no long-term prospective assessment designs available in the literature. In addition, the measures used were often primarily cognitive-verbal, to the exclusion of the more functional adaptive skill assessments. There are major problems with sample selection since the majority of these longitudinal studies are from large institutionalized populations. In this respect, there has been subject attrition due to the so-called brain drain out of the more competent, who are released from placement, and furthermore, problems exist in sample interpretation because of the "survivor effect" as well. That is, only the best or most capable (more healthy) adults are left for later repeated intellectual assessment.

2. The data based on early diagnostic labels (idiot, imbecile, and moron) in these studies of older adults with mental retardation was generated from nosological models from the 1920s and 1930s. These data are suspect because of their general impreciseness.

3. No studies are available in the literature that examine the limitations of experiential or language stimulation as a factor in long-term placement and subsequent cognitive decrements.

4. The majority of studies on cognitive status over time have, as noted earlier, indiscriminately mixed groups with diverse health and ongoing disease conditions. To conclude that such data represent a normative outcome of cognitive changes in the aging person with mental retardation is questionable (Burack et al., 1988). This is a major confound in the literature as it now exists.

### Summary of Cognitive IQ Studies on Adults and Mental Retardation

Despite the obvious shortcomings of the literature on the intellectual change and cognitive status of aging mentally retarded adults, some findings can be reported:

1. The existing data on cognitive status changes over time appear to be primarily applicable to those individuals with a mild to moderate level of mental retardation. These studies were summarized by Walz et al. (1986), who used cross-sectional study methods, and date to cohorts from the late 1920s to the more contemporary age groups. These studies (Kaplan, 1943; Bell & Zubek, 1960; Demaine & Silverstein, 1978; Fenner, Hewitt, & Tropy, 1987; Fisher & Zeoman, 1970; Harper & Wadsworth, 1990; Hewitt, Carter, & Jancar, 1985; Hewitt, Fenner, & Tropy, 1986) collectively indicated, for non–Down syndrome older adults, that general intellectual capacity remains intact until approximately age sixty-five. Change in these studies, primarily using global measures (IQ and Mental Age) was gradual over time. The degree to which cognitive decline is known in those with severe to profound mental retardation remains equivocal at present. It should also be emphasized that these are group findings and do not necessarily reflect individual declines related to specific disease or psychiatric processes.

2. Specific and more marked declines may be evident in some; however, these are likely to be related to particular illness factors or disease, the iatrogenic effects of medication treatments, and generally unstimulating environments.

3. Those with initially lower functional levels may appear to drop sooner in cognitive and adaptive functioning with advancing age (Janicki & Jacobson, 1986).

4. Evidence is accumulating that Down syndrome has a unique pattern of cognitive deterioration in aging (Dalton & Crapper-MacLachlan, 1984, 1986; Dalton & Wisniewski, 1990) as contrasted with older adults without Down syndrome and with mental retardation. Cognitive changes that are gradual appear sometime after the age of fifty. A larger subgroup (compared to non-Down subjects), however, evidence a dementing disorder and also some sensory-related decrement in test performance (Cooke, 1988). As

Dalton and Wisniewski (1990) noted, results of studies on cognitive change are difficult to interpret since other authors have not reported a unity between signs of Alzheimer's disease and cognitive functioning. Performance on all evaluations of older adults with Down syndrome is obscured by the "floor effects" associated with more severe handicapping conditions. Larger test batteries consolidating to global outcomes clearly miss subtle changes in these adults.

5. Deficits on general IQ tests are often masked by specific and more pervasive problems in cognitive functioning in the elderly with mental retardation. It is quite possible that a more basic (or specific and underlying) change is occurring in attention or arousal states in these elders with mental retardation rather than just deficits in isolated memory or global cognitive capabilities.

6. Decline in cognitive skills, especially abstract cognitive skills, may not be as directly parallel with consequent changes in adaptive functional skills. This particularly depends on the structure of the living environment where the elder with mental retardation has been living for several years (Kleban et al., 1976).

7. Neuropsychological studies of aging and mental retardation—that is, efforts to study more specialized cognitive factors—have revealed age decrements in measures of orientation, attention, digit span, and delayed matching-to-sample tasks for those with Down syndrome but little difference across ages in those without Down syndrome (Thase et al., 1982, 1984). Dalton and Crapper-McLachlan (1984) also reported specific memory deterioration in adults with Down syndrome over forty years of age. Muir et al. (1988) evaluated cortical evoked-auditory-response potential in several different (etiology) groups of adults with mental retardation and noted a unique (P500) response in Down syndrome, which may signal dementia related to aging.

## Adaptive Behavior Changes in Aging and Mental Retardation

Changes specific to adaptive functioning as elders with mental retardation age have received considerable attention in the last several years. Since there is a documented and unique pattern of aging associated with Down syndrome (Wisniewski, Wisniewski, & Wen, 1985), conclusions on adaptive change and behavioral regression are reported separately for this group. *Adaptive functioning* in the majority of studies has referred to coping with daily environmental demands and the basics of self-care, usually communication, general mobility (ambulation), eating, toileting, dressing, and grooming.

1. Consistent or uniform age-related changes in adaptive behavior as a direct function of Alzheimer's disease in Down syndrome remains controversial (Harper, 1991). In fact, Wisniewski and Rabe (1986) reported significant discrepancies between the neuropathology of Alzheimer's disease in adults with Down syndrome and the actual prevalence (6 to 75 percent, depending on age) of clinical dementia. Behavioral regression is not axiomatic, since there are substantial numbers of elders with Down syndrome in their seventh and eight decades who are symptom-free (Dalton & Wisniewski, 1990).

2. Recent studies (Brown et al., 1990; Evinhuis, 1990; Loi & Williams, 1989); utilizing cross-sectional, longitudinal, and prospective designs have identified age-related decrements in all areas of adaptive functioning for adults with Down syndrome. Age-associated deficits were more common after age fifty.

3. Many of the studies of adaptive age changes with Down syndrome and those without Down syndrome are potentially confounded by issues related to varying decrements at different levels of mental retardation, precipitous changes associated with "terminal drop" (Schupf et al., 1989), and younger-older cohort effects associated with different access and experience in special educational and vocational opportunities.

4. Older adults (non-Down syndrome) living in institutional settings display a higher prevalence of problems with activities of daily living and possibly more precipitous decline than those residing in community settings (Hauber, Rotegard, & Bruininks, 1985; Haveman, Maaskent, & Sturmans, 1989; Janicki & Jacobson, 1986). Specific findings of adaptive deficits across age (that is, in toileting, grooming, and so on) are much less robust. Mobility and motor functioning appear to decline rather consistently with age in most studies.

5. Janicki and Jacobson (1986) provided compelling and detailed information on the adaptive functioning (cross-sectional design; 10,532 adults with mental retadation, aged forty-five and older; all levels of functioning; residential and community settings) and age-related changes. Their data suggest that adults with mild to moderate deficits evidence a decline in adaptive skills after age fifty and maintain their cognitive integrity until late in the seventh decade; adults with severe to profound deficits remained stable in both areas (adaptive and cognitive) into their early seventies and then displayed gradual decline.

All the studies of age-specific changes in adaptive behavior are subject to confounds associated with cohort uniqueness, robust survivor effects, brain drain out, and mixed etiologies of mental retardation, often with associated multiple health and physical problems. Clearly, a decline in adaptive function occurs in elders with mental retardation, but as in the "normal" elderly population, "growing old" and "growing infirm" are highly variable.

## Part II: Aging, Mental Retardation, and Dementia—
## Clinical Findings and Applications

*Psychiatric Disorders and Dementia in Elders with
Mental Retardation*

The phenomenon of dual or multiple diagnosis is brought into focus for
the elder with mental retardation in whom we suspect some specific decline but who may also have a concurrent psychiatric disorder (Harper,
1987b). Apparent intellectual impairment or dementia associated with
psychiatric disorders has been traditionally considered under the category
of pseudodementia. *Pseudo* seemingly implies something false in the mental status of an individual. This is a questionable assumption, as noted by
Cummings and Benson (1983). Associated psychiatric disorders clearly
occur in concert with organic disease and the presence of long-standing
mental retardation. Such additional intellectual compromise in the course
of psychiatric disease must be identified and treated since it may often be
possible to reverse or lessen it. This is an extremely important point for elders with mental retardation and concurrent psychiatric disease. The question with respect to adults with long-standing mental retardation and
psychiatric disorder is clearly one of differential diagnosis and a sorting
out of the multiple effects of disease and environmental deficits.
Diagnostic statements need to be placed within a probable hierarchical
framework, that is, an assessment of the likelihood of a number of events
(for example, the development of organic dementia, a history of psychiatric disorder, chronic health status, and psychotropic drug use) in a priority ranking rather than any definitive statement regarding etiology.
Interactions among events are the reality for the elderly person with mental retardation because of the complex interrelated nature of concurrent
psychiatric problems, organic disease, psychoactive medications, and mental retardation, all within the context of an aging central nervous system.
As noted by Holland (1990), aging adults with mental retardation represent a mixture of "hazards of life and hazards of birth." Ascertaining the
degree to which psychiatric disorders may mimic or be associated with dementia with concurrent degenerative disorders of the central nervous system is a formidable task for clinicians and, as yet, is not well understood
beyond a descriptive level. We simply do not understand the neuropathology of psychiatric disease and concurrent dementia conditions in older
adults with significant mental retardation.

The dilemma of pseudodementia requires careful attention to many de-
tails. The term *pseudodementia* is applied to at least two different groups of
individuals. The first group typically includes depressed individuals whose
cognitive impairment improves when the depression is successfully treated
or remits. *Pseudodementia* has also been used as a more inclusive term to

refer to all individuals with apparent cognitive impairment secondary to major psychiatric disorders, whether it be transient or chronic. Caine (1981) suggested four criteria for defining and diagnosing pseudodementia or psychiatric-related cognitive and functional regression in adults. First, there has to be intellectual impairment with a primary psychiatric disorder. Second, the syndrome must resemble similar impairments in other central nervous system diseases. This usually means that the syndrome is characterized by some type of memory impairment or disorientation. Third, intellectual change is viewed as reversible. Clearly, this latter status or cognitive issue relates to a time frame and whether or not the person is followed long enough so that it can be determined if such changes have occurred. Fourth, the individual must have no primary neurological disease that can account for the cognitive changes. Clearly, the last two criteria are inconsistent with defining dementia or pseudodementia in elders with mental retardation.

As Caine (1981) noted for the nonretarded elderly and Sovner and Hurley (1983) and Menolascino (personal communication, 1988) noted for the mentally retarded elderly, unipolar depression appears to account for the majority of the so-called pseudodementias. However, numerous other psychiatric disturbances can account for dementialike changes. These psychiatric disturbances usually include disorders with some type of psychosis. The apparent dementia (behavioral regression) may represent a general loss of contact with reality and consequent behavioral regression during the more active phase of the psychiatric disorder, which clears or remits when this phase is treated or passes. The dementia changes may also reflect currently undefined and unknown neuropathological changes in the central nervous system that are enduring and are related to the psychotic disorder. Caine (1981) also noted that, as age increases, depression and/or mood disorder is a more likely etiological disorder than dementia. Reid (personal communication, 1987) noted that this is also true in mentally retarded elders. However, the frequency of pseudodementia varies greatly depending on the method of ascertainment. As noted by Cummings and Benson (1983), of all persons (all patient types) admitted to neurological services, estimates on pseudodementia vary between 2 and 32 percent. Most surveys put the outcome at 10 percent, again with depression as the most frequently associated psychiatric disorder as age advances. However, follow-up studies of nonmentally retarded elders have suggested that dementia is often overdiagnosed (20 to 50 percent of the time), and that most patients actually suffer from a primary psychiatric disorder unspecified on follow-up (Tyler & Tyler, 1984).

In sum, the term *pseudodementia* appears to refer to a question of time-referenced etiology, not false dementia. The literature and the comments of numerous investigators and contemporary clinicians suggest a high rate of false-positives for dementia in the general elderly population. Such false-positives are frequently later diagnosed as displaying a primary psychiatric disorder (Cummings & Benson, 1983). At present, we have no solid base-rate figures on associated psychiatric disease as a primary cause of dementia in the mentally retarded elderly. Future studies need to be done in this area. Pseudodementia suggests many factors to be considered in the process of diagnosing dementia in elders with mental retardation. Clearly, dementia is a general condition of deterioration in behavioral competence based on clinical and neurological observations and laboratory findings. Diagnosis must be placed in both a behavioral and a medical framework. Dementia may be organic—that is, cortical or subcortical—and may be associated with a psychiatric disease. In this latter case, however, the possibility of reversibility may be greater but not axiomatic. Some subtypes of schizophrenia display persistent neurocognitive deficits beyond the bizzare episodes of the disorder (Cummings & Benson, 1983). Dementia associated with concurrent psychiatric disorder may now represent a not-yet-recognized altered brain state. Contemporary research in neuroimaging (positron emission tomography) may provide data on these hypothesized but unknown relationships. Dementia may present as a relative combination of organic and psychiatric disease. The latter is probably the more likely case in elders with mental retardation because of the increased prevalence of psychiatric disorders. Depression is generally underdiagnosed in mental retardation (Szymanski, 1988; Yapa & Roy, 1990) because of a limited or unusual presentation of the symptoms of depression. Most important, dementia does not appear to be axiomatic in elders with mental retardation with or without Down syndrome. Differential-diagnosis becomes a formidable task but is feasible within a medical and behavioral framework.

*Literature on Dementia in Aging Adults with Mental Retardation*

The literature on dementia in mental retardation has been accumulating (Harper, 1991) rather dramatically. Much of the attention in the newer literature has focused on Down syndrome and its association with Alzheimer's disease. The following comments address the literature on dementia separately for those elders with and without Down syndrome.

Although there are references to dementia in the literature on elders with mental retardation, contemporary findings on those without Down syndrome date to the study by Reid and Aungle in 1974. This seminal paper acknowledges the difficulty of identifying dementia in patients of low initial intelligence and with limited adaptive skills. Reid and colleagues assessed 155 people (63 males, 92 females), forty-five years of age and older, for the condition of dementia. The diagnosis was based on data collected for age, sex, chromosomal analysis, level of retardation, and intelligence, in addition to direct clinical interviews. Diagnosis was facilitated primarily by the behavioral observations of the caretakers. Those with suspected dementia were reevaluated at least six months after their initial assessment, and a final diagnosis was completed. These data reveal an overall prevalence rate of dementia of 71 per 1,000 for those over age forty-five and 136 per 1,000 for those over age sixty-five. These respective rates of 7 and 13 percent have become a standard of comparison for future studies. It was concluded that a diagnosis of dementia could be assessed in this population with adequate reliability, as well as in those with severe mental retardation. Standard psychiatric criteria were employed in this diagnostic process.

Tait (1983) reported an investigation examining factors associated with mortality and dementia in aging individuals with mental retardation. This study carefully examined 382 cases of subjects with an intellectual quotient of 50 or less. Of these individuals, 277 were residing in hospitals, and 105 in community settings. At follow-up on the 137 survivors, Tait reported a prevalence rate by examination for dementia of 10 to 17 percent for those over age sixty-five.

Janicki and Jacobson (1986) sampled from 10,532 adults with mental retardation born between 1890 and 1939 and known to the New York State service system. Between 1978 and 1984, these investigators determined the status of these multiple cohorts at follow-up by file review in a number of specific areas. Their data (adaptive and cognitive) reveal a marked or greater degree of decline for individuals with higher intellectual capacity: "The more you have, the more you lose." Earlier general decline was associated with motor skill decline in those with severe to profound deficits, but not in those with higher (moderate plus) intellectual and functional levels. The profile of decline became more variable as age increased, with the mid-fifties as a reasonable empirically supported starting point for defining the onset of aging in this group on the basis of the data available. Finally, differential rates of change were evident in the groups from each setting, with those in community settings maintaining their skills better. Again, this outcome appears to be related to sampling and the fact that larger residential settings are known for assisting those with more severe and multiple physical and behavioral problems.

Kleban and colleagues (1976) evaluated 64 aged females (all had very significant moderate to severe organic impairment and limited IQ functioning; mean age = 83) who were living in a supervised residential environment. An eight-category behavioral rating system of functional behaviors was employed, and indivduals' ratings, based on caretakers' observations, were completed on a repeated basis for two years. The behavioral outcomes for this population were highly predictable, given the availability of baseline measures of initial levels of cognitive and behavioral functioning. The "stable group" evidenced less serious medical conditions, had better "initial cognition," were more socially responsive to their environment, displayed fewer psychiatric conditions, and initially displayed greater control over their impulses and aggression. The declining group (37 percent) displayed more serious morbidity (all types) and less comprehension of the institutional environment at the outset of the study. The authors noted that psychiatric variables (particular behaviors) and medical variables (specific conditions) were particularly effective in differentiating the "stable" and "decline" categories. Control of aggression, impulsivity, psychiatric behaviors, and seriousness of medical condition explained 90 percent of the variance between those who declined and the stable group. Lower levels of initial baseline function appeared to be associated with earlier mortality. Finally, the authors reported that cognition appeared to decline more than functional behavior.

Hewitt et al. (1986) reported on the effects of aging and cognitive and behavioral functioning in a developmentally disabled group that were seventy-three years of age on average and very low in general functioning. Cognitive levels were measured by repeated administrations of the Stanford-Binet Intelligence Scale (the mean number of assessments was seven). These adults had been in a residential hospital for the majority of their lives. Orientation for time, place, and person was reassessed before each direct assesment. The results revealed that mental age continued to rise into late middle age in the majority of the population. This rise was generally followed by an intellectual decline at approximately age sixty that affected 18 percent of the individuals significantly. Cognitive decline was accompanied by an associated deficit in self-care skills and orientation. Behavioral disturbance did not necessarily accompany this decline, although behavioral disturbance was noted in about half of the sample at the time of the direct psychological assessments. Hewitt et al. (1986) noted that their data supported the fact that a majority of elders with mental retardation are capable of self-care in advancing age, as is true of their age-peers in the general population.

Day (1985) reported a retrospective survey of psychiatric disorder in the United Kingdom of two groups of adults with mental retardation, forty years of age and older. One group consisted primarily of long-term in-hospital residents, and the other group represented a series of psychiatric first admissions to the same hospital. All subjects were assessed by means of the standard international diagnostic nomenclature (World Health Organization, 1991). Day (1985) reported that between 7 and 9 percent of these adults had dementia, depending on whether presenile states (that is, early changes) were included. Day interpreted these data as indicating that senile dementia is neither more nor less prevalent in those with mental retardation than in the nondisabled older adult population. By Day's own acknowledgment, the population in this study may have been somewhat atypical. Fewer seriously impaired were included, and there appeared to be more individuals with "neurotic and adjustment disorders" in the more recent admissions to the hospital grouping.

In a 1985 Danish study on the prevalence of psychiatric morbidity, Lund studied 302 adults with mental retardation using a well-designed sampling procedure. Specific psychiatric criteria developed by Lund also utilized a computerized hierarchical probability classification system for diagnosis. Individuals were specifically examined in a direct interview with proven reliability. The overall prevalence rates of dementia were reported as follows: 1 percent at ages 30–44; 6 percent at ages 45–64; 22 percent at age 65 and over. Lund noted that the sex ratio was unaffected. Lund further clarified that the larger number of demented individuals (22 percent) compared to Ried and Aungle data (1974) was very likely due to the presence of more individuals with Down syndrome in his study, as well as differences in Reid's cohorts' mortality rate compared to the Lund's rate.

Barcikowska et al. (1989) conducted a retrospective study focusing on the relationships (postmortem) between the presence of plaques, tangles, amyloid angiopathy (Alzheimer neuropathology), and dementia in 70 deceased adults over sixty-five and without Down syndrome. A comprehensive record review also identified (1) gender; (2) age at death; (3) cause of death; (4) etiology of mental retardation; (5) initial IQ; (6) physical status affecting deterioration; and (7) cardiovascular status. In 22 of the 70 cases (31 percent) Alzheimer's neuropathology was noted, and in the majority, at least some Alzheimer-specific lesions were noted. Age-related data from the clinical histories lacked fidelity and were difficult to evaluate. For those adults without concurrent physical problems, a documented 10-point or greater drop in IQ was a likely predictor of Alzheimer's disease. The estimate of the prevalence of Alzheimer-type neuropatholgy among these adults with mental retardation appeared to be comparable to that for non-mentally-retarded people. Barcikowska et al. (1989) outlined an emerging set of risk factors associated with Alzheimer's disease based on empirical data.

Jacobson and Harper (1989) reported on a large national U.S. survey of the mental health of elders with mental retardation in residential care facilities. The focus of the study was on older mental-retardation–developmental-disability persons (over age fifty-five) as residents in special and nursing facilities (269 different locations). The comprehensive survey included current diagnosis (medical and psychiatric), cognitive level, activities of daily living, behavior problems and symptoms, changes in functional status over time, medications, and interventions. The focus was elders with psychiatric diagnoses. The response rate was 20.7 percent for ($N$ = 397 individuals). Among these elders, 21.6 percent (ages 55–75+) exhibited a current diagnosis of specific mental disorder, with 8.5 percent evidencing a progressive neurological disorder. Advancing age was associated with a higher prevalence of progressive neurological disorder. Combining the categories identifying neurological disease and changes revealed an increase (from 12 percent at 55–59 years to 13.8 percent at 75 years and over) for dementia-like conditions.

Harper and Wadsworth (1990) reviewed the problems of evaluating dementia within the context of depression in adults with mental retardation over the age of forty-five. Physical disorders were common in this group, with 90 percent having concurrent and frequently multiple medical diagnoses, and 10 percent displaying a psychiatric diagnosis. Multiple measures were used to evaluate these 90 adults, who were a convenience sample. The findings revealed that decreasing cognitive skills were associated with higher rates of depression and reported behavior problems. Trends approaching statistical significance suggested that, at older ages, more depressive behaviors, high use of psychotropic medication, and cognitive decline were more common with lower initial intellectual status. This Iowa pilot study was among the first reported that attempted to sort out the complexities of identifying dementia in older adults with preexisting mental retardation and depression.

Most recently, Popovitch et al. (1990) carried out an extensive postmortem study of the brain tissue of 385 adults with mental retardation, aged twenty-three to ninety. These were adults without Down syndrome and without metabolic disorders or hydrocephalus. The authors sought to provide data on the relationship between indicators of Alzheimer's neuropathology and selected clinical variables. The data presented are rather compelling, since the presence of one or more neurofibrilary tangles (NFTs) and/or neuritic plaques (NPs) was noted in 63.4 percent of all cases and varied with age. The prevalence of positive cases (presence of NFTs and/or NPs) was higher when mental retardation was due to head trauma, congenital malformation, or familial factors and a positive history of seizures. The presence of NPs was associated with advancing age, and NFT counts varied by location. NFTs were more prevalent in those with low IQ (20 or less); however, because of the imprecision of such cognitive estimates, this finding remains equivocal, requiring replication. The authors acknowledged the predisposition of Alzheimer pathology in those elders without Down syndrome. Furthermore, the data suggest that lesions often associated with Alzheimer's disease may represent a more general "end response" of the brain to some injury (for example, trauma, congenital dysfunction, or seizures).

## Down Syndrome and Dementia

The growing literature on Down syndrome and dementia is too voluminous to allow a comprehensive review in this chapter. Several key studies are highlighted here, particular summaries are referenced, and the more current findings are noted.

The historical identification of Down syndrome and dementialike changes dates to Fraser and Mitchell (1876), well over one hundred years ago. Struwe (1929) identified senile plaques in the postmortem brains of individuals with Down syndrome, and Jervis (1948) provided initial clinical descriptions of the dementing course. By the mid-1960s, Heston, Lowther, and Leventhal (1966) had suggested a familial link between Down syndrome and Alzheimer's disease. As adults with trisomy 21 increased their longevity, the morbidity of Alzheimer's-related dementia began to increase as well. Adults with Down syndrome became the study of many neurologists, geneticists, and gerontologists because of their known early characteristics of premature aging. Subsequent research (Evenhuis, 1990; Lai & Williams, 1989; Malamud, 1972; Wisniewski, Wisniewski, & Wen, 1985) has consistently supported the presence of Alzheimer's pathology in the vast majority of Down syndrome adults over age thirty-five. However, there is considerable debate (Dalton & Wisniewski, 1990) on the prevalence associated with the frequency (Murphy et al., 1990), the location (Mann, Royston, & Ravindra, 1990), the method of ascertainment and staining procedures (Rabe et al., 1990), and the biological significance (Pearlson et al., 1990; Wisniewski, Robe, & Wisniewski, 1987) of particular signs of Alzheimer's disease (plaques and tangles) and, most important, the clinical expression of dementia in adults with Down syndrome. For a comprehensive review of these issues, see Rabe et al. (1990).

Lai and Wiliams (1989) completed a comprehensive study of 96 adults with Down syndrome (DS), exploring their clinical and neuropathological status in relation to Alzheimer's disease by using prospective longitudinal data collection. A detailed study was completed on all individuals (76 institutionalized; 23 in the community), and appropriate conditions were screened (hypothyroidism, syphilis, $B_{12}$ deficiency, CNS tumor, and depression) with repeated neuropsychological and laboratory examinations (electroencephalogram and computereized axial tomography). The authors identified dementia (a functional decline in orientation, memory, verbal, motor, and self-care skills) in 49 adults with DS, with an average age at onset of $54.2 \pm 6.1$ years. The prevalence of dementia (in the institutionalized group) was 8 percent between ages 35 and 49, 55 percent between 50 and 59, and 75 percent in those over 60 years of age. These data are consistent with those of Thase et al. (1982). A high number (84 percent) developed seizures, suggesting additional neuropathology superimposed on a developmentally atypical CNS. Ten (20 percent) displayed Parkinsonian motor changes. In the 23 patients who died, the average duration of dementia was $4.6 \pm 3.2$ years from diagnosis. Neuroimaging evidenced pronounced temporal-lobe tissue loss, and the autopsied brains showed a high frequency of plaques and tangles. The discrepancy in identified clinical dementia in relation to Alzheimer's neuropathology among studies, according to Lai and Williams (1989), may reflect a latent "incubation period" of up to three decades between neuropathological evidence and functional dementia. Lai and Williams presented three phases of clinical decline: an initial phase of memory drop, decreasing orientation, and reduced verbal output in higher functioning individuals with DS, and apathy, inattention, and decreased social interactions in low functioning individuals; a second phase of loss of adaptive skills, gait changes, work level drops, and some onset of seizures; and a final phase of nonambulation, flexed postures, incontinence, and pathological neurological reflexes; aspiration pneumonia and intercurrent infection preceded death. These data of Lai and Williams (1989) were further corraborated by Evenhuis (1990) in a similar prospective study of individual with DS in the Netherlands. This author provided additional clinical data to assist in identifying adults who were declining in cognitive status by relying on careful observations of daily life from parents and caregivers. These data also confirmed the presence of earlier dementia in those with DS as compared with non-DS adults.

Pearlson et al. (1990) compared the computer axial tomography (CAT) scans of 18 individuals with DS, aged 26 to 70, with normal volunteer CAT scans to examine evidence of cortical and subcortical atrophy. All scans were analyzed as a function of age and cognitive status. Specific data were obtained by use of the *Mini Mental Status Examination* (MMSE), the *Adaptive Behavior Scale*, and the *Disability Assessment Schedule*. The suprasellar cistern ratio, presumed to measure mesial temporal-lobe atrophy was correlated (;ms.91) with the severity of cognitive impairment on the MMSE, with age partialed out. The suprasellar cistern ratio predicted dementia status with an accuracy of more than 75 percent. The authors noted that specific brain measurements on the CAT scans showed a distinct pattern of increased abnormality with age in those with DS that differed from that of normal volunteers. These data demonstrated significant anatomical brain change in DS during life and were present in most subjects studied by age thirty.

Finally, the leading authorities on Down syndrome and dementia of the Alzheimer type, Wisniewski and Dalton (1990), reviewed the state-of-the-art knowledge in the area. While echoing the findings of others reported in this section, these authors raised several important points on the differential diagnosis of dementia changes in those with DS. More precise (specific measures) and repeated neuropsychological assessment is needed to identify early signs of dementia in DS. Subtle psychiatric, personality, and motivational changes (irritability, fear, lability, and reduced initiation of activities) are often the early prodromes of dementia and are rarely recognized. Finally, dyspraxic features, sensory deficits, and EEG abnormalities that appear to be changes caused by dementia are often associated with the fundamental DS developmental anomaly rather than with the progress of dementia. This is a very complicated task of neuropsychological evaluation in adults who display limited functional differences on most standard psychological measures.

## Conclusions Offered on the State of Knowledge on Dementia and Mentally Retarded Elders

Some conclusions can be offered regarding our present knowledge of dementia in elders with mental retardation. These are summarized here and are based on material reviewed previously in this chapter.

No investigators currently report dementia rates associated with concurrent psychiatric disease in elders with mental retardation. Such definitions of so-called pseudodementia are complicated to define, but these conditions do exist (Harper & Wadsworth, 1990). Because of the higher incidence of emotional disorders in mental retardation (Menolascino, 1987), there is likely to be a greater number of individuals with dementias associated with psychiatric disease than in the non-mentally-retarded elderly population. Dalton and Wisniewski (1990) noted that the evaluation of dementia in adults with Down syndrome is often complicated by psychiatric disease.

The dementia rates, as reported, appear to fall between 6 and 20 percent in the majority of studies, depending on the age groups and the etiologies included. Reid & Aungle 1974 data of approximately 13 to 14 percent for mentally retarded adults over age sixty-five appear to have become the standard. Menolascino (1987) reported a 19 percent incidence of dementia for adults over age fifty-five. Barcikowska et al. (1989) noted that motor deterioration, an onset of behavior problems, and a documented 10-point or larger IQ drop (without other physical disease) was associated with Alzheimer's-related dementia. The prevalence of Alzheimer's pathology in non-Down-syndrome adults with mental retardation was reported as being similar to that in the general adult population. In all of these studies, morbidity outcomes for dementia were slightly different because of the different age groups, the different methods of ascertainment, the various settings studied, and, in some cases, particular sample features (e.g., more individuals with Down syndrome). Down syndrome dementia rates (Evenhuis, 1990; Lai & Williams, 1989) are generally 6 to 8 percent at ages 35–49; 50 to 55 percent at ages 50–59, and 70 percent or more for those 60 or older.

The etiological factors, reported by Barcikowska et al. (1989), Corbett (1985), Eaton and Menolascino (1982), Lund (1985), Reid & Aungle (1974), and Wisniewski (1982) as a basis for dementia, appear to be similar to those found in non-mentally-retarded aging groups. This is true with the exception of Down syndrome (Dalton & Wisniewski, 1990; Evenhuis, 1990; Lai & Wililams, 1989; Wisniewski et al., 1978). However, since the health and frequency of illness (physical and mental), the use of psychoactive medications, and the presence of CNS deficits are all higher in those with more severe forms of mental retardation (Haveman et al., 1989), general behavioral regression and dementialike conditions are more likely (Harper, Wadsworth, & Michael, 1989; Harper & Wadsworth, 1990). The dementia rates may be somewhat higher than in the nonretarded elderly, but the specific reasons remain unclear at this time (Jacobson & Harper, 1989). Multiple factors, as previously noted, are likely to interact to an unknown degree.

Dementia associated with certain psychiatric disorders may be reversible to some unknown degree (Cummings & Benson, 1983); however, we have no data on this reversibility in populations with mental retardation. The diagnosis of dementia in individuals (with and without Down syndrome) with intelligence below an IQ of 25 remains equivocal (Reid & Aungle 1974), and its relationship to specific neuropathology indicators is difficult to ascertain (Dalton & Wisniewski, 1990; Popovitch et al., 1990). This is especially true if no prior test data are available for comparison. Decline in individuals with very low cognitive functioning is often reflected in changes in adaptive self-help behavior or the onset of physical changes (for example, the loss of continence or a reduction in motor or ambulation skills) than in a cognitive decline. The diagnosis of dementia in these cases is clearly facilitated by repeated behavioral observations over time provided by knowledgeable caretakers (Evenhuis, 1990; Harper, 1991; Reid & Aungle 1974). Dementia assessment must be evaluated within a medical and an adaptive and behavioral framework and must be documented with observations of changes in daily skill functioning (Harper, 1987a). As noted by Reid (1982), the differential diagnosis of dementia may be aided by the use of serial EEGs. These are especially useful in diagnosis at the early stages of dementia for individuals who are very low functioning and severely multiply impaired. Popovitch et al. (1990) noted that the presence of NFTs and NPs was higher when mental retardation was associated with head trauma, congenital malformation, and a positive history of seizures. Pearlson et al. (1990) clearly emphasized the diagnostic use of neuroimaging in those with Down syndrome and identified early (prior to age thirty) signs of progressive anatomical brain changes.

Standard clinical psychiatric criteria with modifications, as noted by Reid (1982), Ballinger et al. (1975), and Lund (1985), are applicable in diagnosing older adults with mental retardation in the mild and moderate range. However, many researchers (Harper, 1987b; Levitas, 1987; Menolascino, 1987; Szymanski, 1987) have raised serious questions about the applicability to individuals with significant mental retardation of the standard criteria in the revised third edition of the American Psychiatric Association (APA, 1987) *Diagnostic and Statistical Manual* (DSM-III-R). Standard psychiatric nomenclature is rarely precise in describing the often subtle atypical behavioral features and occasionally "primitive" characteristics of nonverbal older adults with severe to profound mental retardation. The multiplicity of categories in the DSM-III-R seemingly implies a precision of defining mental disorders that does not currently fit with the known etiologies of mental retardation or its current treatment. Harper (1987b), in a pilot diagnostic field study, reported that, for a group of older adults with moderate mental retardation, the standard DSM-III-R diagnoses were applicable to only about 30 percent of the study sample. Multiple medical conditions (convulsive disorder) and multiple physical and sensory impairment in this population make the application of the standard diagnostic criteria very difficult or moot. The presentation of psychiatric disorders in those with significant mental retardation is heavily influenced by their functional skill levels, the expertise of the diagnostician, and the examiner's patience with older persons.

Disorientation alone may not be a stable predictor of early dementia according to Reid & Aungle (1974) early studies. Psychiatric episodes (transient) may portend dementia, especially in Down syndrome (Dalton & Wisniewski, 1990; Reid, 1982). Janicki and Jacobson (1986) reported that individuals with a higher initial baseline of intellectual functioning appeared to lose more cognitive status over time. This finding documents the well-known phenomenon of "The more you have, the more you lose."

The type, pattern, rate, and degree of decline that an individual displays may be somewhat different at different levels of intellectual and adaptive functioning. Suggestions in this area have been noted by Reid (1987). Psychiatric disorders in combination with organic problems are helpful in discriminating those who remain stable into later years from those who are likely to decline precipitously. This pattern has been noted in elders with mental retardation and has been supported by the work of Kleban et al., (1976). Finally, cognitive decline is not axiomatic with adaptive decline. However, most individuals decline from the "top down," that is, memory to motor, cortical to subcortical. The more abstract cognitive skills appear to drop off more than the adaptive function skills (Kleban et al., 1976). This latter conclusion may be based on the relative precision of cognitive and adaptive tests. Much work has been accomplished on the relationship between Down syndrome and dementia, specifically Alzheimer's disease. Although a high percentage of Alzheimer neuropathology is present in adults with Down syndrome, the expression of functional dementia is highly variable, and its latent nature is a cause of major debate (Dalton & Wisniewski, 1990). The average longevity of adults with Down syndrome and identified Alzheimer's-related dementia is between fifty-one and fifty-five years of age. Earlier identification of more subtle cognitive, personality, and adaptive changes associated with dementia in adults with Down syndrome is possible by the use of experimental learning-task paradigms, repeated neuropsychological assessment, and careful observations of daily behavior by knowledgeable care providers (Dalton & Wisniewski, 1990; Harper & Wadsworth, 1990).

Table 1 presents a partial summary of the signs and symptoms that reflect impending dementia or behavioral regression in elders with mental retardation. These "signs" may occur in all older adults; they are also in some cases etiologically specific to those with Down syndrome. Such a list or individual items should be viewed in a context with other factors known

# Table 1
## Practical Conclusions: Signs and Symptoms of Possible Impending Dementia in Elders with Mental Retardation

*Changes from baseline functional behavior in the following:*

1. Changes in routine behavior (cannot follow directions or simple instructions as before)
2. Decreasing orientation broadly defined (may be eqivocal in some instances, but this area is important to note from a baseline for all individuals)
3. Nocturnal confusion
4. Abrupt aggressiveness (usually unprovoked), irritability, fearfulness
5. Transient psychotic episodes.
6. Inconsistent neuropsychological performance on direct assessment (or a 10-point or greater loss of general cognitive function)
7. Lack of attention (lower arousal—level of fluctuating arousal)
8. Cannot learn new simple tasks
9. Beginning posturing (heretofore absent)
10. Gait imbalance, falling more
11. Slurred speech
12. Reduced verbal output
13. Memory changes
14. Inability to initiate activities or actions as before
15. More labile emotions
16. Withdrawing from social contact

*Physiological risk factors*

1. Intermittent incontinence
2. History of high blood pressure
3. History of ischemic episodes
4. Seizure onset
5. Onset of motor tremors, rigididy, myoclonus
6. Focal neurological signs
7. Head trauma
8. Congenital malformations of CNS

*Genetic risk factors*

1. Family history of psychiatric disease
2. Family history of dementia (all types)
3. Family history of ischemic attacks
4. Family history of Down syndrome

*Medication risk factors*

Chronic use of the following medications have been shown to affect the higher functioning of the central nervous system:

1. Psychotropics
2. Anticholinergic agents
3. Antihypertensive agents
4. Anticonvulsants
5. Antineoplatic agents
6. Selected antibiotics
7. Miscellaneous drugs (e.g., steroids, contraceptives)

*Assorted risk factors or predictive factors*

1. Unresponsiveness to psychotropics
2. Age 55+
3. Down syndrome

*Psychiatric-associated risk factors*
(Psychiatric disorders, transient or chronic, may and often present with behavioral regression reflecting dementialike states. Such pseudodementia conditions should be noted. Their validity as "true dementias" is not well understood clinically or from a neuropathological standpoint.)

*Schizophrenic and psychotic disorders*
*Depression and affective disorders*

about an individual. This compilation draws heavily from the work of Barcikowska et al. (1989); Cummings and Benson (1983); Dalton and Wisniewski, 1990; Lai and Williams (1989); Popovitch et al. (1990); and Thase et al. (1984). The reader is also referred to the following: *Psychopharmacology Bulletin,* "Special Feature: Assessment in Diagnosis and Treatment of Geropsychiatric Patients" (1988), Volume 24, Number 4. This is a comprehensive compendium reviewing many issues and assessment methods for dementia. It is applicable to adults with mental retardation. Also, Aman (1991) prepared an excellent text, *Assessing Psychopathology and Behavior Problems in Persons with Mental Retardation: A Review of Available Instruments.*

# References

Aman, M. G. (1985). Drugs in mental retardation: Treatment or tragedy? *Aus. N. Z. J. Devel. Disabilities, 10*(4), 215–226.

Aman, M. G. (1990). Considerations in the use of psychotropic drug use in elderly mentally retarded persons. *J. Ment. Defic. Res., 34,* 1–10.

Aman, M. G. (1991). *Assessing psychopathology and behavior problems in persons with mental retardation. A review of available instruments.* Washington, D.C.: Department of Health and Human Services.

American Medical Association. (1986). *Dementia* (Council on Scientific Affairs Report. *J. Am. Med. Assoc., 256*(16), 2234–2238.

American Psychiatric Association. (1987). *Diagnostic and statistical manual of mental disorders* (3rd ed., rev.: DSM-III-R). Washington, DC: Author.

Ballinger, B. R., Armstrong, J., Presly, A. S., & Reid, A. H. (1975). Use of standardized psychiatric interview in mentally handicapped patients. *Br. J. Psychiatr., 127,* 540–544.

Barcikowska, M., Silverman, W., Zigman, W., Kozlowski, P. B., Kujawa, M., Rudelli, R., & Wisniewski, H. M. (1989). Alzheimer-type neuropathology and clinical symptoms of dementia in mentally retarded people without Down syndrome. *Am. J. Ment. Retard., 93*(5), 551–557.

Bell, A., & Zubek, J. (1960). The effect of age on intellectual performance of mental defectives. *J. Gerontol., 15,* 285–295.

Benton, A., & Sivan, A. (1984). Problems and clinical issues in neuropsychological research in aging and dementia. *J. Clin. Neuropsychol., 6*(1), 56–63.

Botwinick, J. (1984). *Aging and behavior.* New York: Springer.

Brown, F. R., Geer, M. K., Aylward, E. H., & Hunt, H. H. (1990). Intellectual and adaptive functioning in individuals with Down syndrome in relation to age and environmental placement. *Pediatrics, 85,* 450–452.

Burack, J. A., Hodapp, R. M. & Zigler, E. (1988). Issues in the classification of mental retardation: Differentiating among organic etiologies. *J. Child Psychol. Psychiatr., 29,* 765–779.

Caine, E. D. (1981). Pseudodementia. *Arch. Gen. Psychiatr., 38,* 1359–1364.

Cooke, L. (1988). Hearing loss in the mentally handicapped: A study of its prevalence and association with ageing. *Br. J. Ment. Subnorm., 34,* 112–116.

Corbett, J. A. (1985). Aging and mental retardation: A new challenge. *J. R. Soc. Med., 78,* 166–168.

Cummings, J. L., & Benson, D. F. (1983). *Dementia: A clinical approach.* Boston: Butterworths.

Dalton, A. J., & Crapper-McLachlan, D. R. (1984). Incidence of memory deterioration in aging persons with Down syndrome. In J. M. Berg (Ed.), *Perspectives and progress in mental retardation: Vol. 2. Biomedical aspects* (pp. 55–62). Baltimore: University Park Press.

Dalton, A. J., & Crapper-McLachlan, D. R. (1986). Clinical expression of Alzheimer's disease in Down's syndrome. *Psychiatr. Persp. Ment. Retard.: Psychiatr. Clinics N. Am., 2,* 43–52.

Dalton, A. J. & Wisniewski, H. M. (1990). Down's syndrome and the dementia of Alzheimer disease. *Int. Rev. Psychiatr., 2,* 43–52.

Day, K. (1985). Psychiatric disorder in middle-aged and elderly mentally handicapped. *Br. J. Psychiatr., 147,* 660–667.

Demaine, G. C., & Silverstein, A. B. (1978). MA changes in institutionalized Down's syndrome persons: A semi-longitudinal approach. *Am. J. M. Defic., 82,* 429–432.

Dickerson, M., Hamilton, J., Huber, R., & Segal, R. (1979). *The aging mentally retarded—The invisible client: A challenge to the community.* Presented at the 98th Annual Meeting of the American Association on Mental Deficiency, Toronto, Canada.

Eaton, L., & Menolascino, F. J. (1982). Psychiatric disorders in mentally retarded: Types, problems, and challenges. *Am. J. Psychiatr., 139,* 1297–1303.

Evenhuis, H. M. (1990). The natural history of dementia in Down's syndrome. *Arch. Neurol., 47,* 263–267.

Fenner, M. E., Hewitt, K. E., & Tropy, D. M. (1987). Down's syndrome. Intellectual and behavioral functioning during childhood. *J. Ment. Defic. Res., 31,* 241–249.

Fisher, M. A., & Zeaman, D. (1970). Growth and decline of retardate intelligence. In N. R. Ellis (Ed.), *International review of research in mental retardation* (Vol. 4, pp. 151–191). New York: Academic Press.

Fraser, J., & Mitchell, A. (1876). Kalmuc idiocy: Report of a case with autopsy with notes on 62 cases. *J. Ment. Sci., 22,* 161.

Goldman, R. (1984). The epidemiology and demography of dementia. *Psychiatr. Ann., 14,* 169–174.

Goodman, J. (1977). IQ decline in the mentally retarded: A matter of fact or methodological flaw. *Am. J. Ment. Defic., 21,* 199–203.

Harper, D. C. (1987a, June). *Dementia in elders with mental retardation.* Presented at the First International Conference on the Mental Health Aspects of Mental Retardation, Evanston, Illinois.

Harper, D. C. (1987b, August). *Evaluating depression in elders with mental retardation.* Presented at the Annual Meeting of the American Psychological Association, New York.

Harper, D. C. (1989). Aging and mental retardation. *Current Opinion Psychiatr., 2,* 603–606.

Harper, D. C. (1991). *Aging and psychiatric problems in persons with mental retar-*

*dation.* Edited proceedings of the Consortium on Aging and Developmental Disabilities, University Affiliated Cincinnati Center, Cincinnati, Ohio.

Harper, D. C. (1991). Aging and mental retardation. *Current Opinion Psychiatr., 4,* 717–721.

Harper, D. C., & Wadsworth, J. S. (1990). Dementia and depression in elders with mental retardation: A pilot study. *Res. Devel. Disabilities, 11,* 177–198.

Harper, D. C., Wadsworth, J. S., & Michael, A. L. (1989). Psychotropic drug use in older develoepmentally disabled with behavioral difficulties. *Res. Devel. Disabilities, 10,* 53–60.

Hauber, F. A., Rotegard, L. L., & Bruininks, R. H. (1985). Characteristics of residential services for older/elderly mentally retarded persons. In M. P. Janicki & H.M. Wisniewski (Eds.), *Aging and developmental disabilities: Issues and approaches* (pp. 327–350). Baltimore: Brookes.

Haveman, M., Maaskant, M. A., & Sturmans, F. (1989). Older Dutch residents of institutions, with and without Down syndrome: Comparisons of mortality and morbidity trends and motor/social functioning. *Aus. N. Z. J. Devel. Disabilities, 15,* 241–255.

Henderson, A. S. (1983). The coming epidemic of dementia. *Aus. N. Z. J. Psychiatr., 17,* 117–127.

Heston, L. L., Lowther, D. L., & Leventhal, C. M. (1966). Alzheimer's disease: A family study. *Arch. Neurol., 47,* 263–267.

Hewitt, K. E., Carter, G., & Jancar, J. (1985). Ageing in Down's syndrome. *Br. J. Psychiatr., 147,* 58–62.

Hewitt, K. E., Fenner, M. E., & Tropy, D. (1986). Cognitive and behavioral profiles of the elderly mentally handicapped. *J. Ment. Defic. Res., 30,* 217–225.

Holland, A. J. (1990). Ageing and mental retardation. *Current Opinion Psychiatr, 3,* 591–594.

Hurley, A., & Sovner, R. (1986). Dementia, mental retardation, and Down's syndrome. *Psychiatr. Aspects Ment. Retard. Rev., 5*(8), 1–6.

Jacobson, J. W., & Harper, M. S. (1989). Mental health status of older persons with mental retardation in residential care settings. *Aus. N. Z. J. Devel. Disabilities, 15*(3, 4), 301–309.

Janicki, M. P., & Jacobson, J. (1986). Generational trends in sensory, physical, and behavioral abilitites among older mentally retarded persons. *Am. J. Ment. Defic., 90*(5), 495–500.

Janicki, M. P., & Wisniewski, H. M. (1985). *Aging and developmental disabilities: Issues and approaches.* Baltimore: Brookes.

Jervis, G. A. (1948). Early senile dementia Mongoloid idiocy. *Am. J. Psychiatr., 105,* 102–106.

Kaplan, O. (1943). Mental decline in older morons. *Am. J. Ment. Defic., 91,* 237–243.

Kiloh, L. G. (1961). Pseudo-dementia. *Acta Psychiatr. Scand, 37,* 336–351.

Kleban, M. H., Lawton, P., Brody, E. M. & Moss, M. (1976). Behavioral observations of mentally impaired aged: Those who decline and those who do not. *J. Gerontol., 31,* 333–339.

Lai, F., & Williams, R. S. (1989). A prospective study of Alzheimer disease in Down syndrome. *Arch. Neurol., 46,* 849–853.

Levitas, A. (1987). *Psychiatric diagnosis.* Presented at the International Research

Conference on the Mental Health Aspects of Mental Retardation, Evanston, Illinois.

Lund, J. (1985). The prevalence of psychiatric morbidity in mentally retarded adults. *Acta Psychiatr. Scand., 72,* 563–570.

Malamud, N. (1972). Neuropathology of organic brain syndromes associated with aging. In Gaitz, C. M. (ed.), *Aging and the Brain.* New York: Plenum, p. 63.

Mann, D. M. A., Royston, M. C., & Ravindra, C. R. (1990). Some morphometric observations on the brains of patients with Down syndrome: Their relation to age and dementia. *J. Neurol. Sci., 99,* 153–164.

Menolascino, F. J. (1987). *Diagnostic clarity in dual diagnosis.* Presented at the International Research Conference on the Mental Health Aspects of Mental Retardation, Evanston, Illinois.

Mortimer, J. A. (1981). *The epidemiology of dementia.* New York: Oxford University Press.

Muir, W. J., Squire, I., Blackwood, D. H. R., Speight, M. D., St. Clair, D. M., Oliver, C., & Dickens, P. (1988). Auditory P300 response in the assessment of Alzheimer's disease in Down's syndrome: A 2-year follow-up study. *J. Ment. Defic. Res., 32,* 455–463.

Murphy, G. M., Eng, L. G., Ellis, W. G., Perry, G., Meissner, L. C., & Tinklenberg, J. (1990). Antigenic profile of plaques and neurofibrillary tangles in amygdala in Down sydnrome: A comparison with Alzheimer's disease. *Brain Res., 537,* 102–108.

National Institute of Mental Health. (1988). *Special feature: Assessment in diagnosis and treatment of geropsychiatric patients* (Vol. 20, No. 4). Rockville, MD: U.S. Department of Health and Human Services.

Office of Technology Assessment (1987). U.S. Congress. Losing a million minds: Confronting the tragedy of Alzheimer's disease and other dementias. OTA-BA-323. Washington, DC: Supt. of Docs., U.S. Govt. Print. Off.

Pearlson, G. D., Warren, A. C., Starkstein, S. E., Alyward, E. H., Kumar, A. J., Chase, G. A., & folstein. M. F. (1990). Brain atrophy in 18 patients with Down syndrome: A CT study. *Am. J. Neuroradiol., 11,* 811–816.

Plum, F. (1979). Dementia: The approaching epidemic. *Nature, 279,* 372–373.

Popovitch, E. R., Wisniewski, M. M., Barcikowska, M., Silverman, W., Bancher, C., Sersen, E., & Wen, G. Y. (1990). Alzheimer neuropathology in non-Down's syndrome mentally retarded adults. *Acta Neuropathol., 80,* 362–367.

Rabe, A., Wisniewski, K., Schupf, N., & Wisniewski, H. M. (1990). Relationship of Down's syndrome to Alzheimer's disease. In S. I. Deutch, A. Weizman, & R. Weizman (Eds.), *Application of basic neuroscience to child psychiatry* (pp. 325–340). New York: Plenum Press.

Reid, A. H. (1982). The psychiatry of mental handicap. Oxford: Blackwell Scientific.

Reid, A. H. (1987). *Schizophrenia and mental retardation.* Presented at the International Conference on the Mental Health Aspects of Mental Retardation, Evanston, Illinois.

Reid, A. H., & Aungle, P. G. (1974). Dementia in aging mental defectives: A clinical psychiatric study. *J. Ment. Defic., 18,* 15–23.

Schupf, N., Silverman, W. P., Sterling, R. C., & Zigman, W. B. (1989). Down syndrome, terminal illness, and risk for dementia of the Alzheimer type. *Brain Dysfunction, 2,* 181–188.

Small, G. W., & Jarvik, J. F. (1982). The dementia syndrome. *Lancet, 2,* 1443–1445.

Sovner, R., & Hurley, A. D. (1983). Do the mentally retarded suffer from affective illness? *Arch. Gen. Psychiatr., 40,* 61–67.

Struwe, F. (1929). Histopathologische untersuchengen uber eststehung and wesen der senilen paques. *Z. Gesamte Neurol. Psychiatr., 122,* 291.

Szymanski, L. S. (1987). *Psychiatric diagnosis.* Presented at the International Conference on the Mental Health Aspects of Mental Retardation, Evanston, Illinois.

Szymanski, L. S. (1988). Integrative approach to diagnosis of mental disorders in retarded persons. In J. Stark, F. J. Menolascino, et al. (1988), *Mental retardation and mental health: Classification, diagnosis, treatment, services.* Berlin: Springer-Verlag.

Tait, D. (1983). Mortality and dementia among aging defectives. *J. Ment. Defic. Res., 27,* 133–142.

Thase, M. E., Liss, L., Smeltzer, D., & Matson, J. (1982). Clinical evaluation of dementia in Down's syndrome: A preliminary report. *J. Ment. Defic. Res., 26,* 239–244.

Thase, M. E., Tigner, R., Smeltzer, D. J., & Liss, L. (1984). Age-related neuropsychological deficits in Down syndrome. *Biol. Psychiatr., 19,* 571–585.

Tyler, K. L., & Tyler, H. R. (1984). Differentiating organic dementia. *Geriatrics, 39,* 38–52.

Walz, T., Harper, D. C., & Wilson, J. (1986). The aging developmentally disabled person: A review. *Gerontologist, 26,* 622–629.

Wisniewski, H. (1982). Aging and developmental disabilities. *Gerontologist, 22(5),* 250.

Wisniewski, H. M., & Rabe, A. (1986). Discrepancy between Alzheimer-type neuropathology and dementia in persons with Down syndrome. *Ann NY Acad. Sci., 477,* 247–259.

Wisniewski, K., Howe, J., Williams, D., & Wisniewski, H. M. (1978). Precocious aging and dementia in patients with Down's syndrome. *Biol. Psychiatr., 13(5),* 619–627.

Wisniewski, H. M., Rabe, A., & Wisniewski, K. E. (1987). Neuropathology and dementia in people with Down's syndrome. In *Molecular neuropathology of aging* (Bunberg Report 27, pp. 399–408). Cold Spring Harbor, NY: Cold Spring Harbor Laboratory.

Wisniewski, K. E., Wisniewski, H. M., & Wen, G. Y. (1985). Occurrence of neuropathological changes and dementia of Alzheimer's disease in Down syndrome. *Ann. Neurol., 17,* 278–282.

World Health Organization (1991). *International Classification of Diseases,* Ninth Revision (ICD-9). Washington, DC: U.S. Department of Health and Human Services.

Yapa, P., & Roy, A. (1990). Depressive illness and mental handicap: Two case reports. *Ment. Handicap, 18,* 19–21.

Zigman, W. B., Schupf, N., Lubin, R. A., & Silverman, W. P. (1987). Premature regression in adults with Down syndrome. *Am. J. Ment. Defic., 92,* 161–168.

# Part III
# Treatment Approaches

The editors of this book thought that a parallel presentation of the diagnostic and treatment views of the same authors would be the most suitable format for use in practical work.

Most authors favor the multidimensional treatment of a particular disorder. As Gardner and Graeber stress, the multimodal behavioral treatment approach is based on a multidisciplinary biopsychosocial and function-analysis diagnosis; therefore, their behavioristically oriented treatment leans toward the medical, psychiatric, and socioenvironmental modes. Other authors, like Reid and Ruedrich, also accentuate a multidimensional approach.

The psychopharmacological treatment of some disorders receives much attention, not because of the predominantly pharmacological orientation of the authors, but because these disorders, owing to their pathophysiological background, require pharmacological treatment in the first instance. The sort of treatment that comes first depends not on the preference of the therapist, but on the factors causing the disorder. A good illustration of this attitude is Dosen and Petry's chapter on the treatment of depression.

Dana's broad orientation toward treatment is undoubtedly a consequence of a more keen assessment and more differentiated diagnostics. When the causal factors are differentiated, the treatment approach can be more target-directed. The complexity of the disorder calls for combined treatment. However, all the treatment methods that are used in a case should be integrated so that they support and amplify each other. The treatment of personality disorder is an example of such an approach.

The treatment of self-injurious behavior (SIB) presented by Verhoeven, Tuinier, and Sijben is based exclusively on a biological point of view. This approach should be understood as one in a range of treatment possibilities for SIB. In practice, this treatment may be applied in cases in which the diagnostician presumes a biological aberration. The current attitude of scientists in this field is that the use of drugs should be target-directed. At the same time, however, other treatment techniques directed to other important pathogenetic factors may be recommended as well. The approach described by Gardner and Graeber, for example, would combine well with the pharmacological treatment of Verhoeven and colleagues. Other approaches like psychotherapeutic and pedagogical treatment (not described in this book) may also be combined with aforementioned treatment techniques.

# 10

# Treatment of Severe Behavioral Disorders in Persons with Mental Retardation: A Multimodal Behavioral Treatment Model

*William I. Gardner*
*Janice L. Graeber*

A s noted in Chapter 3, hypotheses about contributing factors are used to select the specific procedures that make up a psychosocial treatment program addressing these client-specific influences. An illustration of this process is provided by the adolescent who demonstrates an increased set to aggress following the nonattainment of a valued reward and whose assessment data reveal deficit coping skills under these conditions of provocation. A program designed both to teach alternative means of coping with this failure and to provide the personal motivation to use these skills to replace aggression would be offered. If physical factors or specific psychological-psychiatric disorders are also hypothesized to contribute to the aggressive episodes, an integrated treatment program would be designed to ensure a close interface among the different treatment modalities.

The following provides a more detailed illustration of the translation of assessment information into intervention approaches:

> Jack, a young adult with profound mental retardation and severe physical disabilities, regurgitated his food following every meal. Observation of Jack in his living area indicated that, immediately following each meal, he would sit in the dayroom across from the staff office and would stick his hand into his throat until he regurgitated a small amount of his meal. He would then rub the vomitus on his face and hands and finally wipe it on his clothing. After chewing the remaining vomitus for a few minutes, he would reswallow it. These activities were repeated until staff intervened or until he had vomited four or five times. Eventually, staff would approach Jack, make some comment about his mess, and then take him to his room to clean and change him. At other times, Jack was typically ignored, as he appeared content to sit in his chair and observe staff

and peers. Jack responded positively when he was provided attention by staff or peers but made minimal attempts to initiate or maintain interaction.

These observations suggested an intervention program of consistent structured program experiences immediately following each meal, frequent social attention throughout the waking hours, regular participation in structured programs away from the living area that provided valued sensory and social stimulation and taught Jack alternative means of obtaining valued social feedback.

## Treatment, Management, and Control

Before we discuss intervention, let us make a distinction between procedures designed to produce enduring behavior change and those designed to manage the occurrence, intensity, or duration of specific episodes of aberrant behaviors. Let us also make a distinction between these treatment and management procedures and those used to control specific episodes.

### Psychosocial Treatment

*Psychosocial treatment* refers to the use of procedures designed to reduce the frequency, duration, and/or intensity of excessive behaviors (such as physical aggression, property destruction, and taunting peers), and to increase the strength of positive alternative skills (such as interacting with peers in a socially appropriate manner or expressing anger through appropriate verbal means). The major objective of the treatment is producing *enduring* behavior change that will persist across time and situations. The treatment program is designed to change the person's responsiveness to the external and internal conditions that instigate aberrant symptoms, and to teach new, socially appropriate emotional and behavioral skills that will replace these (Gardner & Cole, 1987).

The specific treatment procedures selected should have both conceptual and, whenever available, empirical support for enduring behavior change. As an example, a young man with moderate mental retardation who engages in frequent aggressive and related agitated and disruptive outbursts may be provided a skills training program designed to teach him to cope with peer conflict (Cole, Gardner, & Karen, 1985). As a second example, persons with severe developmental disabilities may be taught communication skills as replacements for tantrum, self-abusive, and aggressive behaviors for use in instructional demand situations (Bird et al., 1989; Carr & Durand, 1985; Durand, 1990).

*Behavior Management*

*Behavior management* refers to those procedures that (1) eliminate or minimize specific stimulus conditions likely to instigate problem behaviors; (2) present or emphasize specific stimulus conditions that increase the likelihood of competing prosocial behaviors; (3) present or emphasize specific stimulus conditions that inhibit the occurrence of aberrant behaviors; and (4) minimize the duration and intensity of these behaviors following their initiation. The initial three procedures are *proactive* in nature, as they involve changing the antecedents that precede problem behavior and are designed to encourage the alternative prosocial actions currently available in the person's repertoire.

The fourth behavior management procedure is *reactive* in nature, as it is initiated following the occurrence of aberrant responding. Even though reactive, this management procedure may prove quite valuable in minimizing the effects of any specific act. These management procedures as a group support active treatment efforts but differ critically in function and effect, as they do not by themselves produce durable changes in behavior strength.

**Proactive Management Procedures.** In the first proactive approach, management procedures are initiated that serve to *remove* or *minimize* the effects of specific preceding conditions that instigate problem behaviors (such as reassigning a staff member who consistently provokes a particular trainee) (Gardner et al., 1986).

In the second proactive behavior-management approach, stimulus conditions are presented that increase the likelihood of competing prosocial adaptive, instead of aberrant, behaviors. As an example, Carr, Newsom, and Binkoff (1980) demonstrated that providing strongly preferred reinforcers for correct responding under aversive demand conditions resulted in an increase in prosocial behavior and a concomitant abrupt decrease to a low level in the previously observed high-rate aberrant behaviors. The reinforcers served as discriminative events for prosocial behaviors that successfully competed with the aberrant responses.

In the third proactive behavior-management procedure, inappropriate behaviors are inhibited by the presentation of stimulus conditions that signal the potential occurrence of aversive consequences contingent on an aberrant act. In illustration, a reminder that the occurrence of a specific aggressive behavior will result in the loss of valued privileges may serve to inhibit the occurrence of the aberrant behavior.

**Reactive Behavior Management.** The final behavior management procedure is reactive and is used after aberrant behavior has begun. This procedure is designed to terminate or decrease the duration and/or intensity of this current episode. Such specific approaches as redirection, removing the instigating conditions, ignoring the behavior when acknowledging it would serve to intensify it, and removing the person from the source of instigation (for example, removing the person to a quiet area away from the provoking, noisy environment) illustrate the types of reactive tactics that may serve this management function.

As indicated, the objective of use of management procedures is *not* the teaching of alternative competency skills or of producing durable behavior change across time and changing conditions. As an example, a diagnostic assessment of agitated and disruptive behaviors in children with severe developmental delays may reveal an increased likelihood of disruptive outbursts under conditions of specific task demands or under conditions of reduced social attention (Carr & Durand, 1985). With this diagnostic information, one may reduce or even eliminate the occurrence of disruptive behaviors by removing these controlling conditions, that is, by never presenting task demands and/or by continually providing a rich schedule of social attention. Under these conditions of managing the specific stimulus conditions that instigate the disruption, the inappropriate behavior may not occur. However, whenever the controlling stimulus events of task demands and reduced social attention are reintroduced, the problem behavior reappears. The strength of agitated and disruptive behaviors in the presence of these controlling conditions has not been altered by the use of the management procedures. Durable changes can be enhanced when active treatment procedures are included that teach alternative responses to these controlling events.

As a second example, assessment may reveal that a person's episodes of agitation and self-injury can be minimized in intensity and duration if, immediately following the initial signs of agitation, the person is redirected into alternative activities. The strength of these problem behaviors is not altered by this management procedure; rather, its disruptive features are minimized. With consistent use of this management procedure, the person more quickly becomes available to participate in whatever treatment experiences are provided. From a treatment perspective, this management program would be improved considerably by addition of procedures that, for example, would teach the person (1) to recognize his own early signs of agitation and then (2) to self-initiate alternative activities that will reduce or remove his agitation and the consequent self-injury.

## Medical Management

As an example of medical management, psychopharmacological intervention, including lithium or carbamazepine, may reduce aggression and self-injury in a person with profound mental retardation and irritability or generalized restlessness by raising the person's threshold to aggressive responding (Sovner & Hurley, 1984). On termination of the drug regimen, however, the person's aggressive and self-injurious acts may return to the preintervention level. The drug regimen thus serves to reduce the aggression and self-injury by managing a component of the stimulus complex involved in instigation. However, as the person's anxiety or irritability level is not reduced in an enduring manner, the person's inclination toward aggression or other aberrant behaviors in the absence of the medication is not reduced. Combining the drug intervention with a psychological treatment program designed to teach the client to cope both with the factors producing the anxiety and with the specific factors instigating the aggression and self-injury offers better promise of an enduring treatment effect following withdrawal of the medication.

## Behavior Control

*Behavior control* refers to the use of procedures in a behavioral crisis to deal with out-of-control behaviors that pose a potential danger to the person and/or to others in the environment. These control procedures include the use of various *physical restraints* (such as isolating the person in a locked space, physically holding the person, and using mechanical devices such as leather belts or cuffs) and *chemical restraints* (such as the use of neuroleptic medication to physiologically immobilize the person). These procedures are used in emergency situations for the sole purpose of immobilizing the individual for the duration of a current crisis and are used only after other *treatment* and *management* procedures have failed. The purpose is neither to produce durable behavior change nor to reduce the likelihood that a current behavior episode will escalate to out-of-control status (that is, to serve as a management procedure). Rather, behavior control procedures are used to protect the person who is out of control by restraining his or her actions to minimize the possibility of injury to self or others.

It is, of course, possible that some behavior control procedures for some individuals (such as placing an out-of-control person in a locked isolation room or physically restraining a person's movement until control is regained) may have a treatment effect (that is, a reinforcing or punishing effect) of increasing, or reducing, the future probability of the out-of-control behavior. However, a particular control procedure used with a specific person is neither selected nor used to produce this effect.

## Interrelations of Procedures

Intervention programs for aberrant behaviors should have the dual objectives of teaching and/or strengthening the discriminated occurrence of personally satisfying and socially appropriate adaptive behaviors and of reducing or eliminating excessively occurring aberrant behaviors. To accomplish these objectives, active treatment programs most frequently include, in addition to therapeutic procedures designed to produce durable changes, (1) those supportive behavior-management procedures designed to facilitate the occurrence of problem behavior and to minimize the occurrence of problem behavior and, (2) when needed for those persons inclined to demonstrate out-of-control behaviors, behavior control components. With effective treatment procedures, however, these supportive management and control components are faded as treatment goals are accomplished and as the person is able to adapt appropriately under the normal or usual conditions of his or her everyday living environment.

## Purpose and Focus of Treatment

The primary purpose of a psychosocial intervention program, as noted, is to teach appropriate coping skills that will replace recurring problem reactions and not merely to reduce or eliminate excessively occurring problem behaviors such as aggression or self-injury or emotional expressions such as anxiety or depression. In most instances, a cluster of problems is seldom symptomatic of some single, specific biological or psychological pathology that then becomes the sole focus of treatment. Rather, the complex of problem behavioral and/or emotional reactions represents the focus of intervention, and, as noted, a variety of potentially contributing physical, psychological, and socioenvironmental influences are assessed to provide a basis for identifying the areas of needed intervention.

From a biopsychosocial perspective, the intervention focus may be on changing (1) *biological* factors, such as those contributing to pain, overarousal, or emotional liability; (2) the *person's* psychological status, through teaching skills that can be used to cope with changing conditions across different environments; (3) the *environment,* to remove physical and psychosocial conditions that are not conducive to promoting positive mental health and to replace these with conditions that consistently encourage more appropriate adaptive skills; and (4) the *interactions* between the person and his or her physical and social environments.

When aberrant behaviors are symptomatic of various physical, neurological, or biochemically based mental disorders, these become a focus of treatment. In the majority of cases, especially among those people who are more severely handicapped, recurring behavioral symptoms are independent of identifiable physical and psychiatric disorders and typically are not drug-responsive (Reid, Ballinger, & Heather, 1978; Gualtiere, Matson, & Keppel, 1989; Thompson, 1988). Psychosocial treatment thus becomes the focus. In fact, even in those instances in which a drug-responsive mental disorder is present, additional interventions of a psychosocial nature are required to decrease the person's vulnerability to the recurrence of the mental disorder or to provide means of better coping with pathological physical, psychological, and/or environmental conditions.

*Staging of Treatment Focus*

As the factors influencing problem behaviors and emotions vary in their relative potency, as well as in the ease or difficulty with which change in these factors may be accomplished, intervention must occur in stages. Thus, the primary focus of interventions at any given time varies, depending on the nature of the factors presumed to contribute to the person's difficulties. This staging of intervention primacy is depicted in Figure 1.

> If Harry, an adult with profound mental retardation, has increased self-injurious episodes that are presumed to be influenced by an acute ear infection, the initial primary intervention may focus on reducing or removing the abnormal physical conditions (Time 1 in Figure 1). After this is accomplished, the primary treatment may shift to teaching Harry to communicate his physical discomfort in ways other than face slapping and head banging (Time 2 in Figure 1). After the teaching of this alternative mode of communication, the primary intervention focus may move to the social environment to ensure that Harry is prompted to use and is reinforced for using his newly acquired communication skills (Time 3 in Figure 1).

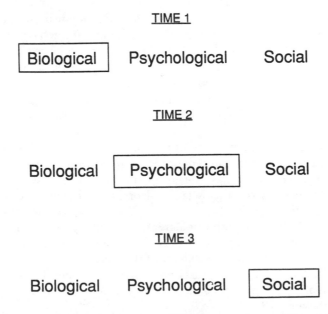

**Figure 1. Depicting the Staging of Treatment Across Time Periods**

*Treatment Focus: Biological*

A variety of biological conditions—some temporary, such as a person's menses, and others more enduring, such as neurological damage—may represent a focus of treatment. In most instances, these biological factors produce abnormal internal states that increase the likelihood of inappropriate behavior, cognitions, and emotions. Various writers have suggested that neurological damage may contribute to such personal features as levels of activity, elevated mood, emotional lability, distractibility, and general irritability (Kastner et al., 1990). These emotional and activity-level difficulties may in turn increase the likelihood of problem behaviors. These conditions may also interfere with the person's learning and using adaptive skills. Thus, biological intervention is designed to reduce or remove such abnormal conditions as a biochemical imbalance, infections, organic overarousal, or constipation, which may contribute to the person's psychosocial difficulties.

As an illustration, an adult with a moderate level of mental retardation who, under stress conditions, displays physical aggression and other impulse control difficulties may be provided drug therapy, under the assumption that the problems are symptoms of organic impairment and overarousal or perhaps an underlying major mental disorder such as schizophrenia or depression (Lowry & Sovner, 1991). Medication is provided as a treatment for these internal, biologically based abnormalities, which are assumed to contribute to the overt behavior problems. To elaborate, the thought and perceptual difficulties of persons with a schizophrenic disorder may impair their judgment about the consequences of their aberrant behaviors. This impairment, in combination with emotional lability and impaired impulse control, may result in severe aggressive and self-injurious behaviors when the person is confronted with provocative external conditions. Drug treatment is directed at the presumed underlying biochemical abnormalities (Sovner & Hurley, 1984). The biological model of mental disorders is depicted in Figure 2.

As noted earlier, examples of other medical conditions that may influence behavioral and emotional symptoms are provided by persons with temporal lobe epilepsy, who may engage in episodes of assaultive behaviors, and by individuals with other seizure disorders or hyperthyroidism, who may present with generalized irritability (Gedye, 1989; Kastner et al., 1990). This organically based irritability increases the susceptibility of the person to responding inappropriately to external sources of provocation or stress. The medical treatment or management of these and other mental and physical disorders, such as mania, agitated depression, generalized anxiety, or akathisia, may result in a concomitant decrease in the behavioral symptoms (Lowry & Sovner, 1991).

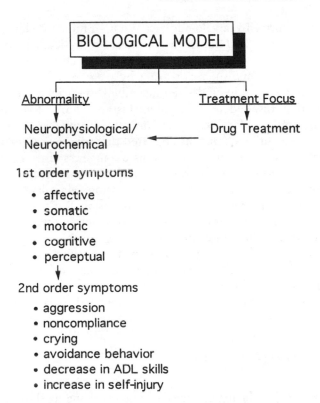

Figure 2. Depicting the Treatment Focus of the Biological Model

*Treatment Focus: Psychological*

When the primary focus of intervention is on changing psychological features of the person, the therapeutic program should be designed to teach socially appropriate behaviors as replacements for inappropriate ones or to influence the person's motivational and cognitive states to ensure the selection of coping skills currently in his or her repertoire. In this endeavor, interventions would be designed to change specific behaviors as well as related cognitions and emotions. If an adolescent with severe mental retardation is displaying excessive temper tantrums in his home, he is taught not merely to "control his temper," but also to identify and express his emotions in a more acceptable manner. If a child is physically aggressive when she becomes "jealous" of the attention provided her peers and as a result has been isolated by her peers, the child is taught appropriate means of actively relating to her feelings and her peers in a more socially appropriate and personally enhancing manner.

Mary, a thirteen-year-old adolescent with a moderate level of mental retardation, had numerous episodes of physical and verbal aggression in her school program and at home. During assessment, a number of events, such as teasing by peers, teacher instructions, and delay in obtaining desired incentives, were identified as situations that resulted in a heightened state of negative emotional arousal. When Mary was upset, any minor provocation resulted in aggressive outbursts. It thus appeared that a variety of experiences produced such emotional reactions as anger, sadness, loneliness, disappointment, or embarrassment. These emotions, in turn, contributed to a common reaction of aggression. Mary had not learned to respond differently to different emotions. Rather, any state of negative emotional arousal was likely to result in the single reaction of aggression. Instead of the use of a treatment approach designed merely to suppress her aggression, the therapeutic program was designed to teach Mary to (1) recognize the label different emotions; (2) relate these different emotions to the different precipitating conditions; and (3) use a variety of self-managed socially appropriate behaviors to replace the generalized aggressive reaction.

## Treatment Focus: Environment

In other instances, the major focus may be on changing those aspects of the environment that may be influencing the problem behaviors. An environment that is devoid of interesting materials, that is excessively crowded and does not permit privacy, or in which negative feedback is the predominant mode of managing a group of adolescents may result in excessive behavior problems. Providing a more stimulating and positive physical and psychosocial environment may result in the reduction or elimination of problems.

## Treatment Focus: Interactions

The focus of interventions may also address the nature of the interactions between the person and his or her social environment. Teaching house parents and other staff to listen to clients and at the same time teaching clients to cooperate with reasonable requests may both be necessary to reduce the frequency of negativism and related agitated and disruptive outbursts in a group home for persons with severe mental retardation and challenging behaviors.

## Summary

The behavioral approach based on a biopsychosocial model treats problem behaviors and emotions directly and attempts to change those current physical, psychological, and environmental factors assumed to contribute to the person's difficulties. As noted, any consistently occurring behavioral characteristics of a person, appropriate or inappropriate, represent the end results of a history of experiences and a current set of environmental conditions, as these have and do interact with specific physical and psychological characteristics of the person.

## Functional Interrelationships of Problems

The behavioral approach recognizes the interrelationships of various patterns or clusters of behavioral and emotional difficulties. Some problem behaviors and emotions may have a functional relationship to other problem clusters and thus, by their presence, may influence the likelihood of the occurrence of these other problem behaviors. To illustrate:

> An adolescent with mild mental retardation may become highly emotional and disruptive in a range of situations in which she does not "have her way." These reactions may effectively block the occurrence of the more appropriate prosocial behaviors available in her repertoire. These disruptive outbursts also may interfere with participation in various prosocial experiences with peers, and this interference may, in turn, impede the learning of more complex and appropriate modes of behavior. The intervention program in this instance would focus on reducing the disruptive emotional outbursts and on teaching alternative coping skills involving appropriate emotional expression and social interaction.

## Clinical Applications

The following sections provide illustrations of the range of behavioral interventions used successfully with a range of behavior problems. Consistent with the individualized diagnostic perspective described, the selection of any one or a combination of these behavioral intervention procedures is based on the functional hypotheses deemed most pertinent for an individual client. As the level of health risk associated with such problems as self-injury, pica, or aggression varies from client to client, the selection of intervention approaches is influenced somewhat by the severity and specificity of the aberrant and related collateral behaviors. Suppressive procedures may be selected to inhibit health-threatening actions and may be combined with positive procedures to ensure the development and maintenance of alternative skills for gaining valued sensory and social stimulation and for coping with various aversive conditions.

*Treatment: Aggression*

**Reinforcement-Motivated Aggression.** *Extinction and Reinforcement.* After demonstrating in an individualized diagnostic behavioral assessment that aggression in a fifteen-year-old developmentally disabled male increased under a social disapproval contingency, Mace et al. (1986) selected a treatment program consisenting of differential reinforcement and extinction procedures. During treatment, social attention in the form of conversation was provided on a variable schedule contingent on the absence of aggression. Incidents of aggression were ignored. This treatment resulted in levels of aggression that were approximately one-third those observed when aggression was followed by social disapproval.

*Differential Reinforcement.* Luiselli and Slocumb (1983) demonstrated the successful use of a differential reinforcement procedure in reducing the aggressive behaviors of a nine-year-old girl with severe mental retardation and a diagnosis of autism. Her behaviors consisted of hitting, kicking, hair pulling, spitting, and tantrumming; were directed at peers and instructional staff; and occurred in the absence of any clearly discernible antecedent events. During treatment, reinforcement was provided following a seven-minute period of no aggression. This interval was gradually increased. The target behaviors decreased to 1 per day from a preintervention rate of 17.8 per day.

*Combined Reinforcement and Punishment.* Friman et al. (1986) successfully treated the aggressive pinching of a ten-year-old girl with severe mental retardation and a deteriorating neurological condition. The child could not self-feed and had no speech. At program initiation, both the mother's and the teachers' arms had scratch marks, scabs, and bruises resulting from the child's pinching. A differential reinforcement procedure was combined with a response prevention procedure of holding the child's hands for two minutes following attempts at pinching. This program, used in home and at school, produced a rapid reduction in pinching in both settings. Similar results were reported by Luiselli and Greenidge (1982) and St. Lawrence and Drabman (1984). In both studies of multi-handicapped children presenting persistent conduct difficulties, reinforcement-based interventions were effective in eliminating problem behaviors when used in combination with punishment procedures of time-out or facial screening.

**Escape-Motivated Aggression** *Teaching Communicative Skills.* Carr and Durand (1985) illustrated this treatment approach in a series of studies demonstrating the teaching of alternative communicative skills to children with developmental disabilities who engaged in aggressive and related disruptive behaviors under aversive conditions. These newly acquired communicative behaviors served a functionally equivalent role for the children, thus reducing the necessity of the aggressive responding. Using a similar paradigm, Bird et al. (1989) reported the successful use of communication training to teach alternatives to aggression in an adult with autism and profound mental retardation. Assessment suggested that the aggression was motivated by escape from demands and a desire to obtain preferred tangible rewards. Following teaching the client to communicate these needs, the aggression was reduced.

## Treatment: Pica

**Environmental Enrichment: Providing Alternative Activities.** Based on the supposition that pica in some individuals may serve the purpose of providing gustatory sensory stimulation, Favell, McGimsey, and Schnell (1982) demonstrated a substantial reduction in pica in three persons with profound developmental disabilities by providing large rubber toys (balls, squeak toys, and rubber rings) on which they could chew. Two of the clients, both aged nineteen, were confined to wheelchairs and constantly chewed on and ingested their clothing and bed linen. The third client, aged sixteen, scooted along the floor in a seated position and constantly picked up and ingested small objects such as paper and pieces of toys from floors, bulletin boards, and table surfaces. When provided an alternative means of obtaining oral self-stimulation, all three clients replaced the pica with toy chewing. Also, when they were provided popcorn, this form of oral activity was preferred over toy chewing and pica. Finally, the therapists demonstrated that appropriate toy usage would occur in these clients when this activity was reinforced with popcorn.

**Environmental Enrichment: Providing Noncontingent Social Stimulation.** Mace and Knight (1986) demonstrated that an increase in staff-provided noncontingent social interaction (talking to and/or touching) with a nineteen-year-old male who was nonverbal and profoundly mentally retarded, with moderate, spastic quadriplegia, resulted in a significant reduction in pica. Pica was the man's dominant behavior during periods of minimal staff supervision. Additionally, combining this increased schedule of social interaction with the removal of a protective helmet with a face shield, which was worn to discourage pica, resulted in even lower levels of pica.

**Extinction** Frieden and Johnson (1979) reported the successful treatment of feces smearing and coprophagy in a boy with profound mental retardation by removing the positive social and sensory feedback that had previously occurred during showering and cleanup.

**Differential Reinforcement.** Smith (1987) successfully reduced pica in a twenty-three-year-old nonverbal male with profound mental retardation and autism. The client, who was living in a community-based group home and who was provided supported employment in the stockroom of a local department store, exhibited a high frequency of pica, consisting of the ingestion of paper clips, bottle caps, paper, and other nonfood items. Previous pica incidents had resulted in hospitalization.

The treatment consisted of reinforcement with food, drink, and activity reinforcers on an average of every fifteen minutes for such incompatible behaviors as keeping his hands on his work, remaining in his work area and working, and keeping his mouth clear. Additionally, verbal praise was provided approximately every fifteen minutes for the same behaviors. Redirection or removal of pica items was followed to prevent or manage pica attempts. Prior to treatment with these differential reinforcement procedures, his pica behaviors averaged twenty-one episodes per day. During the initial treatment of approximately one month, pica was reduced to an average of approximately six incidents daily. At one-year follow-up, pica averaged less than one incident per day. Because of staff reluctance to terminate it, the treatment program had continued throughout the interim period.

**Differential Reinforcement and Time-Out.** Ausman, Ball, and Alexander (1974) used a time-out procedure combined with consistent tangible and social reinforcement for periods of no-pica behavior to treat the life-threatening pica behavior of a fourteen-year-old male with severe mental retardation. The pica involved the ingestion of such objects as string, candy wrappers, and syringe needle covers. The procedure involved the removal of the inedible object, informing the client, "Don't eat that, Mike," and then placing a time-out helmet over the boy's head for fifteen minutes following each occurrence of pica. In addition, food was provided initially following five minutes of nonpica behavior and then gradually following longer periods of time in which pica behavior had not occurred. Twenty-four-hour observation and treatment were required to accomplish generalized pica reduction across settings in his residential placement.

**Differential Reinforcement and Overcorrection.** Kalfus et al. (1988) reported success with the use of a DRO procedure combined with overcorrection in the treatment of a four-year-old nonverbal boy with moderate mental retardation. The treatment occurred at home and in a special-education classroom. The boy tended to put all objects in his mouth upon contact and was likely to ingest small items. When he put an object in his mouth, the treatment agent (that is, his mother or the classroom staff) would (1) loudly and firmly present the reprimand "no"; (2) remove the object from the boy's lips or mouth; and (3) wash the boy's lips and mouth area with a damp cool washcloth for fifteen seconds. Eye contact was avoided. In addition, physical affection and verbal praise were provided every fifteen seconds for behavior other than pica. His mother provided food reinforcers in the home. The procedure was later modified so that the overcorrection procedure was replaced with a brief fifteen-second time-out consisting of removal of attention and all toys and objects contingent on mouthing or pica. The treatment effects had been maintained at follow-up approximately forty-nine weeks after the treatment had been begun.

**Visual Screening.** Singh and Winton (1984) used a visual screening procedure to eliminate pica in a twenty-four-year-old woman with profound retardation. On her ingestion of such substances as cigarette butts, string, or soil, staff instructed and physically assisted the client to remove the inedible object from her mouth and then covered her eyes with a blindfold for one minute. Removal of the blindfold was contingent on a one-minute period of nondisruptive behavior. Rapid suppression was noted following the initiation of the procedure in three different settings. It was also noted that her picking up and handling of inedible objects were markedly reduced even though never explicitly treated. Maintenance of suppression at near-zero levels was noted at six-month follow-up.

**Overcorrection.** Foxx and Martin (1975) and Mulick et al. (1980) demonstrated the use of various overcorrection procedures in successfully treating pica and coprophagy in persons with profound mental retardation. Following each occurrence of pica or coprophagy, Foxx and Martin used an overcorrection program consisting of oral hygiene, personal hygiene, and restitutional procedures, combined with positive practice and graduated guidance. Briefly, following ingestion or attempts to ingest such substances as feces, cigarette butts, paper clips, rocks, coins, or screws, the client was (1) instructed to spit out and throw away the inedible objects; (2) provided five minutes of graduated manual guidance of mouth and teeth cleansing; (3) required to spend the next five minutes in cleaning up all debris from the floor; and finally, (4) was guided in five minutes of handwashing with soap and water.

It was reported that (1) pica behavior was reduced by 90 percent within four days of treatment and remained at near-zero levels throughout the intervention periods; (2) overcorrection was more effective than a physical restraint procedure; (3) long-standing *Trichuris trichuria* was eliminated in the three clients who had demonstrated coprophagy; (4) the treatment effects were situation-specific and required the extension of treatment to other settings in which the clients functioned; and (5) the positive side effects included increased awareness of and responsiveness to the environment, the learning of new skills from the hygienic program, and increased appetites, resulting in a thirty-pound weight gain for an individual who had previously been described as "gaunt and emaciated."

Mulick et al. (1980), using similar overcorrection procedures, demonstrated generalization effects across settings and trainers. However, the effectiveness of overcorrection was greater in a dayroom environment, where reinforcing alternative social activities were more available, than in a less socially stimulating classroom environment.

**Physical Restraint and Verbal Reprimand.** Bucher, Reykdal, and Albin (1976) used a thirty-second physical restraint and a verbal reprimand to reduce the pica and coprophagy behaviors of two children with profound retardation. Following the ingestion of grass, stones, dirt, or food off the floor, staff shouted, "No!" and restrained the child's arms beside or behind him for thirty seconds. An extension of the treatment across physical and social settings was necessary to ensure generalization. Elimination of pica in one of the children was accomplished only after the punishment contingency was applied at the earliest detectable response (that is, picking up food debris) in the chain of behaviors resulting in the pica response.

In a similar demonstration, Winton and Singh (1983) found a ten-second physical restraint in the absence of a verbal reprimand sufficient to control pica. Release from the restraint was contingent on a ten-second period of nondisruptive behavior.

**Water Mist and Aromatic Ammonia.** Rojahn et al. (1987) compared the relative effects of contingent aromatic ammonia and water mist procedures on the pica behavior of a sixteen-year-old adolescent with autism and severe retardation. The pica included ingesting tacks, staples, crayons, strings, woven materials, paper, and cigarette butts. The initial treatment occurred in an inpatient psychiatric facility, and follow-up was provided both in the adolescent's classroom and at her group home. Attempts to ingest a nonnutritive item resulted either in a crushed ammonia capsule's being held directly under the adolescent's nose for three seconds or a mist of water sprayed in a her face. The water mist procedure proved to be the most effective, producing a rapid reduction in the pica behavior. Three months of daily follow-up sessions in the client's natural environment revealed almost complete suppression of pica.

*Treatment: Psychogenic Vomiting*

**Structuring Antecedent Stimulus Events** *Food Satiation.* Based on the hypothesis that ruminative vomiting in two men with profound mental retardation was being maintained by the reinforcing qualities of reconsumption of the vomitus because of a state of food deprivation, Jackson et al. (1975) provided the adults with double portions of their meals, including milk shakes, cereal, and ice cream, as well as a milk shake between meals, to maintain the effect of satiation throughout the day. A 94 percent reduction in the frequency of rumination was obtained in one adult and a 50 percent improvement in the other.

Success with this procedure of food satiation was also reported by Clauser and Scibak (1990) in their treatment of three males with profound mental retardation, by Libby and Phillips (1979) in their treatment of a seventeen-year-old adolescent, and by Rast et al. (1981) in their treatment of adults with severe and profound mental retardation. Each treatment ensured satiation by providing unlimited quantities of such high-caloric carbohydrates as Cream of Wheat, bread, and potatoes. Rast et al. (1981) reported success in reducing the frequency and duration of rumination as well as significant weight gains (thirty to forty pounds) in previously underweight adults.

Lobato, Carlson, and Barrera (1986) provided a possible solution to this problem by offering adults with severe and profound mental retardation unlimited quantities of low-calorie foods and liquids following the completion of their standard diets of sixteen hundred to eighteen hundred calories. Foods and liquids, including such items as fresh vegetables, fresh fruits, low-sugar canned fruits, diluted fruit juices, diet soda, and D-Zerta gelatins and puddings, were available until ten minutes had elapsed during which the food was not approached. Additionally, each person was offered unlimited quantities of the satiation foods at hourly intervals between meals. Significant reductions in ruminative vomiting were obtained, while body weight remained in the middle of the ideal weight ranges.

A second procedure for controlling for the possibility of excessive weight gain following the initiation of a food satiation procedure was reported by Yang (1988). Chronic and health-threatening rumination was terminated in a seventeen-year-old male with profound mental retardation following the initiation of a procedure of providing up to twenty slices of bread daily following the completion of his regular meals. After a rapid reduction in rumination and desirable weight gains had been attained, the extra food was gradually faded over a seven-week period. Results had been maintained at twelve-week follow-up. It was reported that the adolescent, after eating his entire meals plus the twenty slices of bread during the first few meals, quickly reduced his amount of food intake without intervention. Using satiation and fading procedures with persons with profound mental retardation, Clauser and Scibak (1990) reported similar results. Of interest also was the finding that other self-stimulatory behaviors decreased with the reduction in rumination.

This food satiation and fading procedure was offered as a desirable treatment alternative for the elimination of chronic rumination as it (1) involves no potential side effects; (2) can be implemented without unusual demands on staff time or coverage; (3) requires minimal expertise in behavior technology; (4) produces results in a short period of time; (5) produces rapid body weight gains that offset the nutritional risks resulting from chronic rumination; (6) does not interfere with routine habilitation training programs;

and (7) meets the least-restrictive-alternative criterion of legal and ethical mandates.

*Food Satiation and Overcorrection.* Foxx, Snyder, and Schroeder (1979), successfully used food satiation in combination with an oral hygiene over-correction procedure.

*Food Satiation and Time-Out.* The chronic rumination of a male with pro-found mental retardation was treated successfully by the use of a combined procedure of food satiation and time-out from tactile stimulation provided by the therapist. The combination of the procedures was more effective than either used in isolation (Borreson & Anderson, 1982).

*Multicomponent Program.* As a final example of structuring antecedent stimulus events, the chronic vomiting of a twenty-seven-year-old individual with profound mental retardation was eliminated by a multicomponent pro-gram that included satiation (Pickup & Arsenault, 1976). The client was taught to feed himself slowly with a small spoon, using only one hand. If he stole food, used the wrong hand, or did not slow down, a one-minute time-out was instituted. He was allowed to eat all he wanted in the early treat-ment sessions and was later faded to five servings per meal. Following completion of the meal, he was taken for a one-hour walk based on the as-sumption that his living area served as a discriminative cue for vomiting. After the vomiting was reduced, the man was transferred to another living area that provided more regular activities. The walks and food intake were faded over the following six months. The therapists attributed the success of the program to the increased gustatory stimulation and satiation during meals, the increased stimulation associated with the walks, and improved digestion related to the slower eating.

*Type of Program Experiences.* Humphrey et al. (1989) reported that the ru-minative vomiting of a twelve-year-old boy with cerebral palsy and pro-found mental retardation was lower during school hours than during nonschool hours, greatest on weekends and lowest on school days, lower during classroom activities in which individual attention was provided, higher during independent play with toys, and lowest when one-to-one in-struction was provided. Finally, rumination was lower when interactions were provided by staff who liked the boy than when provided by those who expressed less fondness of him. The program implications of these findings are obvious.

*Premeal Chewing.* Rast et al. (1988) demonstrated a modest reduction in rumination in three female adults with profound mental retardation by pro-viding varying amounts of premeal chewing of sugarless gum. These findings lend support to the relationship between oral stimulation and satiation. These writers suggested a variety of ways to increase oral stimulation, including the teaching of slower eating and more chews per bite of food, providing food of normal consistency as a replacement for diced or pureed food, eating meals with a small spoon, and providing after-meal sugarless chewing gum or suckers.

*Role of Stomach Distension, Caloric Intake, and Satiation.* Rast et al. (1985) evaluated the relative effects of stomach distension (provided by adding wheat bran to the diet), number of calories ingested, and a starch-satiation diet on ruminative behaviors in four adults with profound mental retardation. Although each method produced some effects, the large and immediate effects of a starch-satiation procedure (described above under "Food Satiation") were not obtained.

**Reinforcement of Alternative Behaviors.** Barmann (1980) successfully eliminated life-threatening ruminative vomiting in a six-year-old boy with profound mental retardation and no functional vision through a procedure of providing positive reinforcement for periods of time in which hand mouthing, a prevomiting response, did not occur. Vibratory stimulation, an experience that the child enjoyed, was provided during therapy sessions for having "dry hands." The treatment gains generalized to nontreatment settings and were maintained over a one-year follow-up period.

**Withholding or Removing Reinforcement.** *Extinction and Positive Reinforcement.* Wolf et al. (1970) provided one of the initial examples of the successful use of behavior therapy with a clinical problem presented by a nine-year-old child who was nonverbal and had been diagnosed as "suffering from mental retardation, cerebral palsy, aphasia, hyperirritability, and brain damage." Within three months of her being enrolled in a school program, her vomiting had become almost an everyday occurrence. Drug therapy had no effect on the problem. Further, the medical staff did not view the vomiting as being due to physical factors.

Noting that the child frequently was returned to her living area following a vomiting episode in the classroom, the therapists hypothesized that these consequences were reinforcing and thus maintaining the vomiting behavior. The behavior therapy program consisted of keeping the child in the classroom for the scheduled period regardless of her vomiting. The extinction procedure removed the possible sources of positive and/or negative reinforcement that the vomiting had previously produced. Additionally, the teacher provided the child with tangible and social reinforcers following a variety of appropriate classroom behaviors. The vomiting behavior was eliminated within a month. The other behaviors that occurred with virtually every vomiting episode—screaming, clothes tearing, and destruction of property—also disappeared. The therapists noted that productive class-room behavior and responsiveness to teacher requests improved markedly. These rather severe "emotional" problems were dealt with by developing hunches about the environmental factors contributing to the problems and by restructuring the child's experiences in the natural settings in which the problems were occurring.

*Time-Out from Positive Reinforcement.* Davis, Wiesler, and Hanzel (1980) eliminated rumination in a twenty-six-year-old male with profound mental retardation through the contingent removal of music. Music was played continuously throughout treatment. Rumination resulted in a loud sharp "No" from the therapist and the absence of the music for short periods of time. In this manner, a long-standing pattern of ruminatory behavior was controlled.

**Presentation of Aversive Consequences.** *Overcorrection.* Azrin and Wesolowski (1975) and Duker and Seys (1977) demonstrated the usefulness of behavioral programs using positive practice, self-correction, and restitutional overcorrection combined with a procedure of differentially re-inforcing appropriate behavior to eliminate vomiting in adults with profound mental retardation. As an illustration, in the Duker and Seys report, the person was shown, with verbal disapproval and physical guidance, the results of the vomiting (dirty bib, vomit on the floor, and soiled clothes). During the next twenty minutes, the person was required to wash her face with cold water, to clean the vomit from the floor, and then, in addition, to clean part of the floor, the window sill, and the walls not soiled by the vomit. Following this restitution, she was then required to remove her soiled clothing and to redress in clean clothes. During this process, instructions were provided in a neutral manner. At other frequent times, the person was reinforced with attention and physical contact.

*Aversive Electrical Stimulation.* Luckey, Watson, and Musik (1968) and Kohlenberg (1970) used a punishment procedure involving aversive electrical stimulation to reduce signifiantly the persistent vomiting of clients with severe mental retardation. Luckey et al. (1968) successfully eliminated the life-threatening ruminative behavior of a six-year-old by providing electrical stimulation immediately following the observation of vomiting and ruminating behavior. A marked reduction in these behaviors was evident by the fifth day of treatment. A general improvement in overall behavior was also noted. In treating a woman with severe mental retardation whose progressive weight loss due to vomiting after every meal had become a serious medical problem, Kohlenberg (1970) reasoned that the vomiting behavior was the last response in a chain of behaviors. Contingent aversive electrical stimulation was provided following the occurrence of stomach tensions, a prevomiting response that consisted of an overt abdominal movement. A rapid reduction in vomiting was obtained, with a resulting weight gain. Similar results were reported by Gilbraith, Byrick, and Rutledge (1970) and Bright and Whaley (1968).

*Lemon Juice Therapy.* Becker, Turner, and Sajwaj (1978) reported the successful reduction of chronic and high-rate rumination in a thirty-six-month-old child with profound mental retardation following the initiation of a procedure that involved the injection of lemon juice into the child's mouth contingent on rumination. Also noted following the reduction in the rumination was an increase in the child's social behaviors and language, along with a greater interest in manipulating objects.

## Treatment: Sterotyped Behavior

**Increasing General Stimulation.** Under the assumption that stereotyped behaviors in some individuals result from conditions of low stimulation, Repp, Felce, and Barton (1988) increased the rate of contact between young children with severe mental retardation and the training environment. Under these conditions of increased stimulation, stereotyped responding was reduced to a low level of occurrence.

**Providing Physical Exercise.** Some clinicians, because of their observation that stereotyped behaviors are correlated with periods of inactivity, have evaluated the effects of regular physical exercise on stereotypy. As an illustration, Baumeister and MacLean (1984) reported the successful use of an exercise program in reducing the high rates of stereotyped mannerisms and self-injurious behaviors of two adults with severe mental retardation. The program consisted of a one-hour jog every afternoon. The fact that the aberrant behaviors again increased when the program was terminated emphasized the importance to these adults of the added physical and sensory stimulation.

**Self-Management Procedures.** Koegel and Koegel (1990) used a self-management treatment package to virtually eliminate high-rate stereotypical behaviors in nine- to fourteen-year-old students with severe autistic disabilities, including moderate to severe levels of cognitive retardation. Initially, the students were taught to discriminate their stereotypical and appropriate behaviors. Following discrimination training, the students were taught to self-record on a card after periods of time without stereotypical behavior. The time interval was cued by the chronograph alarm on a watch worn by the student. Self-recorded marks on the card could be exchanged for reinforcers. Following use of the self-management procedures, stereotypical behaviors in classroom and community settings showed a rapid and substantial reduction (from 80 to 100 percent prior to treatment to virtual no occurrence following treatment). Although generalization of effects did not occur in the untreated settings, rapid reduction in these settings occurred on the initiation of self-management (use of the watch and the card for recording). The results of this demonstration suggest that the self-management treatment package provides an effective and efficient method of reducing stereotypical behaviors in some persons with severe disabilities.

**Differential Reinforcement Procedures.** *Reinforcement and Verbal Reprimand.* Repp, Deitz, and Speir (1974) demonstrated the value of a DRO procedure by providing positive reinforcement for increasingly longer periods of time in which no stereotyped behaviors occurred. During the treatment of three persons with severe levels of mental retardation who exhibited high rates of various stereotyped behaviors, a timer was set for a predetermined brief period of time. If stereotyped behavior did not occur during the interval, a bell rang, and the teacher hugged and verbally praised the client for a few seconds. Also, each occurrence of stereotypy was followed by a loud "No." The stereotyped behavior was rapidly reduced to a near-zero occurrence.

*Reinforcement of Specific Alternative Behavior.* Favell (1973), Mulick et al. (1978), Eason, White, and Newsom (1982), and Greer et al. (1984) provided reinforcement for the specific alternative behavior of toy play for children and adults who demonstrated severe and profound levels of mental retardation. With this procedure, high-rate stereotyped actions decreased and appropriate toy play increased. These results were observed even when the trainers were absent and were maintained during two- and six-month follow-up periods.

*Reinforcement of Alternatives for Escape-Motivated Stereotyped Behavior.* After demonstrating that the stereotyped behavior of four children with developmental disabilities was functional in terminating difficult task demands, Durand and Carr (1987) taught the children a communicative alternative. Each child was taught to say the words "Help me" whenever he incorrectly responded to a task-related request. Teaching this alternative social behavior produced a substantial reduction in stereotyped body rocking and hand flapping.

*Reinforcement, Verbal Reprimand, and Physical Interruption.* Azrin and Wesolowski (1980) reduced to infrequent occurrence the stereotyped behaviors of seven adults with profound mental retardation who attended a group-classroom training program. Prior to treatment, these adults had spent 40 percent or more of their time in stereotyped movement. Each client was initially provided intensive individual training in the adaptive behaviors (such as a table task, eye contact, and following instructions) included in the classroom program. Appropriate behaviors were reinforced by praise, stroking, and snack items. When stereotyped acts occurred, the client was reprimanded verbally, the behavior was interrupted, and the client was required to place his hands in his lap or on the edge of the table for two minutes. Each client was returned to the group-classroom setting, and the interruption procedure was gradually faded as the stereotyped behavior was reduced to infrequent occurrence.

**Withholding or Removing Reinforcement.** *Sensory Extinction.* Because of the notion that self-stimulation in some persons is intrinsically reinforced by the resulting auditory, visual, vestibular, or proprioceptive sensory stimulation, Rincover (1978) and Rincover et al. (1979) eliminated the high-rate self-stimulatory behaviors of children with developmental disabilities by removing or minimizing the sensory consequences of such actions. These therapists then used the preferred sensory stimulation of each child to establish appropriate toy play by selecting toys that provided this reinforcing consequence. A music box and an autoharp were selected for the child whose self-stimulatory behaviors produced auditory stimulation; building blocks and stringing beads were selected for proprioception; and a bubble-blowing kit was selected for visual stimulation. After each child was trained to play with the toys until he or she spontaneously played correctly, stereotyped behavior remained at a low level as the appropriate toy play replaced it. These therapists emphasized the potential value of such procedures by noting that they require virtually no staff training, are relatively convenient, and have immediate effects.

*Time-Out.* Mattos (1969) decreased facial tics and finger sucking by stopping music, which a child enjoyed, contingent on self-stimulation. Greene, Hoats, and Hornick (1970) reduced body rocking in a severely visually impaired boy with severe mental retardation who enjoyed listening to music. Whenever he began to body-rock, the music was distorted. An immediate decrease in inappropriate rocking was observed.

**Presentation of Aversive Consequences.** *Overcorrection.* A number of reports have demonstrated the potential usefulness of overcorrection in suppressing the stereotyped behavior of some clients with mental retardation. As an illustration, Foxx and Azrin (1973) used the procedure to virtually eliminate the stereotyped behaviors displayed by four children with profound levels of mental retardation. For children who repetitively mouthed objects, a toothbrush immersed in an oral antiseptic was brushed in the child's mouth, and the child's lips were wiped with a washcloth. To decrease head weaving, the therapist restrained the child's head and then instructed her to hold her head either up, down, or straight ahead for fifteen seconds. The positions were randomly changed for five minutes, and manual guidance was provided as necessary to ensure that the child performed as required. As a second example of the effectiveness of overcorrection, Matson and Stephens (1981) used "hand overcorrection" to treat a variety of stereotyped behaviors of long standing in adults with severe mental retardation. Such behaviors as wall patting, face patting, hair flipping, and head rubbing were followed by a five-minute overcorrection procedure requiring the client to hold his hands either over his head, straight out, or at his sides. The client held each position for fifteen seconds before proceeding to the next position.

*Other Aversive Consequences.* A number of other aversive consequences have been used in successful programs for reducing stereotyped behaviors. These include such events as *facial screening* for repetitive finger sucking and *depressing the tongue with wooden blade* for tongue protrusion (Barrett et al., 1981); *physical punishment combined with a differential reinforcement of alternative behaviors procedure* (Cavalier & Farretti, 1980); *physical restraint* (Salzberg & Napolitan, 1974; Luiselli et al., 1976); and *slaps on the hand* (Koegel & Covert, 1972; Koegel et al., 1974). Charlop et al. (1988) demonstrated the superiority of varying the type of punishers used (that is, verbal reprimand, overcorrecting, or time-out) over the use of a single punisher for a child with autism and profound mental retardation. Although each punisher resulted in a decrease in the child's stereotypy, the behavior frequency was consistently lower when varied punishers were used.

*Treatment: Self-Injury*

**Structuring Antecedent Stimulus Events.** Based on the observation that self-injurious behavior (SIB) is more prevalent in some situations than others, Favell et al. (1982) and Lockwood and Bourland (1982) successfully reduced SIB in young adults with profound retardation by providing access to those conditions associated with little or no self-injury. When provided objects that could be manipulated and that provided preferred sensory stimulation, these adults with long histories of various SIBs replaced the self-injurious activities with more appropriate object manipulation and play.

**Teaching the Skills for Communicating Needs.** Carr and Durand (1985) initially observed that children with developmental disabilities who were provided task demands in an educational setting frequently engaged in the self-injurious behaviors of head hitting and hand biting. The SIBs were most likely when these children were presented difficult task demands or when teacher support was decreased to a minimal level. The SIBs were reduced to infrequent occurrence after each child was taught functional communication skills that involved soliciting assistance from the teacher or the living-area staff or soliciting attention from the teacher whenever it was desired. Teaching the children alternative means of communicating their individual needs under an aversive or stress condition thus served as a functional equivalent to the SIBs.

**Providing Sensory Stimulation via Gross Motor Activities.** Lancioni et al. (1984) were successful in reducing the self-injurious tantrums of three adolescents with multiple handicaps by providing daily periods of gross-motor activities designed to provide a variety of sensory input. These periods lasted about fifteen to twenty minutes each and totaled from one to three hours daily. The tantrums occurred infrequently but were severe and appeared to be unrelated to specific environmental events. The gross-motor activities were selected as the therapeutic approach because of the assumption that the self-injurious tantrums were being maintained by the sensory consequences produced. When a more acceptable means of obtaining sensory stimulation was provided through various gross-motor activities, the tantrums apparently became less functional and were reduced in frequency and duration.

Similar reductions of SIBs and stereotypical responding were reported by Baumeister and MacLean (1984) in two young adult males with severe mental retardation. Neither had responded significantly to previously provided behavior-modification programs involving a range of reinforcement and punishment procedures or to various drug therapies. Both were provided an exercise program consisting of a daily one-hour jog. The distance covered increased from one mile per hour during the first week to three miles per hour during a six-week period. Self-injurious responding and stereotyped movements systematically decreased over the course of the exercise program. These therapeutic effects were lost, however, on termination of the exercise program, a finding suggesting a need for a long-term and routine program.

**Reinforcement of Alternative Behaviors.** The procedure of differential reinforcement involves providing more frequent and valuable consequences for appropriate behaviors and reducing or removing the reinforcement associated with SIBs. An extinction procedure that weakens the SIBs is combined with a differential reinforcement procedure designed to strengthen appropriate alternative behaviors. The differential reinforcement procedure may consist of a DRO (reinforcement provided immediately following periods of time in which no self-injury occurs) or differential reinforcement provided for specific behavior that is both appropriate and incompatible with self-injury).

Lovaas et al. (1965) reduced the high-rate self-hitting behavior of a nine-year-old boy to near zero after systematically reinforcing him with smiles and praise for clapping his hands to music, an appropriate use of his hands that replaced the SIBs. Weiher and Harman (1975) using a DRO procedure, reduced to zero the chronic head banging of a fourteen-year-old boy with severe mental retardation by providing applesauce at the end of the various time intervals during which the SIBs did not occur. Regain and Anson (1976) used food reinforcers in a DRO procedure with a twelve-year-old girl with severe retardation who, prior to intervention, spent much of her time engaging in self-scratching and head-banging behaviors. Although not totally eliminated, these SIBs were significantly reduced under the DRO contingency. Tarpley and Schroeder (1979), in the treatment of three profoundly retarded adults, found a DRI procedure (that is, providing ice cream or orange juice following periods of play activity and no SIB) to be more useful than DRO (that is, providing ice cream or orange juice following periods of no SIB) in effectively reducing head banging.

As a final illustration of the reinforcement of alternatives incompatible with SIBs, Tierney (1986) taught a fourteen-year-old male with profound mental retardation to sit calmly in a chair on the initiation of any SIBs. A significant reduction in SIBs—consisting of slapping and punching his head and hitting his fingers and hands, and often accompanied by screaming, jumping, running, and/or clinging to the nearest person—coincided with reinforcement of the incompatible behavior of sitting calmly in a chair with his hands resting on his knees. Twelve-month follow-up revealed maintenance of the treatment gains.

In a novel approach to producing alternatives to SIBs, Schroeder et al. (1977) demonstrated that the relaxation training of two adolescents with severe mental retardation and chronic high-rate head banging resulted in a physiological state that was incompatible with occurrence of the SIBs. The effects were short-lived, however, a result suggesting a more comprehensive intervention program for effective and durable effects.

**Differential Reinforcement and Physical Interruption.** Differential reinforcement has also been used in combination with other procedures to treat SIBs. Azrin, Besalel, and Wisotzek (1982) and Azrin et al. (1988) reduced the severe and chronic self-injurious behaviors of adolescents and adults with severe and profound mental retardation to near-zero levels in both school and living settings. In the use of a DRI-plus-physical-interruption procedure, reinforcement was provided following periods of no self-injury and occurrence of play, social, or other appropriate behaviors. This reinforcement procedure was combined with interrupting each self-injurious episode and requiring the person to rest his or her hands in the lap for two minutes. In the 1988 report, Azrin et al. demonstrated the superiority of this DRI-plus-interruption procedure over other procedures involving social extinction, DRO and DRI used alone, and interruption used alone. In addition, treatment effects were obtained in each person's living area following the initiation of the DRI-plus-interruption procedure by the living area staff.

**Withholding or Removing Positive Reinforcement.** *Extinction.* In treating young children with profound mental retardation whose self-injury appeared top be self-stimulatory and thus maintained by the *sensory stimulation* produced, Rincover and Devany (1982), demonstrated the value of a sensory extinction procedure in immediately and substantially reducing SIBs. In this procedure, the sensory stimulation associated with the specific SIBs of each child was removed. As an illustration, one boy who engaged in head banging was provided a helmet that attenuated the tactile sensory consequences of the SIB. Another child, who engaged in self-injurious face scratching, was required to wear thin rubber gloves, which prevented her from damaging her skin but, although significantly reducing the sensory stimulation, did not prevent her from scratching.

Blankenship and Lamberts (1989) provided further support for the utility of removing the sensory stimulation involved in SIBs. These therapists reported a rapid and significant reduction in self-injurious cheek gouging and face slapping in two women with profound mental retardation through the contingent of a five-minute application of a helmet with an opaque face screen. The results were maintained at low levels over six months. These treatment effects were viewed as supporting the hypothesis that the SIBs were being maintained by the reinforcing properties of the heightened sensory input resulting from the SIBs.

*Time-Out.* A time-out procedure, consisting of removing the person from the opportunity to obtain reinforcement immediately following each occurrence of SIB, has been used successfully in reducing SIBs in some individuals. This procedure obviously would not be appropriate for those persons whose SIBs are related to boredom and a need for increased social or sensory stimulation, or for SIBs that are reinforced negatively, as these function to remove aversive conditions.

An underlying assumption in the use of a time-out procedure is that the person, at the time of removal, is in an environment that is positively reinforcing. Contingent removal from this reinforcing environment is aversive and should suppress the SIBs. A report by Solnick, Rincover, and Peterson (1977) illustrates the need to ensure, prior to selecting this treatment procedure, that reinforcing conditions are in fact present. The self-injury of an adolescent with severe retardation was not reduced significantly following the initiation of a time-out contingency until the environment from which the person was removed was enriched through increased stimulating and reinforcing activities and objects. Following enrichment, the time-out was effective in suppressing the SIBs. Typically, the time-out procedure is used in combination with the reinforcement of alternative behaviors.

Hamilton, Stephens, and Allen (1967) demonstrated the effectiveness of a time-out in eliminating the head and back banging behaviors of adults with severe levels of mental retardation. Following treatment, the SIBs had not recurred at follow-up checks several months later. Similar results were reported by Wolf, Risley, and Mees (1964), who used time-out in both a hospital and a home setting to eliminate the self-destructive behavior of a 3 1/2-year-old boy with mental retardation. Wolf et al. (1967) reported that three years later, the same child's SIBs were again eliminated by time-out, this time in a school setting. The SIBs were eliminated following a small number of time-out experiences in this second setting, a result suggesting that the child's prior experience with the time-out contingency had increased its effectiveness. Finally, in a study by Lucero et al. (1976), the self-injurious behaviors of three girls with profound mental retardation were markedly reduced by the withdrawal of food on each occurrence of the behavior.

*Movement Suppression Time-Out.* Matson and Keyes (1990) demonstrated the effectiveness of a version of time-out that involved directing the client to remain in a designated motionless position (movement suppression) for a specified period of time following self-injury. One adult with severe mental retardation who displayed a moderate rate of self-injury was required to stand still with his arms extended out to the sides. A second adult with a low rate of self-slapping was required to stand quietly in a corner with feet together, hands to sides, and face to the corner for one minute. Both had been unresponsive to previous treatments involving DRO and verbal reprimand. The addition of the movement-suppression time-out resulted in a rapid reduction to nonoccurrence of the self-injury. The treatment effects were maintained in one client over an eight-month follow-up period.

**Presentation of Aversive Consequences.** A final procedure in the behavioral treatment of SIBs consists of presenting an aversive or punishing event contingent on each occurrence of self-injury. When punishment effects are obtained, empirical studies report rapid and clinically significant results. However, as noted in the earlier discussion of punishment, if it is used in isolation or as the major intervention procedure, its therapeutic suppressive effects often lessen. Additionally, because of the highly specific discrimination frequently made by the client, generalization across settings typically does not occur. For maximum therapeutic effectiveness, punishment procedures, when used, should thus be combined with procedures designed to teach and/or strengthen alternative behaviors that will produce readily available and naturally reinforcers in the person's environments.

*Overcorrection.* Several reports have demonstrated the usefulness of over-correction procedures in reducing SIBs. The most common form of overcorrection used with SIBs involves training in which the part of the client's body (for example, head or the arm) involved in the SIBs is moved to a series of positions where it is held for several seconds (Foxx & Bechtel, 1983). Harris and Romancyzk (1976) applied this type of overcorrection to treat the chroinc head and chin banging of an eight-year-old boy in both home and school settings. An immediate reduction in SIBs was obtained following the implementation of overcorrection, initially in the school and later in the home. The SIBs remained at near-zero levels in both settings at nine-month follow-up. Using a similar procedure of "forced arm exercise," deCatanzaro and Baldwin (1978) eliminated the head-hitting behaviors of young boys with profound levels of mental retardation. The overcorrection procedure produced an initial reduction in SIB to near-zero levels. The overcorrection effects were generalized by the extension of the intervention to several different settings.

Overcorrection, used in combination with other procedures, has been favored by a number of therapists. Measel and Alfieri (1976) demonstrated the efficacy of a combination of DRI and overcorrection in eliminating the hand-slapping and head-banging behaviors exhibited by two boys with profound mental retardation. Johnson et al. (1982) successfully reduced a variety of SIBs in adults with profound retardation through overcorrection and differential reinforcement procedures. These therapists observed, however, that overcorrection alone produced most of the therapeutic effects. Azrin et al., (1988) combined three overcorrection approaches (autism reversal, required relaxation, and hand-awareness training) to significantly decrease the SIBs of eleven clients, ten of whom exhibited severe or profound mental retardation. An analysis of the benefits indicated that the SIBs had been reduced by 99 percent. However, the therapists speculated that this multicomponent approach would be most effective (1) with a client who had possessed a high level of outward-directed behavior prior to intervention, or (2) if the social environment was one that strongly encouraged outward-directed activity.

*Aversive Electrical Stimulation.* Butterfield (1975) described this technique as delivering a physically harmless but psychologically aversive electrical stimulus to the person's limb or back for a brief duration immediately following the occurrence of self-injury. This procedure is the most widely researched and generally effective method of intially suppressing self-injury. The only published exceptions to the effectiveness of shock are with persons presenting the Lesch-Nyhan syndrome (Favell, 1982).

Following the implementation of a shock contingency, Tate and Baroff (1966) virtually eliminated the high-rate SIBs (head banging, self-biting, and self-kicking) of a nine-year-old boy who was severely visually impaired. These therapists reported the positive side effects of increased eating and decreased posturing, saliva saving, and clinging behaviors. Similar results were obtained by Lovass and Simmons (1969) with boys with severe levels of mental retardation. The desirable side effects following the reduction of SIBs included reduced exploration of the environment. Finally, Merbaum (1973) described the use of electrical stimulation by a mother in the treatment of the SIBs of her twelve-year-old son. SIB was reduced in both home and school settings. A one-year follow-up indicated maintenance of the SIBs at near-zero levels, with the mother reporting that her son was "quieter, happier, and wonderful around the house."

*Additional Punishment Procedures.* Oher procedures have been reported as effective in reducing self-injurious behavior: *facial screening,* in which the person's face is briefly covered with a terry-cloth bib following the SIBs (Watson, Singh, & Winton, 1986; Lutzker, 1978); *water mist,* in which the mist is sprayed in the person's face following SIBs (Dorsey et al., 1980); *aromatic ammonia,* in which the ammonia is held briefly under the person's nose following SIBs (Altman, Haavik, & Cook, 1978); *aversive tickling,* in which the person is tickled for a prolonged period following SIBs (Greene & Hoats, 1971); and a *rage reduction technique* in which the person is physically restrained and forced to hit the therapist's hand (Saposnek & Watson, 1974).

*Conditioned Avoidance.* When punishment procedures are used, the therapist may pair "no" or a similar stimulus with the presentation of the aversive consequences. In this manner, "no" may acquire sufficient conditional aversive properties to maintain suppression of the behavior when presented in the absence of the primary aversive event. This effect was illustrated by Lovaas and Simmons (1969), who, following the pairing of "no" with electrical stimulation, found that "no" presented in isolation served to maintain suppression.

## Case Illustration

This case study illustrates the assessment and treatment procedures described. In this case, Rebecca, a fourteen-year-old adolescent with mild mental retardation, and her family had been seen on an outpatient basis for a few weeks prior to placement for inpatient treatment in a short-term psychiatric facility. As a result, some initial behavioral assessment data were obtained in the home and school settings. Both Rebecca's mother and her special-education teacher completed a behavioral recording form during a three-week period. Interviews with the mother and the teacher and a problem-focused interview with the young adolescent also were conducted. Prior to initiation of the behavior therapy program, the adolescent assaulted her mother while in a fit of rage and was hospitalized because her "mother could no longer manage her." These assessment data, combined with those obtained following psychiatric placement, were most valuable to our understanding of the case and in the development of short- and long-term goals for Rebecca.

Rebecca was an only child who lived with her mother. She was physically incapacitated because of a childhood injury and required some assistance with mobility, dressing, and toileting. Her father had died of a heart attack when she was ten years old. Her mother reported a history of acting-out behaviors that had begun shortly after the death of Rebecca's father, who was the disciplinarian in the family. Rebecca was described as demanding and impatient, and as depending excessively on her mother to entertain her at home. The mother admitted that she had spoiled Rebecca but frequently was unable to manage her unless she gave in to her demands. Rage reactions consisting of screaming, swearing, physical assault, property destruction, and self-abuse were likely to occur if her demands were not met. These tantrums had continued for extended periods of time when the mother had attempted to "wait Rebecca out." Following these episodes, Rebecca frequently expressed remorse and resolved to control her temper in the future. Mother and daughter had participated in an insight-based counseling experience for over a year prior to Rebecca's hospitalization. Although some initial improvement was noted, the problems had intensified in the few months prior to hospitalization. Rebecca's mood, while variable, was generally negative or neutral. Although her mother and her teacher described Rebecca as sociable, she had few friends because of her disruptive and demanding actions. She was described by the teacher as an overanxious child who excessively sought approval and reassurance and who was overly sensitive to criticism.

Following her placement in the psychiatric treatment facility, Rebecca's defiant, oppositional, and conduct problems continued. Her problem behaviors, defined by the facility staff, included verbal and physical aggression toward peers and staff, uncooperativeness in following living-area routine and in complying with reasonable staff requests, refusal to attend and participate in the educational and therapy programs provided, excessive demands on staff time and services, prolonged periods of excessive negative emotionality, prolonged temper outbursts, and frequent negative self-statements. She also displayed both nocturnal and diurnal enuresis, a problem that had been present on an irregular basis for about three years. The behavior recording form completed by the living-area and program staff, direct observation of and interaction with Rebecca by the behavior therapists in the living and program areas, and interviews with Rebecca relative to her problems were used to obtain the assessment data.

On the basis of these data, supported by the preadmission information, a number of program hypotheses were developed relative to factors that instigated and contributed to the functionality of her acting-out and oppositional behaviors:

1. The aggressive behaviors were functional in that they resulted in
   a. compliance with her demands
   b. valuable staff and peer attention
   c. distress in staff who ignored her demands
   d. the removal or postponement of requests or directives that she did not find to her liking

2. Rebecca required a frequent schedule of social interaction with staff and frequent feedback relative to her acceptability. If these were not provided, she ensured attention through her acting-out behavior.

3. Her remorse and apologies following her disruptive actions, while reflecting guilt and shame, were also functional in that they resulted in valued affectionate reactions from others.

4. The prolonged tantrum behavior had been shaped by Rebecca's mother and was currently being maintained by intermittent positive and negative reinforcement.

5. The acting-out behaviors were more likely to occur under conditions of negative emotional arousal (such as anxiety, anger, and jealousy).

6. Various frustrations produced in Rebecca by her physical limitations and her dependency on others produced frequent negative emotional arousal. When negatively aroused, she showed an increased likelihood of responding disruptively to minor sources of aggravation.

7. Rebecca had a limited repertoire of socially appropriate means of obtaining and maintaining positive social interaction and feedback from adults or peers.

8. Rebecca had a limited repertoire of skills for coping with frustration, peer conflict, or anxiety.

9. As a result of her physical limitations and deficit social skills, Rebecca was limited in the ways in which she could control or exert influence over her physical and social environments. Her experiences had taught her that various of her disruptive behaviors did result in her exercising control over others.

10. Rebecca's physical limitations resulted in poor self-esteem and generaized anxiety over her competency. She was likely to react in an impulsive and disruptive manner to any criticism or failure.

These hypotheses next were translated into program implications and then into detailed program approaches. These approaches were followed by living-area and program staff as they interacted with Rebecca throughout the day. The following program excerpts illustrate the focus on teaching and strengthening a variety of social, coping, and self-management skills designed to replace the acting-out behaviors and to provide Rebecca with increased positive social and emotional experiences.

1. Provide Rebecca with a schedule card of her daily activities. Review the schedule with Rebecca each morning and at times throughout the day prior to each activity. Prompt Rebecca to describe the program activity, and remind her of some positive features of program attendance and participation. Use the card to emphasize that she is managing aspects of her own life, for example, "Rebecca, what program are *you* attending this afternoon?"

2. Provide lead time when reminding Rebecca of her scheduled activities, especially prior to activities that she does not prefer. Avoid confrontation to arguments. Staff interactions should reflect interest and positive concern.

3. Following each period or activity, prompt Rebecca to label her social behaviors relative to those expected in the setting, to decide if she "did meet" or "did not meet" the expected behaviors, and then to self-record her evaluation on her schedule card. Staff will initial the card to verify its correctness and to record any differences in opinion relative to the appropriateness of her behavior. Staff will prompt Rebecca to describe her behaviors that resulted in her evaluation. Praise her for prosocial behaviors. Do not reprimand or otherwise react to inappropriate behaviors. Rebecca will keep her schedule card with her throughout the day.

4. Staff are encouraged to prompt Rebecca to show her schedule card and describe what she is doing. Comment on the positive behavior marks and ignore the negative ones. Our strategy is to focus her attention on prosocial behaviors and to minimize attention for inappropriate actions.

5. Prior to bed each evening, Rebecca will count the number of marks attained for prosocial behaviors throughout the day. She will transfer these to a reinforcer preference card (RPC). These cards, depicting the backup reinforcers previously selected by Rebecca and the cost (number of positive evaluations) of each, will be placed in a three-ring binder located in Rebecca's room. Rebecca will deposit the earned marks on the RPC of her choice.

6. After the transfer has been completed, staff will describe the number of marks on each card needed for exchange for the depicted reinforcer. Provide a casual, noncritical comment about the number of "did-not-meet" marks obtained that day. Follow this with a comment of encouragement relative to earning a large number of marks for expected behaviors during the next day.

7. After an RPC has been completed, Rebecca may exchange the card for the depicted item or activity. A range of backup reinforcers reflecting her

preferences will be available for exchange. This is especially essential during the early weeks of the program to ensure adequate incentives for her to inhibit her inappropriate behaviors and to select desired ones.

8. It is essential that staff interactions with Rebecca be as positive as possible. Model desired behavior and a positive demeanor, and demonstrate a helpful attitude. Label appropriate behaviors (such as positive affect, initiating positive peer and staff interactions, following staff requests, and being independent) and express your satisfaction. To enhance her self-esteem, use positive self-labels, such as, "Wow, Rebecca, *you* did it," "That's really using *your* head," "*You* really worked hard on that one," and "I'll bet *you're* proud of yourself."

Also, provide Rebecca with frequent opportunities to make choices, and to be in a position of being in charge and having specific personal responsibility. Make such statements as "Rebecca, *you* decide," or "What would *you* choose to do?" Label and praise appropriate choices and independent actions.

9. Provide Rebecca with specific routine responsibilities in the living and program areas. These resonsibilities will provide her experiences of being in charge of and influencing aspects of her environment. A positive sense of personal value and accomplishment should develop.

10. Relate to Rebecca in a *calm* manner, even when she is being inappropriate. A reprimand, a sharp tone of voice, a criticism, an aggravated grimace, or a sign of despair will serve to provoke, and potentially reinforce, inappropriate behavior. When she is disruptive, be as calm and deliberate as possible. Demonstrate that her inappropriate demands, yelling, or swearing will not have a negative effect on you.

11. As there is a correlation between her negative, depressivelike moods and her disruptive behaviors, it is essential that we provide Rebecca with numerous mood-elevating positive experiences. A predominant positive mood state serves as an emotional background for a range of prosocial behaviors that currently are in her repertoire. Approach Rebecca positively, prompt positive affect, interact with her in a personable manner, and spend individual time with her. Vary conversational topics to ensure that she will focus on activities and events other than her own limitations. Label positive affect and express your delight, for example, "Rebecca, what a pretty smile! Did you know that your brown eyes sparkle when you smile?" . . .

12. Identify specific situations that result in negativistic and other acting-out behaviors. Use these in developing training scenes for use in desensitization, cognitive restructuring, and social skills training. An emphasis will be placed on such interpersonal behaviors as initiating and maintaining appropriate peer and adult interactions, coping with frustration, expressing emotions, making friends, expressing disagreements, handling criticism, and pursuing leisure skills involving peers. Basic self-management skills of self-labeling, evaluating behaviors as appropriate or inappropriate, self-rein-

forcement, self-punishment, standard setting, and self-instruction will be taught and used in training the interpersonal social skills. Psychological services staff will consult with living- and program-area staff in developing specific training experiences.

13. Following training, staff will be in a position to anticipate problem situations and prompt Rebecca to use appropriate social skills. Also, when observing Rebecca behaving negatively, staff can prompt Rebecca to *label* her behavior ("Rebecca, what are *you* doing?"); *evaluate* it ("Rebecca, is that appropriate or not appropriate?"); *describe its consequences* ("Rebecca, what happens when you threaten your peers?"); and *self-instruct* and *demonstrate* more appropriate behaviors ("Rebecca, what is a better way to show your anger? Please show me."). If successful, staff will be in a position to provide positive feedback and prompt Rebecca to self-reinforce with positive self-statements. . . .

The program also included specific rocedures for managing episodes of physical aggression and prolonged tantrums. These involved prompting Rebecca to remove herself to a quiet area until she had calmed herself. She then was prompted to describe and demonstrate alternative means of expressing her frustrations and concerns.

Rebecca responded quite positively to the program and was returned to the community within three months following hospitalization. Her mother was provided training in the rationale and procedures of the program. Additionally, the behavior therapist consulted with the public school system and provided a set of guidelines for managing any recurrence of her acting-out problems and for support of her newly developed social, coping, and self-management skills.

## Summary

Diagnostically based behavioral interventions for behavior disorders presented by those with mental retardation have been demonstrated to be effective therapeutic approaches. As is emphasized in this chapter, such interventions must be closely interfaced with medical, psychiatric, and socioenvironmental treatment modes to ensure maximum curative effects.

## References

Altman, K., Haavik, S., & Cook, J. W. (1978). Punishment of self-injurious behavior in natural settings using contingent aromatic ammonia. *Behav. Res. Ther.*, 16, 85–96.

Ausman, J., Ball, T. S., & Alexander, D. (1974). Behavior therapy of pica in a profoundly retarded adolescent. *Ment. Retard.*, 12(6), 16–18.

Azrin, N. H., Besalel, V. A., Jamner, J. P., & Caputo, J. N. (1988). Comparative study of behavioral methods of treating severe self-injury. *Residential Behav. Treat., 3,* 119–152.

Azrin, N. H., Besalel, V. A., & Wisotzek, I. E. (1982). Treatment of self-injury by a reinforcement plus interruption procedure. *Anal. Intervention Devel. Disabilities, 3,* 105–113.

Azrin, N. H., & Wesolowski, M. D. (1975). Eliminating habitual vomiting in a retarded adult by positive practice and self-correction. *J. Behav. Ther. Exp. Psychiat., 6,* 145–148.

Azrin, N. H., & Wesolowski, M. D. (1980). A reinforcement plus interruption method of eliminating behavioral stereotypy of profoundly retarded persons. *Behav. Res. Ther., 18,* 113–119.

Barmann, B. C. (1980). Contingent vibration for hand-mouthing and rumination. *J. Behav. Ther. Exp. Psychiatr., 11,* 307–311.

Barrett, R. P., Matson, J. L., Shapiro, E. S., & Ollendick, J. H. (1981). A comparison of punishment and DRO procedures for treating stereotypic behavior of mentally retarded children. *Appl. Res. Ment. Retard., 2,* 247–256.

Baumeister, A. A., & MacLean, W. E. (1984). Deceleration of self-injurious and stereotypic responding by exercise. *Appl. Res. Ment. Retard., 5,* 385–393.

Becker, J. V., Turner, S. M., & Sajwaj, T. E. (1978). Multiple behavioral effects of the use of lemon juice with a ruminating toddler-age child. *Behav. Modif., 2,* 267–268.

Bird, F., Dores, P. A., Moniz, D., & Robinson, J. (1989). Reducing severe aggressive and self-injurious behaviors with functional communication training. *Am. J. Ment. Retard., 94,* 37–48.

Blankenship, M. D., & Lamberts, F. (1989). Helmet restraint and visual screening as treatment for self-injurious behavior in persons who have profound mental retardation. *Behav. Residential Treat., 4,* 253–265.

Borreson, P. M., & Anderson, J. L. (1982). The elimination of chronic rumination through a combination of procedures. *Ment. Retard., 20,* 34–48.

Bright, G. O., & Whaley, D. L. (1968). Suppression of regurgitation and rumination through a combination of procedures. *Mich. Ment. Health Bull., 2,* 17–20.

Bucher, B., Reykdal, B., & Albin, J. (1976). Brief restraint to control pica in retarded children. *J. Behav. Ther. Exp. Psychiat., 7,* 137–140.

Butterfield, W. H. (1975). Electric shock-safety factors when used for the aversive conditioning of humans. *Behav. Ther., 6,* 98–110.

Carr, E. G., & Durand, V. M. (1985). Reducing behavior problems through functional communication training. *J. Appl. Behav. Anal., 18,* 111–126.

Carr, E. G., Newsom, C. D., & Binkoff, J. A. (1980). Escape as a factor in the aggressive behavior of two retarded children. *J. Appl. Behav. Anal., 13,* 101–117.

Cavalier, A. R., & Farretti, R. D. (1980). Stereotyped behavior, alternative behavior and collateral effects: A comparison of four intervention procedures. *J. Ment. Defic. Res., 24,* 219–230.

Charlop, M. H., Burgio, L. D. Iwata, B. A., & Ivancic, M. T. (1988). Stimulus variation as a means of enhancing punishment effects. *J. Appl. Behav. Anal., 21,* 89–96.

Clauser, B., & Scibak, J. W. (1990). Direct and generalized effect of food satiation in reducing rumination. *Res. Devel. Disabilities, 11,* 23–36.

Cole, C. L., Gardner, W. I., & Karen, O. C. (1985). Self-management training of mentally retarded adults presenting severe conduct difficulties. *Appl. Res. Ment. Retard., 6,* 337–347.

Davis, W. B., Wiesler, N. A., & Hanzel, T. E. (1980). Contingent music in management of rumination and out-of-seat behavior in a profoundly mentally regarded institutionalized male. *Ment. Retard., 18,* 43–45.

deCatanzaro, D. A., & Baldwin, G. (1978). Effective treatment of self-injurious behavior through a forced arm exercise. *Am. J. Ment. Defic., 82,* 433–439.

Dorsey, M. F., Iwata, B. A., Ong, P., & McSween, T. E. (1980). Treatment of self-injurious behavior using a water mist: Initial response suppression and generalization. *J. Appl. Behav. Anal., 13,* 343–353.

Duker, P. C., & Seys, D. M. (1977). Elimination of vomiting in a retarded female using restitutional overcorrection. *Behav. Ther., 8,* 255–259.

Durand, V. M. (1990). *Severe behavior problems: A functional communication training approach.* New York: Guilford Press.

Durand, V. M., & Carr, E. G. (1987). Social influences on "self-stimulatory" behavior: Analysis and treatment application. *J. Appl. Behav. Anal., 20,* 119–132.

Eason, L. J., White, M. G., & Newsom, C. (1982). Generalized reduction of self-stimulatory behavior: An effect of teaching appropriate play to autistic children. *Anal. Intervention Devel. Disabilities, 2,* 157–169.

Favell, J. E. (1973). Reduction of stereotypes by reinforcement of toy play. *Ment. Retard., 11,* 21–23.

Favell, J. E. (Task Force Chairperson). (1982). The treatment of self-injurious behavior. *Behav. Ther., 13,* 529–554.

Favell, J. E., McGimsey, J. F., & Schnell, R. M. (1982). Treatment of self-injury by alternate sensory activities. *Anal. Intervention Develop. Disabilities, 2,* 82–104.

Foxx, R. M., & Azrin, N. H. (1973). The elimination of autistic self-stimulatory behavior by overcorrection. *J. Appl. Behav. Anal., 6,* 1–14.

Foxx, R. M., & Bechtel, D. R. (1983). Overcorrection: A review and analysis. In S. Axelrod & J. Apsche (Eds.), *The effects of punishment on human behavior* (pp. 227–228). New York: Academic Press.

Foxx, R. M., & Martin, E. D. (1975). Treatment of scavenging behavior (coprophagy and pica) by overcorrection. *Behav. Res. Ther., 13,* 153–162.

Foxx, R. M., Snyder, M. S., & Schroeder, F. (1979). A food satiation and oral hygiene punishment program to suppress chronic rumination by retarded persons. *J. Autism Devel. Disorders, 9,* 399–412.

Frieden, B. D., & Johnson, H. K. (1979). Treatment of a retarded child's feces smearing and coprophagic behavior. *J. Ment. Defic. Res., 23,* 55–61.

Friman, P. C., Barnard, J. D., Altman, K., & Wolf, M. M. (1986). Parent and teacher use of DRO and DRI to reduce aggressive behavior. *Anal. Intervention Devel. Disabilities, 6,* 319–330.

Gardner, W. I., & Cole, C. L. (1987). Behavior treatment, behavior management and behavior control. *Behav. Residential Treat., 2,* 37–53.

Gardner, W. I., Cole, C. L., Davidson, D. P., & Karan, O. C. (1986). Reducing aggression in individuals with developmental disabilities: An expanded stimulus control, assessment, and intervention model. *Educ. Training Ment. Retard., 21,* 3–12.

Gedye, A. (1989). Extreme self-injury attributed to frontal lobe seizures. *Am. J. Ment. Retard., 94,* 20–26.

Gilbraith, D. A., Byrick, R. J., & Rutledge, J. T. (1970). An aversive conditioning approach to the inhibition of chronic vomiting. *Can. Psychiatr. Assoc. J., 15,* 311–313.

Greene, R. J., & Hoats, D. L. (1971). Aversive tickling: A simple conditioning technique. *Behav. Ther., 2,* 389–393.

Greene, R. J., Hoats, D. L., & Hornick, A. J. (1970). Music distortion: A new technique for behavior modification. *Psychol. Record, 20,* 107–109.

Greer, R. D., Becker, B. J., Soxe, C. D., & Mirabella, R. F. (1984). Conditioning histories and setting stimuli controlling engagement in stereotypy or toy play. *Anal. Intervention Devel. Disabilities, 5,* 269–284.

Gualtieri, C. T., Matson, J. L., & Keppel, J. M. (1989). Psychopathology in the mentally retarded. In American Psychiatric Association, *Treatment of Psychiatric Disorders* (Vol. 1, pp. 4–8). Washington, DC: Author.

Hamilton, H., Stephens, L., & Allen, P. (1967). Controlling aggressive and destructive behavior in severely retarded institutionalized residents. *Am. J. Ment. Defic., 71,* 852–856.

Harris, S. L., & Romanczyk, R. G. (1976). Treating self-injurious behavior of a retarded child by overcorrection. *Behav. Ther., 7,* 235–239.

Humphrey, F. J., Mayes, S. D., Bixler, E. O., & Good, C. (1989). Variables associated with frequency of rumination in a boy with profound mental retardation. *J. Autism Devel. Disorders, 19,* 435–447.

Jackson, G. M., Johnson, C. R., Ackron, G. S., & Crawley, R. (1975). Food satiation as a procedure to decelerate vomiting. *Am. Assoc. Ment. Defic., 80,* 223–227.

Johnson, W. L., Baumeister, A. A., Penland, M. J., & Inwald, C. (1982). Experimental analysis of self-injurious, stereotypic, and collateral behavior of retarded persons: Effects of overcorrection and reinforcement of alternative responding. *Anal. Intervention Devel. Disabilities, 2,* 41–66.

Kalfus, G. R., Fisher-Gross, S., Marvullo, M. A., & Nau, P. A. (1988). Outpatient treatment of pica in a developmentally delayed child. *Child Family Behav. Ther., 9,* 49–63.

Kastner, T., Friedman, D. L., O'Brian, D. R., & Pond, W. S. (1990). Health care and mental illness in persons with mental retardation. *Habilitative Ment. Healthcare Newsl., 9,* 17–24.

Koegel, R. L., & Covert, A. (1972). The relationship of self-stimulation to learning in autistic children. *J. Appl. Behav. Anal., 5,* 381–387.

Koegel, R. L., Firestone, P. B., Kramme, K. W., & Dunlop, G. (1974). Increasing spontaneous play by suppressing self-stimulation in autistic children. *J. Appl. Behav. Anal., 7,* 521–528.

Koegel, R. L., & Koegel, L. K. (1990). Extended reductions in stereotypic behavior of students with autism through a self-management treatment package. *J. Appl. Behav. Anal., 23,* 119–127.

Kohlenberg, R. J. (1970). The punishment of persistent vomiting: A case study. *J. Appl. Behav. Anal., 3,* 241–245.

Lancioni, G. E., Smeets, P. M., Ceccarani, P. S., Capodaglio, L., & Companari, G. (1984). Effects of gross motor activities on the severe self-injurious tantrums of multihandicapped individuals. *Appl. Res. Ment. Retard., 5,* 471–482.

Libby, D. G., & Phillips, E. (1979). Eliminating rumination behavior in a profoundly retarded adolescent: An exploratory study. *Ment. Retard., 17,* 94–95.

Lobato, D., Carlson, E. L., & Barrera, R. D. (1986). Modified satiation reducing ruminative vomiting without excessive weight gain. *Appl. Res. Ment. Retard., 7,* 337–347.

Lockwood, K., & Bourland, G. (1982). Reduction of self-injurious behaviors by reinforcement and toy use. *Ment. Retard., 20,* 169–173.

Lovaas, O. I., Freitag, G., Gold, V., & Kassorla, I. (1965). Experimental studies in childhood schizophrenia: Analysis of self-destructive behavior. *J. Exp. Child Pyschol., 2,* 67–84.

Lovaas, O. I., & Simmons, J. Q. (1969). Manipulation of self-destruction in three retarded children. *J. Appl. Behav. Anal., 2,* 143–157.

Lowry, M., & Sovner, R. (1991). The functional significance of problem behavior: A key to effective treatment. *Habilitative Ment. Health Newsl., 10,* 59–63.

Lucero, W. J., Frieman, J., Spoering, K., & Fehrenbacher, J. (1976). Comparison of three procedures in reducing self-injurious behavior. *Am. J. Ment. Defic., 80,* 548–554.

Luckey, R. E., Watson, C. M., & Musik, J. N. (1968). Aversive conditioning as a means of inhibiting vomiting and rumination. *Am. J. Ment. Defic., 73,* 139–142.

Luiselli, J. K., & Greenidge, A. (1982). Behavioral treatment of high-rate aggression in a rubella child. *J. Behav. Ther. Exp. Psychiatr., 13,* 152–157.

Luiselli, J. K., Reisman, J., Helfen, C. S., & Pemberton, B. W. (1976). Control of self-stimulatory behavior of an autistic child through brief physical restraint. *School Appl. Learning Theory, 9,* 3–13.

Luiselli, J. K., & Slocumb, P. R. (1983). Management of multiple aggressive behaviors by differential reinforcement. *J. Behav. Ther. Exp. Psychiat., 14,* 343–347.

Lutzker, J. R. (1978). Reducing self-injurious behavior by facial screening. *Am. J. Ment. Defic., 82,* 510–513.

Mace, F. C., & Knight, D. (1986). Functional analysis and treatment of severe pica. *J. Appl. Behav. Anal., 19,* 411–416.

Mace, F. C., Page, T. J., Ivancic, M. T., & O'Brien, S. (1986). Analysis of environmental determinants of aggression and disruption in mentally retarded children. *Appl. Res. Ment. Retard., 7,* 203–221.

Matson, J. L., & Keyes, J. B. (1990). A comparison of DRO to movement suppression time-out and DRO with two self-injurious and aggressive mentally retarded adults. *Res. Devel. Disabilities, 11,* 111–120.

Matson, J. L., & Stephens, R. M. (1981). Overcorrection treatment of stereotyped behaviors. *Behav. Modification, 5,* 491–502.

Mattos, R. L. (1969). *Operant control of facial ticking finger sucking in a severely retarded child.* Paper presented at the annual convention of the American Association on Mental Deficiency, San Francisco.

Measel, C. J., & Alfieri, P. A. (1976). Treatment of self-injurious behavior by a combination of reinforcement for incompatible behavior and overcorrection. *Am. J. Ment. Defic., 81,* 147–153.

Merbaum, M. (1973). The modification of self-destructive behavior by a mother-therapist using aversive stimulation. *Behav. Ther., 4,* 442–447.

Mulick, J. A., Barbour, R., Schroeder, S. R., & Rojahn, J. (1980). Overcorrection of pica in two profoundly retarded adults: Analysis of setting effects, stimulus and response generalization. *Appl. Res. Ment. Retard., 1,* 241–252.

Mulick, J. A., Hoyt, P., Rojahn, J., & Schroeder, S. R. (1978). Reduction of a nervous habit in a profoundly retarded youth by increasing toy play. *J. Behav. Ther. Exp. Psychiat., 9,* 381–385.

Pickup, J., & Arsenault, P. (1976). The reduction of chronic regurgitation in a profoundly retarded individual using a multi-therapeutic paradigm. *Res. Retard., 3*(3), 82–88.

Rast, J., Johnston, J. M., Drum, C., & Conrin, J. (1981). The relation of food quality to rumination behavior. *J. Appl. Behav. Anal., 14,* 121–130.

Rast, J., Johnston, J. M., Ellinger-Allen, J., & Drum, C. (1985). Effects of nutritional and mechanical properties of food on ruminative behavior. *J. Exp. Anal. Behav., 44,* 195–206.

Rast, J., Johnston, J. M., Lubin, D., & Ellinger-Allen, J. (1988). Effects of premeal chewing on ruminative behavior. *Am. J. Ment. Retard., 93,* 67–74.

Regain, R. D., & Anson, J. E. (1976). The control of self-mutilating behavior with positive reinforcement. *Ment. Retard., 14,* 22–25.

Reid, A. H., Ballinger, B. R., & Heather, B. B. (1978). Behavioural syndromes identified by cluster analysis in a sample of 100 severely and profoundly retarded adults. *Psychol. Med., 8,* 399–412.

Repp, A. C., Deitz, S. M., & Speir, N. C. (1974). Reducing stereotypic resonding of retarded persons by the differential reinforcement of other behavior. *Am. J. Ment. Defic., 79,* 279–284.

Repp, A. C., Felce, D., & Barton, L. E. (1988). Basing the treatment of stereotypic and self-injurious behaviors on hypotheses of their causes. *J. Appl. Behav. Anal., 21,* 281–289.

Rincover, A. (1978). Sensory extinction: A procedure for eliminating self-stimulatory behavior in psychotic children. *J. Abnorm. Child Psychol., 6,* 299–310.

Rincover, A., Cook, R., Peoples, A., & Packard, D. (1979). Sensory extinction and sensory reinforcement principles for programming multiple adaptive behavior change. *J. Appl. Behav. Anal., 12,* 221–223.

Rincover, A., & Devany, J. (1982). The application of sensory extinction procedures to self-injury. *Anal. Intervention Devel. Disabilities, 2,* 67–81.

Rojahn, J., McGonigle, J. J., Curcio, C., & Dixon, M. M. (1987). Suppression of pica by water mist and aromatic ammonia. *Behav. Modification, 11,* 65–74.

St. Lawrence, J. S., & Drabman, R. S. (1984). Suppression of chronic high frequency spitting in a multiply handicapped and mentally retarded adolescent. *Child Fam. Behav. Ther., 6,* 45–55.

Salzberg, B., & Napolitan, J. (1974). Holding a retarded boy at a table for two minutes to reduce inappropriate object contact. *Am. J. Ment. Defic., 78,* 748–751.

Saposnek, D. T., & Watson, L. S., Jr. (1974). The elimination of the self-destructive behavior of a psychotic child: A case study. *Behav. Ther., 5,* 79–89.

Schroeder, S. R., Peterson, C. R., Salomon, L. J., & Artley, J. J. (1977). EMG feedback and the contingent restraint of self-injurious behavior among the severely retarded: Two case illustrations, *Behav. Ther., 8,* 738–741.

Singh, N. N., & Winton, A. S. W. (1984). Effects of a screening procedure on pica and collateral behaviors. *J. Behav. Ther. Exp. Psychiatr., 15,* 59–65.

Smith, M. D. (1987). Treatment of pica in an adult disabled by autism by differential reinforcement of incompatible behavior. *J. Behav. Ther. Exp. Psychiatr., 18,* 285–288.

Solnick, J. V., Rincover, A., & Peterson, C. R. (1977). Some determinants the reinforcing and punishing effects of timeout. *J. Appl. Behav. Anal., 10.,* 415–424.

Sovner, R., & Hurley, A. D. (1984). The role of the medical model in psychiatry. *Psychiat. Aspects Ment. Retard. Rev., 5,* 51–55.

Tarpley, H., & Schroeder, S. (1979). A comparison of DRO and DRI procedures in the treatment of self-injurious behavior. *Am. J. Ment. Defic., 84,* 188–194.

Tate, B. G., & Baroff, G. S. (1966). Aversive control of self-injurious behavior in a psychotic boy. *Behav. Res. Ther., 4,* 281–287.

Thompson, T. (1988). Prevention and early treatment of behavior disorders of children and youth with retardation and autism. In J. A. Stark, F. J. Menolascino, M. H. Albarelli, & V. C. Gray (Eds.), *Mental retardation and mental health: Classification, diagnosis, treatment, services* (pp. 98–105). New York: Springer-Verlag.

Tierney, D. W. (1986). The reinforcement of calm sitting behavior: A method used to reduce the self-injurious behavior of a profoundly retarded boy. *J. Behav. Ther. Exp. Psychiatr., 17,* 47–50.

Watson, J., Singh, N. N., & Winton, A. S. (1986). Suppressive effects of visual and facial screening on self-injurious finger sucking. *Am. J. Ment. Defic., 90,* 526–534.

Weiher, R. G., & Harman, R. E. (1975). The use of omission training to reduce self-injurious behavior in a retarded child. *Behav. Ther., 6,* 261–268.

Winton, A. S. W., & Singh, N. N. (1983). Suppression of pica using brief-duration physical restraint. *J. Ment. Defic. Res., 27,* 93–103.

Wolf, M. Risley, T., Johnston, M., Harris, F., & Allen, E. (1967). Application of operant conditioning procedures to the behavior problems of an autistic child. A follow-up and extension. *Behav. Res. Ther., 5,* 103–111.

Wolf, M., Risley, T., & Mees, H. (1964). Application of operant conditioning procedures to the behavior problems of an autistic child. *Behav. Res. Ther., 1,* 305–312.

Wolf, M. M., Birmbrauer, J., Lawler, J., & Williams, T. (1970). The operant extinction, reinstatement and re-extinction of vomiting behavior in a retarded child. In R. Ulrich, T. Stanick, & T. Mabry (Eds.), *Control of human behavior: From cure to prevention* (Vol. 2, pp. 146–149). Clearview, IL: Scott Foresman.

Yang, L. (1988). Elimination of habitual rumination through the strategies of food satiation and fading: A case study. *Behav. Residential Treat., 3,* 223–224.

# 11

# Treatment of Depression in Persons with Mental Retardation

*Anton Dosen*
*Detlef Petry*

The challenge of treating behavioral and psychiatric disorders among the mentally retarded is a topic that has recently taken on increased importance in society's care of these citizens. With the recent move of the mentally retarded from institutions to the mainstream of community life, the increased needs of caregivers to influence and change maladaptive and abnormal behavioral patterns and to treat salient psychiatric symptoms have become more pronounced.

The diagnosticians of the mentally retarded have been spurred on to discover more about the internal world of the mentally retarded and to understand their psychological needs, the patterns of onset of their psychic problems, and their conflicts with the surroundings. These developments have resulted in changes in the attitude of professionals with regard to various issues. The views on normal and abnormal behavior as manifested in this population have changed as the personality of the mentally retarded and their motivations for behavior have been understood better.

The psychiatric diagnostics of the mentally retarded has received more attention and has become increasingly more differentiated by including more specific diagnostic categories (like depression, anxiety disorder, and borderline disorder). Etiological insights into behavioral as well as psychiatric disorders have become more profound as various approaches specifically geared to the needs of this population have been used to search for the roots of mental illness.

The improvement of diagnostics has had a stimulative effect on the development of a number of new treatment approaches. On the one hand, attempts have been made to apply the same treatment methods to this population as to nonretarded individuals with similar disorders. On the other hand, new methods and approaches specific to the life problems of the mentally retarded have been developed.

Recent developments in the treatment of depression are also characterized by these two sorts of approaches. There are clinicians like Reid (1982),

Day (1990), and Sovner and Hurley (1990) who have stressed that the major treatment methods used with nonretarded depressed individuals are also applicable to patients who are mentally retarded. At the same time, these authors have pointed out that there are specific features of the mentally retarded that deserve the special attention of the clinician. There are others who have emphasized the essential differences in the reactions of mentally retarded patients as compared to the nonretarded (for example, Aman et al., 1986). Finally, there are investigators who have continually searched for new methods of treatment, particularly for treating personality development problems and for improving the poor social skills of the mentally retarded and intervening in their vulnerability to depression caused by unfavorable social interactions (for example, Benson, 1990; Gaedt and Gärtner, 1990).

Various recent treatment approaches to depression among the mentally retarded are presented here. Three main dimensions of disturbances are the guidelines:

- disturbance in vitality
- disturbance in inner world experiences
- disturbance in interaction with the surroundings

These three dimensions of disorders reflect the disorders at three levels: somatic, psychological, and social (Dosen, 1990b). In cases of severe forms of affective disorder, disturbances at all three levels are evident. In the lighter forms, problems at the somatic level are minimal or not present at all.

## Treatment at the Somatic Level: Disturbed Vitality

As stressed earlier, Chapter 4, among the mentally retarded, especially those at very low developmental levels, a depressed mood is a less constant symptom than is a disturbance in vitality. The following symptoms may be considered disturbances in the level of vitality: sleeping and eating disorders, loss of pleasure and energy, motor retardation, loss of diurnal-rhythm, constipation, loss of libido, and vegetative lability. Mood disorder may be present, but not in all cases. In particular cases, the mood may be dysphoric or rather indifferent or apathetic.

Various authors have agreed that, for the patients exhibiting these symptoms and diagnosed as suffering from depression, the treatment indicated first is specific antidepressant medication or electroconvulsive treatment (Day, 1990; Reid, 1982; Sovner & Hurley, 1990; Lund, 1990).

With regard to the use of antidepressant drugs with the mentally retarded, most authors have described their experiences with tricyclic antidepressants like imipramine, amitriptyline, clomipramine, and desipramine.

The effects of these compounds have been described for both psychotic and neurotic forms of depression (Reid, 1972; Szymanski & Biederman, 1984; Field at al., 1986; James, 1986; Warren, Holroyd, & Folstein, 1989). Most of these studies are case reports of uncontrolled clinical trials providing little basis for drawing firm conclusions about the effects of these drugs on the mentally retarded. The dosage of drugs used has varied from 50 mg. to 200 mg./day (Reid, 1982; Lund, 1990; Warren et al., 1989). Tricyclic antidepressants have also been described as being effective with mentally retarded children (Dosen, 1990B). The dosage of amitriptyline used was not higher than 2.5 mg./kg./day.

Most investigators agree that the administration of tricyclics to the mentally retarded should follow the same general principles that apply to the intellectually normal. According to clinical experience, some compounds have a better effect on some symptoms; for example, with marked anxiety and agitation, amitriptyline may give good results, and when there is motoric retardation, imipramine or nortriptyline may be effective. It usually takes several weeks for the therapeutic effect to be seen. The drug should be continued at the therapeutic dosage for six to eight months after full recovery (Day, 1990) and should be withdrawn slowly over a number of weeks. Severe withdrawal symptoms have been reported when high doses were stopped abruptly (Paykel, 1979).

Side-effects of tricyclic antidepressants, like dry mouth, constipation, urinary retention, cardiac toxicity, orthostatic hypotension, and precipitation of convulsions, have been described in all sorts of patients, nonretarded as well as retarded, and adults as well as children. Some authors have stressed that, when using psychopharmaceuticals, mentally retarded patients are more side-effect-prone than nonretarded patients (Dosen, 1990B; Sleator & Sprague, 1978; Snaith, James, & Winokur, 1979; Donaldsen, 1984).

Mainly, authors have described their experiences with neuroleptic drugs for the mentally retarded. Adverse reactions of the mentally retarded when given minor tranquilizers and some sedatives have also been reported. These experiences point to the general need for caution when using psychotropic drugs with the mentally retarded. Thus, despite what some authors (Lund, 1990; Day, 1990) have said, when using antidepressants, there is no evidence that the mentally retarded would experience more side effects than the nonretarded. A low initial dose, slowly increased until an optimal effect has been reached, as well as a moderate maximal dose, has been recommended.

According to some investigators, the usefulness of tricyclic antidepressants in severely and profoundly retarded persons may be questionable. Aman et al. (1986) described a number of profoundly retarded persons who reacted to the imipramine dosage of 3 mg./kg./day with an increase in behavioral difficulties like irritability, social withdrawal, and hyperactivity. These findings correspond with our own clinical experiences with a number of mentally retarded children. Increased aggression and self-injurious behavior were marked in these individuals.

Administrating other sorts of antidepressants to mentally retarded individuals has only rarely been described in the professional literature. The reason may be the rather conservative attitudes of psychiatrists, who seem to feel that the new antidepressants are not more effective than the old ones (Lund, 1990). However, because of the possibility that the mentally retarded are more susceptible to side effects, it would be reasonable to pay more attention to research on new-generation antidepressants particularly because they are less likely to cause certain side effects.

Monoamine oxidase inhibitors (MAOIs) are considered useful in the treatment of neurotic depression. Day (1990) recommended these drugs as the second choice in the treatment of neuroses and as the third choice in cases of psychotic depression (after trials with tricyclics and electroconvulsive therapy have failed).

Tryptophan has also been used alone or in combination with other drugs in the treatment of the depressive mentally retarded (Dosen, 1990A; Day, 1990). The minimal amount of side effects is an important advantage of this compound. However, the efficacy of this drug is still questionable.

As mentioned earlier, antidepressant drugs are being used not only in cases of psychotic forms of depression with clear symptoms of vitality disturbances, but also, sometimes, in cases of neurotic depression with less pronounced or no vital symptoms relating to vitality. In our opinion, in these cases, antidepressants should be seen as the second choice, and other treatment forms, like psychotherapy or counseling, should be tried first. Usually, in these cases, these drugs are administered to support other forms of treatment.

The combination of antidepressants and neuroleptics has been recommended in cases of psychotic delusions and hallucinations.

When antidepressants alone are not responded to, a combination with lithium carbonate may yield good results.

Electroconvulsive therapy (ECT) may also be indicated for depressive mentally retarded patients (Day, 1990; Lund 1990). Despite the serious discussions that have been taking place since the early 1970s concerning the scientific aspects, the ethics, and the clinical value of ECT in treating depression, recently a more positive attitude toward this therapy form has apparently been evolving. However, the acceptance as well as the frequency of application of ECT varies from country to country.

In view of the high prevalance of structural brain abnormalities among the mentally retarded, various psychiatrists are cautious about using ECT with this population because of the possible risk of precipitating epileptic seizures in previously nonepileptic persons (Reid, 1972). In more recent studies, however, some authors (Day, 1990; Lund, 1990) have stressed that, even for the mentally retarded, ECT may be useful when the indication is examined carefully and the procedure is carried out judiciously. Indications for ECT are a life-threatening depression or a resistant depression for which all other treatment methods have failed. Day (1990) recommended using ECT six to eight times at the rate of two to three per week and extending it, if necessary, to a maximum of twelve to fourteen times.

Some authors (Warren et al., 1989; Lazarus, Jaffe, & Dubin, 1990) have reported favorable results when using ECT with depressed Down syndrome patients. They have speculated that Down syndrome individuals may respond better to ECT than other populations because, usually, the psychomotor retardation is more pronounced (Lazarus et al., 1990). The combination of ECT and antidepressant drugs has been recommended.

For a manic-depressive psychosis, the professionals prefer compounds that influence both the manic and the depressive state at the same time. Lithium carbonate has this effect. Recently there have been reports of a number of drugs that exhibit similar effects, for example, carbamazepine, valproic acid, clonazepam, and clonidine. A rapidly-cycling manic-depressive psychosis may be resistant to treatment and may call for a combination of drugs.

Lithium carbonate has been used for both treatment and prophylaxis. For treatment, blood levels of 0.9–1.0 mmol/l and for prophylaxis 0.5–0.8 mmol/l have been recommended. Lithium is usually indicated when there have been frequent episodes of either mania or depression. According to Lund (1990), two severe episodes within five years may be seen as the criterion. Before administering lithium, a careful physical examination is necessary, and particular attention must be paid to the kidney and thyroid function. In addition to its usefulness in depressive and manic-depressive illness, lithium has also been indicated for use during manic episodes. In these cases, some authors have preferred lithium to neuroleptics because there is no risk of drug-induced Parkinsonism, akathisia, or tardive dyskinesia (Sovner & Hurley, 1985). The side effects of lithium (within therapeutic blood levels) may be divided into adverse effects in the first week of treatment (nausea, diarrhea, hand tremor, and incoordination); in the first six months of therapy (increased thirst and urination, weight gain, acne, and swelling of the feet and ankles); and after six months (decreased thyroid and kidney functioning) (Sovner & Hurley, 1985). Among the mentally retarded with damaged brain tissue, a state of confusion has been reported as well. Also, a decrease in seizure threshold and an increase in seizure frequency have been described (Sovner & Hurley, 1985). When the therapeutic blood level is exceeded (above 1.5 mmol/l), symptoms of toxicity may occur: drowsiness, tremors, incoordination progressing to hyperactive deep-tendon reflexes, muscle fasciculations, confusion, seizures, coma, and, if left untreated, possibly death.

Unfavorable interactions between lithium and other antipsychotic agents, particularly haloperidol, have been described as causing high fever, confusion, dyskinesias, and even coma. This toxic reaction is seldom seen.

Carbamazepine has been used for the treatment of various sorts of affective disorders, depression, manic-depressive psychosis, and manic psychosis. Carbamazepine is indicated for the treatment of depression in cases of chronic depressive psychosis, when typical antidepressants have had no effect (Raptis, Enrich, & Stoll, 1989). Rapidly cycling manic-depressive psychoses may react favorably to carbamazepine alone or in combination with lithium (Sovner, 1990b). Also, chronic manic states, often characterized by severe behavioral disorders, may indicate the prescription of carbamazepine. There are reports of positive outcomes with carbamazepine when treating depression or other types of affective disorders of the mentally retarded who are epileptic or autistic or have other forms of organic CNS disorders (Reid, 1982; Sovner, 1990a, Bellaire, Caspari, & Gawlitza, 1989). Aggressive and self-injurious behavior, which are often symptoms of these affective disorders, may be favorably influenced by this drug (Bellaire et al., 1989). The dosage used is higher than the usual therapeutic rage for epileptic disorder. The blood level recommended is between 8.5 and 12.0 mmol/l. The effects of the drug may be visible within one or two weeks. Since affective disorders tend to relapse, preventive therapy with carbamazepine is usually needed. A drug-free trial may be indicated when there are no seizures.

The side effects of carbamazepine are liver damage, bone marrow suppression, allergic skin reactions, and, sometimes, neurological symptoms like incoordination, double vision, and muscle spasms. Also, paradoxical behavioral reactions and even sedation have been reported (Sovner, 1990a).

Valproic acid (VPA) has been described as being effective in rapid-cycling illness and in chronic mania (Sovner, 1989). The blood levels are within the usual therapeutic range of 50 to 100 mg/l. Apparently, this drug may also yield good results in cases of combinations of affective disorders with organic disorders of the CNS. These side effects may occur: neurological (dizziness, sedation, and incoordination), allergic reaction, and gastrointestinal problems (nausea, vomiting, liver toxicity, and diarrhea).

## Treatment of Disturbances of the Inner World Experience

The usual symptoms of disturbances in the inner world experience of depressive persons are low self-esteem, death wishes, feelings of guilt, loss of initiative, passivity, dysphoria, somatic complaints, various anxieties, delusions, hallucinations, autoaggression, and suicidal tendencies. Different approaches are currently being used to treat these disorders, like psychotherapy, counseling and support, the application of behavioral and cognitive strategies, social skills training, and social rehabilitation.

A *psychotherapeutic approach* for the mentally retarded is a subject that triggers vehement discussions among professionals. There are authors who have doubts about the usefulness of psychotherapy with persons having an IQ lower than 50 (Bicknell, 1979; Rubin, 1983). Others (Monfils & Menolascino, 1984) believe that the intellectual level in and of itself is an insufficient criterion for determining suitability for psychotherapy. Any individual who is able to respond to a warm, supportive relationship and who possesses a minimal desire to effect change should, according to these authors, be considered for psychotherapy. Persons at higher levels, who may, additionally, be capable of using the therapist as a role model, can learn to recognize and verbally communicate their feelings (Szymanski, 1980), while those at lower levels can use play as a tool for communication with the therapist (Corbett, 1987).

Many psychotherapeutic methods—psychoanalytic, client-centered, developmental, and other—are currently being used in the treatment of mentally retarded children and adults. A common feature of all these methods is that, in addition to the traditional vehicle for communication between therapist and client—language—other communication channels, like kinesthesia, play, music, and drama, are being used with the mentally retarded.

The goal of psychotherapy for depressed mentally retarded children is to help the child develop a sense of a personal ability to be autonomous and competent in accordance with his or her own needs and capabilities. This so-called developmentally oriented psychotherapy focuses on the child as a developing organism whose needs and sensitivities vary with his or her developmental level, and whose course of development is, to a large extent, determined by the biological substrate and interaction with the environment. Keeping the child's developmental needs in mind, a developmentally oriented psychotherapist not only helps the child with the situational and personal conflicts that are present at the moment but actively stimulates psychosocial development by intervening in the child's environmental experiences and influencing those experiences in such a way that the child's adaptation can be facilitated (Dosen, 1984; O'Quinn, 1988; Gaedt & Gärtner, 1990).

Favorable results have been reported in the treatment of depressive mentally retarded children with the method of developmentally oriented relationship therapy (Dosen, 1984, 1990b). In this treatment approach, the affective positive relationship between the therapist and the child is dually utilized, as both therapeutic tool and therapeutic aim. This treatment method is a derivative of the psychodynamic and cognitive theories of development and of Bowlby's attachment theory (1973). This theory states that human beings have an existential need for bonding with others in order to establish a psychological security base that enables them to learn to explore and master their surroundings. "Giving the child a hand," the therapist attempts to free him or her from isolation, fears, and conflicts and helps him or her to adapt to and cope with the present situation (Dosen, 1992).

Another form of treatment for depressed mentally retarded children used in the developmental approach is the reeducation of psychomotoricity (Bojanin & Ispanovic-Radojkovic, 1990). In this method, movement is the most elementary form of communication. By means of sensorimotor activity, the child learns to find his or her own way in space, experiences safety in familiar circles, and learns about the material world. By means of motoric interactions, the therapist interprets and reveals to the child the world that he or she has abandoned through depressive withdrawal or chaos.

There are authors such as Sand et al. (1990) who have been successful in applying psychodynamic developmental therapy and in combining it with pedagogical and milieu treatment for depressed children and adults as well. The focus of this therapeutic approach is on the weakness of various aspects of the self that usually characterizes a depressed mentally retarded person. According to these authors, the main difference between this form of psychotherapy and psychoanalysis is the attitude of the therapist. The therapist does not maintain a therapeutic distance; on the contrary, she or he is actively involved in affective interactions with the client. When patients have speech impediments, it is important to pay attention to their facial expressions, gesticulations, and movements, which may express their affective state. The reaction of the therapist to these emotional signals depends on his or her diagnostic insight into the emotional problems of the client. The therapist makes a developmentally oriented diagnosis and interacts with the client at the developmental level that the client is at. In doing so, the therapist attempts to avoid interactions that confirm the patient in the pathological state and directs the interaction to more appropriate experiences. In teaching the client to become aware of his or her own needs, the therapist attempts to heighten the level of interaction and to further stimulate the client's emotional development.

By making use of pedagogical and milieu strategies, we attempt to strengthen the effects of our psychotherapeutic work and to facilitate the adaptation of the mentally retarded person to the living environment.

The client-centered approach has, until recently, been limited to the nonretarded population. Prouty (1976) examined client-centered theory and concluded that the major theoretical limitation relating to retarded persons centered on Rogers's concept of "psychological contact." Introducing Roger's "pretherapy" as a method of achieving psychological contact with mentally retarded persons, Prouty and Cornwall (1990) reported favorable results with a client-centered approach to mentally retarded depressive clients.

Psychoanalytic psychotherapies have also recently been applied to the mentally retarded (Sinason, 1990; Ruth, 1992; Hollins, 1992). Verbal communication is not considered essential. Other communication channels and the ability to create an emotional relationship form the basis of the use of individual as well as group psychoanalytic treatment even with the severely and profoundly mentally retarded.

Grief therapy has been recommended by Hollins (1990, 1992) in cases of depression following bereavement caused by the loss of relatives, friends, or staff. The expression of emotions through color, gesture, and other non-verbal forms of communication has proved helpful. In addition, bereavement counseling and mourning guidance may yield good results.

Various other psychotherapeutic methods have been utilized in treating depressive mentally retarded individuals. So-called symbolic interactional therapy (Caton, 1990) combines learning techniques with fantasy play, as employed by the psychodynamic approach, in a cognitive-behavioral mode. The therapist uses symbols, in the form of toys or figurines, as a basis for concrete communication. Unconditional acceptance, warmth, and empathy toward the client are accentuated in this approach.

*Counseling and support* may be a useful approach in cases in which constant conflicts between the client and the surroundings play an important role. By counseling or management of daily living problems directed toward solving adaptation difficulties, rather than attempting to change the client's personality, the mentally retarded individual may be helped to interact with the surroundings in a manner that is more satisfying to herself or himself as well as to others. Counseling must not, however, be confused with therapy. The term *therapy* should be reserved for treatment targeted at achieving changes in basic ways of feeling and thinking. To attain these results, other methods and techniques are used than those applied in counseling (Dosen & Day, 1992; Hollins, 1992). There are various *behavioral and cognitive methods* for treating depressive mentally retarded persons. Behaviorists assume that, if the behaviors associated with depression are modified, the symptoms will decrease and the desired behavior will increase. Matson (1982) described the good results achieved when several patients were treated by having their depressive behaviors corrected and their non-depressive behavior reinforced with tokens. Other authors have also reported favorable results when reinforcing behavior that was incompatible with depression (Boyd & Lewis, 1980).

Cognitive therapies for treating depression focus on the negative patterns of thinking and attitudes in depressives. Authors applying this approach (Beck et al., 1979) focus on the negative views the client has of his or her existence. A depressed patient has a negative view of the world as well as of the self and of the future. The therapist's task is to teach the client to think in another way. Despite previous ambiguity concerning the use of this method with the mentally retarded, recent results have been encouraging. Hurley (1989) reported the successful treatment of a Down syndrome depressed adult by means of cognitive therapy. Benson (1990) described the advantages of the cognitive-behavioral model in the treatment of depression among the mentally retarded. Schneider (1992) pointed to the favorable effects of the so-called rational-emotive therapy, formally introduced by Ellis (1962), in the treating of nonretarded clients. When modified, this mode of treatment may be effective in building peer support systens as well as independence and reality testing among the mentally retarded.

According to some investigators, the poor social skills of the mentally retarded may play a role in depression (Reiss & Benson, 1985; Laman & Reiss, 1987). *Social skills training* may therefore be of importance in the treatment of depression (Griffiths, 1990). The methods of training social skills vary from the shaping of target behaviors by means of simple reinforcement schemes to more complex techniques. Benson (1990) suggested the following stages: instruction (defining the focus of training), modeling (demonstrating the appropriate behavior), role playing (the supervised practice of behavior), feedback (constructive criticism by the trainer), reinforcement, and homework.

Besides treatment and training efforts undertaken to ameliorate the personal qualities of the depressed individual, it is important to work on his or her *social rehabilitation* as well. Whenever possible, the patient should be gradually reintroduced into his or her former milieu. In cases in which this is not possible, patients should be given guidance and support in creating other living space for themselves and another milieu in which they can make appropriate use of their own capabilities.

## Treatment of Impaired Interaction with the Surrounding Milieu

Treatment involving interactions with one's surroundings deals with both animate and inanimate objects. The disorders include aggression, destructiveness, negativism, attention deficit, hyperactivity, hypoactivity, passivity, withdrawal, and other adaptation and reaction disorders. These difficulties may be seen partially as learned behavioral patterns that occur as maladjusted reactions in particular circumstances. It is important to analyze the circumstances in which such behaviors occur in order to alter the reaction patterns of persons in the client's surroundings and to prevent the maintenance of maladaptive development. Furthermore, a feature common to these depressed mentally retarded persons is that they show a lack of interest in material objects and creativity. Their real performance level is often lower than their potential cognitive ability. In treatment, they should be stimulated to explore and to experience their own power in altering their surroundings in a purposeful manner. It is important to stress that the material that makes up their environment has to be carefully chosen so that it suits the developmental level and the stimulation needs of the individual.

The treatments of choice for this purpose are the behavioral and cognitive therapies described earlier. Furthermore, it is essential to plan the daily activities well and to involve the patient in such activities as music and dance.

The training of social interactions is also an important aspect of the treatment. Further, the methods already mentioned in connection with the treatment of disturbances in inner world experience may also be applied in the treatment of impaired interactions; group therapy may be very useful in this regard. It is worth noting, too, that pedagogical treatments are reported to have been successful as well. The pedagogical schools in the Dutch, Swiss, and German traditions have extensive experience in the directive pegagogical treatment of the mentally retarded (Gennep, 1990; Reukauf, 1985; Bradl, 1987). From this point of view, the problem behavior is seen as being a call for help, and its treatment focuses on the real-life situation. Three elements of this approach are of essential importance: creating a therapeutic climate, structuring the activities, and establishing an appropriate relationship (Gennep, 1990). In this approach, the totality of the person's existence may be involved in a process aimed at modifying some behaviors and helping patients to acquire more adaptive behaviors and skills. The relationships between the client, on the one hand, and the caregiver and others in the living milieu, on the other hand, are an important aspect of the pedagogical approach. Responsibility for one's own behavior and respect for other people form the core of the treatment (Gemert, 1990; Sand et al., 1990). In developing a sense of responsibility and an awareness of the consequences of one's own behavior, the client is being taught to be as competent and independent as her or his abilities permit. All this happens within an individually tailored, "normalized" pedagogical situation that encompasses as many real-life aspects as is possible. This treatment may be combined with individual psychotherapies aimed at dealing with other aspects of depression (Reukauf & Herzka 1990).

## Practical Issues of Treatment

As stressed earlier, treatment should be closely linked to diagnostic insights concerning the type and severity of the disorder. Information about possible etiological factors—such as precipitating events, familial predisposition, specific biological impairments, personality problems, and specific developmental difficulties—may have an important influence on the choice of treatment. To be taken into acount, too, are such factors as: the level of retardation, the presence of comorbid states, previous treatment efforts, and social circumstances (Ruedrich et al., 1992). Because of the complexity of the disorder in mentally retarded individuals, their treatment may call for the use of a combination of various approaches. From the practical point of view, however, it is important to make schemata of treatment combinations for particular clinical pictures. An insight into the etiological factors is particularly important in such schematizations.

In our clinical practice (Dosen, 1990a), with psychotic forms and with the symptoms of disturbance in vitality mentioned earlier, we usually start with psychotropic medication. However, this intervention is always combined with one or more of the other treatment approaches, like psychotherapy and behavioral and cognitive therapies. Also, especially for prophylactic purposes, guidance for rehabilitation and adequate social involvement in the structures of the living milieu are essential.

> Jonathan is a thirty-eight-year-old severely retarded man, living together with seven other mentally retarded individuals with severe behavioral disturbances. He has been diagnosed as having pervasive developmental disorder (PDD) and exhibits no speech. Medically, he has cerebral paraparesis and prebirth hypothyroidism. Because of his PDD, Jonathan shows marked stereotyped fluttering movements of the legs and arms. Sometimes, psychotic features are in evidence.
>
> Until his eleventh year, Jonathan stayed within his family. Descriptions by his parents make clear that, in those years, Jonathan and his mother almost formed a kind of dual unit: His mother has been described in the image of a "livery," always gushing over her son and following in his footsteps.
>
> On admission to an institution for the mentally retarded, Jonathan displayed severe behavioral disturbances: autoaggression, throwing objects, tearing up clothes, and so on. In the course of the following years, it became more and more clear that episodes of this sort were accompanied by various somatic symptoms, such as looking grayish in the face, eczema, constipation, poor appetite, irregular sleep, and crying fits. These episodes sometimes alternated with calm periods, and also with short periods marked by motoric excitation, laughing fits, running around in the nude, fluttering, and so on. Jonathan's diagnosis was manic-depressive psychosis, superimposed on pervasive developmental disorder. He proved resistant to lithium prophylaxis.
>
> A combination of lithium carbonate and carbamazepine gave favorable results. Jonathan's psychotic episodes disappeared, but the periods of problem behavior persisted. Besides medications, Jonathan was treated by a developmentally based approach focused on the achievement of a constancy of space, time, and persons and on a reduction of sensory stimuli (see Chapter 4). He also received special attention from a member of the nursing staff.
>
> Further, Jonathan was trained to perform particular activities of social significance for other persons in the group. The developmental approach was targeted to meet his basic psychological needs. Stated differently, we regarded this man as suffering primarily from a pervasive developmental disorder. His inability to cope

with intensive stimuli and changing environmental and personal circumstances within the group had an adverse effect, comparable to recurring of chronic stress, that made him vulnerable to psychotic episodes. When placed in a minimally changing milieu and when the stimuli were reduced, Jonathan was given an opportunity to consolidate the psychological processes he needed to find a new homeostasis. He was also given affective support by one particular person in order to compensate for his loss of basic emotional security (which he suffered on separation from his mother). Treating the primary disorder was considered basic to the treatment of the secondary illness.

In other forms of depression, such as reactive neurotic or developmentally determined depressive conditions, we used psychotherapeutic treatment, behavioral and cognitive approaches, or other forms of treatment, separately or in combination. Psychotropic medication is also used, but usually as a support for the other methods. It would not be correct to call this method of treatment eclectic. Rather, it is a multidimensional and multifocal approach that offers more possibilities for combating the disorder on a wider front, which is commensurate with the multifeatured complexity of the disturbances of the depressed individual.

Deborah is a twenty-seven-year-old woman with mild cognitive impairment. During childhood and adolescence, she maintained a passively dependent and docile relationship with her parents. When Deborah was seventeen, she struck up a friendship with a boy. This seems to have changed her life: Suddenly, she no longer wanted to be awakened by her mother in the morning, she wanted to prepare her own breakfast, and she wanted to travel to a sheltered workshop independently. After a courtship of five years, Deborah insisted on living with her boyfriend independently.

In Deborah's strivings for independence, her sister, who is four years older, had always functioned as a model that had to be copied. Her sister represented the idealized image of autonomy, independence, and adulthood that Deborah strove to emulate.

After nine months of living with her boyfriend, the relationship broke down and Deborah returned to her parents. Some months afterward, she was admitted to a community group-home for the mildly and moderately retarded. However, three months after admission, Deborah slipped into a psychosis with depressive features and suicidal ideation. After four years of inpatient care at different institutions, Deborah was placed in a live-in group of mildly retarded young adults with mental illness or behavioral problems. She still is there.

At the beginning, strong passivity and inactivity dominated her clinical picture. She demonstrated no intrinsic pleasure or interest in daily activities. Her participation in playing games was minimal. Her dependence on the instructions of her caregivers was very obvious. As a result, Deborah gained much attention and sought physical and psychological proximity, a proximity that seemed to offer her some existential reassurance.

In the course of time, however, Deborah began to seek independence and to make demands that were far beyond her socioemotional developmental level. This tendency was accompanied by various behavioral peculiarities: running away, sulking and pouting behavior, strong passivity, provocations, and thwarting. She made false accusations about the caregivers, and they were forced to take corrective action to put an end to her outbursts of aggression.

When Deborah's parents went on vacation, she reproached them for letting her down by making verbal threats of committing suicide and making them responsible for that. As Deborah noted, "Nobody cares for me. My life isn't worth anything. I am a good-for-nothing. I am a bad and worthless girl. I'd rather be dead." These remarks alternated with utterances to the effect that their departure for vacation did not bother her at all and that she could easily do without them!

From the psychodynamic point of view, Deborah's behaviors seemed to represent some of the characteristics of the separation–individuation phase. Her feelings of omnipotence, her obstinacy, and her role-playing developments centered on gender identity and reflected the first hallmark of striving for individuation. However, her relationships with her caregivers and especially with her parents seemed to reflect much more the characteristics of the rapprochement phase. Moreover, Deborah's self-representation still depended largely on the continuous proximity of her bonding figures, the continuity of her environment, and predictability in her daily activities. Once she felt a slight experience of loss of a sense of selfhood (due either to the excessive demands of her self-ideal or to her sensed loss of the bonding figures), her behavioral tendencies to cling to the bonding figures were mobilized.

Based on developmental diagnosis concerning her psychological needs and the level of her emotional development, a psychotherapeutic developmentally oriented treatment was recommended. Also an antidepressant medication was prescribed to support the psychotherapy. Further, Deborah was brought under a well-structured daily program within which clear limits were set forth concerning tolerated and nontolerated behavior. At the same time, her parents were given guidance in understanding the signals their daughter sent by her inappropriate behavior, and in learning how to react to meet her needs.

Except for some particular differences, the treatment of depression in the general population of mentally handicapped people is globally and principally the same. A comprehensive treatment plan should be formulated before treatment begins. It should include the management of any associated factors and should take into account any wider or general issues that require further assessment. A full explanation of the nature of the illness and the proposed treatment plan and its rationale should be given to the patient and his or her relatives and caregivers. Relatives and caregivers play a crucial role in securing adherence to the course of treatment, and it is important that their confidence and cooperation be obtained.

The treatment setting is also of great importance. Less severe forms of depression can usually be successfully treated on an outpatient basis. Extra support in the form of home help or care attendant services, community-nursing or social-work input, or day hospital attendance may be required, particularly in the early stages of the illness. Frequent psychiatric review is essential, and hospitalization may become necessary if the patient's condition deteriorates or if other problems arise. Inpatient treatment may be called for under such conditions as severe depression, diagnostic uncertainty, inadequate community support, or inability of the family or caregivers to cope with the situation.

In addition to specific treatment to be targeted on the depression, a full program of daily activities should be made available, and the patient should be encouraged to participate in it. Less taxing and more recreational activities, like art therapy, are the best in the early stages, but during recovery, patients should be reintroduced, as far as is possible, to the types of activities they had been undertaking prior to the illness.

The discharge and aftercare of hospital inpatients should be properly planned and coordinated. Wherever possible, the patients should be restored to their former state of mental health before discharge; releasing a patient in a fragile mental state can lead to rapid deterioration, readmission, and loss of confidence in the treatment program. After a major illness, the patient should gradually be reintroduced into the community through a process of weekend and extended leaves. Some patients are unable to return to their former place of residence because they need more support than can be provided there or because the previous environment is wanting or otherwise a major causative factor in the illness (Day, 1985).

Community mental-handicap nurses who are appropriately trained and experienced should play an important role in aftercare, such as in ensuring treatment compliance, monitoring progress, and providing support, guidance, advice, and access to psychiatric intervention when necessary. Relatives and caregivers should always be informed about signs and symptoms that may indicate a relapse and should be instructed to seek psychiatric advice accordingly.

The question still persists as to whether or not it is essential that mentally handicapped people with a psychiatric illness be treated in services properly geared to meet their particular needs. While there are those who argue—from normalization principles—that mentally handicapped people with mental illness should be treated in the generic psychiatric services (Melin, 1988), the majority view is in favor of specialized services, as reflected in the services developed throughout different Western countries (Zarfas, 1988; Dosen, 1988). The arguments in support of a specialized service have been detailed by Day (1988). They relate to the difficulties of diagnosis, the overall pattern of disease, and the need to take into account the underlying mental handicap, dependency levels, and coexisting physical handicaps in treatment rehabilitation and aftercare. Another argument is that, in a generic setting, where mentally retarded people would be in the minority, the main emphasis is on the care of nonhandicapped patients; this emphasis implies that there would be little opportunity for the staff to gain the necessary experience, knowledge, and skills or to establish a cadre of experts to teach, train, and carry out the much needed research.

Specialized psychiatric services should be comprehensive and should include a sufficient number of treatment settings to provide specialized programs and care for the spectrum of problems presented and to take into account the client's range of intellectual level, age, and sex. Special facilities for rehabilitation and continuing care in the community are also needed, as mentally handicapped people with psychiatric or behavior problems do not always fit well into regular community facilities.

## Summary

The treatment of depression in the mentally retarded is, globally speaking, the same as the treatment for the nonretarded population. However, because of the multiplicity and specificity of factors playing a role in the mentally retardation, the treatment approach calls for a multidimensional and selectively specific approach. A plan of treatment should be made according to the clinical picture and the prevalence of disturbances in a particular client's existential life. For a disturbance in vitality, for example, psychotropic medications are the first treatment line. Personality problems, on the other hand, may call for an accentuation of psychotherapeutic treatment in the first line. Various other approaches are being developed for the treatment of the mentally retarded. Most of these treatment methods are actually adaptations of treatment approaches usually used with the nonretarded population. There are, however, also treatment methods that have been developed specially for mentally retarded individuals. Increased sophistication in diagnosis and more refined insight into etiological factors make possible the development of new treatment forms or a combination of different forms suited to this particular population. Recent developments in this field make clear the necessity of creating special services for this population and of providing special education for professionals in this field. The growing interest of a widening circle of professionals and the increased attention to scientific investigations in this area are promising.

# References

Aman, M., White, A., Vaithiantan, C., & Techan, C. (1986). Preliminary study of imipramine in profoundly retarded residents. *J. Autism Develop. Disorders, 16*(3) 263–273.

Beck, A. T., Rush, A. J., Shaw, B. F., & Emery, G. (1979). *Cognitive therapy of depression.* New York: Guilford Press.

Bellaire, W., Caspari, D., & Gawlitza, M. (1989). (Eds.), Carbamazepin bei Oligophrenen. In B. Múller-Oerlinghausen, S. Haas, K. D. Stoll. *Carbamazepin in der psychiatrie.* Stutgart, New York: Georg Thieme Verlag.

Benson, B. A. (1990). Behavioral treatment of depression. In A. Dosen & F. J. Menolascino (Eds.), *Depression in mentally retarded children and adults.* Leiden: Logon.

Bicknell, D. J. (1979). Treatment and management of disturbed mentally handicapped patients. In F. E. James & R. P. Snaith (Eds.), *Psychiatric illness and mental handicap.* London: Gaskell.

Bojanin, S., & Ispanovic-Radojkovic, V. (1990). Treatment of depression in mentally retarded children: A developmental approach. In A. Dosen & F. J. Menolascino (Eds.), *Depression in mentally retarded children and adults.* Leiden: Logon.

Bowlby, V. (1973). *Attachment and loss: Vol. 1. Attachment.* New York: Basic Books.

Boyd, T. L., & Lewis, D. J. (1980). Depression. In R. J. Daitzamn (Ed.), *Clinical behavior therapy and behavior modification* (Vol. 1). New York: Garland STPM Press.

Bradl, Ch. (1987). *Geistegbehinderte und Psychiatrie.* In W. Dreher, Th. Hofmann & Ch. Bradl (Eds.), *Geistig behinderte zwischen Pädagogik und Psychiatrie.* Bonn: Psychiatrie Verlag.

Caton, J. B. (1990). Symbolic interactional therapy: A treatment intervention for depression in mentally retarded adults. In A. Dosen & F. J. Menolascino (Eds.), *Depression in mentally retarded children and adults.* Leiden: Logon.

Corbett, J. (1987). Mental retardation, psychiatric aspects. In M. Rutter & L. Hersov (Eds.), *Child and adolescent psychiatry.* London: Blackwell.

Day, K. (1985). Psychiatric disorder in the middle-aged and elderly mentally handicapped. *Br. J. Psychiatr., 147,* 660–667.

Day, K. (1988). Service for psychiatrically disordered mentally handicapped adults: A U.K. Perspective. *Aust. N.Z. J. Develop. Disabilities, 14,* 31–35.

Day, K. A. (1990). Treatment, care and management—A general overview. In A. Dosen & F. J. Menolaschino (Eds.), *Depression in mentally retarded children and adults.* Leiden: Logon.

Donaldson, J. Y. (1984). Specific psychopharmacological approaches and rationale for mentally ill mentally retarded children. In F. J. Menolascino & J. A. Stark (Eds.), *Handbook of mental illness in the mentally retarded* (pp. 172–181). New York: Plenum Press.

Dosen, A. (1984). Experiences with individual relationship therapy within a therapeutic milieu for retarded children with severe emotional disorders. In J. Berg (Ed.), *Perspectives and progress in mental retardation* (Vol. 2). Baltimore Univ. Park Press.

Dosen, A. (1988). Community care for people with mental retardation in The Netherlands. *Aust. N.Z. J. Develop. Disabilities, 14,* 15–18.

Dosen A. (1990a): *Psychische en gedragsstoornissen bij zwakzinnigen.* Amsterdam: Boom.

Dosen, A. (1990b). Psychotherapeutic approaches in the treatment of depression in mentally retarded children. In A. Dosen & F. J. Menolascino (Eds.), *Depression in mentally retarded children and adults,* Leiden, Logon.

Dosen, A. (1992). Psychodynamically oriented relationship therapy. In A. Dozen, K. Day (Eds.), *Treatment of mental illness and behavioral disorders in mentally retarded children and adults.*

Dosen, A., Day, K. (1992). Survey of treatment methods for the mentally retarded. In A. Dosen, K. Day (Eds.), *Treatment of mental illness and behavioral disorders in the mentally retarded.*

Ellis, A. (1962). *Reason and emotion in psychotherapy.* New York: Lyle Stuart.

Field, C. J., Aman, M. G., White, A. J., & Vaithianathan, C. (1986). A single-subject study of imipramine in a mentally retarded woman with depressive symptoms. *J. Ment. Defic. Res., 30,* 191–198.

Gaedt, Ch., Gärtner, D. (1990): Depressive Grundprozesse—Reinszenifrungen der Selbstenwertung. Neuerkerode: Neuerkeröder Forum 4.

Gemert, G. H. van. (1990). An educational approach to behavioral disorders. In A. Dosen, A. van Gennep, G. Zwanikken. (Eds.), *Treatment of mental illness and behavioral disorders in the mentally retarded.* Leiden: Logon.

Gennep, A. van. (1990). Treatment of persons with a mental handicap: Trends in orthopedagogy. In A. Dosen, A. van Gennep, G. Zwanikken (Eds.), *Treatment of mental illness and behavioral disorders.* Leiden: Logon.

Griffiths, D. (1990). The social skills game, Parts 1 and 2. *Habilitative Ment. Healthcare Newslett., 9,* 1–13.

Hollins, S. C. (1990). Grief therapy for people with mental handicap. In A. Dosen, A. van Gennep, G. Zwanikken (Eds.), *Treatment of mental illness and behavioral disorders in the mentally retarded.* Leiden: Logon.

Hollins, S. C. (1992). Psychotherapeutic methods. In A. Dosen & K. Day (Eds.). *Treatment of mental illness and behavioral disorders in mentally retarded children and adults.*

Hurley, A. D. (1989). Behavior therapy for psychiatric disorders in mentally retarded individuals. In R. J. Fletcher & F. J. Menolascino (Eds.), *Mental retar-*

dation and mental illness: Assessment, service and treatment for the dually diagnosed. Lexington, MA: Lexington Books, D. C. Health.

James, D. H. (1986). Psychiatric and behavioral disorders amongst older severely mentally handicapped inpatients. *J. Ment. Defic. Res., 30,* 341–345.

Laman, D. S., & Reiss, S. (1987). Social skill deficiencies associated with depressed mood of mentally retarded adults. *Am. J. Ment. Defic., 92,* 224–229.

Lazarus, A., Jaffe, R. L., & Dubin, W. R. (1990). Electroconvulsive therapy and major depression in Down's syndrome. *J. Clin. Psychiatr., 51,* 422–425.

Lund, J. (1990). Psychopharmacological approaches to the treatment of depression in the mentally retarded. In A. Dosen & F. J. Menolascino (Eds.), *Depression in mentally retarded children and adults.* Leiden: Logon.

Matson, J. (1982). Treatment of the behavioral characteristics of depression in the mentally retarded. *Behav. Ther., 13,* 209–213.

Melin, L. (1988). Services and provisions for persons with mental retardation in Sweden. *Aust. N.Z. J. Devel. Disabilities, 14,* 37–42.

Monfils, N. S., & Menolascino, F. J. (1984). Modified individual and group treatment approaches for the mentally retarded mentally ill. In F. J. Menolascino & J. Stark (Eds.), *Handbook of mental illness in the mentally retarded.* New York: Plenum Press.

O'Quinn, L. (1988). Medical treatment of psychiatric disorders in the handicapped. In J. Gering & L. McCarthy (Eds.), *The psychiatry of handicapped children and adolescents.* Boston: College Hill.

Paykel, E. S. (1979). Management of acute depression. In E. S. Paykel & A. Coppen (Eds.), *Psychopharmacology of affective disorders.* Oxford: Oxford University Press.

Prouty, G. F. (1976). Pre-therapy: A method of treating pre-expressive psychotic retarded patients. *Psychother. theory res. pract., 13,* 290–294.

Prouty, G. F., & Cronwall, M. (1990): Psychotherapeutic approach in the treatment of depression in mentally retarded adults. In A. Dosen & J. Menolascino (Eds.), *Depression in mentally retarded children and adults.* Leiden: Logon.

Raptis, H., Emrich, M., & Stoll, D. K. (1989). Antidepressive Wirkung von Carbamazepin. In B. Müller-Oerlinghausen, S. Haas, K. D. Stoll (Eds.), *Carbamazepin in der psychiatrie.* Stutgart, New York: Georg Thieme Verlag.

Reid, A. H. (1972). Psychosis in adult mental defectives: Manic depressive psychosis. *Br. J. Psychiatr., 120,* 205–212.

Reid, A. H. (1982). *The psychiatry of mental handicap.* London: Basil Blackwell.

Reiss, S. & Benson, B. A. (1985). Psychosocial correlates of depression in mentally retarded adults: Minimal social support and stigmatization. *Am. J. Ment. Defic., 89,* 331–337.

Reukauf, W. (1985). Zur Praxis der Kooperation zwischen Psychotherapeuten und Heilpädagogen aus psychologischer Sicht. *Schweiz. Heilpäd. Rundsch., 7*(11), 265–268.

Reukauf, W., & Herzka, H. S. (1990). Aspect of integration and dialogical co operation between therapeutic pedagogues and psychotherapists in working with the mentally retarded. In A. Dosen, A. van Gennep, G. Zwanikken (Eds.), *Treatment of mental illness and behavioral disorders.* Leiden: Logon.

Rubin, R. L. (1983). Bridging the gap through individual counseling and psychotherapy with mentally retarded people. In F. Menolascino & B. McCann (Eds.), *Mental health and mental retardation.* Baltimore: University Park Press.

Ruedrich, S. L., Des Noyers, Hurley A., & Sovner, R. (1992). Treatment of mood disorders in mentally retarded persons. In A. Dosen, K. Day. (Eds.), *Treatment of mental illness and behavioral disorders in mentally retarded children and adults.*

Ruth, R. (1992). Psychoanalytic therapies. In A. Dosen & K. Day (Eds.), *Treatment of mental illness and behavioral disorders in mentally retarded children and adults.*

Sand, A., Ohmes, J., Gartner-Peterhoff, D., & Nierste, E. (1990). Therapeutische umgang mit Entwertungsprozessen. In Ch. Gaedt (Ed.), *Selbstentwertung-depressive Inszenierungen bei Menschen mit geistiger Behinderung.* Neuerkeröde: Neuerkeröder Beitrage.

Schneider, N. (1992). A rational emotive group treatment approach with dually diagnosed adults. In A. Dosen & K. Day (Eds.), *Treatment of mental illness and behavioral disorders in mentally retarded children and adults.*

Sinason, V. (1990). Individual psychoanalytic psychotherapy with severely and profoundly mentally handicapped patients. In A. Dosen, A. van Gennep, & G. Zwanikken (Eds.), *Treatment of mental illness and behavioral disorders in the mentally retarded.* Leiden: Logon.

Sleator, E. K., & Sprague, R. L. (1978). Pediatric psychopharmacology. In E. K. Sleator, R. L. Sprague (Eds.), *Principles of psychopharmacology* (pp. 573–591). New York: Academic Press.

Snaith, R. P., James, F. E., & Winokur, B. (1979). The drug treatment of mental illness and epilepsy in the mentally handicapped patient. In F. E. James & R. P. Snaith (Eds.): Psychiatric illness and mental handicap, London, Gaskal.

Sovner, R. (1989). The use of valproate in the treatment of mentally retarded persons with typical and atypical bipolar disorders. *J. Clin. Psychiatr., 50*(3, Suppl.), 40–43.

Sovner, R. (1990a). Bipolar disorder in persons with developmental disorders: An overview. In A. Dosen & F. Menolascino (Eds.), *Depression in mentally retarded children and adults* (pp. 175–197). Leiden: Logon.

Sovner, R. (1990b). Developments in the use of psychotropic drugs. *Cur. Opinion Psychiatr., 3,* 606–612.

Sovner, R., & Hurley, A. (1985). Drug profiles: 1. Lithium: *Psychiatr. Asp. of Ment. Retard. Rev., 4,* 6.

Sovner, R., Hurley, A. (1990). Affective disorder update. *Habilit. Ment. Health Care Newsl., 9,* 12.

Szymanski, L. S. (1980). Individual psychotherapy with retarded persons. In L. Szymanski & P. Tanquay (Eds.), *Emotional disorders of mentally retarded persons.* Baltimore: University Park Press.

Szymanski, L. S., & Biederman, J. (1984). Depression and anorexia nervosa of persons with Down syndrome. *Am. J. Ment. Defic., 89,* 246–251.

Warren, A. C., Holroyd, S., & Folstein, M. F. (1989). Major depression in Down's syndrome. *Br. J. Psychiatr., 155,* 202–205.

Zarfas, D. E. (1988). Mental health systems for people with mental retardation: A Canadian perspective. *Aust. N.Z. J. Devel. Disabilities, 14,* 3–7.

# 12

## Treatment of Schizophrenic and Paranoid Syndromes in Persons with Mental Retardation

*Andrew Reid*

There is some evidence that the natural history of schizophrenia has changed over the last one hundred years and that it is now running a more benign course. Kraepelin (1919), for example, concluded that only 17 percent of his patients in Heidelberg were socially well adjusted several years later. In 1932, Mayer-Gross reported social recovery in about 30 percent of patients after sixteen years. By 1966, Brown et al. had reported social recovery in 56 percent of patients after five years.

In a rather different study, Manfred Bleuler (1974), reporting on his twenty-year follow-up of 208 schizophrenics at the Burgholzli clinic in Zurich, noted that approximately one-third of his patients had made a stable recovery, many had run an intermittent course with acute episodes followed by improvement, and only 10 percent had run a chronically progressive course necessitating long-stay care in the hospital. He also noted that, with the advent of neuroleptics, virtually no cases of schizophrenia ran the catastrophic course of earlier years resulting in the syndrome of dementia praecox. Bleuler's message was, therefore, one of hope. Even so, schizophrenia remains a most distressing disease, and we know that up to 10 percent of schizophrenics die by suicide (Roy, 1982).

It is against this background that the success or failure of treatment approaches has to be considered. Contemporary treatment approaches are two-pronged and rely on neuroleptic drugs and social and psychological measures.

### Neuroleptic Medication

Most of the effective neuroleptics appear to exercise their effect through the dopamine receptors of the nigrostriatal system and are believed to act by increasing dopamine turnover. Antipsychotic drugs also affect cholinergic, alpha-adrenergic, histaminergic, and serotonergic receptors. The main therapeutic action of antipsychotic drugs is to reduce hallucinations, delusions, agitation, and psychomotor excitement in schizophrenia, organic psychosis, and mania. To refer to these drugs as *antischizophrenic agents* implies a more specific action than can be justified (Gelder, Gath, & Mayou, 1989).

The compounds available fall into three main groups: phenothiazines, thioxanthenes, and butyrophenones. The phenothiazines themselves fall into three subgroups according to their side chains: the aliphatic, piperidine, and piperazine compounds. In general, the aliphatic compounds, such as chlorpromazine, are more sedating and have moderate extrapyramidal effects; the piperidine compounds, such as thioridazine, have the least extrapyramidal effects; and the piperazine compounds, such as trifluoperazine and fluphenazine, are the least sedating, the most likely to produce extrapyramidal effects, and the most potent therapeutically. The thioxanthenes are similar in structure and properties to the phenothiazines. The butyrophenones are powerful antipsychotics, have little sedative effect, and are particularly prone to producing extrapyramidal side effects. The butylpiperidines, of which pimozide is the most often used in clinical practice, are related to the butyrophenones but have a longer half-life and can be administered on a once-only daily oral basis. The slow-release depot preparations, such as fluphenazine, flupenthixol, and clopenthixol, can be administered in an intramuscular depot form on a variable time scale from once weekly to once monthly, according to individual patient responsiveness and the side effect profile. The depot preparations are largely effective in overcoming problems with compliance.

In general, chlorpromazine is the first-line choice of drug when a sedative effect is required, trifluoperazine or haloperidol when sedation is undesirable or unnecessary, and fluphenazine decanoate when a depot preparation is required. Thioridazone is probably the drug of choice in elderly patients in whom it is desirable to reduce the incidence of extrapyramidal or anticholinergic side effects.

The many different antipsychotic drugs share a broad spectrum of unwanted side effects that are mainly related to their antidopaminergic, antiadrenergic, and anticholinergic properties.

**Antidopaminergic Side Effects.** These include acute dystonia, akathisia, the Parkinsonian syndrome and, tardive dyskinesia. Acute dystonia is rare; it tends to occur in young men shortly after the onset of treatment, especially with the butyrophenone or piperazine group of phenothiazines, and presents with involuntary postural distortions. Akathisia is an unpleasant feeling of physical restlessness. The Parkinsonian syndrome includes akinesia, facial immobility, lack of associated movements when walking, rigidity, and tremor. Tardive dyskinesia, consisting of forced buccolingual masticatory movements may be particularly distressing because, unlike the other extrapyramidal syndromes, it may not remit when neuroleptic drugs are discontinued.

**Antiadrenergic Effects.** These include postural hypotension and inhibition of ejaculation.

**Anticholinergic Effects.** These include dry mouth, urinary hesitancy and retention, constipation, reduced sweating, blurred vision, and, rarely, the precipitation of glaucoma.

**Other Effects.** These include cardiac arrhythmias, weight gain, galactorrhea and amenorrhea in some women, hypothermia (especially in the elderly), photosensitivity, retinal degeneration (especially with thioridazine in high dosage), and, rarely, cholestatic jaundice and blood dyscrasias. Most neuroleptics are also mildly epileptogenic.

Finally, neuroleptics can produce the neuroleptic malignant syndrome, consisting of hyperthermia, fluctuating levels of consciousness, muscular rigidity, and autonomic dysfunction with pallor, tachycardia, labile blood pressure, sweating, and urinary incontinence. This syndrome is a rare but potentially fatal side effect (British National Formulary, 1992).

Most extrapyramidal side effects, with the exception of tardive dyskinesia, are either reversible on stopping the drug or can be controlled by anti-Parkinsonian agents. Discontinuation of drug therapy is essential in the neuroleptic malignant syndrome, and supportive measures may be necessary.

It is these side effect profiles that have led many clinicians to place an emphasis on using medication in the minimal clinically effective dosage, to keep the need for ongoing medication under continuing review, and to explore such possibilities as "drug holidays" (Kirman, 1975). It is timely to recall Bleuler's observation (1974) that, of all his patients who achieved a stable remission, "not one was on longstanding neuroleptic medication" (p. 246). The clinician aims, therefore, to discontinue medication wherever possible, mindful always that noncompliance and defaulting are probably the main precipitants of relapse in neuroleptic-responsive schizophrenics, and that for many patients a certain level of side effects is preferable to ongoing active schizophrenic symptomatology.

## Drug Treatment of Acute Schizophrenia

Schizophrenia frequently presents with acute symptomatology, including restlessness, excitement, impulsivity, a florid hallucinosis, and disorganized and irrational behavior. The mainstay of treatment of these acute schizophrenic episodes is the phenothiazine compounds, such as chlorpromazine, which possesses useful calming and sedative, as well as antipsychotic, properties. Chlorpromazine can be administered orally up to a dose of around 1 g per day in divided doses, or intramuscularly if there are problems with compliance. Usually an oral dose in the range of 100–400 mg per day will suffice, however. An alternative phenothiazine preparation is thioridazine in a comparable oral dose range; it may be preferred for its lesser extrapyramidal side effects, although it is less potent than chlorpromazine. Haloperidol at an oral dose range of up to 20 mg daily in divided doses is another alternative that may be useful in the management of acute psychomotor agitation and excitation, or of violent and dangerously impulsive behavior. In case of urgent need, it may be administered at considerably higher dose levels. It is less sedative than chlorpromazine, but extrapyramidal and dystonic reactions and akathisia may be particularly troublesome. Clopixol acuphase injection, which has a duration of action of two to three days, is a useful alternative where a rapid calming and antipsychotic effect is required. In addition to neuroleptic medication, it may be necessary to prescribe night sedatives, for example, of the benzodiazepine group, such as temazepam (10–20 mg nocte), chlormethiazole, or chloral derivatives.

Very occasionally, a patient with an acute schizophrenic episode may be so disturbed and psychotic that he or she may not respond to neuroleptic medication. He or she may be so dominated by delusional beliefs—for example, that the food and water is poisoned—that there may even be a risk to life through refusal to eat and drink. Under such circumstances, it may rarely be necessary to administer electroconvulsive therapy (ECT) in an endeavor to disrupt the psychotic process.

## Drug Treatment of Chronic Schizophrenia

Many patients are prepared to continue on a maintenance dose of oral neuroleptic medication, for example, with chlorpromazine or trifluoperazine, once the acute symptomatology has subsided. If their compliance can be relied on and the remission is satisfactorily sustained, this treatment is perfectly acceptable. There are preparations such as pimozide or trifluoperazine in spansule form that are suitable for administration on a once-daily oral basis, which may simplify matters. Pimozide has been claimed to be particularly effective in maintaining normal social responsiveness in successfully treated patients (Falloon, Watt, & Shepherd, 1978). There are concerns, however, about its potential cardiotoxicity.

More often, a depot preparation is considered preferable because of the compliance problem and also because there is the built-in requirement of regular professional contact with patients on depot medication. Depot antipsychotics are administered by deep intramuscular injection at intervals of one to four weeks. There may be a higher incidence of extrapyramidal side effects with them, so it is advisable first to administer a small test dose. Table 1 gives approximately equivalent doses of depot antipsychotics.

There is no clear-cut division in the choice of antipsychotics, but zu-

### Table 1
### Equivalent Dosages of Depot Antipsychotics

| Antipsychotic | Dose (mg) | Interval |
|---|---|---|
| Flupenthixol decanoate | 40 | 2 weeks |
| Fluphenazine decanoate | 25 | 2 weeks |
| Haloperidol decanoate | 100 | 4 weeks |
| Zuclopenthixol decanoate | 200 | 2 weeks |

clopenthixol may be more suitable for the treatment of agitated or aggressive patients. Flupenthixol may have a useful excitatory and mood-elevating effect in patients who are depressed and withdrawn. Fluspirilene is an alternative preparation with an intermediate duration of action of around one week, which may sometimes be advantageous.

In earlier years there were doubts and anxieties about the safety of using depot preparations in retarded people with schizophrenia, but Craft and Schiff (1980) showed that these drugs have an acceptable margin of safety in appropriately selected mentally retarded patients.

## Social and Psychological Treatment

An acute schizophrenic psychosis may remit completely, and the patient may be able to pick up the threads of his or her previous lifestyle and responsibilities without any continuing support or input. More often, however, there is a certain blunting of drive and motivation through time, with the emergence of some personality eccentricities and intermittent periods of acute symptomatology. The change in a schizophrenic person's nature may be difficult to accommodate in a family setting, and we know from the work of Brown, Birley, and Wing (1972) that high emotional involvement may be inimical to recovery and may trigger relapses. It may be possible to minimize this pattern through family therapy (Leff et al., 1982), but at times, a more neutral and less emotionally charged living environment may be required, for example, a hostel, a group home, or a sheltered housing placement. In some patients with continuing active symptomatology, ongoing residential or hospital care may even be necessary.

Many patients also require retraining and rehabilitation to help them regain, or approach, their previous level of functioning. These involve a multidisciplinary treatment program with input by clinical psychology, occupational and recreational therapy, and social work, aimed at time structuring, help with daily living skills, social skills training, and back-to-work or sheltered-work programs. There is a key role here for the community psychiatric nurse, who, by virtue of his or her community base, is particularly well placed to support and inform family and carers, and to monitor the client's progress through depot clinics and the administration of depot neuroleptics.

All in all, therefore, there is nothing unique or idiosyncratic about the treatment of schizophrenia in people who are mentally retarded. The underlying level of diminished intelligence, along with the severity and the treatment responsiveness of the psychosis, does, however, influence the outcome in terms of independence and level of functioning.

## Note

No guarantee is given by the author about the accuracy or comprehensiveness of the psychopharmacological and neuroleptic information in this chapter. In particular, the names and doses of drugs should be checked against national formularies in all cases.

## References

Bleuler, M. (1974). The long-term course of the schizophrenic psychoses. *Psychol. Med., 4,* 244–54.

*British National Formulary,* No. 22 (1991, September), British Medical Association and Royal Pharmaceutical Society of Great Britain. London.

Brown, G. W., Birley, J. L. T., & Wing, J. K. (1972). Influence of family life on the course of schizophrenic disorders: A replication. *Br. J. Psychiatr., 121,* 241–258.

Brown, G. W., Bone, M. Dalison, G., & Wing, J. K. (1966). *Schizophrenia and social care,* Maudsley Monograph No. 17. London: Oxford University Press.

Craft, M. J. U., & Schiff, A. A. (1980). Psychiatric disturbance in mentally handicapped patients. *Br. J. Psychiatr.,* 250–255.

Falloon, I., Watt, D. C., & Shepherd, M. (1978). The social outcome of patients in a trial of long-term continuation therapy in schizophrenia: Pimozide vs. fluphenazine. *Psychol. Med., 8,* 265–274.

Gelder, M., Gath, D., & Mayou, R. (1989). Schizophrenia and schizophrenia-like disorders. In *Oxford Textbook of Psychiatry* (2nd. ed.). London: Oxford University Press.

Kirman, B. (1975). Drug therapy in mental handicap. *Br. J. Psychiatr., 127,* 545–549.

Kraepelin, E. (1919). *Dementia praecox and paraphrenia.* (trans. R. M. Barclay). Edinburgh: Livingstone.

Leff, J., Kuipers, L., Berkowitz, R., Eberlein-Vries, R., & Sturgeon, D. (1982). A controlled trial of social intervention in the families of schizophrenic patients. *Br. J. Psychiatr., 141,* 121–134.

Mayer-Gross, W. (1932). *Die Schizophrenie.* In *Bumke's Handbuch der Geisteskrankheiten* (Vol. 9) Berlin: Springer.

Roy, A. (1982). Suicide in chronic schizophrenia. *Bri. J. Psychiatr., 141,* 171–177.

# 13

## Treatment of Bipolar Mood Disorders in Persons with Mental Retardation

*Stephen Ruedrich*

A review of the literature surrounding the treatment of bipolar mood disorder (BMD) in retarded persons quickly reveals much less breadth and depth than the corresponding information regarding the diagnosis of these disorders. A number of possible explanations for this imbalance may be relevant. Generally, information regarding the treatment of medical conditions follows the characterization of the pathology or illness itself; in mentally retarded persons, it may be that the difficulty previously discussed (Chapter 6) regarding accurate descriptive diagnosis means that information about treatment must wait until these parameters are more fully detailed. It may just be that issues of diagnosis are globally more intrinsically interesting to the field, occupying researchers and clinicians at this stage of development of our discipline. An unlikely explanation would hold that, once a diagnosis of BMD is endorsed, the treatment is clearly defined, well established, and not controversial. This does *not* appear to be the case. Repeatedly, the literature in this area describes mentally retarded bipolar patients as "atypical," in both their diagnostic *and* their therapeutic circumstances (Sover, 1991). Finally, it is generally accepted that the difficulties inherent in mounting research programs of all kinds, including research into therapeutics, are magnified in work with developmentally disabled persons, for a host of reasons (Tanguay & Szymanski, 1984). The summation of these forces, therefore, has resulted in significantly less attention overall to the treatment of BMD in retarded persons, particularly when one compares the volume and magnitude of research and clinical efforts directed at BMD in the general population.

Nevertheless, there does exist a body of work addressing the therapeutic approach to BMD occurring in retarded individuals. This statement is actually somewhat confusing, or at least misleading, in that the treatment of BMD actually incorporates several different forms and goals of treatment approach:

268

1. acute treatment of specific depressive episode in a bipolar individual
2. acute treatment of a specific manic episode in a bipolar patient
3. acute treatment of mixed symptomatology of mania and depression occurring simultaneously
4. following acute treatment, long-term or prophylactic treatment of BMD, with the aim of preventing subsequent mood episodes, which is necessarily for both typical and rapid-cycling forms of BMD
5. psychosocial approaches to all of the above, with the goal of ensuring compliance with therapy, enhancing quality of life, and addressing educational, vocational, and social developmental opportunities

It is sometimes unclear, when one is addressing the literature in these areas, which situations reflect treatment that is considered acute and which is considered prophylactic. For practical purposes, the major distinction in approach appears to be between the treatment of acute depressive episodes and all other treatments, in that the major pharmacological methods used to treat acute mania are also useful in subsequent prophylaxis, and in the treatment of mixed states. Each is reviewed here in turn.

## Acute Treatment of Depressive Symptoms in BMD Patients

The therapeutic approach to depressive symptomatology in bipolar retarded persons is not significantly different from similar approaches to unipolar depression and should combine somatic and psychosocial elements for optimal success. In Chapter 11, Dosen and Petry comprehensively outline these issues and emphasize that it is insufficient to rely on biological or psychosocial approaches in isolation, in that retarded persons with depressive illness bring to their symptoms that same complex biochemistry, as well as internal psychic and external social experiences, as do their nonretarded peers.

Regarding the former, it is clear that somatic treatments, including both pharmacological agents and electroconvulsive therapy (ECT), are effective and necessary in addressing major depressive symptoms in retarded patients (Day, 1990; Lund, 1990). When depression occurs in the context of BMD, the same is true, but additional caution must be exercised in view of the bipolar nature of the patient's illness. McLaughlin (1987) and Day (1990) have reported possible or confirmed exacerbations or changes from depression to mania in bipolar retarded patients treated with tricyclics and/or ECT. This "switch" phenomenon has been well described in thenonretarded population with BMD (Baldessarini, 1977). Although controversial, it is likely that the fourth edition of the American Psychiatric Association (APA, 1991) Diagnostic and Statistical Manual (DMS- IV) will define these so-called treatment-induced manias not as substance-induced, but as evidence of BMD. As noted by Lund (1990), the pharmacological approaches to depressive illness in retarded persons are not unlike those in the nonretarded, and anecdotally, most standard antidepressants have been utilized with success. There is little systematic research involving the treatment of depression in retarded individuals, nor many reports of utilization of new or novel antidepressant medications, such as sertraline, fluoxetine, and clomipramine, in these patients. Ruedrich and Wilkinson (1992) described two patients with moderatel mental retardion, self-injurious behavior (SIB), and apparent depressive illness who were treated successfully with amoxapine, after the failure of adequate treatment with other antidepressants. These authors speculated that the combined antidepressant and antipsychotic properties of this compound may have aided in treatment.

## Treatment of Acute Mania in BMD Retarded Persons

For over two decades, the mainstay of the pharmacologic treatment of acute mania has been lithium, alone or in combination with neuroleptic treatment. Its utilization in this regard in retarded patients dates back nearly as far. Reid (1972) alluded to lithium treatment in his benchmark article describing twenty-one patients with BMD, and Reid and Naylor (1976) presented four BMD persons who were intensively studied biochemically and clinically. All four were treated with lithium; two of the four responded, one did not, and the fourth could not tolerate the neurotoxicity associated with the medication.

In a rare nonanecdotal report in this area, Naylor et al. (1974) treated fourteen BMD retarded patients in a double-blind long-term trial of lithium. All patients were given lithium or placebo, in blind fashion, for one year and were then crossed over to the other treatment group for the second year. Adequate treatment (levels between 0.6 and 1.0 mEq/l) was maintained by treatment personnel not related to the study. Other psychotropic drugs were used at the discretion of the non-blind clinical assessor. The authors reported that the number of weeks of illness (ongoing symptomatology) was significantly lower in the lithium treatment group than in the placebo group, but that the actual "episodes" of illness differed little between the groups. This finding seems to suggest that lithium was successful in the treatment of acute mania, but less successful in preventing breakthroughs of mood symptomatology. In a separate report, Reid and Leonard (1977) reported that lithium successfully decreased the cyclic vomiting associated with depressive episodes in a woman with moderate mental retardation and BMD, and Lesage and Chouinard (1978) reported a good response to lithium in a young man with borderline mental retardation and Klinefelter's syndrome.

In an often-quoted report, Rivinus and Harmatz (1979) described their treatment of five retarded persons with BMD. All five were given lithium for one year, followed by placebo. All five had a reemergence of mania within 5½ months of the discontinuation of lithium, and none displayed either manic or depressive symptoms during the lithium treatment. At the appearance of mania while on placebo, lithium was restarted, and all five entered another lengthy remission. The authors concluded that lithium was clearly effective in both the treatment of acute mania *and* prophylaxis against subsequent episodes, and they noted that the lithium had been well tolerated by their patients, without signficant side effects or toxicity. Hasan and Mooney (1979) presented three more retarded individuals with BMD who were lithium responders, and they agreed that lithium was effective as a prophylactic agent, particularly in the prevention of manic episodes in such patients. In separate case reports, Kadambari (1986) and Linter (1987) presented, respectively, an elderly woman and a prepubertal male with BMD who were both lithium responders. The former patient had been treated over many years with ECT and neuroleptics for a presumed diagnosis of schizophrenia, but she maintained a significant remission of symptoms with lithium (she had one manic exacerbation in ten months, which responded to an addition of low-dose thioridazine to the lithium).

In two additional separate reports, four patients with autism, mental retardadtion, and BMD were reported to be lithium responders. (Steingard & Biederman, 1987; Kerbeshian, Burd, & Fisher, 1987). In two patients, lithium was added to antipsychotic medications, and dramatic improvement resulted; however, subsequent attempts to taper off or discontinue the antipsychotic were not successful, and the manic symptoms returned (Steingard & Biederman, 1987). In the other two patients, Kerbeshian et al. (1987) also noted significant improvement with lithium but noted that serum levels above 1.0 mEq/l were necessary for sustained improvement. Finally, Arumainayagam and Kumar (1990) presented a woman with mild mental retardation and BMD whose clearly seasonal mood disturbances were eliminated by lithium treatment, following previous failures with antipsychotics.

Based on these and other reports, it appears that lithium is beneficial— and, at times, dramatically useful—in the treatment of BMD in retarded patients (Crabbe, 1989). With the exception of the report by Naylor and coauthors, however, all of these have been single or multiple case reports of clinical or limited uncontrolled treatment. For this reason, Pary (1991) recently reviewed the use of lithium in retarded persons with BMD and other disorders, in order to characterize what guidelines may exist to aid the clinician in this area. In the first review, the author outlined the components of adequate psychopharmacological trials, including rationale, contraindications to treatment, treatment goals, monitoring procedures and treatment parameters, and a plan for discontinuation. A lithium trial was thought to be clearly indicated for any retarded individual with BMD, and also for aggressive retarded patients with a strong family hisory of bipolar disorder or lithium response, or with behavioral problems characterized by cyclicity or strong affective flavor.

Pary (1991) noted the need for following treatment response in a systematic manner (generally lacking in the literature) but reported that little information exists attempting to characterize an "adequate trial" of lithium (in terms of either dose, serum level, or duration of treatment) for BMD in retarded persons. As a result, most clinicians treat using guidelines developed for nonretarded manic or bipolar patients, seeking lithium levels in the 0.8–1.2-mEq/l range for acute mania, and in the 0.5–0.8-mEq/l range for BMD prophylaxis, and continuing treatment for at least several weeks at adequate levels before determining efficacy. Finally, Pary outlined the side effects that may result from a cessation of therapy with lithium, including neurotoxicity (ataxia, drowsiness, tremor, vomiting, seizures, and coma), rare cardiac arrhythmias, hypothyroidism, severe gastrointestinal problems, psoriasis, and significant polyuria with incontinence. He noted that, although lithium can clearly cause seizures when given in toxic doses, the literature is unclear regarding whether lithium at therapeutic doses worsens preexisting seizure disorders, and he recommended that patients with known seizure disorders not discontinue lithium if a breakthrough seizure occurs. In a subsequent report, Pary (1991) noted that ten out of fifteen (67%) retarded patients receiving lithium in a clinic setting had side effects (tremor, GI irritation, rash, sedation, thirst, and polyuria) that necessitated discontinuation of the medication. This percentage was noted to be at least as high in retarded persons as in patients with normal intelligence.

In summary, there is no doubt that lithium is effective as both an antimanic and a prophylactic medication in mentally retarded persons with BMD, either alone or in combination with antipsychotic or other psychotropic medication. Guidelines for its utilization have been nicely detailed by Gaultieri (1989) and Sovner and Hurley (1985), who have highlighted the need to monitor serum levels, and to observe and monitor the patient closely for signs of side effects and/or significant toxicity.

Turning to another area, there is now evidence that several anticonvulsant medications have psychotropic properties and can often serve as substitutes or adjuncts of lithium in the treatment of acute mania or the prophylaxis of BMD. The two most commonly employed agents in this area are carbamazepine and valproic acid. Reid, Naylor, and Kay (1981) compared carbamazepine to placebo in a double-blind crossover fashion, in twelve severely retarded overactive adults. Those patients who were described as having elevated moods and distractibility were found to respond with a decrease in overactivity on the carbamazepine treatment, whereas overactive patients with no mood abnormalities did not. One can speculate, based on these symptoms, that the individuals who responded may have had BMD although no specific psychiatric diagnoses were given. The presence or absence of epilepsy was not related to the response, and the carbamazepine was well tolerated by all the recipients.

Signer, Benson, and Rudnick (1986) described a moderately retarded man with BMD whose recurrent depressive and hypomanic episodes were dampened with carbamazepine after thioridazine failure. Glue (1988) reported on ten retarded adults with rapid- cycling BMD, who were treated sequentially with lithium, lithium plus carbamazepine, or carbamazepine alone. Only five of the ten responded favorably: two to lithium alone and three to the combination treatment. No patient responded to carbamazepine alone.

Sovner (1989) reported on five retarded individuals with BMD (two with chronic mania, two with rapid-cycling BMD, and one with BMD and autism) who responded to standard treatment with divalproex sodium, a valproic acid derivative. Four had a dramatic and the fifth a moderate response. All had failed in previous neuroleptic and/or carbamazepine treatment. Sovner particularly noted the marked response in two individuals with rapid-cycling BMD, a condition that has been less than optimally responsive to lithium in both retarded and nonretarded persons (Keck & McElroy, 1988).

In a similar report, three children with retardation and BMD were successfully treated with valproic acid (Kastner et al., 1990). All three had had previous trials of both lithium and carbamazepine, either without clinical efficacy or with intolerable side effects. Kastner et al. noted that they had found lithium to be associated with many side effects in retarded children with mood disorders and concurrent cerebral palsy, movement disorders, and incontinence, and they felt that either carbamazepine or valproic acid should be preferred over lithium for these reasons.

In a comprehensive review of the use of anticonvulsants in developmentally disabled patients, Sovner (1991) summarized the available information regarding their use in BMD and concluded that carbamazepine and valproic acid may be considered a primary therapy choice in retarded patients with BMD, because of the difficulties associated with lithium (unreliable response and side effects). Sovner also noted that clonazepam (a benzodiazepine anticonvulsant) has been used to treat BMD in the general population, but that its use has not been reported so far in retarded persons. He concluded that carbamazepine is useful singly or in combination with lithium in "typical" BMD; that valproic acid should be considered the treatment of choice for "atypical" or rapid-cycling forms; and that successful treatment may require serum levels above 100 mg/l, higher than those usually considered therapeutic in the use of this anticonvulsant. Finally, although other pharmacological agents (calcium channel blockers and clonidine) have been employed in treating acute mania and BMD in nonretarded persons, there has been little or no research, or even case reports, of their use in retarded persons with BMD (Sovner, 1990).

## Psychosocial Treatments of Bipolar Disorders

Reports of *nonpharmacological* treatment approaches to retarded individuals with acute mania or BMD are rare to nonexistent. Decidedly, the opposite is true of the treatment of depression, or depressive equivalents, in the developmentally disabled. Virtually all forms of psychosocial treatment utilized for nonretarded depressives have been applied to retarded depressed persons (Ruedrich, Des Noyers-Hurley, & Sovner, in press). These include individual therapies (psychodynamic, psychoanalytic, client-centered, interactional, directive, play, supportive, and cognitive-behavioral) and group therapies, as well as social skills training. Authors in this area have emphasized that specific psychosocial treatments often need to be modified to accommodate the developmental level of the patient (Monfils & Menolascino, 1984). Such accommodation usually takes two primary forms. First, there is often increased utilization of nonspeech (and sometimes nonlanguage) forms of communication, such as play, movement, music, modeling, and role- playing therapies (see Chapter 11). Second, the therapist must assume a much more "active" directive treatment stance than may be the case in work with persons without language or communication difficulties (Hurley, 1989; Benson, 1990; Bojanin & Ispanovic-Radojkovic, 1990). These approaches, as well as their rationale and success are reviewed in detail in Chapter 11.

It should be noted that psychosocial therapies applicable to unipolar depressed retarded persons are also quite likely to succeed in addressing depressive episodes occurring in bipolar patients. Of significant interest, however, is the dearth of reports of psychosocial approaches to patients in the manic phase of BMD. Several would appear to have potential clinical utility, particularly those that include cognitive-behavioral and/or directive elements. Cognitive therapy, which posits that mood symptomatology and the consequent behavior is based on misperception and/or cognitive distortions, may be applied to the manic patient with elevated mood and grandiosity. Such an approach may be considered mildly controversial when *broadly viewed,* however, in light of what is clearly known regarding the often-fragile development of esteem and self-worth in developmentally disabled persons. Similarly, social skills training, which has been successfully used to alter depressive disorders in retarded individuals (Griffiths, 1990), may also benefit those with manic (or at least hypomanic) symptoms. This approach, outlined by Benson (1990), would include, first, a demonstration of expected (nonmanic) behavior, followed by directed practice while the client is observed by the therapist, and finally feedback to the patient regarding the appropriate exercise of self-control. Although this approach probably characterizes most milieu treatment of manic or hypomanic patients (particularly in inpatient settings), its utilization in specific forms or prescribed sequences is usually not carried out and may be a focus for further study. Group psychotherapy, although obviously not without difficulty with manic, overactive, overtalkative individuals, may have similar, although probably less satisfactory, applications.

Finally, comprehensive psychosocial treatment in BMD would include support (frequent contact, opportunities to ventilate, and reassurance) of the individual as he or she is reintegrated into the premorbid environment(s), as well as psychoeducational approaches (need for treatment compliance and observation for symptom recurrence) directed at both the patient and the family or other caregivers.

## Recommendations

1. In the consideration of psychopharmacological treatment, an initial goal must be identifying the target symptoms and signs that are the focus of treatment, as well as organizing a systematic method of assessment of the response. Sovner and Hurley (1985) and Keppel and Gaultieri (1989) have outlined methodologies for assessing the qualities of psychotropic regimens and monitoring psychopharmacology practices. These include the need for accurate diagnosis, regular and systematic monitoring of response and side effects, the avoidance of polypharmacy when possible, the use of the lowest *effective* dose, a consideration of drug discontinuation when appropriate (certainly when there is no clear evidence of efficacy), and a reduction in or an avoidance of drugs with a long duration of action, if at all possible. These general guidelines apply to all medications used to treat BMD.

2. Lithium is the psychotropic most studied (most reported) in the treatment of acute mania and in the prophylaxis of BMD in retarded persons. The available literature supports its utilization in retarded persons with BMD for both acute mania and prophylaxis against subsequent episodes. It is also the only medication that has been studied in a methodologically sound manner, and that, in these studies, was found to be effective in decreasing the number of weeks of illness compared to placebo (Naylor et al., 1974), and in reversing manic symptoms before and after placebo crossover (Rivinus & Harmatz, 1979). In the case report literature, it is often apparently combined with antipsychotic medication in the treatment of acute mania.

When lithium is utilized, the treatment guidelines for retarded persons are not notably different from those applied elsewhere in practice. Patients should undergo a comprehensive evaluation before therapy is initiated, including a complete blood count, a chemistry profile, thyroid functions, and an electrocardiogram. Conservatively, therapy should start with slightly lower initial doses in retarded persons, based on the presence of structural brain abnormalities in many patients, as well as on the anticipated difficulties that some patients may have in reporting side effects. Dosage increases should follow, with an assessment of serum levels, aiming for levels in the 0.8–1.2-mEq/l range for acute mania and the 0.5–0.8-mEq/l range for prophylactic treatment (Pary, 1991). The side effects include thirst, polyuria with new-onset incontinence, tremor, sedation, hypothyroidism, and nausea, occasionally with vomiting. Several authors have noted that retarded patients may be particularly susceptible to the polyuric and neurotoxic side effects of lithium (Kastner et al., 1990; Pary, 1991). Observation for an exacerbation of preexisting seizure disorders or predispositions is widely cautioned, but not widely reported. Clearly this form of neurotoxicity may occur when lithium is given in toxic doses. Once a therapeutic response has been obtained, long-term monitoring should begin, not only for the return of manic or depressive symptoms, but also for the metabolic effects of lithium on several organ systems. This stage entails regular monitoring (at least every six months) of a complete blood count and renal and thyroid functions. Because the response to lithium is clearly associated with providing a therapeutic level in the serum, lithium doses should be maintained to ensure these levels and should not be tapered off during symptom-free intervals, as is occasionally practiced with psychotropics (particularly antipsychotics) when they are used non-specifically for behavioral problems.

3. As outlined above, the anticonvulsants carbamazepine and valproic acid have also demonstrated efficacy in treating acute mania, and in subsequent BMD prophylaxis, in retarded patients. Although they represent a clear addition to the options available for these patients, it should be noted that these drugs have not been studied systematically in retarded bipolar persons to date. Interestingly, reports of a clear efficacy of carbamazepine when used alone are infrequent; more commonly, it is combined with lithium or valproic acid for optimal success. So far, there are no known reports of direct comparison studies involving patients treated with lithium versus carbamazepine that have used blind or placebo-control methodology for retarded bipolar patients. The closest approximation is the study by Reid, Naylor, and Kay (1981), reported above, in which carbamazepine was utilized for overactive severely retarded patients, some of whom may have had bipolar symptomatology.

Like most anticonvulsants, carbamazepine is given in divided doses, the total dose gradually being increased every two to four days so as to produce a serum level consistent with efficacy. This range has not been established for carbamazepine given to treat BMD, so that the usual anticonvulsant range of 8–12 mg/dl is usually substituted. Common side effects include drowsiness, nausea, ataqxia, rash, blurred vision, and, *rarely,* dangerous hematopoietic suppression (Sovner & Hurley, 1988). When utilized at the usual clinical doses, carbamazepine is not thought to cause cognitive dysfunction (Evans, Aman, & Gaultieri, 1989). Decreased serum sodium has been described in up to 20 percent of retarded patients receiving carbamazepine; however, in a recent report, this decrease was seen in only two of forty (5%) patients treated (Kastner, Friedman, & Pond, 1992) and may be more prevalent in individuals with schizophrenic psychosis rather than BMD. The same group of clinicians also reported a 9 percent incidenc of "behavioral" side effects in sixty-five retarded patients receiving carbamazepine, and they noted that such an effect (hallucinations, mania, overactivity, and self-injury) was more common in those receiving carbamazepine for behavior problems than in those receiving it for epilepsy (Friedman, et al., 1992).

Valproic acid may be specifically useful in BMD patients with "atypical" presentations, including those with rapid-cycling disorder or chronic mania. It is given in divided doses, and serum levels between 50 mg/dl and 100 mg/dl are thought to be therapeutic. These levels have been standardized for valproic acid, as they have been for carbamazepine, when valproic acid is used as an anticonvulsant, and there are no controlled studies addressing serum levels in BMD retarded patients. In several anecdotal reports, however, levels above 100 mg/dl have been necessary for successful remission (Sovner, 1989). The side effects include sedation, rash, fatigue, alopecia, nausea, and vomiting; rarely, valproic acid produces liver dysfunction, pancreatitis, and decreased white-blood-cell and platelet counts (Sovner & Hurley, 1988). Serious liver failure has been seen with valproic acid, but apparently only in young children. For this reason, however, it is usual to check the complete blood count, the chemistry profile, and the serum amylase and lipase prior to initiating treatment, and regularly thereafter.

4. Other anticonvulsants and psychotropic agents other than antipsychotics, lithium, carbamazepine, and valproic acid cannot currently be recommended as treatments for retarded persons with BMD.

5. Pharmacological treatments, however successful, make up only one aspect of comprehensive management. Psychosocial treatments, including individual, group, and family therapy, must be added. Individual cognitive-behavioral therapy, as well as social skills paradigms, may be applicable in the treatment of acute manic or hypomanic symptomatology. Other directive, supportive, and psychoeducational approaches may be traditionally beneficial in ensuring compliance with the treatment and the prevention of future mood episodes.

## Summary

As stated at the outset, the treatment of BMD in retarded persons may present a daunting challenge to the clinician and the multidisciplinary treatment team, and it requires a comprehensive and integrated approach, involving multiple caregivers and treatment strategies. The first step is a rigorous diagnostic formulation, utilizing one or more of the currently available assessment instruments, and involving a review of not only recent but also remote history (age of onset, previous symptomatology, cyclical pattern, and treatment type and response), as well as accurate information regarding similar disorders in the biological family. Once a diagnosis of BMD has been established, the treatment team must then address multiple treatment parameters, including the locus of the treatment (Is a psychiatric hospitalization useful or necessary? Can the individual be managed in her or his current residential setting?); the form of approach (psychopharmacology, psychotherapy, or social-vocational therapy); and individualized needs (What are the wishes, psychosocial issues, and psychoeducational needs of the individual and his or her family?). Only after these circumstances are globally addressed can the clinician(s) involved have realistic confidence regarding the treatment plan prescribed for the current acute symptomatology, as well as for prophylaxis against subsequent illness episodes.

# References

American Psychiatric Association. (1991). *DSM-IV Options Book: Work in Progress.* Washington, DC: *Task Force on DSM-IV.*

Arumainayagam, M., & Kumar, A. (1990). Manic-depressive psychosis in a mentally handicapped person. Seasonality: A clue to a diagnostic problem. *Br. J. Psychiatry., 156,* 886–889.

Baldessarini, R. J. (1977). *Chemotherapy in psychiatry* (pp. 75–125). Cambridge: Harvard University Press.

Benson, E. (1990). Behavioral treatment of depression. In A. Dosen & F. J. Menolascino (eds.). *Depression in mentally retarded children and adults* Leiden: Logon. pp. 309–330.

Bojanin, S. E., Ispanovic-Radojkovic, V. (1990). Treatment of depression in mentally retarded children: A developmental approach. In A Dosen & F. J Menolascino (eds.) *Depression in mentally retarded children and adults.* Leiden: Logon.

Crabbe, H. F. (1989). *Lithium: A guidebook for the use of psychotropic medication in persons with mental illness and mental retardation.* Connecticut Dept. Mental Retardation.

Day, K. A. (1990). Treatment, care and management. In A. Dosen & F. J. Menolascino (eds.), *Depression in mentally retarded children and adults* (pp. 235–254). Leiden: Logon.

Evans, R. W., Aman, M. D., & Gualtieri, C. T. (1989). Anticonvulsant drugs. In (pp. 94–99). *Treatments of psychiatric disorders* Karasu, T. (ed.), American Psychiatric Press, Washington, D.C.

Friedman, D. L., Kastner, T., & Plummer, A. T., Ruiz, M. Q., Henning, D. (1992). Adverse behavioral effects in individuals with mental retardation and mood disorders treated with carbamazepine. *Am. J. Ment. Retard., 96(5),* 541–546.

Gaultieri, C. T. (1989). Antidepressant drugs and lithium. In *Treatment of psychia-*

*tric disorders*, (pp. 77–84). Washington, D.C.: American Psychiatric Association.

Glue, P. (1989). Rapid cycling affective disorders in the mentally retarded. *Biol. Psychiatr., 26,* 250–256.

Griffiths, D. (1990). The social skills game, Parts 1 and 2. Halsilitative Ment. *Healthcare Newsl. 9,* 1–13.

Hasan, M. R., & Mooney, R. P. (1979). Three cases of manic- depressive illness in mentallyretarded adults. *Am. J. Psychiatr., 136,* 1069–1071.

Hurley, A. D. (1989). Behavioral therapy for psychiatric disorders in mentally retarded individuals. In R. J. Fletcher & F. J. Menolascino (eds.), Mental retardation and mental illness: Service and treatment for dually diagnosed. Lexington, MA: Lexington Books.

Kadambari, S. R. (1986). Manic-depressive psychosis in a mentally handicapped person: Diagnosis and management. *Br. J. Psychiatr., 148,* 595–596.

Kastner, T., Friedman, D. L., Plummer, A. T., Ruiz, M. Q., & Henning, D. (1990). Valproic acid for the treatment of children with mental retardation and mood symptomatology. *Pediatrics, 86*(3), 467–472.

Kastner, T., Friedman, D. L., & Pond, W. S. (1992). Carbamazepine-induced hypnoatremia in patients with mental retardation. *Am. J. Mentl. Retard., 96*(5), 536–540.

Keck, P. E., & McElroy, S. L. (1988). Anticonvulsants in the treatment of rapid-cycling bipolar disorder. In S. L. McElroy & H. G. Pope (Eds.), *Use of anticonvulsants in psychiatry: recent advances* Oxford Health Care, Inc., Clifton, NJ: (pp. 117–126).

Keppel, J. M., & Gualtieri, C. T. (1989). Monitoring psychopharmacology in programs for the retarded. In Karasu, T. (ed.) *Treatments of psychiatric disorders,* Washington, DC: (pp. 68–70). American Psychiatric Press.

Kerbeshian, J., Burd, L., & Fisher, W. (1987). Lithium carbonate in the treatment of two patients with infantile autism and atypical bipolar of symptomatology. *J. Clin. Psychopharmacol., 7*(6), 401–405.

Lesage, J., & Chouinard, G. (1978). Manic-depressive illness associated with Klinefelter's syndrome and essential tremors. *Am. J. Psychiatr.,135*(6), 757–758.

Linter, C. M. (1987). Short-cycle manic-depressive psychosis in a mentally handicapped child without family history. *Br. J. Psychiatr., 151,* 554–555.

Lund, J. (1990). Psychopharmacological approaches in treatment of depression in the mentally retarded. In A. Dosen & F. J. Menolascino (Eds.), *Depression in mentally retarded children and adults* Lieden, Netherlands, Logon Publication (pp. 331–340).

McLaughlin, M. (1987). Bipolar affective disorder in Down's syndrome. Br. J. Psychiatr., 151, 116–117.

Monfils, M. J., & Menolascino, F. J. (1984). Modified individual and group treatment approaches for the mentally retarded-mentally ill. In F. J. Menolascino & J. A. Stark (Eds.), *Handbook of mental illness in the mentally retarded* (pp. 155–170). New York: Plenum Press.

Naylor, G. J., Donald, J. M., Le Poidevin, D., & Reid, A. H. (1974). A double-blind trial of long-term lithium therapy in mental defectives. *Br. J. Psychiatr., 124,* 52–57.

Pary, R. (1991). Side effects during lithium treatment for psychiatric disorders in adults with mental retardation. *Am. J. Ment. Retard., 96(3),* 269–279.

Pary, R. (1991b). Towards defining adequate lithium trials for individuals with mental retardation and mental illness. *Am. J. Ment. Retard.,* 95(6), 681–691.

Reid, A. H., (1972). Psychoses in adult mental defectives: 1. Manic depressive psychosis. *Br. J. Psychiatr.,* 120, 205–212.

Reid, A. H., & Leonard, A. (1977). Lithium treatment of cyclic vomiting in a mentally affective patient. *Br. J. Psychiatr., 125,* 316.

Reid, A. H., & Naylor, G. J. (1976). Short cycle manic depressive psychosis in mental defectives: A clinical and psychological study. *J. Mentl. Defic. Res., 20(1),* 67–76.

Reid, A. D., Naylor, G. J., & Kay, D. (1981). A double-blind placebo controlled crossover trial of carbamazepine in overactive severely mentally handicapped patients. *Psychol. Med., 11,* 109–113.

Rivinus, T. M., & Harmatz, J. S. (1979). Diagnosis and lithium treatment of affective disorder in the retarded: Five case studies. *Am. J. Psychiatr., 136,* 551–544.

Ruedrich, S. L., & Wilkinson, L. (1992). Atypical unipolar depression in mentally retarded patients: Amoxapine treatment, *J. Nerv. Ment. Dis. 180(3),* 206–207.

Ruedrich, S. L., DesNoyers-Herley, A. D., & Sovner, R. (in press). Treatment of mood disorders in mentally retarded persons. In Dosen, A. & Day6, K. (eds.), *Treatment of mental illness and behavioral disorders in mentally retarded children and adults.*

Signer, S. F., Benson, D. F., Rudnick, F. D. (1986). Undetected affective disorders in the developmentally retarded., *Am. J. Psychiatr. 143(2) 259.*

Sovner, R. (1989). The use of valproate in the treatment of mentally retarded persons with typical and atypical bipolar disorders. *J. Clin. Psychiatr., 50(3,* Suppl.), 40–43.

Sovner, R. (1990). Bipolar disorder in persons with developmental disorder: An overview. In A. Dosen & F. J. Menolascino (Eds.), *Depression in Mentally Retarded Children and Adults* (pp. 175–198). Leiden: Logon.

Sovner, R. (1991). use of anticonvulsant agents for treatment of neuropsychiatric disorders in the developmentally disabled. In Ratey, J. J. (ed.), *Mental Retardation: Developing Pharmacotherapies,* Washington, DC: American Psychiatric Press. pp. 83–106.

Sovner, R., & Hurley, A. D., (1985). Assessing the quality of psychotropic drug regiments prescribed for mentally retarded persons. *Psychiatr. Aspects Ment. Retard. Rev., 8/9,* 31–38.

Sovner, R., & Hurley, A. D. (1988). Drug profiles: 4. carbamazepine and valproate, *Psychiatr. Aspects Ment. Retard. Rev., 7(12) 74–83.*

Steingard, R., & Biederman, J. (1987). Lithium responsive manic- like symptoms in two individuals with autism and mental retardation. *J. Am. Acad. Child Adol. Psychiatr.,26,* 932–935.

Tanguay, P. E., & Szymanski, L. S. (1984). Psychiatric research in mental retardation: Current status and future dirctions in F. J. Menolascino & J. A. Stark (Eds.), *Handbook of mental illness in the mentally retarded* (pp. 403–416). New York: Plenum Press.

# 14

## Treatment of Personality Disorder in Persons with Mental Retardation

*Laurence Dana*

The treatment of persons with personality disorders is an extremely challenging assignment for any clinician.

The literature on personality disorder in the general population is full of conflicting theories about both what constitutes a personality disorder and what actually is meant by the word *personality*. An excellent summary of the past fifty years or so of literature was provided by Rutter (1987) in his speech to the Royal College of Psychiatrists in London.

He described personality as "the coherence of functioning that derives from how people react to their given attributes, how they think about themselves, and how they put these together into some form of conceptual whole." He went on to say that some forms of personality disorders "are characterized by a persistent, pervasive, abnormality in social relationships and social functioning generally. . . . They deserve much greater attention than they have received in the past" (454).

This definition, quite similar to the definition in the revised third edition of the American Psychiatric Association (APA, 1987) *Diagnostic and Statistical Manual* (DSM-III-R) (see Chapter 7), is as good a definition as we are likely to get. Once again quoting Rutter, "there is no way of measuring personality" (454).

Given the conflicting theories about the etiology, course, and treatment of personality disorder among persons without cognitive loss, it should not be surprising that the literature is not very helpful to the clinician desiring to treat a person with coexisting developmental disabilities.

First, there is little or no established "standard of care" for developmentally disabled persons with diagnosed personality problems. Reid and Ballinger (1987) correctly cited and agreed with Corbett (1979), stating, "very little attention has been devoted to the problems of personality in the population, and research in this field has tended to be impressionistic and inadequate" (p. 983). Two five-year literature searches produced only seventeen references to personality disorder among the developmentally disabled. And in these papers, very little was said about treatment strategies; the articles focusing primarily on incidence or diagnosis.

So, lacking a literature reflecting established treatment protocols and standards (as exists, for example, for schizophrenia or bipolar disorders), treatment providers are largely left to their own devices. There is great potential for mischief here, given the extremely volatile nature of the behaviors associated with many of these personality disorders (Reid & Ballinger, 1987; Mawson, 1985).

As was emphasized in chapter 7, the clinician is strongly cautioned to reevaluate the diagnosis of personality disorder periodically. This diagnosis can become an all-too-easy "garbage-pail" label developmentally disabled persons, who cannot be expected to have the same level of social sophistication and communication abilities that nonhandicapped persons have.

Since the treatment literature is so sparse, the diagnosis of personality disorder may become a convenient excuse to give up all positive treatment efforts and consign the person to a life of heavy medication, personal and mechanical restraints, needless "time-out" episodes, and even aversive conditioning.

Although there are times when a firm stand must be taken, it is my contention that even persons with severe personality disorders can be successfully treated. And this treatment can (and must) remain within the boundaries of culturally acceptable and normative interventions.

## Antisocial Personality Disorder

Let us begin with the diagnosis most clinicians tend to have in mind when they use the term personality disorder.

The most difficult challenge facing the clinician attempting to serve this group is the virtual impossibility of forming any kind of true therapeutic alliance. Such an alliance is crucial in the thinking of virtually all schools of psychotherapy (Corsini, 1984), and most therapists feel lost when such an alliance cannot be achieved (Carkhuff, 1987). This sense of frustration is compounded when the individual needing service is also borderline or mildly retarded and may not possess the ability to use symbolic or abstract concepts in counseling.

Given these very unusual constraints, the treatment strategy designed to serve this group should consider the following:

*Get control.* Control may be the poor cousin of rapport, but without either, there is no point in reading further. This may sound cynical, but persons with antisocial personality disorder are unstable and potentially dangerous. A controlled situation is the absolute minimum requirement for any positive change.

In many cases control comes through the courts, and therapists should not feel uncomfortable gaining support through court actions (Griffin, Steadman, & Heilbreen, 1991).

At a minimum, clinicians should familiarize themselves with the criminial procedure law in their state regarding persons with developmental disabilities. Familiarity with such tools as the Rogers Criminal Responsibility Assessment Scales (Rogers, 1984) would also be most helpful.

This approach is recommended because persons with antisocial personality disorder very frequently run afoul of the law (or are inappropriately shielded from the law). The clinician should develop a comfortable working relationship with the local police, the probation department, the local magistrate, the district attorney, and the Legal Aid services. This group of persons is likely to be called on to aid the clinician in managing the key components of the rest of the plan.

*Establish a prosocial pattern of behavior either with or* (if necessary) *for the individual.* A plan based solely on punishment for misdeeds is doomed to failure. Rather, a schedule of *activities* designed to engage the person and integrate her or him into the natural environment must be established. This pattern may have to be part of a plea bargain, a condition of probation or parole, (in New York State) part of an Adjoinment in Contemplation of Dismissal, or part of a privilege schedule of a person committed to a state agency pending forensic services.

A key element here is the clinician's understanding that a person with antisocial personality disorder will initially resist all attempts to conform his or her behavior to societal rules. One can expect the full range of the antisocial repertoire as an initial response to imposed controls. Thus, for a program to successfully get through the first phase of services to these people, much thought and planning must be done about handling the inevitable deceptive and even aggressive behaviors that will almost certainly ensue.

*Establish a control stimulus.* This is a staff person whom the individual perceives as powerful, and who can dispense both rewards and punishments. Respect for power is very much part of the personality structure of people with antisocial personality disorder (Doren, 1987). The staff person who is to act as a control stimulus needs to be carefully selected and highly trained. Such a person must be able to model responsible, mature, and even-tempered behavior in the face of sometimes extreme provocation. Although imposing physical size is sometimes a helpful attribute in such a staff person, it also sometimes actually interferes with long-range outcomes. The reason is that the client may come to respond only to physically large caregivers and to lose behavioral control when these people are not immediately present.

My preference is to use two such staff persons, working different shifts.

Whenever possible, one should be a woman of normal size. This choice is meant to prevent sending the wrong message to the client that only large men must be respected.

The key, here, is that this staff member has the final word on both rewards and punishments. The whole program must be designed to empower this staff person so that decisions can be made on the spot and no "end runs" are possible.

The reader is reminded that persons with antisocial personality disorder respect persons who they feel are more powerful than themselves. So the initial treatment strategy must create one or two caregivers who present themselves as having near-total control over the life of the person served.

*Arrange for counseling and supervision.* The person acting as a control stimulus should meet often with the client and set forth specific expectations. Consequences, both negative and positive, should be explained to the person and should be enforced rigidly.

The key to success here is not simply to supervise and counsel, but to engage the person in a full day's activity that *precludes* the opportunity for maladaptive behaviors. This means an hourly schedule of required on-task behavior (including recreational activities) in which the assigned staff person is giving very frequent reinforcement to the individual.

When it becomes necessary to mete out punishment, the policies governing such consequences must be crystal clear to both the staff and the person served.

There is a raging controversy among professionals serving developmentally disabled persons regarding the appropriateness of using punishment as part of a treatment plan. A fair treatment of both sides of this controversy can be found in the National Institute of Mental Health (NIMH) publication 91-2410, *Treatment of Destructive Behaviors in Persons with Developmental Disabilities*. Readers are encouraged to write NIMH and secure a copy.

This material, as well as a review that I have made of the last ten years of literature on the subject of punishment, suggests the following guidelines.

1. Punishment must be predictable. This means the individual knows the rules and clearly has the capacity to avoid punishment by not engaging in the target behavior.
2. It must be fair.
3. It should be of sufficient intensity to be, in fact, punishing.
4. It should be brief and clearly associated with the target behavior.
5. Only agreed-upon alternatives or compensatory behavior should permit an avoidance of the punishment.

6. The punishment should not model the very behaviors that are being punished.

7. All punishments must be consistent with cultural norms and must be periodically reviewed by a responsible "due-process" system.

8. Punishments may not be the lead component of the treatment plan.

*Stage surveillance.* The individual's behavior has to be monitored to ensure compliance as the level of supervision is gradually reduced. Persons known, and unknown, to the individual should make frequent and random behavior probes. These are absolutely necessary, because persons with antisocial personality disorder cannot be relied on to give honest accounts of their own behavior. In fact, relying on such accounts may actually set the person up for failure.

*Remain vigilant for positive growth.* Sometimes "repatterning" people helps them reexamine their lives. One should always be prepared to look for signs that moral values are starting to develop, and to reach out with an appropriate response.

Persons with personality disorder who are developmentally disabled generally need active treatment programs that are designed to focus on increasing their successful interpersonal relationships with both peers and caregivers.

I am familiar with two very successful community-based programs serving developmentally disabled persons with antisocial personality disorder. Both programs serve persons with serious forensic problems and behaviors that include sexual assault, fire setting, alcohol abuse, and potentially lethal violent attacks. These programs are successful because they offer their people a wide variety of positive, active, attractive alternatives to antisocial behavior. The staff are also not afraid to deal swiftly and firmly, with even a small violation of the rules, and they do so in a way that models prosocial behavior.

One of these programs has the concept of *moral training* built into its counseling methodology. Despite the poor prognosis for persons with antisocial personality disorder to internalize moral values, many of the program participants have surprised the staff and have shown considerable growth in this area. Once again, this is a reminder to us all to be open to the possibility of positive change.

## Other Personality Disorders

For persons (unlike those with antisocial personality disorder) in whom the clinician is not concerned about dangerous or criminal behavior, the following treatment approaches are suggested.

For many developmentally disabled persons with personality disorder, especially those with avoidant or schizoid personality disorder, having even *one* friend is quite an accomplishment. Those with a history of institutional living may have been repeatedly betrayed by persons claiming to be friends. As a result, making the distinction between these two types of personality disorders may have to wait until the response to an intensive treatment plan has been attempted. In fact, persons with many forms of personality disorder can benefit from programs based on increasing the likelihood of developing a bond with someone.

*Use a formal counseling paradigm with a trained counselor.* One excellent paradigm for such a series of counseling sessions can be found in Robert Carkhuff's structured "helping" material (Carkhuff, 1987).

The goal here is to start the "bonding" process by encouraging the person to develop feelings of *trust* in at least one person, the therapist. This may be a breakthrough for the person that then facilitates the development of these feelings with others.

This bonding may be a very long-term process. Working with a middle-aged, mildly retarded man who had spent his whole life in institutions (he was actually *born* in one!), I have, after many years, seen him start to reach out and form similar trusting relationships with a few others. He still has no friends among his peers and trusts very few professionals, but now there is more than one person he will trust and share his confidences with.

*Use structured social skills training.* Even persons who are quite handicapped can learn what to say and when (Hunt, Atwell, & Goetz, 1988). By techniques used for more severely handicapped retarded persons, even persons with schizoid personality disorder can be trained to model behaviors similar to those of nonhandicapped persons (Hornstein et al., 1980; Fox et al., 1984; Lamon & Reiss, 1987).

Consider creating an environment that *rewards* interpersonal relationships. Make every attempt to set up living alternatives and program designs that reinforce a shared or joint activity. Two-person tasks and small-group recreational activities should be encouraged whenever possible. Sadly, too many vocational programs serving the developmentally handicapped discourage human interaction. I find it troubling to see, both in sheltered workshops and in (so-called) day treatment programs, people sitting in front of a task they are forced to do, alone, over and over again.

One common problem I have found among developmentally disabled persons with personality disorder is a high level of disorganization—a sort of disintegration of the core personality. This feature, virtually the hallmark of the dreaded borderline personality disorder among cognitively normal people, makes retarded people seem even more retarded.

Here are some suggested interventions that both the literature (what little exists) and my experience suggest.

*Bring order out of chaos.* These people need gentle discipline and order.

Since many of these people have a pathological fear of abandonment, consider "private time" a major reinforcer to shape adherence to a schedule. The term *private time* refers to using a very potent reinforcer—a coffee break with a staff member—as a reward for following even a rudimentary schedule. The key, here, is encouraging the person to develop a much better sense of, or orientation to "time." So many people with disorganized personality structure have terrible problems with time management. Sometimes, even transposing a written schedule into actual behavior is a skill that needs to be developed.

Sometimes, it becomes evident that the individual is simply *never* going to get the abstraction of following a schedule. The best you can do is to try to keep the person *engaged* with a menu of activities.

Keep in mind that persons with poorly organized personality structure cannot tolerate idle time well and are likely to lapse into stereotypical and self-stimulatory behaviors if left to their own devices too long. They are not likely to self-initiate or even to request certain activities.

*Develop a unifying theme.* Developmentally disabled persons with borderline personality disorder (and similar "disorganizing" features) lead lives with few opportunities for "meaning" or fulfillment. Although it can be quite a challenge, it is important to help these individuals find *something* with which they can define themselves as something other than "clients."

Since most normal people find their sense of identity through their personal relationships and their jobs, imagine the vacuum created when someone has neither.

The "cluster C" (avoidant, dependent, obsessive-compulsive, passive-aggressive) personality disorders deserve special treatment because they frequently become a "problem" when a developmentally disabled person is placed in a normalized environment. In fact, dependent and obsessive personality traits are probably adaptive and valued traits in many congregate care centers.

The reader may find the last group of suggested intervention strategies helpful with this group.

*Create an emotionally safe environment.* The pump needs to be primed for these people by setting up an environment in which it is OK to assert a need with *no* fear of consequences. Using a "psychodrama" approach is a good way to start, since the person can read ahead in the script and know that all will turn out OK.

Using humor, especially allowing someone to make a joke at a staff member's expense, is a good beginning. This can sometimes lead to surprising exchanges, if the trust is there. On one occasion, I was chiding a person with whom this approach was being used, and he retorted with "The hell with you. You're not a *real* doctor."

*Make choices part of the natural environment.* Rather than artificially "teaching" choices, make functional decision making a part of the daily routine (Dana Henning, personal communication, 1992). This means taking people to places where choices are *naturally made,* such as at a McDonald's. The person should be taught that it is OK to choose from a menu, rather than have an authority person always make the selection. This theme of encouraging independent choice making should be an objective integrated into every naturally occurring situation in which choices are possible.

*Help the person communicate his or her needs better.* One potentially promising approach for this group is functional communication training (Durand, 1985). Certainly, people with, for example, dependent personality disorder have a much greater chance of becoming more independent if they can communicate better their needs.

Teaching people specific conversational skills can also work toward reducing behaviors that make them more staff-dependent (Hunt et al., 1988).

*Use status and title.* Sometimes, a symbol of authority, such as a nametag or a special title, helps a person more clearly define his or her role. Try to find a reassuring structure within a residence or day program that allows a person to act with autonomy by virtue of a *title,* and without having to make a verbal request each time.

*Use specific treatments for compulsive rituals.* Many treatments for obsessive-compulsive disorder are also effective for some of the behaviors seen in people with obsessive-compulsive personality disorder. An excellent resource describing such techniques as response prevention and flooding, as well as biological treatments, can be found in a monograph by Turner and Beidel (1988).

*Train for compliance.* Passive-aggressive personality disorder, or at least passive-aggressive behavior, is hardly foreign to those working with the developmentally disabled. The challenge here is to help someone who has developed a sometimes amazing repertoire of techniques for avoiding compliance with requests without ever having a direct confrontation.

I have found that one of the most effective techniques for this group is an adaptation of an approach used for people who use tantrum behavior (or an increase in stereotypy) to avoid tasks. This technique is to request that a person do something she or he is about to do *anyway* and then heavily reinforce the notion of compliance. After a while, the person begins to seek out ways to gain reinforcement by finding requests that he or she can comply with. Two examples in the literature that describes this approach are articles by Mace and Belfiore (1990) and Davis (1992).

## Summary

There are many obstacles in the path of the clinician trying to develop an effective treatment protocol for persons with personality disorder who are also developmentally disabled. Not only is making a precise diagnosis very difficult, but there is very little consensus on the very concept of *personality* itself among providers of mental health services.

Complicating matters even more is the fact that persons with the combined effect of both disorders tend to be extremely treatment-resistant. Persons in this situation are commonly rejected from entire service systems and may find themselves on the streets or in correctional facilities.

In fact, the future for persons with this dual diagnosis need not be so bleak. With creative planning that includes a variety of agency partners, and by constant redirection to the right path, most of these persons can be served in normalized community-based settings.

It is almost a cliché to end a chapter like this by suggesting more research. In this instance, the abject paucity of solid clinical research and the virtual absence of generally agreed-upon treatment paradigms make the call for more research in this area very valid indeed.

# References

American Psychiatric Association. (1987) *Diagnostic and statistical manual of mental disorders* (3rd ed., rev.), DSM- III-R). Washington, DC: Author.

Carkhuff, R. (1987). *The art of helping (Vol. 6.)* Amherst, MA: Human Resource Development Press.

Corbett, J. A. (1979). Psychiatric mortality and mental retardation. In F. E. James & R. P. Smith (Eds.), *Psychiatric illness and mental handicap.* London: Gaskell.

Corsini, R. J. (1984). *Current psychotherapies.* ITASCA: Peacock.

Davis, C. A. (1992) Effects of high probability request on the acquisition and generalization of responses to requests in young children with behavior disorders. *J. Appl. Behav. Anal., 25,* 905–916.

Doren, D. M. (1987). *Understanding and treating the psychopath.* New York: John Wiley & Sons.

Durand, M. (1985). Reducing behavior problems through functional communication training. *J. Appl. Behav. Anal., 18,* 111–126.

Foxx, R., McMorrow, M., Storey, K., & Rogers, B. (1984). Teaching social/sexual skills to mentally retarded adults. *Am. J. Ment. Defic., 89,* 9–15.

Griffin, P. A., Steadman, H. J., & Heilbreen, K. (1991). Designing conditional release systems for insanity acquitees. *J. Ment. Health Admini., 18,* 231–241.

Hornstein, P., Bach, P., McFall, M., Friman, P., & Lyons, P. (1980). Application of a social skills training program in the modification of interpersonal deficits among retarded adults: A clinical replication. *J. Appl. Behav. Anal., 13,* 171–176.

Hunt, P., Atwell, M., & Goetz, L. (1988). Acquisition of conversational skills and the reduction of inappropriate social interaction behaviors. *J. Assoc. Persons with Severe Handicaps, 13,* 20–27.

Lamon, D. S., & Reiss, S. (1987). Social skill deficiencies associated with depressed mood of mentally retarded adults. *Am. J. Ment. Defic., 92*(2), 224–229.

Mace, F. C., & Belfiore, P. (1990). Behavioral momentum in the treatment of escape motivated stereotypy. *J. Appl. Behav. Anal., 23,* 507–514.

Mawson, D., Grounds, A., & Tantan, D. (1985). Violence and Aspergers Syndrome: A case study. *Br. J. Psychiatr., 147,* 566–569.

Reid, A. H., & Ballinger, B. R. (1987). Personality disorder in mental handicap. *Psychol. Med., 17,* 983–987.

Rogers, R. (1984). *Rogers Criminal Responsibility Assessment Scales.* Odessa: Psychological Assessment Resources.

Rutter, M. (1987). Temperament, personality and personality disorder. *Br. J. Psychiatr., 150,* 443–458.

Turner, S. M., & Beidel, D. C., (1988). *Treating obsessive compulsive disorder.* New York: Pergamon Press.

# 15

# Biological Aspects and Pharmacological Treatment of Self- Injurious Behavior in Persons with Mental Retardation

*Willem M. A. Verhoeven*
*Siegfried Tuinier*
*No E. S. Sijben*

Self-injurious behavior (SIB) is a common problem among the retarded population, particularly in residential institutions, and can be defined as the commission of deliberate harm to one's own body. The injury is done to oneself, without the aid of another person, and is severe enough for tissue damage to result (Winchel & Stanley, 1991). In more restrictive terms, SIB can be defined as a chronic repetitive behavior, causing external trauma on a mechanical basis and occurring mostly in a cognitively impaired patient. Common forms of SIB include cutting and burning the skin, banging the head and limbs, picking at wounds, and chewing fingers and lips. Estimates of the incidence of SIB among mentally retarded patients range from 8 to 14 percent for institutionalized persons and from 1.7 to 2.6 percent for those living not in residential facilities (Singh & Millichamp, 1985; Rojahn, 1986; Griffin et al., 1987; Oliver, Murphy, & Corbett, 1987).

In the diagnosis of SIB, environmental and medical causes that may underlie this type of behavioral disorder should be considered first, followed by specific neurological and psychiatric assessment, and then the delineation of specific syndromes that are associated with SIB. The aim of adequate diagnosis is not only to establish treatment guidelines but also to improve subject homogeneity and therefore enhancing the reliability of clinical studies (Gualtieri, 1989, 1991). Regarding the treatment of SIB, in general two strategies have been followed: medication with psychotropics or other psychoactive compounds and behavior modification techniques. The literature on behavioral approaches to SIB has yielded some positive findings from these techniques, but most of the studies deal with case reports, do not follow a controlled design, are highly labor-intensive, and lack a good long-term follow-up (Tarnowski et al., 1989). The interest in the pharmacological treatment of behavior disorders, particularly SIB, in the mentally retarded has recently been renewed, not only because at least 40 to 50 percent of institutionalized mentally retarded persons receive psychotropic drugs (Singh & Millichamp, 1985; Stone et al., 1989) but because of the increasing insights into the putative etiopathogenesis of SIB and the general risk of effective treatment. An analysis of the relevant pharmacological literature, however, shows that the bulk of the research is clinical in nature, and that few of the necessary methodological controls have been employed.

In this chapter, we summarize the current knowledge about the effects of pharmacotherapy on SIB based on a critical evaluation of the clinical and empirical literature and, where possible, in relation to the pathogenetic views that are now under investigation. In addition, we discuss some methodological aspects that are of importance in performing clinical trials as well as in interpreting the results.

## Methodological Issues

Regarding the findings discussed in this chapter, it is obvious that the research on SIB has yielded only a very limited amount of valid data that seem to be consistent (Gualtieri & Schroeder, 1990). There are several reasons.

First, it is extremely difficult to operationalize the concept of mental retardation and SIB. In the revised third edition of the American Psychiatric Association (APA, 1987) *Diagnostic and Statistical Manual* (DSM-III-R), mental retardation is defined as a disturbance in development before the age of eighteen, with an IQ below 70 and concurrent deficits or impairments in adaptive behavior, considering age. The criteria IQ below 70 and impairments of adaptive behavior are especially difficult to measure. Most of the intelligence tests are not adequate for the low-IQ range, so it is very difficult to determine an IQ below 70 and to discriminate among the different stages of mental retardation. In the DSM-III-R, a differentiation is made between the IQ levels 50–70, 35–49, 20–34, and less than 20. In the lowest ranges, it is impossible to assess the level of intelligence. The tests currently used to assess the level of intelligence can also be criticized for their content as well as their practice. These tests are developed for normal subjects, so the tasks cannot be applied to mentally retarded persons, and the norm scores do not match new insights into the developmental model of retardation (Dosen & Bojanin, 1990). In addition, the test situation is often too rigid to be useful for these subjects.

The second criterion is maladaptiveness of behavior. This criterion is also difficult to measure. Several observation scales have been developed, such as the Vineland Social Maturity Scale (Doll, 1965) and the Adaptive Behavioral Scale (Nihira et al., 1974). The shortcomings of these observation scales are, among others, low reliability, subjective interpretations, and the impossibility of quantifying relatively complex behavior.

These two difficulties in the operationalization of the criteria imply that the selection and identification of a specific level of mental retardation cannot meet the standards for research criteria. Thus, the fact that patient groups are not homogeneous with respect to the main criteria may explain some of the contradictory results found in the literature.

Similar arguments can be applied to the measurement of SIB. As mentioned previously, there is a large variety of symptoms, and it is questionable whether or not these are relevant and have a common etiology. In most of the studies, no differentiation in SIB and SIB-related symptoms is made, while no proper criteria are used for the assessment of specific symptoms. Moreover, the methods of assessment vary greatly from one study to another. In order to get a more-or-less objective assessment, standardization of the test situation would be necessary. This standardization, however, can never be achieved in this type of research.

In addition to the abovementioned methodological problems in performing research projects on mentally retarded subjects, including those suffering from SIB, there are the issues of internal and external validity. The factors involved here are (Cook & Campbell, 1979) the following.

**History.** Between the first measurement and the last one, several confounding events may occur, such as a change in the residential situation, a transfer to other wards, or the replacement of staff members. All these events affect the treatment outcome.

**Maturation.** Most of the research on SIB deals with subjects who, in spite of their mental retardation, are still developing. This maturational process may underlie pretest–posttest differences.

**Assessment and Scoring Procedures.** In longitudinal designs, some instruments must be used several times. The rater who applies assessment scales every week becomes familiar with them and less accurate, or he or she may desire to assess changes after several ratings. Also instrumentational effects may occur when the test scale has no equal distance over its whole range, in that the intervals between the scoring categories are different, and the result is a scoring bias, depending on the position on the scale.

**Experimental Dropout.** In longitudinal designs, particularly with the mentally retarded, several factors may cause a premature termination of treatment. If such factors are related to the treatment itself, like side effects or ineffectiveness, the assessment of efficacy is influenced.

If adequate procedures could be developed to solve these problems, there would still be two other problems to be taken into account. First, most of the instruments used are observer rating scales, which hold the implicit risk of contamination because differents variables (level of development, social adaptation, and SIB symptoms) have to be assessed with the same instrument. It is therefore more appropriate to use several methods for the registration of behavior, or at least to use different observers, in order to reach convergent and discriminant validity: The same variables measured by different methods must lead to comparable results, and different variables measured by the same method should yield different results (Campbell & Fiske, 1959). The second problem concerns the statistical evaluation. To compare pre- and postexperimental results, simple statistical procedures are usually applied, like the T test. However, if the variances in the scores are rather small, statistically significant results may not be reached. This is the well-known problem of statistical significance versus clinical relevance. A more appropriate method of statistical evaluation of the results is to specify in advance the expected treatment effects and to measure afterward whether this expectation was justified. This so-called criterion-referenced measurement has been used so far on a very limited scale in research projects on SIB.

## Pathogenetic Hypotheses

### Dopamine

The most logical way to select a medication for SIB would be to determine the cause of the SIB and tailor the pharmacological agent to it. Thus, a considerable amount of the literature deals with the Lesch-Nyhan syndrome (LNS) about whose underlying defect much is already known: an absence of the X-linked enzyme hypoxanthine guanine phosphoribosyltransferase (HGPRT; Lesch & Nyhan, 1964). Based on the observations by Lloyd et al. (1981), who showed a marked reduction of dopamine (DA) and its metabolites in the CNS of patients with LNS, and on those of Castells et al. (1979) and Silverstein et al. (1985), who reported reduced homovanillic acid (HVA) concentrations in the cerebrospinal fluid (CSF) of LNS subjects, it has been hypothesized that SIB in LNS may result from dopaminergic stimulation in a state of receptor supersensitivity (Goldstein et al., 1986). In accordance with this DA-receptor supersensitivity hypothesis are the observations of Sokol et al. (1987), who reported the eliciting of self-biting behavior in four patients with attention-deficit disorder by the administration of DA-agonistic compounds dextroamphetamine and methylphenidate. A promising animal model for SIB was developed by Breese and coworkers (1984, 1986, 1989), who induced a neonatal destruction of DA-containing fibers in the rat brain by treatment with 6-hydroxydopamine. The treatment of these animals as adults with L-dopa resulted in a dose-dependent increase of SIB that could be blocked with the $D_1$-DA-postsynaptic receptor blocker *cis*-flupenthixol, but not with the $D_2$-DA-antagonist haloperidol. Similar findings were reported by Goldstein et al. (1985a, 1985b), who observed the induction of SIB by DA-agonistic drugs in monkeys with ventromedial tegmental lesions, which could be diminished by the administration of $D_1$-DA-receptor blockers like fluphenazine. These observations suggest that the pharmacological basis of SIB may indeed be a $D_1$-DA-receptor supersensitivity state. Goldstein and coworkers hypothesized that the mechanism of the development of supersensitive striatal DA receptors is somehow related to the deficiency of HGPRT acivity in LNS, since their results indicated that HGPRT is localized in intrastriatal neurons that are known to contain $D_1$- and $D_2$-DA receptors. These findings suggest that, in these neurons, the DA receptor may be regulated by nucleotide levels arising from the salvage pathway. The abnormal regulation of affinity states of the DA receptors by the guanine nucleotides may be involved in the pathology of LNS (Goldstein, 1989, 1990). It is therefore conceivable that $D_1$-DA-receptor supersensitivity is related to the occurrence of SIB, although the data from the neonatal 6- hydroxydopamine (6-OHDA) lesioned rat model do not allow conclusions concerning whether activation of DA receptors is the mechanism by which self-biting is induced in LNS. While it seems likely that the increased susceptibility to self-biting in LNS is the result of the reduced neonatal DA function, mechanisms other than the release of DA may be responsible for this symptom in LNS. The data collected in the model of DA related to a neonatal deficiency of DA, even in the absence of HGPRT deficiency as observed in LNS.

The model of DA deficiency, however, is not the only possible explanation of the relation of behavior and biological dysfunction. Jones (1982) suggested that severe forms of SIB may also be provoked by long-term isolation. In their elegant research, Kraemer (1986) and Kraemer and Clarke (1990) demonstrated that there is overwhelming evidence that SIB can emerge in social primate species in the absence of drug treatment and without pre-existing brain damage as a consequence of psychosocial deprivation involving a malfunction of the noradrenalin and serotonin systems. SIB develops when social environmental contingencies are not in place at the right time. In addition, there is some evidence from animal experiments that early prolonged social isolation results in long-term alterations in functional dopamine-receptor supersensitivity (Lewis et al., 1990).

## Serotonin

The serotonin hypothesis of SIB is based on the observation of several investigators that patients with different kinds of violent, impulsive, or (auto)destructive behavior show significantly lower CSF concentrations of the main serotonin metabolite 5-hydroxyindoleacetic acid (5-HIAA). Asberg et al. (1976) were the first to report a bimodal distribution of the levels of CSF 5-HIAA in depressed patients who had made suicide attempts, in that the group of depressed patients who attempted suicide appeared to coincide with the "low" CSF 5-HIAA group. This finding led to the proposal that low CSF 5-HIAA levels may be associated with suicidal behavior. Subsequently, Brown et al. (1979, 1982) reported that patients with a history of suicidal behavior had significantly lower CSF 5-HIAA levels than patients without such a history. Among depressed patients, Van Praag (1982) confirmed the observation that suicide attempts were found significantly more often among patients with low CSF 5-HIAA levels than among people with normal levels. It is of significance that low 5-HIAA levels have been associated in particular with violent suicide attempts. Thus, Traskman et al. (1981) found that CSF 5-HIAA levels were significantly lower only in patients who had made a violent suicide attempt. Moreover, an inverse relationship could be demonstrated between the levels of CSF 5-HIAA and a life history of aggressive-impulsive behavioral disorder (see review and references in Brown et al., 1900; Roy & Linnoila, 1990). In addition, Banki and Arato (1983) reported significantly decreased levels of CSF 5-HIAA in patients suffering from different diagnostic psychiatric entities, a finding that was recently confirmed by Van Praag (1986). These findings indicate that serotonin metabolism is involved in the regulation of aggressive behavior, irrespective of the direction it takes, and that a low CSF 5-HIAA level correlates not only with inwardly directed aggression, like violent suicide and SIB, but also with outwardly directed aggression (Van Praag, 1991).

Concerning SIB, the involvement of serotonin disturbances in the pathogenesis of this symptomatology is based on the inwardly directed aggression model, on the one hand, and the similarity of some of its features to those of obsessive-compulsive disorder (OCD), on the other hand. The evidence for altered serotonergic function in patients with OCD is derived from the efficacy of treatment with serotonin reuptake inhibitors, from studies of CSF 5-HIAA concentrations, and from studies of the serotonin-receptor agonist m- chlorophenylpiperazine (MCPP) (see review and references in Zohar & Zohar-Kadouch, 1991). In children wih disruptive behavior disorders characterized by aggression and impulsivity, Kruesi et al. (1990) found a negative correlation between age-corrected 5-HIAA concentration and some aggression measures. In addition, it has been reported that symptoms of SIB in patients with coexisting OCD respond to treatment with serotonin-reuptake inhibitors (Yaryura-Tobias et al., 1978; Primeau & Fontaine, 1987). In patients with SIB, among other symptoms, Greenberg and Coleman (1973, 1976) reported an association between patterns of behavioral problems, including SIB, and depressed plasma 5-hydroxyindole levels. In these patients with low plasma serotonin levels, elevation of serotonin levels into the normal range by the administration of a variety of psychoactive agents appeared to be associated with an improvement in behavioral disturbances.

In summary, increasing evidence is available that disturbances in central serotonergic mechanisms, as reflected in, among others, lowered CSF 5-HIAA concentrations, are involved in violent, impulsive, and (auto)destructive behavior. The bulk of this evidence has been obtained from clinical studies with non-mentally-retarded psychiatric subjects (Brown et al., 1990). In nonretarded subjects, as well as in mentally retarded subjects, a considerable overlap has been reported of outward aggression and autoaggression, although the mechanisms underlying the direction of this behavior are not yet well understood (Plutchik & Van Praag, 1990). It should be stressed that the amount of aggression displayed in a given situation depends on three factors: the strength of the aggressive impulses, the strength of the countervailing forces, and the ability to control and balance these impulses. The inability of mentally retarded patients to adapt to incoming stressful stimuli is probably one of the important factors in the initiation of SIB.

Preclinical research also shows that serotonergic subsystems have a modulatory influence on several behaviors, including pain, aggression, locomotor activity, and avoidance learning (Azmitia, 1978). Lesions of the raphe nucleus cause hyperactivity and hypersensitivity to external stimuli. In addition, serotonin plays an important role in stress adaptation (Ohi, Mikuni, & Takahashi, 1989; Curzon, 1989), while steroid hormones stimulate serotonin turnover by the activation of tryptophan-hydroxylase, and serotonin on its turn is involved in the steroid-mediated long-term refractoriness of the CNS to subsequent stressful stimuli.

## Endogenous Opioids

Endogenous opioids are neuropeptides that act like morphine in the CNS (see review and references in Akil et al., 1984; Van Ree, Verhoeven, & De Wied, 1987; Mansour et al., 1988). There are three major groups of opioid peptides derived from larger precursor hormones with genetically distinct origins: proopiomelanocortin, from which beta-endorphin and its fragments are derived; preproenkephalin from which met-enkephalin, leuenkephalin, and seven other opioids ae derived; and preprodynorphin, from which dynorphin and neoendorphin peptides are derived. The discovery of these endogenous opioid neuropeptides has given impetus to the formulation of hypotheses about their modulatory effects on brain function and behavior, including, among others, their influences on brain development, plasticity, and functioning (see review and references in Sandman & O'Halloran, 1986; De Wied, 1990; Van Ree, Jolles, & Verhoeven, 1990).

It has been hypothesized that SIB may be due to functional disturbances in the endogenous opioid systems. At this time, two primary biological hypotheses have been formulated. The first is the so-called addiction hypothesis, stating that SIB may be considered a symptom of addiction to endogenous opioid neuropeptides. According to this hypothesis, the release of endorphins is stimulated by SIB, including addictional behavior to endogenous opioids (Van Ree, 1987), and suggesting that individuals may engage in SIB as a method of self-administering endogenous opioids. At present, however, there is no evidence that opioids are released as a consequence of SIB, and the limited studies available so far are flawed by complicated and difficult methodological problems. The second hypothesis was originally proposed by Herman et al. (1985, 1987) and states that enhanced brain opioid activity may underlie SIB, especially given the evidence linking opioids and antinociception. According to this hypothesis, opioid overactivity may be responsible for maintaining a relatively tonic level of pain insensitivity, an idea that is supported by the observation that painful stimulation results in an increased release of endorphins (Willer, Dehen, & Cambier, 1981). Thus, in self-injurious subjects, SIB may not induce pain, since these individuals may be in an opioid analgetic state resulting in little motivation to terminate SIB. Although this hypothesis is capable of explaining why certain individuals may not terminate SIB, it does not explain why the individual would initiate SIB.

Support for the opioid-overactivity hypothesis of SIB can be obtained from animal as well as from human studies. Studies in animals indicate that, in contrast to the effects of opiate antagonists, compounds with an affinity for opiate receptors may induce stereotyped behavior, including self-mutilation. Opiate antagonists appear to reverse all these effects (see review and references in Herman, 1990). In humans, Gillberg, Terenius, and Lunnerholm (1985) found higher concentrations of fractions I and II opioid concentrations in the CSF of twenty-four psychiatric- patient children than in normals. In fact, they demonstrated a positive correlation between fraction II levels and decreased sensitivity to pain as well as a weak trend with respect to high fraction I levels and SIB. Fraction II levels were significantly higher in the group of children with SIB than in non-self- destructive children. In a subsequent study, Ross, Klykylo, & Hitzeman (1987) found increased CSF immunoreactive beta-endorphin concentrations in autistic children compared to sex- and age- matched controls, although they did not analyze separately the concentrations in SIB individuals. Concerning the concentrations of opioid peptides in plasma of SIB individuals, Zelnik et al. (1986) originally described significantly lower plasma immunoreactive beta-endorphin levels in three SIB male children as compared with ten age-matched male controls. Similar findings i.c. decreased plasma beta-endorphin concentration, were reported by Weizman et al. (1988) and Herman et al. (1989) in 8 respectively 7 subjects with SIB as compared to normal controls. In contrast to these observations, Sandman (1988) observed higher levels of plasma beta-endorphin in a group of SIB subjects, that was confirmed by the same investigators (Sandman et al., 1990) in patients with SIB or stereotypy.

Thus, there is circumstantial evidence that opioid CSF concentrations are elevated in subjects with SIB, whereas opioid (immunoreactive beta-endorphin) plasma concentrations are low in SIB as compared with normal control individuals. These seemingly contradictory results concerning CSF opioid levels and plasma opioid levels in SIB individuals may be explained by assuming negative feedback between the hypothalmus and the pituitary in the regulation of the beta-endorphin in the brain and in plasma (Herman, 1990).

## Pharmacological Approaches

### Neuroleptics

As mentioned previously, disturbances in dopamine neurotransmission may be involved in the pathogenesis of SIB, particularly in patients suffering from LNS. If $D_1$-DA-receptor supersensitivity mediates SIB, it may be that patients with SIB, but without LNS, may be treated effectively with a compound that blocks the $D_1$-DA-receptor. Following this hypothesis, Gualtieri and Schroeder (1989, 1990) treated fifteen severely to profoundly mentally retarded subjects, who had a long history of SIB and who had been refractory to alternative treatments, with the neuroleptic fluphenazine (FPZ). FPZ was chosen because it antagonizes both $D_1$- and $D_2$-DA receptors, but preferentially $D_1$ (Seeman, 1981). The starting dose of FPZ was 0.5 mg twice daily, increased weekly until an optimal response was achieved or until side effects developed, up to a maximum of 15 mg per day. In eleven of the fifteen patients some degree of favorable response was observed as measured by the number of tantrums during which SIB occurred and the amount of time in or out of restraints. It appeared that a low dose of FPZ (1.5–8 mg daily) was especially effective, and that, in most cases, higher doses were accompanied by symptoms of akathisia, which actually made the SIB worse after an initial favorable response. From these limited data, the tentative conclusion may be drawn that the efficacy of (low-dose) FPZ is consistent with the receptor supersensitivity hypothesis. Because FPZ is not a pure receptor antagonist, it does, however, not confirm this hypothesis. Thus, further studies are warranted to elucidate this neurochemical hypothesis about SIB by using more selective $D_1$-DA-blocking compounds, such as *cis*-flupenthixol or clozapine. These investigations may yield more information about the relationship between SIB and a dysfunction of the DA neuronal systems. (Kraemer & Clarke, 1990).

Apart from the specific relationship between neuroleptics and DA receptor systems as postulated in LNS, antipsychotics are widely prescribed in facilities for the mentally retarded, although three is only a very limited number of studies of their behavioral effects, and most are vague and uninformative regarding specific symptoms, particularly SIB (Aman & Singh, 1980). There have been evaluations of the effects of several antipsychotics on SIB, including phenothiazines and butyrophenones (see review and references in Farber, 1987; Luchins, 1990). In a double-blind placebo-controlled trial, Singh and Aman (1981) investigated the effectiveness of thioridazine on the symptoms of mental retardation, including SIB. They concluded that, in a standardized dose of 2.5 mg/kg/day, thioridazine induced a reduction of excessive activity and bizarre behavior; SIB was only slightly reduced in a limited number of patients. Other studies using thioridazine have not focused on SIB specifically and have reported a global decrease of stereotyped and hyperactive behavioral patterns (Elie et al., 1980; Breuning et al., 1983). Similar results have been reported with other phenothiazines, like mesoridazine (Lacny, 1973), pericyazine (Tischler et al., 1972), and pipothiazine (Lynch et al., 1985).

The evidence for the efficacy of haloperidol comes from Le Vann (1969), who reported a reduction of SIB. Subsequent studies are anecdotal and suggest general effects only. The same is true of droperidol (Burns, 1980) and pipamperone (Van Hemert, 1975; Deberdt, 1976; Haegeman & Duyck, 1978).

Thus, although neuroleptics are at present the most widely used medications for SIB, the evidence for their effectiveness is more suggestive than conclusive.

## Serotonergic Agents

In view of the animal data that have suggested a relationship between aggression and serotonergic dysfunction and the co-concurrence in patients of outward and autoaggression, Mizuno and Yugari (1975) treated in an open trial four SIB patients with LNS with 6–8 mg/kg/day of 5-hydroxytryptophan (5-HTP), a precursor of serotonin, for 2 to 140 weeks. They reported a complete disappearance of SIB in all four patients within three days of initiating 5-HTP administration. However, within fifteen hours after discontinuation of the 5-HTP treatment, all the patients resumed their self-injurious behavior. These findings have prompted others to administer 5-HTP in the treatment of SIB among LNS patients. As can be inferred from Table 1, however, beneficial effects could not be confirmed in three studies following a double-blind placebo-controlled crossover design (Anderson, Herman, & Dancis, 1976; Frith et al., 1976; Anders et al., 1978). Only two open studies yielded a decrease of SIB on treatment with 5-HTP, followed by tolerance (Nyhan, 1976; Castells et al., 1979). In the study by Perry and Tischler (1964), no effect of 5-HTP administration could be demonstrated in 2 patients with phenylketonuria. It should be stressed, however, that neither of the patients included in the latter study showed any symptomatology of SIB.

The results of these studies with 5-HTP have to be interpreted carefully, not only because of their methodological shortcomings but also since it is well known that 5-HTP influences both serotonin and the catecholaminergic systems, while tryptophan only selectively increases the serotonin turnover

(Van Praag, 1983; Raleigh, 1987; Van Praag et al., 1990). In a primate study by Raleigh (1987), the influence on behavior of the serotonin-reuptake inhibitor fluoxetine and the catecholamine-reuptake inhibitor desmethylimipramine (DMI) or tryptophan and 5-HTP were investigated. Tryptophan produced dose-dependent increases in aggression, vigilance, and locomotion and an additional increase in eating. In contrast, 5-HTP increased aggression and vigilance but did not affect locomotion or eating. Fluoxetine produced effects identical to tryptophan, while DMI resulted in dose-dependent increases in aggression, vigilance, and locomotion. These results suggest that 5-HTP's effects on the catecholaminergic systems may underlie the different behavioral effects of tryptophan and 5-HTP, especially with regard to aggression. In addition, Volavka et al. (1990) found tryptophan to be effective in the treatment of aggressive psychiatric inpatients in that it significantly reduced the need for injections of antipsychotics and sedatives.

Concerning the other limited data on serotonergic compounds, O'Neal et al. (1986) reported on a patient with Cornelia de Lange's syndrome whose SIB was significantly reduced by treatment with the serotonin-reuptake inhibitor trazodone and the serotonin precursor L-tryptophan. In addition, the abnormally low peripheral serotonin levels did markedly increase. In two patients suffering from obsessive-compulsive disorder and associated SIB, Primeau and Fontaine (1987) found a significant decrease of SIB on treatment with the serotonergic antidepressant clomipramine, and Gualtieri (1989) reported a dramatic therapeutic response of SIB on treatment with the specific serotonin-reuptake inhibitor fluoxetine in combination with L- tryptophan. Following an open design, Markowitz (1990) treated eight patients with severe to profound mental retardation with SIB with fluoxetine in a dose of 20–40 mg daily. Their therapeutic response was evaluated by caretaker reports and personal observations of the patients. All patients experienced symptomatic improvement with fluoxetine; it was judged to be marked in five, moderate in one, and mild in two. All improved on the initial 20-mg dose during the first month of treatment; no additional improvement in the two mild responders was noted on the higher dose of 20 mg twice daily. Finally, Geyde (1990) reported a reduction of SIB in a Down syndrome subject by means of dietary increased serotonin availability. Systematic studies on the effectiveness of antidepressants on SIB are not available. The only study is that by Aman et al. (1986), who carried out a double-blind placebo-controlled study with 3 mg/kg imipramine for four weeks in ten subjects with SIB, without demonstrating any therapeutic effects on self-injurious symptoms.

Summarizing, increasing data are available suggesting a therapeutic effect of serotonergic agents on SIB. The most promising future direction may be the administration of specific serotonin-receptor agonistic compounds such as eltoprazine (Rasmussen et al., 1990). So far, only a very limited number of mentally retarded patients with (auto)aggressive behavior have

**Table 1**
**Clinical Studies with 5-HTP and Self-Injurious Behavior (SIB)**

| Author (Year) | N | Dosage | Design | Behavior | Rating of SIB | Baseline | Study Period | Diagnosis | Concurrent Medication | Effects on SIB |
|---|---|---|---|---|---|---|---|---|---|---|
| Perry and Tischler, 1964 | 2 | 50 mg twice daily | Double-blind placebo controlled | Mild degree of mental retardation; no SIB | Naturalistic; four psychometric tests; subjective impression of general behavior | Not specified | 3½ months (two periods; placebo and 5-HTP) 2–140 weeks | Phenylketonuria | Not mentioned | No evidence of any beneficial effect |
| Mizuno and Yugari, 1975 | 4 | 6–8 mg/kg (60–90 mg) | Open | Choreoathetosis; dystonia; SIB | Naturalistic; 6-point symptom-specific scale | Placebo; not specified | | Lesch-Nyhan syndrome | 4–6 mg/kg benz-bromarone; 0.3–0.5 mg/kg diazepam; 1–2 mg/kg chlori-diazepoxide; 5 mg/kg phenobar-bital | Complete disap-pearance during active treatment, starting from days 1 to 3 (no effect on neurological symptoms) |
| Nyhan, 1976 | 1 | Not specified | Open | SIB | Not mentioned | Not mentioned | Not mentioned | Lesch-Nyhan syndrome | Not mentioned | Decrease followed by tolerance |
| Anderson et al., 1976 | 4 | 4 mg/kg daily | Double-blind placebo controlled cross-over | SIB; spasticity | Naturalistic; 6-point symptom-specific scale; 30-min. observation period; 3 times daily | Placebo; 3 days | 21 days (n=3) 33 days (n=1) | Lesch-Nyhan syndrome | Not mentioned | No beneficial effect |

| Study | N | Dose | Design | Target behavior | Measurement | Placebo | Duration | Diagnosis | | Outcome |
|---|---|---|---|---|---|---|---|---|---|---|
| Ciarnello et al., 1976 | 1 | Increasing to maximum 50 mg/kg per day | Open, followed by placebo period | Compulsive SIB | Naturalistic; symptom-specific rating for 3 consecutive 5-min. segments, 2 to 3 times weekly | 3 days | 45 days | Lesch-Nyhan syndrome | Discontinued at least four days prior to trial period | No effect; significantly reduced irritability |
| Frith et al., 1976 | 1 | 100 mg daily | Double-blind placebo controlled crossover | Compulsive SIB; athetoid movements | Naturalistic; 5-point symptom-specific scale, according to Goldberg Psychiatric Scales; 15-min. observation period daily | 2 days placebo | 14 weeks; 7 treatment blocks, 4 on drug and 3 on placebo | Lesch-Nyhan syndrome | Allopurinol 100 mg daily | No effect; slight reduction of involuntary movements |
| Anders et al., 1978 | 1 | Increasing to maximally 1,000 mg per day (50 mg/kg) | Double-blind placebo-controlled crossover | Compulsive SIB choreoathetoid dyskinesia | Naturalistic; symptom-specific rating for 10-min. waking videotapes (frequency not specified) | 2 days | 60 days | Lesch-Nyhan syndrome | Allopurinol (dose unknown) | No effect; decline of choreoathetoid activity |
| Castells et al., 1979 | 1 | 48-96 mg daily | Open | SIB | Not mentioned | Not mentioned | 18 months | Lesch-Nyhan syndrome | Allopurinol 50 mg twice daily | Temporary reduction followed by tolerance (decreased levels of CSF 5-HIAA and HVA concentrations) |

been treated with eltoprazine. In the first placebo-controlled study, fifteen patients were treated with 20–30 mg eltoprazine daily and five with placebo only. Within the eltoprazine-treated patients, a marked and clinically significant reduction in aggressive behavior was apparent. This beneficial effect was obvious on all scales assessing aggressive behavior and was already apparent at the first assessment point in the double-blind phase, indicating a rapid onset of action. After the withdrawal of active medication, a relapse to aggressive behavior was observed, and extended treatment was requested for some patients. No side effects of any importance were observed (Duphar, 1991).

Although the beneficial effects of serotonin (5-HT) agonistic agents are thought to be generated via the 5-HT neuronal systems, other monoaminergic pathways may be involved as well. Accumulating evidence is available suggesting that 5-HT subsystems are functional in a behavioral constraint system in which septohippocampal 5-HT structures inhibit behavior under circumstances of stress, anxiety, and uncertainty, while mesolimbic dopaminergic (sub)systems are involved in mobilizing and orienting goal-directed behaviors and the associated locomotion (Depue & Spoont, 1986; Van Praag et al., 1990). Thus, the serotonin and dopamine hypotheses of aggressive behavior are not mutually exclusive.

### Opiate Antagonists

If there is overactivity in the brain opioid systems in individuals with SIB, then treatment with opioid receptor antagonists should decrease the SIB by blocking the endogenous opioids. The rationale of performing treatment studies with opiate antagonists is that a pharmacological blockade of brain opioid receptors may lower the pain threshold in these individuals and may, in turn, result in a decrease in SIB. Typically, the SIB subjects in these studies were mentally retarded and a small proportion had an additional diagnosis of autism. Two compounds that are potent opioid receptor antagonists that are devoid of opioid agonist effects are naloxone and naltrexone, and both have been investigated in SIB studies. As antagonists, these compounds bind to opioid receptors but do not activate them. Therefore, neither of these compounds is associated with prototypical opioid agonistic effects such as analgesia or addiction. The compounds used are naloxone, which has a restrictive use in neuropsychiatric conditions because of its short duration of action and lack of effectiveness when administered orally, and naltrexone, which is more potent, retains much of its efficacy by the oral route and has a duration of action of approximately twenty-four hours after oral administration.

A number of investigators have studied the effects of the opiate antagonists naloxone and naltrexone in individuals with SIB. The outlines, treatment modalities, and results of these studies are depicted in Table 2. As can be inferred from this table, significant but short-lasting decreasing ef-

fects on SIB have been reported in four out of seven studies using naloxone. In the study by Sandman et al. (1987), however, no incidences of SIB
were present during the trial. Failure of naloxone to attenuate SIB was reported by Davidson et al. (1983) and Beckwith, Couk, and Schumacher
(1986), while Barrett, Feinstein, and Hole (1989) described increased SIB
during the naloxone trial. Interestingly, in the later study, a decrease in
rates of SIB was observed only if the patient had received a placebo injection on the previous day.

Eight more recent investigations used the long-acting opiate antagonist
naltrexone (Table 2). In all but two studies (Szymanski et al., 1987;
Campbell et al., 1988), a significant decrease in the frequency of SIB was reported that appeared to be mostly dose-dependent. In the study of Kars et
al. (1990) the effects of naltrexone in a dosage of 50 mg daily for three con-
secutive weeks following a double-blind placebo-controlled cross-over design were examined in six profoundly mentally retarded subjects with severe
SIB. Naltrexone produced significant decreases in SIB frequency in two subjects and a tendency toward reduction in one, while two did not respond.
These results closely parallel those of Herman et al. (1987, 1989) indicating
an individual variation in response to naltrexone in SIB individuals.
Interestingly, in the study by Herman et al. (1989), the frequency of the
most prominent type of SIB (head and face hitting) was significantly reduced
by naltrexone, while self-biting was not decreased at any dose. These differential effects of naltrexone suggest that decreases in specific SIBs are mediated via blocking opioid receptors in the brain, whereas dopaminergic
systems are involved in self-biting. In summary, these data suggest that the
opiate antagonists naloxone and naltrexone are capable of inducing significant dose-dependent decreases in SIB. Thus, additional studies are warranted using larger numbers of subjects, chronic administration of the
compound and double-blind designs to address more carefully the effects of
opiate antagonists on different symptoms of SIB. Naltrexone seems to be the
most promising opiate antagonist to be further investigated.

## Beta-Blockers

Beta-adrenergic-blocking medications, like propranolol, have been utilized
for a variety of neuropsychiatric disorders (Lader, 1988). Yudofsky, Silver,
and Schneider (1988) and Volavka (1988) concluded from their studies that
enough preliminary evidence exists to use beta-blockers in the treatment of
aggression. In developmentally disabled patients, only a limited number of
reports, dealing with single cases or nonblind open trials, are available describing the use of beta-blockers in the treatment of aggression and, more
specifically, SIB. The studies reported so far that include SIB are listed in
Table 3. In a double-blind placebo-controlled study, Ratey and Lindem
(1991) recently treated fourteen patients with aggression and SIB with the

Table 2
Clinical Studies with Opiate Antagonists and Self-Injurious Behavior (SIB)

| Author (Year) | N | Treatment | Design | Behavior | Etiological Considerations | Rating of SIB | Baseline | Study period | Concurrent Diagnosis | Concurrent Medication | Effects on SIB |
|---|---|---|---|---|---|---|---|---|---|---|---|
| Richardson and Zaleski, 1983 | 1 | Naloxone 1 and 2 mg IV on 2 successive days | Open | SIB | Unknown | Naturalistic 15 min. blocks | 1 day | 4 days | Lesch-Nyhanlike syndrome | Antipsychotics, anticonvulsants, and antidepressants (not specified) | Decrease for 2 days after infusion |
| Sandman et al., 1983 | 2 | Naloxone 0.1, 0.2, 0.4 mg IM on 3 alternate days in 1 week | Double-blind cross-over | SIB | Unknown | Naturalistic; symptom-specific scales; 1-min. samples taken every 10 min. for 90 min. after injection (videotaped) | 5 weeks | 2 weeks | — | Not mentioned | Decrease for 60–90 min. |
| Davidson et al., 1983 | 1 | Naloxone 0.15 and 0.075 mg IM | Double-blind placebo-controlled | SIB | Agnesia corpus callosum | Naturalistic; 5 min. per half hour; 10, 40, and 70 min. following injections | 4 weeks at home and 1 day in hospital | 5 days | — | Not mentioned | No effect |
| Sandyk, 1985 | 1 | Naloxone 1.2 mg IM and IV | Open and double-blind | Aggression, hyperactivity, and SIB | Unknown | Naturalistic | None | 45 min (3x) | Primary generalized epilepsy | Phenytoin, carbamazepine | Decrease for 30 min. after injection |
| Beckwith et al., 1986 | 2 | Naloxone 0.1, 0.2, 0.4 mg IV | Double-blind placebo-controlled | SIB | Not mentally retarded; viral encephalitis | Naturalistic; symptom-specific scales; final 60 sec. of each 5-min. interval during a 120-min. observation period | 2 weeks | 2 weeks | Long-standing seizure disorders ($n=2$) | None | No effect |
| Bernstein et al., 1987 | 1 | Naloxone 0.5 and 1.0 mg/30 min. for 6 hours | Open | SIB | Neonatal asphyxia: 1; prematurity and retrolental fibroplasia: 1 | Naturalistic; counting specific symptoms; data collection for 7 hours/ day on week days (naloxone) and 13 hours/day on weekends (naltrexone) | 3 days 14 days | 10 days 6 periods of 14 days | — | None | Decrease for 30 hours after injection |
| | | Naltrexone 12.5, 25 and 50 mg daily for 14 days | Double-blind placebo-controlled | | | | | | | | Dose-dependent decrease for several days |

| Study | N | Drug/dosage | Design | Target behavior | Etiology | Assessment | Duration | Baseline | Diagnosis | Concomitant medication | Results |
|---|---|---|---|---|---|---|---|---|---|---|---|
| Szymanski et al., 1987 | 2 | Naltrexone 50 mg daily | Double-blind placebo-controlled | SIB | Unknown | Naturalistic; counting during several 30-min. sessions 5 days per week; Nursing Observation Scale for Inpatient Evaluation | 2 weeks | 4 periods of 3 weeks duration each | Mixed seizures (n=1) | Thioridazine 200 mg per day and phenobarbital 300 mg daily (n=1); haloperidol 15 mg daily (n=1) | No effect |
| Sandman et al., 1987 | 1 | Naloxone 0.4, 0.8, 1.2 mg IM | Open (drug-blind rating by videotaping) | SIB | Unknown | Spielberger State-Trait Anxiety Inventory and Conners Parent-Teacher Questionnaire once daily | Several weeks (duration not specified) | 2 periods of 3 days with at least a 3-day interval | Psychotic syndrome; grand mal seizures | Unknown | No incidences of SIB during trial |
| Herman et al., 1987, 1989 | 3 | Naltrexone 0.5, 1.0, 1.5, and 2.0 mg/kg | Open | SIB | Phenylketonuria: 1; unknown: 1 | Symptom-specific; experimental self-injury test; counting by two raters; 10 min. | 30 days (2 sessions) | 6 weeks | Autism (n=2); Tourette's syndrome and periodic depression (n=1) | Discontinued at least 30 days prior to investigation | Significant decrease up to 1.5 mg/kg dosage; no effect on self-biting |
| Campbell et al., 1988 | 8 | Naltrexone 0.5, 1.0, and 2.0 mg/kg/day in 3 consecutive weeks | Open | SIB (n=4) | Unknown | Children's Psychiatric Rating Scale and Clinical Global Impressions scale; twice weekly (videotaped) | 2 weeks | 6 weeks | Autism (n=8) | Discontinued 4 weeks prior to experimentation | No effect |
| Lienemann and Walker, 1989 | 1 | Naltrexone 50 mg per day for 1 year | Double-blind placebo-controlled | Autistic symptoms and SIB | Unknown | Naturalistic | None | 1 year | Autism | Antipsychotics, antidepressants, lithium (not specified) | Marked decrease in severity and frequency (fewer autistic symptoms) |
| Barrett et al., 1989 | 1 | Naloxone SC 0.2 mg for 11 days and 0.4 mg for 9 days | Unknown | Autistic symptoms and SIB | Unknown | Naturalistic; symptom-specific scales, daily 60 min. | 3 days | 30 days | Autism | Chlorpromazine 5.9 mg/kg/day | Increase during active treatment |

**Table 2, Continued**

| Author (Year) | N | Treatment | Design | Behavior | Etiological Considerations | Rating of SIB | Baseline | Study period | Concurrent Diagnosis | Concurrent Medication | Effects on SIB |
|---|---|---|---|---|---|---|---|---|---|---|---|
| | | Naltrexone 50 mg/day for 12 days followed by 3 weeks of open trial | Double-blind placebo-controlled | | | | 3 days | 24 days followed by 3 weeks respite; 22-month follow-up | | | Decrease to zero rating during active treatment and over 22-month follow-up |
| Sandman et al., 1990b | 4 | Naltrexone 25, 50, 100 mg twice weekly | Double-blind Latin-square | SIB | Mental retardation (n=4); Down syndrome: 2; unknown: 2 | Symptom-specific, naturalistic; 5-points scale; all measurements each day during the week (videotaped) | 10 days | 4 weeks | — | Thioridazine 125 mg per day (n=1) | Dose-dependent decrease in 3 patients (maximal effect at the 100-mg dose) |
| Kars et al., 1990 | 6 | Naltrexone 50 mg/day for 3 weeks | Double-blind placebo-controlled crossover | SIB | Down syndrome: 1; neonatal jaundice: 1; Rendu-Osler-Weber syndrome: 1; tuberous sclerosis: 1; birth injury: 1; unknown: 1 | Naturalistic; symptom-specific scales, once or twice daily | 2 weeks | 11 weeks | — | Neuroleptics (n=6) and anticonvulsants (n=3) | Decrease in 2 patients during active treatment |
| Knabe et al., 1990 | 2 | Naltrexone 0.19–2.0 mg/kg increasing over 15 days | Open | SIB | Not mentally retarded | Naturalistic; symptom-specific scales; counting during each quarter of an hour from 9 A.M. to 4 P.M. during all experimental days | 3 days | Not specified (1-month follow-up in 1 patient) | Autism | Not mentioned | After 3 days of naltrexone, marked increase, followed by progressive decrease that persisted during follow-up |
| Walters et al., 1990 | 1 | Naltrexone 50 mg daily | Double-blind placebo-controlled | SIB | Not mentioned | Naturalistic; symptom-specific scales; counting 3 times daily for 30-min. intervals; Real Life Autism Rating Scale and Aberrant Behavior Checklist | Not mentioned | 21-day phases (2 x naltrexone and 2 x placebo) followed by 6-month follow-up | Autism | Not mentioned | Decrease to zero rating, persisting over the follow-up period |

**Table 3**

**Clinical Studies with Beta-Blockers and Self-Injurious Behavior (SIB)**

| Author (Year) | N | Treatment | Design | Behavior | Rating of SIB | Baseline | Study Period | Concurrent Diagnosis | Concurrent Medication | Effects on SIB |
|---|---|---|---|---|---|---|---|---|---|---|
| Ratey et al., 1966 | 19 | Propranolol 120 mg daily | Open | Self-abuse and aggressive SIB (n=12) | Naturalistic; descriptive terms | Not mentioned | 3–18 months | Not specified | Neuroleptics, anticonvulsants, benzodiazepines | Impressive improvement of SIB in all subjects |
| Luchins and Dojka, 1989 | 6 | Propranolol 90–360 mg daily | Open; retrospective | Aggression and SIB | Not specified | 3 months, retrospective | 3 months, retrospective | Not specified | Neuroleptics | Reduction of SIB in 5 out of 6 subjects |
| Rudrich et al., 1990 | 1 | Propranolol 60–120 mg daily | Open; case report | Hyperactivity, aggression, and SIB | Naturalistic; not specified | Not mentioned | 21 months | Microcephaly; major motor seizures | Halperidol 1–1.5 mg daily | Less SIB (not specified) |
| Ratey and Lindem, 1991 | 14 | Pindolol 10–40 mg daily | — | — | Modified overt aggression scale, Nursing Observation Scale for Inpatient Evaluation and Clinical Global Impressions scale once weekly | 4 weeks | 16 weeks | Not mentioned (autistiform disorder?) | Neuroleptics (n=1) | Marked reduction of SIB (40%) |
| | 14 | Nadolol 40–120 mg daily | Double-blind placebo-controlled | Aggression and SIB | | | | | Neuroleptics (n=3) | Reduction of aggression; effects on SIB not mentioned |

beta-blocking compounds pindolol and nadolol. On treatment with pindolol in a dosage of 10–40 mg per day for sixteen weeks, these researchers observed a reduction of nearly 50 percent in SIB. The report about nadolol, however, did not mention the effects on SIB.

In summary of the data on the open or retrospective studies, generally a moderate to marked reduction of SIB was found during treatment with propranolol. The nearly complete absence in the literature of randomized large-scale double-blind placebo-controlled trials of beta-blocking medication for retarded patients, however, necessitates permanent skepticism about the results obtained so far. The mechanism through which beta-adrenergic-blocking medications exert their effect on aggression or SIB remains unclear. Most probably, these compounds induce decreased somatic anxiety or a state of hyperarousal via a peripheral effect, resulting secondarily in decreased aggression and SIB. However, some indications are available that propranolol enhances 5-HT transmission, which may explain its antiaggression effects (Scheinin et al., 1984).

Thus, there are some data suggesting that beta-blocking medications do benefit a certain percentage of aggressive or self-injurious retarded patients who have failed to respond to a multitude of other treatment regimens. More definite conclusions cannot be drawn before the efficacy of these medications is studied in properly designed placebo-controlled studies.

### Anticonvulsants

Since the mid-1970s, a large number of reports have been presented suggesting the psychotropic benefits of some anticonvulsants, particularly carbamazepine (Dalby, 1975). However, most, if not all, studies have dealt with carbamazepine, valproate or clonazepam in the treatment of neuropsychiatric disorders (for example, affective and seizure disorders) in the developmentally disabled (Sovner, 1991). In a recent report, Glue (1989) found carbamazepine to be effective in rapid-cycling bipolar illness, while Gupta, Fish, and Yerevanian (1987) described the antiaggression effectiveness of this compound in patients with intermittent explosive disorder.

None of the reports, however, focused on the effects of anticonvulsants primarily on SIB that was not associated with a cyclic disorder. Thus, there is no evidence at all that anticonvulsants have any beneficial effect on SIB.

### Anxiolytics

Surveys have shown that anxiolytics, specifically the benzodiazepines, are prescribed on a large scale for the institutionalized mentally retarded subjects, although only very limited research has been performed on their indications and effectiveness with special references to SIB.

With respect to SIB, Barron and Sandman (1983, 1985) reported a high incidence of the reaction to paradoxical excitement to sedative-hypnotics in mentally retarded patients with SIB. Although these studies did not specify the different classes of compounds (benzodiazepines?), it should be stressed that sedative-hypnotics can be expected to exacerbate SIB.

Preliminary reports suggest that buspirone, a novel antianxiety agent with serotonergic effects, may be useful in the treatment of SIB. Ratey et al. (1989) described buspirone's efficacy in nine of fourteen aggressive and self-injurious mentally retarded patients. They postulated that the anti-SIB effects of buspirone may be the result of neurochemical changes in the brain that inhibit serotonin metabolism.

In summary, no indications are available suggestive of an anti-actolaggressive effect of anxiolytics. On the contrary, administration of such compounds may increase this type of behavior. Buspirone, however, may have some beneficial treatment effects, but the data are far too limited to allow any conclusions.

## Lithium

Lithium is interesting because it is a pharmacological class by itself and the neurotransmitter role it plays has not been as well worked out as that of other medications, although some evidence is available that lithium treatment alters 5-HT function in animals as well as humans (Price et al., 1989). Recently, Manji et al. (1991) studied the effects of lithium on the serotonergic and noradrenergic systems of normal subjects. They found a marked but quite inconsistent effect of lithium on serotonergic-mediated systems as assessed by a percentage increase in prolactin responses.

Because it is effective in mania, lithium was tried with repeated success for aggressive behavior and subsequently for autoaggressive behavior, that is, SIB (Dostal, 1972; Dale, 1980; Tyrer et al., 1984). From a review of the use of lithium carbonate in mentally handicapped subjects, it cannot be concluded that the compound is effective in reducing aggression and SIB. More controlled studies are needed before any definitive statements about lithium's effectiveness can be made (Sovner & Hurley, 1981). The data reported so far on lithium treatment in SIB, including their methodological shortcomings, are depicted in Table 4.

In two recent clinical studies the use of lithium was analyzed retrospectively (Luchins & Dojka, 1989; Spreat et al., 1989). The results indicated a clear therapeutic effect of lithium on both aggression and SIB in the majority of subjects. These results, however, should be interpreted carefully since both studies assumed implicitly that SIB and aggression are drug-responsive behavior, irrespective of their cause, whereas both forms of behavior may be the result of pathological states, including impulsivity, irritability, and anxiety. In the study of Spreat et al. (1989), evidence was provided that hyperactivity (extreme stimulus sensitivity) may be the mediating variable in

**Table 4**
**Clinical Studies with Lithium and Self-Injurious Behavior (SIB)**

| Author (Year) | N | Treatment | Design | Behavior | Etiological Considerations | Rating of SIB | Baseline | Study Period | Concurrent Diagnosis | Concurrent Medication | Effects on SIB |
|---|---|---|---|---|---|---|---|---|---|---|---|
| Dostal and Zvolsky, 1970 | 14 | Lithium 0.30–0.95 maEq/l | Open | Aggression and hyperactivity; 2 with SIB (?) | Not specified | No rating | 4 months | 8 months | 6 with epilepsy; 4 with paresis; affective disturbances ($n=12$) | Anticonvulsants, not well specified | Reduction of aggressive behavior and affective symptoms; no effect on SIB |
| Micev and Lynch, 1974 | 10 | Lithium | Open | Aggressive behavior and SIB | Not specified | Naturalistic | No baseline | 12 weeks | Not specified | Not specified | Effect on SIB not significant; 5 out of 9 improved significantly |
| Worrall et al., 1975 | 8 | Lithium 0.74–1.38 mmol/l | Double-blind placebo-controlled | Aggression ($n=8$); SIB ($n=1$) | Phenylketonuria; 2; Down syndrome: 1; encephalitis: 1; not specified: 4 | Not specified | Not specified | 16 weeks | Not specified | Not specified | Significantly less aggression; 1 patient less SIB |
| Dale, 1980 | 15 | Lithium 0.4–1.2 mmol/l | Open, retrospective | Aggression and SIB, not specified | Not specified | No rating | Not specified | 3 months to 3 years | 2 epilepsy; 1 tardive; dyskinesia; 1 autism; 1 microcephaly; 1 hydrocephaly | Not specified | Reduction of aggressive behavior in 11; effect on SIB in 1 |
| Sovner and Hurley, 1981 | 2 | Lithium 1.0–1.35 maEq/l | Case reports; open | Hyperactive and assaultive SIB ($N=1$) | 1 unspecified; 1 congenital syphilis | Not specified | Not specified | 98 days and 7 months | Tardive dyskinesia | 1 no medication; 1 primidone 750 mg daily | Effect on SIB not specified; less hyperactive and aggressive behavior |
| Tyrer et al., 1984 | 25 | Lithium 0.5–0.8 mmol/l | Double-blind placebo-controlled crossover | Not specified | Not specified | Visual analogue scale (13 items) | 6 months, retrospective | 5 months (lithium 2 months) | Not specified | Neuroleptics and anticonvulsants, not specified | Marked decrease of aggressive behavior (17 out of 25); no effect on SIB |
| Craft et al., 1987 | 42 | Lithium 0.7–1.25 mmol/l | Double-blind placebo-controlled | Aggression and/or self-mutilation | Not specified | Not specified | 4 weeks | 12 weeks | Not specified | Not specified (tranquilizers and anticonvulsants) | Marked reduction of aggressive behavior; SIB not measured |
| Luchins and Dojka, 1989 | 25 | Lithium 0.6–0.95 maEq/l | Open, retrospective | Aggressive behavior and SIB | Not specified | Monthly counts | 3 months | 3 months | 1 organic affective syndrome; 2 epilepsy | 6 out of 11 with neuroleptics | Decrease of aggressive behavior ($n=7$); decrease of SIB ($n=6$) (?) |

predicting lithium responsiveness. This evidence supports data reported previously (Stewart et al., 1990). Craft et al. (1987) reported the results of a double-blind trial lasting four months in forty-two mentally retarded patients, in which treatment with lithium carbonate (serum levels of lithium: 0.7–1.25 mmol/l) was compared to placebo. In about three-quarters of the patients, a reduction in aggressiveness was observed upon treatment with lithium. SIB, however, was not measured. There was a statistically significant difference between the treatment groups in terms of their weekly mean aggression scores and the weekly counts of their aggressive episodes during the experimental period. Classical side effects were noted in about one-third of the patients in the lithium group, but they were mainly short-lived and in no case necessitated discontinuation of lithium. From Table 4 it can be concluded that, in eight studies, of which three were double-blind, an effect of lithium on SIB has been described in eight patients over a 20-year period. Considering the underreporting of negative results, this means that a demonstrable effect of lithium is almost absent.

## Conclusions

Self-injurious behavior is shown by a substantial percentage of people with mental retardation, and prevalence seems to be related to the severity of the mental retardation and the presence of additional communicational disabilities, sensory or social impairments, and the type of service utilized (Emerson, 1990). Although Winchel and Stanley (1991) recently formulated a broad description of the phenomenon SIB, it is rather questionable whether such a description is at all useful. It is in this respect very doubtful to consider all kinds of deliberate self-harm as manifestations of one fundamental disorder. In addition, it should be emphasized that behavioral approaches can be used in treating SIB and that there is no need to separate pharmacological and behavioral approaches. From animal data, it has been well known for years that there is an important interaction between the response of the organism on drugs and environmental and social factors. Dosen and Bojanin (1990) therefore advocated an integrated approach to the developmental hazards of mentally retarded patients with respect to SIB and stressed the need to use a combined psychological and biological research effort for this specific developmental disorder.

The significant physical and social consequences of this type of behavioral disorder have prompted a large amount of research and debate. In spite of extensive diagnostic efforts, however, generally no specific and treatable etiology for SIB has been found in mentally retarded patients. Thus, behavioral and neurobiological models continue to stimulate theorizing regarding the etiopathogenesis and maintenance of SIB.

Concerning the pathogenetic hypotheses, recent neurobiological models have focused on three areas: disturbances in dopaminergic systems, abnormalities in serotonin metabolism, and disturbed functional activity of the endogenous opioid systems. Tentative evidence in support of the serotonin hypothesis has been provided by the results of investigations in (auto) aggression in psychiatric populations and by data from clinical studies with serotonergic agents like fluoxetine and eltoprazine in mentally retarded patients with SIB. Support for the opioid peptide hypothesis comes from both animal and human studies that suggest that disturbances in the endogenous opioid systems are connected with opioid overactivity. In addition, a number of recent methodologically fairly sound studies have demonstrated the clinically significant effectiveness of the opiate antagonist naltrexone in reducing symptoms of SIB. Concerning this hypothesis, it may even be possible to integrate behavioral and neurobiological processes by assuming that the analgesic effects of opioid peptides may help to reduce the response cost of SIB maintained by environmental effects (Oliver & Head, 1990).

From a review of the literature, it can be concluded that the pharmacological approach should play an important role in the treatment of SIB. Concerning the use of neuroleptics, lithium, beta-blockers, anticonvulsants, and anxiolytics, a restrictive strategy should be used. Almost all of these compounds were evaluated for registration purposes many years ago, when methodological demands were much less strict. After registration, no clear company interest seems to exist in registration for an additional indication, especially because the compounds are already prescribed and the group of patients concerned cannot easily be investigated. The most promising treatment strategies, which are based on pathogenetic hypotheses, seem to be the administration of the opiate antagonist naltrexone or specific serotonergic compounds like reuptake inhibitors and receptor-agonistic agents. By following this type of strategy, including the use of adequate study methodology and rating instruments, may become possible to reconstruct a nosology of SIB. There is, however, so much ambiguity and overlap in the neurochemical effects of the more-or-less specific compounds that can be used at present, that it will be quite impossible to prove behavioral specificity to treatment responses. It is therefore more conceivable to follow a functional approach that tries to correlate psychological and biological dysfunctions in order to achieve, finally, a psychopharmacological strategy that is based on a functional state rather than on a particular diagnosis. An additional important issue to be resolved in future research is the question of whether SIB in mentally retarded patients is just a manifestation of a broad area of behavioral disorders or should be considered a separate dimension. Ongoing validation studies with the Social Dysfunction and Aggression Scale, which is in development for the measurement of inwardly and outwardly directed aggression, show that self-mutilation behavior should be considered a separate dimension within the spectrum of aggression regulation disorders (Wistedt et al., 1990). Moreover, it appears that self-mutilation behavior is correlated negatively with other manifestations of aggression.

# References

Akil, H., Watson, S. J., Young, E., Lewis, M. E., Khachaturian, H., & Walker, J. M. (1984). Endogenous opioids: Biology and function. *Ann. Rev. Neurosci., 7,* 223–255.

Aman, M. G., & Singh, N. N. (1980). The usefulness of thioridazine for treating childhood disorders—Fact or folklore? *Am. J. Ment. Defic., 84,* 331–338.

Aman, M. G., White, A. J., Vaithianathan, C., & Teehan, C. J. (1986). Preliminary study of imipramine in profoundly retarded residents. *Aut. Devel. Disabil., 16,* 203–273.

American Psychiatric Association. (1987). *Diagnostic and statistical manual of mental disorders* (3rd ed., rev.; DSM-III- R). Washington, DC: Author.

Anders, Th. F., Cann, H. M., Ciaranello, R. D., Barchas, D., & Berger, A. (1978). Further observations in the use of 5- hydroxytryptophan in a child with Lesch-Nyhan syndrome. *Neurop;auadiatrie, 9,* 157–166.

Anderson, L. T., Herman, L., & Dancis, J. (1976). The effect of L-5-hydroxytryptophan on self-mutilation in Lesche-Nyhan disease: A negative report. *Neurop;auadiatrie, 7,* 439–442.

Asberg, M., Traskman, L., & Thoren, P. (1976). 5-HIAA in the cerobrospinal fluid: A biochemical suicide predictor? *Arch. Gen. Psychiat., 33,* 1193–1197.

Azmitia, E. C. (1978). The serotonin producing neurons of the midbrain median and dorsal raphe nuclei. In New York/London: Plenum Press. *Handbook of psychopharmacology* (vol. 9, pp. 233–314).

Banki, C. M., & Arato, M. (1983). Amine metabolites and neuroendocrine responses related to depression and suicide. *J. Affect. Disord., 5,* 223–232.

Barrett, R. P., Feinstein, C., & Hole, W. T. (1989). Effects of naloxone and naltrexone on self-injury: A double-blind, placebo-controlled analysis. *Am. J. Ment. Retard., 93,* 644–651.

Barron, J., & Sandman, C. A. (1983). Relationship of sedative- hypnotic response to self-injurious behavior and stereotypy by mentally retarded clients. *Am. J. Ment. Defic., 88,* 177–186.

Barron, J., & Sandman, C. A. (1985). Paradoxical excitement to sedative-hypnotics in mentally retarded clients. *Am. J. Ment. Defic., 2,* 124–129.

Beckwith, B. E., Couk, D. I., & Schumacher, K. (1986). Failure of naloxone to reduce self-injurious behavior in two developmentally disabled females. *Appl. Res. Ment. Retard., 7,* 183–188.

Bernstein, G. A., Hughes, J. R., Mitchell, J. E., & Thompson, T. (1987). Effects of narcotic antagonists on self-injurious behavior: A single case study. *J. Am. Acad. Child Adol. Psychiatr., 26,* 886–889.

Breese, G. R., Baumeister, A. A., McCown, T. J., Emerick, S. G., Frye, G. D., & Mueller, R. A. (1984). Behavioral differences between neonatal and adult 6-

hydroxy-dopamine-treated rats: Relevance to neurological symptoms in clinical syndromes with reduced dopamine. *J. Pharmacol. Exp. Ther., 231,* 343–354.

Breese, G. R., Criswell, H. E., Duncan, G. E., & Mueller, R. A. (1989). Dopamine deficiency in self-injurious behavior. *Psychopharmacol. Bull., 25,* 353–357.

Breese, G. R., Mueller, R. A., Napier, T. S., & Duncan, G. E. (1986). Neurobiology of $D^1$-dopamine receptors after neonatal-6-OHDA-treatment: Relevance to Lesch-Nyhan disease. *Adv. Exp. Med. Biol., 204,* 197–215.

Breuning, S. E., Fergusson, D. G., Davidson, N. A., & Poling, A. D. (1983). Effects of thioridazine on the intellectual performance of mentally retarded drug responders and nonresponders. *Arch. Gen. Psychiatr., 40,* 309–313.

Brown, G., Ebert, M., Goyer, P., Jimerson, D., Klein, W., Bunney, W., & Goodwin, F. (1982). Aggression, suicide, and serotonin: Relationships to CSF amine metabolites. *Am. J. Psychiatr., 139,* 741–746.

Brown, G., Goodwin, F., Ballenger, J., Goyer, P., & Major, L. (1979). Aggression in humans correlates with cerebrospinal fluid metabolites. *Psychiatr. Res., 1,* 131–139.

Brown, G. L., Linnoila, M., & Goodwin, F. K. (1990). Clinical assessment of human aggression and impulsivity in relationship to biochemical meaasures. In H. M. Van Praag, R. Plutchnik, & A. Apter (Eds.), *Violence and suicidality* pp. 184–217) New York: Brunner/Mazel.

Burns, M. E. (1980). Droperidol in the management of hyperactivity, self-mutilation and aggression in mentally handicapped persons. *J. Int. Med. Res., 8,* 31–33.

Campbell, M., Adams, P., Small, A. M., McVeigh Tesch, L., & Curren, E. L. (1988). Naltrexone in infantile autism. *Psychopharamacol. Bull., 24,* 135–139.

Campbell, D. T., & Fiske, D. W. (1959). Convergent and discriminant validity by the multitrait multimethod matrix. *Psychol. Bull., 56,* 81–105.

Castells, S., Chakrabarti, C., Winsberg, B. G., Hurnie, M., Perel, J. M., & Nyhan, W. L. (1979). Effects of L-5 hydroxytryptophan on monoamine and amino acid turnover in the Lesch-Nyhan syndrome. *J. Autism Dev. Disorders, 9,* 95–103.

Ciaranello, R. D., Anders, T. F., Barchas, J. D., Berger, P. A., & Cann, H. M. (1976). The use of 5-hydroxytryptophan in a child with Lesch-Nyhan syndrome. *Child Psychiatr. Human Developm., 2,* 127–133.

Cook, T. D., & Campbell, D. T. (1979). *Quasi-experimentation: Design and analysis issues for field settings.* Chicago: Rand McNally.

Craft, M., Ismail, I. A., Krishnamurti, D., Mathews, J., Regan, A., Seth, R. V., & North P. M. (1987). Lithium in the treatment of aggression in mentally handicapped patients: A double-blind trial. *Br. J. Psychiatr., 150,* 685–689.

Curzon, G. (1989). 5-Hydroxytryptamine and corticosterone in an animal model of depression. *Prog. Neuropsychopharmacol. Biol. Psychiatr., 13,* 305–310.

Dalby, M. A. (1975). Behavioral effects of carbamazephine. In J. K. Penry & D. D. Daly (Eds.), *Advances in neurology* (Vol. 11, pp. 331–334). New York: Raven Press.

Dale, P. G. (1980). Lithium therapy in aggressive mentally subnormal patients. *Br. J. Psychiatr., 137,* 469–474.

Davidson, P. W., Kleene, B. M., Carroll, M., & Rockowitz, R. J. (1983). Effects of naloxone on self-injurious behavior. A case study. *Appl. Res. Ment. Retard., 4,* 1–4.

Deberdt, R. (1976). Pipamperone (dipiperon) in the treatment of behavior disorders: A large-scale multicentre evaluation. *Acta Psychiatr. Belg., 76,* 157–166.

Depue, R. A., & Spoont, M. R. (1986). Conceptualizing a serotonin trait: A behavioral dimension of constraint. *Ann. N.Y. Acad. Sci., 487,* 47–62.

De Wied, D. (1990). Effects of peptide hormones on behavior. In D. De Wied (Ed.), *Neuropeptides: Basics and perspectives* (pp. 1–44). Amsterdam: Elsevier.

Doll, E. A. (1965). *The Vineland Scale of Social Maturity: Condensed Manual of Directions.* American Guidance Service.

Dosen, A., & Bojanin, S. (1990). Developmental and biological factors in the mentally retarded and vulnerability to depression. In A. Dosen and F. J. Menolascino (Eds.), *Depression in mentally retarded children and adults* (pp. 63–79). Leiden: Logon.

Dostal, T. (1972). Antiaggressive effect of lithium salts in mentally retarded adolescents. In A. Annell (Ed.), *Depressive states in childhood and adolescence* (pp. 491–498). Stockholm: Almquist & Wiksell.

Dostal, T., & Zvolsky, P. (1970). Antiaggressive effects of lithium salts in severely mentally retarded adolescents. *Int. Pharmacopsychiat., 5,* 203–207.

Duphar, B. V. (1991). *Eltoprazine information for investigators. A summary on the properties of eltoprazine hydrochloride: Vol. 1. General information and first patient studies,* Solvey/Dupher, Weesp.

Elie, R., Langlois, Y., Cooper, S. F., Gravel, G., & Albert, J. M. (1980). Comparison of SCH-12679 and thioridazine in aggressive mental retardates. *Can. J. Psychiat., 25,* 484–491.

Emerson, E. (1990). Severe self-injurious behavior: Some of the challenges it presents. *Ment. Handicap., 18,* 92–98.

Farber, J. M. (1987). Psychopharmacology of self-injurious behavior in the mentally retarded. *J. Am. Acad. Child Adolesc. Psychiatr., 3,* 296–302.

Frith, C. D., Johnstone, E. C., Joseph, M. H., Powell, R. J., & Watts, R. W. E. (1976). Double-blind clinical trial of 5-hydroxytryptophan in a case of Lesch-Nyhan syndrome. *J. Neurol. Neurosurg. Psychiatr., 39,* 656–662.

Geyde, A. (1990). Dietary increase in serotonin reduces self-injurious behaviour in a Down's syndrome adult. *J. Ment. Defic. Res., 34,* 195–203.

Gillberg, C., Terenius, L., & Lunnerholm, G. (1985). Endorphin activity in childhood psychosis. *Arch. Gen. Psychiatr., 42,* 780–783.

Glue, P. (1989). Rapid cycling affective disorders in the mentally retarded. *Biol. Psychiatr., 26,* 250–256.

Goldstein, M. (1989). Dopaminergic mechanisms in self-inflicting biting behavior. *Psychopharmacol. Bull., 25,* 349–352.

Goldstein, M. (1990). Dopamine agonist induced dyskinesias, including self-biting behavior in monkeys with supersensitive dopamine receptors. In H. M. Van Praag, R. Plutchnik, & A. Apter (Eds.), *Violence and suicidality* (pp. 316–323). New York: Brunner/Mazel.

Goldstein, M., Anderson, L. T., Reuben, R., & Dancis, J. (1985a). Self-mutilation in Lesch-Nyhan diseases is caused by dopaminergic denervation. *Lancet, 1,* 338–339.

Goldstein, M., Kuga, S., Kusano, N., Meller, E., Dancis, J., & Schwarcz, R. (1986). Dopamine agonist induced self-mutilative biting behavior in monkeys with unilateral ventromedial tegmental lesions of the brain stem: Possible pharmacological model for Lesch-Nyhan syndrome. *Brain Res., 367,* 114–120.

Goldstein, M., Kuga, S., Schmiza, Y., & Meller, E. (1985b, December). *The pathophysiological functions mediated by D;i1 dopamine receptors.* Maul: American College of Neuropsychiatr.

Greenberg, A. G., & Coleman, M. (1973). Depressed whole blood serotonin levels associated with behavioral abnormalities in the de Lange syndrome. *Pediatrics, 51,* 720–724.

Greenberg, A. S., & Coleman, M. (1976). Depressed 5-hydroxyindole levels associated with hyperactive and aggressive behavior: Relationship to drug response. *Arch. Gen. Psychiatr., 33,* 331–336.

Griffin, J. C., Ricketts, R. W., Williams, D. E., Locke, B. J., Altmeyer, B. K., & Stark, M. T. (1987). A community survey of self-injurious behavior among developmentally disabled children and adolescents. *Hosp. Community Psychiatr., 9,* 959–963.

Gualtieri, C. Th. (1989). The differential diagnosis of self- injurious behavior in mentally retarded people. *Psychopharmacol. Bull., 25,* 358–363.

Gualtieri, C. T. (1991). The measurement of self-injurious behavior. *J. Neuropsychiatr., 3,* S30–S39.

Gualtieri, C. Th., & Schroeder, S. R. (1989). Pharmacotherapy for self-injurious behavior: Preliminary tests of the D;i2 hypothesis. *Psychopharmacol. Bull., 25,* 364–371.

Gualtieri, C. T., & Schroeder, S. R. (1990). Phyarmacotherapy for self-injurious behavior: Preliminary tests of the D;i1 hypothesis. *Prog. Neuropsychopharmacol. Biol. Psychiatr., 14,* S81–S107.

Gupta, B. K., Fish, D. N., & Yerevanian, B. I. (1987). Carbamazepine for intermittent explosive disorder in a Prader-Willi syndrome patient. *J. Clin. Psychiatr., 48,* 423.

Haegeman, J., & Duyck, F. (1978). A retrospective evaluation of pipamperone (Dipiperon) in the treatment of behavioral deviations in severely mentally handicapped. *Acta Psychiatr. Belg., 78,* 392–398.

Herman, B. H. (1990). A possible role on proopiomelanocortin peptides in self-injurious behavior. *Prog. Neuropsychopharmacol. Biol. Psychiatr., 14,* S109–S139.

Herman, B. H., Hammock, M. K., Arthur-Smith, A., Egan, J., Chatoor, I., Boeckx, R., Zelnik, N., Jack, R., & Rosenquist, J. (1985). Naltrexone induces dose dependent decreases in self- injurious behavior. *Soc. Neurosci. Abst., 11,* 468.

Herman, B. H., Hammock, M. K., Arthur-Smith, A., Egan, J., Chatoor, J., Werner, A., & Zelnik, N. (1987). Nelatrexone decreases self-injurious behavior. *Ann. Neurol., 22,* 550–552.

Herman, B. H., Hammock, M. K., Egan, J. Arthur-Smith, A., Chatoor, I., & Werner, A. (1989). Role for opioid peptides in self-injurious behavior: Dissociation from autonomic nervous system functioning. *Devel. Pharmacol. Ther., 12,* 81–89.

Jones, I. H. (1982). *Self-Injury: Toward a biological basis.* Persp. Biol. Med., 26, 137–150.

Kars, H., Broekema, W., Glaudemans-van Gelderen, I., Verhoeven, W. M. A., &

Van Ree, J. M. (1990). *Naltrexone attenuates self-injurious behavior in mentally retarded subjects.* Biol. Psychiatr., 27, 741–746.

Knabe, R., Schulz, P., & Richard, J. (1990). Initial aggravation of self-injurious behavior in autistic patients receiving naltrexone treatment. *Autism Dev. Disorders, 20,* 591–592.

Kraemer, G. W. (1986). Causes of changes in brain noradrenaline systems and later effects on responses to social stressors in rhesus monkeys: The cascade hypothesis. In R. Porter, G. Boek, & S. W. Clark (Eds.), Antidepressant and receptor function (pp. 216–233). Chichester: Wiley.

Kraemer, G. W., & Clarke, A. S. (1990). The behavioral neurobiology of self-injurious behavior in rhesus monkeys. *Prog. Neuropsychopharmacol. Biol. Psychiatr., 14,* 141–168.

Kruesi, M. J. P., Rapoport, J. L., Hamburger, S., Hibbs, E., & Potter, W. Z. (1990). Cerebrospinal fluid monoamine metabolites, aggression, and impulsivity in disruptive behavior disorder of children and adolescents. *Arch. Gen. Psychiatr., 47,* 419–426.

Lacny, J. (1973). Mesoridazine in the care of disturbed mentally retarded patients. *Can. Psychiatr. Assoc. J., 18,* 389–391.

Lader, M. L. (1988). B-Adrenoceptor antagonists in neuropsychiatry: An update. *J. Clin. Psychiatr., 49,* 213–223.

Lesch, M., & Nyhan, W. L. (1964). A familial disorder of uric acid metabolism and central nervous system function. *Am. J. Med., 36,* 561–570.

Le Vann, L. J. (1969). Haloperidol in the treatment of behavioral disorder in children and adolescents. *Can. Psychiatr. Assoc. J., 14,* 217–220.

Lewis, M. H., Gluck, J. P., Beauchamp, A. J., Keresztury, M. F., & Mailman, R. B. (1990). Long-term effects of early social isolation in Macaca mulatta: Changes in dopamine receptor function following apomorphine challenge. *Brain Res., 513,* 67–73.

Lienemann, J., & Walker, F. (1989). Naltrexone for treatment of self-injury. *Am. J. Psychiatr., 146,* 1640.

Lloyd, K. G., Hornykiewicz, O., Davidson, L., Shannak, K., Farley, I., Goldstein, M., Shibuya, M., Kelley, W. N., & Fox, I. H. (1981). Biochemical evidence of dysfunction of brain neurotransmitters in the Lesch-Nyhan syndrome. *N. Engl. J. Med., 305,* 1106–1111.

Luchins, D. J. (1990). A review of pharmacological agents for self-injurious behavior. *Prog. Neuropsychopharmacol. Biol. Psychiatr., 14,* 169–179.

Luchins, D. J., & Dojka, D. (1989). Lithium and propranolol in aggressive and self-injurious behavior in the mentally retarded. *Psychopharmacol. Bull., 25,* 372–375.

Lynch, D. M., Eliatamby, C. L. S., & Anderson, A. A. (1985). Pipothiazine palmitate in the management of aggressive mentally handicapped patients. Br. J. Psychiatr., 146, 525–529.

Manji, H. K., Hsiao, J. K., Risby, E. D., Oliver, J., Rudorfer, M. V., & Potter, W. Z. (1991). The mechanisms of action of lithium. Arch. Gen. Psychiatr., 48, 505–512.

Mansour, A., Khachaturian, H., Lewis, M. E., Akil, H., & Watson, S. J. (1988). Anatomy of CNS opioid receptors. *Trends Neurosci., 77,* 306–314.

Markowitz, P. I. (1990). Fluoxetine treatment of self-injurious behavior in mentally retarded patients. *J. Clin. Psychopharmacol., 10*, 299–300.

Micev, V., & Lynch, D. M. (1974). Effect of lithium on disturbed, severely mentally retarded patients. *Br. J. Psychiatr., 125*, 1–10.

Mizuno, T. I., & Yugari, Y. (1974). Self-mutilation in Lesch-Nyhan syndrome. *Lancet, I, 761.*

Mizuno, T., & Yugari, Y. (1975). Prophylactic effect of L-5- hydroxytryptophan on self-mutilation in the Lesch-Nyhan syndrome. *Neurop;auadiatrie, 6*, 13–23.

Nihira, K., Foster, R., Shellhaas, N., Leland, H. (1974). AAMD adaptive behavior scale (rev.). Washington: American Association of Mental Deficiencies.

Nyhan, W. L. (1976). Behavior in the Lesch-Nyhan syndrome. *J. Autism Childhood Schizophrenia, 3*, 235–252.

Ohi, K., Mikuni, M., & Takahashi, K. (1989). Stress adaptation and hypersensitivity in 5-HT neuronal systems after repeated foot shock. *Pharmacol. Biochem. Behav., 34*, 603–608.

Oliver, C., & Head, D. (1990). Self-injurious behavior in people with learning disabilities: Determinants and interventions. *Int. Rev. Psychiatr., 2*, 101–116.

Oliver, C., Murphy, G. H., & Corbett, J. A. (1987). Self- injurious behavior in people with mental handicap: A total population study. *J. Mentl Defic. Res., 31*, 147–162.

O'Neal, M., Page, N., Atkins, W. N., & Eichelmann, B. (1986). Troptophantrazedone treatment of aggressive behavior. *Lancet II*, 859–860.

Perry, T. L., & Tischler, B. (1964). 5-Hydroxytryptophan administration in phenylketonuria. *Am. J. Dis. Children, 107*, 586–589.

Plutchik, R., & Van Praag, H. M. (1990). Psychosocial correlates of suicide and violence risk. In H. M. Van Praag, R. Plutchik, A. Apter (Eds.), *Violence and suicidality* (pp. 37–65). New York: Brunner/Mazel.

Price, L. H., Charney, D. S., Delgado, P. L., & Heninger, G. R. (1989). Lithium treatment and serotonergic function: Neuroendocrine and behavioral responses to intravenous tryptophan in affective disorder. *Arch. Gen. Psychiatr., 46*, 13–19.

Primeau, F., & Fontaine, R. (1987). Obsessive disorder with self-mutilation: A subgroup responsive to pharmacotherapy. *Can. J. Psychiatr., 32*, 699–700.

Raleigh, M. J. (1987). Differential behavioral effects of tryptophan and 5-hydroxytryptophan in vervet monkeys: Influence of catecholaminergic systems. *Psychopharmacoly, 93*, 44–50.

Rasmussen, D. L., Olivier, B., Raghoebar, M., & Mos, J. (1990). Possible clinical applications of serenics and some implications of their preclinical profile for their clinical use in psychiatric disorders. *Drug Metabolism and Drug Interactions, 8*, 159–186.

Ratey, J. J., & Lindem, K. J. (1991). ß-Blockers as primary treatment for aggression and self-injury in the developmentally disabled. In J. J. Ratey (Ed.), *Mental retardation: developing pharmacotherapies* (pp. 5–81). Washington: American Psychiatric Press.

Ratey, J. J., Mikkelsen, E. J., Smith, G. B., Upadhyaya, A., Zuckerman, H. S., Martell, D., Sorgi, P., Polakoff, S., & Bemporad, J. (1986). B-Blocker in the severely and profoundly mentally retarded. *Psychopharmacol., 6,* 103–107.

Ratey, J. J., Sovner, R., Mikkelsen, E., Chmielinski, H. E. (1989). Buspirone therapy for maladaptive behavior and anxiety in developmentally disabled persons. *J. Clin. Psychiat., 50,* 382–384.

Richardson, J. S., & Zaleski, W. A. (1983). Naloxone and self-mutilation. *Biol. Psychiatr., 18,* 99–131.

Rojahn, J. (1986). Self-injurious and stereotypic behavior of noninstitutionalized mentally retarded people: Prevalence and classification. *Am. J. Ment. Defic., 91,* 268–276.

Ross, D. L., Klykylo, W. M., & Hitzeman, R. (1987). Reduction of elevated CSF beta-endorphin by fenfluramine in infantile autism. *Pediatr. Neurol., 3,* 83–86.

Roy, A., & Linnoila, M. (1990). Monoamines and suicidal behavior. In H. M. Van Praag, R. Plutchnik, & A. Apter (Eds.), *Violence and suicidality (pp. 141–183). New York: Brunner/Mazel.*

Ruedrich, S. L., Grush, L., & Wilson, J. (1990). Beta adrenergic blocking medications for aggressive or self-injurious mentally retarded persons. *Am. J. Ment. Retard., 95,* 110–119.

Sandman, C. A. (1988). b-Endorphin disregulation in autistic and self-injurious behavior: A neurodevelopmental hypothesis. *Synapse, 2:* 193–199.

Sandman, C. A., Barron, J. L., Chicz-Demet, A., & Demet, E. M. (1990a). Plasma ß-endorphin levels in patients with self-injurious behavior and stereotypy. *Am. J. Ment. Retard., 95,* 84–92.

Sandman, C. A., Barron, J. L., & Colman, H. (1990b). An orally administered opiate blocker, naltrexone, attenuates self-injurious behavior. *Am. J. Ment. Retard., 95,* 93–102.

Sandman, C. A., Barron, J. L., Crinella, F. M., & Donnelly, J. F. (1987). Influence of naloxone on brain and behavior of a self injurious woman. *Biol. Psychiatr., 22,* 899–906.

Sandman, C. A., Datta, P. C., Barron, J., Hoehler, F. K., Williams, C., & Swanson, J. M. (1983). Naloxone attenuates self-abusive behavior in developmentally disabled clients. *Appl. Res. Ment. Retard., 4,* 5–11.

Sandman, C. A., & O'Halloran, J. P. (1986). Pro-opiomelancortin, learning, memory and attention. In D. De Wied, W. H. Gispen, Tj. B. Van Wimersma Greidanus (Eds.), *Encyclopedia on pharmacology and therapeutics* (pp. 399–420). New York: Pergamon Press.

Sandyk, R. (1985). Naloxone abolishes self-injuring in a mentally retarded child. *Ann. Neurol., 17,* 520.

Scheinin, M., Van Kammen, D. P., Ninan, P. T., & Linnolla, M. (1984). Effect of propranolol on monoamine metabolites in cerebrospinal fluid of patients with chronic schizophrenia. *Clin. Pharmacol. Ther., 36,* 33–39.

Seeman, P. (1981). Brain dopamine receptors. *Psychol. Reviews, 32,* 229–313.

Silverstein, F. S., Johnston, M. V., Hutchinson, R. J., & Edwards, N. L. (1985). Lesch-Nyhan syndrome: CSF neurotransmitter abnormalities. *Neurology, 6,* 907–911.

Singh, N. N., & Aman, M. G. (1981). Effect of thioridazine dosage of the behavior of severely mentally retarded persons. *Am. J. Ment. Defic., 83,* 580–587.

Singh, N. N., & Millichamp, C. J. (1985). Pharmacological treatment of self-injurious behavior in mentally retarded persons. *J. Autism Dev. Disorders, 15,* 257–267.

Sokol, M. S., Campbell, M., Goldstein, M., & Kriechman, A. M. (1987). Attention deficit disorder with hyperactivity and the dopamine hypothesis: case presentations with theoretical background. *J. Am. Acad. Child. Adol. Psychiatr., 26,* 428–433.

Sovner, R. (1991). Use of anticonvulsant agents for treatment of neuropsychiatric disorders in the developmentally disabled. In J. J. Ratey (Ed.). *Mental Retardation: Developing pharmacotherapies* (pp. 83–106). Washington: American Psychiatric Press.

Sovner, R., & Hurley, A. (1981). The management of chronic behavior disorders in mentally retarded adults with lithium carbonate. *J. Nerv. Ment. Dis., 169,* 191–195.

Spreat, S., Behar, D., Reneski, B., & Miazzo, P. (1989). Lithium carbonate for aggression in mentally retarded persons. *Compr. Psychiatr., 30,* 505–511.

Stewart, J. T., Myers, W. C., Burket, R. C., & Lyles, W. B. (1990). A review of the pharmacotherapy of aggression in children and adolescents. *J. Am. Acad. Child Adol. Psychiatr., 29,* 269–277.

Stone, R. K., Alvarez, W. F., Ellman, G., Horn, A. C., & White, J. F. (1989). Prevalence and prediction of psychotropic drug use in California, Developmental Centers. *Am. J. Ment. Retard., 93,* 627–632.

Szymanski, L., Kedesky, J., Sulkes, S., & Catler, A. (1987). Naltrexone in treatment of self-injurious behavior: a clinical study. *Res. Devel. Disabilties, 8,* 179–190.

Tarnowski, K. J., Rasnake, L. K., Mulick, J. A., & Kelly, P. A. (1989). Acceptability of behavior interventions for self-injurious behavior. *Am. J. Ment. Retard., 93,* 575–580.

Tischler, B., Patriasz, K., Beresford, J., & Bunting, R. (1972). Experience with pericyazine in profoundly and severely retarded children. *C.M.A. J., 106,* 136–141.

Traskman, L., Asberg, M., Bertilsson, L., & Sjostrand, L. (1981). Monoamine metabolites in CSF and suicidal behavior. *Arch. Gen. Psychiatr., 38,* 631–636.

Tyrer, S. P., Walsh, A., Edwards, D. E., Berney, T. P., & Stephens D. A. (1984). Factors associated with a good response to lithium in aggressive mentally handicapped subjects. *Prog. Neuropsychopharmacol. Biol. Psychiatr., 8,* 751–755.

Van Hemert, J. C. J. (1975). Pipamperone (Dipiperon, R3345) in troublesome mental retardation: a double-blind controlled cross-over study with long-term follow up. *Acta Psychiatr. Scand., 52,* 237–245.

Van Praag, H. M. (1982). Depression, suicide and the metabolism of serotonin in the brain. *J. Affect. Disorders, 4,* 275–290.

Van Praag, H. M. (1983). In search of the mode of action of antidepressants: 5-HT tyrosine mixtures in depressions. *Neuropharmacoly., 22,* 433–440.

Van Praag, H. M. (1986). (Auto)aggression and CSF 5-HIAA in depression and schizophrenia. *Psychopharmacol. Bull., 22,* 669–673.

Van Praag, H. M. (1991). Serotonergic dysfunction and aggression control: Serotonin and (auto)aggressive behavior. *Psychol. Med., 21,* 15–19.

Van Praag, H. M., Asnis, G. M., Kahn, R. S., Brown, S. L., Korn, M., Harkavy Friedman, J. M., & Wetzler, S. (1990). Monoamines and abnormal behavior. A multi-aminergic perspective. *Br. J. Psychiatr., 157,* 723–734.

Van Ree, J. M. (1987). Reward and abuse: Opiates and neuropeptides. In J. Engel &

L. Oreland (Eds.), *Brain reward systems and abuse* (pp. 75–88). New York: Raven Press.

Van Ree, J. M., Jolles, J., & Verhoeven, W. M. A. (1990). Neuropeptides and psychopathology. In D. De Wied, (Ed.), *Neuropeptides: Basics and perspectives* (pp. 313–351). Amsterdam: Elsevier Science.

Van Ree, J. M., Verhoeven, W. M. A., & De Wied, D. (1987). Animal and clinical research on neuropeptides and schizophrenia. In E. R. De Kloet, V. M. Wiegant, D. De Wied (Eds.), *Progress in brain research* (Vol. 72, pp. 249–267). Amsterdam: Elsevier Science B.V. (Biomedical Division).

Volavka, J. (1988). Can aggressive behavior in humans be modified by beta blockers? *Postgrad. Med., 163* 168.

Walters, A. S., Barrett, R. P., Feinstein, C., Mercurio, A., Hole, W. T. (1990). A case report of naltrexone treatment of self-injury and social withdrawal in autism. *J. Autism Dev. Discord., 20:*169–176.

Weizman, R., Gil-Ad, I., Dick, J., Tyano, S., Szekely, G. A., Laron, Z. (1988). Low plasma immunoreactive beta-endorphin levels in autism. *J. Am. Acad. Child Adolesc. Psychiatry, 27:*430–433.

Willer, J. C., Dehen, H., Cambier, J. (1981). Stress induced analgesia in humans. *Science, 212:*680–691.

Winchel, R. M. and Stanley, M. (1991). Self-injurious behavior: a review of the behavior and biology of self mutilation. *Am. J. Psychiatry, 148:*306–317.

Wistedt, B., Rasmussen, A., Pedersen, L., Malm, L., Wakelin, J., & Bech, P. (1990). The development of an observer-scale for measuring social dysfunction and aggression. *Pharmacopsychiatr., 23,* 249–252.

Worrall, E. P., Moody, J. P., & Naylor, G. J. (1975). Lithium in non-manicdepressive: Antiaggressive effect and red blood cell lithium values. *Br. J. Psychiatr., 126,* 464–468.

Yaryura-Tobias, J. A., & Neziroglu, F. (1978). Compulsions, aggression and self-mutilation: A hypothalmic disorder? *J. Orth. Psychiatr., 7,* 114–117.

Yudofsky, S. C., Silver, J. M., & Schneider, S. E. (1988). The use of beta blockers in the treatment of aggression. *Psychiatry Letter,* 15–23.

Zelnik, N., Herman, B. H., Hammock, M. K., Arthur-Smith, A., Egan, J., Chatoor, I., Werner, A., Boecky, R. L. (1986). Role of opioid peptides in self-injurious behavior. *Abstract Annual Meeting Society for Neuroscience, Washington,* 12:412.

Zohar, J., & Zohar-Kadouch, R. C. (1991). Is there a specific role for serotonin on obsessive compulsive disorder? In S. L. Brown, H. M. Van Praag (Eds.), *The role of serotonin in psychiatric disorder: Clinical and experimental psychiatry monograph no. 4.* (pp. 161–182). New York: Brunner/Mazel.

# Part IV
# Specific Methods

There has recently been a revival of the treatment of behavioral and psychiatric disorders in the mentally retarded. New techniques and methods have been developed, some founded on the basic knowledge of therapeutical methods as used with the population in general, and others based on practical experiences in work with mentally retarded individuals. These methods have been attuned to an understanding of the specificities of the psychosocial development and the social life of mentally retarded individuals. Not only should the psychosocial needs of the mentally retarded be appropriately understood, but the involvement of their surroundings and accompanying changes also require the understanding of the helpgivers.

John McGee has developed a philosophy in which the basic human qualities of mentally retarded persons are appreciated, and respect for such a person is implemented. Gentle teaching is not only a teaching method for the mentally retarded individuals but also a school of thought presented to their caregivers, who learn how to understand the mentally retarded individual and how to develop a meaningful relationship with such a person.

Individual and group treatment techniques are powerful tools in treating various intrapsychic problems of the mentally retarded. The techniques described by Robert Fletcher and Thomas Duffy have been developed on the basis of extensive experience in practical work with mentally retarded individuals.

The systems therapy described by Klaus Hennicke is a promising approach. Apparently, system-theoretical thinking is applicable to the mental health care of the mentally retarded in a similar way as it is to the nonretarded population. However, until recently, this approach was seldom utilized in the field of the mentally retarded. Hopefully, Hennicke's contribution will stimulate the introduction of this method into the treatment arsenal for the mentally retarded and their milieus.

All these methods are applicable to the treatment of different disorders. Nevertheless, in order to guarantee the appropriate use of these treatment methods for particular persons, an indication for a particular therapy should be established not by the therapist but by the diagnostician or by the diagnostic team. The combination and integration of a particular treatment method with other treatment methods should be possible and is even desirable.

# 16

## Individual Psychotherapy for Persons with Mental Retardation

*Robert J. Fletcher*

Mental health needs of persons who exhibit severe behavioral problems or psychiatric disorders have been increasingly recognized in recent years (Stark et al., 1988; Matson & Barrett, 1993). This recognition is evidenced by burgeoning literature on the psychiatric diagnoses and treatment of mental disorders in mentally retarded persons (Menolascino & Stark, 1984; Fletcher & Menolascino, 1989; Dosen & Menolascino, 1990; Nezu, Nezu, & Gill-Weiss, 1992). Also, the founding of the National Association for the Dually Diagnosed (NADD) has been instrumental in marshaling professional interest in the mental health issues concerning persons with a dual diagnosis (Fletcher & Menolascino, 1989; Nezu et al., 1992).

Historically, persons with mental retardation were believed by many professionals to enjoy immunity from emotional distress and psychiatric disorders (Nezu et al., 1992). Maladaptive behaviors were perceived as a manifestation of the condition of mental retardation, rather than as possibly being driven by a psychiatric disorder (Menolascino, 1983). The mildly retarded were characterized as worry-free and thus mentally healthy, and the severely retarded did not verbally express feelings and thus were thought to be exempt from emotional stress (Fletcher, 1988). The distinction of mental retardation from mental illness and the separation of their respective service systems contributed to the paucity of individual therapy available to persons with mental retardation. However, knowledge is increasing, and professional attitudes are changing regarding the efficacy of therapy with persons who have both mental retardation and mental health problems.

This chapter describes and illustrates the usefulness of psychotherapy with persons who have mental retardation and mental illness. The chapter describes several key concepts, such as the therapeutic relationship, boundary setting, directiveness, and the interagency team approach. Stresses in the lives of persons who have mental retardation are described along with the implications for the need for psychotherapy. Last, the chapter describes the dynamic, supportive, and counseling approaches, along with case illustrations.

In the last few years, the term *psychotherapy* with mentally retarded people who have emotional problems has appeared with increased frequency in the literature (Sinason, 1992) and has gained increased acceptance as a viable form of treatment for this population (Hellendoorn, 1990). However, disagreement remains among theoreticians and clinicians about how to conceptualize and treat the full range of psychopathology exhibited by persons with mental retardation (Pfadt, 1990).

Until recently, the psychotherapeutic schools held that persons with mental retardation were incapable of benefiting from psychotherapy (Szymanski, 1980; Sinason, 1992). There is still a debate about this issue. For example, psychoanalytically oriented therapists generally consider the lack of abstract conceptual skills and language deficiency major obstacles to the development of insight into mentally retarded persons. Reid (1982) contended that these people do not have the intellectual resources to benefit from in-depth psychotherapy; others have disagreed with this perspective. For example, Sinason (1992), Hollins (1990), and Ruth (1990) have argued that psychoanalytical psychotherapy can be effective with this population.

According to the client-centered theoretical perspective, retarded people lack the psychosocial autonomy, verbal communication skills, and other elements of inherent normal intelligence necessary for client-centered therapy (Rogers, 1942). This assumption has been refuted by Prouty (1976, 1990, 1991), who has used a client-centered theoretical base in his pretherapy approach with mentally retarded–mentally ill persons. Others have argued that normal intelligence is not necessary for therapy (Sternlicht, 1965; Szymanski, 1980; Rubin, 1983; Dosen, 1990; Sinason, 1992). Although there are unique constructs in each theoretical school of therapy (that is, psychoanalytical, relationship, client-centered, and supportive), all have one fundamental concept in common: unconditional valuing of the client (Sinason, 1992).

The literature reviews on therapy with mentally retarded persons (Jakab, 1970; Lott, 1970; Sternlicht, 1965; Albini & Dinitz, 1965; Szymanski, 1980) demonstrate that psychotherapy with persons who have mental retardation is both feasible and successful. Furthermore, these reviews do not advocate any particular theoretical framework; rather, they describe the benefits derived from multiple forms of clinical orientation (Rubin, 1983). It is interesting that these reviews were done as long ago as 1965, and the practice of psychotherapy with mentally retarded persons has steadily increased.

## Toward a Definition of Psychotherapy

Mental health practitioners commonly divide individual approaches into three theoretical orientations: (1) psychodynamic psychotherapy, which focuses on changing abnormalities within the individual personality; (2) supportive psychotherapy, which seeks to strengthen the person's existing personality skills for managing life problems; and (3) counseling, which stresses practical living and social skills. As pointed out by Rubin, "These are methods that fit a modern counseling therapy definition and are applicable to a modern definition of mental health problems that focuses on the individual thoughts and emotions, as distinguished from education and training modalities for learning and adaptive problems" (p. 120). Since various therapeutic schools of thought apply to mentally ill–mentally retarded persons, how can therapy be adequately defined? Rubin (1983) offered a definition that applies to differing therapy approaches and psychological theories: "Counseling-therapy consists of a professionally trained practitioner who uses a systematic method and a cooperative relationship to achieve goals of change in another person's emotions, thoughts or behavior" (p. 120).

There has been ambiguity within the professional community as to what constitutes psychotherapy versus counseling (Szymanski, 1980; Perkins, 1991). The term that is applied may be related to the setting in which the therapy or counseling takes place. For example, a school social worker typically uses the term *counseling*. A psychiatric social worker in a clinic setting uses the term *therapy*. The terms may also be influenced by one's professional discipline. A psychiatrist or a psychologist is likely to prefer the term *psychotherapy*. Others make a distinction based on the nature of the presenting problems or the severity of the symptoms. For example, issues concerning change of living or work environment and other here-and-now themes may be viewed as being in the realm of counseling. On the other hand, internal conflicts may be considered issues in the domain of psychotherapy.

There is no qualitative or quantitative distinction between the two terms (Perkins, 1991). The terms *counseling* and *psychotherapy*, therefore, should be interchangeable; they have essentially the same meaning: a relationship between a client and a therapist who engage in an interpersonal process through a systematic method to achieve the goals of change in the client's emotions, thoughts, or behavior.

## Attitudes and Values

A practitioner's attitudes and values will influence who receives therapy and how therapy will be conducted. Some mental health professionals possess a negative disposition toward providing therapy for individuals who have limited intellectual capacity (Sinason, 1992; MacKinnon & Frederick, 1970; Fletcher, 1988). Mentally retarded persons are often denied adequate mental health services because of negative attitudes of mental health professionals (Walker, 1980; Stark et al., 1988; Nezu, Nezu, & Gill-Weiss, 1992). These negative attitudes are associated with both ignorance and bias. Ignorance plays a major role in the formulation of attitudes toward the mentally retarded and are frequently based on misunderstandings, myths, and unfounded beliefs (Fletcher, 1988). Prejudice and negative attitudes toward persons with mental retardation may impede the development of a therapeutic relationship (Monfils & Menolascino, 1984).

It is important that we be fully aware of our attitudes and values with respect to the provision of psychotherapy to clients who have both mental retardation and mental illness. The correct professional posture is a prerequisite for effective psychotherapy (Monfils & Menolascino, 1984). All human interactions are influenced by attitudes, beliefs, and moral judgments. These represent a set of values that can be referred to as *professional posture*. Clinicians need to examine their own attitudes, feelings, and prejudices about working with persons who have mental retardation (McGee et al., 1987). It is important for practitioners to have a strong commitment to the dignity and value of each individual, a pre-requisite in working with persons with a dual diagnosis (Monfils & Menolascino, 1984). McGee et al. (1987) reflected on the concept of posture and stated, "It is different from, but includes, our theoretical orientation and intervention strategies. It is not an abstraction. Our posture, defined or not, shapes what we do, how we do it, and why we do it" (p. 30).

Our values influence the people we treat, the techniques we select, and the manner in which they are implemented. Our posture also influences the goals established for the clients we have in therapy.

## Goals of Psychotherapy

The goals of psychotherapy with persons who have mental retardation and mental illness are actually no different from those for nonretarded persons (Szymanski, 1980). Goals are the intended outcome of the therapy in a desired direction in change of thought, feelings, and/or behaviors.

The goal of psychotherapy is often not clear at the time of referral (Monfils & Menolascino, 1984; Levitas & Gilson, 1989). Most mentally retarded persons are referred for therapy by care providers (that is, family, workshop, or hospital) because of a variety of behaviors that are perceived as maladaptive. Additionally, most referrals are based on observed behaviors rather than on the underlying causes of the behavior. For example, disruptive or even assaultive behavior is often perceived as a "behavioral problem," rather than as an expression of inner feelings, although misdirected. The referring person or agency often has a goal "behavioral compliance." The client being referred may have a different goal, of course, or may not even know why he or she is being referred for mental health services.

Frequently, referrals for therapy are made by care providers because of perceived maladaptive behaviors exhibited by mentally retarded persons. The referring person or agency has as a goal a quick solution to a manifest problem. The complaint from the referring agency may reflect the caregivers' discomfort rather than the client's maladjustment (Szymanski, 1980). Also, it is not uncommon for the problem to be rooted in the system in which the client lives or works (Beasly & Kroll, 1992).

The first step in the process of establishing goals in psychotherapy is to determine whether the problem lies with the identified client or with the systems in which she or he is involved (Levitas & Gilson, 1989). A multimodel diagnostic and treatment model can help the clinician to focus on the psychosocial and physical environmental influences that may instigate or otherwise increase the likelihood of occurrence of maladaptive behaviors (Gardiner & Graeber, 1990).

Early in the treatment process the therapist and the client should establish goals, which they mutually agree upon, rather than relying on the therapist's unilateral perception of the client's needs (Monfils & Menolascino, 1984). The therapist, after an initial rapport has been developed, may ask the client what he or she would like to accomplish in the therapy. The goal may then be put into a contract or treatment plan that spells out the desired outcome of the therapy (goals) and the steps toward achieving the outcome (objectives). The goals and objectives should be clear, realistic, measurable, and mutually agreed upon.

Including the client in the treatment-planning process is essentially a method of achieving client-based decision making (Stohlman, 1992). The process of developing a treatment plan or a goal plan between the client and the therapist provides a way for any ambiguity to be resolved in a way that is beneficial to the client (Zastrow, 1981). Mentally retarded–mentally ill persons are a population at risk of being denied the opportunity to make decisions affecting their own lives because they are assumed by many mental health professionals to be incapable of making rational decisions (Levitas & Gilson, 1989). A mutually agreed-upon treatment plan that articulates goals and objectives may be therapeutic in itself, as it provides an opportunity for the client to take an active role in the goal-planning process. Client input from the beginning stage of goal setting empowers the client.

Although goals are individualized, some commonly encountered goals are appropriate for a large number of mentally ill–mentally retarded persons. Szymanski (1980) pointed out the following goals: understanding and accepting one's disability; improving impulse control and frustration tolerance; expressing feelings and emotions in socially acceptable ways; increasing independent decision making and self-reliance; improving self-esteem and self-image; improving interpersonal relationship skills; learning to cope with stressful situations; improving social skills; and resolving the conflicts of dependency and guilt.

McGee and Menolascino (1990) stated: "The challenge is not only to effectuate modified behavior, but rather to enhance the meaning of life, to re-establish feelings of self-esteem and union with others, to encourage self-empowerment and to expand meaningful relationships in order to counteract death, loss and existential aloneness" (p. 109).

How do we know when a goal has been achieved? It is useful to state in the contract or treatment plan what behaviors directly reflect goal achievement. This clarification enables both the therapist and the client to monitor and assess progress.

John is a thirty-six-year-old mildly retarded individual who recently moved into a group home after living with his parents. He was referred for mental health services because of a recent onset of aggressive and assaultive behavior at the group home. He was diagnosed with adjustment disorder. He is experiencing an adjustment reaction to the residential change, which is a traumatic event in his life. He is suffering from anxiety, fear, and confusion. He became assaultive as a way to communicate his feelings. The goal of therapy was for John to adjust to his new living environment by expressing his feelings regarding the change effecting his life. John's behavior improved after he had been in weekly therapy for two months. In therapy, he was able to share his feelings of fear of the new living arrangement and his perceived loss of his family. He was able to benefit from short-term therapy and evidenced a significant decrease in aggressive behavior and a corresponding increase in prosocial behavior. John obtained goal achievement.

## Therapeutic Relationship

A relationship between a client and therapist is foremost and paramount the nearly all theoretical orientations and practice models of therapy. The value and importance of the relationship is at the heart of a therapeutic process and is based on the fact that all people have an existential need for bonding with other people (Bowlby, 1971; McGee, 1989). This bonding provides a psychologically secure base from which a person can explore and master his or her surroundings (Dosen, 1990).

Establishing a therapeutic relationship with a mentally retarded–mentally ill person is the first step in the treatment process (Menolascino, 1989);

it is fundamental to the therapy. The relationship should be based on mutual trust and respect. The therapist needs to communicate such qualities as concern, acceptance, empathy, and genuineness to the client as a basis for their relationship (Monfils & Menolascino, 1984). A working alliance creates the framework for future growth and development.

Establishing positive rapport with a client is fundamental in nearly all theoretical orientations and applies to all client populations. However, never is such rapport more important than in a therapeutic process with persons who have a developmental disability (Landsell, 1990). The effectiveness of therapists or counselors in working with dually diagnosed persons is dependent on their ability to form effective professional relationships (Vernikoff & Dunayer, 1992). The initial stages of treatment need to focus on fostering this alliance. Once this key process has been completed, the client can work toward specific goals and objectives.

The client's relationship building with the clinician takes time, and the clinician needs to be patient. Establishing a therapeutic relationship with a mentally retarded–mentally ill person may take longer than with a nonretarded person. Many of these individuals have justifiable reasons for not trusting others—from lifelong experiences of rejection, from having been denied access to services and supports, from having been bounced back and forth between one agency and another (Fletcher, 1988; Nezu, et al., 1992). Many have never experienced nurturing, supportive, and stable relationships. The therapist needs to be a "real person" and a direct role model by demonstrating to the client qualities such as warmth, respect, empathy, and compassion (McGee et al., 1987; Perkins, 1991).

The therapist's qualities needed for establishing a relationship with the client can be summarized by the term *empathetic understanding:* understanding the inner world of the client from his or her perspective, understanding the perceived reality experienced by the client. Developmentally disabled individuals with significant mental health problems often perceive the world around them differently from nonretarded individuals. It is important for the therapist to make every attempt to demonstrate understanding of the client from the client's perspective of the world, even if that perspective is distorted.

An important consideration in developing a therapeutic relationship is demonstrating respect. It is important for the therapist to provide "unconditional positive regard" (Rogers, 1957) for the client, independent of the person's behaviors. This regard requires the therapist to perceive the client as a whole person rather than merely as a collection of behaviors. This approach is sometimes difficult for clinicians who work with individuals exhibiting severe behavioral problems. Rather than being viewed as first a person, a client may have a reputation as being a behavioral problem. As clinicians, we must be aware of how we perceive the clients with whom we work to ensure that we will provide the full level of dignity and respect that each individual deserves and has a right to expect. The central question is: Does the *client* feel that she or he is receiving the clinician's respect? The therapist is therefore challenged to keep his or her perceptions in accordance with those of the client. The therapist must be perceived by the client as one who demonstrates value, human potential, and high regard.

It is important in the therapeutic relationship for the clinician to allow themselves to be comfortable with being "real persons" (Szymanski, 1980). A clinician should not merely be a neutral "therapeutic mirror." Therapeutic genuineness is being authentically oneself within the context of the relationship (Perkins, 1991). The therapist working with a person who has a dual diagnosis provides more than traditional one-to-one therapy. The therapist also needs to be a resource finder, an advocate, a consultant, and, in essence, a case manager. Therapeutic genuineness is congruent with the multiplicity of the therapist's role. It is my experience that developing a relationship with a client who has both mental illness and mental retardation is not always optimally established in an office setting. Sometimes "seeing" a client in his or her own natural environment is safer and more comfortable for the client, and is more conducive to creating a bonding relationship. Other authors have had similar experiences. Landsdell (1990) noted: "While the principle of bonding, unconditional positive regard, etc., remain the same, the method of creating such feelings may vary from one individual to another. For example, I have often found that a cup of coffee at the corner donut shop is far more effective than sitting in my counselling room" (p. 3).

> Albert is a twenty-two-year-old young man who recently "aged out" of a residential school for the mentally disturbed. He was diagnosed with personality disorder with antisocial features and mild mental retardation (IQ 68). His case history reflects that he was abandoned by his mother at age three months, has no known father, and was raised by his maternal grandmother until her death when he was eight years old. Subsequently, he was in three different foster homes for a period of about three years. His aggressiveness and difficult-to-manage behaviors resulted in his being removed from these homes. At age eleven, he entered a residential school facility for emotionally disturbed children. He remained at the facility until he "aged out" of the school system and was placed in a group home. He was referred for evaluation and treatment services because of assaultive and threatening behaviors at the group home. Records indicate that he was aggressive with antisocial behaviors and with a poor self-image. Albert found himself in an adult world with adult expectations. He did not know how to relate appropriately to other adults. He had not developed appropriate interpersonal relationship skills. He

denies responsibility for his impulsive and aggressive behaviors, is often suspicious, is easily agitated, and has low self-esteem. All his life, he has used his "machismo" as a defense against developing meaningful human engagement.

Demonstrating sympathetic understanding, respect, and therapeutic genuineness took time and patience. During the first year, we worked on building a relationship. In this particular case, the relationship was the method and goal of therapy. Most of our sessions focused not on a specific maladaptive behavior to be altered, but on developing a trusting relationship. Albert had a great deal of difficulty trusting others. He had internalized feelings of rejection, abandonment, and distrust. Developing a therapeutic relationship with him was critically important, as it enabled him to view himself as a person who could trust another. He was able to gain an understanding of a trusting relationship between himself and the therapist, and this enabled him to begin to experience trust in others. Now, three years later, he is in a supportive work environment and is living in his own apartment. He has learned the meaning of human engagement and the value of a therapeutic relationship. The consistent and supportive therapeutic relationship helped this individual establish a positive self-concept and a belief in his capacity to develop intimacy with others.

## Boundaries and Directiveness

### Setting the Boundaries

Most professionals agree that appropriate limits are sometimes necessary in psychotherapy with mentally retarded persons who have emotional problems (Szymanski, 1980). Setting limits and establishing boundaries are often helpful in maintaining focus on the therapeutic material (Hinsburger, 1987). Some therapists, especially those who are psychoanalytically or client-centered-oriented, may feel that any limits stifle the client's spontaneity and put the therapist in the position of a rejecting parent. However, there is a consensus in the field of dual diagnosis that setting limits is necessary and therapeutic. The therapist needs to establish limits and provide sufficient structure to permit therapy to proceed (Monfils & Menolascino, 1984). Some clients benefit from this type of structure because of low frustration tolerance or distractibility, or they simply may not know how to act in a client–therapist situation (Szymanski, 1980). Establishing limits and boundaries, when needed, should be communicated during the initial stage of treatment. Issues of limits and boundaries may be developed as part of a treatment plan or contract.

Barbara is a twenty-seven-year-old female who has mild mental retardation and borderline personality disorder with disturbed interpersonal relationships. She lives with her mother and was recently terminated from a supported employment situation because she yelled at her employer when he criticized her work. She was referred for evaluation and treatment services because of a long-term pattern of losing control of her angry feelings, not taking responsibility for her behavior, and blaming others. During the initial stage of psychotherapy, Barbara would start each session by blaming her mother, her boyfriend, or other people for her problems. A verbal contract was established between the client and her therapist that allowed Barbara to talk about whatever she pleases during the first ten minutes of the session; the remainder of the session focused on other specific issues that were related to the treatment.

This limit- and boundary-structured situation is therapeutic for three reasons: First, it provides time for the client to "unload" and gain a cathartic effect by expressing her immediate issues. Second, it enables the therapist to acknowledge the feelings, thoughts, and emotions that the client brings to the session, even if they are distorted or disturbed. Third, it provides the framework for moving toward the treatment goals.

## Directiveness

It is generally accepted that therapy with persons who have both mental retardation and mental illness is more directive than with nonretarded persons (Hurley, 1989; Hurley & Hurley, 1986). These individuals are frequently brought into therapy because they are distractible, are injurious to others or themselves, and tolerate frustration poorly. Directiveness in a therapy context means establishing a direction, as necessary, to facilitate a treatment focus on the therapeutic interaction about the relevant issues. The therapist must take an active role in initiating and facilitating interaction and communicating the procedure and process of therapy at the appropriate level of intellectual and interpersonal development (Hurley, 1989; Rubin, 1983).

Bob is a thirty-one-year-old moderately retarded male who moved into a community residence about one year ago. Prior to this, he lived with his mother, who had died of cancer several months before he moved into the community residence. He was referred for treatment services because of a recent onset of self-abusive behavior. The treatment focused not on this self- abusive behavior per se, but on the underlying forces that drive this behavior. Bob initially did not know why he was in treatment, and therefore, he did not know how he could benefit from seeing a therapist. The therapist hypothesized that Bob was suffering from depression associated with a complicated bereavement over the significant loss of his mother. The therapist needed to take an active role in directing the treatment process on Bob's relationship with his mother and eventually on acceptance of her loss. Bob's self-abusive behavior decreased as he began to understand and accept the death of his mother.

This process went on over a two-year period. The therapist needed to bring focus to the treatment issues during each therapy session. Bob was also treated with an antidepressant medication for one year while in therapy. The therapist took an active role in soliciting his feelings and thoughts. Death and dying are abstractions that needed to be translated so that they were comprehensible to Bob. The therapist used concrete examples and frequently prompted Bob to respond.

## Interagency Team Approach

Regular contact with family members and other care providers is an essential aspect of the therapeutic change process (Levitas & Gilson, 1989; Fletcher, 1988). Psychotherapy cannot be done in a vacuum; it must be part of the larger, comprehensive support system involved with the client. The emotionally disturbed and retarded client needs multiple services to address her or his multiple problems. The components of residence, vocation, family, case management, and psychotherapy need to interact in a process that makes all participants members of an interdisciplinary team, the effect of which is synergistic rather than additive (Szymanski, 1980).

The application of this principle requires a great deal of interagency coordination. Case conferences and treatment planning should be done in the context of an interagency team approach (Fletcher, 1990). Mental health clinicians, vocational counselors, residential staff, family members, and the client need to be aware of the general issues and broad goals that are developed within these various components. This team approach facilitates the communication of the relevant issues and provides a forum so that each service component is knowledgeable about and supportive of the others. Confidentiality needs to be respected, and therefore, the client needs to give permission for the release of any information to be shared among the players on the team.

David is a thirty-year-old person who has been diagnosed with schizophrenia and mild mental retardation (IQ 58). He recently moved into this area with his family as a result of the job relocation of his father. This is the first time David has moved. He was referred to a sheltered workshop because he had previously been successful in this kind of work environment. However, he was referred for therapy because he had difficulty adjusting to his new work experience. He experienced decompensation, which was manifested by an increase in his psychiatric symptomatology (that is, auditory hallucinations, delusions, and distorted thought processes). The therapist needed to work with the client, the psychiatrist, and the work supervisor in conjunction with David's parents. Supportive therapy and the team approach helped David to cope with the high level of stress associated with the environmental changes in his employment and living. Key players were involved and necessary in the therapeutic process.

## Stress and Implications for Therapy

People with mental retardation may experience more stress than their nonretarded peers. Deutsch (1989) pointed out three sources of stress experienced by mentally retarded persons: (1) ordinary stress; (2) difficult-to-manage stress; and (3) unique stress.

### Ordinary Stress

Nonretarded people buffer themselves against everyday stress through the development of coping mechanisms through years of experience and exposure to normal stressful situations. Mentally retarded persons and those with a dual diagnosis do not generally have a sophisticated coping mechanism to help them deal with the stress they encounter in their daily lives. The inability to defend against ordinary stress can contribute to low self-esteem, anxiety, confusion, depression, and psychotic behavior. Therapy may buffer them against ordinary stress: The client can interact on an ongoing basis with someone who will listen respectfully and empathetically.

> Glenn is a thirty-year-old mildly retarded individual who has also been diagnosed with schizotypal disorder. He has been a client of the community mental-health center for many years and is seen for therapy at least weekly by a psychiatric social worker. Glenn frequently experiences stress, and if he is not able to ventilate his feelings, he tends to behave in peculiar ways. During a recent therapy session, Glenn was very upset because his roommate smoked a cigarette in the off-limits area of their shared bedroom in a community

residence. Rather than confront the individual involved or talk to staff about the incident, he held this stress inside his inner world. The stress was manifested by pacing behavior and sleeping difficulty during the night of the incident. During the therapy session, he was able to describe the situation, and the therapist elicited Glenn's feelings regarding the incident. Without ongoing and frequent support and intervention, Glenn would be confronted with daily stressful situations that would inevitably lead to an increase in his anxiety, agitation, and psychotic thinking.

### Difficult-to-Manage Stress

Stress associated with life events is difficult to cope with for all people. Major life changes, such as the death of a loved one, a change in employment, and a relocation in living space are examples of life events that may contribute to great anxiety and depression (McGee et al., 1987). These dramatic events are more difficult for persons with mental retardation or dual diagnosis because of their limited capacity to comprehend and cope with such circumstances. Because of limited life experience and exposure to dramatic events, many mentally retarded people are not prepared to adjust easily to major life changes.

> Frank is a sixty-five-year-old mildly retarded man who, until recently, has lived all his life with his mother and his alcoholic brother. Like many persons who are mentally retarded, Frank has a very small social network, and his life has revolved around his interactions with his mother and attending a sheltered workshop five days a week. Frank moved into a community residence becuase of the ill health and age of his mother. When his mother died after a long illness, he became depressed. He stopped going to work and lost a considerable amount of weight. He was left with no one to fill the void; the death of his mother left him with deep feelings of confusion, emptiness, and isolation. Frank was referred for therapy to help him cope. The course of bereavement therapy took several years. During the first several months of treatment, Frank said very little, and his inner feelings of despair and loneliness were evidenced by his nonverbal communication. In time, he developed a good relationship with his therapist, who acted as a "real" person. The therapist was empathetic, warm, and sensitive and shared her own experiences of death, dying, loss, and grief. Eventually, Frank came out of his state of despair and depression, reconnected with work, and developed social relationships.

## Unique Stress

Some persons who have moderate to mild developmental handicaps are cognizant of their differences from their nonhandicapped peers. They are aware of the lifestyle of nonretarded counterparts and often aspire to the same goals and hopes. However, anxiety and depression may occur when their self-identity is not congruent with a realistic expectation of themselves (Panagua & DeFazio, 1989). They see that their age-peers pass through developmental milestones such as dating, marriage, having a family, and owning their own cars and homes—symbols of "normal" adulthood that represent independence and normality. They aspire to these same symbols, yet many live in supervised residences and are employed in supervised work environments. This stark contrast in lifestyle causes unique stress and may lead to low self-esteem.

Jane is a forty-year-old female with an IQ of 64 and a coexisting bipolar psychiatric diagnosis. She receives weekly therapy and is on lithium medication. She has been living in a group home for the past five years, after living with her natural family. She was in special education classes until her senior year of high school, at which time she was mainstreamed. For her, mainstreaming was a "godsend." It was an opportunity for her to interact with nonretarded people. Mainstreaming reaffirmed her ability to effectively communicate with nonretarded people and culminated in a long-awaited personal goal achievement. The advent of mainstreaming for Jane had a marked positive effect on her self-esteem. When she is interacting with nonretarded people, she feels "normal" and derives a great deal of satisfaction.

These normalizing experiences have a positive effect on her self-esteem. However, there is a down side to this situation. Jane experiences a great deal of anxiety when she is unable to participate in the socially normalizing experiences of her nonretarded age-peers. For example, she does not currently have a boyfriend, and this causes her emotional pain. She becomes intensely jealous when she observes others displaying signs of affection toward each other. A major problem is that she has a tendency to become infatuated with single men on the staff. The course of treatment over the past few years has focused on this issue. One treatment goal is for her to have a better understanding and acceptance of the nature, boundaries, and differentiation of relationships, that is, friendships, staff–client relationships, intimate relationships, and so on. A long-term goal is for her to accept herself with all her strengths and limitations and to develop meaningful relationships with her peers.

## Therapy Approaches

Several therapy concepts were mentioned earlier in this chapter: therapeutic relationships, empathetic understanding, and therapeutic genuineness; setting boundaries; and directiveness. Although these are conceptual considerations, they may also be applied as techniques. Individual therapy approaches may be broken down into three orientations: psychodynamic psychotherapy, supportive psychotherapy, and counseling. Each of these approaches is described here as it applies to mentally ill–mentally retarded persons.

### Dynamic Approaches

Present behavior is often rooted in past experience. How we think, feel, and behave today is a result of many past experiences. The key to a dynamic approach is to understand how past experiences are influencing present behavior. This technique has been demonstrated to be effective with mildly retarded persons (Szymanski, 1980; Jakab, 1982; Levitas & Gilson, 1989; Sinason, 1992).

Historically, psychodynamic psychotherapy with persons who have mental retardation has not been widely used (Sinason, 1992). One explanation is the misconception that emotional problems are a function of mental retardation (Phillips, 1966). Nevertheless, there have been some efforts to apply psychoanalytic knowledge to therapy with retarded persons (Rank, 1949; Lott, 1970; Greyson & Akhtar, 1977; Sinason, 1992).

In general, a dynamic approach uses material about defensive operations and transference. A dynamic psychotherapy approach may use techniques ranging from projective, expressive play to verbal interaction. The treatment focus should be more on immediate life experiences than only on historical review, as self-reflection occurs better with fresh observations and reactions than with recall (Rubin, 1983).

In therapy, the clinician helps to draw the connection between meaningful events and relationships that occurred in the past and events and relationships being experienced in the present. The course of treatment may uncover painful experiences that occurred during the childhood years. Some mentally retarded individuals come from dysfunctional families. Sexual and physical abuse in their early childhood is not uncommon. Early-childhood emotional deprivation is very common.

> Jim is a forty-year-old mildly retarded individual who lives independently in the community with his wife, who also has mild mental retardation. He has been involved with mental health services intermittently since he was six years old. He was first referred when he was in the first grade because he did not verbalize in school, al-

though his mother reported that at times he talked excessively at home. School records indicate he was very withdrawn.

Except for the interaction with his wife, he tends to be a loner. His diagnosis is personality disorder with schizoid feathers.

His most recent referral for mental health services was made by the county adult protective services because he was allegedly physically abusive toward his wife. Jim is very guarded and at times paranoid. Because of a recent physical attack on his wife, she asked him to leave. After a therapeutic relationship was developed with Jim (this process took six months), he began to disclose issues surrounding his abusive behavior. Until this time, he had avoided discussing the subject, often stating, "I don't want to talk about it." As the therapeutic relationship developed, Jim began to talk about the physical abuse his father inflicted on him when he was a child. He had great difficulty in expressing the pain he had experienced as a result of his own physical abuse. Eventually, he was able to express the relationship between the pain he had experienced as a child and the pain he had inflicted on his wife. This insight was a significant milestone in his treatment.

## Supportive Therapy

A supportive therapy approach with mentally ill–mentally retarded persons may be effective in addressing a variety of emotional problems (Monfils & Menolascino, 1984; McGee, 1989). Techniques such as encouragement, reassurance, ventilation, and guidance are useful and are described in the following section.

Encouragement and reassurance are two techniques frequently used in a supportive therapy approach. Clients need to be encouraged and reassured to develop optimal levels of independence. These two techniques are employed when the clinician accentuates the positive in helping clients achieve their potential. Encouragement and reassurance helps clients with their self-esteem, which is critically important for people who have experienced failure, frustration, and despair. Instilling self-confidence and a sense of hope is aided by using encouragement and reassurance techniques.

Sometimes, the opportunity to talk with someone who listens respectfully is a very effective therapeutic tool. Supportive therapy is often a "here-and-now" approach. It allows clients to discuss the issues of immediate concern. This approach to therapy provides an avenue for ventilation, which enables the client to express her or his thoughts and feelings rather than keeping them inside.

Supportive therapy assists the client by providing guidance. In this method, the clinician uses the tools of communication to help the client identify important events or people affecting the client's behavior. The techniques of advice or option coaching may be effective. Option coaching helps the client identify several ways to approach poblem solving. This is a useful technique, as mentally retarded–mentally ill persons are rarely afforded the opportunity to develop a body of alternative behaviors. Not only are their choices limited, but their ability to make judgments is also underdeveloped (Schulman, 1980).

Some individuals with mental retardation do not know how to express feelings appropriately; others have difficulty in identifying a feeling state. Supportive therapy helps clients to identify and express their feelings in ways that are socially beneficial and individually rewarding. The purpose is to help clients express their feelings appropriately, rather than to act them out inappropriately (Fletcher, 1990; McGee & Menolascino, 1990). In supportive therapy, clients learn how to express their feelings verbally and how to acquire adaptive ways to deal with daily stress. The clients may not have had successful experiences in channeling emotions in socially acceptable ways. Supportive therapy is a cogent way to work with clients on identifying and expressing emotions.

If feelings are not communicated either verbally or nonverbally, anger and aggression may be triggered (McGee et al., 1987). Difficulties with obstructions and information processing make it difficult for mentally handicapped persons to understand and express feelings. When nonretarded people feel sadness, they have the opportunity to express this emotion to significant others in their lives. Mentally retarded persons, on the other hand, do not always have significant others in their lives. Care providers do not always allow mentally retarded individuals to express their feelings, such as sadness, and even less often encourage such expression. Inappropriate expression of anger may emerge if the feeling of sadness is not expressed.

> Pam is a twenty-eight-year-old woman with borderline intellectual functioning (IQ 75). She was referred for mental health services by her vocational counselor, who noticed she was crying a lot at work, to the point where her crying interfered with her productivity. She is the youngest of six brothers and sisters, and she continues to reside with her mother and father. Her family history reveals the presence of bipolar disorder in her maternal grandmother. She complains of depression, with crying spells and frightening dreams. She exhibits an anxious and depressed mood, with occasional suicidal thoughts. Her medical history includes lifelong hypothyroidism, which is being treated with Synthroid. She also suffers from severe arthritis. When feeling anxious or depressed, she becomes self-abusive by hitting herself in the abdominal area.
>
> Pam is being treated with supportive psychotherapy. During the first year, she was also treated with an antidepressant medica-

tion, but because of significant improvement, this was discontinued. During her weekly sessions, she has an opportunity to ventilate, at which time she discusses thoughts and feelings rather than keeping them bottled up. Weekly supportive therapy has given her the opportunity to discuss psychosocial stressors, interpersonal relationships, work-related issues and problems, and living at home with her parents. Supportive therapy has helped her to discover how her body and mind affect one another. The treatment has also involved Pam's emerging need for separation from her family and for increased independence. Most of the therapy with Pam involves real-life issues that are of immediate concern to her. Supportive therapy provides her with an opportunity to ventilate, disclose, and express her inner feelings in a safe, therapeutic environment. Pam has been in therapy for four yeras. She no longer requires antidepressant medication. Although she continues to exhibit disphoria, she no longer shows suicidal ideation or self-abusive behavior.

## Counseling

There is an apparent lack of consensus regarding the definition of counseling (Perkins, 1991). How does counseling differ from psychotherapy? The term *counseling* has been applied to the process of training (Matson, 1986) and is an approach that deals with information giving (Perkins, 1991). Counseling is concerned with information giving on the part of the counselor and knowledge and skills acquired on the part of the client. Counseling as a therapeutic method addresses issues such as skill development, social skills training and sexuality.

Social learning methods have been increasingly emphasized and include the modeling of appropriate skills, role playing as a means of practicing specific skills, social reinforcement, feedback on the performance of desired behaviors, and instruction on how to effectively perform a particular skill (Matson, 1989).

Reeducation is often an integral part of a counseling approach (Monfils & Menolascino, 1984). Some mentally ill–mentally retarded persons have acquired maladaptive behaviors as a means of managing stressful situations. At times, the counselor teaches constructive patterns of behavior. The subject of human sexuality is one area in which mentally retarded persons frequently need (re)education and counseling.

There are a variety of techniques of sex education. These techniques vary from loosely structured discussion to more structured approaches provided by instructional aids such as slides, models, drawings, and other audiovisual aids. Sexual education and behavior should not be separated from a consideration of interpersonal skills. Walker-Hirsch & Champagne (1992) state, "The tangled web of emotions and reactions that is sometimes created by inappropriate social/sexual interactions can require individual counseling either as a 'teachable moment' or on a longer-term basis" (p. 3).

## Conclusions

A variety of theoretical orientations and therapy techniques have been developed and adapted for use with persons who have mental retardation (Szymanski, 1980: Rubin, 1983; Monfils & Menolascino, 1984). It is my opinion, based on eighteen years of experience of psychotherapy with mentally retarded–mentally ill persons, that the practitioners should have a diverse theoretical orientation and practice skills in order to use a variety of therapy approaches. As pointed out by Monfils and Menolascino (1984), "Because the needs of clients are so diverse, professionals should not rely solely on any one technique or therapeutic school. Rather, a flexible, eclectic approach is indicated, in which the therapist possesses a multiplicity of skills and techniques" (p. 159). Therapists therefore should have a theoretical knowledge base and practice skills in a variety of therapy approaches in the treatment of mentally ill–mentally retarded people. The clinical skill is identifying what approach will be most effective at a given time in the therapeutic process.

## Summary

Individual psychotherapy with persons who have both mental illness and mental retardation is an important approach to meeting the mental health needs of these individuals. Mental health clinicians can provide a valuable service in reducing feelings of confusion, anxiety, loneliness, and despair. Psychotherapy with this population is very similar to psychotherapy with the nonretarded, although the techniques are modified according to the client's language and psychosocial development. A correct professional posture and the ability to communicate therapeutic empathy and respect are critical concepts, and when applied to mentally retarded individuals, they are cogent tools. The concepts, clinical skill, and knowledge that have proved to be effective with nonretarded people may also be effective with persons who have mental retardation and mental illness. A variety of theoretical orientations and practice skills has proved to be effective, including the psychodynamic, supportive, and counseling approaches. An eclectic approach that uses the knowledge base and practice skills of a variety of theoretical orientations is most effective.

# References

Albini, J. L., & Dinitz, S. (1965). Psychotherapy with disturbed and defective children: An evaluation of changes in behavior and attitudes. *Am. J. Ment. Def., 69,* 560–567.

Beasley, J., & Kroll, J. (1992). Who is in crisis: The consumer or the system? *NADD Newsl., 9,*(6), 1–5.

Bowlby, J. (1971). *Attachment and loss: Vol. 1. Attachment.* London: Hogarth Press.

Deutsch, H. (1989). Stress, psychological defense mechanisms, and the private world of the mentally retarded: Applying psychotherapeutic concepts to habilitation. *Psychiatr. Aspects Ment. Retard. Rev., 8*(4).

Dosen, A. (1990). Developmental-dynamic relationship psychotherapy." In A. Dosen, A. van Gennep, & G. J. Zwanikken (Eds.), *Treatment of mental illness and behavioral disorder in the mentally retarded: Proceedings of the International Congress,* May 3–4, 1990. Leiden: Logon.

Dosen, A., & Menolascino, F. J. (Eds.) (1990). *Depression in mentally retarded children and adults.* Leiden: Logon.

Fletcher, R. (1988). County systems model: Comprehensive services for the dually diagnosed. In J. A. Stark, F. J. Menolascino, M. H. Albarelli, & V. C. Gray (Eds.), *Mental retardation and mental health: Classification, diagnosis, treatment, services.* New York: Springer-Verlag.

Fletcher, R. (1990). Mental health services for mentally ill/mentally retarded persons: A community mental health center model. In A. Dosen, A. van Gennep, & G. J. Zwanikken (Eds.), *Treatment of mental illness and behavioral disorder in the mentally retarded: Proceedings of the International Congress,* May 3–4. Leiden: Logon.

Fletcher, R., & Menolascino, F. (Eds.) (1989). *Mental retardation and mental illness: Assessment, treatment and services for the dually diagnosed.* Lexington, Ma: Lexington Books.

Gardner, W. I., & Graeber, J. L. (1990). People with mental retardation and severe behavioral disorders: Multi-modal behavioral, diagnostic and treatment model. *NADD Newsl., 7*(3), 1–4.

Greyson, B., & Akhtar, S. (1977). *Erotomanic delusions in mentally retarded in a group home.* Springfield, ILL.

Hellendoorn, J. (1990). Indications and goals for play therapy with the mentally retarded in Holland. In A. Dosen, A van Gennep, & G. J. Zwanikken (Eds.), *Treatment of mental illness and behavioral disorder in the mentally retarded: Proceedings of the International Congress,* May 3–4. Leiden: Logon.

Hingsburger, D. (1987). Sex counseling with the developmentally handicapped: The assessment and management of seven critical problems. *Psychiatr. Aspects Ment. Retard. Rev., 6,* 41–46.

Hollins, S. C. (1990). Group analytic therapy with people with mental handicap. In A. Dosen, A van Gennep, & G. J. Zwanikken (Eds.), *Treatment of mental illness and behavioral disorder in the mentally retarded: Proceedings of the International Congress,* May 3–4. Leiden: Logon.

Hurley, A. D. (1989). Individual psychotherapy with mentally retarded individuals: Review and call for research. *Res. Devel. Disabilities, 10,* 261–275.

Hurley, A. D., & Hurley, F. J. (1986). Counseling and psychotherapy with mentally retarded clients: 1. The initial interview. *Psychiatr. Aspects of Ment. Retard. Rev., 5,* 22–23.

Jakab, I. (1970). *Psychotherapy of the mentally retarded child.* In N. R. Bernstein (Ed.), *Diminished people.* Boston: Little, Brown.

Jakab, I. (1982). Psychiatric disorders in mental retardation: Recognition, diagnosis and treatment. In I. Jakab (Ed.), *Mental retardation.* New York: Kaiser.

Lansdell, C. (1990). Psychotherapy with persons who have developmental disorders: Biopsychosocial model. *NADD Newsl., 7*(2); 1–5.

Levitas, A. & Gilson, S. F. (1989). Psychodynamic psychotherapy with mildly and moderately retarded patients. R. Fletcher & F. Menolascino (Eds.), *Mental retardation and mental illness. Assessment, treatment and services for the dually diagnosed.* Lexington, MA: Lexington Books.

Lott, G. (1970). Psychotherapy of the mentally retarded: Values and cautions. In F. J. Menolascino (Ed.), *Psychiatric approaches to mental retardation.* New York: Basic Books.

Mackinnon, M. C., & Frederick, B. (1970). A shift of emphasis for psycho-psychiatric social work in mental retardation. In F. J. Menolascino (Ed.), *Psychiatric approaches to mental retardation.* New York: Basic Books.

Matson, J. L. (1986). Psychotherapy with persons who are mentally retarded. *Ment. Retard., 22,* 170–175.

Matson, J. L. (1989). Social learning approaches in the treatment of emotional problems. In R. Fletcher & F. J. Menolascino (Eds.), *Mental retardation and mental illness: Assessment, treatment and service for the dually diagnosed.* Lexington, MA: Lexington Books.

Matson, J. L., & Barrett, R. P. (1993). *Psychopathology in the mentally retarded.* Boston: Allyn and Bacon.

McGee, J. (1989). *Being with others: Toward a psychology of interdependence.* Omaha, NE: Creighton University Press.

McGee, J., Menolascino, F. J., Hobbs, D. C., & Menousek, P. (1987). *Gentle teaching.* New York: Human Sciences Press.

McGee, J. J., & Menolascino, F. (1990). Depression in persons with mental retardation: Toward an existential analysis. In A. Dosen & F. J. Menolascino (Eds.), *Depression in mentally retarded children and adults.* Leiden: Logon.

Menolascino, F. (1977). *Challenges in mental retardation: Progressive ideology and services.* New York: Human Sciences Press.

Menolascino, F. (1983). Overview: Bridging the gap between mental retardation and mental illness. In F. J. Menolascino & B. McCann (Eds.), *Bridging the gap.* Baltimore: University Park Press.

Menolascino, F. (1989). Overview: Promising practices in caring for the mentally retarded-mentally ill. In R. Fletcher & F. Menolascino (Eds.), *Mental retardation and mental illness: Assessment, treatment and service for the dually diagnosed.* Lexington, MA: Lexington Books.

Menolascino, F., & Stark, J. A. (1984). *Handbook of mental illness in the mentally retarded.* New York: Plenum Press.

Monfils, M., & Menolascino, F. (1984). Modified individual and group treatment approaches for the mentally retarded-mentally ill." In F. Menolascino & J. Stark (Eds.), *Handbook of mental illness in the mentally retarded.* New York: Plenum Press.

Nezu, C. M., Nezu, A., & Gill-Weiss, M. J. (Eds.) (1992). *Psychopathology in persons with mental retardation: Clinical guidelines for assessment and treatment.* Champaign, IL: Research Press.

Panagua, C., & DeFazio, A. (1989). Psychodynamics of the mildly retarded and borderline-intelligence adult. In R. Fletcher & F. Menolascino (Eds.), *Mental retardation and mental illness: Assessment, treatment and service for the dually diagnosed.* Lexington, MA: Lexington Books.

Perkins, D. M. (1991). Counseling and psychotherapy for persons with developmental disabilities. In *Rush to the Rockies: Maximizing the individual through the state of the art in mental health and mental retardation. Proceeding of the National Association for the Dually Diagnosed 9th Annual National Conference in Denver, Colorado, December 2–5.* Kingston, NY: National Association for the Dually Diagnosed.

Pfadt, A. (1990). Diagnosing and treating psychopathology in clients with dual diagnosis: An integrative model in treatment of mental illness for behavioral disorder in the mentally retarded. In A. Dosen, A van Gennep, & G. J. Zwanikken (Eds.), *Treatment of mental illness and behavioral disorder in the mentally retarded: Proceedings of the International Congress, May 3–4.* Leiden: Logon.

Phillips, I. (1966). *Children, mental retardation and emotional disorder in prevention and treatment of mental retardation.* New York: Basic Books.

Prouty, G. (1976, Fall). Pre-therapy, a method for treating pre-expressive psychotic and retarded patients. *Psychother.: Theory, Res. Prac., 13,* 290–294.

Prouty, G. (1990). Pre-therapy: A theoretical evolution in the person-centered/experiential psychotherapy of schizophrenia and retardation. In G. Lietaer, J. Rombauts, & R. Van Balen (Eds.), *Client centered and experiential psychotherapy in the nineties.* Leuven, Belgium: Leuven University Press.

Prouty, G. (1991). Pre-therapy: A treatment for the dually diagnosed-schizophrenic/retarded. *NADD Newsl., 8*(6), 1–3.

Rank, B. (1949). Adaptation of the psychoanalytic technique for the treatment of young children with atypical development. *Am. J. Orthopsychiatr., 19,* 130–139.

Reid, A. (1982). *The psychiatry of mental handicap.* Oxford: Blackwell.

Rogers, C. (1942). *Counseling and psychotherapy.* New York: Houghton-Mifflin.

Rogers, C. (1957). The necessary and sufficient conditions of therapeutic personality change. *J. Consult. Psychol., 21,* 95–103.

Rubin, R. L. (1983). Bridging the gap through individual counseling and psychotherapy with mentally retarded people. In F. J. Menolascino & B. McCann (Eds.), *Bridging the gap.* Baltimore: University Park Press.

Ruth, R. (1990). Some trends in psychoanalysis and their relevance for treating people with mental retardation. In A. Dosen, A van Gennep, & G. J. Zwanikken (Eds.), *Treatment of mental illness and behavioral disorder in the mentally retarded: Proceedings of the International Congress, May 3–4.* Leiden: Logon.

Schulman, E. D. (1980). *Focus on the retarded adult: Programs and services.* St. Louis: C. V. Mosby.

Sinason, V. (1992). *Mental handicap and the human condition.* London: Free Association Books.

Stark, J., Menolascino, F., Albarelli, H., & Gray, U. (1988). *Mental retardation and* mental illness: Classification, diagnosis, treatment, services. New York: Springer-Verlag.

Sternlicht, M. (1965). Psychotherapy techniques useful with mentally retarded: A review and critique. *Psychiatr. Q., 39,* 84–90.

Stohlman, H. T. (1992). Use of contracts in psychotherapy with people with mental retardation. *Rush to the Rockies: Maximizing the individual through the state of the art in mental health and mental retardation. Proceedings of National Association for the Dually Diagnosed 9th Annual National Conference in Denver, Colorado December 2–5.* Kingston, NY: National Association for the Dually Diagnosed.

Szymanski, L. (1980). Individual psychotherapy with retarded persons. In L. Szymanski & P. Tanguay (Eds.), *Emotional disorders of mentally retarded persons.* Baltimore: University Park Press.

Vernikoff, S., & Dunayer, R. (1992). Counseling and psychotherapy: Techniques of relationship building as a tool for change. *Rush to the Rockies: Maximizing the individual through the state of the art in mental health and mental retardation. Proceedings of National Association for the Dually Diagnosed 9th Annual National Conference in Denver, Colorado December 2–5.* Kingston, NY: National Association for the Dually Diagnosed.

Walker, P. (1980, July). Recognizing the mental health needs of the developmentally disabled people. *Nat. Assoc. Social Workers,* 293–297.

Walker-Hirsch, L., & Champagne, M. P. (1992). "The circles for use as a counseling strategy: An old dog learns new tricks." *NADD Newsl., 9*(5) 3.

Weber, H. (1953). Borderline defective delinquent. *Br. J. Delinquency, 3,* 173–184.

Zastrow, C. (1981). *The practice of social work.* Homewood, IL: Dorsey.

# 17

# Gentle Teaching for Persons with Mental Retardation: The Expression of a Psychology of Interdependence

*John McGee*

Gentle teaching (McGee et al., 1987; McGee & Menolascino, 1991) is a nonviolent intervention strategy for those who care for and about children and adults who reside on the very edge of family and community life. It is for those who want not only to help these distanced individuals, but also to change themselves in the process. It is for those who want to strive for interdependence and uncover ways to express and practice a spirit of companionship instead of control. It is about children and adults who live in marginalized conditions—pushed and pulled away from feelings of union and hurting themselves and others, or simply giving up. It is for those who live and work among the mentally retarded, the mentally ill, the aged, the homeless, and the poor.

To be marginalized is to be controlled, isolated, and segregated. And to be a caregiver is more than caring; it is to enter into a mutual change process with the person, in which both become more instead of less—the parent embracing the crying child instead of yelling, the teacher befriending a lonely child instead of punishing, the psychiatric nurse sitting with the confused and belligerent patient instead of opening the heavy seclusion-room door, the social worker creating circles of friends around the homeless person instead of simply dishing out soup.

## A Psychology of Interdependence

Interdependence is a way of looking at ourselves and those who cling to the slippery edges of family and community life. It views us and others as equals, as a people who long for companionship, as a people in pain, and as a people who hunger for justice and union. It is a life-long project that brings about healing and affirmation in us and those whom we serve. It involves purposes different from those that are typically thought of. Instead of focusing on getting rid of aggression or self-injury, it starts us on a road toward feelings of companionship and solidarity—the beginning of the fulfillment of the longing for union. Instead of worrying about compliance or obedience, it calls on us to teach new ways of interacting. Instead of seeing ourselves as those who control, it asks us to struggle to create community. Interdependence leads us to bring about feelings of union, emotional well-being, and the instillation of hope at the center of our lives and of those whom we serve.

A psychology of human interdependence concerns itself with the whole being—mind, body and spirit, not just observable behavior, but also the inner nature of the human condition. It focuses on the marginalized person as well as on the caregiver. We are the ones who have to initiate it. It calls for transformation in our inner lives, a change in the way we see ourselves and others, and the recognition that unfolding interdependence is a vital and central dimension of our life condition. It is based on the belief that all of us long to be companions in this life and that this feeling for being-with-others and a sense of belonging resides in all of us.

## Gentle Teaching as a Way to Support Interdependence

Gentle teaching is an intervention approach designed to help caregivers find an alternative to punishment practices. The challenge is not just to find nonaversive behavioral techniques, but to formulate and put into practice a psychology of interdependence that goes against the grain of modifying the other and asks for mutual change. This approach presents a major challenge to parents, professionals, and advocates. It requires an awakening of our values and our putting them into practice in the most difficult situations.

> Patrick is a 6-year old boy who has his loving parents and teacher almost pulling out their hair. At home and school, he is a terror—throwing everything in sight onto the floor, tantrumming, hitting, scratching, and spitting at their faces when nothing else seems to insult them. He has become the school's "spitter." Everyone knows him by that name. When extremely mad, his last resort is to insult, with a sally of spit, anyone asking him to do anything. He knows that this is the last straw. The teacher calls the mother almost every morning to pick him up because of his extreme disruptiveness. The mother goes through the same thing at home. The family are at their wit's end and are about to send him to a special live-in school for disturbed children. They have been nurturing, affectionate, and warm toward him; yet, he acts as though they are his enemies.

How can these caregivers reach Patrick and help him feel at-home. They need first to look at themselves. More than simply ignoring these behaviors and redirecting him so that they can reward him, his caregivers need to express ongoing warmth and unconditional valuing. They have to find ways to protect him and others without domineering over him. They need to enable him to feel that it is good to be with them. At the same time, they have to look at the subtle ways they signal fear and demands and have to dramatically decrease any expressions of coldness and superiority.

Patrick's mother and father think about this possibility: increasing their valuing of him, making sure that it is unconditional, and also seeking to draw it from him. They realize that it will be a long and energy-consuming process, but perhaps worth it. That morning, the mother sits with her son in the kitchen. He is bawling and screaming. The mother has some silverware and a tray on the table and wants to use these objects to structure the time. Patrick wants nothing to do with sitting there, doing a task, or even being with his mother. She feels horrible about this rejection, which is like rubbing salt more deeply into her emotional wound; yet, she has decided to teach him that he is safe with her. Her hands and words will not signal violence or force; rather, they will represent valuing and doing things together.

Patrick's parents and teacher went through this questioning process and persevered with him. He slowly began to accept and even seek out being with them, his brothers and sisters, and his schoolmates.

In the first days, they fight against the urge to control and dominate him. Patrick does everything he can to shove them away physically and emotionally. But as the spit flies from his mouth and lands right on his teacher's face, she continues to give him value and focus on the goodness of being together. As the week progresses, the mother and the teacher feel slightly more at ease and start to ask for hugs. And after an hour of screaming, tossing objects, and spitting, he runs toward his mother, smiles, and embraces her. She feels relieved and senses that they are on the road to a different relationship. Yet, she and the teacher recognize that this will be a difficult process and that they will need to endure more onslaughts.

Change in Patrick means change in his caregiver. Gentle teaching provides the supportive techniques that his caregivers can use to help the child. But these have to be driven by a psychology of interdependence that puts companionship at the heart of caregiving's purpose so that we enter into a new relationship with others.

## The Establishment of Companionship

The central purpose of caregiving is to establish a feeling of companionship with the marginalized other. Bringing about a mutually valued relationship means that we need to help Patrick and others to feel safe and secure with us, to become engaged with us, and to feel valued by us. We have to be careful that our presence does not signal fear. When we approach the person with behavioral difficulties, we need to concentrate on nurturing rather than demands. Our hands and our words should be not instruments of terror, but signs of valuing.

Feelings of safety and security converge with the growing recognition that being with and participating side by side with others is inherently good. Participation can lead to skill acquisition and productive work, but the development of a feeling of engagement is much more basic. It means the growing acceptance and understanding of the significance of being with others. The acceptance of human presence and the engagement with others are the cornerstones of companionship, along with the recognition of the power of unconditional valuing.

### Safety and Security

A profound meaning rests in our very presence. Our hands and words yield much meaning to a marginalized person. They are like instruments that symbolize either warmth and affection or oppression and control. When we raise our hands to help, this movement may generate fear, not because we consciously intend it, but because the person lives in a culture in which our hand is just one more among many violent ones. Our words of affection are just so many more syllables in a litany of orders and denigrations. These words and movements converge into a perception of what our presence so often means: fear. One of the most essential initial challenges confronting us is to teach the person that our presence, in spite of a world of control and domination, represents safety and security. When we speak, it is to create dialogue. When we reach out, it is to warmly help or give value. As caregivers, we have to remember that our very presence conveys strong messages. Before we utter a word or open our hands, the alienated person begins to feel who we are and what we represent. Imagine that you are a lonely and scared child in school. The teacher approaches. What does it mean to feel in danger?

> Mary is sitting in school, and the teacher coldly says, "Do your puzzle now, Mary!" The teacher has not said much of anything to the child all day except ordering her what to do. The child sees the teacher as a stern authority figure: "Do this! Do that!" Mary becomes more frightened of her, not because the teacher is deliberately

cruel, but because Mary sees in her little more than demanding words.

Is it possible that a simple thing like telling a child to do something will teach the child to have fear? The answer is "yes" if this happens day after day, year after year, in a world where the child is valued only for deeds done. It is not just the spoken words, but also the tone, the superiority, and the coldness. The teacher becomes a commandant instead of a friend. There is a deterioration of the human spirit over time. Our interactions are like drops of water falling on a rock. One or two drops do not make much difference, but constant drops, time after time, year after year, take their toll. Our words and acts become symbols of oppression.

Harsh words often turn into grabbing when the person does not do whatever she or he is supposed to do. Our hands are like our words. They can be instruments of valuing or domination. Caregiving is filled with euphemisms that mask violence: Physical help is often a charade for force, escorting often equates with pushing and pulling another person like a bag of garbage, and compliance often means "Do this, or else!" The person quickly learns to fear us or rebel against us. We begin to represent feelings of danger and insecurity that distance us from the person. The gap widens.

> When Mary does not start to do her task after having been told several times, the teacher gives her a "physical prompt," taking her by the hand and moving her through the motions of compliance. This action results in an emotional and physical tug-of-war, and both become more resistant. Mary sees the caregiver approach and her heart cringes. This fear soon translates into aggression or withdrawal.

If we want to teach feelings of safety and security, we need to question what we are doing and how we are doing it. The key is to look at ourselves and ask, "What do we represent to this person: valuing or domination?" If we see the person as our equal and if we define our relationship as one of brotherhood and sisterhood, then the answer becomes more obvious. We commit ourselves to making certain that our presence signifies feelings of safety and security. Yet, we need to deal with the irony of representing these feelings while face to face with rejection, disruption, or even violence.

### Human Engagement

Along with safety and security, it is critical to establish a sense of human engagement. As the person draws near, we need to enable the feeling that being with us and mutually participating brings us closer together, opens up ongoing opportunities for sharing, and sets a backdrop for dialogue. Caregivers who are bent on bringing about behavioral control often push to have the marginalized person acquire skills based on a rationale that human value is found only in the ability to be independent.

A central question is not what we can do, but who we are. Our assumption is that our life takes on meaning based on our relatedness to others. The development of our particular talents is important, but secondary to human engagement. Self-reliance leaves already alienated people more isolated in a dog-eat-dog world. Our option is to teach the meaning of human engagement: that it is good to be with and participate with us and others. The central factor in human engagement is an evolving desire to be with us, not interest in a task. It is not some magical process involving finding something interesting to do, but the person's perception of who we are and what we represent.

To be engaged is to feel that it is good to be with the other, to interact, to share, and to give and receive human valuing. Being together and being engaged in the flow of ordinary life communicates feelings of union. Engagement is a relationship based not on manipulation or control, but on an affirmation of the other through mutual participation. For those who are marginalized, it is a critical dimension in the elaboration of companionship since it creates a common ground for being together. Yet, alienated individuals have no reason to be with us. So, a basic caregiving role is to bring about engagement. This is facilitated by doing activities with the person and using such a structure to express unconditional valuing.

> The teacher decides to convey a spirit of friendship to frightened Mary. Instead of ordering her to do her task, she sits beside her, reaches her hand out, and offers words of valuing while also putting the puzzle together with her. She does not mind that Mary is not "complying;" she is focused on having the child feel that it is good to be near her and knowing that she will help her. Mary's fear begins to diminish as she senses that her teacher recognizes her value and understands her human condition. She slowly begins to participate.

In the beginning, we have to enable the elaboration of participation. Putting aside the drive to demand compliance, we have to be present with the individual and avoid domineering commands. When the person refuses to participate, the focus cannot be on "Do this, or else!" As in teaching safety and security, we need to concentrate our efforts on valuing, moving toward the person without conveying fright, and being with the other, whether or not the person does a particular activity or not.

*Unconditional Valuing*

The driving force behind the newly emerging meaning of our presence with others and our engagement with them is our unconditional valuing. To value another is to uplift, to honor, to respect, to listen, and to reflect and share feelings—whether with words or with other humanizing expressions. To do this unconditionally is to express it regardless of deeds done.

It is common for persons who have been exploited and rejected, or who are simply vulnerable to emotional devastation because of handicapping or marginalizing conditions, to shun our valuing. Most of them are accustomed to the experience of being rewarded only for deeds well done, and since they do few things that meet the criterion for reward within this culture, they not only have little opportunity to "earn" it but also find little meaning in it because it is perceived as inauthentic and mechanistic. Or they have been pushed and pulled so much to perform "good" behaviors that they rebel against our very presence, let alone doing something with us.

The unfolding of the feeling of being valued and valuing others is the central dimension in the establishment of feelings of companionship. It can be taught only through our giving and eliciting it frequently and unconditionally. We are confronted with the initial meaninglessness of our relationship—not only in the eyes of the other, but sometimes in our own. It is impossible to give genuine value if we do not feel it ourselves, and it is difficult to express it when it falls on seemingly deaf ears. Yet, the act of giving genuine value, and giving it frequently, regardless of what the person may be doing or not doing, is our central task. This process deepens its meaning for us and shares its power with the marginalized person.

> When Mary refuses to participate or throws something to the floor, the teacher does not reprimand her. She approaches Mary as a friend. She sits down with the child and does the particular task with her—even if she has to do everything. All the while, the teacher talks with the child, gives value, and gradually creates a feeling of safety and security. The child's cries lessen; the teacher feels more affectionate. She slips a puzzle piece into the girl's hand and helps her. The child gazes and smiles at the teacher.

Someone might say, "Well, I interact a lot and give positive reinforcement, but she still does not comply, and she still won't do anything. In fact, whenever I ask her to do something, she starts to throw the material on the floor or to scream or hit herself." The problem does not lie in positive reinforcement because such a reward has to be earned and Mary earns little. We are not behavioral accountants dispensing loans. Valuing someone does not depend on contingencies. It is given because the person is a full human being with a hunger and longing for warmth and affection.

*The Central Task of Caregiving*

When our interactions revolve around unconditional valuing, then our feelings and actions also reflect a full acceptance of the person, tolerance of violent or recalcitrant acts, and empathy for the life condition of the individual. The central caregiving paradigm involves all caregiver interactions, beginning with, centering on, and effectuating unconditional valuing.

But this is no easy task. It requires a sharp consciousness that our most subtle, and seemingly irrelevant, interactions have a tremendous impact on the person's ability to accept us. A solitary neutral gaze, a demanding word, or a cold touch may shout out to the already suspicious person that we are nothing more than oppressors, even when our intention is to value. Our interactions need to start with valuing, including the manner in which we physically and emotionally approach, look at, reach out to, and speak to the person. Every move, step, and expression has to summon up a strong feeling of genuine warmth and exude unconditional valuing.

Within this process, we also need to seek valuing from the person. Besides giving it, we have to seek its reciprocation. The elicitation of valuing is a process that needs to be woven into value giving through nonforceful attempts that indicate that it is fulfilling to give and to receive. As we elicit and receive valuing, we also generate encouragement to persevere in our efforts, since the slightest signs of companionship multiply our own feelings of mutuality and instill hope in us as well as in the other. We need to seek this reciprocation slowly, yet perseveringly, since so many marginalized persons fear our touch, words, or gestures.

The power of what it means to give and receive unconditional valuing is a learning process. It cannot be given and then withdrawn. Imagine that you are starving and someone gives you food and then takes it away, for whatever reason. How would you feel? The homeless person in the shelter needs comradeship, not damnation. The adult in the mental hospital needs intense and warm regard, not isolation. The child needs our embrace, not abuse. Valuing starts with our beliefs and is seen in our commitment to the person during the very worst moments.

> Out of the blue, Ted screams, "No!" several times. His size and loudness intimidate everyone. The sound echoes through the community work place. Everybody looks. They see his large body moving. His caregiver becomes nervous, afraid, and embarrassed. Ted goes beyond yelling. He tears his shirt off, pounds his fists on the table, stands up, and hovers over the caregiver with his fists flying. The caregiver stands behind Ted, wraps his arms around his chest, and brings him to the floor. Another caregiver straddles Ted's prone body "until he is calm for three minutes." Ted is sweating, and so

are the caregivers. He is scared, and so are the caregivers. He is dominated, and so are the caregivers.

Yet, we say that in this most difficult moment we need to center our interactions on valuing. Instead of overpowering Ted, there is another option: expressing unconditional valuing through dialogue. For us to do this takes the best that we can give.

Later on in the day, another caregiver decides to value Ted as he begins another fury. As he stands, this caregiver stands and makes sure that his slightest movements express calming, nonviolence, and nurturing. As Ted screams, the caregiver's warm and soothing words of value are heard. As he flails his arms, the caregiver, even with great difficulty, continues to engage him in the particular task. As Ted catches his breath, the caregiver places his hand in Ted's for a handshake. Ted slaps him away, but the caregiver says, "I know you are scared. I will not hurt you." At the same time, the caregiver is ready to protect himself from blows without doing violence or increasing fear. Any focus on compliance is avoided. The center of all interactions is to give Ted value and even to elicit it from him. Throughout forty minutes, Ted has had brief moments of calmness—catching his breath, rocking, and looking around. The caregiver has stood and sat with him. He has done a task for him and then with him. All along, he has conversed with him about friendship, doing things together, and feeling safe. Ted increasingly senses the warmth of the tone and starts to scream and thrash less. Instead of hitting the caregiver's hand, he starts to let him touch his, and a faint smile emerges.

As caregivers, we can represent either domination or valuing. We can teach either apartness or union. Domination is most frequently shown in almost unnoticeable acts, such as coldness and detachment in our words and deeds. Perhaps domination seems to be too strong a term for that cold gaze or uninterested conversation. Yet, every interaction matters. Interactions have a cumulative effect over days, months, and years. Likewise, valuing is often silent and is delicately woven into the fabric of our interactions—the way we move, our tone, and our touch. Fortunately, these fragile threads become stronger as we weave them into laces of affection.

## Value-Centered Interactions

Before worrying about others' actions and interactions, our initial task is to question what we do and how we do it. Our challenge is to dramatically increase our value-centered interactions and to decrease domineering ones. At the same time, we have to help the person move toward feelings of union with us. Several critical caregiver interactional patterns help bring us to a spirit of unconditional valuing.

## Value Giving

*Value giving* refers to any action on the part of the caregiver that recognizes and expresses the dignity, worth, presence, and participation of the other person. It conveys genuineness, sincerity, and honesty. It represents solidarity with the person. It is given through words, touches, gestures, and any other form of verbal or nonverbal expression. Indeed, most often, what we "say" is expressed in our warmth, authenticity, and caring—the tone of our voice, the softness of our gaze, and the serenity of our movements. These are interactions that prize the other with genuine and warm regard. They are honest, direct, and sincere, not mere role playing. They are given at any time, not just contingently. In fact, most frequently, valuing is given regardless of any particular behavior. It is given for who the person is, not for what she or he does. It requires a deep commitment on our part to perceive the wholeness of the other, a commitment that propels us to give respect and friendship regardless of what may be transpiring. Its expression emanates from our whole being. It can be seen in our physical, verbal, and gestural interactions.

Value giving tells the other person that we represent safety and security. It conveys the recognition that our interactions express warm and genuine feelings of oneness. These are more than a mere reward because positive reinforcement is given only for deeds done according to preordained norms. These interactions are given rather than earned. They are expressed in even the most difficult moments. They are more than just praise. They are an ongoing dialogue with the person that demonstrates, through words, gestures, and touch, the acceptance of the wholeness of the other in spite of ongoing rejection. These interactions are the center of what we do.

## Reciprocity Eliciting

Even if caregivers give plenty of reward, they often leave the person in a passive and dependent state since rewarding is a lopsided process. We view the marginalized individual as the receiver and ourselves as the givers. This attitude places us in an unjustly powerful position and leaves the dispossessed more powerless. The center of the human condition is not only our valuing others, but their empowerment to value us. We need to avoid being "nice" and to focus on being with one another. It is reciprocation that draws us into equality. So, we have to teach the goodness of being valued as well as of valuing. *Reciprocity eliciting* refers to any interaction on the part of the caregiver that has as its expressed purpose the evocation of the expression of valuing on the part of the person toward the caregiver. It is meant to encourage and teach the person to return and initiate value giving toward others. It is as significant as any valuing that the caregiver conveys. Like value giving, we need to elicit these interactions from the person in a spirit of companionship, avoiding force or a condescending attitude. These interactions initially depend on our seeking them from the person.

Reciprocity eliciting is intended to draw valuing toward ourselves and then toward others. It indicates to the person that relationships are not paternalistic, nor based on authoritarian attitudes. Rather, they are founded on equality and solidarity. Reciprocity eliciting involves any caregiver contacts that are designed to help the person learn to return valuing interactions.

## Helping Warmly

*Helping warmly* refers to any caregiving interaction done in a patient and tolerant manner to effectuate mutual participation and a shared spirit of engagement without causing any violence. It involves the process of teaching or utilizing concrete skills that enable increased opportunities for engagement and also the expression of friendship in the helping relationship. Warmly helping includes interactions that prevent disruption or that maintain or increase the person's capacity to participate. These interactions convey a spirit of mutuality, not the imposition of demands seen in physical or emotional tugs-of-war. Warmth is conveyed in the caregiver's nurturing tone, softness of touch, and kindness of presence. The person learns that being with and participating with the caregiver are good. Warmth can be seen in empathy, caring, respectfulness, and trust. It reflects solidarity with the person, not overprotection or bossiness. The frequent linking of engagement with unconditional valuing generates an understanding and feeling that these phenomena are of the same cloth.

Warmly helping involves a broad range of interactions. The expression of warmth is the critical dimension in this variable. It includes the expression of words that are not commands, a touch that is not forceful, and gestures that are not mechanistic. For a person who has trouble doing tasks, it may mean a parent working hand-over-hand with a child, but taking extreme care to use his or her hands as instruments of affection. For a caregiver working among the homeless, it may mean inviting the person into the kitchen to be not a passive recipient of charity, but an active participant in justice making: organizing the street people, running the shelters and soup kitchens, publishing a newsletter, and speaking for himself or herself. For a person living with someone who is mentally disorganized, it may mean the avoidance of words, sitting down and doing the task together, and making sure that the pace of the help is congruent with the person's mood. If the person refuses to participate, the caregiver may go ahead and do the task for the person. Remember that the main intent of this variable is human engagement, not skill acquisition or compliance.

## Protecting

*Protecting* refers to those caregiving interacations that are used to prevent actual or possible harm to the person or to anyone else, whether through acts of self-injury, aggression, or property destruction. The primary factor involves the avoidance of any immobilization, even for a split second. Protection includes actions such as shadowing a person's movements to prevent being hit and blocking hits or any form of contact that occurs at a particular moment when harm is imminent. Protecting also includes actions that prevent disruptiveness. It does not include any form of restraint or forced movements. It does not include those packaged approaches that make caregivers appear to be boot camp instructors. It prevents the escalation of violence. It neither immobilizes nor humiliates the person. It is brief and must be accompanied by engagement and valuing. An irony is that, during the worst moments, caregivers need to be the most valuing and to help with the greatest degree of warmth.

While valuing and warm help occur, caregivers also have the responsibility to protect. The very nature of behavioral difficulties implies that someone can be hurt by acts of aggression or self-injury. Caregivers need to do everything possible to avoid harm while simultaneously valuing the other. It is critical to avoid the use of restraint and any physical immobilization, since one of our primary duties is to help the person feel safe with us. Nonviolence is a basic rule in caregiving. Nevertheless, the first rule of caregiving is that harm come to no one. If any momentary immobilization is necessary, it should be used to prevent immediate harm and then should be avoided in the future through the prevention of causes that might lead to such dangerous interactions. The most useful form of protection is prevention.

## Dominative Dimension

It is ironic that we often "treat" violence with violence, distance ourselves further from those who are already apart, and express coldness to those who need warmth. Death comes to the human spirit in many ways, often through subtle interactions that rust away at our being. Most often, we do these actions without even knowing it, not only through punishment but through expressions that signal indifferentness, lessened value, and compliance as life's purpose rather than a deep desire to relate to others in a spirit of solidarity. These expressions are as destructive as the more obvious practices that prevail, such as time-out, taking away privileges, spankings, electric shock, seclusion, locking up people, and a host of other control mechanisms. All such interactions need to be eliminated if we want to teach feelings of companionship. The most common ones relate to the making of demands and any interactions that are contingent and reflect a superior attitude.

### Assisting Demandingly

*Assisting demandingly* refers to any caregiving interactions whose aim is to "help but that are done in a cold, mechanistic, or authoritarian manner. They express a hierarchical, nonfraternal relationship toward the person. They indicate a degree of intolerance, impatience, and disregard. They give the feeling that control is the purpose rather than engagement. They are typically forceful in nature and overfocus on the mechanics of compliance instead of a flow of mutual participation. The caregiver feels compelled to make the person respond rather than to empower mutual participation. These actions symbolize a desire to impose correction and correctness rather than the use of participatory interactions as a means toward human valuing.

These interactions are probably the most common reason why we sense fear and even loathing in vulnerable people. They are generally very subtle things that we do, such as grabbing people, taking their hands and forcing them to do something, verbally ordering people, giving demeaning or condescending instructions, and other interactions indicative of a feeling of apartness. Even when these actions are done in the name of helping the person, they send clear messages that we are in authority and that the focus is on obedience and compliance instead of companionship. They gnaw away at the human spirit and make the person feel that life is nothing more than rote compliance. Instead of creating a mutually valuing relationship, they place the caregiver over the person.

### Restraint, Reward, and Punishment

*Restraint, reward, and punishment* refer to physical, verbal, or environmental actions that result in any immobilization of the person by the caregiver or forced movements based on any form of compliance, treating the person as a being who has to earn a reward, or treating the person as a being who can be controlled or modified through reward or punishment. The purpose of these actions is to control the person based on contingency. These three types of interactions arise out of the belief that the powerful must modify the powerless. The caregiver operates in the belief that the vulnerable human being is simply a mechanism that responds to the carrot and the stick: "If you do good things, you will be rewarded; if you do bad things, you will be punished." Restraint is often the last hope when the other two fail. It essentially says, "Since you do not respond to reward or punishment, we must lock you up, tie you up, or drug you." Reward is viewed as the negation of the human condition when it is the basic procedure used to "modify" the other's behavior. Everything has to be earned, and the reward is "delivered" in a robotlike manner. Punishment is reward's twin. It is the bleaker side of the family of control.

Restraint is any use of any part of the caregiver's body or the surrounding environment to stop a person's movement through grabbing or containing the person. It includes the use of any contingent orders designed to immobilize the person, such as orders to put one's hands down or in one's pockets, the use of time-out rooms, or the use of the environment to jail a person. It is also seen in the use of mechanical devices such as helmets and straitjackets.

Reward and punishment are characterized by any caregiver interactions that are based on the view that the person is nothing more than a machine, what some term mere sets of stimuli and responses. It is dehumanizing to base our interactions on the notion that the center of the human condition is reward and punishment, and that this rule is what brings about learning, including behavioral change. Doubtless, these often work, but whether something works or not is not the issue. The central question is what kind of relationship we want to create. Reward is different from valuing the person. It is scheduled and earned. It is applied to the person in a prescriptive format. It often involves giving material things, such as food or tokens. It distances the caregiver from the person and emanates from an attitude that we are superior and have the power to modify the behavior of those who are alienated. Punishment is similar to reward. It is given for deeds done and is scheduled and applied as in a prescription. It involves verbal, physical, and gestural reprimands delivered in a broad number of ways. Most punishment is also accompanied at some point by various types of contingent reward. The idea is to use the "carrot" as much as possible but, when that does not work, to use the "stick." Either view devalues the person. A life made up primarily of reward or punishment is a life devoid of meaning.

## Union versus Apartness

For the marginalized person, aggression, self-harm, and withdrawal represent apartness—a surrender to anguish, meaninglessness, and choicelessness. Our central role is not to find ways to get rid of behavior problems, but to enable the learning of accepting and returning unconditional valuing and engagement. The world takes on distinct meanings depending on each person's reality, vulnerabilities, talents, history, and support networks. These meanings are filled with signs and symbols. To resignify is to give new meanings. We need to initiate a process in which the meaning of companionship takes root, and apartness disappears. A homeless person may see most others as oppressors; an abused child may cringe when just seeing an adult approach. A retarded adult, on seeing others working and playing, may feel saddened because such fulfillment is beyond his or her reach. These old meanings need to be discarded. We have the responsibility to introduce new feelings through our interactions so that the marginalized person begins to feel one with us—united instead of apart, embracing instead of avoiding, engaged instead of obedient, and valued instead of controlled. Our reality and that of the other person need to be given new meanings. Different signs and symbols need to fill an absurd world. These meanings are embedded within and between people and translate into how we perceive ourselves and others, how the other sees us, and how their interpretations transform themselves into actions. When we feel no companionship toward the aggressive person, our interactions cannot convey warmth and authenticity. Our words reflect apartness, and our hands are seen as aggressive. Likewise, the marginalized person has deeply rooted meanings. These weigh on the person like stones. The person views herself or himself as worthless and looks on us as agents of force and control. When the person sees us, it seems better to avoid than to reach out or simply to obey rather than communicate.

In order to bring new meanings to the human condition, we need to assume the responsibility for our own change as well as an initial commitment to enabling feelings of union in the other. This interpretation of behavioral difficulties leads us to see the other in the shadow of anguish. Even if aggression, self-injury, or withdrawal appears to be volitional, we need to understand each person's history and to translate it into the here and now. The new meanings that we elicit are indicative of companionship—a relationship based on mutuality, marked by warmth and openness, and centered on unconditional valuing. The challenge is not only to modify observable behaviors, but to transform the very essence of the human condition and to change the reality of marginalization.

*Feelings of Union*

We have seen the principle value-centered interactions that we need to be committed to. Now, let us examine the other side of the interactional nature of caregiving. These factors help the person learn to express companionship and create these new meanings. They represent our helping others center their own valuing, and this is what brings about union. These factors necessitate active caregiver involvement. They do not simply evolve; rather, we have to teach each one. To establish feelings of union, we need to concentrate our efforts on teaching the person to reciprocate our valuing, to initiate it on their own, to become engaged with us, and to share these feelings with others.

## Value Reciprocation

*Value reciprocation* refers to any interactions on the part of the person that express or indicate the person's return of valuing to the caregiver who is eliciting it. These interactions are related to the caregiver's seeking smiles, handshakes, hugs, and any facial, corporal, or verbal expressions related to giving back signs of union. They help to equalize and democratize the relationship so that the other is not a perpetual recipient, but an active participant in a value-centered life condition. Our task is not only to give valuing, but to teach its return.

Giving value to the other person also assumes a commitment to eliciting it. As we do this, we are teaching the person to return our valuing. This return results in the emergence of a mutual relationship in which the other begins to express signs of bonding. It conveys the feeling that the person is entering into a spirit of dialogue. In the beginning, reciprocation is often minute movements away from previous patterns.

## Value Initiating

*Value initiating* refers to the same phenomena as the above, except these interactions are initiated spontaneously. They may appear apart from value reciprocation or within it. They often start to occur once the person begins to sense the meaning of the elicited reciprocation and to indicate an internalization of the goodness of being with the caregiver. When we ask for a handshake and the person also responds with a warm gaze, the gaze would be interpreted as the initiation of a form of value giving. This is no small matter; it signals the start of a different relationship, one based on emerging companionship.

This element indicates that the person is moving beyond mere reciprocation and starting to naturally express warmth, affection, and authentic friendship. These interactions arise on their own and do not require the caregiver's seeking them. They mean that feelings of safety and security are emerging, that engagement with the caregiver is becoming an important and significant dimension in the person's life, and that being valued and giving value are starting to take root at the center of the human condition. They are the clearest sign and symbol of the formation and equalization of the relationship and signal the advent of interdependence. We have to take care to be sensitive to these expressions and to be aware of their importance so that we continue to enable and encourage them.

## Engagement

*Engagement* refers to the person's willingness and desire to be with and participate with the caregiver. It is conveyed in interactions such as moving closer, paying attention longer, working together, playing together, listening intently, and using one's talents. It relates secondarily to the acquisition of skills and fulfilling responsibilities. These begin to emerge as the person feels secure and accepts our unconditional valuing. Engagement enables the person to express feelings about being with the other. It is like a bridge that links us with marginalized others. This bridging is often done in the face of rebellion or near-total withdrawal. So, we need to effectuate it by putting aside any focus on compliance. The fact that a person may know how to do a task is irrelevant. The desire to participate with us is the key element. If we react with observations such as, "He knows how to do this, so he should!" then we leave the person floundering in the backwaters of isolation. Our task is to enable engagement regardless of the person's abilities or skills. If the person refuses to cook supper, the question here is not culinary skills, but being-with-us. We need to give whatever help is necessary to bring about participation so we can nurture this feeling.

Tasks are a vehicle for enabling engagement. In essence, as we seek to bring about participation, day-to-day activities serve as the structure within which engagement occurs, such as when the mother invites the child to wash dishes with her, when the father helps his child clean his bedroom, when the teacher sits with the student, or when the group home worker goes shopping with the resident. Each of these activities has the potential of bringing the other closer to us. However, if this does not happen, we must go to the person. Engagement is broken into two subvariables: with help and without help. We encourage maximum personal development; yet, especially at the start, it is critical that we lend as much help as necessary, even if we do nearly everything.

By enabling and facilitating participation, we help the person to start to perceive being with others as a central part of the human condition. A feeling of solidarity emerges. The person begins to participate in activities and tasks throughout the flow of the day, not because of any feeling of compliance, but because of the evolution of a spirit of being together. Its strongest indicator is when we are with the person, doing a task together, and talking. These activities signify that companionship is solidifying.

Most hospitals, institutions, work-training centers, shelters, and special schools focus on rehabilitation through learning an occupation or acquiring skills. Indeed, it is good to work and to develop and express our talents. But for most marginalized people, work or schooling is, at best, secondary. Low pay, no benefits, and long hours of heavy work do little to lift up the human spirit. More important, a life without significant others shatters the person's ability to develop individual talents. Sitting in a classroom and becoming literate are important, but they should be considered within the context of the person's emotional needs. Houses, cottages, and special residential units devoid of friendship do little to spark the human spirit. These are made of bricks and mortar; a home is made of love and companionship. It does little good to teach someone to wash clothing or prepare meals if that person cannot reach out and honor those around him or her.

What about someone with severe disabilities who can hardly move or understand the surrounding world? Is it possible to establish a feeling of engagement and to bring about participation in those with the profoundest mental retardation?

> Kathleen was born with profound mental retardation and died when she was two years old. She was unable to suck, chew, or swallow. She was blind and deaf. She would never be able to sit up by herself. She frequently spent her time arched in a state of seizure. Yet, her mother and father assumed that she could learn to participate in life in her own unique way. They embraced her as a full human being and taught their two other children that Kathleen was equal to everyone. They understod that their baby's worth would have to be seen in another dimension, but that she was a full, giving human being. Her parents taught her to move her tiny hand when it was in theirs and to smile and move her tongue as if kissing. This was her embrace and her demonstration of affection—not much, but more than many humans achieve. Her struggle to do these deeds surpassed the expression of affection of most other people and were her labored way of being engaged. This mutuality ended with her death, but while living, she was able to show oneness with her parents and siblings.
>
> How did her parents teach her this? They spent hours with the baby, placing their fingers in her hand, valuing her, caressing her, and encouraging the slightest movement. They kissed her on her cheek and encouraged the tiniest expressions of warmth and love. They touched her lips and helped her move them over their fingers as her kiss. Her sounds also began to speak nonverbal messages of the desire for and affirmation of union. This infant required much but also gave much. Her mother said, "She is both a burden and a joy: a burden because of the constant care; a joy because the slightest sign of her affection, her acknowledgment of our presence, and her movement toward us was a moment of celebration."

The desire to be with us and to reach out toward us indicates that the person feels safe and secure. The act of participating with us is a sign of companionship. It is a moving toward the other in a spirit of solidarity. Human engagement means that the other is entering into our life space because there is an emerging sense of oneness. Without it, valuing occurs in a vacuum and is one-sided. We need to be at the person's side not because we are important, but because we are equal. Learning to be with us is learning to become engaged—both for the other and for ourselves.

## Sharing

We need to expand this initial relationship to others by bringing our newly forming relationship to a broader number of other individuals. Sharing generates this process. Instead of downward relationships, as seen in a staff-to-client world, the purpose of sharing is to create a circle of friends that expands outward. Old-fashioned sewing circles are examples of this process. People come together to make a beautiful quilt, but all the while the group is communicating. In barn raising, farmers came together to help a neighbor in distress by using construction to express unity. Or in urban settings, volunteers join hands to rehabilitate deserted buildings for human habitation. Or the teacher asks her students to show and tell about their prized possessions. The busy hands, the productivity, and the telling are reasons to come together. Sharing breaks up the tendency to live independent, but parallel, lives. It is the soup kitchen where the homeless work together, the group home where all are learning to live together, and the classroom where the children are helped to reach out to one another.

Emotional strength and stability increase as the circle of companions broadens. A key factor is to teach the other to share and reach out, first to us, then to others. Sharing involves any interactions on the part of the person that indicate participation with or that express value toward persons other than the primary caregiver. These may be self-initiated or elicited. We have the responsibility to expand friendship with the person to others since it does not automatically transfer to others; it needs to be extended. Additionally, we need to avoid an overdependence on ourselves since this stagnates maximum fulfillment.

Sharing can occur in two ways: through doing tasks together and through valuing others. In the first, we use common activities as vehicles to bring others around us and the person whom we are helping. This concrete approach is a good way to start the sharing process. The second way is more complex and involves teaching the group to value one another. These two processes are often combined—the first giving a structure and the second deepening the meaning.

> Little Kathleen learned to share and move her sharing beyond her parents by reaching out to her brother and sister. Her mother would often have them help in feeding, bathing, and dressing Kathleen. More important, during these times, she made sure that their interactions were similar to hers: valuing Kathleen with caresses, hugs, and kisses; encouraging the baby to make slight movements to show her love; and teaching the other family members these nuances. As simple as these movements were, they were Kathleen's way of showing love and sharing her fullness.

As we teach value-centered interactions, the person begins to learn to reject violence, disruptiveness, and destruction in his or her relationships with those who are just. We need to be keenly aware of the importance of extending these feelings beyond our relationship in order to construct the strongest social network possible. The ability to reach out toward others strengthens emotional fortitude and the ability to face life's vicissitudes. The first steps toward sharing are difficult. The person often passes through the same fear, distancing, and meaninglessness with others as with the first caregiver.

## Apartness

A culture of death gives birth to isolation, loneliness, and marginalization. These are expressed in violence—the hatred and fear conveyed through aggression, the suicidal attempts of self-injury, and the despair of withdrawal. *Apartness* is what behaviorists would term maladaptive behaviors, but it is much deeper than what we observe. It resides in the inner heart and eats away at the anguished spirit. Getting rid of observable behaviors does not solve the mysteries of the heart; it only serves to mask them, often in a frozen state of obedience. Apartness comes from ordinary moment-to-moment, gnawing-away feelings such as those seen in a focus on obedience. "Hands down! Sit!" might seem like a good thing to demand, but for the marginalized person, such commands add to the other fear that multiply and accumulate until their weight crushes any desire to be with others. Our dominating interactions accumulate in a pattern that tells the person that there is no hope of union, and that aggression or self-injury is the best way to deal with increasing isolation.

Distancing behaviors are any actions or interactions that cause or may cause physical or emotional harm to oneself or others. They indicate emotional homlessness in that they serve to remove the person from engagement and participation, whether through withdrawal, self-injury, or aggression. They connote a fear of others and loudly proclaim the lack of adequate valuing. These behaviors are signs and symbols of the lack of union and the presence of feelings of oppression. Our task is to take away their meaning through our value-centered interactions. Our designification of these behaviors gives more power to our valuing. Again, we can get rid of such behaviors through force or control, but our option is to create new interactional patterns. These behaviors, then, are replaced by valuing, its reciprocation, and engagement.

We are called on to fulfill a twofold responsibility: to decrease our domination and to increase our valuing. In this way, we help others move away from feelings of apartness and toward those of union. This mutual change

process is complex, and our responsibility is great. We are enablers and fa-
cilitators in the marginalized person's movement toward companionship.
Our central concern should revolve not around the behavior problem, but
around the reciprocation of our valuing, engagement with us, and sharing
with others. A psychology of interdependence encompasses interactional
change, a process in which our interactions are interwoven with the marginalized person's. Obviously, control and contingency procedures can
bring about changes in observable behaviors, but our purpose is the elaboration of feelings of companionship and the bringing about mutual change
in what is seen and felt within and between ourselves and marginalized
people.

## Facilitating Change

Several supportive techniques can be mobilized to effectuate and intensify
the change process. The formation of feelings of companionship is easier
said than done, but the mastery of these skills will enable us to move more
closely to this spirit. Unlike many current practices, these techniques are applied in varying mixes, at different moments. It is not just a matter of "Do
this, then that." The change process involves arduous work, flexibility, and
creativity. It is not just a matter of desiring interdependence or trying to represent new meanings. We need to be ready to spend time, exert much effort,
and apply a range of techniques that highlight unconditional valuing, support the resignification process, and help create engagement. Some of the
techniques help to prevent or diminish behavioral problems. Others help to
increase participation. And still others help to center our interactions on
valuing. There is no cookbook formula.

### Supportive Techniques

Most of the supportive techniques are common psychological and educational practices, and their worth lies in their use as ways to support valuing the person in need, preventing violence, and promoting engagement.
Errorless teaching enables us to bring about participation by presenting
interactions and activities in such a way that the person does not fail.
The key is to bring about engagement. Any way we can prevent confusion or frustration helps maintain the focus on coming together. This
process involves split-second decisions and changes. In the beginning, the
slightest error may be frustrating and may lead to violence. We have to
be ever ready to ensure a smooth flow in our interactions. Task analysis
supports errorless learning. It involves breaking down tasks and activities
so that we can proceed more easily and need not be concerned about

what comes next. It facilitates participation. The more we can enable a smooth flow to doing things together, the more likely it is that engagement with us will come about. A basic technique involves doing activities with the person to ensure a flow. It is within the structure of coparticipation that we are more readily seen as equal and that we can more naturally enter into a dialogue. Making sure the environment is conducive to participation and preventing aggression and self-injury are important and include such considerations as where we sit or stand, how we approach the person, how we offer warm help, how we enable participation, and how we give and elicit valuing. These arrangements may change from one second to the next. In warmly helping the individual, we concentrate on our words and touch so that they are as supportive and nondemanding as possible. Since the person is likely to be fearful, we need to express warmth, especially in those interactions that have historically been equated with demands.

Indeed, our helping needs to border on our valuing in a spirit of "We are doing this together as friends." If we are handing an item to someone, our movements are meant to help, but the way we do it can be interlaced with valuing. The warmth of helping relates to our manner and how the person interprets our relationship and purpose. The soundest way to help someone is through coparticipation. Instead of standing over someone with our arms folded as a straw boss, we need to sit down and accomplish the activity together. We should always keep in mind that one of our primary purposes is to teach human engagement, and that no matter what we are doing, the task at hand is simply a vehicle for enabling participation and a means to structure our valuing.

## Conclusion

Fortunately, even in the midst of oppression, men and women of values emerge—rejecting a culture of death and seeking out ways to give life and hope, some quietly, some loudly, some behind closed doors, some publicly. Each of us is challenged to assume a posture of solidarity, to break away from acts of marginalization, and to rupture the culture of death. Caregiving is an act of social justice, the instillation of hope, and entering a journey toward home. It is the teacher who befriends the slow or recalcitrant child. It is the tired parent who stays awake in the night and gives affection to the crying child. In the group home, it is welcoming the stranger and making friendship. In nursing, it is staying with the frightened patient. In advocacy it is sitting and sharing a meal with the homeless person.

We can refuse to marginalize. We can elect to become companions. The establishment of justice knows no limits if dialogue is at the center. Our challenge is to reflect on and practice a psychology of human interdependence in which feelings of safety and security replace those of fear and loathing, in which the feeling of being with the other replaces the absurdity of isolation and withdrawal, and in which the expression of unconditional valuing overcomes the driven desires for compliance, obedience, and control.

> Brian reaches out to Mary, his adopted child, only to receive deep scratches in return. He does not recoil in fear or retribution. He stays by her side. He soothes rather than yells; he values rather than castigates. At first, she runs, screams, and flails her arms. But Brian approaches and reaches out. The child's fingernails gouge deeply into his outstretched arms. She stops and looks as if asking herself whether he will retaliate or endure. For a split second, she pauses and almost smiles. Brian stays with her. He knows his commitment is to give value to her and that someday she will give it back. And that day comes with amazing haste, for Mary's heart, like everyone's, longs for feelings of being-at-home.

Interdependence is a psychology of life in which we recognize that we all long for union and a feeling of being at home in spite of the crusted layers of ice that sometimes cover our hearts. The warmth that thaws this ice is what we can bring to the emergent relationship with the marginalized person. Just like those whom we serve, we have an inner hope to be one with others and, at the same time, a fear of self-surrender. Likewise, we struggle with those around us in a battle between domination and union. It is a difficult life project that requires mutual change, since it is not only the other person who is emotionally frozen. This can befall all who walk the face of the earth. As caregivers, we have a special responsibility to recognize the meaning of the human condition and to find ways to reveal and express the feeling of being at home while bringing the warmth of companionship to those who await it. No change in the other will transpire until it occurs in us. We are the ones who need to make the commitment to reach out, but this extension of ourselves cannot occur until we begin to question our values and put them into practice. Our inner struggle between the fear of giving and the hope of companionship is where we need to start. This struggle creates uneasiness. It is a process in which we need constantly to engage ourselves with marginalized people, to persevere in the difficult moments of rejection, and to know that mutual change will come. Ongoing battles between the urge for compliance and the pursuit of companionship symbolize this inner struggle. We are confronted with institutionalized violence, whose cold blood circulates through service programs. We have to ask ourselves which is our role: to dominate or to value? If we opt for the latter, we then choose to enter into a process of human interdependence.

Each of us is on a journey. Some move along the road with more ease and comfort. As on journeys, there are detours and barriers. Some become lost; others are not certain of where they are going. All of us need direction and help, some more than others. This life project requires purposefulness defined and questioned, and it calls for endurance and patience. It is always wiser to move in the company of others, for during the dark nights of the spirit, it is safer and more secure to be with those whom we love than to be alone. Nobody wants to be pushed or dragged down this road. Nobody chooses to wander aimlessly. But, everyone can become lost. Coming together makes the road less dangerous, less lonely, and less detoured. It is what can guide us home.

The feeling of being at home is much more than the arrival at a destination; it is the journey itself. It is the companionship of others and their support throughout life. It is warmth on the cold days of the spirit and hands united during stormy moments. It is laughter and tears. It is an ongoing and expanding coming together. It is not merely the strong helping the weak nor the fast accompanying the slow. It has nothing to do with charity; it has to do with the struggle for union through justice. Coming home is the process of the human condition. It is not a point at which we ever arrive; rather, it is the horizon toward which we move and on the way gather others. And this gathering helps the dawn move closer.

To give care is to instill hope, to question and change reality, and to form a life of companionship. Throughout the world, children and adults by the hundreds of thousands live apart. Some have been abandoned out of hopelessness. Others live in hunger imposed by unjust social and economic structures. Others are scooped up and placed in multi-million-dollar warehouses. Others are segregated like lepers. And some are lost at home. Yet, as caregivers, we are asked to enter these worlds and generate feelings of friendship and justice with one, then two, and then untold numbers of those who are marginalized.

> Panchito lived in a world caved in by the weight of personal, political, and economic abandonment. He had been abandoned in a city garbage dump and lived among other abandoned children and stray pigs. He became know as Panchito of the Pigs after someone placed him in a local asylum. By then, he had become blind from head banging. Nobody knew how to care for him. Yet, one caregiver, Maria, was able to begin to bring him and others hope. She knew, as we do, that she had to enter a life project with him and eventually find ways to help other nameless children.

Our challenge, like Maria's, is to enter the darkened world of the abandoned, the forgotten, and the segregated. Maria's struggle was perhaps more difficult than that of many caregivers, but we can begin to accompany her and Panchito with those whom we serve. Her reality was one of near hopelessness; yet, she instilled hope. It was one of abandonment; yet, she brought companionship.

> Christ, atop the highest hill,
> Looks upon the city,
> Arms of stone opened
> Toward the housed and the fed,
> Eyes fixed firmly
> On the land of the living.
>
> The sun shines on His face,
> Casting a cascading shadow
> Behind and down the darkened hillside,
> Impacting on white tombstones,
> Each rising from the ground
> Like rectangular scars.
>
> At the bottom,
> On the opposite side of the Street of Tears,
> On the darkened plain,
> The earth has opened up,
> Pushing out a tomb for the abandoned,
> For twenty-seven children
> Frozen between life and death,
> Chilled by the lengthening shadow,
> Forgotten by the fattened city dwellers
> On the other side of the hill.
>
> Child Salvador,
> Body black,
> Arms outstretched,
> Approached,
> Sucking a red plastic cord,
> His lips never having touched
> A mother's breast.
>
> Juan Luis,
> Pale face,
> Eyes moving from side to side
> Like rounded ice,
> Stands alone,
> Frozen in time,

An infant child
Imagining what he has never seen.

Claudia
Sits on a wooden stool,
Lips moving,
Whispering, crying,
"Come, come, come!,"
Words not answered.

And Panchito,
Head cast downward,
Rocks himself,
His blinded eyes fixed
On his tiny strapped arms
Listening to an unsung song.

And twenty-three others
Are twisted images of these four.
Though named,
They are nameless.
Though gowned,
They are naked.
Though living,
They are dead.
Until someone is touched
By the twenty-seven.

Maria, warm-hearted
In the midst of coldness,
Reaches down,
Unties Panchito,
And lifts him up,
The beginning of the instillation
Of hope.

Each of us is called on to walk into these worlds. Some glisten with ceramic tiles. Some reek with odors. We do want to live not in a culture of death, but in one of life. Like Maria, we can reach into these tombs of nothingness, refuse to opt for the darkness of the night, and help create human interdependence. And one day, our Panchito will look warmly at us, reach his hands out, and embrace us.

## References

McGee, J., & Menolascino, F. J. (1991). *Beyond gentle teaching: A nonviolent way to help those in need.* New York: Plenum Press.

McGee, J., Menolascino, F. J., Hobbs, D., & Menousek, P. (1987). *Gentle teaching: A nonaversive approach for helping persons with mental retardation.* New York: Human Sciences Press.

# 18

# Group Therapy for Persons with Mental Retardation

*Robert J. Fletcher*
*Thomas H. Duffy*

G roup therapy is an underestimated treatment modality for persons who are mentally retarded (intellectually challenged) and have mental health problems. Many mental health practitioners do not believe that persons who have mental retardation are suitable candidates for group therapy (Monfils, 1989). Historically, these practitioners have largely avoided therapy with this population because of the misconception that an intellectual deficit would preclude its use (Szymanski, 1980).

In recent years, however, there has been a growing interest in this treatment approach, with positive results. Group treatment can be valuable in addressing the habilitative and mental health needs of mentally retarded persons (Monfils & Menolascino, 1984), or it can be used as just one part of the overall habilitation plan along with other mental health approaches, such as individual therapy and/or pharmacotherapy.

The purpose of this chapter is to discuss the role of group therapy in treating people who are intellectually challenged and have mental health problems to demonstrate that it is a useful treatment approach. The chapter reviews the literature, presents a therapeutic rationale for group therapy, and presents common clinical themes. Also included is a section on leadership style and interventions, as well as practical group issues that need to be considered when developing a group therapy approach. Additionally, the stages of group development as they apply to this population are enumerated.

## Survey of the Literature

The literature reveals that group therapy has been used with persons who have mental retardation since the 1940s, across treatment settings. Cotzin (1948) reported on behavioral improvement after ten group sessions in an institutional setting. Several studies during the 1950s used control groups and a rating scale to measure improvement in the experimental clients. In a literature review of group therapy with mentally retarded persons, Szymanski and Rosefsky (1980) reported that four out of five studies demonstrated improvement in the experimental groups: Yonge and O'Connor (1954); O'Connor and Yonge (1955); Wilcox and Guthrie (1957); and Snyder and Seshrest (1959). The literature published in the 1950s on group therapy with persons who have mental retardation came mainly from institutions where clients demonstrated beneficial effects through improved communication and social skills and heightened self-esteem, self-control, and responsibility, as well as relief from anxieties (Sternlict, 1966). Slavson (1952) reported that the value of group therapy for mentally retarded persons is the discharge of emotions through anger, rage, disgust, and quarreling because their inability to express themselves verbally requires the acting out of their feelings.

During the 1960s, innovative and, at times, nonverbal approaches were used and studied. Gorlow et al. (1963) employed role playing, psychodrama, and active structuring in treating female residents in an institutional setting. Sternlicht (1964) used a variety of nonverbal techniques in establishing rapport with mentally retarded adolescents. Miezio (1967) used the group discussion of daily problems and feelings with a group of adolescent inpatients.

Group therapy was reported on by several people during the early 1970s. Mowatt (1970) reported on conducting a group with young adults in a sheltered workshop setting for persons who had mental retardation and/or a physical handicap. Members of the group discussed practical concerns as well as deeper clinical issues, such as the lack of freedom of choice and sexuality. The benefits of the group experience as reported by Mowatt (1970) were mutual support, sharing of feelings, alternatives to suggestions, relieved anxiety, and improved self-esteem.

Richards and Lee (1972) reported on groups that used verbal expression in topical discussions such as of family issues or behavior problems. These groups were usually open-ended, with no set agenda.

Slicken and Bernstein (1970) reported positive results of group therapy for mentally retarded adolescents with IQs ranging from 45 to 75. They found that group psychotherapy diminishes hyperactivity in response to emotional stress, thus helping the institutionalized clients to avoid the rejections that further impoverish their personalities.

Since the mid-1970s, there has been a growing use of group work with mentally retarded persons. Group work has been used as a treatment modality for social skills training for the more severely handicapped persons. Zistein and Roen (1974) reported on the effect of personal adjustment training through group work. Richards and Lee (1972) described the effects of group work in social rehabilitation. Perry and Cerroto (1977) described successful group work experience employing a structured social-skills-training approach.

The 1980s was an era that witnessed the use of group therapy with mentally retarded persons who had significant mental health needs. Szymanski and Rosefsky (1980) wrote about types of group therapy and techniques. Fletcher (1984a) described the therapeutic gains of decreasing feelings of isolation, rejection, and defeat with individuals who had a dual diagnosis of mental illness and mental retardation. Monfils and Menolascino (1984) stated that group treatment approaches played a valuable and effective role in the habilitation of mentally retarded citizens who had mental health problems. Fletcher (1984b) reported that group therapy as part of a day treatment program with mentally ill–mentally retarded adults fostered social interaction and increased problem-solving skills. Monfils (1989) wrote about the advantages and techniques of group psychotherapy with mentally retarded persons who have psychiatric disorders. Benson (1986) discussed an anger management group that used faces to represent feeling states to monitor the group members' moods. Glatt and Eustace (1986) described a program developed by a community mental-health center (CMHC) in which mental health professionals conducted group therapy services for dually diagnosed clients in settings outside the CMHC, that is, in sheltered workshops.

The professional literature in the 1990s continues to reflect group therapy as an effective treatment approach with mentally retarded persons who have mental health needs. Hurley and Sovner (1991) reported that group work can help depressed clients identify negative cognitions and substitute positive ones. Duffy (1991) described how group counseling can be an effective intervention in work with people who have a dual diagnosis of mental illness and mental retardation.

## Therapeutic Rationale for Group Therapy

Group treatment approaches for people who are intellectually challenged and have mental health problems offer several advantages. In many ways, group intervention may be more effective than an individual treatment approach. Group members have an opportunity to discuss, listen, and observe others who have similar circumstances, feelings, and goals. This commonality is experienced in group therapy and helps to reduce feelings of isolation, defeat, and inadequacy. Another therapeutic advantage of a group as a modality of treatment is that participation with peers fosters a sense of security, trust, and a feeling of belonging (Fletcher, 1984a).

Many persons who are intellectually challenged experience pervasive feelings of abandonment, exclusion, and rejection, and frequently do not have the supports necessary to develop a strong and healthy sense of self because of ego deficits. Negative feelings among people who are intellectually challenged may contribute to the chronicity and severity of superimposed psychiatric disorders, such as depression and anxiety states (Reiss & Benson, 1985). A group offers a safe environment in which a sense of belonging becomes the norm.

Many persons who are intellectually challenged and who have significant mental health problems have enormous difficulty in interpersonal and intrapersonal problem solving. Many do not have the skills for effective problem solving because of limited experience and opportunity in this area. Emotionally disturbed–intellectually challenged persons are often dependent on others to meet their daily needs and to make important decisions for them. The majority of people who are intellectually challenged live within a web of relationships in which their ability to change their behavior is limited by the capacity of their care providers to respond to such changes (Levitas & Gilson 1989). Many have not had the experience and exposure to acquire problem-solving skills because their care providers have made decisions and "solved conflicts" for them. Group therapy provides an opportunity to learn the important skills necessary to the process of problem solving.

Members can practice new skills in a group setting. They often have a greater chance to generalize new skills to situations outside the group than in one-to-one counseling. A group can be a more accurate sample of reality than an individual therapy modality. The group experience is a prototype of other life experiences.

Members may also learn to offer others encouragement. Many people who are dually diagnosed learn, through role modeling, how to give encouragement and support to their peers. Many need to help as well as to be helped. Being needed and wanted fosters self-esteem and decreases self-absorption. Providing support is often a new skill for this population. Group therapy presents opportunities for interactions that permit receiving support from and giving support to others. This support in turn, increases skills in interpersonal transactions. Group therapy often promotes the establishment of natural support systems (something that is particularly missing with this population). In addition, group therapy affords clients the opportunities to correct their own misconceptions, by listening to others and observing how others act and interrelate with one another. An opportunity for the members to examine and perhaps modify their own values and behaviors by conforming to a group norm can be provided through a group experience.

Persons who are intellectually challenged and have mental health problems are more vulnerable to stress than their non-disabled peers. Many have poor coping skills and lack experience in dealing with situations causing stress. Deutsch (1989) described three sources of stress experienced by mentally retarded persons:

1. *Stress from ordinary situations.* All people experience varying levels of stress in their daily lives. Through exposure and experience, we have learned coping mechanisms to deal with everyday stress. However, persons

who have mental retardation typically have not developed adequate defenses against everyday stressful situations. The stress caused by the inability to defend oneself against it contributes to negative self-esteem. For example, nondisabled people usually learn, over a period of years, how to cope in social situations (for example, asking someone out for a date). Persons who have mental retardation often have limited opportunities to experience and to learn to cope with social situations of this kind.

2. *Stress from difficult-to-manage situations.* All people experience very stressful circumstances during dramatic life changes. The death of a loved one, moving, and changing jobs are examples that cause enormous stress, even for people who have an intact ego and adequate defense mechanisms. Community-based persons with mental retardation are moved relatively frequently in the context or continuum of residential care, from most to least restrictive. If nonretarded people experience a great deal of stress during a move, what would the impact of a move be on people who are dually diagnosed?

3. *Unique stress.* Mentally retarded people experience stress that is unique to them involving internal and external events. It is not uncommon for a mildly retarded young adult to have the same aspirations, goals, and hopes as their nonretarded counterparts (for example, dating, marriage, owning a home, and having an independent job). These goals are often viewed as symbols of success. The aspirations of the mentally retarded are within sight but often out of grasp, and this situation is anxiety-producing. Mildly mentally retarded individuals usually have insight into their exceptionality. However, their awareness of its realistic implications is anxiety-provoking (Paniaque & DeFazio 1989).

The three types of stress experienced by mentally retarded persons pointed out by Deutsch (1989) also apply to persons who have mental illness coexistent with intellectual challenges. Our clinical experience indicates that dually diagnosed persons are even more vulnerable to these types of stress than are people who are intellectually challenged and who do not have significant mental health problems.

Group therapy can be a cogent treatment approach to addressing the issues mentioned above: stress from ordinary situations, stress from difficult-to-manage situations, and the unique stress experienced by persons who are intellectually challenged. A group is a social unit where, in a safe atmosphere, members can acquire new social skills, learn how to problem-solve, and learn to feel good about who they are.

Another value of group therapy as contrasted to individual therapy is that it is more cost-efficient (West & Richardson, 1981; Monfils, 1989). Group treatment requires one or two trained personnel for six to ten individual group members. A group approach maximizes the use of the few skilled therapists to work effectively with this population.

## Common Clinical Themes

Several themes are common in group treatment with people who are intellectually challenged and have mental health problems. Several of the clinical themes are described in this section and include problem solving, human sexuality, social skills training, interpersonal relationships, the identification and expression of feelings, and death, dying, and grief.

### Problem Solving

Individuals who are intellectually challenged are often referred to mental health services because of inappropriate problem-solving behaviors. These poor coping strategies are frequently expressed as maladaptive behaviors. Rarely are mentally retarded persons offered opportunities to develop a body of effective coping and problem-solving skills (Levitas & Gilson, 1989). Not only are their choices limited, but their ability to make judgments is underdeveloped. They do not have a wealth of experience in making decisions and choices on wants affecting their own lives. Group therapy is useful in helping clients develop a wider range of coping skills in response to anxiety or stress (Monfils, 1989).

*Case Example:* Mary, a twenty-seven-year-old female with mild mental retardation and a dependent personality disorder discussed in group the difficulty she had in confronting her boyfriend for fear of being rejected by him. Group members understood her feelings of abandonment, and at the same time, they were able to give her constructive feedback. One member said, "Mary, if he loves you, he will not leave just because you express yourself to him." Another member chimed in and said, "Mary, if he does leave you, which I don't think he will, he would show that he is not worth loving anyway." Another member added, "Take control of your life and stand up to him." Several others pointed out that they cared for Mary and did not want to see her being "used as a puppet" by the boyfriend. Still other members gave some concrete ways that Mary could assert herself. A role play was conducted to demonstrate alternative coping mechanism related to this issue. The group was supportive of Mary, yet they confronted her and presented constructive alternative coping skills to address her problem.

### Social Skills

Group work can be a viable approach to teaching and learning social skills. The acquisition of social skills is important to success in community-based living for people who are intellectually challenged. Successful community living has been correlated with social skills (Schalock & Harper, 1978). Additionally, research has demonstrated that the minimal social support of mentally retarded persons is related to depression (Reiss & Benson, 1985). In recent years, there have been structured group methods designed to teach social skills in a group setting (Foxx, McMorrow, & Mannemeier, 1984; Quinsy & Varney, 1977; Griffiths, 1990a&b).

Social skills training can occur as an adjunct to a group therapy approach. For example, in a group discussion on the topic of being as independent as possible, one group member mentioned that he would like to learn how to cook. This led to a discussion of how to cook spaghetti, and another group member offered her apartment to the group to prepare and have a spaghetti dinner. The group discussed what ingredients are needed to make a spaghetti dinner and offered to bring the necessary ingredients (spaghetti sauce, ground beef, onions, and so on). The group members decided what each would bring. They then discussed who would do what in the meal preparation. The higher functioning members offered to do the more complex tasks, such as making meatballs, and the lower functioning members offered to do other tasks, such as setting the table and cleaning the dishes.

The following week, they had a dinner together in the group member's apartment. In the subsequent group session, the members expressed feelings on this experience and shared its meaningfulness and how much they had enjoyed it. They talked about the concrete skills that they had learned from each other as well as the socialization, which they had enjoyed very much. This was not a structured social skills program. Nevertheless, a great deal of social skills training occurred. In addition, the members learned and shared with each other in a way that was very meaningful, therapeutic, and skill building.

This *in vivo* experience was an adjunct to and emanated from group therapy. It provided an opportunity to use social skills in a real-life situation. It also provided the group work leader an opportunity to observe and assess the members' social behaviors outside the formal group setting.

Other group methods teach appropriate social and sexual behavior to people who are intellectually challenged. One such approach is referred to as the *circle concept*, which teaches boundaries, that is how close a person should come in terms of proximity (Champagne & Walker-Hirsch, 1987). Valenti-Hein (1990) described a dating-skills program that moves beyond just teaching the anatomy and physiology of sexuality. In a group setting, all social behaviors relevant to establishing close interpersonal relationships are dealt with by means of a problem-solving format. As the group progresses, the members work on higher level intimacy skills. The group may begin to work on basic social skills (for example, active listening and understanding emotions). As they develop these social skills, they may move on to dealing with interpersonal skills (such as asking for a date and dealing with rejection), and then to intimacy skills (such as compromising and setting limits on sexuality).

## Human Sexuality

Persons who are intellectually challenged have the same candid and complete facts about human sexuality as the nonintellectually challenged and should have an opportunity to discuss sexually related topics. This discussion may include such topics as basic anatomy, contraception, pregnancy, sexually transmitted diseases, masturbation, homosexuality, and heterosexuality.

Persons who are intellectually challenged are like all other persons in regard to the occurrence of sexual development. The stages may be delayed, but the people exhibit the same needs for belonging and intimacy. They are sexual persons like all others. Unfortunately, because of the restrictions that are imposed on them, they often do not have interpersonal experiences to augment their knowledge of and skills in sexual relationships. The consequences are inept development and ineffectual interpersonal relationships (Schulman, 1980).

Group therapy is an effective treatment modality for teaching and discussing issues related to human sexuality. A group format provides an open and free climate of acceptance within which issues of sexuality can be discussed in a reassuring manner. In this context, the therapist has the dual role of educator and therapist. He or she presents factual information on topics such as sexual anatomy, birth control, and masturbation as well as facilitates the group process. The group leader can provide information on a particular area of human sexuality and then facilitate group discussion concerning the topic. Group members learn from the information being presented and have an opportunity to discuss their knowledge, experiences, and feelings.

## Interpersonal Relationships

Interpersonal relationships are often difficult to develop and maintain for people who are intellectually challenged and present a special challenge for those who also have a psychiatric disorder. Many of these people feel isolated, defeated, and alone. They have not had much opportunity to develop meaningful friendships. Some come from dysfunctional family or institutional environments, where they have not been exposed to normal interpersonal relationships. Group therapy offers opportunities to learn how to make friends and how to engage in meaningful interpersonal relationships. The group can also provide a vehicle for developing meaningful friendships among the group members. Group therapy offers an avenue for giving and receiving support, and this kind of interpersonal transactions can help to break down social fears and barriers.

It is not uncommon for group members to develop friendships with each other outside the group. For example, this situation has occurred in a group we have been conducting for over a year. Prior to the formation of the group, none of the members had known each other. The group consists of eight members who have mild mental retardation and a mental health diagnosis. Over time, several of the members have developed close relationships outside the group. The group has offered an opportunity to meet people, to learn to make friends, and to develop meaningful relationships.

## Death, Dying, and Grief

Grief is a universal experience that occurs for all persons who endure a significant loss when separated from another to whom strong feelings of attachment have developed over time (Worden, 1982). In most respects, people with a developmental disability experience grief the same way as others experience grief. This is a common theme with which many people who are dually diagnosed have to deal. The individuals develop close relationships not only with family members but also with other care providers, as well as with peers. Grief and feelings of loss manifest themselves in many ways in this population. Obviously, the death of a parent or other loved one evokes these feelings, but so can separation from the family. Experiences that cause feelings of loss include the death of a loved one, moving away from one's family, and separating from caregivers because of change of residence or a change in the caregiver's situation. Any of these experiences can cause feelings of loss. Kübler-Ross (1969) discussed the stages of the grieving process: (1) denial; (2) anger; (3) negotiation; and (4) acceptance. It is important for developmentally disabled people to be assisted through the grieving process (Warren, Bradbury, & Bruno, 1991). The movement through the stages is rarely straightforward; more typically, it is back-and-forth. In an article entitled "Grief Counseling with the Mentally Retarded," Deutsch (1985) identified four tasks of mourning:

1. to accept the reality of the loss
2. to experience the pain of grief
3. to adjust to an environment in which the deceased is missing
4. to withdraw emotional energy and reinvest it in another relationship

If the individual with a developmental disability does not progress through the stages of mourning, feelings of alienation, loneliness, and depression may continue for years after the loss of a loved one. Inadequate or incomplete mourning may have severe consequences, including a denial of the reality of the loved one's death, idealization of the loved one, a decrease in self-esteem, and feelings of guilt (Deutsch, 1985).

Group therapy can be an effective way to help developmentally disabled adults deal with issues of death and dying. McDaniel (1989) discussed how a group experience with this population can be useful in supporting group members in coping with loss and with the grieving process. In this situation, the group was established in a group home following several deaths of family members or friends over the past year. Although the group was time-limited and focused, the depth and abundance of feelings were evident from the first session.

Process groups, as opposed to short-term focused groups, can also be effective in dealing with issues of loss and grieving. Recently, one of our group members in a process-oriented group lost his mother, with whom he had lived most of his life. The group members provided support and helped the individual through the grieving process. They discussed significant loss experiences and were able to share their inner feelings and emotions. The common ground of sharing feelings around death and dying helps group members to cope with the death of a loved one (McDaniel, 1989).

### Identification and Expression of Feelings

Many persons who are intellectually challenged and have a mental health problem need to learn how to identify and verbalize their feelings rather than act them out impulsively. Group therapy provides a treatment vehicle for this process (Slivkin & Bernstein, 1970). Many of these people do not have the experience or understanding how to express themselves in socially acceptable ways. Their feelings states may not be easily recognized or expressed appropriately. Group therapy can help identify feeling states and help the members express them in a therapeutic manner.

For example, a member arrived at the group session with a frown on his face and his hands crossed. During the initial part of the session, this member was silent. Another group member stated to him, "John, you are quiet and look sad. Are your feelings bad today?" John responded, "Yes, I feel depressed." A group process followed that helped to identify the cause of his sadness. John was then able to identify and express his feeling of sadness, that is, the reality that another person had called him a "retard" earlier in the day and that this was why he was feeling sad. Other group members then expressed how they felt when others make derogatory remarks to them. Through the group process, the members expressed feelings related to stigmatization and benefited by the peer interaction and the sharing of common concerns and mutual support.

## Leadership Style and Interventions

One of the major roles of a group leader is to facilitate interactions among the group members. That is, a leader must be willing to be very active and, at times, directive with this population. Unfortunately, a lot of people who are intellectually challenged have been trained to rely heavily on authority figures for support and direction. As a result, a lot of the interactions within the group are initiated by the group leader.

It is not uncommon for the leader to be the center of attention. The leader must be aware that a lot of the interactions will tend to flow through him or her rather than between group members (especially in the early stages of a group). A major task for any group leader when working with this population is to teach the group members to interact positively with the other members. The leader needs to gradually redirect the interactions around him or her so that the discussion flows among the members. Whenever appropriate interactions occur between members, the leader should underscore the importance of the interaction. As a group develops, the leader may be able to be less active.

In order to make a group a truly worthwhile and rewarding group for all concerned, it is important that the leader enjoy the group. The members, no matter what their functioning level, will pick up on whether or not the leader is truly enthusiastic and committed to the group or simply going through the motions. A healthy sense of humor certainly helps out in group work with this population. The group leader is the most effective tool that the group has. Supplies, setting, and group structure are all important, but the effective group leader is the one who brings it all together.

A group leader needs to be flexible to be effective. Of course, the leader has a goal and agenda for every group but should be able to deviate from that agenda when appropriate. For example, if the group is working on an issue related to appropriate social skills but a couple of members bring up their anger when called a "retard," it may be beneficial to explore their feelings regarding that label.

The group leader should be willing to work in the here and now. Getting too caught up in a member's past may be unproductive. A focus on what is happening with the person and the group at the present point is especially important for people who have developmental or mental disabilities. Difficulty in generalizing information and skills from one situation to another is common in this population. Therefore, staying in the here and now with such questions as "How are you feeling now?" is very important. Of course, the group will also deal with issues from the past, but if the members can learn to focus more on the here and now, they can also learn to be more effective in the here and now.

Maintaining a therapeutic level of leader self-discipline is an issue in any group. The leader needs to balance his or her expression of self-disclosure: too much, and the group may stop working; too little, and the group members may find it hard to connect with the leader. The members may have difficulty seeing the leader as a viable role model or a real person. This balance is crucial to group work with this population, as the members tend to be more dependent longer than other populations. The cause is their learned dependence on helpers. When self-disclosing, the leader should take care to reframe his or her experiences into ones to which the members can relate. For example, instead of stating, "When I was driving my car . . . ," use something like "When I was walking down Main Street . . ." As another example, instead of saying, "When I was in graduate school . . . ," the leader may say, "When I was in McDonald's . . ." Examples that group members can identify with help the members identify more with the leader and the group.

Should the group use a coleader? The answer depends on the size and purpose of the group. Large groups (eight to ten) may benefit from having two leaders. Before a group begins, the respective roles of the coleaders should be established. There are a lot of dynamics overlooked when one leader runs a group. Leaders from various facets of the members' life may be effective (for example, the community residence, the worksite, and the mental health center). This teamwork may reveal a clear picture of the "whole" member and may promote generalization outside the group. One word of caution: If the leaders' styles or personalities do not mesh, they may not work well together and may actually be destructive for the group.

### Group Activities and the Use of Concrete Aids

When doing group work with this population, the leader(s) needs to go beyond the traditional verbal therapy that is used with other populations. Many people who are intellectually challenged or dually diagnosed have difficulty expressing themselves. Therefore, a variety of possible avenues of expression should be used in a group. "Hands-on" activities that reinforce group discussions should be used whenever possible.

An anger management group may use faces to represent feelings such as happy, sad, angry, and neutral to monitor group members' moods (Benson, 1986). Drawing these faces on a blackboard helps the members learn to identify the feelings. This use of visual, combined with auditory, stimuli may increase group members' chances of learning and retaining material.

Drawing pictures or cutting out pictures from magazines may also be a way for group members to express themselves. Using a concrete aid such as a Nerf Ball may help with traffic directing in a group. The member who has the Nerf Ball in her or his possession is the only member who can talk. Thus, the member has a chance to express herself or himself uninterrupted. When the member wishes to hear from another member, she or he passes the ball to that member.

Group rules should be developed with input from the group members, whenever possible. Putting the rules in basic terms or symbols on a "rule board" that is reviewed by the group is frequently helpful. Having the members participate in setting up the group rules helps to increase their feelings of ownership of the group.

The use of videotaping may be effective, as the group members have an opportunity to see themselves as others see them. Also, the members can see themselves and the other group members improve their skills over time. Often, group members become involved in learning to use the video equipment. This involvement helps to facilitate sharing and ownership of the group.

There is a lot of latitude for creativity when designing group activities with this population. Not only is it fun for the group, but presenting material and making points in a concrete way may help the members learn more effectively.

## Group Process Problems

Any group is bound to have its challenging members and process difficulties. Some examples follows.

A monopolizer tends to ramble, go on tangents from the group, and interrupt other members. The leader should attempt to determine what purpose this behavior serves in the group. Does the group protect the monopolizer? He or she may take the pressure off the rest of the group and reduce their anxieties so they do not have to take as many risks. What is unfortunate is that the monopolizer is often unable to hear others and pick up on group norms. The monopolizer who is confronted may be surprised and may respond harshly or explosively.

With this population, a real emphasis needs to be placed on taking turns. Individual work with a monopolizer, dealing with sharing and listening, may be fruitful. The leader needs to be more active, setting limits with the monopolizer and redirecting him or her. The leader also needs to draw others into the group. If the monopolizer has a strong need for attention and the spotlight, perhaps there are ways that the monopolizer can retain status. Can he or she write notes on the board for the group? His or her concentrating on the notes and spelling may give others an opportunity to interact.

Silent members sometimes benefit from the group vicariously, but often they limit the group process. Silence is behavior, so the reasons for the passivity need to be explored. Are the silent members responding to internal stimuli? Is the group overwhelming or threatening? Are they threatened by a particular member? Are their verbal skills poor, and are they afraid of expressing their weaknesses? Individuals working concurrently can be helpful. The passive members may be set up for success by exploring issues ahead of time. Let them know you will be calling on them ahead of time so they can be prepared.

Group pressure may produce positive changes in people; however, a difference must be made between the encouragement or feedback and demands from the group.

Beware of scapegoating. A scapegoat may help the others escape some of the pressures within the group. Gossiping is also counterproductive. The rule should be to talk about group members only when they are present.

If members are anxious, shaping their behavior by gradually building up their tolerance for the group may be useful. If the group has an open-door policy, it may be possible for them to attend small portions of the group and increase their time gradually.

An aggressive or psychotic person should be dealt with in a way that keeps everyone safe. Rules for dealing with aggression are important to establish at the beginning of the group.

### "Typical" Group Session

If there is such a thing as a "typical" group session, it would go as follows. The leader checks in with each member. Each member is acknowledged for her or his input and support. Who is not here? An emphasis on the importance of each member, even those who may not be present, is made. The members are asked to review the last meeting. The leader runs with the agenda, unless an important issue arises that must be dealt with immediately. Review at the end. Develop "homework" assignments whenever possible to help the members generalize the material covered.

## Practical Group Issues

When developing group therapy for persons who have a dual diagnosis of mental illness and mental retardation, it is important to consider several key issues. This section reviews the issues of purpose, composition, selection, size, the length of the group, location, and open versus closed groups.

### Purpose of the Group

The purpose of a group should be understood by all group participants. Group leaders need to clearly conceptualize the nature and purpose of the group and communicate them to the group members. It is also important for the group leader to be flexible and to allow for changes as clinically indicated during the group process.

There are essentially two types of groups, each having a different purpose. One is a process-oriented group, and the other is a theme-centered group.

A process-oriented group has a global purpose of growth and development. This type of group usually does not have a single focus or theme. The group members may discuss, for example, issues of independence, relationships, improvement in interpersonal communication, and alternative behaviors to acting out. The overall goals are to increase emotional maturity and independence and to develop a repertoire of problem-solving skills. In this type of group, the members learn to identify and express their feelings, to work on the resolution of conflicts, and generally to improve their self-esteem. A process-oriented group is beneficial for individuals who have moderate or mild mental retardation. The full range of the psychiatric disorders that coexist with this range of mental retardation is usually appropriate for a process-oriented group. However, an actively psychotic person or an individual who is constantly disruptive would not be appropriate.

The other type of group is a theme-centered group. Such groups generally have a focused purpose and are frequently time-limited. This type of group addresses a single theme which becomes the focal point of group interaction.

Theme-centered groups may focus on things such as human sexuality, conflicts with parents, or group-home residency. Monfils (1989) pointed out that a theme-centered group may be useful for instructing severely handicapped clients in basic social and adaptive skills or for allowing persons with mild to moderate mental retardation to explore interpersonal relationships.

### Group Composition

Who is to be part of this group? Is this group going to be homogeneous or heterogeneous? The members of a homogeneous group have some major similarity or similarities. It is easier to establish cohesion in this type of group because some important commonalities have already been established. A heterogeneous group consists of a wider range of people. This type of group offers its members a greater opportunity to experience new ideas and behaviors. It is also more representative of society.

Even if the group is fairly heterogeneous, the basis of homogeneity for the group must be identified. The common threads may be age, sex, living arrangement (for example, living in the same community residence), working arrangement (for example, being in the same work group), similar problems, and/or the same functional level. Look for compatibility: Is there potential for cohesiveness in this group?

A mix of people is usually therapeutic. Mixing higher and lower functioning members who have similar problems may be effective. A "buddy system" can be developed in which the higher functioning members have an opportunity to help the lower functioning members. The lower functioning members would, in turn, have an opportunity to interact successfully with their higher functioning peers.

Developing a group with five or six actively acting-out individuals would not be very productive. A group may be able to effectively handle one or two of this type of individual. On the other hand, six withdrawn people would be a difficult group to run. A mix may draw the more withdrawn people out of their shells, while giving the more verbal or active members a chance to share their time with the quiet members.

The intellectual level of an individual should not be used as the only criterion in the group selection process. Rather, the therapist must consider a range of variables in determining group selection, such as verbal abilities, motivation, and degree of insight. Groups composed of individuals with disparate diagnoses have been useful. The members can learn about various mental health problems and diagnoses in this type of heterogeneous group. A group composed of men and women may also be beneficial. In discussing a range of issues, such as dating, having both sexes present may be clinically relevant and therapeutic.

### Selection of Group Members

A general rule when selecting group members is that people should not be placed in the group if they are likely to be deviant. A group deviant is someone who is unable to participate in the group task (Yalom, 1985).

Every effort should be made to include people in the group who have a potential for cohesion. These members should be able to tolerate some healthy conflict and to grow. The perfect mix is not possible because there is not usually a large number of people from which to choose. Also, there may be pressure by referral sources, administration, and even group members to get started.

Another "rule" to keep in mind is to exclude people who are in the midst of a life crisis that may be more efficiently addressed in other ways (Yalom, 1985). Otherwise, the group may be dominated by this individual's issues and needs, and the other group members' needs may not be met.

Attention should be given to preparing the members for the group, if possible. Expanding on the pretherapy concept described by Prouty and Kubiak (1988), it can be argued that some skills must be developed and deficits addressed prior to the person's becoming a group member. Can the person attend to and relate to others enough to be successful in a group setting, or does the person need work prior to group to develop bonds with others? If consideration is given to the readiness of the person to be a productive group member, it may help to reduce your group dropout rate.

After a group begins, the leader(s) should expect to spend time establishing group norms and relationships and helping members understand how to truly be part of a group. Sometimes, learning how to be effective in a group setting is more important than the original goal of the group experience. Also, sufficient time should be spent by the group leader(s) in reviewing the potential members' backgrounds, strengths, and deficits.

### Size of the Group

How large should the group be? The size depends on the purpose of the group, on whether or not a coleader is being utilized, and on the people in the group. The group should be small enough so that each member can contribute and feel part of the group. It should be large enough to facilitate a variety of interactions among members. Yalom (1985) recommended five to ten members. Generally, a group of six to eight is a good range. Avoid large groups (ten plus) whenever possible, as the competition to be part of the group will be nonproductive. People will either interrupt constantly or withdraw. The group leader will expend all of his or her energy directing traffic, and group issues will rarely be resolved.

### Length of Group

Groups involving people who are dually diagnosed should meet once or twice a week to increase the retention of material and group processes. Meeting once a month may make it difficult to retain skills and maintain cohesion.

Groups of short duration (thirty to forty-five minutes) are most effective; they maximize the shorter attention span of many people who are dually diagnosed. Also, look at the time of day when the group meets. A group is probably not going to be most effective just before the bus or van transports the members home. A clean break at the end is helpful for the members to make a transition to their next activity.

The leader and the members should be committed to the group for the long haul (six months or longer), as it takes that long for cohesion and other group dynamics to take hold. Three or four sessions are not effective for most issues that persons with both mental illness and intellectual challenges face.

### Location of Group Sessions

Group therapy can be held at the workshop, at the community residence, or in a private practice office.

Glatt and Eustace (1986) described a program developed by the Dutchess County (New York) Community Mental Health Center in which the CMHC staff provided group therapy services to clients in settings outside the CMHC (for example, in sheltered workshops or primary-care programs). The CMHC staff worked closely with outside staff to tailor the program to the needs of both the dually diagnosed clients and the primary-care staff. Groups can be held in the members' natural environment, and multiple opportunities to practice skills learned in the group should be provided. Many people who have both mental illness and intellectual challenges have difficulty generalizing material from one setting to another. Inform other key staff of progress in the group (respecting the limits of confidentiality, of course). Key staff can then reinforce material covered in the group in other settings.

### Open versus Closed Group

The determination to have an open versus a closed group depends on the purpose and length of the group. If the purpose is to develop a process-oriented group that focuses on areas such as problem solving, relationship building, or developing alternative coping strategies, then an open group would be beneficial. Also, open groups work well with groups that are long-term. On the other hand, closed groups are useful for specific topics that are time-limited. For example, a group developed to explore and discuss issues related to death and dying may lend itself to the time-limited closed-group format.

It should be determined prior to starting a group whether it is to be open or closed. In a closed group, the members and the leader remain the same for some agreed-upon portion of time. The stages that the group progresses through are much clearer than in an open group. A closed group can offer stability and an opportunity for cohesion to occur more quickly. However, if too many members drop out, the group process may be drastically effected.

An open group can replace members if they leave. It may be more difficult to attain cohesion in an open group than in a closed group. When a new member joins an existing group, the members have an opportunity to review material and to teach the new member. In an open group, members get a chance to deal appropriately with termination issues.

## Stages of Groups

Yalom (1985) and Corey (1990) described the stages of group development. We have attempted to comment on how these stages, in a modified framework, emerge in groups that consist of mentally retarded persons who have significant mental health problems.

An important point to emphasize is that, even though groups involving people who are dually diagnosed go through these stages, the process is slower because of the developmental delays and mental health problems of the group members.

It takes longer for trust and cohesion to develop in a group with this population than in groups that are nonintellectually challenged. The members may initially find it difficult to understand how to use the group therapeutically. In group therapy, there is not usually a clear and identifiable transition from one stage to another (Yalom, 1985). The stages of group therapy with mentally retarded–mentally ill persons usually overlap. Szymanski and Rosefsky (1980) pointed out that an overlapping of group stages occurs in groups composed of mentally retarded persons because of their tendency toward regression, their distractibility, and their need for repetition.

The following section describes the five stages of group development: (1) pregroup affiliation; (2) orientation and exploration; (3) transition; (4) working; and (5) consolidation and termination.

### Stage 1: Pregroup Affiliation

Pregroup affiliation issues should be seriously considered when one is developing a group with this population. Planning goals and taking the time to prepare the members for group can pay off in the form of a successful group. The prospective group members should be interviewed before the formation of the group. This interview provides an opportunity for both the therapist and the group member to assess whether group therapy is an appropriate treatment modality. This is the time to discuss the purpose of group therapy and the role of the group members. The group affiliation process also allows an opportunity for the therapist to develop an initial relationship with each group member.

### Stage 2: Orientation and Exploration

During this initial stage, the members learn how the group functions and look for their place in the group. For many individuals, this may be the first experience of being a member of a group, and it may take some time and effort on everyone's part before they "settle in." Some questions that members may ask themselves during this stage are

- Do I fit in and belong here?
- Can I really trust these people?
- Whom do I like and whom do I dislike?
- Will I be accepted or rejected?

A major task of the group at this stage is to establish trust. This is often a difficult task, given the members' disabilities and past experiences, but trust is the foundation of any successful group. For this population, it is important to do as much work as possible prior to the start of the group with individual members to prepare them for the group. If the members enter the group with a preexisting rapport with the leader and perhaps a few group members, the group can get off the ground sooner and more easily.

Individuals who are intellectually challenged and have a mental health problem often come to therapy sessions with a history of mistrust and sometimes hostility because of the lack of trusting relationships in their previous personal experience. For this reason, it is initially difficult for them to verbally express their feelings. Developing an initial therapeutic alliance with the group is important. The leaders need to demonstrate understanding, acceptance, and respect. This is what Menolascino (1989) referred to as a "professional posture." A group leader can help to establish trust by modeling appropriate behaviors and showing empathy with and respect for each member.

In a "typical" group, the members are very dependent on the leader at this stage. Unfortunately, many people who are dually diagnosed have been trained by the "system" to be dependent on their caretakers. Many interactions tend to go through the leader instead of among the members. The leader should be very active at this stage in modeling and teaching appropriate group behavior and in establishing trust.

During the early phases of group development, the group leader(s) needs to take an active role in developing structure. The directive and active role of the leader(s) helps to decrease the anxiety of the group members (Slivkin & Bernstein, 1970), while establishing structure (Monfils, 1989). The group leader needs to facilitate a discussion on the purpose of the group and to help the group develop a set of "ground rules." The ground rules usually focus on the issues of confidentiality, taking turns to talk, and being on time, among others. The group leader(s) may need to define confidentiality or simply clarify the term. The leader(s) can begin this ground rule discussion by asking if someone can define the concept of confidentiality. The leader(s) can promote structure by initially going around the circle and asking the members to introduce themselves and say something about themselves. The leader can begin as a role model. It is important for the leaders to "share" themselves and to be genuine. After each person has introduced himself or herself, the leader(s) should thank him or her for sharing the information with the group. This sets a tone of trust and provides structure. It also is nonthreatening, and at the same time, it encourages disclosure. The disclosure is likely to be superficial during the initial stage, laying the foundation for deeper issues later in group development.

### Stage 3: Transition

The members continue to learn how to function in a group setting during the transition stage. However, by this stage, some trust has been established, and members can take more risks and even withstand some conflict (among members and challenging the leader). The members can learn appropriate ways to express themselves and to listen to others' concerns. Some struggle for control may occur within the group as the members' roles within the group begin to take shape.

For members who are dually diagnosed, this stage may offer an opportunity to learn to tolerate and cope with conflict, to begin to work with other people toward a common goal, and to be able to express their feelings and concerns.

The leader is still very active at this stage, directing traffic, assisting in the resolution of conflicts, and encouraging members to express themselves. The content of the group's discussions at this stage differs from that at the initial stage, as the topics are not as surface-oriented and do deal more with self-disclosure. Many members who have both intellectual challenges and mental health problems continue to need assistance to learn appropriate group behavior and how to express their emotions.

### Step 4: Working

A sign that the group has enter the working stage is that interactions now go among members more frequently and less often through the leader. Cohesion begins to develop. Members begin to show empathy, caring, and support to their fellow members.

Important events that take place during this stage are teaching members to confront others with respect and more willingness to take risks both in self-disclosure and in turning insight into action by attempting new behaviors.

Many people who are dually diagnosed may need assistance and support outside the group in trying out new behaviors, but this support from the group during this period can be very powerful. Members can (maybe for the first time) help other members by offering support and encouragement, instead of always being on the receiving end of assistance.

### Step 5: Consolidation and Termination

The consolidation and termination stage is particularly important for people who are dually diagnosed, as just the word *termination* has connotations of failure for them. Often, people who deal with these disabilities have little control over the way people come and go in their lives. Through changes in residential and vocational placements, moving between inpatient care and the community, many of them have had to say good-bye to people in a haphazard and very unsatisfying way. A successful termination offers a therapeutic way for members to end their group treatment and move on with their lives in more adaptive ways. Generalizing what has been learned from a group setting to the real world is often difficult, especially for a person who has a dual disability. Members who are leaving a group (as in an open-ended group) should be encouraged to "take stock" and share with the group the gains they have made. Departing members should also be encouraged to disclose their feelings about leaving the group. Those who remain in the group should also be encouraged to disclose their feelings about the impending loss of the member who is leaving.

The use of occasional maintenance or "booster" groups may help the members to review the skills they have developed in group and to maintain the gains made by the group.

## Summary

In this chapter, we began with an examination of the professional literature concerning group therapy with persons who are intellectually challenged. There is a paucity of literature on group therapy with persons who have a dual diagnosis of mental illness and mental retardation. This paucity points to the need for more research and clinical practice in using group therapy with this population. The therapeutic rationale for and value of using group therapy have been explored. We have noted the advantages of using a group approach in helping individuals with a dual diagnosis cope with a variety of challenges. A number of common clinical themes have been articulated, such as human sexuality, expression of feelings, problem solving, and grieving.

The chapter also offers a section on leadership style and intervention. In this section, we noted that leaders need to take a directive approach, yet be flexible enough to respond to the changing dynamics and needs of the group. Also noted was the importance of the group leader's working with a "here-and-now" approach. The next section addresses practical group variables that one needs to consider in developing group therapy with this population, and the last section of the chapter discusses five stages of group development.

Group therapy can indeed be an effective intervention in work with persons who have a dual diagnosis. This treatment modality can also be part of an overall treatment and habilitative approach in helping to meet the mental health needs of persons who are intellectually challenged.

## References

Beeber, Alan R. (1988). A systems model of short-term open-ended group therapy. *Hosp. Comm. Psychiatr., 39*(5), 537–542.

Benson, B. (1986). Anger management training. *Psychol. Aspects Ment. Retard. 5,* 51–55.

Benson, B. (1992). *Teaching anger management to persons with mental retardation.* Worthington, Ohio: International Diagnostic Systems, Inc.

Champagne, M., & Walker-Hirsch, L. (1987). Circles: A self-organization system for teaching appropriate social/sexual behavior to mentally retarded/developmentally disabled persons. *Sexuality and Disability, 5*(3),

Corey, G. (1990). *Theory and practice of group counseling.* (3rd ed.) Pacific Grove, CA: Brooks/Cole.

Corey, G.; Corey, M. S.; Callanan, P; & Russell, J. M. (1992). *Group techniques* (2nd edition). Pacific Grove, California: Brooks/Cole Publishing Co.

Cotzin, M. (1948). Group psychotherapy with mentally defective problem boys. *Am J Ment. Defic., 53* ,268–283.

Deutsch, H. (1985). Grief counseling with the mentally retarded client. *Psychol. Aspects Ment. Retard. Rev., 4*(5), 17–20.

Deutsch, H. (1989). Stress, psychological defense mechanisms, and the private world of the mentally retarded: Applying psychotherapeutic concepts to habilitation. *Psychol. Aspects Ment. Retard. Rev., 8*,(4), 25–30.

Duffy, T. (1991). Group counseling issues with people who are dually diagnosed. *NADD Newsl., 8*(2), 1–5.

Fletcher, R. (1984a). Group therapy with mentally retarded persons with emotional disorders. *Psychol. Aspects Ment. Retard., 3* , 21–24.

Fletcher, R. (1984b). A model day-treatment service for the mentally retarded–mentally ill population. In F. Menolascino & J. Stark (Eds.), *Handbook of mental illness in the mentally retarded.* New York: Plenum Press.

Foxx, R., McMorrow, M., & Mannemeier, M. (1984). Teaching social/vocational skills to retarded adults with a modified table game: An analysis of generalization. *J. Appl. Behav. Anal., 17,* 343–352.

Glatt, K., & Eustace, A. (1986). On-site mental health care for the retarded. *Hosp Comm. Psychiatr., 37*(9), 972.

Gorlow, L., Butler, A., Einig, K., & Smith, J. (1963). An approach of self attitudes and behavior following group psychotherapy with retarded young adults. *Am. J. Ment. Defic., 67,* 892–898.

Griffiths, D. (1990a). Teaching social competency: 1. Practical Guidelines. *Habilitative Ment. Health Care Newsl., 9*(1), 1–5.

Griffiths, D. (1990b). Teaching social competency: Part 2. The social life game. *Habilitative Ment. Health Care Newsl., 9*(2), 9–13.

Hurley, A., & Sovner, R. (1991). Cognitive behavioral therapy for depression in individuals with developmental disabilities. *Habilitative Ment. Healthcare Newsl., 10*(7), 8.

Kübler-Ross, E. (1969). *On death and dying.* New York: Macmillan.

Levitas, A., & Gilson, S. (1989). Psychodynamic psychotherapy with mildly and moderately retarded patients. In R. Fletcher & F. Menolascino (Eds.), *Mental retardation and mental illness: Assessment, treatment and services for the dually diagnosed.* Lexington, MA: Lexington Books.

McDaniel, B. (1989). A group work experience with mentally retarded adults on the issues of death and dying. *J. Gerontol. Soc. Work, 13*(3/4), 187–191.

Menolascino, F. (1989). Overview: Promising practices in caring for the mentally retarded-mentally ill. In R. Fletcher & F. Menolascino (Eds.), *Mental retardation* and mental illness: Assessment, treatment and service for the dually diagnosed. Lexington, MA: Lexington Books.

Miezio, S. (1967). Group therapy with mentally retarded adolescents in institutional settings. *Int. J. Psychother.*, *17*, 321–327.

Monfils, M. (1989). Group psychotherapy. In R. Fletcher & F. Menolascino (Eds.), *Mental retardation and mental illness: Assessment, treatment and service for the dually diagnosed.* Lexington, MA: Lexington Books.

Monfils, M., & Menolascino, F. (1984). Modified individual and group treatment approaches for the mentally retarded-mentally ill. In F. Menolascino & J. Stark (Eds.), *Handbook of mental illness in the mentally retarded.* New York: Plenum Press.

Mowatt, M. (1970). Group therapy approach to emotional conflicts of the mentally retarded and their parents. In F. Menolascino (Ed.), *Psychiatric approaches to mental retardation.* New York: Basic Books.

O'Connor, N., & Yonge, K. A. (1955). Methods of evaluating the group psychotherapy of unstable defective delinquents. *J. Gen. Psychol.*, *87*, 89–101.

Panagua, C., & De Fazio, A. (1989). Psychodynamics of the mildly retarded and borderline-intelligence adults. In R. Fletcher & F. Menolascino, (Eds.), *Mental retardation and mental illness: Assessment, treatment and services for the dually diagnosed.* Lexington, MA: Lexington Books.

Perry, M. A., & Cerreto, M. C. (1977). Structured learning training of social skills for the retarded. *Ment. Retard.*, *15*, 31–34.

Quinsey, V., & Varney, G. (1977). Social skills game: A general method for the modeling and practice of adaptive behaviors. *Behav. Ther.*, *2*, 279–281.

Reiss, S., & Benson, B. (1985). Psychosocial correlates of depression in mentally retarded adults. 1. Minimal social support and stigmatization. *Am. J. Ment. Defic.*, *89*, 331–337.

Richards, L. D., & Lee, K. A. (1972). Group process in social habilitation of the retarded. *Soc. Casework*, *53*, 30–37.

Schalock, R., & Harper, R. (1978). Placement from community-based mental retardation programs: How well do clients do? *Am. J. Ment. Defic.*, *83*, 240–247.

Schulman, E. D. (1980). *Focus on the retarded adult: Programs and services.* St. Louis: C. V. Mosby.

Slavson, S. R. (1952). *Child psychotherapy.* New York: Columbia University Press.

Slivkin, S. E., & Bernstein, N. R. (1970). Group approaches to treating retarded adolescents. In F. J. Menolascino (Ed.) *Psychiatric approaches to mental retardation.* New York: Basic Books.

Snyder, R., & Sechrest, L. (1959). An experimental study of directive group therapy with defective delinquents. *Am. J. Ment. Defic.*, *64*, 117–123.

Sternlicht, M. (1964). Establishing an initial relationship in group psychotherapy with delinquent retarded male adolescents. *Am. J. Ment. Defic.*, *69*, 39–41.

Sternlicht, M. (1966). Treatment approaches to delinquent retardates. *Int. J. Group Psychother.*, *16*, 91–93.

Szymanski, L. (1980). Individual psychotherapy with retarded persons. In L. Szymanski & P. Tanguay (Eds.), *Emotional disorders of mentally retarded persons.* Baltimore: University Park Press.

Szymanski, L., & Rosefsky, B. (1980). Group psychotherapy with retarded persons.

In L. Szymanski & P. Tanguay (Eds.), *Emotional disorders of mentally retarded persons*. Baltimore: University Park Press.

Valenti-Hein, D. C. (1990). A dating skills program for adults with mental retardation. *Habilitative Ment. Healthcare Newsl.*, 9(6), 47–50.

Warren, B., Bradbury, S., & Bruno, P. (1991). On death and dying: The grieving process. *Info Fact—OMRDD. Series 91-1.*

West, M. A., & Richardson, M. (1981). A statewide survey of CMHC programs for mentally retarded individuals. *Hosp. Comm. Psychiatr.*, 32, 413–416.

Wilcox, G. T., & Guthrie, G. M. (1957). Changes in adjustment of institutionalized female defectives following group psychotherapy. *J. Clin. Psychol.*, 13, 9–13.

Worden, J. (1982). *Grief counseling and grief therapy*. New York: Springer.

Yalom, I. D. (1985). *The theory and practice of group psychotherapy* (3rd ed.). New York: Basic Books.

Yonge, K. A., & O'Connor, N. (1954). Measurable effects of group psychotherapy with defective delinquents. *J. Ment. Sci.*, 100, 944–952.

Zisfein, L., & Rosen, M. (1974). Effects of a personal adjustment training group counseling program. *Ment. Retard.*, 12, 50–53.

# 19

# Systems Therapy for Persons with Mental Retardation

*Klaus Hennicke*

Encounters with mentally retarded persons, especially with those who are disruptive, act strangely, or behave destructively, are complicated for everyone: family, acquaintances, and any member of the social system. Systems theory helps us structure the complexity of the relationships in which mentally retarded persons live. Our encounters with the mentally retarded become more open and clear, and we can at the same time overcome unconstructive traditional reactions.

An open systems approach to therapy is not a new method for treating families and groups in addition to or in lieu of individual therapy. It is, instead, a perspective that encompasses not only personal structures and psychopathological symptoms but also the larger social manifestations. Systems theory has implications for all methods of treatment (Simon, 1991; Rotthaus, 1990; Selvini-Palazzoli, 1988; Boese & Schiepek, 1989). It projects the case history of a single person onto his or her primary group: the family and its context as a sum of the extrapersonal, socioeconomic, and political conditions. Instead of dealing with simple cause-and-effect relationships, systems theory deals with complex, mutually influencing connections.

Systems therapy means

> to induce changes by . . . disrupting dysfunctional patterns or restrictive ideas and to introduce ideas and perspectives that will open up new options and start new development to broaden the possibilities for freedom on an individual as well as a systemwide basis. Thus, the therapist helps the system to organize itself in a new way. The existing structures and patterns are revealed as sources of disruption and as developmental blocks not only in

the formation of symptoms but also in the use of system resources. The question now is: How can we use these resources in a therapeutic way? Otherwise, if we typically use the resources only impulsively, we can expect only sudden and discontinuous changes. (Stierlin, 1988, p. 56)

The aim of systems therapy is to "lead to creative problem solving, previously unavailable possibilities, and successful adaptation" (Imber-Black, 1987, p. 429).

"Examining the entire social system with the relevant diagnostic therapeutic process, we can construct a new reality no matter which cognitive systems we use" (Schiepek, 1986, p. 4)—that is how we can define *systems diagnosis.* The diagnosis must clarify whether treatment is necessary and which treatment is appropriate, must define the specific problems and the desired results, and must identify the responsible people and social systems (Hoffman, 1991; Imber-Black, 1990).

In defining the problem, the therapist is actually *part* of the problem and, in a way, its creator. In the systems perspective, diagnosis and the therapy itself cannot be seen as isolated processes. The skill of the therapist is not seen as being in managing dysfunctional structures but "in preparing a context in which communication leading to the evolution of a different reality is possible" (Goolishian, 1987, p. 109). Thus, the term *therapist* is unsuitable; we should use *consultant* instead. The consultant is more able to be in a "metaposition," perceiving the interdynamics of the system, and will not be expected to treat or heal.

Systems theories are derived from biological systems theories as well as from communication-systems and scientific-engineering theories. On the one hand, this is a very fruitful development, especially for a (clinical) theory of the family; on the other hand, this is a problematic transplanting of scientific laws onto social circumstances. For example, the historical changes of form and function of the family clearly show its social and political significance. But the premises of a (radical) constructivism that deny the possibility of an objective knowledge and therefore also deny any objective reality can easily be misused as a convenient, unethical expedient (Groell & Koerner, 1991; Hoffman, 1991). It is beyond the scope of this chapter to explore exhaustively the doubtless important problems of power, control, and the (manipulative) misuse of systems intervention within all the different schools and trends of systems therapies.

Obviously, the way we look at mental retardation is being critically modified by its historical, social, and political context. This is true, by the way, of all biologically transmitted problems. Systems therapy with mentally retarded people and their families is not a new therapeutic approach but a reflexive incorporation of the social, biological, and psychosocial situation.

## A Systems Evaluation of a Mentally Retarded Person

### Description of a Mentally Retarded Person

Mental retardation is a possible human state that becomes an actual disability only in the context of society, that is, through the mentally retarded person's being ostracized and isolated from ordinary social intercourse (Jantzen, 1987; Bradl & Hennicke, 1990). Though mental retardation originates in biology, it "becomes subjectively important only through social communication and interaction, especially when we consider emotional experiences" (Jonas, 1990, p. 23).

Every mentally retarded person is at the same time the subject and the object of his or her experience; he or she is both the doer and the done unto. Also, retarded persons' past actions influence their present circumstances in a recursive manner, both within themselves and within their social system. They also construct their reality as explorers and discoverers of their own objective environment. Permanently recursive processes of assimilation and accommodation occur (in the sense of Piaget) in which the mentally retarded revise their perception of reality. They adapt their individual interpersonal limitations according to their own socialization history on the continuum between openness and self-absorption (Rotthaus, 1990).

Retarded persons are usually regarded as trapped in their condition, with no potential for self-guided development. They are regarded as objects and as victims of circumstances. It is very hard for parents and their helpers to accept that the disabled child is actually an active person, with individual resources and an accountability of her or his own, that retarded persons can control themselves and can deal with family and society in a certain critical way, and that this ability is important for future personal development.

### The Biological Context

To look at mental retardation as a biological fact is important in many ways. Dosen and Bojanin (1990) referred to the concepts of Luria and Piaget:

> The development of a mentally retarded person is characterized by insufficient integration of functions of the CNS, the striking feature of which is the lack of dominance of the cortex as the highest integrative neural structure. The result of this dysfunction is immaturity of neuromuscular structures, a weak differentiation of gnostic functions, and shortages of emotional and social development which lead to disharmonious personality development. (p. 64)

This limitation in taking in the environment becomes a matter of subjective importance only in the social context. (This is also true of healthy children.)

We are gradually beginning to understand the social context through parents and such social institutions as schools and preschools. The daily interaction of mentally retarded persons—that is, their interacations with the intrafamily and extrafamily help systems—has, of course, a direct impact on the type, extent, and severity of the retardation. Different biological deficits call for different social values and implications, which are reflected in the reactions of the world at large and thus are an important part of intrafamily and extrafamily interactions and patterns of communication (Imber-Black, 1987; Sloman & Konstantareas, 1990; Sorrentino, 1988).

An important intrafamily factor is how the impairment of the child is discovered and dealt with. A great deal of literature addresses this process, especially the aspects of grief and loss (for example, Balzer & Rolli, 1975; Dornette, 1984; Goerres, 1987). Sorrentino (1988) stressed that the confrontation of the disabled with the efficiency of the healthy inevitably leads to a "loss in their relationship" and provokes many different psychological strategies in the disabled.

## The Social Context

A family with a mentally retarded member does not appear to be any different from other families at first glance; it must struggle with the same normative developmental processes. But there are additional conditions, of course:

- biological prerequisites and the nature of the impairment
- the vagueness or uncertainty of the diagnosis or other assessments
- the prolonged and often lifelong dependency of the child upon his or her parents
- the confrontation of such feelings as shame, guilt, grief, and denial (here social class and social patterns play an important role)
- the social isolation and stigmatizing of the family
- the official separation from real life of the retarded person, who is kept in a special world of his or her own
- inadequate help from social systems

Through all this, a family with a retarded member carries additional, long-lasting burdens that force adjustments that are naturally far more demanding than life would have been without the retarded member. Without additional psychiatric, physical, social, and material resources, a family cannot cope, and crises are much more likely to occur—and more often—than in a so-called normal family. This does not mean that the family is weak or inadequate, or even pathological; rather, it means that the continuous stress that the family must endure while it is giving its "all" pushes it to the edge of burnout (Bradl & Hennicke, 1990; Hennicke & Bradl, 1990–1991).

The mentally retarded person and the family must deal with political and economic changes in society and in the social helping services in often contradictory ways. Opinions, views, diagnoses, and problem-solving strategies from different social networks and experts converge on the problem in unrelated bursts, adding to the confusion. There is very little cooperation among the organizations set up to care for the disabled (Imber-Black, 1990; Schiller, 1987).

If we mention stress, we must note that its perception is relative (McCubbin et al., 1983). There is not always a linear, positive correlation between the weight of one's disability or other disorders and the extent of distress. Moreover, we must consider the context as well as the reliability and clarity of the diagnosis. Especially in borderline cases, the strain on the entire situation, including personal relationships resulting from an ambiguous assessment may be more severe than that resulting from an unequivocal assessment of an unmistakable disability (Boss, 1988).

## Mental Retardation and Mental Illness

The vulnerability of mentally retarded people to psychological disorders is not a natural consequence of their organic impairment (see, for example, Dosen & Bojanin, 1990; Menolascino, 1990); rather, it is due to an active subjective adaptation to, and is therefore a logical by-product of, social strains and isolation (Hennicke, 1987; Feuser, 1987). Mentally retarded people are typically faced with the same physical and psychological choices of perception, experience, and sensation as nonretarded people. There is no question that they experience psychological conflicts stemming from their interaction and communication with other people, and from being at the mercy of social norms, values, and rules. The conflicts arise from their trying to adapt and from their failure to do so. Therefore, psychological events unrelated to any primary sickness can occur in a retarded person, events that require help and support from the outside (Bradl & Hennicke, 1990; Hohn, 1989).

Disturbing, weird, or destructive behaviors are inevitably both the cause and the result of a certain, specific condition; these behaviors can be explained within this context. They are expressions of a person in his or her concrete historical context.

## The Medical-Psychiatric Model of Mental Retardation

The medical model of mental retardation in German psychiatry is of an incurable defect or a sickness that defines all outward manifestations of the thinking, experiencing, behavior, and entire personality system of the mentally retarded person. These psychological or behavioral manifestations are regarded as the state of mental retardation. This fundamental error still dominates the overall thinking in German psychiatry (Hennicke, 1987) and is seen in principle in German psychology and special education as well (Feuser, 1987). The consequence of this error is the lack of a developed psychopathology, of a differentiated diagnostic arsenal, and of appropriate methods of treatment. The medical model implies a qualitative difference between "retarded" and "nonretarded," analogous to the understanding of healthy and sick, normal and disturbed (Zygowski, 1991).

Out of this concept, the therapeutic practice offers procedures that treat the defect or deficit of an individual disabled person, who is regarded as an object.

## Systems Therapy in the Context of Mental Retardation

I want to show that the systemic approach provides therapeutic and pedagogical strategies that make the disabled person the central focus and organizing factor, and that make the entire social system a source of stimulating activities that will help in his or her development. The systems approach extends far beyond the medical-psychiatric model.

### Our Therapeutic Context: Psychiatry

Every family has its own "historical context," which has evolved out of its experiences with any helping institutions in the past (Imber-Black, 1987); each institution puts its own stamp on the evolving context.

As an employee in a psychiatric institution for children and adolescents, I see our service as the last link in a chain of helper and expert contacts. The German psychiatric institution is where long-lasting therapeutic attempts or the well-known "shopping" for diagnoses or "right" therapies find their temporary end.

Clients often have high expectations, because all prior attempts have been useless or ineffective. Or there is no consciousness of a problem at all, because the helpers have taken care of everything, including the transferral into the institution. It is usually very difficult to deal with the diagnostic appraisals and the very determined expectations of the transferrer. For example, on the transferral you may read: "Therapy is possible only on an inpatient basis; extreme, until now therapy-resistant; needs drugs; very difficult family relations," and so on. The more specialists who have been consulted, the more complicated the problem proves to be, or the more likely it is that the problem has proved to be insoluble. A process of pathologicizing takes place and leads the family and helpers to a dead end (Boeckhorst, 1991).

Therapy can make good use of this state of contradictions because it allows diverse views of the problem. If therapy does not use this confusion, the only result is a fight around the question of who is the best or who is the stronger. Senseless treatments will result, because the subject matter, the path, or the developmental aim has not been agreed upon.

### The Setting and Aim of the First Contact

Minuchin (1984) used the term *joining* to describe the first contact of the family and the therapist. The successful "joining" of the therapist with the existing system transforms the system into a new and purposive social system that aims to make changes. The basic structure of a "therapeutic system" assigns certain roles to the participants and determines strict limits of competence and responsibility up front.

The therapist must recognize that, within "systems therapy," he or she never has absolute control over the clients. It is therefore impossible to plan therapies with a definite aim. Clients will go where *they* want to go. It is important to note that therapists themselves become part of the problem while they elaborate on diagnoses and therapy recommendations based on their personal problem definition. Good-bye to the notion that there are certain indications for special problems!

Therapists should adopt an even-tempered calmness; they should allow themselves a distance for observation and patience. They should not expect quick success in treatment or problem solving, nor should they feel pressure from others to accomplish quick feats. It will be difficult for therapists to drop the professional dialogue of helping and healing and to give up their expertise. They should let themselves fantasize, that is, have alternative, spontaneous, and uncommon thoughts beyond the pale of their own patterns and the patterns of the institution.

This all seems much easier to imagine for use in an ambulant (outpatient) or community-based setting, but on closer examination, we can see its applicability to a stationary (inpatient), institutional setting. It is important to define for all the participants the subjective, social, and ethical limits from the viewpoint of all concerned, not just of the experts. A central therapeutic event occurs here that preconditions all other developments. In German, the event is called *Vorschaltambulanz*, and it occurs before a person is accepted for stationary treatment. In *Vorschaltambulanz*, we clarify the zones of responsibility: institution, family, parents, helpers—all concerned. Together, we lay out a clear therapy plan and commit someone to responsibility for the patient during the whole time of his or her stationary treatment. This is possible only if there is a supportive, equal alliance between the institution and the family or friends of the patient (Rotthaus, 1990).

Here, it becomes evident that the problems remain where they originate, and where they should remain, and that the institution can only support efforts to solve the problems. We are not willing to put a label on a psychiatric disorder in the form of a certain sickness or on a problem of the family in the form of guilt. The opening of the perspective through systems thinking also means embracing the whole social context as an effective, responsible frame of conditions and to change them.

Through interfamily mechanisms and stigmatizing processes in the society, families with handicapped members often feel some security in fixating on the "identified patient." The opening up of the perspective by the use of systems therapy may lead to insecurity in the family structure. Perhaps this insecurity will cause the therapeutic relationship to end. Or perhaps, after the first meeting, the original reason for starting therapy is no longer important. Or perhaps the therapy will indeed concentrate on the "identified patient," as is the case in many crisis interventions, to the great relaxation and relief of the family.

## Special Problems and Themes

In this section, I sketch problems and themes that are more in the foreground, or have a bigger impact, in families with mentally retarded persons than in other families. The impression may arise that I am describing pathological structures in a family that are meant to be changed through therapy. But all we do is observe the background family patterns and systems. The bottom line of the therapy is that only the agreed-upon part of the behavior or setup that was determined to be changeable will be dealt with and will become the theme in consultation. The themes exemplify where communication and interaction, relationship and structure, can be seen and changed. The themes change in their emotional intensity according to the structure of the current problems, the family situation, and the flow of the therapy.

**Interfamily Boundaries.** In structured family therapy, the condition of the system boundaries and their clarity are the central point. The pertinent question is how the subsystem limits are defined and how the individual fits into the whole system. As a rule, the limits are clear, open, and flexible. Contact beyond the limits is possible and does occur. Mutual penetration across each other's boundaries, however, is forbidden, or at least very difficult. The establishment of boundaries within the family is usually based on a constant enmeshment and disengagement or isolation (Minuchin, 1984). *Enmeshment* means that the limits are diffuse, unclear, blurred, or too open. Frequent intervention occurs, which inhibits autonomy and allows little opportunity for personal development. Separation brings on the severest anxiety. *Disengagement* means that the limits are very rigid, and that little communication or interaction occurs. There is little awareness of each other as well, and feelings of relationship are lacking. Here, getting too close to each other brings on great anxiety (von Schlippe, 1986; Minuchin, 1984).

Many of the problems in families with handicapped children are problems with boundaries and can be defined as structural hypotheses (Schubert, 1987). The following typical descriptions are hardly unique; they can be seen as specific results of basic boundary struggles. I am describing inter-family struggles here, but I have to point out that the same structural hypotheses apply to the interactions between family and helpers outside the family.

*Symbiosis* is defined as a system relationship in which one system member cannot exist without the other. This relationship typically crosses generational boundaries. Many families with retarded members are characterized by symbiotic parent–child (usually mother–child) structures that are manifested in intense and enduring worry about the retarded child. A symbiotic relationship is vital and practical during the child's infancy, but its continuation beyond infancy leads to the development of dysfunctional family structures. This continuation inhibits the child's striving for autonomy, and it isolates the other parent. Since the symbiosis is artificially maintained with great force, it leads to burnout. Symbiosis represents an extreme variation of emotional enmeshment. Because it is derived from a natural bond and a high moral value is usually attributed to it, it is difficult to perceive as a problem. It is usually another family member—a sibling who feels neglected or the "peripheral father"—who complains of a problem in the family and thus initiates change.

*At the periphery of the family system* is the person who fails to fulfill the expected roles and so is no longer functioning within the system. Very often, it is the father, who is dealing with external matters and long-range plans and delegating (or abdicating) to his wife the day-to-day caring for the re-tarded child, who feels cut off. A *family division* occurs, with two rigid sub-systems confronting each other. Conflicts then develop between these *coalitions*: e.g., father and sibling against mother and retarded child.

A third person involved in the coalitions and alliances may easily be-come a scapegoat. In the so-called *triangulation,* or *conflict diversion*, one system member acquires significance through the tensions between the other members, but then the others "gang up on" this member. In the triad mother–father–child, the retarded child absorbs relationship problems be-tween the father and the mother or differences with the in-laws. It seems to be a special triangulation game, where one system member is *delegated* the specific tasks of another.

The retarded child is often found in the center of the family because of her or his intensive need for help and attention. These growing requirements force more assistance, and the child may control and dominate all family ac-tions. It is therefore justified to speak of a *reverse hierarchy*, in which the parents are powerless. A "negative interaction spiral" may develop, "with paradoxical effects. The person we objectively regard as having the reduced capacities to control relationships is actually the one in charge, directing the lives of those on whom his own life depends" (Sorrentino, 1988, p. 43).

This "power of impotence" (Sorrentino, 1988) is a central mechanism in the context of mental retardation.

The child in the center usually weighs heavily on the relationship of the parents, both as parents and as a couple. There is a need to develop and strengthen the autonomy of the principal caretaker, on the one hand, and for each spouse to reassume mutual responsibilities for the other spouse, on the other hand. The aim should be to enable a functioning partnership, not to create an ideal marriage; obviously, a functioning partnership can go a long way toward solving the problems and alleviating the hardships. The development of functioning parental and marital systems reduces the danger of symbiotic structures and diminishes the unwarranted power of the retarded child. It should be noted, however, that the retarded child will not necessarily allow a structural change without a struggle; quite possibly her or his behavioral problems will become more severe.

**Symptom Origins and Functional Effects.** If we accept that the symptoms we observe are spontaneous (not put on), we have to take them seriously as a legitimate expression of the person (that is, give them a positive connotation as *Lebensaeusserung*, or life expression and manifestation). We should ask how a symptom functionally affects the family (or larger) system:

- What does the symptom do in the structure of the family system? Why is the symptom necessary?
- What message does the therapist receive from the system? Is it more a signal for the family or for external systems? Is it more to break out of family patterns or to stabilize them? Every system has this double character; what is important is the prevailing tendency.

There are many therapeutic techniques: talking to the family about the symptoms and speculating about them, for example, reframing it, making paradox assignments, transposing it into the future (what would happen if . . . ?), and formulating circular questions. The main leads in the controlled interaction with the family are guesses about the function of the symptom in specific contexts.

The search for ultimate causes has many pitfalls. Because most of the assumptions cannot be clarified or proved, there is a great danger of unjustified guilt proclamations (conflicts within the family, symbiotic enmeshment, and so forth) or of diffuse imputations about medication and the type of the disability. "Cause" explanations by the parents (or even by helpers) have an important function in a concrete context that may help in consciously dealing with the symptom or problem. They may even make the symptom visible to start with. Thus, such constructions of reality reveal the cold, hard facts, which must simply be accepted. It is not advisable to regard the search for ultimate causes as a therapy, but it can help to dismantle the family's construction of blame for the dysfunction. At the same time, it is important to have an open and critical dialogue about diagnoses and treatment methods with the family and to be competent as a therapist, that is, to understand the scientific ramifications of the biological problem, including the latest trends and miracle healing methods. It should be clear that all of these possibilities are optional for the family. Diagnosis should not just be an ongoing discussion with the family: It can change, and the family struggling with their child's disability changes, too (Sloman & Konstantareas, 1990). In the therapeutic setting, it is important to make use of, as well as to respect, the knowledge of the family and their expertise on their retarded child. Their value system must be respected as well.

**Significant Differences of Perception.** Differences among all the family (and the larger system) participants concerning educational measures, techniques, and principles; differences in assessment of the seriousness, extent, and curability of the disability (its "nature" and its associated behavior problems), and especially differences in future perspectives for the retarded person—all are almost always topics of discussion in therapy. All these factors may be an expression of a specific critical family situation, or they may point to a crisis between the family and the larger system. They may cause the family to expect an authority to tell them what is right or wrong. We have discussed this dead end before. On the other hand, differences always offer a chance for a creative solution; they are the condition for a consensual resolution on a new basis. They offer all involved the insight that the same things are still different according to perspective and context. To pinpoint such differences is to create boundaries and to stimulate different behaviors, which may lead to solutions.

**Life-Cycle Transitions.** The three most difficult phases in the life of a family with a retarded person are his or her starting in a special school for the retarded, puberty, and leaving home. These phases have one thing in common: Each involves decisions that are final. Clinical practice shows that the crisis in the family escalates through expansive behavioral problems, on the one hand, and through syndromes of exhaustion (burnout), on the other. Imber-Black (1987) pointed out that quickly changing and contradictory opinions and attitudes toward residential institutions make families insecure. There are no recognized social rituals for slowly granting independence to mentally retarded people. In the possible conflict between institution and family, it is easy to forget that it is the family that has been supplying "intensive" care up to this point and has been looking for an alternative to fill the vacancy. But every new organization of the relationship with other social systems is a transition that raises the possibility of a crisis and of a development that may be useful for therapy.

**Impact of Nonfamily Systems.** The interactions between the family of the retarded person, the enlarged social system (helpers, the social system, and the society at large), and the retarded person himself or herself are extremely important, often for the life span of the retarded person, during which all kinds of alliances and coalitions are possible. Contradictory and diffuse triadic relationship patterns, both creating and increasing problems, are very likely (Imber-Black, 1990). Boundary violations within the intimacy of the family are frequent from both sides. It is possible that the helpers will take on family-specific roles, placing them overtly or covertly in certain functions that they are not even aware of (Sorrentino, 1988).

If bringing this context into the base of individual therapy activities is impossible, making the consultations helpful in the development of the retarded person will be difficult. If different organizations work with the retarded person or the family, "helper conferences" may give some insight into assignments, responsibilities, and perspectives. The clearer the assignments are, the simpler it will be to define the respective responsibilities and competences, and the smaller is "the possibility, indeed, the probability for misunderstanding, mishandling, and attribution of blame" (Imber-Black, 1987, p. 437). The clarification itself is already a therapeutic act (see above the concept of the *Vorschaltambulanz*).

### Decision to Pursue Therapy

The therapist must decide whether to start unfolding activities even though the final go-ahead awaits the family's consensus. The criteria for starting are the extent and structure of the family crisis, measured by the family's immobility and inability to make decisions; the family's cohesion or lack of it; its dysfunctionality or instability; and evidence that the well-being of the family is in acute jeopardy. The therapist must also assess the availability of family resources for coping with and mastering the critical situation. Effective treatment involves only actions that direct the family toward positive changes. The therapist should not look for a hard-to-define psychiatric need to treat the "identified patient." He or she should instead look for what the family has to change structurally in order to overcome the critical situation. It is necessary to develop realistic and concrete steps to overcome acute problems by means of internal or external resources. It is important to clarify the relationship to the larger context (see above), for example, through helper conferences. Necessary long-term changes should be started in an assertive, supportive, and informative way. I must stress how important an effective advocacy can be. In the context of mental retardation as a lifelong process, it is appropriate to speak of management rather than of therapy (see, for example, Sloman & Konstantareas, 1990; Imber-Black, 1987).

## Relationship with Other Methods of Treatment

Disability-centered and context-oriented approaches do not exclude one another. Selvini-Palozzoli (1988) put it this way: "The quality of the relationship in which the retarded child lives, acts, and interacts reflects his development and determines the efficiency of the rehabilitation. The most elaborate pedagogical and rehabilitative program is doomed if it is embedded in a system of dysfunctional relationships" (in Sorrentino 1988). (p. 4).

In the framework of systems therapy, virtually all forms of pedagogical and therapeutic activities are possible if they occur within a consensual context, with clearly defined responsibilities and competences. The aim of systems therapy is often just that: to bring about this clarification, to define who is responsible and who is competent. In this case, systems therapy is a superordinate hierarchical program.

## Treatment Outcomes

Apparently family systems therapy is as effective as other psychotherapeutical methods (Heekerens, 1991). Our clinical experience leads us to the certain conclusion that systems therapy in the context of mental retardation represents an important and effective expansion of the traditional therapeutic efforts of psychiatry and psychotherapy. We still await scientific proof. As a matter of fact, it is very difficult to determine which aspect systems therapy is to be measured against. Certainly, any reduction of the measurement only to healing—that is, only to the removal or the amelioration of the symptoms of the "identified patient"—is inappropriate. The improvement of the quality of life and/or the consciousness raising of all concerned, as well as the duration of therapy, the small number of dropouts, the subjective happiness of the participants, and the feeling of success that the family gets from taking responsibility in the therapy—all are important factors that must be considered in the context of mental retardation (Heekerens, 1991).

## References

Balzer, B., & Rolli, S. (1975). *Sozialtherapie mit Eltern Behinderter* (Social therapy with parents of retarded children. Basel: Beltz, Weinheim.

Boeckhorst, F. (1991). *Stagnierende Hilfesysteme* (Stagnating helper systems). Cologne: unpublished paper.

Boese, R., & Schiepek, G. (1989). *Systemische Theorie und Therapie: Ein Handwoerterbuch* (Systems theory and therapy: A handbook). Heidelberg: Asanger.

Boss, P. (1988). *Family stress management*. London: Sage, Newbury Park.

Bradl, C., with Hennicke, K. (1990). Familien mit einen geistig behinderten Mitglied:

Ein systemisch-sozialwissenschaftlicher Ansatz (Families with a mentally retarded child: A systems social scientific approach). In W. Dreher (Ed.), *Geistigbehindertenpaedagogik* (Teaching the mentally retarded), pp. 145–167. Guetersloh: Van Hoddis-Verlag.

Dosen, A., & Bojamin, S. (1990). Developmental and biological factors in the mentally retarded and vulnerability to depression. In A. Dosen & F. J. Menolascino (Eds.). *Depression in mentally retarded children and adults.* pp. 63–79. Leiden: Logon.

Feuser, G. (1987). Zum Verhaeltnis von Geistigbehindertenpaedagogik und Psychiatrie (On the relationship of training for the mentally retarded and psychiatry). In W. Dreher, T. Hofmann, & C. Bradl (Eds.), *Geistigbehinderte zwischen Paedagogik und Psychiatrie* (The mentally retarded between training and psychiatry), pp. 75–92. Bonn: Psychiatrie-Verlag.

Gaedt, C. (Ed.). (1987). Psychotherapie bei geistig Behinderten: Beitraege der psychoanalytischen Entwicklungspsychologie (Psychotherapy for the mentally retarded: Essays to the psychoanalytical developmental psychology). Lectures at the Neuerkeroeder Forums, Neuerkerode.

Goerres, S. (1987). *Leben mit einem behinderten Kind* (Life with a retarded child). Munich: Piper.

Goolishian, H. A. (1987). Jenseits von "Jenseits von" (Beyond from "Beyond from"). *Z. system Th. 5,* 107–142.

Groell, J., & Koerner, W. (1991). Klinisch-psychologische Systemkonzepte (Clinical psychological systems concepts). In G. Hoermann & W. Koerner (Eds.), *Klinische Psychologie* (Clinical psychology), pp. 107–142. Reinbek bei Hamburg: Rowohlt.

Heekerens, H.-P. (1991). Familientherapie auf dem Pruefstand (Family therapy on trial). *Acta Paedopsychiatrica 54,* 56–67.

Hennicke, K. (1987). Ist "die Psychiatrie" an allem schuld? Ueberlegungen zu einer alternativen Praxis in der Kinder- und Jugendpsychiatrie (Is psychiatry to blame? Thoughts concerning an alternative practice in child and adolescent psychiatry). In W. Dreher, T. Hofman, & C. Bradl (Eds.), *Geistigbehinderte zwischen Paedagogik und Psychiatrie* (The mentally retarded between training and psychiatry) (pp. 154–165). Bonn: Psychiatrie-Verlag.

Hennicke, K. & Bradl, C. (1990–1991). Familien mit einem geistig behinderten Mitglied (Families with a mentally retarded member). 1st and 2nd scientific research projects (unpublished), Viersen.

Hennicke, K. & Bradl, C. (1990). Systemic family therapy and mental retardation. In A. Dosen, A. VanGennep, & G. Zwanikken (Eds.), *Treatment of mental illness and behavioural disorder in the mentally retarded, Proceedings of the International Congress,* pp. 225–232. May 3–4, Amsterdam. Leiden: Logon.

Hoffman, L. (1991). Das Konstruieren von Realitaeten eine Kunst der Optik (Construction of realities, an art of perception). *Familiendynamik 16*(3), 207–225.

Hohn, Ernst. (1989). Zu dumm, um verrueckt sein zu duerfen? Geistige Behinderung und Psychose (Too stupid to be able to be crazy? Mental retardation and psychosis). In W. Rotthaus, (Ed.), *Psychotisches Verhalten Jugendlicher* (Psychotic behavior of adolescents), pp. 150–173. Dortmund: Modernes lernen.

Imber-Black, E. (1987). The mentally handicapped in context. *Family Sys Med 5*, 428–445.

Imber-Black, E. (1990). *Familien und groessere Systeme: Im Gestruepp der Institutionen* (Families and larger systems: In the labyrinth of the institutions). Heidelberg: Auer. (American original title: *Families and larger systems: A family therapist's guide through the labyrinth*. New York: Guilford Press, 1988.)

Jantzen, W. (1987). *Allgemeine Behindertenpaedagogik* (General training for the retarded), Vol. 1. *Sozialwissenschaftliche und psychologische Grundlagen* (Social scientific and psychological fundamentals). Basel: Beltz, Weinheim.

Jonas, M. (1990). *Trauer und Autonomie bei Muettern schwerstbehinderter Kinder: Ein feministischer Beitrag* (Grief and autonomy in mothers of very retarded children: A feminist contribution). Mainz: Fischer.

McCubbin, H. I., (Eds.), (1983). *Social stress and the family: Advances and developments in family stress theory and research*. New York: Haworth Press.

Menolascino, F. J. (1990). "Mental Retardation and the Risk, Nature and Types of Mental Illness." In A. Dosen & F. J. Menolascino (Eds.), *Depression in mentally retarded children and adults*, (pp. 11–34). Leiden: Logon.

Minuchin, S. (1984). *Familie und Familientherapie: Theorie und Praxis struktureller Familientherapie* (The family and family therapy: Theory and practice of structured family therapy). Freiburg: Lambertus. (American original title: *Families and family therapy*. Cambridge, Harvard University Press, 1976).

Rotthaus, W. (1990b) Diagnostische und therapeutische Sichtweisen in Wandel: Die systemische Perspektive (Changing diagnostic and therapeutic views: The systems perspective). *Praxis Kinderpsychol. Kinderpsychiat. 39*, 361–364.

Rotthaus, W. (1990a). Stationaere systemische Kinder- und Jugendpsychiatrie (Institutional systemic child and adolescent psychiatry). *Modernes lernen* Dortmund: 1990.

Schiepek, G. (Ed.), (1986). *Systeme erkennen Systeme* (Systems identifying systems). Weiheim: Beltz.

Schiller, B. (1987). *Soziale Netzwerke und behinderte Menschen* (Social networks and retarded people). Frankfurt-am-Main: Lang.

Schlippe, A. von. (1986). *Familientherapie im Ueberblick: Basiskonzepte, Formen, Anwendungmoeglichkeiten* (Family therapy overview: Basic concepts, types, possibilities for application). Paderborn: Junfeimaun.

Schubert, M. T. (1987). *System Familie und Geistige Behinderung* (The system family and mental retardation). Springer, Vienna, New York 1987.

Selvini-Palazzoli, M. (1988). Vorwort zu A. M. Sorrentino, "Behinderung und Rehabilitation: Ein systemischer Ansatz" (Foreword to A. M. Sorrentino, "Retardation and rehabilitation: A systemic approach." Dortmund: *Modernes lernen* (1991).

Simon, F. B. (1991). *Meine Psychose, mein Fahrrad und ich* (My psychosis, my bicycle, and me). Heidelberg: Auer.

Sloman, L., & Konstantareas, M. M. (1990). Why families of children with biological deficits require a systems approach. *Family Process, 29*, 417–429.

Sorrentino, A. M. (1988). Behinderung und Rehabilitation: Ein systemischer Ansatz (Retardation and rehabilitation: A systemic approach). Dortmund: *Modernes lernen*.

Stierlin, H. (1988). Prinzipien der systemischen Therapie (Principles of systems theory. In F. Simon (Ed.), *Lebende Systeme* (Living systems) pp. 54–65. Berlin: Springer.

Zygowski, H. (1991). "Modelle psychischer Stoerungen [Models of psychological disturbance]." In G. Hoermann & W. Koerner (Eds.), Klinishche Psychologie (Clinical psychology), pp. 39–61. Reinbek bei Hamburg: Rowohlt.

———————

Many of the thoughts represented in this article are developed from my collaboration with Dr. Christian Bradl in our research project "Familien mit einem geistig behinderten Mitglied" (Families with a mentally retarded member) and from discussions with our coworkers in the clinic, especially J. Kleemann. My sincerest thanks to all of them.

# Summary and Conclusion

A s mentioned in the introduction, the editors have asked scientists from different countries to contribute topics to this volume for two main reasons:

- to shed light on particular issues from the standpoint of scientists at a geographical and cultural distance from each other
- to create an opportunity for the dissemination of knowledge beyond national frontiers

The authors were not chosen by chance; the criterion was being the most prominent scientist in a particular country and on a particular topic. The results show that there are far more similarities than differences in the approaches of different authors. Some of the important similarities are

- In different countries, the necessity of forming adequate mental health care is evident.
- Different authors preach a cautious approach to the assessment and diagnosis of psychopathology in the mentally retarded, pointing to the complexity of the disorder and to the need for multidisciplinary cooperation and multidimensional views.
- The symptomatology found in this population does not often fit within the diagnostic systems used for the general population.
- A proper understanding not only of biological determinants but also of the intrapsychic world, the manner of communication, and the interpersonal relationships of the client is necessary before one can give any judgment concerning the normality or psychopathological condition of these individuals.
- Special knowledge is necessary for proper assessment and diagnosis.

419

From the assessment and diagnostic considerations presented by some authors, it is apparent that, at this moment, integrative thinking prevails in both diagnostic and treatment approaches. The differences between various theoretical schools, as represented by cognitive theorists, biologically oriented authors, and psychodynamically oriented scientists, diminish significantly when a person and his or her environment are thought of as a whole. The complexity of the disorders encountered in this population is of such an order that only a combination of these theoretical approaches can give a meaningful explanation and an understanding of the processes and mechanisms involved. However, in this conglomeration of factors, the reconstruction of an aberrant process is necessary in order to determine the priorities and sequence of therapeutic intervention. A proper diagnosis is thus essential to decisions about what treatment method should be used.

Assessment instruments are, however, still underdeveloped and insufficient. Most of these tools have been extrapolated from the existing instruments or constructs used for the assessment of the population in general and do not correspond to the specificities of development and the life of the mentally retarded. Not only the screening lists of behavioral symptoms but also the biological parameters relevant to the mentally retarded may differ in many respects from those applicable to the general population.

Gardner and Graeber (chapter 3) have made an important contribution to a better understanding of the complexities in the psychiatric and behavioral disorders of the mentally retarded. These authors stress that the interaction of different nosological factors is so complicated that, in our present state of knowledge, there is no theoretical nor practical value in making an exclusive diagnosis of a behavioral or a psychiatric disorder. In most cases, a person develops psychiatric as well as behavioral aberrations. Nevertheless, the diagnostician must try to gain a proper insight into all the factors and to make a diagnosis in which the causes of emergence and maintenance may sufficiently come to light. The picture presented should be the beginning point for intervention plans are made and therapeutic approaches.

For such diagnoses, different professionals have to work together, not only to add to each other's findings, but also to integrate them into an understandable totality. A team of examiners is usually needed for such a task, coordinated by a professional with the ability to place different factors in the appropriate perspective and to delineate the relationships between them.

The treatment described in this volume has characteristics of integrative thinking. The descriptions of some of the treatment forms is very thorough and may not be completely clear to professionals in other disciplines. It may be encouraging, however, for workers in day-to-day practice to become better informed about the different possibilities for treating particular disorders. It is also important to know that many of these treatment forms are just developing.

Advances in assessment and diagnostics are stimulating the development of various treatment approaches. It is important that the choice of a particular treatment form be made not by the therapist, but by the diagnostician. Because of the complexity of the clinical picture of a disorder, an integratively oriented diagnostician can appropriately judge which particular treatment is indicated. The therapist, when playing the role of the diagnostician, may be inclined to view the disorder from his or her own perspective and to overestimate the contribution and importance of the his or her profession.

The treatment methods specially developed for the mentally retarded are not applicable to all disorders. A correct appraisal of the situation is necessary here as well. As is the case with diagnostics and assessment, most treatment approaches used with the mentally retarded have also been derived from the therapeutic methods applied to the nonretarded population. There is a danger that particular techniques have still not been sufficiently adapted to the different levels of developmental disorder. A keen consideration of whether these techniques are applicable to all levels of mental retardation is necessary. The intensity and the length of the treatment are still disputable issues in various treatment methods. The effects of treatment have still not been matched objectively. The results of studies of these treatments have mostly been anecdotal. Also, clear indicators for the application of particular methods are missing. Combinations with other methods are usually not described or evaluated. All these deficits make it clear that these techniques need further development and maturation.

For future development, it is important to focus on the further elaboration of the concept of the mental health of the mentally retarded. A positive attitude toward the mental health construct would make the progress of the normalization movement easier. This change in thinking and attitude is particularly important with respect to prevention. With this aim in mind, various developmental and social aspects of the mentally retarded should be pondered. Until recently, the attention of the scientist has been predominantly on the cognitive aspects of the mentally retarded. Although the biological and social aspects have received some attention, too, other psychosocial aspects, like emotional development, personality formation and awareness of one's own existence, have received hardly any attention from investigators. Research on these aspects as well as on the issues of biological development and the consequences of the interaction between biological and socioemotional development deserves priority in the development of mental health care for these persons.

The diagnostic problems encountered in this population require alternative or additional diagnostic approaches. It is necessary not to change the existing diagnostic classification systems but to adapt them to persons at lower developmental levels who have particular symptoms, or to create additional diagnostic categories that are specific to the problems of these individuals. The search for particular pathogenetic mechanisms is even more pressing because of an increased insight into the characteristics of biological and psychosocial development in particular sorts of mental retardation.

Instruments yielding an accurate assessment should be developed. As mentioned before, the utility of the tools developed for the general population is questionable. Also, new advances in biological examination technology, like the MRI scan and the PET scan, can reveal important information and help us to discover disorders early in biological development.

There is an acceleration in the development of different treatment techniques. A lot of systematic and scientific work is needed to make these techniques optimally applicable to mentally retarded individuals. Even traditional psychopharmacological treatment needs to be specially adapted to this population. Only recently, investigators have been focusing on the specific effect of psychotropic drugs on the mentally retarded. Not only must there be a clear indication or target that is to be effected, but the consequences of treatment must also be closely monitored. Even the dosage needed and the side effects of these drugs on the mentally retarded at lower levels are still not completely clear.

Also, the behavioristic approach is currently changing and promises a better link to other methods. The further development of multidimensional treatment is a challenging. This approach may bring about new treatments that are suitable for application to particular disorders.

All these problems await further investigation. International cooperation in this area would be very welcome. The sharing of ideas and experiences by professionals in different countries is very important for a sophisticated approach to all these problems and for the stimulation of research.

The editors of this book hope that they have succeeded in informing the reader of the international developments currently taking place in the mental health care of the mentally retarded. When even more knowledge has been accumulated in this area, we hope to address you again.

# Index

# About the Editors

**Robert J. Fletcher, D.S.W., A.C.S.W.,** is the founder and executive director of the National Association for the Dually Diagnosed (NADD). He has committed his professional career to the field of mental health care for persons with mental retardation.

Dr. Fletcher received his masters in social work from Washington University and his doctorate at Hunter College, City University of New York. For nearly two decades, he has been working in clinical, programmatic, and policy areas concerning mental health aspects of mental retardation. He has published numerous articles and book chapters and has coedited one other book, along with Frank J. Menolascino, entitled *Mental Retardation and Mental Illness*. As an expert in the field, he frequently consults in the areas of mental health services and systems development. He has presented at numerous state, national, and international conferences. Dr. Fletcher is also director of adult services for Ulster County Mental Health Services in New York State. In this capacity, he developed an out-patient mental health service model for persons who have mental retardation and mental illness. He has been instrumental in the design and implementation of a comprehensive service system for this population.

**Anton Dosen, M.D., Ph.D.,** is psychiatrist and medical director of the Clinic for Behavioral and Psychiatric Disorders in the Mentally Retarded, Nieuw Spraeland, Oostrum, The Netherlands.

For over eighteen years Dr. Dosen has been actively involved in the development of mental health care for mentally retarded citizens in The Netherlands. As a specialist in child psychiatry he has advocated the introduction of a developmental psychiatric approach to the diagnosis and treatment of mentally retarded children and adults. On these issues he has published approximately one hundred scientific articles in various Dutch and international journals. He is also the author and coeditor of several books on the subject of mental health problems in mentally retarded persons. He is actively involved in supporting the development of mental health care for the mentally retarded in several European countries and serves as president of the European Association for Mental Health in Mental Retardation. Currently Dr. Dosen lectures at several universities in The Netherlands and teaches post-graduate courses. He has recently served as chairman of Section Mental Retardation of the World Psychiatric Association as well as chairman of Section Mental Retardation of Dutch Psychiatric Association.

# About the Contributors

**Lawrence Dana, Ph.D.,** is chief psychologist at the Wilton Developmental Disabilities Service Office. He received his Ph.D. in psychology at Hofstra University. He is a diplomate of the American Board of Behavioral Psychology. Dr. Dana conducts seminars for professionals working with dually diagnosed persons, and is a consultant to provider agencies serving this population.

**Thomas H. Duffy, M.S.Ed., N.C.C.,** obtained his master of science in education degree in community counseling from St. Bonaventure University, and received his certification as a National Certified Counselor in 1986. He has worked with dually diagnosed persons in a variety of settings, including as an outpatient mental health therapist. He is program director for the continuing treatment program at the Rehabilitation Center in Olean, New York, a mental health day program designed specifically to meet the needs of people who are dually diagnosed. He has presented workshops on group counseling issues with this population. He is also an adjunct professor in the graduate community counseling program at St. Bonaventure University.

**Mark H. Fleisher, M.D.,** is director of outpatient services for mentally retarded–mentally ill patients at the combined Creighton–Nebraska department of psychiatry. He is also a staff psychiatrist in that department. Dr. Fleisher has published nationally and internationally on a variety of topics dealing with issues of mental retardation.

**William I. Gardner, Ph.D.,** is a professor and chairperson of the department of rehabilitation psychology and special education and is a member of the treatment processes faculty, Walsman Center on Mental Retardation and Human Development, University of Wisconsin-Madison. He currently serves on the board of directors of the National Association for the Dually

Diagnosed and is a past president of Division 33 (Mental Retardation and Developmental Disabilities), American Psychological Association. His publication, research, and clinical activities are concerned with the assessment and treatment of behavioral and emotional difficulties presented by persons who are dually diagnosed.

**Jan J. M. Gielen, Ph.D.,** is a clinical psychologist at Eckartdal, a general institution for the mentally retarded in the city of Eindhoven, The Netherlands. He is also a consultant for diagnosis and treatment of the mentally ill–mentally retarded in the region. Research and teaching interests include a hermeneutic approach of diagnostics of mental illness in this group.

**Janice L. Graeber** is completing her doctoral dissertation research in rehabilitation psychology at the University of Wisconsin–Madison. Prior to doctoral studies, Janice was a staff member of a psychology department in a residential facility providing services to persons with a dual diagnosis of mental retardation and mental disorders. Her current studies include a focus on substance abuse issues as a co-existing disability. Her previous publication topics include habilitation of the offender with mental retardation, multimodal diagnostic and treatment approaches, and enhancing the personal competency of persons with a dual diagnosis.

**Dennis C. Harper, Ph.D.,** is a professor of psychology in the divisions of developmental disabilities and pediatric psychology at the department of pediatrics of the University of Iowa College of Medicine. He received his Ph.D. from the University of Iowa, Iowa City, and was an intern in pediatric psychology in the department of pediatrics. His research and clinical interests include aging-related decline and psychiatric disorders in adults with developmental disabilities, crosscultural attitudes of children toward disabilities, and functional pain in children. He continues to function as a child psychologist as well for children with psychosomatic disorders.

**Klaus Hennicke, M.D.,** is a child psychiatrist and sociologist. He is a medical chief of a great institution for mentally retarded persons in Germany. He received his M.D. at the University of Heidelberg and Berlin. His interests include family structure under stress, family therapy and psychopharmacology of the mentally retarded. The last two years he realized an empirical study about families with a mentally retarded member.

**John McGee, Ph.D.,** is an associate professor in the department of psychiatry at Creighton University. He received his Ph.D. from Kansas University. Research and clinical interests include helping children and adults with severe behavioral problems. He also provides help to numerous programs and serves across the Americas and Europe. His most recent research includes the validation of "gentle teaching" as well as the development of a psychology of human interdependence.

**Frank J. Menolascino, M.D.,**\* is a professor and chairman of the combined departments of psychiatry for Creighton University School of Medicine and the University of Nebraska College of Medicine. He has authored hundreds of articles and numerous books on the nature and types of mental illness in persons with mental retardation. His research and scholarly writings laid the scientific foundation for others to build upon in the diagnosis and treatment of mental illness in persons with mental retardation.

**Detlef Petry, M.D.,** is a psychiatrist working for the Section Rehabilitation of Psycho Medisch Streekcentrum "Vijverdal," a general psychiatric hospital in Maastricht, The Netherlands. He is interested in the rehabilitation of the chronic psychiatric patient, especially in the "hard core" of the population of a general psychiatric hospital. One group of this hard core are mentally retarded persons with mental or psychiatric problems. He is also interested in other long-term psychiatric problems such as schizophrenia and depression in the context of their biography, development, and environmental circumstances.

**Andrew Reid, M.D., Ph.D.,** is a consultant psychiatrist in the Dundee Psychiatric Service, based at the Royal Dundee Liff Hospital near Dundee, Scotland. He is a medical graduate of the University of St. Andrews and also holds a doctorate from the University of Dundee. He is a fellow of the Royal College of Psychiatrists and of the Royal College of Physicians of Edinburgh. He has had a longstanding interest in the psychiatry of the mentally handicapped. He is the author of many publications on the subject, including a monograph.

**Stephen Ruedrich, M.D.,** is an associate professor of psychiatry at Case-Western Reserve University in the school of medicine, where he is the director of psychiatry residency training at MetroHealth Medical Center. He received his M.D. and psychiatric residency education at Ohio State University. Research interests include psychiatric aspects of mental retardation, with emphasis on psychopharmacologic approaches to mental disorders and behavioral problems in such individuals, as well as issues in the education of psychiatrists in general, and in developmental disabilities in particular.

---

\*Dr. Menolasino passed away on April 3, 1992, shortly after completing the chapter co-authored with Mark Fleisher, M.D. (see dedication).

No E.S. Sijben, Ph.D., is a psychologist/methodologist at the Vincent van Gogh Institute for Psychiatry in Venray. He received his Ph.D. in program evaluation from the University in Nijmegen. Research and teaching interests include the further implementation of program evaluation, the development of scales to measure abnormal behavior and the assistance of residents with respect to research activities.

Siegfried Tuinier, M.D., Ph.D., is a psychiatrist in the Vincent van Gogh Institute for Psychiatry in Venray. He completed his training in psychoanalysis and received his Ph.D. from the Free University in Amsterdam in the phenomenon of aggression, both clinically and biologically. His main interests include psychotherapy on analytic lines and the biology of aggression regulation disorders.

Willem M.A. Verhoeven, M.D., Ph.D., was formerly an associate professor of biological psychiatry at the University Hospital in Utrecht. Since January 1989 he has worked at the Vincent van Gogh Institute for Psychiatry in Venray as director of residency training and head of the department of biological psychiatry. He received his Ph.D. in endogenous opiates and schizophrenia from the University in Utrecht. His research interests include the atypical antipsychotics in schizophrenia, monamines in depression, and impulse control disturbances in mentally retarded subjects.